The SOURCE

for Effective Church Service Planning

Unleashing the Power of the Creative Arts in Your Church

The

SOURCE

for Effective Church Service Planning

REVISED & UPDATED

Compiled by

Scott Dyer

ZONDERVAN™

GRAND RAPIDS, MICHIGAN 49530 USA

WILLOW CREEK
RESOURCES

We want to hear from you. Please send your comments about this book to us in care of zreview@zondervan.com. Thank you.

ZONDERVAN™

The Source for Effective Church Service Planning
Copyright © 1996, 2003 by Willow Creek Association

Requests for information should be addressed to:
Zondervan, *Grand Rapids, Michigan 49530*

Library of Congress Cataloging-in-Publication Data
  Dyer, Scott.
  The source for effective church service planning : unleashing the power of the creative arts in your church / compiled by Scott Dyer.—Rev. and updated.
      p. cm.
  Rev. ed. of: The source. c1996.
  Includes indexes.
      ISBN 0-310-22878-6
  1. Public worship—Audio-visual aids. 2. Drama in public worship. 3. Church music.
I. Dyer, Scott. II. Title: Source.
BV288.S68   2003
246'.7—dc21
                                                          2003002409

Interior design by Nancy Wilson

Printed in the United States of America

03 04 05 06 07 08 09 /❖ VG/ 10 9 8 7 6 5 4 3 2 1

Contents

Life Issues

Relationship with God

Relationships

Seeker Issues

Social Issues

Introduction

By the time this book is released, it will have been seven years since the first edition, called *The Source,* was published. Our world has changed so much in that time. The events of September 11, 2001, and the resulting instability in the world have shaken our very foundations as a nation and have caused many to search earnestly for meaning, purpose, and security, and, ultimately, for God. In the weeks and months following the tragedies, people flocked to churches, desperate for hope. For many, their openness and hunger for God has persisted. The opportunity for the church to reach people with the gospel message is perhaps greater right now than at any time in the last fifty years.

If our churches are indeed going to bring the grace and peace of God to a world in critical need of it, our use of the arts will be vitally important. In order to reach any community with the message of Christ, we first need to learn to speak its language. My best friend from college is today a missionary to a part of Russia that has not yet had the Bible translated into its dialect. He spent years in training in linguistics and many more years living among the people so that he could not only learn the language, but also understand all of the nuances of the dialect. In America, the language of our culture is the arts, and the church must learn to speak it well.

We form our opinion of what truth is through the arts. Music, newspapers, television, movies—they all influence how and what we think. If we are to lead this generation to the cross, we will need to use every cultural tool at our disposal to do so. While the foundational need for compelling and sound biblical teaching has not changed, the need for music, drama, video, dance, and other artistic elements that effectively communicate the life-changing message of the gospel has perhaps never been greater. I say all of this to underscore the reality that what you do in your church is vitally important. God can use you and your team to change hearts and lives. Because the church is God's primary mouthpiece for his message of grace to this world, the church is the hope of the world. And you, as artists, can be the carriers of that hope.

It is vital to understand that our culture has been changing and that we must therefore be students of our culture. Biblically functioning churches have purposes that are central to their existence. These purposes are universal and timeless. For example, one of the primary reasons the church exists is to reach lost people—*evangelism.* This will always be true for every church from Australia to Zimbabwe. However, not all churches use the same methods to communicate the gospel, nor should they. Each church's individual approach to spreading the gospel will depend on the community it is trying to reach as well as the talents and resources it has available. What works in suburban Chicago probably won't be as effective in Southern California. In fact, what works in the northwest suburbs of Chicago, where Willow Creek Community Church is, will be different from what works in the northern or western suburbs. The communities are very different in their economic, social, and ethnic makeup. Every church has to go through the hard work of determining what it needs to do to reach friends and neighbors who are facing a Christless eternity.

Purposes are timeless, but methods should not be. At Willow Creek our primary method for doing evangelism is our weekly Seeker Service, at which we use contemporary music, drama, video, and other creative elements, combined with a topical message to present Christianity on an introductory level. The value that "lost people matter to God and should matter to us" will always be at the very core of our church as it should be in every church. But when the Seeker Service in its current form loses effectiveness, we will adapt our methodology. When we hold too tightly to our methods, we sometimes lose sight of the very purposes they initially were designed to accomplish. For example, when we wage battles over which worship style is "best," we often are drawn away from the real issue: Are people's hearts vitally connected with God, and are we really lifting him up to the place he deserves?

We have been doing a lot of experimenting with our seeker services at Willow Creek over the last two or three years and have been finding that people are not content just to be spectators anymore. For many years, the people in our largely unchurched community wanted to come in, be anonymous, not have to participate, and just let us present something to them. But that has been changing. Today people are longing for experience and community. They want to be part of something and not merely be observers.

Our knee-jerk reaction at Willow Creek to this changing reality was to add more worship to our weekend services. What we found after about a year of increasing the number of choruses from one to four or five was that it wasn't very effective. Our seekers were confused by it—they didn't understand it and they didn't like singing that much. I know of many churches in more churched regions, such as the Deep South, Western Michigan, and Southern California, where this approach has been very effective. I also know of other churches in areas that culturally are much like South Barrington that tried more worship in their evangelistic services and also found it to be ineffective for similar reasons.

Yet other things we have tried to increase the level of interactivity worked very well. We started an entirely new service, which ran for about a year, called "The Seven." It featured more alternative-sounding worship, a weekly testimony called "My Story" from someone in the congregation, and a shortened message followed by Q and A with the pastor. The My Story segment had high impact for people, and we have regularly incorporated it into our current weekend services. We have also been using "Spiritual Direction" moments, in which one of our pastors leads the congregation through a brief spiritual exercise, perhaps identifying an area of need or sin and talking to God about it, sometimes followed by a congregational song of response. We continue to try new things even to this point. One of our current understandings is that people are not as impressed or interested in highly polished presentations as they once were, so we are experimenting with being more spontaneous without lowering the bar of excellence. Time will tell where that leads us.

What we have learned is that it is important to hold fiercely to our purposes but to hold loosely to our methods and be willing to alter or replace them as our culture changes. We must never compromise the message, nor would we ever need to. At Willow Creek one of our core values is "to be culturally relevant but doctrinally pure." We know that God is the same yesterday, today, and forever, and his gospel needs no alterations. But he is also the God of creativity, and he can give us fresh new ways to communicate the good news of his amazing grace.

My hope is that this book will help you to unleash that creativity in your church in a way that ultimately leads to changed lives and eternities. But creative ideas are only a part of what is necessary to plan and execute powerful church services. You also need to have a great process. In this introduction I will share with you our current service planning and evaluation process and the roles of the people involved in making it happen. In doing so, I also want to thank all of the people at Willow Creek who play critical roles in this process, because they are the ones who really wrote this book. Their ideas and the work of their minds and hearts are represented here.

Our **programming director, Nancy Beach,** is the overall leader of our department. She is the primary visionary leader for the use of the arts at Willow Creek. She works with our **senior pastor, Bill Hybels,** on the overall direction of the services, both weekend and New Community. Nancy has done much to unleash the power of the arts in the church, not only at Willow Creek, but in countless other churches that have been influenced by her vision and passion.

The **executive producer,** or creative team leader, in our case, is ultimately responsible for what happens at our services. In the case of our weekend services (evangelistic seeker services designed to present Christianity on a "101" level to unchurched people), that person is **Corinne Ferguson.** Corinne is responsible to work with Bill and Nancy to determine the overall vision for the seeker services and to carry out that vision through the creative team. The content of this book is largely the result of her tremendous leadership and the countless hours she has spent making sure the services are as effective as they possibly can be. On a weekly basis, Corinne is the main point of connection with the teaching pastor. She receives a basic outline of the message about four and a half weeks before the services and talks it through with the teacher to make sure our team has the information we need. She also periodically touches base with the teacher to make sure he or she is aware of what we are doing and also to get his or her feedback after the first service (we have four identical weekend services, two on Saturday and two on Sunday). The **executive producer** for our midweek New Community services (identical worship services Wednesday and Thursday designed for believers), is **Pam Howell.** Pam has also contributed heavily to this book through her leadership of the New Community team.

Once the executive producer has the information for the service, we go into the brainstorming process. Our planning process starts with a **brainstorming meeting** held for three hours every Thursday. This meeting happens about four weeks before the service we are planning. The leader of the entire planning process is the **producer.** The producer is responsible for overseeing every aspect of the individual service we are planning. He or she leads the brainstorming meeting and is responsible for working with each point person, or **area director,** to make sure the ideas the planning team agrees on are executed with excellence. During the services, the producer is in the sound booth calling cues and making sure everything runs smoothly. He or she also oversees the final rehearsal on Saturday afternoon and works with the area directors during rehearsals to make final refinements. Our weekend producers, who have led the process that resulted in most of the ideas listed in this book, are **Chuck Spong, Larry Dahlenberg,** and **Lori Finnegan. Mark Bernardo** also led several of the brainstorming sessions represented here. Our primary producers for New Community, besides Pam, are **Sheri Meyer** and **Kristin Smith.**

The planning processes for the weekends and New Community differ slightly because the nature and purposes of the two are different. The process I will describe here is for our weekend services. The **planning team** is made up of several people. The producer leads the meeting, but Corinne is always there to provide overall leadership, and Nancy is there when she can be, contributing ideas and vision. At least one area director for drama and instrumental and vocal music is always at the meetings—whoever is responsible for that particular service.

The **drama director** is responsible for working with script writers on new scripts and for working with the actors to make the sketch come to life. **Steve Pederson** has been the drama director at Willow Creek for many years and has become one of the primary pioneers for the use of drama in the local church. Drama has been a powerful tool for life change at Willow Creek from the beginning, and Steve has been its champion. **Mark Demel** and **Rod Armentrout** are our other drama directors.

The **music director** is responsible for writing charts and rehearsing the band for the weekend services. We currently have three weekend music directors, **Rory Noland, Tom Vitacco,** and **Steve Myers.** Rory is also our overall music director and oversees the entire music department. He is a tremendously godly man who has greatly influenced the spiritual development of our staff and volunteers. If you haven't read his book *The Heart of the Artist,* I would highly recommend taking your team through it. Rory is also present at as many brainstorming meetings as possible and has contributed heavily to this book. **John Carlson, Steven Claybrook, Todd Hiller, Paul Langford,** and **Jason Sirvatka** have also served as music directors in the past, and, along with Tom and Steve, have made significant contributions to this book. **Randy Pearce** has been our primary New Community music director and has also made a huge mark on our church and on this material.

The **vocal director** makes vocal casting decisions and works with the singers to get the most out of each song stylistically and from a spiritual/communication standpoint. We have two vocal rehearsals for each song, both on Tuesday nights—the first is one and a half weeks out, for learning parts, and the second is the week of the service, to refine style and to help the vocalists internalize the songs and truly minister, not just perform. **Vonda Dyer** is our vocal director, and she has not only contributed many great ideas listed in this book, she is also my wife and has loved and greatly supported me through the writing of it.

We also have **creative consultants** who come to as many planning meetings as possible, whether they are involved in the actual services or not. **Greg Ferguson, Mark Demel,** and I serve in these roles. Greg is a phenomenal songwriter and singer, but he contributes to much more than just the musical side of things—he has great insight into what works for seekers and has often helped to craft the entire creative package. Mark is much the same way—he is a great script writer and actor but adds much more than that. He is a real out-of-the-box thinker, and he often helps to shape the feel and direction of the services. He is also a great illustrator and sometimes draws pictures during meetings to capture an idea or a thought.

At Willow Creek we have the blessing of multiple programming staff, and I recognize that most churches don't have that luxury. But I wanted to outline who is at our brainstorming meetings so that you can get a picture of the players you will need in your own process. I led programming teams in our youth ministries for many years, and I was the only staff person, but our process and planning team was similar. I led the band, so I served as executive producer and music director, but I had a volunteer drama director, producer, and vocal director, and the four of us made up the planning team.

The key concepts here are to create your services in a *team*—don't be a lone ranger service planner—and to give yourself and your volunteer teams enough time to make the service a strong one. As leaders, we are responsible for equipping our volunteers to do what God has called and gifted them to do. When vocalists, band members, and actors get their songs and scripts at the last minute, they will be more concerned with remembering lines and lyrics than with authentically communicating the message. Do whatever it takes to work with your pastor and your team to set your creative process far enough ahead so that you will free your people to truly minister from their hearts.

At our brainstorming meetings, we try to create a safe place for people to throw out ideas: "No idea is a bad idea" is one of our key values for that meeting. We also come prepared with ideas whenever possible. Our drama people come with script ideas or possibilities for repeat scripts, and our music people come with songs they think will work for the topic for which we're planning. We continually experiment with *how* we brainstorm, but in general we try to identify what our purpose is for the service, gather as many ideas around that topic and purpose as we can, and then get a consensus from the team on what elements will be most effective for that service. We also try to plan out the flow of the service, walking through different orders to get a sense of what feels right to us.

On the Friday before the weekend service, we have a **technical meeting.** This meeting involves the producer, area directors, and each of our key technical leaders—sound person, lighting director, video director, and stage manager. They meet to walk through the service and to make sure everyone is on the same page. I won't go into detail on what happens at that meeting, but, as an example, the music and vocal directors will talk through each song with the group—where instrumental breaks and solos are, who sings when, and so on so that the sound person knows how to mix the song, so the lighting director knows who to highlight at what point, and so the video director knows how to plan the camera shots.

On the Tuesday following the weekend services, we have an **evaluation meeting.** We watch the video of the service as a team and comment on what worked and what could have been better. If you have the capability of video taping your service, even if it's just with a camcorder, it will be a great help to your evaluation process. Celebration is also a key part of this meeting. Although it's important for us to learn from things that don't go particularly well and to talk through what might have gone awry, it is also essential to recognize and applaud the great things people on the team accomplished and celebrate what God did through them.

That's our process in a very small and abridged nutshell. I would encourage you to think through your process, to make sure it's serving you and your volunteers well. Your process should reflect your own objectives and realities, but the elements of brainstorming, technical preparation, and evaluation are important for any process.

My prayer for you is that God will unleash the power of the arts in your church and touch countless lives through you. Your church is unique in all the earth because of the people in it and the place you live in, and God can use you to bring hope and peace to your community like nothing else will. I hope that this book will help you in your creative process and inspire you to create powerful, life-changing moments. God bless you as you serve him. He can do marvelous things through you!

How to Use This Book

The Purpose

The creative process can be one of the most rewarding and exciting things one can do in ministry, but it can also be agonizing and frustrating. Sometimes great ideas flow like streams of inspiration. At other times the "right" ideas seem to be lost behind an impenetrable wall. The purpose of this book is to provide a source of ideas for people responsible for programming "relevant" church services. My desire is that it would become a useful part of your creative arsenal—a place to start when you need an idea, a place to turn when you're stuck.

The word *relevant* can be interpreted many different ways, and because this is a Willow Creek resource, you might be inclined to assume that "relevant" refers only to seeker services. While many of these ideas came from Willow Creek's seeker services, This book can be helpful to many different churches with many different styles. A song or a drama that works well in a seeker service might also have tremendous ministry impact in a service geared more toward believers. The common denominator is that these elements seek to relate biblical truth and wisdom to specific aspects of life.

The Blanks

This book is intended to be a supplement to your creative process, not a substitute for it. After each series of ideas, you will find some blanks for you to fill in your own ideas. At Willow Creek we are very aware that we are not the end-all when it comes to creative ideas. *A Source . . .* would probably be a more accurate title for this book; it will only become *The Source . . .* for you when you add your input. You and your creative team know your specific church audience better than anyone, and it is your ability to come up with fresh ideas and innovations that will ultimately make the biggest difference in your ministry.

The Content

The ideas listed in this book represent the creative programming elements that have been used effectively at Willow Creek Community Church over the past five to seven years in both the weekend seeker services and the believer-oriented New Community worship services, combined with just a few of my own ideas. The content is organized in five specific element categories: Message Titles, Dramas, Songs, Worship Choruses, and Movie Clips.

Message Titles

This is a listing of many of the titles that Willow Creek's teaching pastors have used over the years. We hope they will be useful to you, perhaps just to spur a thought for your pastor regarding his message title. The message titles are coded according to how they were used at Willow. All actual message titles are listed in normal type. If a title is preceded by another title in italics, it means that the message was part of a series (the series title is in italics). For example, a listing such as "*Seven Wonders of the Spiritual World:* God Can Be Trusted" means that the message "God Can Be Trusted" was one message in a series entitled Seven Wonders of the Spiritual World. Titles in boldface indicate that all of the following message titles were a part of the same series (the series title is in boldface). For example, the series **Faith Has Its Reasons** consisted of five messages, all of which are listed afterward. A message title not preceded by another title indicates a stand-alone message, one that was not part of a series.

Dramas

All of the sketches listed are available through Willow Creek Resources online at www.willowcreek.org. Next to each drama title, you will find three other pieces of information: Tone, Characters, and Topics. The Tone refers to the general mood of the drama. Characters are listed by gender, although with some scripts one or more characters may work in either gender. The Topics will help you to determine whether a drama deals with the aspect of the subject you are exploring. For example, *Faith* can be a fairly broad topic. If you are dealing with the specific aspect of having reasoning behind your faith, the sketch "Reason Enough" would probably be a good one to consider, based on the Topics listing.

Additional information about each sketch, including a brief synopsis of each one, can be found in the **Drama Index** at the back of the book.

Songs

There is probably no matter of greater diversity among churches than music. Consequently, you may have found recording artists or writers not listed here whose songs work very well in your church setting. The blanks are for your suggestions. We have listed some recommended songs to consider for each topic, and we hope that the combination of our ideas and your ideas will give you a much larger pool of quality music from which to choose. The songs listed in this section are presentational in nature— "specials"—as opposed to worship choruses, which are more congregational in nature and have their own listing in this edition.

The song entries are coded according to a couple of distinguishing factors. Songs in bold type have been particularly effective at Willow Creek for the topic under which they are listed. This is not to say that the songs not listed in boldface are not strong songs. All of them have merit, or they would not be listed, but the songs in boldface have typically had great impact at our services. Songs in *italics* are songs that are Willow Creek originals. Many of these songs were written specifically for our services, and we use them often. Because of that, you may find that some of them fit a particular topic exceptionally well. The instrumental and vocal charts for most of the Willow Creek songs and many others listed are available through the Willow Creek Association at www.willowcharts.com. If the album listed is a Willow Creek CD, it is available at www.willowcreek.org.

Beside each song are four other categories: Artist, Style, Tempo, and Seeker-Sensitivity Rating. The first three are self-explanatory. The Seeker-Sensitivity Rating is very important. This is a scale from 1 to 10, 10 being the most seeker-oriented. The rating is not a quality rating, but rather a gauge for how relevant a song is to seekers and how understandable the language and concepts are to the heart and mind of someone who doesn't know Christ. Be cautious about using any song under a 6 or 7 in a seeker-targeted or seeker-sensitive service. However, a high Seeker-Sensitivity Rating should not preclude your using a song in a believer-oriented service. A song with a 10 rating might be very effective in any type of service. With all music, use your own judgment.

More information about each song, including the album, record label, and comments, is included in the Song Index at the back of this book. We recommend that you review the index information for any song you are seriously considering for a service.

Worship Choruses

This is a new section for this edition and is probably the most significant addition to the book's content. We had many requests to include worship songs in this update. This book was never intended to help churches plan evangelistic services only, and since just about every church has a weekly worship service, this seemed like a natural and essential piece to include this time around. My desire is that this book would be a great resource for as many churches as possible—churches of all denominations, philosophies, and worship styles.

The worship chorus entries are identical to the song listings except that no song titles are in boldface. This is because we use all of the worship choruses listed here regularly at Willow Creek, so almost every song would be in bold type. Songs written by Willow Creek writers are in italics as they are in the song section. This is not an exhaustive list of choruses by any means, but it does represent the base of what we currently use at Willow Creek to plan our midweek worship services. For a much larger list, you might want to reference the Christian Copyright Licensing, Inc. website, www.ccli.com.

Movie Clips

We do not use a lot of movie clips at Willow Creek, and many of the clips included here have not been used at Willow Creek. When we do use movie clips, they are sometimes used in the message as an illustration of a particular point and sometimes presented as an element in the program itself.

Several pieces of information are given for each clip: Movie Title, Specific Topic, Clip Description, Start Time, Start Cue, End Time, End Cue, and Comments (where applicable). The Start and End Times are measured from the point in each film when the movie studio's header fades to black (In other words, when the Universal Globe fades to black), and the main titles begin. The Start and End Cues refer to suggested points in the dialogue or action to begin and end each clip.

Some clips have language that may or may not be acceptable in your church service. I have noted these instances in the Comments section, with the understanding that you will use discernment according to your church's standards. At Willow Creek we take a conservative approach to this issue. Also, some churches may have editing systems that allow you to "bleep" certain words.

Always make sure that you secure copyright clearance before you use a movie clip.

Package Suggestions

One of the things we have found particularly effective at Willow Creek is to use songs, dramas, and occasionally movie clips in a "package," in which one element immediately follows another. Many programs need bridging elements, such as a Scripture reading, to maintain creative and emotional flow; by contrast, when it fits, a drama/song package can be a powerful and moving tool for ministry. Where appropriate, we have inserted packages for you to consider.

The Future

One thing inherent in creative programming is change. A drama that was great four years ago might not work as well now, for any number of reasons. Musical styles change, important issues change, trends in theater and movies and culture in general change. If we are to be truly "relevant," it is important to be aware of these things and make appropriate adjustments in the creative elements we choose.

With this in mind, our plan at this point is to update the book from time to time to keep it current and fresh. We hope to continually expand and improve upon the material in this edition.

May God inspire you and use the gifts he has given uniquely to you to bring honor and glory to him and to help bring a world that is lost back home to him.

—Scott Dyer

Faith

Topic title

Related topics not given an individual listing in the book

Cross-reference: Related topics that are included in the book

Might also include: *Trusting God*

See also: **God's Faithfulness**

Message Listing

MESSAGE TITLES

Stand-alone message title

- ❑ Can I Trust a Silent God?
- ❑ Developing a Daring Faith
- ❑ Faith's First Steps
- ❑ Mind-Expanding Faith
- ❑ *Making Life Work:* Trust God
- ❑ *Seven Wonders of the Spiritual World:* God Can Be Trusted
- ❑ *What Money Can't Buy:* Conviction
- ❑ **Faith Has Its Reasons:** Reasons for Believing in God • Reasons for Believing in the Bible • Reasons for Believing in Jesus Christ • Reasons for Believing in the Resurrection • Reasons for Believing in Heaven and Hell

Message title within a series

Series title

List of messages in the series

Package Suggestion

Drama:
Straight-Jacketed

Song:
Take My Hand

A possible package of a drama going directly into a song

Blanks for your ideas

Drama Listing

DRAMAS

Title	Tone	Characters	Topics
In … We Trust	Serious, not heavy	1 male	Trust; Difficulty trusting God
Just in Case	Humorous	1 male, 1 female	Trusting God; God's faithfulness
Plane Talk	Humorous	2 males, 1 offstage voice (pilot)	Doubt; Skepticism; God's presence
The Quagmire	Serious	1 male or female	Failure; Self-esteem; Being "stuck"; Trusting God
Reason Enough	Mixed, mostly serious	1 male, 1 female	Importance of faith grounded in reason
Seeing Is Believing	Humorous	1 male, 1 female, 1 narrator	A Savior you can trust; Easy faith
Straight-Jacketed	Serious	1 male	Bondage to past and to sin; Anger toward God

SONGS

Song Listing

Willow Creek original (indicated by italics)

Song that has worked well at Willow Creek (indicated by boldface)

Title	Artist	Style	Tempo	Seeker-Sensitivity Rating
All the Faith You Need	*Greg Ferguson*	*Bluesy rock*	*Up*	*10*
Dive	**Steven Curtis Chapman**	**Pop/rock**	**Up**	**9**
Facts Are Facts	Steven Curtis Chapman	Rock/pop	Up	4
Found a Way	*Greg Ferguson*	*Ballad*	*Slow*	*9*
God Is in Control	Twila Paris	Pop/rock	Up	1
I Choose to Follow	Al Denson	Ballad	Slow	5
In My Father's Hands	Susan Ashton	Folk pop	Mid	9
Live Out Loud	**Steven Curtis Chapman**	**Pop**	**Up**	**9**
Seize the Day	**Carolyn Arends**	**Folk pop, in 3**	**Mid**	**8**
Take My Hand	The Kry	Acoustic ballad	Mid/slow	9
There Is a Love	Michael English	Pop	Up	9

Worship Choruses

Chorus Listing

Title	Artist	Style	Tempo	Seeker-Sensitivity Rating
All the Power You Need	Hillsongs	Pop worship	Up	5
Be Still My Soul	*Willow Creek Music*	*Worship ballad*	*Slow/mid*	*4*
I Will Bless You, Lord	Hillsongs	Worship ballad, in 3	Mid	3
Jesus, You're the Answer	Tommy Walker	Soulish worship ballad	Slow	5
Joy, Joy, Joy	Tommy Walker	Rock shuffle	Up	5
Lord, I Believe in You	Tommy Walker	Worship power ballad	Slow/mid	4
My Redeemer Lives	Hillsongs	Pop/rock	Up	3
Still I Will Worship You	*Willow Creek Music*	*Pop/rock worship*	*Up*	*3*
With Our Hearts	Lenny LeBlanc	Pop worship, in 3	Mid/up	3
You Are Worthy of My Praise	Passion	Rock/pop	Up	3

Blanks for your ideas

MOVIE CLIPS

Title: Chariots of Fire

Topic: Christian life; Endurance

Description: Eric Liddell gives a sermonette about running the race of faith.

Start Time: 0:25:35

Start Cue: "You came to see a race today."

End Time: 0:27:20

End Cue: "That is how you run a straight race."

Comments: _____
_____
_____

Title: Indiana Jones and the Last Crusade

Topic: Faith; Trusting God when circumstances are confusing

Description: Indiana Jones faces a seemingly uncrossable chasm but takes a "leap of faith" and steps onto an invisible bridge. Illustrates faith, believing what can't be seen.

Start Time: 1:46:50

Start Cue: Indiana Jones walks through cave to the chasm.

End Time: 1:48:45

End Cue: Indy throws sand on bridge to mark it (can be cut earlier).

Comments: _____
_____
_____

Title: _____

Topic: _____

Description: _____

Start Time: _____

Start Cue: _____

End Time: _____

End Cue: _____

Comments: _____
_____
_____

Blanks for your ideas

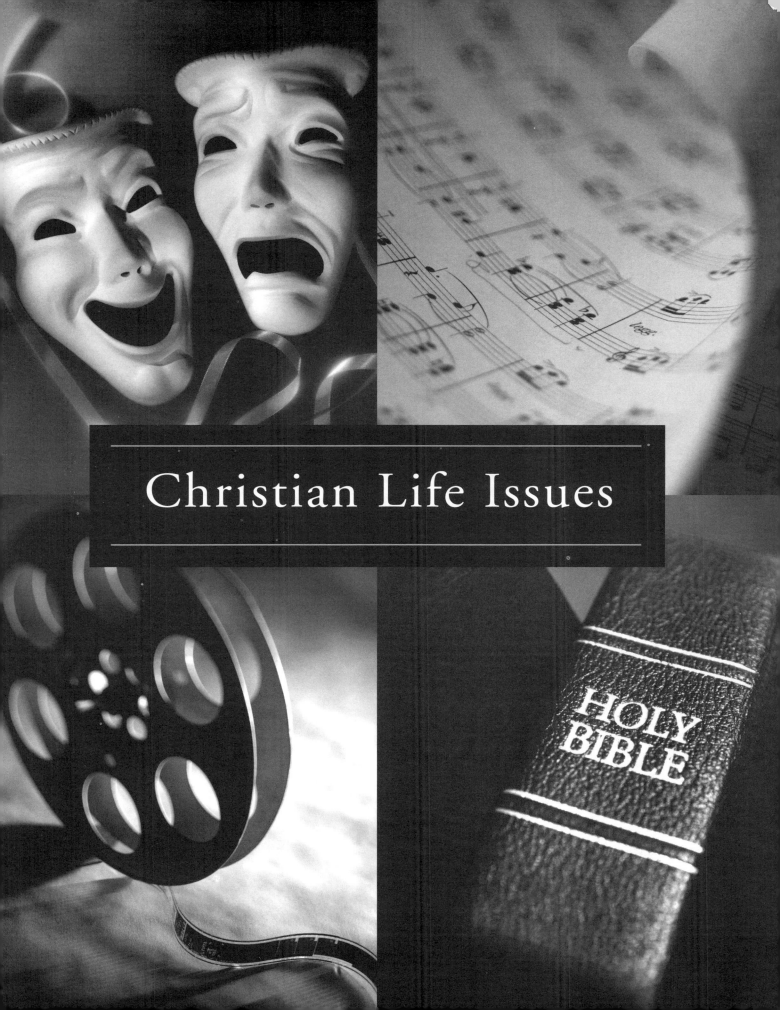

Christian Life Issues

Authenticity

Refers to living out what you believe

Might also include: *Integrity*

MESSAGE TITLES

- ❏ Cosmetic Christianity
- ❏ Habits of Highly Ineffective Christians
- ❏ *Becoming a Contagious Christian:* Authenticity
- ❏ *A Faith That Works—The Book of James:* Doers or Hearers
- ❏ *Living Excellent Lives:* Morally
- ❏ *Living Excellent Lives:* Spiritually
- ❏ *Truths That Transform:* Shine Like the Stars in the Heavens
- ❏ *What Jesus Would Say to . . .* Billy Graham

DRAMAS

Title	Tone	Characters	Topics
A Day in the Life	Humorous	5 males	Christians in the marketplace; New Christian
Getting the Nod	Mixed	2 males, 1 either male or female	Honesty; Integrity; Business ethics; Handling failure
Impressions, Inc.	Humorous	2 males, 1 female	Skin-deep Christianity
Man of the Year	Serious	5 males, 1 female	Moralism; Our need for Christ
The Mystery of Robert Richardson	Mixed	3 males, 2 females, 1 narrator	Living the Christian life
The Neighborhood	Mixed	3 males, 3 females	Small groups; Relationships; Getting deeper; Authenticity
One Step Up, One Step Down	Serious	4 males (1 can be female)	Ambition; Priorities

SONGS

Title	Artist	Style	Tempo	Seeker-Sensitivity Rating
All I Ever Wanted	Margaret Becker	Pop/rock ballad	Slow/mid	4
Audience of One	*Willow Creek Music*	*Power ballad*	*Slow*	*8*
Casual Christian	**DeGarmo & Key**	**Power ballad**	**Slow**	**6**
For Who He Really Is	Steven Curtis Chapman	Folk pop ballad	Mid/slow	1
From the Heart	**Scott Krippayne**	**Pop/rock**	**Up/mid**	**7**
Heart's Cry	**Steven Curtis Chapman**	**Acoustic ballad**	**Mid/slow**	**7**
If That's What It Takes	*Willow Creek Music*	*MOR pop*	*Mid/slow*	*5*
Life Means So Much	**Chris Rice**	**Folk pop**	**Mid**	**7**
Man of God	*Greg Ferguson*	*Pop/rock*	*Mid/up*	*7*
No More Pretending	**Scott Krippayne**	**Pop ballad**	**Slow**	**7**
Show Yourselves to Be	Steven Curtis Chapman	Acoustic ballad	Slow/mid	4
There Is a Line	Susan Ashton	Folk pop	Mid	6
We Can Make a Difference	Jaci Velasquez	Pop	Up	8
What if I?	*Willow Creek Music*	*Piano ballad*	*Slow/mid*	*8*
Whatever You Ask	Steve Camp	Power ballad	Slow	5
Would I Know You?	Wayne Watson	Ballad	Slow	3
You've Got to Stand for Something	Aaron Tippin	Country	Up	10
_____	_____	_____	_____	_____
_____	_____	_____	_____	_____
_____	_____	_____	_____	_____
_____	_____	_____	_____	_____

Worship Choruses

Title	Artist	Style	Tempo	Seeker-Sensitivity Rating
Everyone Arise	Tommy Walker	Pop/rock	Up	3
Heart of Worship	Matt Redman	Worship ballad	Slow	2
_____	_____	_____	_____	_____
_____	_____	_____	_____	_____

MOVIE CLIPS

Title: Chariots of Fire

Topic: Integrity; Standing up for what you believe in; The Sabbath

Description: Eric Liddell refuses to run on the Sabbath. The English Olympic Committee tries to make him compromise, but he stands firm.

Start Time: 1:28:15

Start Cue: "We decided to invite you in for a little chat."

End Time: 1:30:00

End Cue: "But I can't make that sacrifice."

Comments: _____

_____

_____

Title: Finding Forrester

Topic: Friendship; Keeping promises

Description: William, a reclusive author, comes to the aid of his young friend Jamal, who has been accused of cheating at a writing contest. In coming out of his seclusion, a very big step for him, he clears Jamal's name and honors a promise Jamal kept to him.

Start Time: 1:58:04/DVD Ch. 26

Start Cue: "Professor Crawford, may I read a few words?"

End Time: 2:02:35 or 2:04:02

End Cue: "I didn't write them. . . . Jamal Wallace did" (applause). Or William and Jamal leave together to applause.

Comments: _____

_____

_____

Title: _____

Topic: _____

Description: _____

Start Time: _____

Start Cue: _____

End Time: _____

End Cue: _____

Comments: _____

_____

_____

Being Salt and Light

See also: **Evangelism**

MESSAGE TITLES

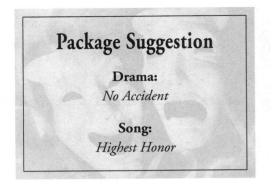

Package Suggestion

Drama:
No Accident

Song:
Highest Honor

DRAMAS

Title	Tone	Characters	Topics
Buy One, Get One Free	Mixed, moving	1 male, 1 female	The joy of giving
A Day in the Life	Humorous	5 males	Christians in the marketplace; New Christian
First-Day Jitters	Humorous	1 female	New Christian; Obeying God
Here to Help	Mixed	6 females	Helping those less fortunate; Not giving up; Dealing with difficult people
The Legacy	Touching	1 male, 2 females	Heroes; Character; Christians at work; Serving others; Making a difference
A Little Charity	Humorous	2 males, 3 females	Evangelism, Christian character
Maybe Someday	Mixed, mostly serious	2 males	Evangelism; Success that leaves us empty; Going back to church
No Accident	Mixed, mostly serious	2 females	Forgiveness; Loving your enemies; Growing in Christlikeness
On the Outside	Serious	1 female or male	Being salt and light; Negative church experiences
Parents on the Sidelines	Humorous	2 males, 2 females	Evangelism

Title	Tone	Characters	Topics
Parlor Talk	Mixed	3 males, 2 females	Making a difference with your life; Death; Workaholism
Reason Enough	Mixed, mostly serious	1 male, 1 female	Importance of faith grounded in reason
The Right Thing	Serious	1 male	Costly obedience; Christian character; Persecution
The Story of Rachel	Serious	3 females	Care for the poor; Compassion

SONGS

Title	Artist	Style	Tempo	Seeker-Sensitivity Rating
Broadway	Sherri Youngward	Ballad	Slow	7
Casual Christian	**DeGarmo & Key**	**Power ballad**	**Slow**	**6**
Everything (Apron Full of Stains)	The Normals	Pop/Rock	Mid/up	10
For Who He Really Is	Steven Curtis Chapman	Folk pop ballad	Mid/slow	1
From the Heart	**Scott Krippayne**	**Pop/rock**	**Up/mid**	**7**
Heart's Cry	**Steven Curtis Chapman**	**Acoustic ballad**	**Mid/slow**	**7**
Heaven in the Real World	Steven Curtis Chapman	Pop/rock	Up	7
Highest Honor	**Chris Eaton**	**Ballad**	**Slow**	**7**
Let's Stand Together	The Kry	Rock	Mid/up	1
Live Out Loud	Steven Curtis Chapman	Pop	Up	9
Not Too Far from Here	**Kim Boyce**	**Pop ballad**	**Slow**	**8**
Power of a Moment	Chris Rice	Folk pop	Up	8
Show Yourselves to Be	Steven Curtis Chapman	Acoustic ballad	Slow/mid	4
We Can Make a Difference	Jaci Velasquez	Pop	Up	8

Worship Choruses

Title	Artist	Style	Tempo	Seeker-Sensitivity Rating
Everyone Arise	Tommy Walker	Pop/rock	Up	3
Heart of Worship	Matt Redman	Worship ballad	Slow	2
You Mean the World to Me	*Willow Creek Music*	*Worship ballad*	*Slow/mid*	2
_____	_____	_____	_____	_____
_____	_____	_____	_____	_____
_____	_____	_____	_____	_____
_____	_____	_____	_____	_____

MOVIE CLIPS

Title: Mr. Holland's Opus

Topic: Inspiring others; Leadership; Getting beyond quitting points

Description: A clarinet student who is struggling decides to quit. Her teacher, Mr. Holland, inspires her to stay with it and in the process teaches her the true nature of music and helps her see her own beauty.

Start Time: 0:30:29/DVD Ch. 8

Start Cue: Mr. Holland is playing piano when his student walks in.

End Time: 0:35:02

End Cue: Mr. Holland smiles; scene fades to a concert.

Comments: _____

_____

_____

Title: _____

Topic: _____

Description: _____

Start Time: _____

Start Cue: _____

End Time: _____

End Cue: _____

Comments: _____

_____

_____

The Bible

See also: **Apologetics, God's Wisdom**

MESSAGE TITLES

- ❏ Objections to the Bible
- ❏ *The Case for Christianity:* The Case for the Bible
- ❏ *Defining Family Values:* Origin of Values
- ❏ *Faith Has Its Reasons:* Reasons for Believing in the Bible

DRAMAS

Title	Tone	Characters	Topics
Jeopardized Faith	Humorous	3 males, 1 female	The Bible
Pulpit Talk	Humorous	3 males, 2 females	Stereotypical church experiences; Sermons; Introduction to Sermon on the Mount

SONGS

Title	Artist	Style	Tempo	Seeker-Sensitivity Rating
Take You at Your Word	Avalon	Pop	Up	8
Thy Word	Amy Grant	Ballad	Slow	4

Worship Choruses

Title	Artist	Style	Tempo	Seeker-Sensitivity Rating
Breathe	Michael W. Smith	Worship ballad	Slow	3
Holy and Anointed One	Vineyard	Worship ballad	Slow	3
I Wanna Learn More	Curt Coffield, Ed Kerr	Folk pop worship	Mid	5
Let Your Word Go Forth	*Willow Creek Music*	*Pop worship*	*Up*	*2*
___	___	___	___	___
___	___	___	___	___
___	___	___	___	___
___	___	___	___	___

MOVIE CLIPS

Title: _____

Topic: _____

Description: _____

Start Time: _____

Start Cue: _____

End Time: _____

End Cue: _____

Comments: _____

Christian Character

Compassion

Might also include: *Kindness*

See also: **Caring for the Poor, Comforting Others**

MESSAGE TITLES

- ❏ Building Compassionate Hearts
- ❏ Compassion as a Lifestyle
- ❏ The Many Faces of Compassion
- ❏ Practicing Compassion
- ❏ Random Acts of Senseless Kindness
- ❏ *Becoming a Contagious Christian:* Compassion
- ❏ *A Faith That Works—The Book of James:* Religion According to God
- ❏ *A Faith That Works—The Book of James:* Who Matters?
- ❏ *Making Life Work:* Cultivate Compassion
- ❏ *Making Life Work:* Do Goodness
- ❏ *What Jesus Would Say to . . .* Mother Teresa

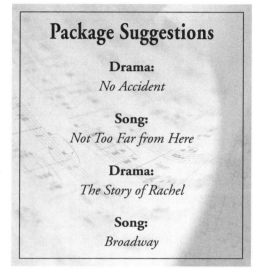

Package Suggestions

Drama:
No Accident

Song:
Not Too Far from Here

Drama:
The Story of Rachel

Song:
Broadway

DRAMAS

Title	Tone	Characters	Topics
The Boy Who Never Got Dirty	Humorous	1 male, 1 female, 1 narrator	Service; Risk taking
Buy One, Get One Free	Mixed, moving	1 male, 1 female	The joy of giving
Character Test	Mixed, moving	2 males, 1 female	Promptings from God; Obedience; Power of encouragement
Family Snapshots—Take IV	Serious	2 males, 3 females, 1 junior high boy	Family; Self-sacrifice
Here to Help	Mixed	6 females	Helping those less fortunate; Not giving up; Dealing with difficult people

Title	Tone	Characters	Topics
Just As I Am	Serious	1 male	Homosexuality
No Accident	Mixed, mostly serious	2 females	Forgiveness; Loving your enemies; Growing in Christlikeness
On the Outside	Serious	1 female or male	Being salt and light; Negative church experiences
The Right Thing	Serious	1 male	Costly obedience; Christian character; Persecution
Simple Gifts	Humorous but touching	2 males (1 teen), 3 females (1 teen and 1 girl)	Caring for others less fortunate; Materialism
The Story of Rachel	Serious	3 females	Care for the poor; Compassion

SONGS

Title	Artist	Style	Tempo	Seeker-Sensitivity Rating
Broadway	Sherri Youngward	Ballad	Slow	7
Everything (Apron Full of Stains)	The Normals	Pop/rock	Mid/up	10
Giving Thing	**Truth**	**Pop**	**Mid/up**	**8**
Heaven in the Real World	Steven Curtis Chapman	Pop/rock	Up	7
Helping Hand	Amy Grant	Pop	Mid/up	10
Not Too Far from Here	**Kim Boyce**	**Pop ballad**	**Slow**	**8**
We Can Make a Difference	Jaci Velasquez	Pop	Up	8

Worship Choruses

Title	Artist	Style	Tempo	Seeker-Sensitivity Rating
The Lord Is Gracious and Compassionate	Vineyard	Worship ballad	Mid/slow	5

MOVIE CLIPS

Title: _____

Topic: _____

Description: _____

Start Time: _____

Start Cue: _____

End Time: _____

End Cue: _____

Comments: _____
_____

Contentment

See also: **Fulfillment, Materialism**

MESSAGE TITLES

- ❏ It All Goes Back in the Box
- ❏ Our Need for Contentment
- ❏ What Can Fill an Empty Frame?
- ❏ When Is Enough Enough?
- ❏ *Rare and Remarkable Virtues:* Contentment

DRAMAS

Title	Tone	Characters	Topics
Catalog-itis	Humorous	1 male, 1 female, 2 junior high girls	Self-control; Contentment
Confessions of an Ad-aholic	Humorous	1 male, 1 female	Materialism; Power of the media; American dream
Early One Morning Just After the Dawn of History as We Know It	Humorous	3 males	Materialism; "Keeping up with the Joneses"

Title	Tone	Characters	Topics
In Pursuit of Happiness	Mixed	1 male, 1 female	Contentment; Possessions
Lifestyles of the Obscure and Indebted	Humorous	4 males, 3 females	Materialism; Coveting
The Mirror Thought of It	Mixed	1 male, 1 female, 1 offstage voice	Materialism; Workaholism; Striving for more
Oh, What a Feeling!	Humorous	2 males, 1 female	Decision making; Self-control; Money management
What's the Ticket?	Mixed	2 females, 4 either males or females	Need for Christ; Contentment; Needs and wants

SONGS

Title	Artist	Style	Tempo	Seeker-Sensitivity Rating
Audience of One	*Willow Creek Music*	*Power ballad*	*Slow*	*8*
How Could I Ask for More?	Cindy Morgan	Piano ballad	Slow	9
Reaching	Carolyn Arends	Ballad	Slow	6

Worship Choruses

Title	Artist	Style	Tempo	Seeker-Sensitivity Rating

MOVIE CLIPS

Title: Cool Runnings

Topic: Success; Ambition

Description: A bobsledder asks his coach why he cheated twenty years ago in the Olympics. The answer has a lot to say about the trap of success and its ultimate lack of fulfillment.

Start Time: 1:25:15

Start Cue: Coach enters hotel room.

End Time: 1:27:15

End Cue: "When you cross that finish line, you'll know."

Comments: _____

_____

Title: _____

Topic: _____

Description: _____

Start Time: _____

Start Cue: _____

End Time: _____

End Cue: _____

Comments: _____

Courage

Might also include: *Confidence*

See also: **Heroes, Risk Taking**

MESSAGE TITLES

❑ Our Need for Confidence

❑ Turning Zeroes into Heroes

❑ *Endangered Character Qualities:* Courage

❑ *A Faith That Works—The Book of James:* Developing Christian Confidence

❑ *No Fear:* Courage for Ordinary People

DRAMAS

Title	Tone	Characters	Topics
The Comfort Zone	Humorous	1 male, 2 females (1 TV announcer on tape)	Risk taking
The Quitter	Serious	2 male, 1 female	Quitting; Failure
The Speculators	Humorous	2 males, 1 female	Risk taking; Missed opportunities

SONGS

Title	Artist	Style	Tempo	Seeker-Sensitivity Rating
For the Sake of the Call	Steven Curtis Chapman	Anthemic pop	Up	3
Man of God	*Greg Ferguson*	*Pop/rock*	*Mid/up*	*7*
Seize the Day	**Carolyn Arends**	**Folk pop, in 3**	**Mid**	**8**
Whatever You Ask	Steve Camp	Power ballad	Slow	5
When You Are a Soldier	Steven Curtis Chapman	Keyboard ballad	Slow/mid	4

Worship Choruses

Title	Artist	Style	Tempo	Seeker-Sensitivity Rating

MOVIE CLIPS

Title: Braveheart

Topic: Leadership; Courage

Description: William Wallace challenges Robert the Bruce, the rightful king of Scotland, to lead the Scottish people to freedom.

Start Time: 1:35:50

Start Cue: "Wait. . . . I respect what you said."

End Time: 1:37:09

End Cue: "And so would I," followed by a close-up of Robert.

Comments: _____

_____

Title: Braveheart

Topic: Courage; Leadership; Freedom

Description: William Wallace exhorts the Scottish army to fight for their freedom. A powerful clip.

Start Time: 1:17:15

Start Cue: "I am William Wallace, and I see a whole army of my countrymen. . . ."

End Time: 1:18:53

End Cue: The Scottish army cheers as Wallace rides around.

Comments: Two cautions here: First, there is mild profanity just before the start cue, so make sure you start at the right place. Second, overall this is a very violent film—the clip, however, is not.

_____

Title: Chariots of Fire

Topic: Perseverance; Determination; Courage

Description: Runner Eric Liddell gets knocked down in a race and comes back to win.

Start Time: 0:34:25

Start Cue: "Gentlemen, get to your marks."

End Time: 0:35:45

End Cue: Liddell falls down in exhaustion at the finish.

Comments: _____

_____

Title: Forrest Gump

Topic: Friendship; Laying down your life for a friend

Description: Forrest goes back into the jungle of Vietnam to find his fallen friend, Bubba, and runs him out of the battle zone.

Start Time: 0:53:30

Start Cue: "I gotta find Bubba!"

End Time: 0:55:00

End Cue: Forrest runs out of frame, with the jungle exploding behind him. Can also end at "That's all I have to say about that."

Comments: _____
_____

Title: Indiana Jones and the Last Crusade

Topic: Faith; Trusting God when circumstances are confusing

Description: Indiana Jones faces a seemingly uncrossable chasm but takes a "leap of faith" and steps onto an invisible bridge. Illustrates faith, believing what can't be seen.

Start Time: 1:46:50

Start Cue: Indiana Jones walks through cave to the chasm.

End Time: 1:48:45

End Cue: Indy throws sand on bridge to mark it (can be cut earlier).

Comments: _____
_____

Title: Men of Honor

Topic: Courage; Friendship; Inspiring others to succeed

Description: Carl Brashear, a navy master diver who lost a leg in an accident, in order to be reinstated to full duty must walk twelve paces in a very heavy diving suit. At a court hearing, his former drill sergeant, a former antagonist, pushes him and challenges him to do it.

Start Time: 1:55:11

Start Cue: Wide shot of the courtroom

End Time: 2:00:30

End Cue: Courtroom erupts in applause.

Comments: There is brief profanity in this clip that must be bleeped, but the power of the clip is worth the extra work.
_____
_____

Title: Rudy

Topic: Quitting; Perseverance

Description: Rudy decides to quit the football team. Fortune, his friend and former boss, challenges him because he used to play for Notre Dame and quit.

Start Time: 1:29:10

Start Cue: Just before "What're you doing here?"

End Time: 1:31:20

End Cue: "Do you hear me clear enough?"

Comments: Two possibly objectional words are used.
_____
_____

Title: _____

Topic: _____

Description: _____

Start Time: _____

Honesty

MESSAGE TITLES

- ❑ Honest to God?
- ❑ Simple Truth Telling
- ❑ Telling the Truth
- ❑ Truth or Consequences
- ❑ *Ninth Commandment:* Refuse to Lie
- ❑ *28 Days of Truth Telling:* Telling the Truth All the Time

_____

_____

_____

DRAMAS

Title	Tone	Characters	Topics
All Gummed Up	Serious	1 male, 1 female, 1 offstage male voice	Adultery; Dealing with past hurts; The pain of lies
Heroic Delusion	Humorous	2 males, 1 female	Self-delusion
Improving Your Lie	Humorous	1 male, 1 female	Truth telling; Marriage
Mr. P. Nocchio	Humorous	2 males or 1 male, 1 female	Honesty

SONGS

*No songs specifically on honesty. Try looking at **Authenticity** or **Truth Telling**.*

Title	Artist	Style	Tempo	Seeker-Sensitivity Rating

Worship Choruses

Title	Artist	Style	Tempo	Seeker-Sensitivity Rating

MOVIE CLIPS

Title: _____

Topic: _____

Description: _____

Start Time: _____

Start Cue: _____

End Time: _____

End Cue: _____

Comments: _____

Purity

See also: **Sex**

MESSAGE TITLES

- ❏ Christians in a Sex-Crazed Culture
- ❏ Defining Our Code of Conduct
- ❏ How to "Affair Proof" Your Marriage
- ❏ Looking, Lusting, or Loving?
- ❏ The Payoff for Sexual Purity
- ❏ The Pornography Problem
- ❏ What Causes Affairs?
- ❏ *Truths That Transform:* Think Excellent Thoughts

DRAMAS

Title	Tone	Characters	Topics
The Big Sell	Humorous	3 males, 2 females	Obsession with sex in society; Effect of the media
It's Only a Movie	Humorous	2 males, 2 females, 1 offstage voice	Power of media; Effects of what we see; Male/female differences
Just Looking	Mixed, light	1 male, 1 female	Eye causing you to stumble; Purity of thoughts

SONGS

Title	Artist	Style	Tempo	Seeker-Sensitivity Rating
Blind Side	Susan Ashton	Folk rock	Up	9
I Am the Man	*Greg Ferguson*	*Piano ballad*	*Slow*	*8*

Title	Artist	Style	Tempo	Seeker-Sensitivity Rating
I Stand, I Fall	*Greg Ferguson*	*Piano ballad*	*Slow*	*7*
Keep My Mind	Margaret Becker	Pop/rock	Up	8
Man of God	*Greg Ferguson*	*Pop/rock*	*Mid/up*	*7*
Miracle of Mercy	Steven Curtis Chapman	Acoustic ballad	Slow	4
Stranger to Holiness	Steve Camp	Ballad	Slow/mid	2
There Is a Line	Susan Ashton	Folk pop	Mid	6
Walk On By	Susan Ashton	Folk pop	Mid/up	8
_____	_____	_____	_____	_____
_____	_____	_____	_____	_____
_____	_____	_____	_____	_____

Worship Choruses

Title	Artist	Style	Tempo	Seeker-Sensitivity Rating
Create in Me	*Willow Creek Music*	*Ballad*	*Slow*	*3*
I Will Never Be	Hillsongs	Worship ballad	Slow/mid	3
My Jesus, I Love You	*Willow Creek Music*	*Worship ballad*	*Slow*	*3*
A Pure Heart	Rusty Nelson	Worship ballad	Slow	4
_____	_____	_____	_____	_____
_____	_____	_____	_____	_____
_____	_____	_____	_____	_____

MOVIE CLIPS

Title: _____

Topic: _____

Description: _____

Start Time: _____

Start Cue: _____

End Time: _____

End Cue: _____

Comments: _____

_____

Self-Control

Refers to being able to control your actions and words—can deal with finances, gossip, physical health, sexuality, etc.

MESSAGE TITLES

❑ *Rare and Remarkable Virtues:* Self-Control
❑ **The Secret of Self-Control:** Your Body • Your Money • Your Passions

DRAMAS

Title	Tone	Characters	Topics
Catalog-itis	Humorous	1 male, 1 female, 2 junior high girls	Self-control; Contentment
Check Mates	Humorous	1 male, 1 female	Personal finances; Debt
Confessions of an Ad-aholic	Humorous	1 male, 1 female	Materialism; Power of the media; American dream
Donuts and Deadbeats	Humorous	1 male, 1 female	Self-control; Physical health
The Killing Spree	Humorous	1 male, 3 females	Sixth commandment; Murder; Gossip
Oh, What a Feeling!	Humorous	2 males, 1 female	Decision making; Self-control; Money management

SONGS

Title	Artist	Style	Tempo	Seeker-Sensitivity Rating
Behind Every Fantasy	*Willow Creek Music*	*Country pop*	*Up*	*10*
There Is a Line	Susan Ashton	Folk pop	Mid	6

Title	Artist	Style	Tempo	Seeker-Sensitivity Rating
Walk On By	Susan Ashton	Folk pop	Mid/up	8
Whatever You Ask	Steve Camp	Power ballad	Slow	5
_____	_____	_____	_____	____
_____	_____	_____	_____	____
_____	_____	_____	_____	____
_____	_____	_____	_____	____

Worship Choruses

Title	Artist	Style	Tempo	Seeker-Sensitivity Rating
I Will Never Be	Hillsongs	Worship ballad	Slow/mid	3
A Pure Heart	Rusty Nelson	Worship ballad	Slow	4
_____	_____	_____	_____	____
_____	_____	_____	_____	____
_____	_____	_____	_____	____

MOVIE CLIPS

Title: _____

Topic: _____

Description: _____

Start Time: _____

Start Cue: _____

End Time: _____

End Cue: _____

Comments: _____

_____

_____

—Christian Life, General—

MESSAGE TITLES

- ❑ **Becoming a Contagious Christian:** Authenticity • Compassion • Sacrifice
- ❑ **Building Bigger Hearts:** Energy Management • Relationship Management • Soul Management
- ❑ **Capturing the Heart of Christianity:** How to Become a Christian • How a Christian Relates to God • Discovering Community • A Day in the Life of a Christian • A Night in the Life of a Christian
- ❑ **Endangered Character Qualities:** Courage • Discipline • Endurance • Vision
- ❑ **Life's Defining Moments:** Defining Our Beliefs • Defining Our Code of Conduct • Defining Our Personal Aspirations
- ❑ **Rare and Remarkable Virtues:** Confidence • Contentment • Patience • Self-Control

DRAMAS

Title	Tone	Characters	Topics
A Day in the Life	Humorous	5 males	Christians in the marketplace; New Christian
First-Day Jitters	Humorous	1 female	New Christian; Obeying God
Impressions, Inc.	Humorous	2 males, 1 female	Skin-deep Christianity
"It"	Humorous	2 males, 1 female	Becoming a Christian doesn't mean no problems; Vulnerability of new believers
The Mystery of Robert Richardson	Mixed	3 males, 2 females, 1 narrator	Living the Christian life
A Problem of Perception	Humorous	3 males, 1 female	Misconceptions about Christianity; Christian life
Seeing Is Believing	Humorous	1 male, 1 female, 1 narrator	A Savior you can trust; Easy faith
Welcome to the Family	Humorous	2 males, 1 female	New Christian; Growing in Christ

SONGS

Title	Artist	Style	Tempo	Seeker-Sensitivity Rating
Ever Devoted	*Willow Creek Music*	*Ballad*	*Slow*	6
From the Heart	**Scott Krippayne**	**Pop/rock**	**Up/mid**	7
Give Me Jesus	**Willow Creek Music**	**Ballad**	**Slow**	7
No Better Place	Steven Curtis Chapman	Pop/folk rock	Up	7
When You Are a Soldier	Steven Curtis Chapman	Keyboard ballad	Slow/mid	4

Worship Choruses

Title	Artist	Style	Tempo	Seeker-Sensitivity Rating
Everyone Arise	Tommy Walker	Pop/rock	Up	3

MOVIE CLIPS

Title: Chariots of Fire

Topic: Christian life; Endurance

Description: Eric Liddell gives a sermonette about running the race of faith.

Start Time: 0:25:35

Start Cue: "You came to see a race today."

End Time: 0:27:20

End Cue: "That is how you run a straight race."

Comments: _____

_____

_____

Title: _____

Topic: _____

Description: _____

Start Time: _____

Start Cue: _____

End Time: _____

End Cue: _____

Comments: _____

_____

_____

_____

Title: _____

Topic: _____

Description: _____

Start Time: _____

Start Cue: _____

End Time: _____

End Cue: _____

Comments: _____

_____

_____

_____

The Church

Can refer to the biblical model for the church as well as issues within the church or between churches.

Might also include: *Denominational Differences*

See also: **Community**

MESSAGE TITLES

- ❑ Loving Sundays
- ❑ The Soul of Willow Creek (insert your church's name)
- ❑ What Catholics Can Learn from Protestants
- ❑ What Protestants Can Learn from Catholics
- ❑ *Changing Times*: The Changing American Church
- ❑ *Life at Its Best*: The Church at Its Best
- ❑ **From the Beginning:** Reach Your Friends • Unleash the Arts • Serve Each Other • Become Fully Devoted Followers • Invest in the Next Generation
- ❑ **The Story of Seven Churches (Rev. 2–3):** The Heartless Church • The Tested Church • The Compromising Church • The Church of the Open Door • The Lukewarm Church

_____

_____

_____

DRAMAS

Title	Tone	Characters	Topics
Differences	Humorous	2 males, 1 female	Catholicism vs. Protestantism
Maybe Someday	Mixed, mostly serious	2 males	Evangelism; Success that leaves us empty; Going back to church
On the Outside	Serious	1 male or female	Being salt and light; Negative church experiences
Pastor General	Humorous	2 males, 2 females	Leadership; Church life; Serving others
Pastor General: Evaluation Time	Humorous	4 males, 2 females	Authoritarian leadership; How not to do program evaluations; Church programming/worship teams
Pastor General: Resource Allocation	Humorous	4 males, 2 females	Providing for volunteers; Bad leadership styles

Title	Tone	Characters	Topics
Pulpit Talk	Humorous	3 males, 2 females	Stereotypical church experiences; Sermons; Introduction to Sermon on the Mount
Truthful Words	Serious	1 male, 1 female	Leadership; Pride; Truth telling

 S O N G S

Title	Artist	Style	Tempo	Seeker-Sensitivity Rating
At the Foot of the Cross	*Willow Creek Music*	*Pop*	*Mid*	*7*
Bridge between Two Hearts	Bob Carlisle	Pop	Up	9
Holy Flame	Ken Medema	Gospel shuffle	Mid	3
Leave a Light On	*Greg Ferguson*	*Ethereal pop ballad*	*Slow/mid*	*8*
Let's Stand Together	The Kry	Rock	Mid/up	1
Revive Us	Anointed	R & B/gospel	Up	3
Undivided	First Call	Ballad trio	Slow	5

Worship Choruses

Title	Artist	Style	Tempo	Seeker-Sensitivity Rating
Build Your Church into My Heart	*Greg Ferguson/Willow Creek Music*	*Pop*	*Up*	*2*
How Good and Pleasant	Tommy Walker	Pop/rock	Up	5
I Do Believe	*Willow Creek Music*	*Pop*	*Up*	*3*
Let the Walls Fall Down	Student Impact	Pop worship	Up	6
Shout to the North	Student Impact	Rock, in 3	Up	4
You Have Been Given	Willow Creek Music	Worship ballad, in 3	Slow	3

Title	Artist	Style	Tempo	Seeker-Sensitivity Rating

MOVIE CLIPS

Title: Sister Act

Topic: The church; Reasons people don't go to church

Description: Humorous clip of a boring preacher and a horrible choir, illustrating a couple of reasons why people don't go to church.

Start Time: 0:30:25

Start Cue: "We are a small congregation this morning. . . ."

End Time: 0:32:25

End Cue: Whoopi Goldberg winces.

Comments: _____

_____

_____

Title: _____

Topic: _____

Description: _____

Start Time: _____

Start Cue: _____

End Time: _____

End Cue: _____

Comments: _____

_____

_____

Evangelism

Primarily intended for a Christian audience, this refers to the importance of evangelism.

For evangelistic ideas, see: **Baptism, Grace, Salvation**.

Package Suggestion

Song:
Dear God

Drama:
Maybe Someday

Song:
Leave a Light On

MESSAGE TITLES

❏ Becoming a Contagious Christian
❏ People Matter to God
❏ **Adventures in Personal Evangelism:** The Motivations for Evangelism
  • The Mind-Set of an Evangelist • The Message of an Evangelist • The Style of an Evangelist
❏ **Stronger Salt, Brighter Light:** Assessing Your Savor Factor • Increasing Your Candle Power • Impacting the Irreligious • Discovering Your Evangelism Style • Communicating the Message of Hope • Enfolding New Believers • Coping with Questions

DRAMAS

Title	Tone	Characters	Topics
The Lane of Life	Serious; Mime	5 either males or females, 1 offstage narrator	Salvation; Our value to God; Self-esteem
Life Cycle	Humorous	2 females	Evangelism
A Little Charity	Humorous	2 males, 3 females	Evangelism; Christian character
Maybe Someday	Mixed, mostly serious	2 males	Evangelism; Success that leaves us empty; Going back to church
Parents on the Sidelines	Humorous	2 males, 2 females	Evangelism
Reason Enough	Mixed, mostly serious	1 male, 1 female	Importance of faith grounded in reason
Trying Time	Serious	1 male, 2 females	Marriage; Spiritual mismatch
Wait 'Til Half-Time	Mixed	1 male, 1 female	Eternity; Heaven and hell; Evangelism

SONGS

Title	Artist	Style	Tempo	Seeker-Sensitivity Rating
Dear God	**Midge Ure**	**Rock**	**Mid/up**	10
For Who He Really Is	Steven Curtis Chapman	Folk pop ballad	Mid/slow	1
Leave a Light On	*Greg Ferguson*	*Ethereal pop ballad*	*Slow/mid*	8

Worship Choruses

Title	Artist	Style	Tempo	Seeker-Sensitivity Rating
As We Worship You	Tommy Walker	Worship ballad	Slow	1
Everyday	Student Impact/Sonlight Band	Rock worship	Up	6
Everyone Arise	Tommy Walker	Pop/rock	Up	3
You Mean the World to Me	*Willow Creek Music*	*Worship ballad*	*Slow/mid*	2

MOVIE CLIPS

*See the *Becoming a Contagious Christian* evangelism training course, available through Willow Creek Resources, for several good video clips illustrating various evangelistic styles.

Title: _____

Topic: _____

Description: _____

Start Time: _____

Start Cue: _____

End Time: _____

End Cue: _____

Comments: _____

_____

Gossip/Slander

See also: **Relational Conflict, Self-Control**

MESSAGE TITLES

- ❏ *Sixth Commandment:* Respect Human Life
- ❏ *What Jesus Would Say to . . .* Rush Limbaugh

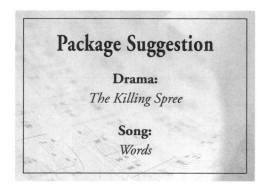

Package Suggestion

Drama:
The Killing Spree

Song:
Words

DRAMAS

Title	Tone	Characters	Topics
The Killing Spree	Humorous	1 male, 3 females	Sixth Commandment; Murder; Gossip

SONGS

Title	Artist	Style	Tempo	Seeker-Sensitivity Rating
Words	Kim Hill	Pop/rock	Up	10

Worship Choruses

Title	Artist	Style	Tempo	Seeker-Sensitivity Rating

MOVIE CLIPS

Title: _____

Topic: _____

Description: _____

Start Time: _____

Start Cue: _____

End Time: _____

End Cue: _____

Comments: _____

_____

_____

Hypocrisy

See also: **Authenticity**

MESSAGE TITLES

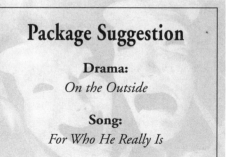

Package Suggestion

Drama:
On the Outside

Song:
For Who He Really Is

❏ Watch Out for Wolves
❏ *Private Conversations:* Jesus Talks to a Religious Person
❏ **Religion Run Amok:** How Good Groups Go Bad • How Good
Christians Go Bad • How (Name of Your Church) Could Go Bad

_____

_____

_____

_____

DRAMAS

Title	Tone	Characters	Topics
Here to Help	Mixed	6 females	Helping those less fortunate; Not giving up; Dealing with difficult people
Impressions, Inc.	Humorous	2 males, 1 female	Skin-deep Christianity
A Little Charity	Humorous	2 males, 3 females	Evangelism; Christian character
On the Outside	Serious	1 male or female	Being salt and light; Negative church experiences
Reason Enough	Mixed, mostly serious	1 male, 1 female	Importance of faith grounded in reason
A Visitor	Serious	2 males, 1 female	Wolves in sheep's clothing; Discernment; Spiritual manipulation

SONGS

Title	Artist	Style	Tempo	Seeker-Sensitivity Rating
Casual Christian	**DeGarmo & Key**	**Power ballad**	**Slow**	**6**
For Who He Really Is	Steven Curtis Chapman	Folk pop ballad	Mid/slow	1
From the Heart	**Scott Krippayne**	**Pop/rock**	**Up/mid**	**7**
No More Pretending	**Scott Krippayne**	**Pop ballad**	**Slow**	**7**
Would I Know You?	Wayne Watson	Ballad	Slow	3
_____	_____	_____	_____	_____
_____	_____	_____	_____	_____
_____	_____	_____	_____	_____
_____	_____	_____	_____	_____

Worship Choruses

Title	Artist	Style	Tempo	Seeker-Sensitivity Rating
Heart of Worship	Matt Redman	Worship ballad	Slow	2
_____	_____	_____	_____	_____
_____	_____	_____	_____	_____
_____	_____	_____	_____	_____

MOVIE CLIPS

Title: _____

Topic: _____

Description: _____

Start Time: _____

Start Cue: _____

End Time: _____

End Cue: _____

Comments: _____

_____

The Joy of the Christian Life

Many seekers have the misconception that Christianity is boring or stifling. This topic addresses that misconception.

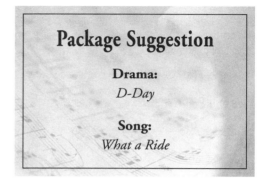

Package Suggestion

Drama:
D-Day

Song:
What a Ride

MESSAGE TITLES

- ❑ The Adventure of Christianity
- ❑ The Benefits of Knowing God
- ❑ The Joy of Christianity
- ❑ *Christianity's Toughest Competition:* Adventurism
- ❑ *A Taste of Christianity:* A Better Kind of Freedom
- ❑ *Three Things God Loves (That Most People Think He Doesn't):* Laughter
- ❑ *Truths That Transform:* Rejoice!
- ❑ *Yeah God:* For Being Joyful

DRAMAS

Title	Tone	Characters	Topics
D-Day	Humorous	2 males, 1 female	Misconceptions about Christianity; Becoming a Christian
The Lures of Life	Mixed, light; Mime	5 males, 1 female	Adventurism; Life fulfillment
Monday Night Meeting	Humorous	4 males	New Christian; Joy of Christian life; Discipleship

SONGS

Title	Artist	Style	Tempo	Seeker-Sensitivity Rating
Change in My Life	John Pagano	Gospel	Mid/up	9
Ever Devoted	*Willow Creek Music*	*Ballad*	*Slow*	6
The Great Adventure	Steven Curtis Chapman	Pop/rock	Up	5
How Could I Ask for More?	Cindy Morgan	Piano ballad	Slow	9
Live Out Loud	Steven Curtis Chapman	Pop	Up	9
No Better Place	Steven Curtis Chapman	Pop/folk rock	Up	7
Smellin' Coffee	Chris Rice	Pop/rock	Up	8
Treasure	**Gary Chapman**	**Acoustic ballad**	**Slow**	**9**
What a Ride	*Willow Creek Music*	*Pop/rock*	*Up*	9

Worship Choruses

Title	Artist	Style	Tempo	Seeker-Sensitivity Rating
Amen	Tommy Walker	Worship shuffle	Up	5
And That My Soul Knows Very Well	Hillsongs	Worship ballad	Slow	5
Better Than	Vineyard	Pop/rock worship	Up	6
Everyone Arise	Tommy Walker	Pop/rock	Up	3
Happy Song	Delirious	Country Rockabilly	Up	5
Joy, Joy, Joy	Tommy Walker	Rock shuffle	Up	5
Mourning into Dancing	Tommy Walker	Pop	Up	5

MOVIE CLIPS

Title: _____

Topic: _____

Description: _____

Start Time: _____

Start Cue: _____

End Time: _____

End Cue: _____

Comments: _____

_____

_____

Servanthood

Refers to serving others and having the attitude and heart of a servant

Might also include: *Self-Sacrifice*

See also: **Compassion, Selfishness/Pride**

MESSAGE TITLES

❑ *Becoming a Contagious Christian:* Sacrifice
❑ *Giving and Receiving Love:* Sacrificial Love
❑ *Truths That Transform:* Look Not to Your Interests Only, but to the Interests of Others As Well
❑ **Serving Lessons:** Exposing the "Me First" Mind-set • Breaking the Back of Self-Centeredness
    • Imagine Everyone Serving • Gifted to Serve • The Servant's Survival Kit • Inspiring Others to Serve
    • Serving through Sharing • The Rewards of Servanthood • My Life, a Living Sacrifice

DRAMAS

Title	Tone	Characters	Topics
Am I Missing Something?	Serious	3 males, 2 females	Attitudes in serving; Giving; Self-deception; Rationalizing
The Boy Who Never Got Dirty	Humorous	1 male, 1 female, 1 narrator	Service; Risk taking
Full-Service Stations and Other Myths	Humorous	1 male, 1 female	Servanthood
Good Friday 1991, Scene I	Serious	Jesus character, 12 disciples, 2 females	Good Friday; Serving others
The Legacy	Touching	1 male, 2 females	Heroes; Character; Christians at work; Serving others; Making a difference
Mr. Hibbs' Day Off	Mixed; Mime	3 males, 1 female, 1 child	Serving others; Self-denial; Being used by God
Parlor Talk	Mixed	3 males, 2 females	Making a difference with your life; Death; Workaholism
Pastor General	Humorous	2 males, 2 females	Leadership; Church life; Serving others

Title	Tone	Characters	Topics
The Story of Rachel	Serious	3 females	Care for the poor; Compassion
Suit and Volly	Humorous	2 males, 2 females	Motives in serving others
The Warrior	Mixed, light	1 female	Prayer; Taking God with you throughout the day

SONGS

Title	Artist	Style	Tempo	Seeker-Sensitivity Rating
Giving Thing	**Truth**	**Pop**	**Mid/up**	**8**
Helping Hand	Amy Grant	Pop	Mid/up	10

Worship Choruses

Title	Artist	Style	Tempo	Seeker-Sensitivity Rating
How Could I But Love You?	Tommy Walker	Worship ballad	Slow	3
I Surrender All	None	Worship ballad	Slow	4
Your Love for Me	Integrity Songwriters	Pop worship	Up	4

MOVIE CLIPS

Title: Mr. Holland's Opus

Topic: Heroes; Honoring people; The fruit of serving others

Description: Mr. Holland, a music teacher whose discontinued program has caused him to retire early, goes to a noisy gym to see what the commotion is. He walks into a celebration in his honor, where he is thanked for the difference he has made in countless lives.

Start Time: 2:06:07

Start Cue: "Now what is that?" Mr. Holland walks toward the gym.

End Time: 2:11:23

End Cue: Close-up of the speaker, Ms. Lang, followed by a close-up of Mr. Holland.

Comments: A bit long, but a great illustration of a well-spent life. This can also be used as a bookend to the other "Mr. Holland" clip listed on page 30, as the speaker is the girl Mr. Holland inspired in the earlier clip. She has now become governor of the state.

_____
_____
_____

Title: _____

Topic: _____

Description: _____

Start Time: _____

Start Cue: _____

End Time: _____

End Cue: _____

Comments: _____

_____

Serving God

Refers to what you do with your gifts to serve God, most likely in the church

Might also include: *Spiritual Gifts*

See also: **Commitment to Christ**

Package Suggestions

Drama:
Suit and Volly

Song:
Audience of One

MESSAGE TITLES

❏ Redefining Commitment
❏ *Discovering the Way God Wired You Up:* Spiritually
❏ *Seven Wonders of the Spiritual World:* God Uses Me
❏ **Values Vital to Our Future:** The Gift of Leadership • The Gift of Evangelism • The Gift of Giving • The Gift of Helps • The Gifts of Exhortation and Mercy • The Gifts of Shepherding and Hospitality

DRAMAS

Title	Tone	Characters	Topics
Call of the Wild	Mixed	1 male, 1 female	Serving God; Serving in a place consistent with your gifts and temperament
Clearing Things Up	Humorous	5 males or females	Balancing life; Priorities
Lifeline	Mixed, touching	1 male, 2 females, 1 small child (no lines)	Serving the church; Life in community; Aging
Pastor General: Resource Allocation	Humorous	4 males, 2 females	Providing for volunteers; Bad leadership styles
Somebody's Got to Do It	Humorous	1 male, 1 female	Spiritual gifts; Serving God
Suit and Volly	Humorous	2 males, 2 females	Motives in serving others
Tired When Needed	Humorous	1 male, 1 female	Burnout; Boundaries; Saying no

SONGS

Title	Artist	Style	Tempo	Seeker-Sensitivity Rating
Audience of One	*Willow Creek Music*	*Power ballad*	*Slow*	*8*
We Can Make a Difference	Jaci Velasquez	Pop	Up	8
Whatever	Steven Curtis Chapman	Rock/pop	Up	8
Whatever You Ask	Steve Camp	Power ballad	Slow	5

Worship Choruses

Title	Artist	Style	Tempo	Seeker-Sensitivity Rating
Everything I Am	*Willow Creek Music*	*Pop/rock*	*Up*	*7*
How Could I But Love You?	Tommy Walker	Worship ballad	Slow	3
I Surrender All	None	Worship ballad	Slow	4
Potter's Hand	Hillsongs	Worship ballad	Slow/mid	3
Spirit of the Living God	NA	Traditional worship song	Slow	4
Take My Life and Let It Be	Paul Baloche	Worship ballad	Mid/slow	3
Your Love for Me	Integrity Songwriters	Pop worship	Up	4

MOVIE CLIPS

Title: Mr. Holland's Opus

Topic: Heroes; Honoring people; The fruit of serving others

Description: Mr. Holland, a music teacher whose discontinued program has caused him to retire early, goes to a noisy gym to see what the commotion is. He walks into a celebration in his honor, where he is thanked for the difference he has made in countless lives.

Start Time: 2:06:07

Start Cue: "Now what is that?" Mr. Holland walks toward the gym.

End Time: 2:11:23

End Cue: Close-up of the speaker, Ms. Lang, followed by a close-up of Mr. Holland.

Comments: A bit long but a great illustration of a well-spent life. This can also be used as a bookend to the other "Mr. Holland" clip listed on page 30, as the speaker is the girl Mr. Holland inspired in the earlier clip. She has now become governor of the state.

_____

_____

_____

Title: Sister Act

Topic: Spiritual gifts; Celebrating uniqueness

Description: Sister Mary Robert confides in Sister Mary Clarence that she wants to give something that's "only me, and nobody else."

Start Time: 0:38:40

Start Cue: After "Have a seat"; Mary Robert sits down.

End Time: 0:40:05

End Cue: "Good night, Mary Robert."

Comments: _____

_____

_____

Title: The Prince of Egypt

Topic: God's power; God's calling on our lives

Description: This film is an animated telling of the story of Moses. This scene shows God's call to Moses through the burning bush.

Start Time: 0:42:50

Start Cue: Lost sheep bleats; Moses goes after him.

End Time: 0:47:50

End Cue: Moses is standing with his staff next to the bush (now not burning).

Comments: Can be used as an illustration much the way the biblical passage itself would be used.

_____

_____

_____

Title: _____

Topic: _____

Description: _____

Start Time: _____

Start Cue: _____

End Time: _____

End Cue: _____

Comments: _____
_____
_____
_____

Title: _____

Topic: _____

Description: _____

Start Time: _____

Start Cue: _____

End Time: _____

End Cue: _____

Comments: _____
_____
_____
_____

Tithing

See also: **Money Management**

MESSAGE TITLES

❏ *Financial Freedom:* Giving Money
❏ *Living Excellent Lives:* Financially
❏ *Making Sense Out of Money:* Giving
❏ *Making Sense Out of Money:* Leveraging Your Money for Eternity
❏ *Your Money Matters:* Discovering the Rewards of Giving

DRAMAS

Title	Tone	Characters	Topics
Am I Missing Something?	Serious	3 males, 2 females	Attitudes in serving; Giving; Self-deception; Rationalizing
Heart Failure	Humorous	1 male	Giving
The Offering	Humorous	3 males, 1 female	Tithing

SONGS

*No songs specifically on tithing. Try looking at **Commitment to Christ, Discipleship, Materialism,** and **Thanksgiving.***

Title	Artist	Style	Tempo	Seeker-Sensitivity Rating

Worship Choruses

Title	Artist	Style	Tempo	Seeker-Sensitivity Rating
Everything I Am	*Willow Creek Music*	*Pop/rock*	*Up*	*7*
I Surrender All	None	Worship ballad	Slow	4
More Precious Than Silver	Don Moen	Worship ballad	Slow	5
Take My Life and Let It Be	Paul Baloche	Worship ballad	Mid/slow	3
_____	_____	_____	_____	___
_____	_____	_____	_____	___
_____	_____	_____	_____	___

 # MOVIE CLIPS

Title: _____

Topic: _____

Description: _____

Start Time: _____

Start Cue: _____

End Time: _____

End Cue: _____

Comments: _____

Holidays/Special Services

Baptism

See also: **Changed Life, New Christians, Salvation**

MESSAGE TITLES

_____

_____

_____

DRAMAS

Title	Tone	Characters	Topics
The Book of Life	Energetic mime; Mixed	3 males, 3 females	Baptism; Faith; Basic Christianity; Eternal life
A Clean Slate	Serious	1 male, 2 or 3 males or females	Forgiveness; Redemption; Guilt
The Lane of Life	Serious; Mime	5 either males or females, 1 offstage narrator	Salvation; Our value to God; Self-esteem
Measuring Up	Mixed; Mime	2 males, 1 female, 1 either male or female	God's acceptance of us; Self-esteem
Milestones	Mixed	1 male	Baptism; New Christian
Sitters, Strivers, Standers, and Saints	Mixed	4 either males or females, 1 narrator	God changing lives; God completing us
The Stickholders	Serious	3 males, 1 female, 1 narrator	Relationship with God; Freedom from rules
"X" Marks the Spot	Serious; Mime	1 male, 1 female, 3 either males or females	Sin; Redemption; Forgiveness; Guilt

SONGS

Title	Artist	Style	Tempo	Seeker-Sensitivity Rating
Cross Medley	*Willow Creek Music*	*Ballad medley—hymns*	*Slow*	*7*
From This Moment On	Newsong	Ballad	Slow	8
Give Me Jesus	**Willow Creek Music**	**Ballad**	**Slow**	**7**
I'm Amazed	*Willow Creek Music*	*Ballad*	*Slow*	*7*
My Life Is Yours	*Willow Creek Music*	*Acoustic ballad*	*Slow*	*10*
What a Good God	**Tommy Walker**	**Worship ballad**	**Slow**	**7**
Who Am I? (Grace Flows Down)	**Watermark**	**Folk pop**	**Mid/slow**	**8**

Worship Choruses

Title	Artist	Style	Tempo	Seeker-Sensitivity Rating
Jesus You're the Answer	Tommy Walker	Soulish worship ballad	Slow	5
Thank You for Saving Me	Delirious	Folk rock worship ballad	Slow/mid	3
Thank You, Lord	Hillsongs	Worship ballad, in 3	Mid	3
What a Good God You've Been	Tommy Walker	Worship ballad	Slow	7
With Our Hearts	Lenny LeBlanc	Pop worship, in 3	Mid/up	3
You Are My King	Passion	Worship ballad	Slow	4

MOVIE CLIPS

Title: _____

Topic: _____

Description: _____

Start Time: _____

Start Cue: _____

End Time: _____

End Cue: _____

Comments: _____

_____

_____

Christmas

MESSAGE TITLES

- ❏ The Aftermath of Christmas
- ❏ Christmas Is More Than Jesus' Birth
- ❏ Christmas of Another Kind
- ❏ The Christmas Story
- ❏ On the Outside Looking In
- ❏ Out of the Ordinary
- ❏ A Promise for Peace
- ❏ Who Is Lying in the Manger?
- ❏ **Getting This Christmas Right:** The Why's of Christmas • The Who in Our Lives
  • How Do You View Gift Giving?

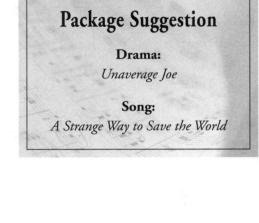

Package Suggestion

Drama:
Unaverage Joe

Song:
A Strange Way to Save the World

DRAMAS

Title	Tone	Characters	Topics
The Best Gift	Humorous, touching	3 males, 4 females	Christmas; Gift giving
Christmas Lite	Serious	3 males (2 teens/preteens), 1 female	Christmas; Faith; Family under stress; Dealing with crisis
Christmas Story	Mixed; End is moving	4 males, 4 females, 12-year-old boy, 10-year-old girl	Christmas; Family
December the 27th		1 male, 1 female	Overcoming regret; Pace of life at Christmas; Finances
Family Snapshots—Take V (Christmas Eve)	Mixed; Touching end	2 males, 2 females, 1 junior high boy	Christmas
Grandma's Recipe	Serious	1 male, 2 females, 2 children	Family struggle during holidays
Little What's His Face	Mixed	3 males, 3 females	Christmas; Parenting

Title	Tone	Characters	Topics
Mistaken Identity	Mixed	3 males, 2 females, 1 young girl	Christmas; Doubting
Self-list Giving	Mixed	2 males, 2 females	Meeting needs; Expressing value; Expectations; Disappointment
Stolen Jesus	Mixed, touching	2 females	Christmas
Unaverage Joe	Mixed	2 males, 1 female	Christmas; Obeying God's call
Wings	Mixed	2 males, 1 female, 1 teen, 1 preteen	Christmas; Family

SONGS

Title	Artist	Style	Tempo	Seeker-Sensitivity Rating
Away in a Manger	Steven Curtis Chapman	Folk pop	Mid	10
Be Not Afraid	**Bridgeway Community Church**	**Ballad**	**Slow**	**9**
Hark Medley	*Willow Creek Music*	*Christmas carol medley*	*Up*	*10*
He Was	*Willow Creek Music*	*Pop/rock, in 6/8*	*Mid*	*10*
Heirlooms	Amy Grant	Ballad	Slow	8
Holy King	*Willow Creek Music*	*Ballad*	*Slow*	*8*
Mary, Did You Know?	Michael English	Pop ballad	Slow	7
Silent Night/All Is Well	*Willow Creek Music*	*A cappella vocal group ballad*	*Slow*	*10*
A Strange Way to Save the World	4Him	Ballad	Slow	7
Welcome to Our World	**Chris Rice**	**Ballad**	**Slow**	**9**
When Love Came Down	Point of Grace	Pop	Up	10
Wonderful Merciful Savior	**Susan Ashton**	**Acoustic ballad, 6/8 feel**	**Mid/slow**	**9**

Worship Choruses

Title	Artist	Style	Tempo	Seeker-Sensitivity Rating
Jesus, What a Beautiful Name	Hillsongs	Worship ballad, in 6/8	Slow/mid	6

MOVIE CLIPS

Title: A Christmas Story

Topic: Christmas memories

Description: A funny clip showing memories of visiting Santa at the department store.

Start Time: 1:09:35

Start Cue: Elf says, "Quit dragging your feet."

End Time: 1:11:40

End Cue: Ralphie goes down the slide after being pushed by Santa.

Comments: It's hard to understand Ralphie's request to Santa. It may need to be explained to the congregation.

Title: A Christmas Story

Topic: Christmas memories

Description: Christmas is over, and Ralphie hasn't gotten the BB gun he wanted. His dad points out one present he hasn't opened yet—it's the BB gun.

Start Time: 1:20:30

Start Cue: Mom says, "Did you have a nice Christmas?"

End Time: 1:22:43

End Cue: "I had one when I was eight years old."

Comments: _____

Title: _____

Topic: _____

Description: _____

Start Time: _____

Start Cue: _____

End Time: _____

End Cue: _____

Comments: _____

Communion

See also: **Salvation, God's Forgiveness of Us, Grace**

MESSAGE TITLES

_____

_____

_____

_____

DRAMAS

We celebrate Communion during our midweek services, where we rarely use drama.

Title	Tone	Characters	Topics
The Wall	Serious	3 males, 2 females, 1 child	Importance of remembering

SONGS

Title	Artist	Style	Tempo	Seeker-Sensitivity Rating
Cross Medley	*Willow Creek Music*	*Ballad medley—hymns*	*Slow*	*7*
Forgive Me	*Willow Creek Music*	*Ballad*	*Slow*	*3*
Miracle of Mercy	**Steven Curtis Chapman**	**Acoustic ballad**	**Slow**	**4**

Title	Artist	Style	Tempo	Seeker-Sensitivity Rating
Remember Your Chains	Steven Curtis Chapman	Acoustic MOR	Mid	2
What a Good God	**Tommy Walker**	**Worship ballad**	**Slow**	**7**
Who Am I?	Margaret Becker	Power ballad	Slow	7
Why Me?	*Willow Creek Music*	*Ballad*	*Slow*	*9*
_____	_____	_____	_____	_____
_____	_____	_____	_____	_____
_____	_____	_____	_____	_____
_____	_____	_____	_____	_____
_____	_____	_____	_____	_____

Worship Choruses

Title	Artist	Style	Tempo	Seeker-Sensitivity Rating
Above All	Paul Baloche/Lenny LeBlanc	Worship ballad	Slow	5
The Beauty of Holiness	Steve Camp	Worship ballad, in 3	Slow	3
Create in Me	*Willow Creek Music*	*Ballad*	*Slow*	*3*
The Cross Has Said It All	Matt Redman	Worship ballad	Mid/slow	2
Do You Know?	Tommy Walker	Worship ballad	Slow/mid	2
Jesus, Lover of My Soul	Hillsongs	Pop worship	Up	3
Lord, I Lift Your Name on High	Maranatha!/Praise Band	Pop worship	Up	6
My Redeemer Lives	Hillsongs	Pop/rock	Up	3
No Greater Love	Tommy Walker	Pop/rock	Up	6
O for a Thousand Tongues	*Willow Creek Music*	*Contemporary arrangement of hymn*	*Up*	*3*
Power of Your Love	Hillsongs	Worship ballad	Slow	6
Still Amazing	Danny Chambers	Worship ballad	Slow	5
Thank You for Saving Me	Delirious	Folk rock worship ballad	Slow/mid	3
Thank You, Lord	Hillsongs	Worship ballad, in 3	Mid	3
That's Why We Praise Him	Tommy Walker	Rock/pop worship	Mid	5
What a Good God You've Been	Tommy Walker	Worship ballad	Slow	7
What the Lord Has Done	Hillsongs	Worship ballad, in 3	Slow/mid	2
You Are My King	Passion	Worship ballad	Slow	4

Title	Artist	Style	Tempo	Seeker-Sensitivity Rating
_____	_____	_____	_____	_____
_____	_____	_____	_____	_____
_____	_____	_____	_____	_____
_____	_____	_____	_____	_____

MOVIE CLIPS

Title: _____

Topic: _____

Description: _____

Start Time: _____

Start Cue: _____

End Time: _____

End Cue: _____

Comments: _____

_____

_____

Easter

See also: **Jesus, Salvation**

MESSAGE TITLES

❑ Easter Celebration
❑ God's Wake-up Calls
❑ People Matter to God
❑ The Relevance of the Resurrection

> ### Package Suggestion
>
> **Drama:**
> *Happy Easter*
>
> **Song:**
> *Love That Will Not Let Me Go*

DRAMAS

Title	Tone	Characters	Topics
The Centerpiece	Humorous	2 males, 3 females, 2 children	Easter; Denial; Not dealing with reality
Easter Snapshots		Multiple, flexible	Easter; Love vs. selfishness
Happy Easter	Humorous	3 males, 5 females, 1 10-year-old girl	Easter
Holy Week	Humorous	1 male, 2 females, offstage girl's voice	Holy Week; Palm Sunday; Easter; The resurrection
Hunting for Easter	Humorous	2 males, 3 females, 2 preteens	Easter
Lonely at the Top	Serious	1 male	Perils of power; Authority; Easter
The Prisoner	Serious	3 males, 1 female	Easter; Freedom from sin; New Christian
The Stickholders	Serious	3 males, 1 female, 1 narrator	Relationship with God; Freedom from rules
These Parts	Mixed	2 males, 1 female, 3 either males or females, 1 child, 1 narrator	The resurrection; Our need for Christ; Easter

SONGS

Title	Artist	Style	Tempo	Seeker-Sensitivity Rating
He Was	*Willow Creek Music*	*Pop/rock, in 6/8*	*Mid*	*10*
I've Been Released	*Willow Creek Music*	*Pop/rock—Chicago sound*	*Up*	*9*
Love That Will Not Let Me Go	**Steve Camp**	**Ballad**	**Slow**	**10**
Via Dolorosa	Sandi Patti	Inspirational ballad	Slow	7

Worship Choruses

Title	Artist	Style	Tempo	Seeker-Sensitivity Rating
Celebrate Jesus Celebrate	Alleluia Music	Pop	Up	6
My Redeemer Lives	Hillsongs	Pop/rock	Up	3
That's Why We Praise Him	Tommy Walker	Rock/pop worship	Mid	5
What the Lord Has Done	Hillsongs	Worship ballad, in 3	Slow/mid	2

MOVIE CLIPS

Title: _____

Topic: _____

Description: _____

Start Time: _____

Start Cue: _____

End Time: _____

End Cue: _____

Comments: _____

_____

Father's Day

MESSAGE TITLES

- ❏ Dads, Whatever You Do
- ❏ Fathers: An Endangered Species
- ❏ Fathers: Heavenly and Otherwise
- ❏ Fathers I Know Best
- ❏ Gracious Fathers
- ❏ Leaving a Living Legacy
- ❏ Phantom Fathers
- ❏ Rediscovering Discipline
- ❏ The Soft Side of Fathering
- ❏ Understanding Dad's Dilemma
- ❏ Unforgettable Fathers

DRAMAS

Title	Tone	Characters	Topics
Definitely Safe	Serious, heartwarming	2 males, 1 female	Father's Day; Prodigal son; Unconditional love
Fishin'	Mixed, touching	2 males	Expressing positive emotions; Father-son relationships
Giving a Blessing Vignettes	Mixed	2 males	Father's Day; Parenting; Giving blessings
I Always Will	Mixed, very moving	3 males, 3 females	Father's Day, Father-daughter relationships
Lucky Day at the Ballpark	Mixed	2 males, 1 boy	Father's Day; Proper priorities
Misjudged Love	Serious	2 males, 1 female	Homosexuality; AIDS; Father-son relationships
Mixed Signals	Mixed	1 male, 1 boy	Encouragement; Fathers; Priorities
Model Behavior	Humorous	1 male, 3 boys (8-year-old, 12-year-old, and 16-year-old)	Fathering; Shortness of the parenting years

Title	Tone	Characters	Topics
One Day at the Zoo	Humorous	1 narrator, 3 males, 2 females, and some offstage voices	Fatherhood
Out of Control	Humorous	2 males, 1 female	Fatherhood; Parenting
Quality Time	Serious	1 male, 1 female, 2 teenage girls	Fatherhood; Workaholism

SONGS

Title	Artist	Style	Tempo	Seeker-Sensitivity Rating
Because You Loved Me	Celine Dion	Pop ballad	Slow	10
Butterfly Kisses	Bob Carlisle	Pop ballad	Slow	10
Father's Love	Bob Carlisle	Ballad	Slow	8
I Want to Be Just Like You	**Phillips, Craig and Dean**	**MOR**	**Mid/slow**	**9**
If I Had Only Known	Reba McEntire	Ballad	Slow	10
The Last Song	Elton John	Ballad	Slow	10
The Living Years	Mike & the Mechanics	Pop	Mid/up	10
Man of God	*Greg Ferguson*	*Pop/rock*	*Mid/up*	*7*
The Measure of a Man	**4Him**	**Pop**	**Up**	**6**
Nothing You Could Do	*Willow Creek Music*	*Ballad*	*Slow*	*10*

Worship Choruses

*See also **God as Father.**

Title	Artist	Style	Tempo	Seeker-Sensitivity Rating
The Lord's Prayer	*Willow Creek Music*	*U2-ish rock/pop*	*Up*	*9*

MOVIE CLIPS

Title: 8 Seconds

Topic: Regret; Communicating love

Description: A father, whose son has recently died in a rodeo accident, breaks down in remorse over not telling his son that he loved him. This short clip probably needs to be set up.

Start Time: 1:27:22

Start Cue: Pallbearers carry the casket out of the church.

End Time: 1:28:44

End Cue: The mother puts her hands on the father's shoulders.

Comments: _____

_____

_____

_____

Title: Dad

Topic: Parenting; Father-son relationship

Description: Ted Danson and Jack Lemmon play a father and son. Lemmon is dying in a hospital bed, and they have a very poignant exchange, ending with Danson crawling into bed with his dad.

Start Time: 1:46:20

Start Cue: "How you feeling?"

End Time: 1:50:35

End Cue: "I must have done something right." End after wide shot.

Comments: _____

_____

_____

_____

Title: Father of the Bride

Topic: Parenthood; Father-daughter relationships

Description: Steve Martin's character plays basketball with his daughter as "My Girl" plays in the background. Shows the warmth and fun of their relationship.

Start Time: 0:14:55

Start Cue: "Suppose you're not in the mood for a little one-on-one?"

End Time: 0:17:00

End Cue: Steve Martin's character and his daughter walk off together.

Comments: _____
_____
_____
_____

Title: Indiana Jones and the Last Crusade

Topic: Father-son relationships

Description: Indiana Jones mildly confronts his father about the lack of a relationship between them.

Start Time: 1:13:45

Start Cue: "Remember the last time we had a quiet drink?"

End Time: 1:15:05

End Cue: "I can't think of anything."

Comments: Conversation is over a drink. May be offensive to some churches.
_____
_____
_____

Title: October Sky

Topic: Parent-child relationships; Father-son relationships

Description: Homer Hikam, a young aspiring rocket scientist comes to his dad's coal mine to talk to him. His dad makes a sarcastic comment about Homer meeting his "hero," Dr. Wernher von Braun. Homer speaks inspiring words to his dad about the man he is and, without saying the words, lets his dad know that he is Homer's real hero.

Start Time: 1:33:00

Start Cue: "Will you let me out?" Homer runs to meet his dad.

End Time: 1:35:08

End Cue: Homer's dad turns his mining light on as he watches Homer walk away.

Comments: Can be ended sooner than the end cue listed above. It can also be extended to show Homer's rocket launch, for which his dad unexpectedly shows up.
_____
_____
_____
_____

Title: Parenthood

Topic: Parenting; Absent fathers

Description: Funny, bittersweet scene where young Gil is taken to a baseball game by his father and then left with an usher. We find out it's actually a combination of memories of his strained childhood.

Start Time: 0:00:05

Start Cue: Start at fade-in. This is the opening scene.

End Time: 0:02:28

End Cue: "Strong, happy, confident kids."

Comments: Profanity immediately follows cutoff point.

_____
_____
_____
_____

Title: Searching for Bobby Fischer

Topic: Fatherhood; Failure; Destructive parenting

Description: Eight-year-old Josh loses a chess match, and his dad angrily confronts him about losing. Illustrates a dad who has too much invested in his son's success.

Start Time: 1:06:30

Start Cue: Shot of clock tower. "Seven moves" is first line.

End Time: 1:08:20

End Cue: "Sorry."

Comments: _____
_____
_____
_____
_____

Title: _____

Topic: _____

Description: _____

Start Time: _____

Start Cue: _____

End Time: _____

End Cue: _____

Comments: _____
_____
_____
_____
_____

Good Friday

MESSAGE TITLES

_____

_____

DRAMAS

Title	Tone	Characters	Topics
Adulterous Woman/Soldier at the Cross	Serious	1 female and/or 1 male	Good Friday
Good Friday 1990	Serious	2 males, 1 female	Good Friday
Good Friday 1991, Scene I	Serious	Jesus character, 12 disciples, 2 females	Good Friday; Serving others
Good Friday 1991, Scene II	Serious	Jesus character, 12 disciples, 2 females	Good Friday
Good Friday Medley	Serious	1 male, 4 females (though some roles are interchangeable)	Good Friday; How we view Jesus
Lonely at the Top	Serious	1 male	Perils of power; Authority; Easter
_____	_____	_____	_____
_____	_____	_____	_____
_____	_____	_____	_____

SONGS

Title	Artist	Style	Tempo	Seeker-Sensitivity Rating
Via Dolorosa	Sandi Patti	Inspirational ballad	Slow	7
What I Wouldn't Give	_Willow Creek Music_	_Acoustic ballad_	_Slow_	_10_
Where Would I Be Now?	_Willow Creek Music_	_Ballad, Broadway feel_	_Slow_	_6_
Why Me?	_Willow Creek Music_	_Ballad_	_Slow_	_9_

Title	Artist	Style	Tempo	Seeker-Sensitivity Rating
_____	_____	_____	_____	_____
_____	_____	_____	_____	_____
_____	_____	_____	_____	_____
_____	_____	_____	_____	_____

Worship Choruses

Title	Artist	Style	Tempo	Seeker-Sensitivity Rating
Above All	Paul Baloche/Lenny LeBlanc	Worship ballad	Slow	5
The Cross Has Said It All	Matt Redman	Worship ballad	Mid/slow	2
Do You Know?	Tommy Walker	Worship ballad	Slow/mid	2
When I Survey the Wondrous Cross	NA	Updated traditional	Slow	3
You Are My King	Passion	Worship ballad	Slow	4
_____	_____	_____	_____	_____
_____	_____	_____	_____	_____
_____	_____	_____	_____	_____
_____	_____	_____	_____	_____

MOVIE CLIPS

Title: _____

Topic: _____

Description: _____

Start Time: _____

Start Cue: _____

End Time: _____

End Cue: _____

Comments: _____

_____

_____

Mother's Day

See also: **Parent-Child Relationships**

MESSAGE TITLES

- ❑ How Much Should Mothers Work?
- ❑ Mindful Motherhood
- ❑ The Nobility of Motherhood
- ❑ Seasons of Motherhood
- ❑ A Tribute to Mothers

DRAMAS

Title	Tone	Characters	Topics
If These Walls Could Speak	Serious, touching	3 females	Mother's Day; Family traditions
Let Me Go	Mixed	2 females	Parenting; Letting go of adult children
The Luncheon	Serious	3 females	Mother-daughter conflict; Honesty in relationships
Maternal Measures	Humorous	3 females	Mother's Day; Pressure on women to measure up
A Mother's Day	Mixed	1 male, 2 females	Mother's Day
The Night Light	Mixed	2 females	Mother's Day; Parenting
Reflections	Mixed	1 male, 2 females, 2 children	Motherhood
The Rest Room	Humorous	1 female, offstage voices: 1 male, 2 children	Boundaries; Taking better care of yourself; Motherhood
Worth Keeping	Mixed, touching	1 male, 2 females	The nobility of motherhood; Single parenting
You and Me	Mixed	2 females	Mother's Day; Family; Rebuilding after divorce; Navigating life's challenges

Title	Tone	Characters	Topics

SONGS

Title	Artist	Style	Tempo	Seeker-Sensitivity Rating
Because You Loved Me	Celine Dion	Pop ballad	Slow	10
When You Come Home	**Mark Schultz**	**Country-tinged ballad**	**Slow/mid**	**9**

Worship Choruses

Title	Artist	Style	Tempo	Seeker-Sensitivity Rating

MOVIE CLIPS

Title:

Topic:

Description:

Start Time:

Start Cue:

End Time:

End Cue:

Comments:

Thanksgiving

See also: **God's Goodness**

MESSAGE TITLES

_____

_____

DRAMAS

Title	Tone	Characters	Topics
Doomed	Humorous	1 male, 1 female, 2 children	Thanksgiving

SONGS

Title	Artist	Style	Tempo	Seeker-Sensitivity Rating
He's Been Faithful	Brooklyn Tabernacle Choir	Ballad with choir	Slow	6
I'm Amazed	*Willow Creek Music*	*Ballad*	*Slow*	7
Thankful	*Willow Creek Music*	*Pop*	*Up*	7
What a Good God	**Tommy Walker**	**Worship ballad**	**Slow**	7
You Have Been Good	Scott Krippayne	Pop ballad	Slow	6

Worship Choruses

Title	Artist	Style	Tempo	Seeker-Sensitivity Rating
Amen	Tommy Walker	Worship shuffle	Up	5
Celebrate Jesus Celebrate	Alleluia Music	Pop	Up	6
Do You Know?	Tommy Walker	Worship ballad	Slow/mid	2
Don't Forget His Benefits	Tommy Walker & the CA Worship Band	Rock/pop	Up	4
For the Beauty of the Earth	*Willow Creek Music*	*Worship ballad*	*Slow*	*5*
Happy Song	Delirious	Country rockabilly	Up	5
Here I Am Again	Tommy Walker/ Willow Creek Music	Pop shuffle	Up	3
How Good You Are	*Willow Creek Music*	*Pop worship*	*Mid/up*	*3*
Lord, I Lift Your Name on High	Maranatha!/Praise Band	Pop worship	Up	6
Love You So Much	Hillsongs	Worship ballad	Slow	5
My Heart Sings Praises	Hillsongs	Pop worship	Mid	4
My Jesus, I Love You	*Willow Creek Music*	*Worship ballad*	*Slow*	*3*
Never Gonna Stop	Tommy Walker/ Willow Creek Music	Pop/rock	Up	3
No Greater Love	Tommy Walker	Pop/rock	Up	6
Pour Out My Heart	Vineyard	Worship shuffle	Mid	4
Reach Down Deep	*Willow Creek Music*	*Pop*	*Up*	*5*
Shout to the Lord	Hillsongs	Worship power ballad	Slow	3
Thank You for Saving Me	Delirious	Folk rock worship ballad	Slow/mid	3
Thank You, Lord	Hillsongs	Worship ballad, in 3	Mid	3
That's Why We Praise Him	Tommy Walker	Rock/pop worship	Mid	5
What a Good God You've Been	Tommy Walker	Worship ballad	Slow	7
_____	_____	_____	_____	____
_____	_____	_____	_____	____
_____	_____	_____	_____	____
_____	_____	_____	_____	____
_____	_____	_____	_____	____
_____	_____	_____	_____	____

MOVIE CLIPS

Title: _____

Topic: _____

Description: _____

Start Time: _____

Start Cue: _____

End Time: _____

End Cue: _____

Comments: _____
_____
_____
_____

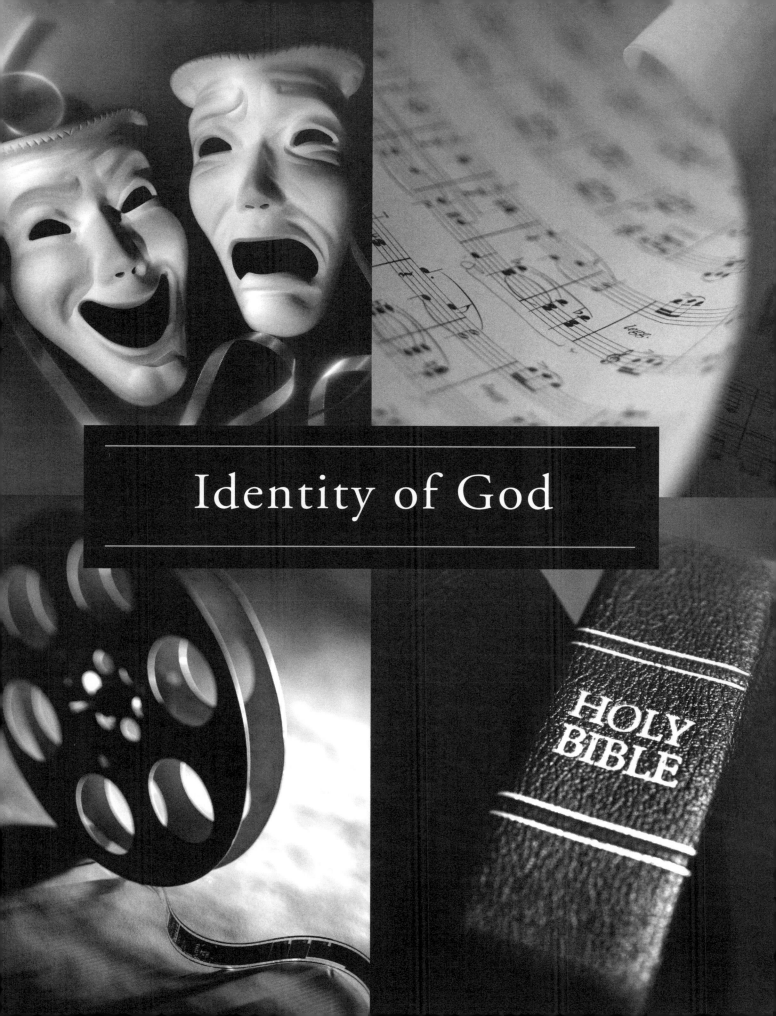

Identity of God

God as a Refuge

Might also include: *God's Protection*

MESSAGE TITLES

- ❏ God Our Refuge
- ❏ The Safest Place
- ❏ *What Would You Ask God?* How Can We Survive Suffering?
- ❏ *When God Shows Up:* The Weary Find Refuge
- ❏ *Yeah God:* For Being a Refuge

DRAMAS

Title	Tone	Characters	Topics
The Stickholders	Serious	3 males, 1 female, 1 narrator	Relationship with God; Freedom from rules

SONGS

Title	Artist	Style	Tempo	Seeker-Sensitivity Rating
Be Still and Know	**Tommy Walker & the CA Worship Band**	**Rock/pop, in 6/8**	**Mid**	**5**
But if Not	*Student Impact*	*Acoustic ballad*	*Slow*	*5*
Can't Live a Day without You	Avalon	Pop ballad	Slow/mid	8

Title	Artist	Style	Tempo	Seeker-Sensitivity Rating
Every Single Tear	Scott Krippayne	Ballad	Slow	10
Found a Way	*Greg Ferguson*	*Ballad*	*Slow*	*9*
God of Wonders	**Various**	**Folk rock**	**Mid**	**7**
Have No Fear	*Willow Creek Music*	*Piano ballad*	*Slow*	*9*
He Knows My Name	**Tommy Walker/Helena**	**Worship ballad**	**Slow**	**9**
Healing Song	Curt Coffield	Ballad, in 3	Slow/mid	7
Here in My Heart	Susan Ashton	Folk rock	Up	8
He's All You Need	Steve Camp	Ballad	Slow	7
He's My Son	Mark Schultz	Ballad	Slow	9
Hiding Place	Steven Curtis Chapman	Pop ballad	Mid/slow	9
His Love Is Strong	Clay Crosse	Pop	Up	10
His Strength Is Perfect	**Steven Curtis Chapman**	**Ballad**	**Slow**	**9**
Hold Me, Jesus	Rich Mullins	Ballad	Slow	7
Hold On	*Willow Creek Music*	*Acoustic rock/pop ballad*	*Slow/mid*	*10*
Hold On to Jesus	Steven Curtis Chapman	Ballad	Slow	8
Holy One	*Helena*	*Ballad*	*Slow*	*7*
Hunger for Healing	*Willow Creek Music*	*Folk ballad*	*Slow*	*10*
I Go to the Rock	Dottie Rambo; Whitney Houston	Swing/big band	Mid	7
I Will Rest in You	Jaci Velasquez	Ballad	Slow	8
If This World	Jaci Velasquez	Pop	Up	9
I'll Find You There	The Kry	Folk rock ballad	Slow	9
Jesus, King of Angels	**Fernando Ortega**	**Ballad**	**Slow**	**6**
Jesus Will Still Be There	Point of Grace	Ballad	Slow	9
Lay Your Burdens Down	*Willow Creek Music*	*Ballad*	*Slow*	*9*
Let the Lord Love You	*Willow Creek Music*	*Acoustic guitar ballad*	*Slow*	*9*
Love That Will Not Let Me Go	**Steve Camp**	**Ballad**	**Slow**	**10**
No One Knows My Heart	Susan Ashton	Folk pop ballad	Slow/mid	9
Peace Be Still	Al Denson	Ballad	Slow	10
A Place to Call Home	*Greg Ferguson/ Willow Creek Music*	*Gospel ballad*	*Slow, in 3*	*10*
Small Enough	Nicole Nordeman	Ballad duet	Slow	6

Title	Artist	Style	Tempo	Seeker-Sensitivity Rating
Strength in You	*Willow Creek Music*	*MOR pop*	*Slow/mid*	*10*
There Is a God	**Tommy Walker**	**Ballad duet**	**Slow**	**8**
There's a Reason	*Willow Creek Music*	*Pop/rock*	*Up*	*9*
Weary Soul	*Helena*	*Tender ballad*	*Slow*	*9*
When You Are a Soldier	Steven Curtis Chapman	Keyboard ballad	Slow/mid	4
You Are with Me Still	*Willow Creek Music*	*Acoustic ballad*	*Slow*	*9*
You Brought My Heart to Life	*Willow Creek Music*	*Ballad*	*Slow*	*9*
Your Love Stays with Me	Gary Chapman	Piano ballad	Slow	10
_____	_____	_____	_____	_____
_____	_____	_____	_____	_____
_____	_____	_____	_____	_____
_____	_____	_____	_____	_____
_____	_____	_____	_____	_____

Worship Choruses

Title	Artist	Style	Tempo	Seeker-Sensitivity Rating
All Things Are Possible	Hillsongs	Pop worship	Up	4
And That My Soul Knows Very Well	Hillsongs	Worship ballad	Slow	5
Be Still My Soul	*Willow Creek Music*	*Worship ballad*	*Slow/mid*	*4*
Better Is One Day	Matt Redman/Passion	Folk worship	Mid	4
Blessed Be the Name	Vineyard	Worship ballad	Slow	4
Breathe	Michael W. Smith	Worship ballad	Slow	3
But if Not	*Student Impact*	*Acoustic ballad*	*Slow*	*5*
God of Wonders	**Various**	**Folk rock**	**Mid**	**7**
Hallelujah (Your Love Is Amazing)	Vineyard—Brenton Brown	Rock/pop worship	Up	4
He Knows My Name	Tommy Walker	Worship ballad	Slow	7
Healing Song	Curt Coffield	Ballad, in 3	Slow/mid	7
He's Here	*Student Impact*	*Worship ballad*	*Slow*	*7*
In Your Loving Arms	*Willow Creek Music*	*Ballad*	*Slow*	*4*
Jesus, Lover of My Soul	Hillsongs	Pop worship	Up	3
Love You So Much	Hillsongs	Worship ballad	Slow	5

Title	Artist	Style	Tempo	Seeker-Sensitivity Rating
My Heart Sings Praises	Hillsongs	Pop worship	Mid	4
O Most High	Mark Altrogge	Pop	Up	3
Power of Your Love	Hillsongs	Worship ballad	Slow	6
Shout to the Lord	Hillsongs	Worship power ballad	Slow	3
You Are with Me Still	*Willow Creek Music*	*Acoustic ballad*	*Slow*	*9*

MOVIE CLIPS

Title: The Prince of Egypt

Topic: The parting of the Red Sea; God's power

Description: Wonderful animated depiction of the parting of the Red Sea, showing the power of God and his deliverance of the people of Israel. It is six minutes long but is powerful.

Start Time: 1:22:20

Start Cue: Man blows the ram's horn.

End Time: 1:28:18

End Cue: Wide shot of the multitude of Israel looking over the Red Sea.

Comments: Can be used as a sermon illustration much the way the biblical passage would be used.

Title: _____

Topic: _____

Description: _____

Start Time: _____

Start Cue: _____

End Time: _____

End Cue: _____

Comments: _____

—God as Creator/Creation—

Might also include: *God's Majesty*

MESSAGE TITLES

- ❑ The Case for Creation
- ❑ *Faith Has Its Reasons:* Reasons for Believing in God
- ❑ *Yeah God:* For Being Expressive

_____

_____

DRAMAS

Title	Tone	Characters	Topics
Is "Nothing" Sacred?	Humorous	3 males and at least 4 others in group	Evolution vs. creation; Modern science
The Nature of Life	Mixed	2 males, 2 females	Wonder of creation; Family

SONGS

Title	Artist	Style	Tempo	Seeker-Sensitivity Rating
Every Season	Nicole Nordeman	Ballad	Slow	8
God of Wonders	**Various**	**Folk rock**	**Mid**	7
Greater Than	Riley Armstrong	Alternative pop/rock	Up	8
Lord of All	First Call	Ballad trio	Slow	6
Mighty Lord	Kathy Troccoli; Ashley Cleveland	Funky pop	Up	8

Title	Artist	Style	Tempo	Seeker-Sensitivity Rating
Praise the King	**Cindy Morgan**	**Ballad**	**Slow**	**4**
This Is My Father's World	Fernando Ortega	Folk ballad	Slow/mid	8

Worship Choruses

Title	Artist	Style	Tempo	Seeker-Sensitivity Rating
Above All	Paul Baloche/Lenny LeBlanc	Worship ballad	Slow	5
All Around	Curt Coffield	Caribbean pop	Up	7
Beautiful God	Vineyard	Pop	Up	5
Faithful to Me	Curt Coffield	Pop worship	Mid	6
For the Beauty of the Earth	*Willow Creek Music*	*Worship ballad*	*Slow*	*5*
God of Wonders	**Various**	**Folk rock**	**Mid**	**7**
Let Everything That Has Breath	Matt Redman	Pop/rock worship	Up	4
Lord Most High	Willow Creek Music	MOR worship	Mid	3
My Glorious	Student Impact	Rock	Mid/up	4

MOVIE CLIPS

Title: _____

Topic: _____

Description: _____

Start Time: _____

Start Cue: _____

End Time: _____

End Cue: _____

Comments: _____

_____

God as Father

MESSAGE TITLES

❏ Father Knows Best
❏ *Our 3-D God:* God as Father

DRAMAS

Title	Tone	Characters	Topics
Definitely Safe	Serious, heartwarming	2 males, 1 female	Father's Day; Prodigal son; Unconditional love
The Intruder	Serious	1 male, 1 female	Self-image; Destructive parenting; God's love in spite of failure

SONGS

Title	Artist	Style	Tempo	Seeker-Sensitivity Rating
Father's Love	Bob Carlisle	Ballad	Slow	8
He Knows My Name	**Tommy Walker/Helena**	**Worship ballad**	**Slow**	**9**
In My Father's Hands	Susan Ashton	Folk pop	Mid	9
A Place to Call Home	*Greg Ferguson/ Willow Creek Music*	*Gospel ballad*	*Slow, in 3*	*10*

Worship Choruses

Title	Artist	Style	Tempo	Seeker-Sensitivity Rating
Everyone Arise	Tommy Walker	Pop/rock	Up	3
He Knows My Name	Tommy Walker	Worship ballad	Slow	7
In Your Hands	Hillsongs	Worship ballad	Slow/mid	4
In Your Loving Arms	*Willow Creek Music*	*Ballad*	*Slow*	*4*
The Lord's Prayer	*Willow Creek Music*	*U2-ish rock/pop*	*Up*	*9*
You Alone	Passion	Folk pop worship, in 6/8	Mid	4
_____	_____	_____	_____	_____
_____	_____	_____	_____	_____
_____	_____	_____	_____	_____
_____	_____	_____	_____	_____

MOVIE CLIPS

Title: _____

Topic: _____

Description: _____

Start Time: _____

Start Cue: _____

End Time: _____

End Cue: _____

Comments: _____

_____

—God's Character, General—

Refers to God's attributes—understanding who God is, to the extent that we can. Attributes that are similar in nature have been combined, so the individual categories are rather broad.

MESSAGE TITLES

❑ **God Has Feelings Too:** What Delights God • What Frustrates God • What Makes God Jealous
❑ **Illustrating the Identity of God:** Our Loving God • Our Forgiving God • Our Attentive God
• Our Providing God • Our Gracious God • Our Giving God • Our Just God
❑ **Our 3-D God:** God as Father • God as Forgiver • God as Friend
❑ **Seven Wonders of the Spiritual World:** God Loves Me • God Can Be Trusted • God Forgives My Failures
• God Transforms Me • God Guides Me • God Uses Me • God Satisfies Me
❑ **Surprised by God:** A Surprising God • Surprised by God's Love • Surprised by God's Truth • Surprised by God's Holiness • Surprised by God's Power • Surprised by God's Satisfaction
❑ **Three Things God Loves (That Most People Think He Doesn't):** Leisure • Laughter • Lovemaking
❑ **Yeah God:** For Being Relational • For Being Expressive • For Being Wise • For Being Joyful • For Being an Equal Opportunity Employer • For Being Patient • For Being a Refuge • For Being Righteous • For Being Gracious • For Being Committed to Me • For Being Generous • For Being a Guide • For Being Powerful
• For Being a Servant

DRAMAS

Title	Tone	Characters	Topics
The Big Question	Mixed, mostly humorous	1 male, 1 female, 1 child	The existence of God
Guess Which God	Humorous	4 males (offstage male and female voices)	Confusion about God; Nature of God
I Am	Serious	4 readers, male or female	Who is Jesus Christ?
I Don't Want to Fight You Anymore	Serious	1 female	Relationship with God; Giving up control; Our value to God
Just in Case	Humorous	1 male, 1 female	Trusting God; God's faithfulness

Title	Tone	Characters	Topics
Will the Real God Please Stand Up?	Humorous	3 males, 1 female	God's character; Second commandment; What is God like?
You Cramp My Style	Serious	1 male, 1 female, 1 either male or female	Reasons people don't believe; Society's view of God
_____	_____	_____	_____
_____	_____	_____	_____

SONGS

Title	Artist	Style	Tempo	Seeker-Sensitivity Rating
Awesome God	Rich Mullins	Pop anthem	Mid/up	1
God of Wonders	**Various**	**Folk rock**	**Mid**	**7**
Greater Than	**Riley Armstrong**	**Alternative pop/rock**	**Up**	**8**
He Was	_Willow Creek Music_	_Pop/rock, in 6/8_	_Mid_	_10_
His Eyes	Steven Curtis Chapman	Acoustic guitar ballad	Mid/slow	9
I Will Worship You	**Matthew Ward**	**Ballad**	**Slow**	**5**
If I Could Look through Your Eyes	_Willow Creek Music_	_Piano ballad_	_Slow_	_10_
I'm Amazed	_Willow Creek Music_	_Ballad_	_Slow_	_7_
Lion and the Lamb	Maranatha! Singers; Crystal Lewis	Ballad trio	Slow	4
Lord of All	First Call	Ballad trio	Slow	6
Love That Will Not Let Me Go	**Steve Camp**	**Ballad**	**Slow**	**10**
Mighty Lord	Kathy Troccoli; Ashley Cleveland	Funky pop	Up	8
More Than Words	Steven Curtis Chapman	Acoustic guitar ballad	Mid/slow	4
My Redeemer Is Faithful and True	**Steven Curtis Chapman**	**Ballad**	**Slow**	**9**
Praise the King	**Cindy Morgan**	**Ballad**	**Slow**	**4**
These Things Are True of You	**Tommy Walker & the CA Worship Band**	**Ballad duet**	**Slow**	**9**
_____	_____	_____	_____
_____	_____	_____	_____

Worship Choruses

Title	Artist	Style	Tempo	Seeker-Sensitivity Rating
Above All	Paul Baloche/Lenny LeBlanc	Worship ballad	Slow	5
God of Wonders	**Various**	**Folk rock**	**Mid**	7
He Is Exalted	Twila Paris	Pop worship, in 3	Mid	3
Shout to the Lord	Hillsongs	Worship power ballad	Slow	3
There Is None Like You	Lenny LeBlanc	Worship ballad	Slow/mid	6
These Things Are True of You	Tommy Walker & the CA Worship Band	Ballad duet	Slow	9
We Praise Your Name	*Willow Creek Music*	*Worship ballad*	*Slow/mid*	*4*
Who Is Like Our God?	Vineyard	Rock/pop worship	Mid	3
You Are Holy	Hillsongs	Worship ballad	Slow	3
_____	_____	_____	_____	_____
_____	_____	_____	_____	_____
_____	_____	_____	_____	_____
_____	_____	_____	_____	_____

MOVIE CLIPS

Title: _____

Topic: _____

Description: _____

Start Time: _____

Start Cue: _____

End Time: _____

End Cue: _____

Comments: _____

_____

_____

God's Faithfulness

Might also include: *God's Trustworthiness*

MESSAGE TITLES

- ❏ *Making Life Work:* Trust God
- ❏ *Seven Wonders of the Spiritual World:* God Can Be Trusted
- ❏ *Truths That Transform:* My God Shall Supply All Your Needs
- ❏ *Yeah God:* For Being Committed to Me

_____

_____

_____

DRAMAS

Title	Tone	Characters	Topics
In . . . We Trust	Serious, not heavy	1 male	Trust; Difficulty trusting God
Just in Case	Humorous	1 male, 1 female	Trusting God; God's faithfulness
Seeing Is Believing	Humorous	1 male, 1 female, 1 narrator	A Savior you can trust; Easy faith

SONGS

Title	Artist	Style	Tempo	Seeker-Sensitivity Rating
Be Still and Know	**Tommy Walker & the CA Worship Band**	**Rock/pop, in 6/8**	**Mid**	**5**
A Beautiful Place	Wayne Watson	MOR ballad	Mid/slow	9

Title	Artist	Style	Tempo	Seeker-Sensitivity Rating
Facts Are Facts	Steven Curtis Chapman	Rock/pop	Up	4
Found a Way	*Greg Ferguson*	*Ballad*	*Slow*	*9*
Foundations	Geoff Moore & the Distance	Folk pop ballad	Slow/mid	8
From This Moment On	Newsong	Ballad	Slow	8
He Knows My Name	**Tommy Walker/Helena**	**Worship ballad**	**Slow**	**9**
He Won't Let You Go	The Kry	Piano ballad	Slow	10
Here in My Heart	Susan Ashton	Folk rock	Up	8
He's All You Need	Steve Camp	Ballad	Slow	7
He's Been Faithful	Brooklyn Tabernacle Choir	Ballad with choir	Slow	6
His Eyes	Steven Curtis Chapman	Acoustic guitar ballad	Mid/slow	9
His Love Is Strong	Clay Crosse	Pop	Up	10
His Strength Is Perfect	**Steven Curtis Chapman**	**Ballad**	**Slow**	**9**
Hold On	*Willow Creek Music*	*Acoustic rock/pop ballad*	*Slow/mid*	*10*
I Go to the Rock	Dottie Rambo; Whitney Houston	Swing/big band	Mid	7
I'll Find You There	The Kry	Folk rock ballad	Slow	9
I'm Amazed	*Willow Creek Music*	*Ballad*	*Slow*	*7*
In My Father's Hands	Susan Ashton	Folk pop	Mid	9
Jesus Will Still Be There	Point of Grace	Ballad	Slow	9
Lay Your Burdens Down	*Willow Creek Music*	*Ballad*	*Slow*	*9*
Lord of All	First Call	Ballad trio	Slow	6
Love Is Always There	Carolyn Arends	Folk pop	Up	9
The Love of God	*Willow Creek Music*	*A cappella vocal group*	*Slow*	*6*
Love That Will Not Let Me Go	**Steve Camp**	**Ballad**	**Slow**	**10**
My Redeemer Is Faithful and True	**Steven Curtis Chapman**	**Ballad**	**Slow**	**9**
Still Listening	Steven Curtis Chapman	Acoustic ballad	Slow/mid	7
Strength in You	*Willow Creek Music*	*MOR pop*	*Slow/mid*	*10*
Take My Hand	The Kry	Acoustic ballad	Mid/slow	9
Take You at Your Word	Avalon	Pop	Up	8
Thankful	*Willow Creek Music*	*Pop*	*Up*	*7*
There Is a Love	Michael English	Pop	Up	9

Title	Artist	Style	Tempo	Seeker-Sensitivity Rating
What a Good God	**Tommy Walker**	**Worship ballad**	**Slow**	7
When You Are a Soldier	Steven Curtis Chapman	Keyboard ballad	Slow/mid	4
You Have Been Good	Scott Krippayne	Pop ballad	Slow	6
Your Love Stays with Me	Gary Chapman	Piano ballad	Slow	10

Worship Choruses

Title	Artist	Style	Tempo	Seeker-Sensitivity Rating
All the Power You Need	Hillsongs	Pop worship	Up	5
Blessed Be the Name	Vineyard	Worship ballad	Slow	4
Faithful to Me	Curt Coffield	Pop worship	Mid	6
Great Is Thy Faithfulness	NA	Traditional worship/hymn	Slow	5
Hallelujah (Your Love Is Amazing)	Vineyard—Brenton Brown	Rock/pop worship	Up	4
I Will Bless You, Lord	Hillsongs	Worship ballad, in 3	Mid	3
In Your Hands	Hillsongs	Worship ballad	Slow/mid	4
Joy, Joy, Joy	Tommy Walker	Rock shuffle	Up	5
Pour Out My Heart	Vineyard	Worship shuffle	Mid	4
What a Good God You've Been	Tommy Walker	Worship ballad	Slow	7
Who Is Like Our God?	Vineyard	Rock/pop worship	Mid	3

MOVIE CLIPS

Title:	Indiana Jones and the Last Crusade
Topic:	Faith; Trusting God when circumstances are confusing
Description:	Indiana Jones faces a seemingly uncrossable chasm but takes a "leap of faith" and steps onto an invisible bridge. Illustrates faith, believing what can't be seen.
Start Time:	1:46:50
Start Cue:	Indiana Jones walks through cave to the chasm.
End Time:	1:48:45
End Cue:	Indy throws sand on bridge to mark it (can be cut earlier).
Comments:	

Title:

Topic:

Description:

Start Time:

Start Cue:

End Time:

End Cue:

Comments:

—God's Forgiveness of Us—

See also: **Grace, Salvation**

MESSAGE TITLES

Package Suggestion

Drama:
A Clean Slate

Song:
Face of Forgiveness

DRAMAS

Title	Tone	Characters	Topics
The Brow Beater	Mixed, mostly serious	1 male, 1 female	Self-esteem; Failures; Forgiveness
A Clean Slate	Serious	1 male, 2 or 3 males or females	Forgiveness; Redemption; Guilt
The Do-Over	Humorous	1 male, 1 female	Longing for second chances; The importance of good choices
A Failure Tale	Mixed	5 males, 1 narrator	Failing; Obeying rules
Forgive Again?	Serious	1 male, 1 female	Forgiving others
Forgiven	Serious	2 females	Forgiving others; God's forgiveness
Only Child	Serious	1 male, 2 females	Grace; Outrageous forgiveness; Doctrine of adoption
The Prisoner	Serious	3 males, 1 female	Easter; Freedom from sin; New Christian
"X" Marks the Spot	Serious; Mime	1 male, 1 female, 3 either males or females	Sin; Redemption; Forgiveness; Guilt

SONGS

Title	Artist	Style	Tempo	Seeker-Sensitivity Rating
Ball and Chain	Susan Ashton	Folk pop	Mid	9
Clumsy	Chris Rice	Pop	Mid/up	8
Could You Believe?	Scott Krippayne	Pop	Up	9
Cross Medley	*Willow Creek Music*	*Ballad medley—hymns*	*Slow*	*7*
Face of Forgiveness	*Willow Creek Music*	*Ballad*	*Slow*	*10*
Farther Than Your Grace Can Reach	**Jonathan Pierce**	**Ballad**	**Slow**	**9**
Forgive Me	*Willow Creek Music*	*Ballad*	*Slow*	*3*
The Great Divide	Point of Grace	Power ballad	Slow	9
He's All You Need	Steve Camp	Ballad	Slow	7
I Am the Man	*Greg Ferguson*	*Piano ballad*	*Slow*	*8*
I Found Myself in You	Clay Crosse	Gospel ballad	Mid/slow	10
I Stand, I Fall	*Greg Ferguson*	*Piano ballad*	*Slow*	*7*
If I Could Look through Your Eyes	*Willow Creek Music*	*Piano ballad*	*Slow*	*10*
I've Been Released	*Willow Creek Music*	*Pop/rock—Chicago sound*	*Up*	*9*
Just Say the Word	*Willow Creek Music*	*Gospel pop, in 3*	*Mid/up*	*4*
Love That Will Not Let Me Go	**Steve Camp**	**Ballad**	**Slow**	**10**
Mercy for the Memories	Geoff Moore & the Distance	Folk pop ballad	Slow	9
My Life Is Yours	*Willow Creek Music*	*Acoustic ballad*	*Slow*	*10*
Naïve	Chris Rice	Folk pop	Mid	8
Never Be an Angel	Margaret Becker	Pop	Mid	4
A Picture of Grace	*Willow Creek Music*	*Medley of ballads*	*Slow*	*9*
Speechless	**Steven Curtis Chapman**	**Acoustic rock**	**Mid/up**	**7**
There Is a God	**Tommy Walker**	**Ballad duet**	**Slow**	**8**
What a Good God	**Tommy Walker**	**Worship ballad**	**Slow**	**7**
Why Me?	*Willow Creek Music*	*Ballad*	*Slow*	*9*
Your Grace Still Amazes Me	Phillips, Craig and Dean	Pop ballad	Slow	7
_____	_____	_____	_____	_____
_____	_____	_____	_____	_____
_____	_____	_____	_____	_____

Worship Choruses

Title	Artist	Style	Tempo	Seeker-Sensitivity Rating
Amazing Love	*Student Impact*	*Rock worship*	*Mid/up*	*6*
The Beauty of Holiness	Steve Camp	Worship ballad, in 3	Slow	3
Create in Me	*Willow Creek Music*	*Ballad*	*Slow*	*3*
The Cross Has Said It All	Matt Redman	Worship ballad	Mid/slow	2
Do You Know?	Tommy Walker	Worship ballad	Slow/mid	2
Don't Forget His Benefits	Tommy Walker & the CA Worship Band	Rock/pop	Up	4
Great Is Thy Faithfulness	NA	Traditional worship/ hymn	Slow	5
Jesus, Lover of My Soul	Hillsongs	Pop worship	Up	3
Just Say the Word	*Willow Creek Music*	*Gospel pop, in 3*	*Mid/up*	*4*
The Lord Is Gracious and Compassionate	Vineyard	Worship ballad	Mid/slow	5
My Redeemer Lives	Hillsongs	Pop/rock	Up	3
Still Amazing	Danny Chambers	Worship ballad	Slow	5
Thank You for Saving Me	Delirious	Folk rock worship ballad	Slow/mid	3
What a Good God You've Been	Tommy Walker	Worship ballad	Slow	7
What the Lord Has Done	Hillsongs	Worship ballad, in 3	Slow/mid	2
When I Survey the Wondrous Cross	NA	Updated traditional	Slow	3
You Are My King	Passion	Worship ballad	Slow	4
_____	_____	_____	_____	_____
_____	_____	_____	_____	_____
_____	_____	_____	_____	_____
_____	_____	_____	_____	_____
_____	_____	_____	_____	_____
_____	_____	_____	_____	_____
_____	_____	_____	_____	_____

MOVIE CLIPS

Title:	Hoosiers
Topic:	Unconditional love; Forgiveness
Description:	Dennis Hopper's character, a recovering alcoholic, is in the hospital drying out. His son visits him and tells him he loves him.
Start Time:	1:30:15
Start Cue:	"No school this small . . ."
End Time:	1:32:30
End Cue:	"Anyway, no school this small has ever been in the state championship!"
Comments:	Needs some setup for those who haven't seen the movie.

_____
_____
_____

Title:	Les Misérables
Topic:	Grace; Forgiveness
Description:	In the first scene of the movie, ex-convict Jean Valjean is welcomed into a church for food and shelter. He steals some silverware, is caught, and in order to model the grace of God to him, the bishop forgives Valjean and gives the silver to him and gives him candlesticks in addition.
Start Time:	0:6:22
Start Cue:	Jean Valjean creeps down the stairs.
End Time:	0:9:53
End Cue:	"Now I give you back to God." Close-up of Valjean, fade to black.
Comments:	Valjean strikes the bishop. It is a bit violent but adds to the power of the bishop's forgiveness of Valjean. One of the bishop's statements sounds as if he bought Valjean's soul, but more likely he is saying that he used the silver essentially to buy him out of the evil he had done so that he could be presented to God. A great picture of grace.

_____
_____
_____

Title:	_____
Topic:	_____
Description:	_____
Start Time:	_____
Start Cue:	_____
End Time:	_____
End Cue:	_____
Comments:	_____

_____
_____

God's Goodness

Might also include: *God's Providence, God's Generosity*

See also: **Thanksgiving**

MESSAGE TITLES

❑ *Illustrating the Identity of God:* Our Giving God

❑ *Truths That Transform:* My God Shall Supply All Your Needs

❑ *Yeah God:* For Being Generous

DRAMAS

Title	Tone	Characters	Topics
Conversations in a Field	Humorous	2 males, 2 females	Anxiety; Worry; God's providence
I Know What You Want	Serious	2 males, 2 females	God's love; Dysfunctional families

SONGS

Title	Artist	Style	Tempo	Seeker-Sensitivity Rating
Enough	*Willow Creek Music*	*Piano ballad*	*Slow*	*7*
Facts Are Facts	Steven Curtis Chapman	Rock/pop	Up	4
Found a Way	*Greg Ferguson*	*Ballad*	*Slow*	*9*
He Knows My Name	**Tommy Walker/Helena**	**Worship ballad**	**Slow**	**9**

Title	Artist	Style	Tempo	Seeker-Sensitivity Rating
I'm Amazed	*Willow Creek Music*	*Ballad*	*Slow*	*7*
Lord of All	First Call	Ballad trio	Slow	6
My Redeemer Is Faithful and True	**Steven Curtis Chapman**	**Ballad**	**Slow**	**9**
Praise the King	**Cindy Morgan**	**Ballad**	**Slow**	**4**
Smellin' Coffee	Chris Rice	Pop/rock	Up	8
Speechless	**Steven Curtis Chapman**	**Acoustic rock**	**Mid/up**	**7**
Thankful	*Willow Creek Music*	*Pop*	*Up*	*7*
What a Good God	**Tommy Walker**	**Worship ballad**	**Slow**	**7**
Who Am I?	Margaret Becker	Power ballad	Slow	7
You Have Been Good	Scott Krippayne	Pop ballad	Slow	6
_____	_____	_____	_____	_____
_____	_____	_____	_____	_____
_____	_____	_____	_____	_____
_____	_____	_____	_____	_____

Worship Choruses

Title	Artist	Style	Tempo	Seeker-Sensitivity Rating
Don't Forget His Benefits	Tommy Walker & the CA Worship Band	Rock/pop	Up	4
Doxology	Tommy Walker	Pop/rock	Mid	6
Everyday	Student Impact/Sonlight Band	Rock worship	Up	6
Everyone Arise	Tommy Walker	Pop/rock	Up	3
Faithful to Me	Curt Coffield	Pop worship	Mid	6
For the Beauty of the Earth	*Willow Creek Music*	*Worship ballad*	*Slow*	*5*
Got the Need	The Parachute Band	Funky R & B/pop	Up	4
Great Is Thy Faithfulness	NA	Traditional worship/hymn	Slow	5
He Knows My Name	Tommy Walker	Worship ballad	Slow	7
How Good You Are	*Willow Creek Music*	*Pop worship*	*Mid/up*	*3*
Joy, Joy, Joy	Tommy Walker	Rock shuffle	Up	5
The Lord Is Gracious and Compassionate	Vineyard	Worship ballad	Mid/slow	5
Pour Out My Heart	Vineyard	Worship shuffle	Mid	4

Title	Artist	Style	Tempo	Seeker-Sensitivity Rating
Revelation 19	Student Impact	Worship ballad	Slow/mid	4
Thank You for Saving Me	Delirious	Folk rock worship ballad	Slow/mid	3
There Is None Like You	Lenny LeBlanc	Worship ballad	Slow/mid	6
Think about His Love	NA	Worship ballad	Slow	6
What a Good God You've Been	Tommy Walker	Worship ballad	Slow	7
Where You Are	Tommy Walker	Pop worship	Mid	5
Who Is Like Our God?	Vineyard	Rock/pop worship	Mid	3
You Alone	Passion	Folk pop worship, in 6/8	Mid	4
_____	_____	_____	_____	_____
_____	_____	_____	_____	_____
_____	_____	_____	_____	_____
_____	_____	_____	_____	_____

MOVIE CLIPS

Title: _____

Topic: _____

Description: _____

Start Time: _____

Start Cue: _____

End Time: _____

End Cue: _____

Comments: _____

_____

_____

God's Holiness

Might also include: *God's Justice, God's Righteousness*
See also: **Praise and Worship**

MESSAGE TITLES

- ❑ *Illustrating the Identity of God:* Our Just God
- ❑ *Surprised by God:* Surprised by God's Holiness
- ❑ *Yeah God:* For Being Righteous

DRAMAS

Title	Tone	Characters	Topics
Everything's Relative	Humorous	3 males, 1 female	God's holiness; Benefits of God's laws

SONGS

Title	Artist	Style	Tempo	Seeker-Sensitivity Rating
The Beauty of Holiness	Steve Camp	Ballad	Slow	1
God of Wonders	**Various**	**Folk rock**	**Mid**	**7**
Holy One	*Helena*	*Ballad*	*Slow*	*7*

Title	Artist	Style	Tempo	Seeker-Sensitivity Rating
Lord of All	First Call	Ballad trio	Slow	6
Stranger to Holiness	Steve Camp	Ballad	Slow/mid	2
_____	_____	_____	_____	_____
_____	_____	_____	_____	_____
_____	_____	_____	_____	_____
_____	_____	_____	_____	_____
_____	_____	_____	_____	_____

Worship Choruses

Title	Artist	Style	Tempo	Seeker-Sensitivity Rating
Above All	Paul Baloche/Lenny LeBlanc	Worship ballad	Slow	5
The Beauty of Holiness	Steve Camp	Worship ballad, in 3	Slow	3
Come Let Us Bow Down	Dennis Jernigan	Worship ballad	Slow/mid	3
God of Wonders	**Various**	**Folk rock**	**Mid**	**7**
High and Exalted	Bob Fitts	Pop worship	Slow/mid	2
Holy and Anointed One	Vineyard	Worship ballad	Slow	3
Holy, Holy, Holy (Gary Oliver)	Alvin Slaughter/ Willow Creek Music	Gospel pop	Up	5
Holy, Holy, Holy (Traditional)	*Willow Creek Music*	*Traditional hymn*	*Mid*	*5*
I See the Lord	Chris Falson, Maranatha! Singers/Willow Creek Music	Worship ballad	Slow/mid	2
Open the Eyes of My Heart	Paul Baloche	Pop/rock worship	Up	5
We Fall Down	Passion	Worship ballad	Slow/mid	3
Who Is Like Our God?	Vineyard	Rock/pop worship	Mid	3
You Are Holy	Hillsongs	Worship ballad	Slow	3
_____	_____	_____	_____	_____
_____	_____	_____	_____	_____
_____	_____	_____	_____	_____
_____	_____	_____	_____	_____
_____	_____	_____	_____	_____

MOVIE CLIPS

Title: The Prince of Egypt

Topic: God's power; God's calling on our lives

Description: This film is an animated telling of the story of Moses. This scene shows God's call to Moses through the burning bush.

Start Time: 0:42:50

Start Cue: Lost sheep bleats; Moses goes after him.

End Time: 0:47:50

End Cue: Moses is standing with his staff next to the bush (now not burning)

Comments: Can be used as an illustration much the way the biblical passage itself would be used.

_____
_____
_____

Title: _____

Topic: _____

Description: _____

Start Time: _____

Start Cue: _____

End Time: _____

End Cue: _____

Comments: _____
_____
_____

God's Love

Might also include: *Unconditional Love*

MESSAGE TITLES

❑ Coming Home (The Prodigal Son's Father)
❑ *Illustrating the Identity of God:* Our Loving God
❑ *The Power of Love:* God's Love
❑ *Seven Wonders of the Spiritual World:* God Loves Me
❑ *Surprised by God:* Surprised by God's Love

DRAMAS

Title	Tone	Characters	Topics
Another Day at the Bus Stop	Mixed	1 male, 1 female	Our relationship with God; Self-esteem
The Black Hole	Serious but light	2 males, 1 female, 1 narrator	Filling the void; Contentment; God's love
I Know What You Want	Serious	2 males, 2 females	God's love; Dysfunctional families
The Intruder	Serious	1 male, 1 female	Self-image; Destructive parenting: God's love in spite of failure
Keeping Tabs	Humorous	1 male, 1 female	Gifts of grace; Undeserved love
The Lane of Life	Serious; Mime	5 either males or females, 1 offstage narrator	Salvation; Our value to God; Self-esteem
Measuring Up	Mixed; Mime	2 males, 1 female, 1 either male or female	God's acceptance of us; Self-esteem
Only Child	Serious	1 male, 2 females	Grace; Outrageous forgiveness; Doctrine of adoption
The Quagmire	Serious	1 male or female	Failure; Self-esteem; Being "stuck"; Trusting God
The Stickholders	Serious	3 males, 1 female, 1 narrator	Relationship with God; Freedom from rules

Title	Tone	Characters	Topics
Take Heart	Mixed; Mime	2 males, 2 females	God heals the brokenhearted; Disappointment
These Parts	Mixed	2 males, 1 female, 3 either males or females, 1 child, 1 narrator	The Resurrection; Our need for Christ; Easter
Tom, Dick, and Mary	Serious	3 males, 1 female, 1 narrator	Hearing God's voice; Crowding God out of your life
"X" Marks the Spot	Serious; Mime	1 male, 1 female, 3 either males or females	Sin; Redemption; Forgiveness; Guilt
_____	_____	_____	_____
_____	_____	_____	_____
_____	_____	_____	_____
_____	_____	_____	_____

SONGS

Title	Artist	Style	Tempo	Seeker-Sensitivity Rating
All Things New	Watermark	Folk pop	Mid	8
At Jesus' Feet	Billy & Sarah Gaines	Ballad	Slow	6
Be Still and Know	**Tommy Walker & the CA Worship Band**	**Rock/pop, in 6/8**	**Mid**	**5**
Bridge between Two Hearts	Bob Carlisle	Pop	Up	9
Clumsy	Chris Rice	Pop	Mid/up	8
Could You Believe?	Scott Krippayne	Pop	Up	9
Cross Medley	_Willow Creek Music_	_Ballad medley—hymns_	_Slow_	_7_
Every Single Tear	Scott Krippayne	Ballad	Slow	10
Face of Forgiveness	_Willow Creek Music_	_Ballad_	_Slow_	_10_
Faith, Hope, and Love Remain	_Willow Creek Music_	_Bluesy pop_	_Up_	_10_
Father's Love	Bob Carlisle	Ballad	Slow	8
Free	Ginny Owens	Folk pop	Mid/up	8
Greater Than	**Riley Armstrong**	**Alternative pop/rock**	**Up**	**8**
He Knows My Name	**Tommy Walker/Helena**	**Worship ballad**	**Slow**	**9**
He Won't Let You Go	The Kry	Piano ballad	Slow	10

Title	Artist	Style	Tempo	Seeker-Sensitivity Rating
Healing Song	Curt Coffield	Ballad, in 3	Slow/mid	7
Here in My Heart	Susan Ashton	Folk rock	Up	8
He's All You Need	Steve Camp	Ballad	Slow	7
His Eyes	Steven Curtis Chapman	Acoustic guitar ballad	Mid/slow	9
His Love Is Strong	Clay Crosse	Pop	Up	10
Holy One	*Helena*	*Ballad*	*Slow*	*7*
I Don't Know Why/Found a Way	*Willow Creek Music*	*Ballad*	*Slow*	*8*
If I Could Look through Your Eyes	*Willow Creek Music*	*Piano ballad*	*Slow*	*10*
If This World	Jaci Velasquez	Pop	Up	9
I'll Find You There	The Kry	Folk rock ballad	Slow	9
I'm Amazed	*Willow Creek Music*	*Ballad*	*Slow*	*7*
Jesus, King of Angels	**Fernando Ortega**	**Ballad**	**Slow**	**6**
Jesus Loves Me	Whitney Houston	R & B/pop	Slow/mid	8
Lay Your Burdens Down	*Willow Creek Music*	*Ballad*	*Slow*	*9*
Let the Lord Love You	*Willow Creek Music*	*Acoustic guitar ballad*	*Slow*	*9*
Lion and the Lamb	Maranatha! Singers; Crystal Lewis	Ballad trio	Slow	4
Lord of All	First Call	Ballad trio	Slow	6
Love Conquers All	Pam Thum	Pop	Up	10
Love Is Always There	Carolyn Arends	Folk pop	Up	9
The Love of God	*Willow Creek Music*	*A cappella vocal group*	*Slow*	*6*
Love That Will Not Let Me Go	**Steve Camp**	**Ballad**	**Slow**	**10**
Mercy for the Memories	Geoff Moore & the Distance	Folk pop ballad	Slow	9
Miracle of Mercy	Steven Curtis Chapman	Acoustic ballad	Slow	4
No One Knows My Heart	Susan Ashton	Folk pop ballad	Slow/mid	9
Nothing You Could Do	*Willow Creek Music*	*Ballad*	*Slow*	*10*
Peace Be Still	Al Denson	Ballad	Slow	10
A Picture of Grace	*Willow Creek Music*	*Medley of ballads*	*Slow*	*9*
A Place to Call Home	*Greg Ferguson/ Willow Creek Music*	*Gospel ballad*	*Slow, in 3*	*10*
Small Enough	Nicole Nordeman	Ballad duet	Slow	6
Speechless	**Steven Curtis Chapman**	**Acoustic rock**	**Mid/up**	**7**
Thankful	*Willow Creek Music*	*Pop*	*Up*	*7*

Title	Artist	Style	Tempo	Seeker-Sensitivity Rating
There Is a Love	Michael English	Pop	Up	9
Treasure of You	Steven Curtis Chapman	Driving rock	Up	10
What a Good God	**Tommy Walker**	**Worship ballad**	**Slow**	**7**
What I Wouldn't Give	*Willow Creek Music*	*Acoustic ballad*	*Slow*	*10*
Who Am I?	Margaret Becker	Power ballad	Slow	7
Who Am I? (Grace Flows Down)	**Watermark**	**Folk pop**	**Mid/slow**	**8**
Why Me?	*Willow Creek Music*	*Ballad*	*Slow*	*9*
You Brought My Heart to Life	*Willow Creek Music*	*Ballad*	*Slow*	*9*
Your Love Stays with Me	Gary Chapman	Piano ballad	Slow	10
_____	_____	_____	_____	_____
_____	_____	_____	_____	_____
_____	_____	_____	_____	_____
_____	_____	_____	_____	_____
_____	_____	_____	_____	_____

Worship Choruses

Title	Artist	Style	Tempo	Seeker-Sensitivity Rating
Above All	Paul Baloche/Lenny LeBlanc	Worship ballad	Slow	5
All Around	Curt Coffield	Caribbean pop	Up	7
Amazing Love	*Student Impact*	*Rock worship*	*Mid/up*	*6*
Amen	Tommy Walker	Worship shuffle	Up	5
Better Than	Vineyard	Pop/rock worship	Up	6
Celebrate the Lord of Love	Paul Baloche	Pop worship	Up	5
Don't Forget His Benefits	Tommy Walker & the CA Worship Band	Rock/pop	Up	4
Faith, Hope, and Love Remain	*Willow Creek Music*	*Bluesy pop*	*Up*	*10*
For the Beauty of the Earth	*Willow Creek Music*	*Worship ballad*	*Slow*	*5*
Hallelujah (Your Love Is Amazing)	Vineyard—Brenton Brown	Rock/pop worship	Up	4
Happy Song	Delirious	Country rockabilly	Up	5
He Knows My Name	Tommy Walker	Worship ballad	Slow	7
He Loves Me	Tommy Walker	Worship ballad	Slow	6
Healing Song	Curt Coffield	Ballad, in 3	Slow/mid	7

Title	Artist	Style	Tempo	Seeker-Sensitivity Rating
He's Here	*Student Impact*	*Worship ballad*	*Slow*	7
Holy, Holy, Holy (Traditional)	*Willow Creek Music*	*Traditional hymn*	*Mid*	5
How Could I But Love You?	Tommy Walker	Worship ballad	Slow	3
I Could Sing of Your Love Forever	Passion	Rock/pop worship	Mid	4
I Will Bless You, Lord	Hillsongs	Worship ballad, in 3	Mid	3
In Your Hands	Hillsongs	Worship ballad	Slow/mid	4
In Your Loving Arms	*Willow Creek Music*	*Ballad*	*Slow*	4
Jesus, Lover of My Soul	Hillsongs	Pop worship	Up	3
Let Your Love Pour	*Student Impact*	*MOR worship*	*Mid*	4
The Lord Is Gracious and Compassionate	Vineyard	Worship ballad	Mid/slow	5
More Love More Power	Jude Del Herro	Worship ballad	Slow	3
My Glorious	Student Impact	Rock	Mid/up	4
My Jesus, I Love You	*Willow Creek Music*	*Worship ballad*	*Slow*	3
No Greater Love	Tommy Walker	Pop/rock	Up	6
Power of Your Love	Hillsongs	Worship ballad	Slow	6
Still Amazing	Danny Chambers	Worship ballad	Slow	5
There Is None Like You	Lenny LeBlanc	Worship ballad	Slow/mid	6
Think about His Love	NA	Worship ballad	Slow	6
We Fall Down	Passion	Worship ballad	Slow/mid	3
We Praise Your Name	*Willow Creek Music*	*Worship ballad*	*Slow/mid*	4
What a Good God You've Been	Tommy Walker	Worship ballad	Slow	7
When I Survey the Wondrous Cross	NA	Updated traditional	Slow	3
Who Is Like Our God?	Vineyard	Rock/pop worship	Mid	3
You Are My King	Passion	Worship ballad	Slow	4
You've Won My Affection	Curt Coffield	Worship ballad	Slow	4
Your Everlasting Love	Student Impact	Rock worship	Up	6
Your Love	Hillsongs	Worship ballad	Slow	4
Your Love for Me	Integrity Songwriters	Pop worship	Up	4
_____	_____	_____	_____	_____
_____	_____	_____	_____	_____
_____	_____	_____	_____	_____

MOVIE CLIPS

Title: Forrest Gump

Topic: Friendship; Laying your life down for a friend

Description: Forrest goes back into the jungle of Vietnam to find his fallen friend, Bubba, and runs him out of the battle zone.

Start Time: 0:53:30

Start Cue: "I gotta find Bubba!"

End Time: 0:55:00

End Cue: Forrest runs out of frame, with the jungle exploding behind him. Can also end at "That's all I have to say about that."

Comments: _____

_____

Title: Forrest Gump

Topic: Love; Friendship

Description: Forrest, driving a shrimp boat, sees his friend Lieutenant Dan and jumps off the boat to greet him.

Start Time: 1:31:10

Start Cue: Shot of Forrest's hands steering the boat.

End Time: 1:32:50

End Cue: "That's my boat." Can end earlier.

Comments: _____

_____

Title: Hoosiers

Topic: Unconditional love; Forgiveness

Description: Dennis Hopper's character, a recovering alcoholic, is in the hospital drying out. His son visits him and tells him he loves him.

Start Time: 1:30:15

Start Cue: "No school this small . . ."

End Time: 1:32:30

End Cue: "Anyway, no school this small has ever been in the state championship!"

Comments: Needs some setup for those who haven't seen the movie.

_____

Title: _____

Topic: _____

Description: _____

Start Time: _____

Start Cue: _____

End Time: _____

End Cue: _____

Comments: _____

God's Majesty

MESSAGE TITLES

_____

_____

DRAMAS

Title	Tone	Characters	Topics
The Nature of Life	Mixed	2 males, 2 females	Wonder of creation; Family

SONGS

Title	Artist	Style	Tempo	Seeker-Sensitivity Rating
Almighty	Wayne Watson	Praise & worship/pop	Up	2
Awesome God	Rich Mullins	Pop anthem	Mid/up	1
God of Wonders	**Various**	**Folk rock**	**Mid**	**7**
Greater Than	**Riley Armstrong**	**Alternative pop/rock**	**Up**	**8**
Lord of All	First Call	Ballad trio	Slow	6
Mighty Lord	Kathy Troccoli; Ashley Cleveland	Funky pop	Up	8
Praise the King	**Cindy Morgan**	**Ballad**	**Slow**	**4**
This Is My Father's World	Fernando Ortega	Folk ballad	Slow/mid	8

Worship Choruses

Title	Artist	Style	Tempo	Seeker-Sensitivity Rating
Above All	Paul Baloche/Lenny LeBlanc	Worship ballad	Slow	5
Awesome in This Place	Dave Billington	Worship ballad	Slow	2
Be Magnified	Don Moen	Ballad	Slow	2
Did You Feel the Mountains Tremble?	Passion	Pop/rock	Mid/up	2
Everyone Arise	Tommy Walker	Pop/rock	Up	3
God of Wonders	**Various**	**Folk rock**	**Mid**	**7**
He Is Exalted	Twila Paris	Pop worship, in 3	Mid	3
High and Exalted	Bob Fitts	Pop worship	Slow/mid	2
Holy, Holy, Holy (Gary Oliver)	Alvin Slaughter/ Willow Creek Music	Gospel pop	Up	5
Holy, Holy, Holy (Traditional)	*Willow Creek Music*	*Traditional hymn*	*Mid*	*5*
I See the Lord	Chris Falson, Maranatha! Singers/Willow Creek Music	Worship ballad	Slow/mid	2
Let Everything That Has Breath	Matt Redman	Pop/rock worship	Up	4
Let It Rise	Praise Band	Rock worship	Up	5
Lift Up Your Heads	Tommy Walker	Rock/pop worship	Up	2
Lord Most High	Willow Creek Music	MOR worship	Mid	3
My Glorious	Student Impact	Rock	Mid/up	4
Open the Eyes of My Heart	Paul Baloche	Pop/rock worship	Up	5
Revelation 19	Student Impact	Worship ballad	Slow/mid	4
Show Your Power	Kevin Prosch, Vineyard	Rock/pop worship	Up	3
Thank You for Saving Me	Delirious	Folk rock worship ballad	Slow/mid	3
Unto the King	Don Moen	Worship ballad, in 3	Slow/mid	3
We Fall Down	Passion	Worship ballad	Slow/mid	3
We Praise Your Name	*Willow Creek Music*	*Worship ballad*	*Slow/mid*	*4*
Who Is Like Our God?	Vineyard	Rock/pop worship	Mid	3
You Have Been Given	Willow Creek Music	Worship ballad, in 3	Slow	3
_____	_____	_____	_____	___
_____	_____	_____	_____	___
_____	_____	_____	_____	___

MOVIE CLIPS

Title:	The Prince of Egypt
Topic:	God's power; God's calling on our lives
Description:	This film is an animated telling of the story of Moses. This scene shows God's call to Moses through the burning bush.
Start Time:	0:42:50
Start Cue:	Lost sheep bleats; Moses goes after him.
End Time:	0:47:50
End Cue:	Moses is standing with his staff next to the bush (now not burning).
Comments:	Can be used as an illustration much the way the biblical passage itself would be used.

_____
_____
_____

Title: _____
Topic: _____
Description: _____
Start Time: _____
Start Cue: _____
End Time: _____
End Cue: _____
Comments: _____
_____
_____
_____

God's Mercy

Might also include: *God's Patience*

MESSAGE TITLES

❑ *Yeah God:* For Being Patient

DRAMAS

Title	Tone	Characters	Topics
Another Day at the Bus Stop	Mixed	1 male, 1 female	Our relationship with God; Self-esteem
Measuring Up	Mixed; Mime	2 males, 1 female, 1 either male or female	God's acceptance of us; Self-esteem
Take Heart	Mixed; Mime	2 males, 2 females	God heals the brokenhearted; Disappointment
"X" Marks the Spot	Serious; Mime	1 male, 1 female, 3 either males or females	Sin; Redemption; Forgiveness; Guilt

SONGS

Title	Artist	Style	Tempo	Seeker-Sensitivity Rating
At Jesus' Feet	Billy & Sarah Gaines	Ballad	Slow	6
Be Still and Know	**Tommy Walker & the CA Worship Band**	**Rock/pop, in 6/8**	**Mid**	**5**
Farther Than Your Grace Can Reach	**Jonathan Pierce**	**Ballad**	**Slow**	**9**

Title	Artist	Style	Tempo	Seeker-Sensitivity Rating
Lay Your Burdens Down	*Willow Creek Music*	*Ballad*	*Slow*	*9*
Let the Lord Love You	*Willow Creek Music*	*Acoustic guitar ballad*	*Slow*	*9*
Lord of All	First Call	Ballad trio	Slow	6
Love Is Always There	Carolyn Arends	Folk pop	Up	9
Mercy for the Memories	Geoff Moore & the Distance	Folk pop ballad	Slow	9
Miracle of Mercy	Steven Curtis Chapman	Acoustic ballad	Slow	4
My Redeemer Is Faithful and True	**Steven Curtis Chapman**	**Ballad**	**Slow**	**9**
Naïve	Chris Rice	Folk pop	Mid	8
Remember Your Chains	Steven Curtis Chapman	MOR acoustic	Mid	2
Speechless	**Steven Curtis Chapman**	**Acoustic rock**	**Mid/up**	**7**
Who Am I?	Margaret Becker	Power ballad	Slow	7
Why Me?	*Willow Creek Music*	*Ballad*	*Slow*	*9*
Your Grace Still Amazes Me	Phillips, Craig and Dean	Pop ballad	Slow	7
____	____	____	____	____
____	____	____	____	____
____	____	____	____	____
____	____	____	____	____

Worship Choruses

Title	Artist	Style	Tempo	Seeker-Sensitivity Rating
Above All	Paul Baloche/Lenny LeBlanc	Worship ballad	Slow	5
Be Still My Soul	*Willow Creek Music*	*Worship ballad*	*Slow/mid*	*4*
Faithful to Me	Curt Coffield	Pop worship	Mid	6
Great Is Thy Faithfulness	NA	Traditional worship/hymn	Slow	5
He Knows My Name	Tommy Walker	Worship ballad	Slow	7
Holy, Holy, Holy (Traditional)	*Willow Creek Music*	*Traditional hymn*	*Mid*	*5*
Let Your Love Pour	*Student Impact*	*MOR worship*	*Mid*	*4*
Lord, I Lift Your Name on High	Maranatha!/Praise Band	Pop worship	Up	6
The Lord Is Gracious and Compassionate	Vineyard	Worship ballad	Mid/slow	5
No Greater Love	Tommy Walker	Pop/rock	Up	6

Title	Artist	Style	Tempo	Seeker-Sensitivity Rating
O Most High	Mark Altrogge	Pop	Up	3
We Fall Down	Passion	Worship ballad	Slow/mid	3
Who Is Like Our God?	Vineyard	Rock/pop worship	Mid	3
You Are My King	Passion	Worship ballad	Slow	4
Your Love for Me	Integrity Songwriters	Pop worship	Up	4

MOVIE CLIPS

Title: Les Misérables

Topic: Grace; Forgiveness

Description: In the first scene of the movie, ex-convict Jean Valjean is welcomed into a church for food and shelter. He steals some silverware, is caught, and in order to model the grace of God to him, the bishop forgives Valjean and gives the silver to him and gives him candlesticks in addition.

Start Time: 0:6:22

Start Cue: Jean Valjean creeps down the stairs.

End Time: 0:9:53

End Cue: "Now I give you back to God." Close-up of Valjean, fade to black.

Comments: Valjean strikes the bishop. It is a bit violent but adds to the power of the bishop's forgiveness of Valjean. One of the bishop's statements sounds as if he bought Valjean's soul, but more likely he is saying that he used the silver essentially to buy him out of the evil he had done so that he could be presented to God. A great picture of grace.

Title: _____

Topic: _____

Description: _____

Start Time: _____

Start Cue: _____

End Time: _____

End Cue: _____

Comments: _____

God's Power

Might also include: *God's Strength*

MESSAGE TITLES

❏ Connect with the Source of Strength
❏ *A Faith That Works—The Book of James:* All Things Are Possible
❏ *God's Outrageous Claims:* Unlocking Our Power
❏ *Surprised by God:* Surprised by God's Power
❏ *Truths That Transform:* I Can Do All Things

_____

_____

_____

_____

DRAMAS

Title	Tone	Characters	Topics
The Quagmire	Serious	1 male or female	Failure; Self-esteem; Being "stuck"; Trusting God
The Safe	Mixed	1 male, 1 female, 3 either males or females	Inner strength; Needing God's strength
These Parts	Mixed	2 males, 1 female, 3 either males or females, 1 child, 1 narrator	The Resurrection; Our need for Christ; Easter

SONGS

Title	Artist	Style	Tempo	Seeker-Sensitivity Rating
Almighty	Wayne Watson	Praise & worship/pop	Up	2
Awesome God	Rich Mullins	Pop anthem	Mid/up	1
Be Still and Know	**Tommy Walker & the CA Worship Band**	**Rock/pop, in 6/8**	**Mid**	**5**
God Is in Control	Twila Paris	Pop/rock	Up	1
God of Wonders	**Various**	**Folk rock**	**Mid**	**7**
Greater Than	**Riley Armstrong**	**Alternative pop/rock**	**Up**	**8**
Have No Fear	*Willow Creek Music*	*Piano ballad*	*Slow*	*9*
His Love Is Strong	Clay Crosse	Pop	Up	10
His Strength Is Perfect	**Steven Curtis Chapman**	**Ballad**	**Slow**	**9**
Hold On	*Willow Creek Music*	*Acoustic rock/pop ballad*	*Slow/mid*	*10*
Hold On to Jesus	Steven Curtis Chapman	Ballad	Slow	8
I Go to the Rock	Dottie Rambo; Whitney Houston	Swing/big band	Mid	7
Lion and the Lamb	Maranatha! Singers; Crystal Lewis	Ballad trio	Slow	4
Lord of All	First Call	Ballad trio	Slow	6
Mighty Lord	Kathy Troccoli; Ashley Cleveland	Funky pop	Up	8
Strength in You	*Willow Creek Music*	*MOR pop*	*Slow/mid*	*10*
Take My Hand	The Kry	Acoustic ballad	Mid/slow	9
When You Are a Soldier	Steven Curtis Chapman	Keyboard ballad	Slow/mid	4

Worship Choruses

Title	Artist	Style	Tempo	Seeker-Sensitivity Rating
Above All	Paul Baloche/Lenny LeBlanc	Worship ballad	Slow	5
All the Power You Need	Hillsongs	Pop worship	Up	5
All Things Are Possible	Hillsongs	Pop worship	Up	4
And That My Soul Knows Very Well	Hillsongs	Worship ballad	Slow	5
Awesome in This Place	Dave Billington	Worship ballad	Slow	2
Be Magnified	Don Moen	Ballad	Slow	2
Be Still My Soul	*Willow Creek Music*	*Worship ballad*	*Slow/mid*	*4*
Did You Feel the Mountains Tremble?	Passion	Pop/rock	Mid/up	2
God of Wonders	**Various**	**Folk rock**	**Mid**	**7**
He Is Exalted	Twila Paris	Pop worship, in 3	Mid	3
High and Exalted	Bob Fitts	Pop worship	Slow/mid	2
Holy, Holy, Holy (Gary Oliver)	Alvin Slaughter/ Willow Creek Music	Gospel pop	Up	5
Holy, Holy, Holy (Traditional)	*Willow Creek Music*	*Traditional hymn*	*Mid*	*5*
I See the Lord	Chris Falson, Maranatha! Singers/Willow Creek Music	Worship ballad	Slow/mid	2
Jesus, You're the Answer	Tommy Walker	Soulish worship ballad	Slow	5
Let It Rise	Praise Band	Rock worship	Up	5
Let Your Word Go Forth	*Willow Creek Music*	*Pop worship*	*Up*	*2*
Lift Up Your Heads	Tommy Walker	Rock/pop worship	Up	2
More Love More Power	Jude Del Herro	Worship ballad	Slow	3
My Glorious	Student Impact	Rock	Mid/up	4
My Heart Sings Praises	Hillsongs	Pop worship	Mid	4
O Most High	Mark Altrogge	Pop	Up	3
Open the Eyes of My Heart	Paul Baloche	Pop/rock worship	Up	5
Revelation 19	Student Impact	Worship ballad	Slow/mid	4
Shout to the Lord	Hillsongs	Worship power ballad	Slow	3
Show Your Power	Kevin Prosch, Vineyard	Rock/pop worship	Up	3
We Fall Down	Passion	Worship ballad	Slow/mid	3
We Praise Your Name	*Willow Creek Music*	*Worship ballad*	*Slow/mid*	*4*
Who Is Like Our God?	Vineyard	Rock/pop worship	Mid	3

Title	Artist	Style	Tempo	Seeker-Sensitivity Rating
_____	_____	_____	_____	_____
_____	_____	_____	_____	_____
_____	_____	_____	_____	_____
_____	_____	_____	_____	_____
_____	_____	_____	_____	_____
_____	_____	_____	_____	_____

MOVIE CLIPS

Title: The Prince of Egypt

Topic: God's power; God's calling on our lives

Description: This film is an animated telling of the story of Moses. This scene shows God's call to Moses through the burning bush.

Start Time: 0:42:50

Start Cue: Lost sheep bleats; Moses goes after him.

End Time: 0:47:50

End Cue: Moses is standing with his staff next to the bush (now not burning).

Comments: Can be used as an illustration much the way the biblical passage itself would be used.

_____

_____

_____

Title: The Prince of Egypt

Topic: God's power

Description: Powerful depiction of the plagues over Egypt and the struggle between Pharaoh and Moses set to music. The minute and a half before this clip could also be used with it, setting up the plagues.

Start Time: 1:05:08

Start Cue: Zoom in on the temple, leading to frogs climbing the stairs.

End Time: 1:08:00

End Cue: Darkness falls over the city, zooms out to Moses.

Comments: _____

_____

_____

Title: The Prince of Egypt

Topic: The parting of the Red Sea; God's power

Description: Wonderful animated depiction of the parting of the Red Sea, showing the power of God and his deliverance of the people of Israel. It is six minutes long but is powerful.

Start Time: 1:22:20

Start Cue: Man blows the ram's horn.

End Time: 1:28:18

End Cue: Wide shot of the multitude of Israel looking over the Red Sea.

Comments: Can be used as a sermon illustration much the way the biblical passage would be used.

_____
_____
_____

Title: _____

Topic: _____

Description: _____

Start Time: _____

Start Cue: _____

End Time: _____

End Cue: _____

Comments: _____

_____
_____

God's Presence

MESSAGE TITLES

❏ When God Comes Near

❏ **Discovering the Presence of God:** Discovering the Presence of God • Practicing the Presence of God • The Power of the Presence of God

DRAMAS

Title	Tone	Characters	Topics
Chameleon	Mixed	3 males	Controlling our emotions; God's presence in our lives

SONGS

Title	Artist	Style	Tempo	Seeker-Sensitivity Rating
Be Still and Know	**Tommy Walker & the CA Worship Band**	**Rock/pop, in 6/8**	**Mid**	5
Every Season	**Nicole Nordeman**	**Ballad**	**Slow**	8
Have No Fear	*Willow Creek Music*	*Piano ballad*	*Slow*	*9*
He Knows My Name	**Tommy Walker/Helena**	**Worship ballad**	**Slow**	9
His Eyes	Steven Curtis Chapman	Acoustic guitar ballad	Mid/slow	9
I Can Hear You	Carolyn Arends	Folk pop	Mid/up	8

Title	Artist	Style	Tempo	Seeker-Sensitivity Rating
Jesus, King of Angels	**Fernando Ortega**	**Ballad**	**Slow**	**6**
Lord of All	First Call	Ballad trio	Slow	6
Small Enough	Nicole Nordeman	Ballad duet	Slow	6
There Is a God	**Tommy Walker**	**Ballad duet**	**Slow**	**8**
This Is My Father's World	Fernando Ortega	Folk ballad	Slow/mid	8
You Are with Me Still	*Willow Creek Music*	*Acoustic ballad*	*Slow*	*9*
Your Love Stays with Me	Gary Chapman	Piano ballad	Slow	10
_____	_____	_____	_____	_____
_____	_____	_____	_____	_____
_____	_____	_____	_____	_____
_____	_____	_____	_____	_____

Worship Choruses

Title	Artist	Style	Tempo	Seeker-Sensitivity Rating
All Around	Curt Coffield	Caribbean pop	Up	7
Awesome in This Place	Dave Billington	Worship ballad	Slow	2
Beautiful God	Vineyard	Pop	Up	5
Better Is One Day	Matt Redman/Passion	Folk worship	Mid	4
Blessed Be the Name	Vineyard	Worship ballad	Slow	4
Breathe	Michael W. Smith	Worship ballad	Slow	3
Come, Now Is the Time to Worship	Vineyard	Pop/rock	Up	5
For the Beauty of the Earth	*Willow Creek Music*	*Worship ballad*	*Slow*	*5*
Great Is Thy Faithfulness	NA	Traditional worship/hymn	Slow	5
He Knows My Name	Tommy Walker	Worship ballad	Slow	7
He's Here	*Student Impact*	*Worship ballad*	*Slow*	*7*
I Live to Know You	Hillsongs	Worship power ballad	Slow	3
I See the Lord	Chris Falson, Maranatha! Singers/Willow Creek Music	Worship ballad	Slow/mid	2
In Your Hands	Hillsongs	Worship ballad	Slow/mid	4
In Your Loving Arms	*Willow Creek Music*	*Ballad*	*Slow*	*4*
Jesus, Draw Me Close	Willow Creek Music	Worship ballad	Slow	3

Title	Artist	Style	Tempo	Seeker-Sensitivity Rating
Love You So Much	Hillsongs	Worship ballad	Slow	5
Meet with Me	Ten Shekel Shirt	Modern worship	Up	7
Where You Are	Tommy Walker	Pop worship	Mid	5
You Are Holy	Hillsongs	Worship ballad	Slow	3
You Are with Me Still	*Willow Creek Music*	*Acoustic ballad*	*Slow*	9

MOVIE CLIPS

Title: The Prince of Egypt

Topic: The parting of the Red Sea; God's power

Description: Wonderful animated depiction of the parting of the Red Sea, showing the power of God and his deliverance of the people of Israel. It is six minutes long but is powerful.

Start Time: 1:22:20

Start Cue: Man blows the ram's horn.

End Time: 1:28:18

End Cue: Wide shot of the multitude of Israel looking over the Red Sea.

Comments: Can be used as a sermon illustration much the way the biblical passage would be used.

Title:

Topic:

Description:

Start Time:

Start Cue:

End Time:

End Cue:

Comments:

God's Tenderness

Might also include: *God's Gentleness*

MESSAGE TITLES

❑ *Yeah God:* For Being Expressive

_____

_____

_____

DRAMAS

Title	Tone	Characters	Topics
Another Day at the Bus Stop	Mixed	1 male, 1 female	Our relationship with God; Self-esteem
Take Heart	Mixed; Mime	2 males, 2 females	God heals the brokenhearted; Disappointment

SONGS

Title	Artist	Style	Tempo	Seeker-Sensitivity Rating
At Jesus' Feet	Billy & Sarah Gaines	Ballad	Slow	6
Every Single Tear	Scott Krippayne	Ballad	Slow	10
He Won't Let You Go	**The Kry**	**Piano ballad**	**Slow**	**10**
His Eyes	Steven Curtis Chapman	Acoustic guitar ballad	Mid/slow	9
Hold Me, Jesus	Rich Mullins	Ballad	Slow	7
Holy One	*Helena*	*Ballad*	*Slow*	7

Title	Artist	Style	Tempo	Seeker-Sensitivity Rating
I Will Rest in You	Jaci Velasquez	Ballad	Slow	8
If I Could Look through Your Eyes	*Willow Creek Music*	*Piano ballad*	*Slow*	*10*
If This World	Jaci Velasquez	Pop	Up	9
Jesus Loves Me	Whitney Houston	R & B/pop	Slow/mid	8
Jesus Will Still Be There	Point of Grace	Ballad	Slow	9
Lay Your Burdens Down	*Willow Creek Music*	*Ballad*	*Slow*	*9*
Let the Lord Love You	*Willow Creek Music*	*Acoustic guitar ballad*	*Slow*	*9*
Lion and the Lamb	Maranatha! Singers; Crystal Lewis	Ballad trio	Slow	4
The Love of God	*Willow Creek Music*	*A cappella vocal group*	*Slow*	*6*
No One Knows My Heart	Susan Ashton	Folk pop ballad	Slow/mid	9
Peace Be Still	Al Denson	Ballad	Slow	10
A Place to Call Home	*Greg Ferguson/ Willow Creek Music*	*Gospel ballad*	*Slow, in 3*	*10*
Small Enough	Nicole Nordeman	Ballad duet	Slow	6
Treasure of You	Steven Curtis Chapman	Driving rock	Up	10
Weary Soul	*Helena*	*Tender ballad*	*Slow*	*9*
You Brought My Heart to Life	*Willow Creek Music*	*Ballad*	*Slow*	*9*
___	___	___	___	___
___	___	___	___	___
___	___	___	___	___
___	___	___	___	___
___	___	___	___	___

Worship Choruses

Title	Artist	Style	Tempo	Seeker-Sensitivity Rating
Hallelujah (Your Love Is Amazing)	Vineyard—Brenton Brown	Rock/pop worship	Up	4
He Knows My Name	Tommy Walker	Worship ballad	Slow	7
He Loves Me	Tommy Walker	Worship ballad	Slow	6
The Lord Is Gracious and Compassionate	Vineyard	Worship ballad	Mid/slow	5
O Most High	Mark Altrogge	Pop	Up	3

Title	Artist	Style	Tempo	Seeker-Sensitivity Rating
There Is None Like You	Lenny LeBlanc	Worship ballad	Slow/mid	6
Who Is Like Our God?	Vineyard	Rock/pop worship	Mid	3

MOVIE CLIPS

Title: _____

Topic: _____

Description: _____

Start Time: _____

Start Cue: _____

End Time: _____

End Cue: _____

Comments: _____

_____

_____

God's Wisdom

Might also include: *God's Guidance*
See also: **Decision Making**

MESSAGE TITLES

❑ Facing the Fork in the Road
❑ God's Wisdom Works
❑ *The Art of Decision Making:* Father Knows Best
❑ *The Art of Decision Making:* How to Acquire Wisdom
❑ *A Faith That Works—The Book of James:* Finding Direction
❑ *Making Life Work:* Pursue Wisdom
❑ *Seven Wonders of the Spiritual World:* God Guides Me
❑ *Yeah God:* For Being a Guide
❑ *Yeah God:* For Being Wise

DRAMAS

Title	Tone	Characters	Topics
The Advisory Board	Mixed	3 males, 2 females (some characters not gender specific)	Decision making; Finding God's will; Voices in our heads
Permanent Solution	Humorous	4 females	Decision making; Who to listen to
A Second Chance	Mixed, more serious	3 males, 1 female	Decision making; Father-son relationships

SONGS

Title	Artist	Style	Tempo	Seeker-Sensitivity Rating
A Beautiful Place	Wayne Watson	MOR ballad	Mid/slow	9
Found a Way	*Greg Ferguson*	*Ballad*	*Slow*	*9*
In My Father's Hands	Susan Ashton	Folk pop	Mid	9
Lord of All	First Call	Ballad trio	Slow	6
Thy Word	Amy Grant	Ballad	Slow	4
_____	_____	_____	_____	_____
_____	_____	_____	_____	_____
_____	_____	_____	_____	_____
_____	_____	_____	_____	_____
_____	_____	_____	_____	_____

Worship Choruses

Title	Artist	Style	Tempo	Seeker-Sensitivity Rating
He Is Exalted	Twila Paris	Pop worship, in 3	Mid	3
Jesus, You're the Answer	Tommy Walker	Soulish worship ballad	Slow	5
Potter's Hand	Hillsongs	Worship ballad	Slow/mid	3
Step by Step	Rich Mullins	Folk worship	Mid	3
Unto the King	Don Moen	Worship ballad, in 3	Slow/mid	3
Who Is Like Our God?	Vineyard	Rock/pop worship	Mid	3
_____	_____	_____	_____	_____
_____	_____	_____	_____	_____
_____	_____	_____	_____	_____
_____	_____	_____	_____	_____
_____	_____	_____	_____	_____

MOVIE CLIPS

Title: The Prince of Egypt

Topic: God's power; God's calling on our lives

Description: This film is an animated telling of the story of Moses. This scene shows God's call to Moses through the burning bush.

Start Time: 0:42:50

Start Cue: Lost sheep bleats; Moses goes after him.

End Time: 0:47:50

End Cue: Moses is standing with his staff next to the bush (now not burning)

Comments: Can be used as an illustration much the way the biblical passage itself would be used.

_____
_____
_____

Title: _____

Topic: _____

Description: _____

Start Time: _____

Start Cue: _____

End Time: _____

End Cue: _____

Comments: _____

_____
_____

Jesus

See also: **Christmas, Easter, Salvation**

MESSAGE TITLES

- ❏ Jesus, Up Close and Personal
- ❏ The Relevance of Jesus Christ
- ❏ Why the Cross?
- ❏ *The Case for Christianity:* The Case for Christ
- ❏ *Life at Its Best:* Jesus at His Best
- ❏ *Our 3-D God:* God as Friend
- ❏ *Surprised by God:* A Surprising God
- ❏ *What Jesus Would Say to . . . (Various people)*
- ❏ *Yeah God:* For Being a Servant
- ❏ **Private Conversations:** Jesus Talks to a Religious Person • Jesus Talks to a Sinner • Jesus Talks to the Father

_____

_____

_____

DRAMAS

Title	Tone	Characters	Topics
Another Day at the Bus Stop	Mixed	1 male, 1 female	Our relationship with God; Self-esteem
I Am	Serious	4 readers, male or female	Who is Jesus Christ?
Lonely at the Top	Serious	1 male	Perils of power; Authority; Easter
These Parts	Mixed	2 males, 1 female, 3 either males or females, 1 child, 1 narrator	The resurrection; Our need for Christ; Easter

SONGS

Title	Artist	Style	Tempo	Seeker-Sensitivity Rating
Cross Medley	*Willow Creek Music*	*Ballad medley—hymns*	*Slow*	*7*
Give Me Jesus	**Willow Creek Music**	**Ballad**	**Slow**	**7**
He Was	*Willow Creek Music*	*Pop/rock, in 6/8*	*Mid*	*10*
His Eyes	Steven Curtis Chapman	Acoustic guitar ballad	Mid/slow	9
Holy One	*Helena*	*Ballad*	*Slow*	*7*
If That's What It Takes	*Willow Creek Music*	*MOR pop*	*Mid/slow*	*5*
Jesus, King of Angels	**Fernando Ortega**	**Ballad**	**Slow**	**6**
Jesus Loves Me	Whitney Houston	R & B/pop	Slow/mid	8
Lion and the Lamb	Maranatha! Singers; Crystal Lewis	Ballad trio	Slow	4
Mary, Did You Know?	Michael English	Pop ballad	Slow	7
Welcome to Our World	Chris Rice	Ballad	Slow	9
Where Would I Be Now?	*Willow Creek Music*	*Ballad, Broadway feel*	*Slow*	*6*
Why Me?	*Willow Creek Music*	*Ballad*	*Slow*	*9*
Wonderful Merciful Savior	**Susan Ashton**	**Acoustic ballad, 6/8 feel**	**Mid/Slow**	**9**
_____	_____	_____	_____	_____
_____	_____	_____	_____	_____
_____	_____	_____	_____	_____
_____	_____	_____	_____	_____
_____	_____	_____	_____	_____

Worship Choruses

Title	Artist	Style	Tempo	Seeker-Sensitivity Rating
Celebrate Jesus Celebrate	Alleluia Music	Pop	Up	6
Holy and Anointed One	Vineyard	Worship ballad	Slow	3
Jesus Lover of My Soul	Hillsongs	Pop worship	Up	3
Jesus, What a Beautiful Name	Hillsongs	Worship ballad, in 6/8	Slow/mid	6
Lift Up Your Heads	Tommy Walker	Rock/pop worship	Up	2

Title	Artist	Style	Tempo	Seeker-Sensitivity Rating
My Redeemer Lives	Hillsongs	Pop/rock	Up	3
Nothing Is as Wonderful	Vineyard	Worship ballad	Slow	3
Shout to the Lord	Hillsongs	Worship power ballad	Slow	3
Thank You for Saving Me	Delirious	Folk rock worship ballad	Slow/mid	3
That's Why We Praise Him	Tommy Walker	Rock/pop worship	Mid	5
Turn Your Eyes upon Jesus	Hillsongs	Worship ballad	Slow	3
What the Lord Has Done	Hillsongs	Worship ballad, in 3	Slow/mid	2
When I Survey the Wondrous Cross	NA	Updated traditional	Slow	3
You Are My King	Passion	Worship ballad	Slow	4
_____	_____	_____	_____	_____
_____	_____	_____	_____	_____
_____	_____	_____	_____	_____
_____	_____	_____	_____	_____

MOVIE CLIPS

Title: _____

Topic: _____

Description: _____

Start Time: _____

Start Cue: _____

End Time: _____

End Cue: _____

Comments: _____

_____

_____

Life Issues

Death

Might refer to the issue of our own death or the death of people close to us.

MESSAGE TITLES

- ❑ A Better Kind of Grieving
- ❑ The Fear of Death ("What's Going to Happen to You the First 15 Minutes After You Die?")
- ❑ *A Faith That Works—The Book of James:* The Brevity of Life
- ❑ *Truths That Transform:* To Live Is Christ . . . to Die Is Gain
- ❑ **Living with Dying:** Facing Death • Grief • Grieving Process • Heaven and Hell: How to Be Saved • View for True Believers

DRAMAS

Title	Tone	Characters	Topics
After Life	Mixed; Serious ending, sober	1 male	The afterlife; Heaven and hell
In the Dark	Serious	1 male, 1 female	Death of a child; Grief
Mr. Peepers Goes to Sleep	Mixed	1 male, 2 females, 1 child	Death; Facing the truth
New Ball Game	Mixed, very moving	2 males, 1 female	Death; Meaning in life after sorrow
The Old Man and the Laundromat	Mixed, mostly serious	1 male, 1 female, 1 child	Grieving; Dealing with death of a loved one; Letting go
Parlor Talk	Mixed	3 males, 2 females	Making a difference with your life; Death; Workaholism
Playing God	Serious	1 male	Aging parent; Right to die
Time Flies	Mixed	2 males, 1 female, 1 young girl	Honoring parents
What Now?	Serious	2 males, 4 females	Coping with a crisis; Dealing with death

SONGS

Title	Artist	Style	Tempo	Seeker-Sensitivity Rating
Dust in the Wind	Kansas	Acoustic ballad	Slow/mid	10
He Won't Let You Go	**The Kry**	**Piano ballad**	**Slow**	**10**
Healing River	*Willow Creek Music*	*Ballad*	*Slow/mid*	*9*
He's My Son	**Mark Schultz**	**Ballad**	**Slow**	**9**
If I Had Only Known	Reba McEntire	Ballad	Slow	10
If You Could See Me Now	Truth	Ballad	Slow	5
Now That You're Gone	**Fernando Ortega**	**Piano ballad**	**Slow/mid**	**10**
Only Here for a Little While	Billy Dean	Country	Mid/up	10
Treasure	**Gary Chapman**	**Acoustic ballad**	**Slow**	**9**
When You Come Home	**Mark Schultz**	**Country-tinged ballad**	**Slow/mid**	**9**

Worship Choruses

Title	Artist	Style	Tempo	Seeker-Sensitivity Rating

MOVIE CLIPS

Title: 8 Seconds

Topic: Regret; Communicating love

Description: A father, whose son has recently died in a rodeo accident, breaks down in remorse over not telling his son that he loved him. This short clip probably needs to be set up.

Start Time: 1:27:22

Start Cue: Pallbearers carry the casket out of the church.

End Time: 1:28:44

End Cue: The mother puts her hands on the father's shoulders.

Comments: _____

Title: Shadowlands

Topic: Grief; Death; Need for a mother

Description: C. S. Lewis tells Joy Gresham about when his mother died.

Start Time: 0:28:15

Start Cue: "I have been really hurt, you know."

End Time: 0:29:25

End Cue: "Yes, I'd like that."

Comments: _____

_____

Title: Shadowlands

Topic: Death; Sharing the dying process

Description: Jack and Joy talk about her imminent death. She makes a couple of profound statements about sharing the dying process.

Start Time: 1:45:30

Start Cue: "I don't want to be somewhere else anymore."

End Time: 1:47:55

End Cue: Jack and Joy kiss.

Comments: _____

_____

Title: Shadowlands

Topic: Grief

Description: C. S. Lewis talks to his stepson Douglass about his mother dying. Very moving.

Start Time: 2:00:55

Start Cue: Jack walks up behind Douglass, and says "Hi."

End Time: 2:04:00

End Cue: Shot of Jack and Douglass embracing taken from behind them.

Comments: _____

_____

Title: _____

Topic: _____

Description: _____

Start Time: _____

Start Cue: _____

End Time: _____

End Cue: _____

Comments: _____

_____

Decision Making

See also: **God's Wisdom**

MESSAGE TITLES

❑ Facing the Fork in the Road
❑ *A Faith That Works—The Book of James:* Finding Direction
❑ *Making Life Work:* Pursue Wisdom
❑ **The Art of Decision Making:** Decisions, Decisions, Decisions • How to Acquire Wisdom
   • Father Knows Best
❑ **Negotiating the Maze of Life:** Thinkers, Feelers, and Procrastinators • God's Role in Decision Making
   • Developing a Personal Board of Directors

_____

_____

_____

DRAMAS

Title	Tone	Characters	Topics
The Advisory Board	Mixed	3 males, 2 females (some characters not gender specific)	Decision making; Finding the will of God; Voices in our heads
Baby Talk	Humorous	2 males, 2 females	Decision making; Parenting; Decision to have children
Character Test	Mixed, moving	2 males, 1 female	Promptings from God; Obedience; Power of encouragement
The Do-Over	Humorous	1 male, 1 female	Longing for second chances; The importance of good choices
The Fence-Sitter	Mixed	4 males, 1 female	Indecision; Getting involved in ministry; Deciding to become a Christian
The Game of Life	Humorous	1 male, 1 female, 1 narrator	Decision making; Search for meaning
Oh, What a Feeling!	Humorous	2 males, 1 female	Decision making; Self-control; Money management
Permanent Solution	Humorous	4 females	Decision making; Who to listen to

Title	Tone	Characters	Topics
A Second Chance	Mixed, more serious	3 males, 1 female	Decision making; Father-son relationships
The Speculators	Humorous	2 males, 1 female	Risk taking; Missed opportunities
The Waiting Room	Mixed	2 males, 2 females	Fear of decision making; Need to take risks

SONGS

Title	Artist	Style	Tempo	Seeker-Sensitivity Rating
Highest Honor	Chris Eaton	Ballad	Slow	7
Life Means So Much	Chris Rice	Folk pop	Mid	7
Live Out Loud	Steven Curtis Chapman	Pop	Up	9
Seize the Day	Carolyn Arends	Folk pop, in 3	Mid	8

Worship Choruses

Title	Artist	Style	Tempo	Seeker-Sensitivity Rating

MOVIE CLIPS

Title: Indiana Jones and the Last Crusade

Topic: Decision making

Description: Walter Donovan, an evil antiquities collector, has to choose the true holy grail from a roomful of false grails. Because he doesn't know the humble character of Christ, he chooses "poorly."

Start Time: 1:50:35

Start Cue: Elsa and Donovan enter the "grail room."

End Time: 1:53:55

End Cue: "You have chosen wisely." Could also end at "He chose poorly."

Comments: Very gruesome scene when Donovan chooses wrong. Has been shown on network TV but might scare kids and may be judged inappropriate by some churches. We haven't used it in a Willow Creek adult service, though our student ministries have used it.

Title: The Matrix

Topic: Decision making; Spiritual seeking

Description: Metaphors abound in this clip, which shows Morpheus explaining the matrix to Neo. He offers him the choice to stay in the bondage of the world he's in (the matrix) or to know the truth and be set free. Should he take the blue pill or the red pill (the truth)? Neo chooses the red pill.

Start Time: 0:25:42

Start Cue: Neo enters the room where Morpheus is.

End Time: 0:29:50

End Cue: "Follow me."

Comments: The clip probably needs explaining but could easily be used in a sermon to illustrate the choice we make to be free of the slavery of sin through choosing Christ.

Title: _____

Topic: _____

Description: _____

Start Time: _____

Start Cue: _____

End Time: _____

End Cue: _____

Comments: _____

———Emotional Issues———

Anger

See also: **Anger toward God, Bondage to the Past, Relational Conflict**

MESSAGE TITLES

❏ *Making Life Work:* Manage Anger
❏ **The Age of Rage:** The Roots of Rage • Expressing Anger Appropriately • Responding to the Anger of Others

_____

_____

_____

DRAMAS

Title	Tone	Characters	Topics
The Angry Woman	Serious	2 males, 3 females, 1 narrator	The roots of anger
Because I Love You	Serious	1 male, 1 female	Adultery; The consequences of sin
Chameleon	Mixed	3 males	Controlling our emotions; God's presence in our lives
Great Expectations	Mixed; Very serious ending	1 male, 2 females	Unanswered prayer
Missing	Serious	3 males, 1 female	Generational barriers; The church's failure to reach Gen-X
A Problem of Perspective	Humorous	1 male, 1 female, 1 either male or female	Marriage; Marital conflict
Remembrances	Serious	1 male, 1 female	Parent-child relationships; Forgiveness
Richard: 1992	Serious	2 males, 1 female	Anger; Rebellion; Decay of the family
Straight-Jacketed	Serious	1 male	Bondage to past and to sin; Anger at God
Tired of Trying	Serious	1 male, 2 females	Dealing with the anger of others; Confronting injustice

Title	Tone	Characters	Topics
Truthful Words	Serious	1 male, 1 female	Leadership; Pride; Truth telling
Watching from the Window	Serious	1 female, 1 child	Stress of life; Challenge of motherhood; Draining relationships

SONGS

*No songs specifically about anger. Look at **Relational Conflict** and **Anger toward God** for ideas.*

Title	Artist	Style	Tempo	Seeker-Sensitivity Rating

Worship Choruses

Title	Artist	Style	Tempo	Seeker-Sensitivity Rating

MOVIE CLIPS

Title:	City Slickers
Topic:	Dysfunctional families; Friendship
Description:	Three friends share the best and worst days of their lives.
Start Time:	1:12:45
Start Cue:	"All right, I got one."
End Time:	1:14:50
End Cue:	"Same day."
Comments:	Could start earlier, but Billy Crystal's character swears briefly during his worst-day description.

_____
_____
_____

Title:	Forrest Gump
Topic:	Child abuse; Bondage to the past
Description:	Jenny and Forrest walk by the house where Jenny was abused as a child. She throws rocks at it.
Start Time:	1:45:30
Start Cue:	After "Jenny, most of the times was real quiet."
End Time:	1:46:50
End Cue:	"Sometimes, there just aren't enough rocks."
Comments:	_____

_____
_____
_____

Title:	_____
Topic:	_____
Description:	_____
Start Time:	_____
Start Cue:	_____
End Time:	_____
End Cue:	_____
Comments:	_____

_____
_____
_____

Bondage to the Past

Refers to how events in our past still affect us and often keep us from being whole

See also: **Healing, Regret**

MESSAGE TITLES

- ❏ From Stuck to Starting Over
- ❏ Hostility in the Home
- ❏ Life without Regret
- ❏ Resolving Regrets
- ❏ Why Did This Happen to Me?
- ❏ *The Age of Rage:* The Roots of Rage
- ❏ *Life's Too Short* . . . for Unresolved Bitterness
- ❏ *Measuring How Much You Matter to God:* What Scars Self-Esteem

DRAMAS

Title	Tone	Characters	Topics
All Gummed Up	Serious	1 male, 1 female, 1 offstage male voice	Adultery; Dealing with past hurts; The pain of lies
Conversations	Serious	2 males, 1 female, 1 offstage female voice	Self-esteem; Self-criticism; Failure
Funny Girl	Mixed	1 male, 2 females (multiple roles for 1 man and 1 woman)	Self-esteem; Need for acceptance
Honestly Speaking	Mixed	3 males, 3 females	Positive self-talk; Self-esteem
I Don't Want to Fight You Anymore	Serious	1 female	Relationship with God; Giving up control; Our value to God
The Intruder	Serious	1 male, 1 female	Self-image; Destructive parenting; God's love in spite of failure
The Lane of Life	Serious; Mime	5 either males or females, 1 offstage narrator	Salvation; Our value to God; Self-esteem

Title	Tone	Characters	Topics
Make It Happen	Humorous	5 males, 1 female (numerous extras for attendees and security)	Taking responsibility for change; The limits of self-help seminars
Paralyzed	Serious	2 males (1 adult, 1 teen), 2 females (1 adult, 1 teen)	Depression; Prayer; Relationship with God; Family in crisis
The Quagmire	Serious	1 male or female	Failure; Self-esteem; Being "stuck"; Trusting God
Straight-Jacketed	Serious	1 male	Bondage to past and to sin; Anger at God
_____	_____	_____	_____
_____	_____	_____	_____
_____	_____	_____	_____
_____	_____	_____	_____

SONGS

Title	Artist	Style	Tempo	Seeker-Sensitivity Rating
Ask Me	Amy Grant	Pop	Mid	9
Ball and Chain	Susan Ashton	Folk pop	Mid	9
Desperado	Eagles	Ballad	Slow	10
Every Single Tear	Scott Krippayne	Ballad	Slow	10
Free	Ginny Owens	Folk pop	Mid/up	8
Healing Song	Curt Coffield	Ballad, in 3	Slow/mid	7
He's All You Need	Steve Camp	Ballad	Slow	7
Hold Me, Jesus	Rich Mullins	Ballad	Slow	7
Hunger for Healing	*Willow Creek Music*	*Folk ballad*	*Slow*	*10*
I Will Be Free	Cindy Morgan	Ballad	Slow	7
I've Been Released	*Willow Creek Music*	*Pop/rock—Chicago sound*	*Up*	*9*
Lay Your Burdens Down	*Willow Creek Music*	*Ballad*	*Slow*	*9*
Let the Lord Love You	*Willow Creek Music*	*Acoustic guitar ballad*	*Slow*	*9*
Mercy for the Memories	Geoff Moore & the Distance	Folk pop ballad	Slow	9
Now That You're Gone	**Fernando Ortega**	**Piano ballad**	**Slow/mid**	**10**

Title	Artist	Style	Tempo	Seeker-Sensitivity Rating
Take My Hand	The Kry	Acoustic ballad	Mid/slow	9
Weary Soul	*Helena*	*Tender ballad*	*Slow*	*9*
What a Day It Will Be	*Greg Ferguson*	*Flowing ballad*	*Slow/mid*	*8*
You Brought My Heart to Life	*Willow Creek Music*	*Ballad*	*Slow*	*9*

Worship Choruses

Title	Artist	Style	Tempo	Seeker-Sensitivity Rating
Healing Song	Curt Coffield	Ballad, in 3	Slow/mid	7
Let Your Love Pour	*Student Impact*	*MOR worship*	*Mid*	*4*

MOVIE CLIPS

Title: Forrest Gump

Topic: Child abuse; Bondage to the past

Description: Jenny and Forrest walk by the house where Jenny was abused as a child. She throws rocks at it.

Start Time: 1:45:30

Start Cue: After "Jenny, most of the times was real quiet."

End Time: 1:46:50

End Cue: "Sometimes, there just aren't enough rocks."

Comments: _____

_____

_____

Title: Parenthood

Topic: Parenting; Absent fathers

Description: Funny, bittersweet scene where young Gil is taken to a baseball game by his father and then left with an usher. We find out it's actually a combination of memories of his strained childhood.

Start Time: 0:00:05

Start Cue: Start at fade-in. This is the opening scene.

End Time: 0:02:28

End Cue: "Strong, happy, confident kids."

Comments: Profanity immediately follows cutoff point.

Title: Shadowlands

Topic: Grief; Death; Need for a mother

Description: C. S. Lewis tells Joy Gresham about when his mother died.

Start Time: 0:28:15

Start Cue: "I have been really hurt, you know."

End Time: 0:29:25

End Cue: "Yes, I'd like that."

Comments: _____

Title: The Legend of Bagger Vance

Topic: Getting over the past; Quitting; Overcoming fears

Description: Golfer Randolph Junuh, a veteran haunted by his war experiences, hits a ball into the woods. Facing an impossible shot to get back into the tournament, he reaches down to pick up the ball. His caddie, Bagger Vance (who is sort of a mystical God-figure in the movie), helps him to face his fears and overcome them.

Start Time: 1:38:08

Start Cue: Junuh walks down the fairway toward the woods with Bagger behind him.

End Time: 1:42:37

End Cue: Overjoyed look on the boy's face.

Comments: There is mild profanity after the cutoff point. This clip gets borderline New Age, but Bagger's character can be a great metaphor for God helping us through the darkness we face.

Title: _____

Topic: _____

Description: _____

Start Time: _____

Start Cue: _____

End Time: _____

End Cue: _____

Comments: _____

Disappointment

MESSAGE TITLES

- ❑ Dealing with Disappointment
- ❑ When Life Doesn't Turn Out Like You Planned
- ❑ *Strength for the Storms of Life:* Disappointment
- ❑ **Disappointment with God:** What Causes Disappointment? • Where Is God When You Need Him?
  • When God Seems Silent

_____

_____

_____

DRAMAS

Title	Tone	Characters	Topics
Great Expectations	Mixed; Very serious ending	1 male, 2 females	Unanswered prayer
"It"	Humorous	2 males, 1 female	Becoming a Christian doesn't mean no problems; Vulnerability of new believers
Just the Two of Us	Serious	1 male, 2 females	Infertility; Unanswered prayer
Paralyzed	Serious	2 males (1 adult, 1 teen), 2 females (1 adult, 1 teen)	Depression; Prayer; Relationship with God; Family in crisis
A Perspective on Spring	Humorous	1 male	Optimistic/pessimistic views of life; Spring; The spiritual season of spring
Self-list Giving	Mixed	2 males, 2 females	Disappointment; Meeting needs; Expressing value; Expectations
The Surprised Party	Humorous	2 males, 1 female	Disappointments are a part of life
Take Heart	Mixed; Mime	2 males, 2 females	God heals the brokenhearted; Disappointment
Unknown	Serious	1 male, 4 females	Friendship; Loneliness; Small groups
_____	_____	_____	_____
_____	_____	_____	_____
_____	_____	_____	_____

SONGS

Title	Artist	Style	Tempo	Seeker-Sensitivity Rating
A Beautiful Place	Wayne Watson	MOR ballad	Mid/slow	9
But if Not	*Student Impact*	*Acoustic ballad*	*Slow*	*5*
Every Single Tear	Scott Krippayne	Ballad	Slow	10
Found a Way	*Greg Ferguson*	*Ballad*	*Slow*	*9*
His Strength Is Perfect	**Steven Curtis Chapman**	**Ballad**	**Slow**	**9**
Hunger for Healing	*Willow Creek Music*	*Folk ballad*	*Slow*	*10*
Jesus Will Still Be There	Point of Grace	Ballad	Slow	9
Lay Your Burdens Down	*Willow Creek Music*	*Ballad*	*Slow*	*9*
Peace Be Still	Al Denson	Ballad	Slow	10
A Place to Call Home	*Greg Ferguson/ Willow Creek Music*	*Gospel ballad*	*Slow, in 3*	*10*
There Is a Love	Michael English	Pop	Up	9
What a Day It Will Be	*Greg Ferguson*	*Flowing ballad*	*Slow/mid*	*8*
You Are with Me Still	*Willow Creek Music*	*Acoustic ballad*	*Slow*	*9*
_____	_____	_____	_____	___
_____	_____	_____	_____	___
_____	_____	_____	_____	___
_____	_____	_____	_____	___
_____	_____	_____	_____	___

Worship Choruses

Title	Artist	Style	Tempo	Seeker-Sensitivity Rating
But if Not	*Student Impact*	*Acoustic ballad*	*Slow*	*5*
_____	_____	_____	_____	___
_____	_____	_____	_____	___
_____	_____	_____	_____	___
_____	_____	_____	_____	___

MOVIE CLIPS

Title: _____

Topic: _____

Description: _____

Start Time: _____

Start Cue: _____

End Time: _____

End Cue: _____

Comments: _____

Disillusionment

Might also include: _Apathy, Discouragement, Hopelessness_

See also: **Hope**

MESSAGE TITLES

- ❏ From Stuck to Making a Difference
- ❏ From Stuck to Starting Over
- ❏ When Life Doesn't Turn Out Like You Planned
- ❏ _Understanding the Times:_ The '70s

DRAMAS

Title	Tone	Characters	Topics
Grand Canyon	Serious	1 male, 1 female	Marital breakdown
Great Expectations	Mixed; Very serious ending	1 male, 2 females	Unanswered prayer

Title	Tone	Characters	Topics
The Quagmire	Serious	1 male or female	Failure; Self-esteem; Being "stuck"; Trusting God
The Quitter	Serious	2 males, 1 female	Quitting; Failure
Richard: 1974	Serious	5 males, 1 female	Disillusionment; Crumbling dreams
Richard: 1992	Serious	2 males, 1 female	Anger; Rebellion; Decay of the family
_____	_____	_____	_____
_____	_____	_____	_____
_____	_____	_____	_____
_____	_____	_____	_____
_____	_____	_____	_____

 SONGS

Title	Artist	Style	Tempo	Seeker-Sensitivity Rating
Ball and Chain	Susan Ashton	Folk pop	Mid	9
But if Not	*Student Impact*	*Acoustic ballad*	*Slow*	*5*
Desperado	Eagles	Ballad	Slow	10
Eleanor Rigby	Beatles	Acoustic ballad	Slow/mid	10
Every Single Tear	Scott Krippayne	Ballad	Slow	10
Found a Way	*Greg Ferguson*	*Ballad*	*Slow*	*9*
Good News	**Chris Rice**	**Pop**	**Up**	**9**
Heaven in the Real World	Steven Curtis Chapman	Pop/rock	Up	7
His Strength Is Perfect	**Steven Curtis Chapman**	**Ballad**	**Slow**	**9**
Hunger for Healing	*Willow Creek Music*	*Folk ballad*	*Slow*	*10*
Jesus Will Still Be There	Point of Grace	Ballad	Slow	9
Lay Your Burdens Down	*Willow Creek Music*	*Ballad*	*Slow*	*9*
A Place to Call Home	*Greg Ferguson/ Willow Creek Music*	*Gospel ballad*	*Slow, in 3*	*10*
Somebody Make Me Laugh	Patti Austin	Ballad	Slow	10
Treasure of You	Steven Curtis Chapman	Driving rock	Up	10
Weary Soul	*Helena*	*Tender ballad*	*Slow*	*9*
What a Day It Will Be	*Greg Ferguson*	*Flowing ballad*	*Slow/mid*	*8*

Title	Artist	Style	Tempo	Seeker-Sensitivity Rating

Worship Choruses

Title	Artist	Style	Tempo	Seeker-Sensitivity Rating
But if Not	*Student Impact*	*Acoustic ballad*	*Slow*	*5*
Let Your Love Pour	*Student Impact*	*MOR worship*	*Mid*	*4*

MOVIE CLIPS

Title: City Slickers

Topic: Disillusionment; Life fulfillment

Description: Billy Crystal's character speaks at his son's school. Disillusioned with life in general, he gives a very funny, very depressing discourse on the stages of life.

Start Time: 0:44:38

Start Cue: "As Danny said . . ."

End Time: 0:45:30

End Cue: "Any questions?"

Comments: _____

_____

Title: Forrest Gump

Topic: Despair; Disillusionment

Description: Forrest's friend Jenny, in a moment of despair, gets up on the ledge of a tall building, then decides not to jump, collapsing in tears.

Start Time: 1:29:35

Start Cue: Start after Jenny's boyfriend's hand disappears.

End Time: 1:30:55

End Cue: Shot of full moon.

Comments: _____

_____

Title:	_____
Topic:	_____
Description:	_____
Start Time:	_____
Start Cue:	_____
End Time:	_____
End Cue:	_____
Comments:	_____
	_____

Failure

MESSAGE TITLES

- ❏ From Stuck to Making a Difference
- ❏ From Stuck to Starting Over
- ❏ Victim or Victor?
- ❏ When I'm Mad at Myself
- ❏ *Facing Up to Fear:* The Fear of Failure
- ❏ *The God of the Second Chance:* Getting a Second Chance
- ❏ *Learning through Life's Crises:* Learning through Failing
- ❏ *Seven Wonders of the Spiritual World:* God Forgives My Failures
- ❏ *Strength for the Storms of Life:* Failure

DRAMAS

Title	Tone	Characters	Topics
The Brow Beater	Mixed, mostly serious	1 male, 1 female	Self-esteem; Failures; Forgiveness
A Clean Slate	Serious	1 male, 2 or 3 males or females	Forgiveness; Redemption; Guilt
Conversations	Serious	2 males, 1 female, 1 offstage female voice	Self-esteem; Self-criticism; Failure

Title	Tone	Characters	Topics
A Failure Tale	Mixed	5 males, 1 narrator	Failing; Obeying rules
Getting the Nod	Mixed	2 males, 1 either male or female	Honesty; Integrity; Business ethics; Handling failure
Honestly Speaking	Mixed	3 males, 3 females	Positive self-talk; Self-esteem
The Intruder	Serious	1 male, 1 female	Self-image; Destructive parenting; God's love in spite of failure
Measuring Up	Mixed; Mime	2 males, 1 female, 1 either male or female	God's acceptance of us; Self-esteem
A Nice Guy	Serious	2 males	Regret; Admitting failures; Effects of sin; Confession
The Quagmire	Serious	1 male or female	Failure; Self-esteem; Being "stuck"; Trusting God
The Quitter	Serious	2 males, 1 female	Quitting; Failure
"X" Marks the Spot	Serious; Mime	1 male, 1 female, 3 either males or females	Sin; Redemption; Forgiveness; Guilt
_____	_____	_____	_____
_____	_____	_____	_____
_____	_____	_____	_____
_____	_____	_____	_____

SONGS

Title	Artist	Style	Tempo	Seeker-Sensitivity Rating
A Beautiful Place	Wayne Watson	MOR ballad	Mid/slow	9
Bound to Come Some Trouble	**Rich Mullins**	**Ballad**	**Slow**	**10**
Clumsy	Chris Rice	Pop	Mid/up	8
Enough	*Willow Creek Music*	*Piano ballad*	*Slow*	*7*
Face of Forgiveness	*Willow Creek Music*	*Ballad*	*Slow*	*10*
Farther Than Your Grace Can Reach	**Jonathan Pierce**	**Ballad**	**Slow**	**9**
Free	Ginny Owens	Folk pop	Mid/up	8
God of Wonders	**Various**	**Folk rock**	**Mid**	**7**
He's All You Need	Steve Camp	Ballad	Slow	7
His Strength Is Perfect	**Steven Curtis Chapman**	**Ballad**	**Slow**	**9**

Title	Artist	Style	Tempo	Seeker-Sensitivity Rating
Hunger for Healing	*Willow Creek Music*	*Folk ballad*	*Slow*	*10*
I Stand, I Fall	*Greg Ferguson*	*Piano ballad*	*Slow*	*7*
If I Could Look through Your Eyes	*Willow Creek Music*	*Piano ballad*	*Slow*	*10*
I'm Amazed	*Willow Creek Music*	*Ballad*	*Slow*	*7*
Jesus Will Still Be There	Point of Grace	Ballad	Slow	9
Lay Your Burdens Down	*Willow Creek Music*	*Ballad*	*Slow*	*9*
Let the Lord Love You	*Willow Creek Music*	*Acoustic guitar ballad*	*Slow*	*9*
Love That Will Not Let Me Go	**Steve Camp**	**Ballad**	**Slow**	**10**
Mercy for the Memories	Geoff Moore & the Distance	Folk pop ballad	Slow	9
Peace Be Still	Al Denson	Ballad	Slow	10
A Place to Call Home	*Greg Ferguson/ Willow Creek Music*	*Gospel ballad*	*Slow, in 3*	*10*
Stranger to Holiness	Steve Camp	Ballad	Slow/mid	2
Take My Hand	The Kry	Acoustic ballad	Mid/slow	9
You Are with Me Still	*Willow Creek Music*	*Acoustic ballad*	*Slow*	*9*
___	___	___	___	___
___	___	___	___	___
___	___	___	___	___
___	___	___	___	___
___	___	___	___	___

Worship Choruses

Title	Artist	Style	Tempo	Seeker-Sensitivity Rating
God of Wonders	**Various**	**Folk rock**	**Mid**	7
Let Your Love Pour	*Student Impact*	*MOR worship*	*Mid*	*4*
___	___	___	___	___
___	___	___	___	___
___	___	___	___	___
___	___	___	___	___
___	___	___	___	___

MOVIE CLIPS

Title: Chariots of Fire

Topic: Failure

Description: Harold Abrahams loses a race, his first loss ever, then plays it over in his mind. He grieves his failure to his girlfriend.

Start Time: 0:47:50

Start Cue: Begin after the starter walks across the track.

End Time: 0:50:05

End Cue: "If you don't run, you can't win" or "Try growing up."

Comments: _____

_____

Title: Mr. Holland's Opus

Topic: Inspiring others; Leadership; Getting beyond quitting points

Description: A clarinet student who is struggling decides to quit. Her teacher, Mr. Holland, inspires her to stay with it and in the process teaches her the true nature of music and helps her see her own beauty.

Start Time: 0:30:29/DVD Ch. 8

Start Cue: Mr. Holland is playing piano when his student walks in.

End Time: 0:35:02

End Cue: Mr. Holland smiles; scene fades to a concert.

Comments: _____

_____

Title: Searching for Bobby Fischer

Topic: Success; Fear of failure

Description: Josh Waitzkin, a chess prodigy, has a late-night talk with his dad about the possibility of losing. Shows the pressure of staying on top.

Start Time: 1:01:30

Start Cue: Josh's dad is reading him a story.

End Time: 1:03:50

End Cue: "Maybe it's better not to be the best. Then you can lose and it's O.K."

Comments: _____

_____

Title: Searching for Bobby Fischer

Topic: Fatherhood; Failure; Destructive parenting

Description: Eight-year-old Josh loses a chess match, and his dad angrily confronts him about losing. Illustrates a dad who has too much invested in his son's success.

Start Time: 1:06:30

Start Cue: Shot of clock tower. "Seven moves" is first line.

End Time: 1:08:20

End Cue: "Sorry."

Comments: _____

Title:	The Legend of Bagger Vance
Topic:	Getting over the past; Quitting; Overcoming fears
Description:	Golfer Randolph Junuh, a veteran haunted by his war experiences, hits a ball into the woods. Facing an impossible shot to get back into the tournament, he reaches down to pick up the ball. His caddie, Bagger Vance (who is sort of a mystical God-figure in the movie), helps him to face his fears and overcome them.
Start Time:	1:38:08
Start Cue:	Junuh walks down the fairway toward the woods with Bagger behind him.
End Time:	1:42:37
End Cue:	Overjoyed look on the boy's face.
Comments:	There is mild profanity after the cutoff point. This clip gets borderline New Age, but Bagger's character can be a great metaphor for God helping us through the darkness we face.

_____
_____

Title:	_____
Topic:	_____
Description:	_____
Start Time:	_____
Start Cue:	_____
End Time:	_____
End Cue:	_____
Comments:	_____
	_____

Fear

See also: **Courage, God as a Refuge, Risk Taking**

MESSAGE TITLES

❑ _A Faith That Works—The Book of James:_ Developing Christian Confidence
❑ _Truths That Transform:_ Don't Worry . . . Pray
❑ _Truths That Transform:_ My God Shall Supply All Your Needs
❑ **Facing Up to Fear:** The Fear of Failure • The Fear of Living (Being) Alone • The Fear of Death
❑ **No Fear:** No Fear • Courage for Ordinary People • Should I Be Afraid of God?

_____
_____
_____

DRAMAS

Title	Tone	Characters	Topics
The Boy Who Never Got Dirty	Humorous	1 male, 1 female, 1 narrator	Service; Risk taking
Mr. Peepers Goes to Sleep	Mixed	1 male, 2 females, 1 child	Death; Facing the truth
No More Womb	Mixed	1 male, 1 female	State of the world; Fear of the unknown
The Quagmire	Serious	1 male or female	Failure; Self-esteem; Being "stuck"; Trusting God
Straight-Jacketed	Serious	1 male	Bondage to past and to sin; Anger at God
The Waiting Room	Mixed	2 males, 2 females	Fear of decision making; Need to take risks
What If . . .	Humorous	3 males, 1 female	Worry; Anxiety
_____	_____	_____	_____
_____	_____	_____	_____
_____	_____	_____	_____

SONGS

Title	Artist	Style	Tempo	Seeker-Sensitivity Rating
Ball and Chain	Susan Ashton	Folk pop	Mid	9
Be Still and Know	**Tommy Walker & the CA Worship Band**	**Rock/pop, in 6/8**	**Mid**	**5**
Bound to Come Some Trouble	**Rich Mullins**	**Ballad**	**Slow**	**10**
But if Not	_Student Impact_	_Acoustic ballad_	_Slow_	_5_
Desperado	Eagles	Ballad	Slow	10
Dive	**Steven Curtis Chapman**	**Pop/rock**	**Up**	**9**
Found a Way	_Greg Ferguson_	_Ballad_	_Slow_	_9_
Have No Fear	_Willow Creek Music_	_Piano ballad_	_Slow_	_9_
He Won't Let You Go	**The Kry**	**Piano ballad**	**Slow**	**10**
Here in My Heart	Susan Ashton	Folk rock	Up	8
His Love Is Strong	Clay Crosse	Pop	Up	10

Title	Artist	Style	Tempo	Seeker-Sensitivity Rating
Hold Me, Jesus	Rich Mullins	Ballad	Slow	7
Hold On	*Willow Creek Music*	*Acoustic rock/pop ballad*	*Slow/mid*	*10*
Hold On to Jesus	Steven Curtis Chapman	Ballad	Slow	8
I'll Find You There	The Kry	Folk rock ballad	Slow	9
In My Father's Hands	Susan Ashton	Folk pop	Mid	9
Jesus, King of Angels	**Fernando Ortega**	**Ballad**	**Slow**	**6**
Lay Your Burdens Down	*Willow Creek Music*	*Ballad*	*Slow*	*9*
Love Is Always There	Carolyn Arends	Folk pop	Up	9
Peace Be Still	Al Denson	Ballad	Slow	10
Seize the Day	**Carolyn Arends**	**Folk pop, in 3**	**Mid**	**8**
Small Enough	Nicole Nordeman	Ballad duet	Slow	6
Take My Hand	The Kry	Acoustic ballad	Mid/slow	9
What a Day It Will Be	*Greg Ferguson*	*Flowing ballad*	*Slow/mid*	*8*
When You Are a Soldier	Steven Curtis Chapman	Keyboard ballad	Slow/mid	4
Your Love Stays with Me	Gary Chapman	Piano ballad	Slow	10
_____	_____	_____	_____	_____
_____	_____	_____	_____	_____
_____	_____	_____	_____	_____
_____	_____	_____	_____	_____

Worship Choruses

Title	Artist	Style	Tempo	Seeker-Sensitivity Rating
All the Power You Need	Hillsongs	Pop worship	Up	5
All Things Are Possible	Hillsongs	Pop worship	Up	5
And That My Soul Knows Very Well	Hillsongs	Worship ballad	Slow	5
Be Still My Soul	*Willow Creek Music*	*Worship ballad*	*Slow/mid*	*4*
Blessed Be the Name	Vineyard	Worship ballad	Slow	4
But if Not	*Student Impact*	*Acoustic ballad*	*Slow*	*5*
He Knows My Name	Tommy Walker	Worship ballad	Slow	7
He's Here	Student Impact	Worship ballad	Slow	7
In Your Hands	Hillsongs	Worship ballad	Slow/mid	4

Title	Artist	Style	Tempo	Seeker-Sensitivity Rating
Jesus, What a Beautiful Name	Hillsongs	Worship ballad, in 6/8	Slow/mid	6
Let Your Love Pour	Student Impact	MOR worship	Mid	4
Still I Will Worship You	Willow Creek Music	Pop/rock worship	Up	3
You Are with Me Still	Willow Creek Music	Acoustic ballad	Slow	9
_____	_____	_____	_____	_____
_____	_____	_____	_____	_____
_____	_____	_____	_____	_____
_____	_____	_____	_____	_____

MOVIE CLIPS

Title: The Legend of Bagger Vance

Topic: Getting over the past; Quitting; Overcoming fears

Description: Golfer Randolph Junuh, a veteran haunted by his war experiences, hits a ball into the woods. Facing an impossible shot to get back into the tournament, he reaches down to pick up the ball. His caddie, Bagger Vance (who is sort of a mystical God-figure in the movie), helps him to face his fears and overcome them.

Start Time: 1:38:08

Start Cue: Junuh walks down the fairway toward the woods with Bagger behind him.

End Time: 1:42:37

End Cue: Overjoyed look on the boy's face.

Comments: There is mild profanity after the cutoff point. This clip gets borderline New Age, but Bagger's character can be a great metaphor for God helping us through the darkness we face.

Title: _____

Topic: _____

Description: _____

Start Time: _____

Start Cue: _____

End Time: _____

End Cue: _____

Comments: _____

Grief

See also: **Death**

MESSAGE TITLES

- ❑ A Better Kind of Grieving
- ❑ *Disappointment with God:* Where Is God When You Need Him?
- ❑ *Learning through Life's Crises:* Learning through Losing
- ❑ *Living with Dying:* Grief
- ❑ *Living with Dying:* Grieving Process
- ❑ *Strength for the Storms of Life:* Loss

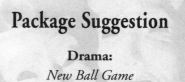

Package Suggestion

Drama:
New Ball Game

Song:
Now That You're Gone

DRAMAS

Title	Tone	Characters	Topics
Attack of the Well-Meaners	Mixed, mostly humorous	1 male, 2 females	Dealing with crisis; Friendship
In the Dark	Serious	1 male, 1 female	Death of a child; Grief
New Ball Game	Mixed, very moving	2 males, 1 female	Death; Meaning in life after sorrow
The Old Man and the Laundromat	Mixed, mostly serious	1 male, 1 female, 1 child	Grieving; Dealing with death of a loved one; Letting go
What Now?	Serious	2 males, 4 females	Coping with a crisis; Dealing with death

SONGS

Title	Artist	Style	Tempo	Seeker-Sensitivity Rating
Be Still and Know	**Tommy Walker & the CA Worship Band**	**Rock/pop, in 6/8**	**Mid**	**5**
Bound to Come Some Trouble	**Rich Mullins**	**Ballad**	**Slow**	**10**
Every Single Tear	Scott Krippayne	Ballad	Slow	10
Healing River	*Willow Creek Music*	*Ballad*	*Slow/mid*	*9*
Healing Song	Curt Coffield	Ballad, in 3	Slow/mid	7
Hunger for Healing	*Willow Creek Music*	*Folk ballad*	*Slow*	*10*
If I Had Only Known	Reba McEntire	Ballad	Slow	10
Lay Your Burdens Down	*Willow Creek Music*	*Ballad*	*Slow*	*9*
Now That You're Gone	**Fernando Ortega**	**Piano ballad**	**Slow/mid**	**10**
Peace Be Still	Al Denson	Ballad	Slow	10
What a Day It Will Be	*Greg Ferguson*	*Flowing ballad*	*Slow/mid*	*8*
You Are with Me Still	*Willow Creek Music*	*Acoustic ballad*	*Slow*	*9*
Your Love Stays with Me	Gary Chapman	Piano ballad	Slow	10
_____	_____	_____	_____	_____
_____	_____	_____	_____	_____
_____	_____	_____	_____	_____
_____	_____	_____	_____	_____

Worship Choruses

Title	Artist	Style	Tempo	Seeker-Sensitivity Rating
He Knows My Name	Tommy Walker	Worship ballad	Slow	7
Healing Song	Curt Coffield	Ballad, in 3	Slow/mid	7
Praise God on High	*Willow Creek Music*	*Worship ballad*	*Slow*	*5*
You Are with Me Still	*Willow Creek Music*	*Acoustic ballad*	*Slow*	*9*
_____	_____	_____	_____	_____
_____	_____	_____	_____	_____
_____	_____	_____	_____	_____

MOVIE CLIPS

Title: Shadowlands

Topic: Suffering; Pain; Why does God allow bad things to happen?

Description: C. S. Lewis delivers a speech about why God allows suffering.

Start Time: 0:10:00

Start Cue: "Yesterday I received a letter."

End Time: 0:11:40

End Cue: "Thank you very much."

Comments: The last line is a bit hard to understand.

Title: Shadowlands

Topic: Grief; Death; Need for a mother

Description: C. S. Lewis tells Joy Gresham about when his mother died.

Start Time: 0:28:15

Start Cue: "I have been really hurt, you know."

End Time: 0:29:25

End Cue: "Yes, I'd like that."

Comments:

Title: Shadowlands

Topic: Grief

Description: C. S. Lewis talks to his stepson Douglass about his mother dying. Very moving.

Start Time: 2:00:55

Start Cue: Jack walks up behind Douglass, and says "Hi."

End Time: 2:04:00

End Cue: Shot of Jack and Douglass embracing taken from behind them.

Comments:

Title:

Topic:

Description:

Start Time:

Start Cue:

End Time:

End Cue:

Comments:

Guilt

See also: **Confession, God's Forgiveness of Us, Grace, Sin**

MESSAGE TITLES

- ❑ *Amazing Grace:* The God of Grace
- ❑ *Seven Wonders of the Spiritual World:* God Forgives My Failures

DRAMAS

Title	Tone	Characters	Topics
A Clean Slate	Serious	1 male, 2 or 3 males or females	Forgiveness; Redemption; Guilt
A Nice Guy	Serious	2 males	Regret; Admitting failures; Effects of sin; Confession
On Vacation	Humorous	2 males, 1 female, 1 either male or female	Leisure time; Guilt; Slowing down
The Prisoner	Serious	3 males, 1 female	Easter; Freedom from sin; New Christian
"X" Marks the Spot	Serious; Mime	1 male, 1 female, 3 either males or females	Sin; Redemption; Forgiveness; Guilt

SONGS

Title	Artist	Style	Tempo	Seeker-Sensitivity Rating
Ball and Chain	Susan Ashton	Folk pop	Mid	9
Face of Forgiveness	*Willow Creek Music*	*Ballad*	*Slow*	*10*

Title	Artist	Style	Tempo	Seeker-Sensitivity Rating
He's All You Need	Steve Camp	Ballad	Slow	7
I Stand, I Fall	*Greg Ferguson*	*Piano ballad*	*Slow*	*7*
If I Could Look through Your Eyes	*Willow Creek Music*	*Piano ballad*	*Slow*	*10*
I'm Amazed	*Willow Creek Music*	*Ballad*	*Slow*	*7*
I've Been Released	*Willow Creek Music*	*Pop/rock—Chicago sound*	*Up*	*9*
Mercy for the Memories	Geoff Moore & the Distance	Folk pop ballad	Slow	9
Never Be an Angel	Margaret Becker	Pop	Mid	4
Why Me?	*Willow Creek Music*	*Ballad*	*Slow*	*9*
_____	_____	_____	_____	___
_____	_____	_____	_____	___
_____	_____	_____	_____	___
_____	_____	_____	_____	___

Worship Choruses

Title	Artist	Style	Tempo	Seeker-Sensitivity Rating
_____	_____	_____	_____	___
_____	_____	_____	_____	___
_____	_____	_____	_____	___
_____	_____	_____	_____	___

MOVIE CLIPS

Title: _____

Topic: _____

Description: _____

Start Time: _____

Start Cue: _____

End Time: _____

End Cue: _____

Comments: _____

_____

_____

Hardship

See also: **Endurance, Healing**

MESSAGE TITLES

- ❏ How to Be Strong When It Counts
- ❏ Victim or Victor?
- ❏ *Restoring Weary Souls:* Overcoming Soul Fatigue
- ❏ *When God Shows Up:* The Weary Find Refuge
- ❏ **Learning through Life's Crises:** Learning through Losing • Learning through Failing • Learning through Falling • Learning through Physical Affliction
- ❏ **Strength for the Storms of Life:** Loss • Betrayal • Failure • Disappointment
- ❏ **Strength for the Storms of Life:** Why Storms Strike • Staying Steady in the Storm • The Strength That Storms Produce

DRAMAS

Title	Tone	Characters	Topics
The Breakfast Club	Mixed, mostly serious	4 males, 1 female	Friendship; Small groups; Friends in crisis
Great Expectations	Mixed; Very serious ending	1 male, 2 females	Unanswered prayer
In the Dark	Serious	1 male, 1 female	Death of a child; Grief
"It"	Humorous	2 males, 1 female	Becoming a Christian doesn't mean no problems; Vulnerability of new believers
New Ball Game	Mixed, very moving	2 males, 1 female	Death; Meaning in life after sorrow
Take Heart	Mixed; Mime	2 males, 2 females	God heals the brokenhearted; Disappointment
The Safe	Mixed	1 male, 1 female, 3 either males or females	Inner strength; Needing God's strength
What Now?	Serious	2 males, 4 females	Coping with a crisis; Dealing with death

Title	Tone	Characters	Topics

SONGS

Title	Artist	Style	Tempo	Seeker-Sensitivity Rating
Ball and Chain	Susan Ashton	Folk pop	Mid	9
Be Still and Know	**Tommy Walker & the CA Worship Band**	**Rock/pop, in 6/8**	**Mid**	**5**
A Beautiful Place	Wayne Watson	MOR ballad	Mid/slow	9
Bound to Come Some Trouble	**Rich Mullins**	**Ballad**	**Slow**	**10**
But if Not	*Student Impact*	*Acoustic ballad*	*Slow*	*5*
Desperado	Eagles	Ballad	Slow	10
Every Single Tear	Scott Krippayne	Ballad	Slow	10
Found a Way	*Greg Ferguson*	*Ballad*	*Slow*	*9*
Good News	**Chris Rice**	**Pop**	**Up**	**9**
Have No Fear	*Willow Creek Music*	*Piano ballad*	*Slow*	*9*
Healing River	*Willow Creek Music*	*Ballad*	*Slow/mid*	*9*
Healing Song	Curt Coffield	Ballad, in 3	Slow/mid	7
Here in My Heart	Susan Ashton	Folk rock	Up	8
He's All You Need	Steve Camp	Ballad	Slow	7
Hiding Place	Steven Curtis Chapman	Pop ballad	Mid/slow	9
His Love Is Strong	Clay Crosse	Pop	Up	10
His Strength Is Perfect	**Steven Curtis Chapman**	**Ballad**	**Slow**	**9**
Hold Me, Jesus	Rich Mullins	Ballad	Slow	7
Hold On	*Willow Creek Music*	*Acoustic rock/pop ballad*	*Slow/mid*	*10*
Hunger for Healing	*Willow Creek Music*	*Folk ballad*	*Slow*	*10*
I Will Rest in You	Jaci Velasquez	Ballad	Slow	8
If This World	Jaci Velasquez	Pop	Up	9

Title	Artist	Style	Tempo	Seeker-Sensitivity Rating
It Will Be Worth It All	Tommy Walker	Guitar ballad	Slow	4
Jesus Will Still Be There	Point of Grace	Ballad	Slow	9
Lay Your Burdens Down	*Willow Creek Music*	*Ballad*	*Slow*	*9*
Love That Will Not Let Me Go	**Steve Camp**	**Ballad**	**Slow**	**10**
No More Pretending	**Scott Krippayne**	**Pop ballad**	**Slow**	**7**
Not Too Far from Here	**Kim Boyce**	**Pop ballad**	**Slow**	**8**
Now That You're Gone	**Fernando Ortega**	**Piano ballad**	**Slow/mid**	**10**
Peace Be Still	Al Denson	Ballad	Slow	10
A Place to Call Home	*Greg Ferguson/ Willow Creek Music*	*Gospel ballad*	*Slow, in 3*	*10*
Small Enough	Nicole Nordeman	Ballad duet	Slow	6
Sometimes He Calms the Storms	Scott Krippayne	Ballad	Slow/mid	6
Strength in You	*Willow Creek Music*	*MOR pop*	*Slow/mid*	*10*
There Is a Love	Michael English	Pop	Up	9
There's a Reason	*Willow Creek Music*	*Pop/rock*	*Up*	*9*
We All Need	Aaron Jeoffrey	Pop	Mid/up	9
Weary Soul	*Helena*	*Tender ballad*	*Slow*	*9*
What a Day It Will Be	*Greg Ferguson*	*Flowing ballad*	*Slow/mid*	*8*
When You Are a Soldier	Steven Curtis Chapman	Keyboard ballad	Slow/mid	4
You Are with Me Still	*Willow Creek Music*	*Acoustic ballad*	*Slow*	*9*
Your Love Stays with Me	Gary Chapman	Piano ballad	Slow	10
_____	_____	_____	_____	_____
_____	_____	_____	_____	_____
_____	_____	_____	_____	_____
_____	_____	_____	_____	_____

Worship Choruses

Title	Artist	Style	Tempo	Seeker-Sensitivity Rating
All Things Are Possible	Hillsongs	Pop worship	Up	5
And That My Soul Knows Very Well	Hillsongs	Worship ballad	Slow	5
Be Still My Soul	*Willow Creek Music*	*Worship ballad*	*Slow/mid*	*4*
Blessed Be the Name	Vineyard	Worship ballad	Slow	4

Title	Artist	Style	Tempo	Seeker-Sensitivity Rating
But if Not	*Student Impact*	*Acoustic ballad*	*Slow*	*5*
He Knows My Name	Tommy Walker	Worship ballad	Slow	7
Healing Song	Curt Coffield	Ballad, in 3	Slow/mid	7
O Most High	Mark Altrogge	Pop	Up	3
Praise God on High	*Willow Creek Music*	*Worship ballad*	*Slow*	*5*
Still I Will Worship You	*Willow Creek Music*	*Pop/rock worship*	*Up*	*3*
You Are with Me Still	*Willow Creek Music*	*Acoustic ballad*	*Slow*	*9*

MOVIE CLIPS

Title: Chariots of Fire

Topic: Christian life; Endurance

Description: Eric Liddell gives a sermonette about running the race of faith.

Start Time: 0:25:35

Start Cue: "You came to see a race today."

End Time: 0:27:20

End Cue: "That is how you run a straight race."

Comments: _____

_____

_____

Title: Shadowlands

Topic: Suffering; Pain; Why does God allow bad things to happen?

Description: C. S. Lewis delivers a speech about why God allows suffering.

Start Time: 0:10:00

Start Cue: "Yesterday I received a letter."

End Time: 0:11:40

End Cue: "Thank you very much."

Comments: The last line is a bit hard to understand.

_____

_____

_____

Title: Shadowlands

Topic: Grief; Death; Need for a mother

Description: C. S. Lewis tells Joy Gresham about when his mother died.

Start Time: 0:28:15

Start Cue: "I have been really hurt, you know."

End Time: 0:29:25

End Cue: "Yes, I'd like that."

Comments: _____
_____
_____

Title: Shadowlands

Topic: Death; Sharing the dying process

Description: Jack and Joy talk about her imminent death. She makes a couple of profound statements about sharing the dying process.

Start Time: 1:45:30

Start Cue: "I don't want to be somewhere else anymore."

End Time: 1:47:55

End Cue: Jack and Joy kiss.

Comments: _____
_____
_____

Title: _____

Topic: _____

Description: _____

Start Time: _____

Start Cue: _____

End Time: _____

End Cue: _____

Comments: _____
_____
_____

Healing

See also **Comforting Others, God's Love, God's Tenderness**

MESSAGE TITLES

- ❏ Connect with the Source of Strength
- ❏ A Hunger for Healing
- ❏ *Measuring How Much You Matter to God:* Rebuilding Self-Esteem
- ❏ *Restoring Weary Souls:* Overcoming Soul Fatigue
- ❏ *Strength for the Storms of Life:* The Strength That Storms Produce
- ❏ *When God Shows Up:* The Weary Find Refuge

DRAMAS

Title	Tone	Characters	Topics
The Angry Woman	Serious	2 males, 3 females, 1 narrator	The roots of anger
Another Day at the Bus Stop	Mixed	1 male, 1 female	Our relationship with God; Self-esteem
Because I Love You	Serious	1 male, 1 female	Adultery; Consequences of sin
New Ball Game	Mixed, very moving	2 males, 1 female	Death; Meaning in life after sorrow
The Old Man and the Laundromat	Mixed, mostly serious	1 male, 1 female, 1 child	Grieving; Dealing with death of a loved one; Letting go
Take Heart	Mixed; Mime	2 males, 2 females	God heals the brokenhearted; Disappointment
Taking Step Four	Humorous	1 female	Self-examination; Self-delusion; Confession of sin
These Parts	Mixed	2 males, 1 female, 3 either males or females, 1 child, 1 narrator	The resurrection; Our need for Christ; Easter

SONGS

Title	Artist	Style	Tempo	Seeker-Sensitivity Rating
Ball and Chain	Susan Ashton	Folk pop	Mid	9
Be Still and Know	**Tommy Walker & the CA Worship Band**	**Rock/pop, in 6/8**	**Mid**	**5**
A Beautiful Place	Wayne Watson	MOR ballad	Mid/slow	9
Bound to Come Some Trouble	**Rich Mullins**	**Ballad**	**Slow**	**10**
Every Single Tear	Scott Krippayne	Ballad	Slow	10
Found a Way	*Greg Ferguson*	*Ballad*	*Slow*	*9*
Good News	**Chris Rice**	**Pop**	**Up**	**9**
Healing River	*Willow Creek Music*	*Ballad*	*Slow/mid*	*9*
Healing Song	Curt Coffield	Ballad, in 3	Slow/mid	7
He's All You Need	Steve Camp	Ballad	Slow	7
He's My Son	Mark Schultz	Ballad	Slow	9
Hiding Place	Steven Curtis Chapman	Pop ballad	Mid/slow	9
His Love Is Strong	Clay Crosse	Pop	Up	10
Holy One	*Helena*	*Ballad*	*Slow*	*7*
Hunger for Healing	*Willow Creek Music*	*Folk ballad*	*Slow*	*10*
I Will Be Free	Cindy Morgan	Ballad	Slow	7
I Will Rest in You	Jaci Velasquez	Ballad	Slow	8
If You Could See Me Now	Truth	Ballad	Slow	5
I'll Find You There	The Kry	Folk rock ballad	Slow	9
Jesus Will Still Be There	Point of Grace	Ballad	Slow	9
Lay Your Burdens Down	*Willow Creek Music*	*Ballad*	*Slow*	*9*
Life Support	*Greg Ferguson*	*R & B/pop*	*Mid/up*	*9*
Mercy for the Memories	Geoff Moore & the Distance	Folk pop ballad	Slow	9
Peace Be Still	Al Denson	Ballad	Slow	10
A Place to Call Home	*Greg Ferguson/ Willow Creek Music*	*Gospel ballad*	*Slow, in 3*	*10*
Sometimes He Calms the Storms	Scott Krippayne	Ballad	Slow/mid	6
There Is a God	**Tommy Walker**	**Ballad duet**	**Slow**	**8**

Title	Artist	Style	Tempo	Seeker-Sensitivity Rating
Weary Soul	*Helena*	*Tender ballad*	*Slow*	*9*
What a Day It Will Be	*Greg Ferguson*	*Flowing ballad*	*Slow/mid*	*8*
You Are with Me Still	*Willow Creek Music*	*Acoustic ballad*	*Slow*	*9*
You Brought My Heart to Life	*Willow Creek Music*	*Ballad*	*Slow*	*9*
Your Love Stays with Me	Gary Chapman	Piano ballad	Slow	10

Worship Choruses

Title	Artist	Style	Tempo	Seeker-Sensitivity Rating
Don't Forget His Benefits	Tommy Walker & the CA Worship Band	Rock/pop	Up	4
He Knows My Name	Tommy Walker	Worship ballad	Slow	7
Healing Song	Curt Coffield	Ballad, in 3	Slow/mid	7
I Could Sing of Your Love Forever	Passion	Rock/pop worship	Mid	4
In Your Hands	Hillsongs	Worship ballad	Slow/mid	4
Let the Peace of God Reign	Hillsongs	Worship ballad	Slow	3
Let Your Love Pour	*Student Impact*	*MOR worship*	*Mid*	*4*
Mourning into Dancing	Tommy Walker	Pop	Up	5

MOVIE CLIPS

Title: _____

Topic: _____

Description: _____

Start Time: _____

Start Cue: _____

End Time: _____

End Cue: _____

Comments: _____

_____

_____

_____

Loneliness

MESSAGE TITLES

❑ God Knows Your Name

❑ Only the Lonely

❑ _Facing Up to Fear:_ The Fear of Living (Being) Alone

❑ _What Jesus Would Say to_ . . . Madonna

_____

_____

_____

DRAMAS

Title	Tone	Characters	Topics
Funny Girl	Mixed	1 male, 2 females (multiple roles for 1 man and 1 woman)	Self-esteem; Need for acceptance
The Quagmire	Serious	1 male or female	Failure; Self-esteem; Being "stuck"; Trusting God

Title	Tone	Characters	Topics
Single?	Mixed	1 male, 1 female	Singleness; Loneliness; Fear of living alone
Unknown	Serious	1 male, 4 females	Friendship; Loneliness; Small groups

SONGS

Title	Artist	Style	Tempo	Seeker-Sensitivity Rating
Change in My Life	John Pagano	Gospel	Mid/up	9
Desperado	Eagles	Ballad	Slow	10
Eleanor Rigby	Beatles	Acoustic ballad	Slow/mid	10
Every Single Tear	Scott Krippayne	Ballad	Slow	10
Found a Way	*Greg Ferguson*	*Ballad*	*Slow*	*9*
He Won't Let You Go	**The Kry**	**Piano ballad**	**Slow**	**10**
Hiding Place	Steven Curtis Chapman	Pop ballad	Mid/slow	9
If This World	Jaci Velasquez	Pop	Up	9
Jesus Will Still Be There	Point of Grace	Ballad	Slow	9
Lay Your Burdens Down	*Willow Creek Music*	*Ballad*	*Slow*	*9*
Peace Be Still	Al Denson	Ballad	Slow	10
A Place to Call Home	*Greg Ferguson/ Willow Creek Music*	*Gospel ballad*	*Slow, in 3*	*10*
Somebody Make Me Laugh	Patti Austin	Ballad	Slow	10
There's a Reason	*Willow Creek Music*	*Pop/rock*	*Up*	*9*
Treasure of You	Steven Curtis Chapman	Driving rock	Up	10
You Are with Me Still	*Willow Creek Music*	*Acoustic ballad*	*Slow*	*9*
You Brought My Heart to Life	*Willow Creek Music*	*Ballad*	*Slow*	*9*
Your Love Stays with Me	Gary Chapman	Piano ballad	Slow	10

Worship Choruses

Title	Artist	Style	Tempo	Seeker-Sensitivity Rating
And That My Soul Knows Very Well	Hillsongs	Worship ballad	Slow	5
He Knows My Name	Tommy Walker	Worship ballad	Slow	7
In Your Hands	Hillsongs	Worship ballad	Slow/mid	4
_____	_____	_____	_____	___
_____	_____	_____	_____	___
_____	_____	_____	_____	___
_____	_____	_____	_____	___
_____	_____	_____	_____	___
_____	_____	_____	_____	___

MOVIE CLIPS

Title: _____

Topic: _____

Description: _____

Start Time: _____

Start Cue: _____

End Time: _____

End Cue: _____

Comments: _____

_____

_____

Title: _____

Topic: _____

Description: _____

Start Time: _____

Start Cue: _____

End Time: _____

End Cue: _____

Comments: _____

_____

_____

Self-Esteem

See also: **Our Value to God**

MESSAGE TITLES

❑ The Curse of Comparison
❑ Truly Significant
❑ *What Jesus Would Say to . . .* David Letterman
❑ *What Jesus Would Say to . . .* Madonna
❑ **Measuring How Much You Matter to God:** The Source of Your Self-Esteem • What Scars Self-Esteem • Rebuilding Self-Esteem • Building Self-Esteem into Others

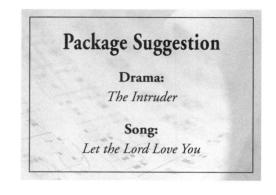

Package Suggestion

Drama:
The Intruder

Song:
Let the Lord Love You

DRAMAS

Title	Tone	Characters	Topics
The Angry Woman	Serious	2 males, 3 females, 1 narrator	The roots of anger
Another Day at the Bus Stop	Mixed	1 male, 1 female	Our relationship with God; Self-esteem
The Brow Beater	Mixed, mostly serious	1 male, 1 female	Self-esteem; Failures; Forgiveness
Call Waiting	Mixed; Serious ending	2 males	Marketplace pressures; Search for significance; Mid-life crisis
Conversations	Serious	2 males, 1 female, 1 offstage female voice	Self-esteem; Self-criticism; Failure
Funny Girl	Mixed	1 male, 2 females (multiple roles for 1 man and 1 woman	Self-esteem; Need for acceptance
Honestly Speaking	Mixed	3 males, 3 females	Positive self-talk; Self-esteem
The Intruder	Serious	1 male, 1 female	Self-image; Destructive parenting; God's love in spite of failure
The Lane of Life	Serious; Mime	5 either males or females, 1 offstage narrator	Salvation; Our value to God; Self-esteem

Title	Tone	Characters	Topics
Masterpiece	Mixed, touching	1 male, 1 female, 2 teenage females	Self-esteem; Parenting
Measuring Up	Mixed; Mime	2 males, 1 female, 1 either male or female	God's acceptance of us; Self-esteem
The Quagmire	Serious	1 male or female	Failure; Self-esteem; Being "stuck"; Trusting God
Wonderfully Made	Serious	2 males, 2 females, 1 narrator	Affirming a child's uniqueness

SONGS

Title	Artist	Style	Tempo	Seeker-Sensitivity Rating
Art in Me	Jars of Clay	Alternative rock	Mid/up	9
Enough	*Willow Creek Music*	*Piano ballad*	*Slow*	*7*
If I Could Look through Your Eyes	*Willow Creek Music*	*Piano ballad*	*Slow*	*10*
If You Could See What I See	Geoff Moore & the Distance	Folk ballad	Slow	10
I'll Find You There	The Kry	Folk rock ballad	Slow	9
I'm Amazed	*Willow Creek Music*	*Ballad*	*Slow*	*7*
Jesus Loves Me	Whitney Houston	R & B/pop	Slow/mid	8
Let the Lord Love You	*Willow Creek Music*	*Acoustic guitar ballad*	*Slow*	*9*
Peace Be Still	Al Denson	Ballad	Slow	10
A Place to Call Home	*Greg Ferguson/ Willow Creek Music*	*Gospel ballad*	*Slow, in 3*	*10*
A Rose Is a Rose	Susan Ashton	Piano ballad	Slow	9
Treasure of You	Steven Curtis Chapman	Driving rock	Up	10
Wanna Be Loved	**DC Talk**	**Funky pop**	**Up**	**10**
You Brought My Heart to Life	*Willow Creek Music*	*Ballad*	*Slow*	*9*

Worship Choruses

Title	Artist	Style	Tempo	Seeker-Sensitivity Rating
He Knows My Name	Tommy Walker	Worship ballad	Slow	7

MOVIE CLIPS

Title: _____
Topic: _____
Description: _____
Start Time: _____
Start Cue: _____
End Time: _____
End Cue: _____
Comments: _____

Worry

Might also include: _Anxiety_
See also: **Faith, God's Faithfulness**

MESSAGE TITLES

- ❏ _If You Only Knew the Father:_ Why Worry?
- ❏ _Illustrating the Identity of God:_ Our Providing God
- ❏ _Truths That Transform:_ Don't Worry . . . Pray

DRAMAS

Title	Tone	Characters	Topics
Conversations in a Field	Humorous	2 males, 2 females	Anxiety; Worry; God's providence
What If . . .	Humorous	3 males, 1 female	Worry; Anxiety

SONGS

Title	Artist	Style	Tempo	Seeker-Sensitivity Rating
Be Still and Know	**Tommy Walker & the CA Worship Band**	**Rock/pop, in 6/8**	**Mid**	**5**
Bound to Come Some Trouble	**Rich Mullins**	**Ballad**	**Slow**	**10**
But if Not	*Student Impact*	*Acoustic ballad*	*Slow*	*5*
Found a Way	*Greg Ferguson*	*Ballad*	*Slow*	*9*
Have No Fear	*Willow Creek Music*	*Piano ballad*	*Slow*	*9*
Hiding Place	Steven Curtis Chapman	Pop ballad	Mid/slow	9
His Love Is Strong	Clay Crosse	Pop	Up	10
Hold On	*Willow Creek Music*	*Acoustic rock/pop ballad*	*Slow/mid*	*10*
Hold On to Jesus	Steven Curtis Chapman	Ballad	Slow	8
I'll Find You There	The Kry	Folk rock ballad	Slow	9
In My Father's Hands	Susan Ashton	Folk pop	Mid	9
Jesus Will Still Be There	Point of Grace	Ballad	Slow	9
Lay Your Burdens Down	*Willow Creek Music*	*Ballad*	*Slow*	*9*
Let the Lord Love You	*Willow Creek Music*	*Acoustic guitar ballad*	*Slow*	*9*
Small Enough	Nicole Nordeman	Ballad duet	Slow	6
Take My Hand	The Kry	Acoustic ballad	Mid/slow	9
Your Love Stays with Me	Gary Chapman	Piano ballad	Slow	10

Title	Artist	Style	Tempo	Seeker-Sensitivity Rating

Worship Choruses

Title	Artist	Style	Tempo	Seeker-Sensitivity Rating
All Things Are Possible	Hillsongs	Pop worship	Up	5
And That My Soul Knows Very Well	Hillsongs	Worship ballad	Slow	5
Be Still My Soul	*Willow Creek Music*	*Worship ballad*	*Slow/mid*	*4*
Blessed Be the Name	Vineyard	Worship ballad	Slow	4
But if Not	*Student Impact*	*Acoustic ballad*	*Slow*	*5*
He Knows My Name	Tommy Walker	Worship ballad	Slow	7
He's Here	*Student Impact*	*Worship ballad*	*Slow*	*7*
O Most High	Mark Altrogge	Pop	Up	3
Still I Will Worship You	*Willow Creek Music*	*Pop/rock worship*	*Up*	*3*
You Are with Me Still	*Willow Creek Music*	*Acoustic ballad*	*Slow*	*9*

MOVIE CLIPS

Title: _____

Topic: _____

Description: _____

Start Time: _____

Start Cue: _____

End Time: _____

End Cue: _____

Comments: _____

_____

Endurance

Might also include: *Quitting* and *Perseverance*
See also: **God's Power, God's Faithfulness**

MESSAGE TITLES

❑ Anyone Can Quit
❑ Quitting Points
❑ Secrets of Surviving
❑ Staying Steady in the Storm
❑ Surviving a Slump
❑ *Endangered Character Qualities:* Endurance
❑ *A Faith That Works—The Book of James:* Developing Endurance
❑ *A Faith That Works—The Book of James:* Press On
❑ *Signs of the Times:* No U-Turn
❑ **Staying Power:** The Power of Perseverance • Power beyond Yourself

_____
_____
_____

DRAMAS

Title	Tone	Characters	Topics
Paralyzed	Serious	2 males (1 adult, 1 teen), 2 females (1 adult, 1 teen)	Depression; Prayer; Relationship with God; Family in crisis
The Quagmire	Serious	1 male or female	Failure; Self-esteem; Being "stuck"; Trusting God
You and Me	Mixed	2 females	Family; Mother's Day; Rebuilding after divorce; Navigating life's challenges
_____	_____	_____	_____
_____	_____	_____	_____
_____	_____	_____	_____
_____	_____	_____	_____

SONGS

Title	Artist	Style	Tempo	Seeker-Sensitivity Rating
A Beautiful Place	Wayne Watson	MOR ballad	Mid/slow	9
A Rose Is a Rose	Susan Ashton	Piano ballad	Slow	9
His Strength Is Perfect	**Steven Curtis Chapman**	**Ballad**	**Slow**	**9**
Weary Soul	*Helena*	*Tender ballad*	*Slow*	*9*
When You Are a Soldier	Steven Curtis Chapman	Keyboard ballad	Slow/mid	4

Worship Choruses

Title	Artist	Style	Tempo	Seeker-Sensitivity Rating
All the Power You Need	Hillsongs	Pop worship	Up	5

MOVIE CLIPS

Title: Chariots of Fire

Topic: Christian life; Endurance

Description: Eric Liddell gives a sermonette about running the race of faith.

Start Time: 0:25:35

Start Cue: "You came to see a race today."

End Time: 0:27:20

End Cue: "That is how you run a straight race."

Comments: _____

_____

_____

Title: Chariots of Fire

Topic: Perseverance; Determination; Courage

Description: Runner Eric Liddell gets knocked down in a race and comes back to win.

Start Time: 0:34:25

Start Cue: "Gentlemen, get to your marks."

End Time: 0:35:45

End Cue: Liddell falls down in exhaustion at the finish.

Comments: _____

Title: Men of Honor

Topic: Courage; Friendship; Inspiring others to succeed

Description: Carl Brashear, a navy master diver who lost a leg in an accident, in order to be reinstated to full duty must walk twelve paces in a very heavy diving suit. At a court hearing, his former drill sergeant, a former antagonist, pushes him and challenges him to do it.

Start Time: 1:55:11

Start Cue: Wide shot of the courtroom.

End Time: 2:00:30

End Cue: Courtroom erupts in applause.

Comments: There is brief profanity in this clip that must be bleeped, but the power of the clip is worth the extra work.

Title: Mr. Holland's Opus

Topic: Inspiring others; Leadership; Getting beyond quitting points

Description: A clarinet student who is struggling decides to quit. Her teacher, Mr. Holland, inspires her to stay with it and in the process teaches her the true nature of music and helps her see her own beauty.

Start Time: 0:30:29/DVD Ch. 8

Start Cue: Mr. Holland is playing piano when his student walks in.

End Time: 0:35:02

End Cue: Mr. Holland smiles; scene fades to a concert.

Comments: _____

Title: Rudy

Topic: Quitting; Perseverance

Description: Rudy decides to quit the football team. Fortune, his friend and former boss, challenges him because he used to play for Notre Dame and quit.

Start Time: 1:29:10

Start Cue: Just before "What're you doing here?"

End Time: 1:31:20

End Cue: "Do you hear me clear enough?"

Comments: The words *crap* and *hell* are used.

Title: The Legend of Bagger Vance

Topic: Getting over the past; Quitting; Overcoming fears

Description: Golfer Randolph Junuh, a veteran haunted by his war experiences, hits a ball into the woods. Facing an impossible shot to get back into the tournament, he reaches down to pick up the ball. His caddie, Bagger Vance (who is sort of a mystical God-figure in the movie), helps him to face his fears and overcome them.

Start Time: 1:38:08

Start Cue: Junuh walks down the fairway toward the woods with Bagger behind him.

End Time: 1:42:37

End Cue: Overjoyed look on the boy's face.

Comments: There is mild profanity after the cutoff point. This clip gets borderline New Age, but Bagger's character can be a great metaphor for God helping us through the darkness we face.

_____
_____
_____

Title: _____

Topic: _____

Description: _____

Start Time: _____

Start Cue: _____

End Time: _____

End Cue: _____

Comments: _____
_____
_____
_____

Heroes

At a time when heroes seemingly fall every day, it's rare to see a truly worthy role model. This topic can be used to inspire people to be difference makers.

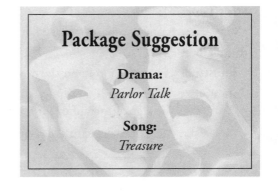

Package Suggestion

Drama:
Parlor Talk

Song:
Treasure

MESSAGE TITLES

❑ Difference Makers
❑ *What Jesus Would Say to . . .* Billy Graham
❑ *What Jesus Would Say to . . .* Michael Jordan
❑ *What Jesus Would Say to . . .* Mother Teresa
❑ **Everyday Heroes:** Hallmarks of a Hero • Heroes of the Heart • Heroes of the Home

_____

_____

_____

DRAMAS

Title	Tone	Characters	Topics
Heroic Delusion	Humorous	2 males, 1 female	Self-delusion
The Legacy	Touching	1 male, 2 females	Heroes; Character; Christians at work; Serving others; Making a difference
Lifeline	Mixed, touching	1 male, 2 females, 1 small child (no lines)	Serving the church; Life in community; Aging
Parlor Talk	Mixed	3 males, 2 females	Making a difference with your life; Death; Workaholism
The Right Thing	Serious	1 male	Costly obedience; Christian character; Persecution
The Story of Rachel	Serious	3 females	Care for the poor; Compassion
Suit and Volly	Humorous	2 males, 2 females	Motives in serving others

SONGS

Title	Artist	Style	Tempo	Seeker-Sensitivity Rating
Audience of One	*Willow Creek Music*	*Power ballad*	*Slow*	*8*
Man of God	*Greg Ferguson*	*Pop/rock*	*Mid/up*	*7*
Treasure	**Gary Chapman**	**Acoustic ballad**	**Slow**	**9**
We Can Make a Difference	**Jaci Velasquez**	**Pop**	**Up**	**8**

Worship Choruses

Title	Artist	Style	Tempo	Seeker-Sensitivity Rating

MOVIE CLIPS

Title: Braveheart

Topic: Leadership; Courage

Description: William Wallace challenges Robert the Bruce, the rightful king of Scotland, to lead the Scottish people to freedom.

Start Time: 1:35:50

Start Cue: "Wait. . . . I respect what you said."

End Time: 1:37:09

End Cue: "And so would I," followed by a close-up of Robert.

Comments: _____

_____

_____

Title: Chariots of Fire

Topic: Perseverance; Determination; Courage

Description: Runner Eric Liddell gets knocked down in a race and comes back to win.

Start Time: 0:34:25

Start Cue: "Gentlemen, get to your marks."

End Time: 0:35:45

End Cue: Liddell falls down in exhaustion at the finish.

Comments: _____
_____
_____
_____

Title: Men of Honor

Topic: Courage; Friendship; Inspiring others to succeed

Description: Carl Brashear, a navy master diver who lost a leg in an accident, in order to be reinstated to full duty must walk twelve paces in a very heavy diving suit. At a court hearing, his former drill sergeant, a former antagonist, pushes him and challenges him to do it.

Start Time: 1:55:11

Start Cue: Wide shot of the courtroom.

End Time: 2:00:30

End Cue: Courtroom erupts in applause.

Comments: There is brief profanity in this clip that must be bleeped, but the power of the clip is worth the extra work.
_____
_____
_____

Title: Mr. Holland's Opus

Topic: Inspiring others; Leadership; Getting beyond quitting points

Description: A clarinet student who is struggling decides to quit. Her teacher, Mr. Holland, inspires her to stay with it and in the process teaches her the true nature of music and helps her see her own beauty.

Start Time: 0:30:29/DVD Ch. 8

Start Cue: Mr. Holland is playing piano when his student walks in.

End Time: 0:35:02

End Cue: Mr. Holland smiles; scene fades to a concert.

Comments: _____
_____
_____
_____

Title: Mr. Holland's Opus

Topic: Heroes; Honoring people; The fruit of serving others

Description: Mr. Holland, a music teacher whose discontinued program has caused him to retire early, goes to a noisy gym to see what the commotion is. He walks into a celebration in his honor, where he is thanked for the difference he has made in countless lives.

Start Time: 2:06:07

Start Cue: "Now what is that?" Mr. Holland walks toward the gym.

End Time: 2:11:23

End Cue: Close-up of the speaker, Ms. Lang, followed by a close-up of Mr. Holland.

Comments: A bit long but a great illustration of a well-spent life. This can also be used as a bookend to the other "Mr. Holland" clip listed on page 204, as the speaker is the girl Mr. Holland inspired in the earlier clip. She has now become governor of the state.

Title: _____

Topic: _____

Description: _____

Start Time: _____

Start Cue: _____

End Time: _____

End Cue: _____

Comments: _____

Leadership

MESSAGE TITLES

- ❏ The Wonder of Leadership
- ❏ *What Jesus Would Say to* . . . Bill Clinton
- ❏ **Bringing Out the Best in People:** Becoming a People Builder • The How-Tos
  • Bringing Out the Best in Yourself

_____

_____

_____

DRAMAS

Title	Tone	Characters	Topics
The Legacy	Touching	1 male, 2 females	Heroes; Character; Christians at work; Serving others; Making a difference
Lightening Leadership	Humorous	2 males, 1 female	Leadership; Work
Lonely at the Top	Serious	1 male	Perils of power; Authority; Easter
Pastor General	Humorous	2 males, 2 females	Leadership; Church life; Serving others
Pastor General: Consultant Visit	Humorous	2 males, 4 females	Leadership; Oppressive managers; Communication
Pastor General: Evaluation Time	Humorous	4 males, 2 females	Authoritarian leadership; How not to do program evaluations; Church programming/worship teams
Pastor General: Resource Allocation	Humorous	4 males, 2 females	Providing for volunteers; Bad leadership styles
Truthful Words	Serious	1 male, 1 female	Leadership; Pride; Truth telling
Wonderfully Made	Serious	2 males, 2 females, 1 narrator	Affirming a child's uniqueness

_____	_____	_____	_____
_____	_____	_____	_____
_____	_____	_____	_____

SONGS

Title	Artist	Style	Tempo	Seeker-Sensitivity Rating
Audience of One	*Willow Creek Music*	*Power ballad*	*Slow*	*8*
Seize the Day	**Carolyn Arends**	**Folk pop, in 3**	**Mid**	**8**
Strength in You	*Willow Creek Music*	*MOR pop*	*Slow/mid*	*10*
You've Got to Stand for Something	Aaron Tippin	Country	Up	10
___	___	___	___	___
___	___	___	___	___
___	___	___	___	___
___	___	___	___	___

Worship Choruses

Title	Artist	Style	Tempo	Seeker-Sensitivity Rating
___	___	___	___	___
___	___	___	___	___
___	___	___	___	___

MOVIE CLIPS

Title: Apollo 13

Topic: Leadership; Trusting people's giftedness

Description: After Apollo 13 is stranded in space, the NASA mission control commander gathers his team together to solve a specific problem. Everyone has an opinion, but ultimately he trusts the entire fate of the mission to the suggestion of one of his engineers. He trusts the engineer's information because of his expertise.

Start Time: 1:15:01

Start Cue: "So you're telling me you can only give our guys forty-five hours?"

End Time: 1:16:18

End Cue: "OK, John, the minute we finish the burn, we'll power down the LEM."

Comments: This clip shows good leadership—knowing your people well enough to know where to turn for information—and is a metaphor for the use of spiritual gifts in the church. Each member of the church plays a vital role—everyone is important. The minute or so after this clip has some good material showing the leader delegating important tasks, but there is profanity in that section.

Title: Braveheart

Topic: Leadership; Courage

Description: William Wallace challenges Robert the Bruce, the rightful king of Scotland, to lead the Scottish people to freedom.

Start Time: 1:35:50

Start Cue: "Wait. . . . I respect what you said."

End Time: 1:37:09

End Cue: "And so would I," followed by a close-up of Robert.

Comments: _____

_____

_____

_____

_____

Title: Braveheart

Topic: Courage; Leadership; Freedom

Description: William Wallace exhorts the Scottish army to fight for their freedom. A powerful clip.

Start Time: 1:17:15

Start Cue: "I am William Wallace, and I see a whole army of my countrymen. . . ."

End Time: 1:18:53

End Cue: The Scottish army cheers as Wallace rides around.

Comments: Two cautions here: First, there is mild profanity just before the start cue, so make sure you start at the right place. Second, overall this is a very violent film—the clip, however, is not.

_____

_____

_____

_____

Title: Hoosiers

Topic: Leadership

Description: A small-town basketball team enters a huge fieldhouse to play the state championship. The players are in awe. The coach has the players measure the basket to show them that it's the same as their gym at home.

Start Time: 1:33:20

Start Cue: Team enters Butler Fieldhouse.

End Time: 1:35:20

End Cue: "It is big."

Comments: _____

_____

_____

_____

_____

Title: Men of Honor

Topic: Courage; Friendship; Inspiring others to succeed

Description: Carl Brashear, a navy master diver who lost a leg in an accident, in order to be reinstated to full duty must walk twelve paces in a very heavy diving suit. At a court hearing, his former drill sergeant, a former antagonist, pushes him and challenges him to do it.

Start Time: 1:55:11

Start Cue: Wide shot of the courtroom.

End Time: 2:00:30

End Cue: Courtroom erupts in applause.

Comments: There is brief profanity in this clip that must be bleeped, but the power of the clip is worth the extra work.

_____

_____

_____

_____

Title: Mr. Holland's Opus

Topic: Inspiring others; Leadership; Getting beyond quitting points

Description: A clarinet student who is struggling decides to quit. Her teacher, Mr. Holland, inspires her to stay with it and in the process teaches her the true nature of music and helps her see her own beauty.

Start Time: 0:30:29/DVD Ch. 8

Start Cue: Mr. Holland is playing piano when his student walks in.

End Time: 0:35:02

End Cue: Mr. Holland smiles; scene fades to a concert.

Comments: _____

_____

_____

_____

Title: Mr. Holland's Opus

Topic: Heroes; Honoring people; The fruit of serving others

Description: Mr. Holland, a music teacher whose discontinued program has caused him to retire early, goes to a noisy gym to see what the commotion is. He walks into a celebration in his honor, where he is thanked for the difference he has made in countless lives.

Start Time: 2:06:07

Start Cue: "Now what is that?" Mr. Holland walks toward the gym.

End Time: 2:11:23

End Cue: Close-up of the speaker, Ms. Lang, followed by a close-up of Mr. Holland.

Comments: A bit long but a great illustration of a well-spent life. This can also be used as a bookend to the other "Mr. Holland" clip listed above, as the speaker is the girl Mr. Holland inspired in the earlier clip. She has now become governor of the state.

_____

_____

_____

_____

Title: Remember the Titans

Topic: Leadership; Respecting authority; Pride; Racism

Description: The Titans' star player confronts the coach and tries to lay down the law about who will play, based on color. The coach puts him in his place.

Start Time: 0:14:21/DVD Ch. 5

Start Cue: The coach starts to walk to the bus.

End Time: 0:16:57

End Cue: "Fix that tie, son." Close-up of the coach.

Comments: If you are using this clip for a message on racism, you may want to use the next minute or so, which shows the coach integrating the two buses.

_____
_____
_____
_____

Title: Remember the Titans

Topic: Truth telling; Racism; Leadership; Friendship

Description: The Titans' two star defensive players, one white and one black, confront each other on their effort and leadership, respectively. They become best friends later in the movie.

Start Time: 0:29:09/DVD Ch. 9

Start Cue: Gary bumps into Julius. "Okay, man, listen. I'm Gary, you're Julius."

End Time: 0:30:48

End Cue: "Attitude reflects leadership, Captain."

Comments: The two scenes following this one are also very strong, and the three scenes combined, though long, would be a great example of leadership and breaking down racial barriers. Gary says "shiver push," and it sounds like profanity because it goes by fast, but it's not.

_____
_____
_____
_____

Title: _____

Topic: _____

Description: _____

Start Time: _____

Start Cue: _____

End Time: _____

End Cue: _____

Comments: _____
_____
_____

Materialism/Greed

Might also include: *Greed*
See also: **Contentment, Fulfillment**

MESSAGE TITLES

- ❏ It All Goes Back into the Box
- ❏ The Power of Money
- ❏ The Profit of Financial Integrity
- ❏ The Truth about Earthly Treasures
- ❏ When Is Enough Enough?
- ❏ You Can't Serve Two Masters
- ❏ *Changing Times:* The Changing American Dream
- ❏ *A Faith That Works—The Book of James:* Destructive Desires
- ❏ *A Faith That Works—The Book of James:* Words to the Rich
- ❏ *Living Excellent Lives:* Financially
- ❏ *Making Sense Out of Money:* The Power of Money
- ❏ *Money, Sex, and Power:* Money
- ❏ *Tenth Commandment:* Restrain Material Desires
- ❏ *Understanding the Times:* The '80s
- ❏ *What Jesus Would Say to . . .* Bill Gates
- ❏ **Financial Freedom:** Earning Money • Managing Money • Giving Money
- ❏ **Testing God's Trustworthiness:** You Can't Out-Give God • It's What You Do with What You Have
- ❏ **Your Money Matters:** Determining a Standard of Living • Developing a Financial Plan • Discovering the Rewards of Giving

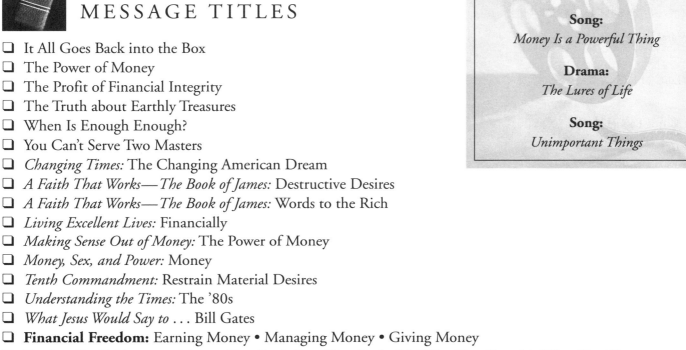

Package Suggestion

Movie Clip:
Wall Street

Song:
Money Is a Powerful Thing

Drama:
The Lures of Life

Song:
Unimportant Things

DRAMAS

Title	Tone	Characters	Topics
All I Want for Christmas	Mixed	3 males, 2 females, 1 female child	Greed; Desire to acquire possessions
Buy One, Get One Free	Mixed, moving	1 male, 1 female	Joy of giving
Catalog-itis	Humorous	1 male, 1 female, 2 junior high girls	Self-control; Contentment

Title	Tone	Characters	Topics
Check Mates	Humorous	1 male, 1 female	Personal finances; Debt
Confessions of an Ad-aholic	Humorous	1 male, 1 female	Materialism; Power of the media; The American dream
Early One Morning Just after the Dawn of History as We Know It	Humorous	3 males	Materialism; Keeping up with the Joneses
Heart Failure	Humorous	1 male	Giving
In Pursuit of Happiness	Mixed	1 male, 1 female	Contentment; Possessions
Lifestyles of the Obscure and Indebted	Humorous	4 males, 3 females	Materialism; Coveting
Lizzy and Leroy	Humorous	1 male, 1 female, piano player (optional)	Life fulfillment; Material things don't satisfy
The Lures of Life	Mixed, light; Mime	5 males, 1 female	Adventurism; Life fulfillment
The Mirror Thought of It	Mixed	1 male, 1 female, 1 offstage voice	Materialism; Workaholism; Striving for more
Oh, What a Feeling!	Humorous	2 males, 1 female	Decision making; Self-control; Money management
One Step Up, One Step Down	Serious	4 males (1 can be female)	Ambition; Priorities
Parlor Talk	Mixed	3 males, 2 females	Making a difference with your life; Death; Workaholism
Richard: 1985	Serious	2 males	Workaholism; Materialism vs. idealism
A Serf's Tale	Humorous	1 male, 1 female	Serving two masters; Materialism
Simple Gifts	Humorous but touching	2 males (1 teen), 3 females (1 teen and 1 girl)	Caring for others less fortunate; Materialism
What's the Ticket?	Mixed	2 females, 4 either males or females	Need for Christ; Contentment; Needs and wants
___	___	___	___
___	___	___	___
___	___	___	___

SONGS

Title	Artist	Style	Tempo	Seeker-Sensitivity Rating
Busy Man	Steven Curtis Chapman	Pop	Mid/up	10
Cat's in the Cradle	Harry Chapin; Ricky Skaggs	Folk	Mid	10
Ever Devoted	*Willow Creek Music*	*Ballad*	*Slow*	*6*

Title	Artist	Style	Tempo	Seeker-Sensitivity Rating
Hold On to Jesus	Steven Curtis Chapman	Ballad	Slow	8
The Measure of a Man	4Him	Pop	Up	6
Money Is a Powerful Thing	*Willow Creek Music*	*Motown/pop*	*Up*	*10*
Only Here for a Little While	Billy Dean	Country	Mid/up	10
Only You	*Willow Creek Music*	*Ballad*	*Slow*	*9*
Strength in You	*Willow Creek Music*	*MOR pop*	*Slow/mid*	*10*
Treasure	**Gary Chapman**	**Acoustic ballad**	**Slow**	**9**
Unimportant Things	**Paul Smith**	**Ballad**	**Slow**	**7**
Walk On By	Susan Ashton	Folk pop	Mid/up	8
_____	_____	_____	_____	____
_____	_____	_____	_____	____
_____	_____	_____	_____	____

Worship Choruses

Title	Artist	Style	Tempo	Seeker-Sensitivity Rating
More Precious Than Silver	Don Moen	Worship ballad	Slow	5
Turn Your Eyes upon Jesus	Hillsongs	Worship ballad	Slow	3
_____	_____	_____	_____	____
_____	_____	_____	_____	____
_____	_____	_____	_____	____

 MOVIE CLIPS

Title: Indiana Jones and the Last Crusade

Topic: Greed

Description: Elsa, Indy's girlfriend, chooses to reach for the grail in a chasm and falls to her death. Indy also reaches for it, but his father persuades him to let it go. Some good imagery.

Start Time: 1:55:50

Start Cue: Elsa grabs the grail.

End Time: 1:57:40

End Cue: Indy's dad pulls him up.

Comments: Elsa's death fall may scare kids.

Title: Lord of the Rings: Fellowship of the Rings

Topic: Greed; Materialism

Description: Short clip that shows Bilbo giving his treasures to Frodo. In the process he sees Frodo wearing his old ring. The ring has a power over anyone who has possessed it—it consumes that person. Bilbo reaches for the ring with a horrible look of greed on his face. The clip is a bit scary, but it is a good illustration of how greed transfigures and consumes us.

Start Time: 1:33:24/DVD Ch. 24

Start Cue: Bilbo uncovers his sword "Sting."

End Time: 1:35:17

End Cue: Bilbo grabs Frodo's hand.

Comments: This clip may be a little scary for children as Bilbo's face turns monstrous for a moment.

_____

_____

Title: She's Having a Baby

Topic: Life in suburbia; Emptiness of suburban life/American dream

Description: Funny parody of suburban life shows men in bad clothes dancing with lawnmowers while their wives dance around them with refreshments.

Start Time: 0:53:00

Start Cue: Start after the bicyclist leaves.

End Time: 0:54:30

End Cue: End when music stops.

Comments: _____

_____

Title: Wall Street

Topic: Greed/materialism; Money

Description: Corporate raider Gordon Gecko addresses a stockholders' meeting by extolling the virtues of greed.

Start Time: 1:17:00

Start Cue: "The new law of evolution in corporate America."

End Time: 1:18:15

End Cue: ". . . that other malfunctioning corporation called the U.S.A."

Comments: _____

_____

Title: _____

Topic: _____

Description: _____

Start Time: _____

Start Cue: _____

End Time: _____

End Cue: _____

Comments: _____

_____

Men's Issues

See also: **Father's Day**

MESSAGE TITLES

- ❏ *The Amazing American Stereotype:* The Amazing American Husband
- ❏ *The Amazing American Stereotype:* The Amazing American Male
- ❏ *Changing Times:* The Changing American Male
- ❏ *Marriagewerks:* When a Man Loves a Woman
- ❏ **The Benefits of Brotherhood:** Overcoming Independence • Superficial or Significant
  • The Cost of Commitment • The Rewards of Relationships

DRAMAS

Title	Tone	Characters	Topics
Any Time?	Mixed, mostly serious	1 male	Making time for God
Call Waiting	Mixed; Serious ending	2 males	Marketplace pressures; Search for significance; Mid-life crisis
Just an Acquaintance	Mixed	2 males, 2 females	Relationships between men; Superficial relationships
Mr. X, Mr. Y, and Mr. Z	Humorous	4 males, 1 female, 1 narrator	Friendship; Intimacy
The Next Step	Humorous	2 males	Authentic community; Positive relational risk taking; Men's relationships
A Real Man	Humorous	4 males, 1 female	The American male; Finding the right man

SONGS

Title	Artist	Style	Tempo	Seeker-Sensitivity Rating
In Christ Alone	**Michael English**	**Power ballad**	**Slow**	**8**
Man of God	*Greg Ferguson*	*Pop/rock*	*Mid/up*	*7*
The Measure of a Man	4Him	Pop	Up	6

Worship Choruses

Title	Artist	Style	Tempo	Seeker-Sensitivity Rating

MOVIE CLIPS

Title: _____

Topic: _____

Description: _____

Start Time: _____

Start Cue: _____

End Time: _____

End Cue: _____

Comments: _____

_____

_____

Money Management

This is different from **Materialism/Greed** in that it refers more to the way we spend and steward our financial resources.

Might also include: *Stewardship*

See also: **Tithing**

MESSAGE TITLES

❑ When Is Enough Enough?
❑ *Living Excellent Lives:* Financially
❑ **Financial Freedom:** Earning Money • Managing Money • Giving Money
❑ **Making Sense Out of Money:** The Power of Money • Mastering Your Money • Leveraging Your Money for Eternity • Giving
❑ **Your Money Matters:** Determining a Standard of Living • Developing a Financial Plan • Discovering the Rewards of Giving

DRAMAS

Title	Tone	Characters	Topics
Catalog-itis	Humorous	1 male, 1 female, 2 junior high girls	Self-control; Contentment
Check Mates	Humorous	1 male, 1 female	Personal finances; Debt
Confessions of an Ad-aholic	Humorous	1 male, 1 female	Materialism; Power of the media; American dream
December the 27th		1 male, 1 female	Overcoming regret; Pace of life at Christmas; Finances
Heart Failure	Humorous	1 male	Giving
Lifestyles of the Obscure and Indebted	Humorous	4 males, 3 females	Materialism; Coveting
The Offering	Humorous	3 males, 1 female	Tithing
Oh, What a Feeling!	Humorous	2 males, 1 female	Decision making; Self-control; Money management

Title	Tone	Characters	Topics

SONGS

*For other songs, look at **Commitment to Christ, Discipleship,** and **Obeying God.***

Title	Artist	Style	Tempo	Seeker-Sensitivity Rating
Highest Honor	**Chris Eaton**	**Ballad**	**Slow**	7
Money Is a Powerful Thing	*Willow Creek Music*	*Motown/pop*	*Up*	*10*
Unimportant Things	**Paul Smith**	**Ballad**	**Slow**	7

Worship Choruses

Title	Artist	Style	Tempo	Seeker-Sensitivity Rating
More Precious Than Silver	Don Moen	Worship ballad	Slow	5

MOVIE CLIPS

Title:

Topic:

Description:

Start Time:

Start Cue:

End Time:

End Cue:

Comments:

Moral Issues

See also: **Sin, Values**

MESSAGE TITLES

- ❏ The High Cost of a Cheap Thrill
- ❏ *A Faith That Works—The Book of James:* Religion according to God
- ❏ *Games We Play:* Scruples
- ❏ *Life's Defining Moments:* Defining Our Code of Conduct
- ❏ *Living Excellent Lives:* Morally
- ❏ *Making Life Work:* Do Goodness
- ❏ *What Money Can't Buy:* Conviction
- ❏ **Modern Day Madness:** The Agony of Escapism • The Pornography Problem • Hope for the Homosexual • Unwanted Pregnancies
- ❏ **Returns on Moral Investments:** The Payoff for Sexual Purity • The Reward of Relational Authenticity • The Benefits of Being a Seeker • The Profit of Financial Integrity

DRAMAS

Title	Tone	Characters	Topics
Attractive Deal	Serious	1 male, 1 female	Convictions, Adultery, Temptation
Because I Love You	Serious	1 male, 1 female	Adultery; Consequences of sin
The Big Sell	Humorous	3 males, 2 females	Obsession with sex in society; Effect of the media
Family Snapshots—Take II	Humorous	2 males, 2 females, 1 junior high boy	Families; Values; Priorities
Finding Evidence	Serious	2 males, 1 female	Trust; Jumping to conclusions
It's Only a Movie	Humorous	2 males, 2 females, 1 offstage voice	The power of media; The effects of what we see; Male/female differences
Just Looking	Mixed, light	1 male, 1 female	Eye causing you to stumble; Purity of thoughts
Man of the Year	Serious	5 males, 1 female	Moralism; Our need for Christ

Title	Tone	Characters	Topics
Man of the Year	Serious	5 males, 1 female	Moralism; Our need for Christ
Mere Technicality	Serious	1 male, 1 female	Living together; The cost of taking a stand for Christ
One Step Up, One Step Down	Serious	4 males (1 can be female)	Ambition; Priorities
Richard: 1992	Serious	2 males, 1 female	Anger; Rebellion; Decay of the family

 S O N G S

Title	Artist	Style	Tempo	Seeker-Sensitivity Rating
Behind Every Fantasy	*Willow Creek Music*	*Country pop*	*Up*	*10*
Man of God	*Greg Ferguson*	*Pop/rock*	*Mid/up*	*7*
There Is a Line	Susan Ashton	Folk pop	Mid	6
Time to Return	*Willow Creek Music*	*Ballad*	*Slow*	*7*
Walk On By	Susan Ashton	Folk pop	Mid/up	8
You've Got to Stand for Something	Aaron Tippin	Country	Up	10

Worship Choruses

Title	Artist	Style	Tempo	Seeker-Sensitivity Rating

MOVIE CLIPS

Title:	City Slickers
Topic:	Adultery; Temptation
Description:	Billy Crystal's character's friend asks him if he would cheat on his wife if no one would ever know. His answer shows integrity.
Start Time:	0:44:38
Start Cue:	"What if you could have great sex . . ."
End Time:	0:45:30
End Cue:	"I wouldn't like myself . . . that's all."
Comments:	May be too straightforward for some. Profanity precedes the clip.

_____
_____
_____

Title:	_____
Topic:	_____
Description:	_____
Start Time:	_____
Start Cue:	_____
End Time:	_____
End Cue:	_____
Comments:	_____

_____
_____
_____

—————Pace of Life/Balance—————

Might also include: *Hurry* and *Living a Balanced Life*
See also: **Workaholism**

Package Suggestion

Drama:
The Plate Spinner

Song:
I'm in a Hurry

MESSAGE TITLES

❑ Balance in Your Life
❑ Called or Driven?
❑ Driven: What Fuels You?
❑ Finding Rest
❑ Lessons from an Hourglass
❑ What Drives the Workaholic?
❑ *A Faith That Works—The Book of James:* No More! The Power to Stop
❑ *Fourth Commandment:* Remember the Sabbath Day
❑ *I Have a Friend Who* Struggles with Balancing Life's Demands
❑ *Life's Too Short . . .* to Work All the Time
❑ *Ordering Your Private World:* Ordering Your Recreational World
❑ *Restoring Weary Souls:* Building Better Boundaries
❑ *Restoring Weary Souls:* Overcoming Soul Fatigue
❑ *Restoring Weary Souls:* Taking Recreation Seriously
❑ *Signs of the Times:* Reduce Speed
❑ *Three Things God Loves (That Most People Think He Doesn't):* Leisure

DRAMAS

Title	Tone	Characters	Topics
Any Time?	Mixed, mostly serious	1 male	Making time for God
The Brotherhood	Humorous	2 males, 4 either males or females	Workaholism; Balancing your life
Clearing Things Up	Humorous	5 males or females	Balancing life; Priorities
December the 27th		1 male, 1 female	Overcoming regret; Pace of life at Christmas; Finances
Distancing	Mixed, mostly serious	1 male, 1 female	Good marriages take work; Demands of life

Title	Tone	Characters	Topics
Driven	Serious	1 male, 1 female	Workaholism; Marriage
Everybody Needs	Mixed	1 female	Being impressed with externals
An Hour on Wednesday	Mixed; Serious ending	1 male, 1 female	Marriage; Damaging effects of a fast-paced life
It's No Picnic	Humorous	3 males, 3 females	Work stress; Surface relationships
Just Below the Jetta	Serious	1 female	Valuing people
Lifetime Deal	Serious	2 males	Workaholism
On Vacation	Humorous	2 males, 1 female, 1 either male or female	Leisure time; Guilt; Slowing down
One Step Up, One Step Down	Serious	4 males (1 can be female)	Ambition; Priorities
One Sunday in the Parking Lot	Humorous	4 males or females	Pace of life; Making changes
The Plate Spinner	Humorous	5 males, 4 females, 1 narrator	Pace of life; Being in control
Quality Time	Serious	1 male, 1 female, 2 teenage girls	Fatherhood; Workaholism
The Rest Room	Humorous	1 female, offstage voices: 1 male, 2 children	Boundaries; Taking better care of yourself; Motherhood
Richard: 1985	Serious	2 males	Workaholism; Materialism vs. idealism
Tired When Needed	Humorous	1 male, 1 female	Burnout; Boundaries; Saying "no"
Up on the Roof	Mixed	1 male, 1 female	Emotional refueling; Building compassion
Vince Bueller's Day Off	Humorous	1 male, 1 female, 1 boy	Workaholism; Importance of rest/leisure
Winning Strategy	Mixed	2 males, 4 males or females	Good vs. evil; Busyness
_____	_____	_____	_____
_____	_____	_____	_____
_____	_____	_____	_____
_____	_____	_____	_____

SONGS

Title	Artist	Style	Tempo	Seeker-Sensitivity Rating
Busy Man	Steven Curtis Chapman	Pop	Mid/up	10
Cat's in the Cradle	Harry Chapin; Ricky Skaggs	Folk	Mid	10
I'm in a Hurry (and Don't Know Why)	Alabama	Country pop	Up	10

Title	Artist	Style	Tempo	Seeker-Sensitivity Rating
King of the Jungle	**Steven Curtis Chapman**	**Pop shuffle with African touches**	**Mid/up**	9
Life Means So Much	**Chris Rice**	**Folk pop**	**Mid**	7
On My Knees	*Willow Creek Music*	*Acoustic guitar ballad*	*Slow*	5
Only Here for a Little While	Billy Dean	Country	Mid/up	10
The Urgency of the Generally Insignificant	Wayne Watson	Pop/rock	Up	9
_____	_____	_____	_____	_____
_____	_____	_____	_____	_____
_____	_____	_____	_____	_____
_____	_____	_____	_____	_____

Worship Choruses

Title	Artist	Style	Tempo	Seeker-Sensitivity Rating
Turn Your Eyes upon Jesus	Hillsongs	Worship ballad	Slow	3
_____	_____	_____	_____	_____
_____	_____	_____	_____	_____
_____	_____	_____	_____	_____
_____	_____	_____	_____	_____

 MOVIE CLIPS

Title: _____

Topic: _____

Description: _____

Start Time: _____

Start Cue: _____

End Time: _____

End Cue: _____

Comments: _____

_____

_____

Power

Refers to the desire for power, control
See also: **Control Issues, Lordship of Christ**

MESSAGE TITLES

❑ *Money, Sex, and Power:* Power
❑ *What Jesus Would Say to . . .* George W. Bush

_____

_____

_____

DRAMAS

Title	Tone	Characters	Topics
The Gardeners	Humorous	1 male, 1 female	New Age movement
Lonely at the Top	Serious	1 male	Perils of power; Authority; Easter
Wheel of Power	Serious	4 males, 1 female, 1 child	Power

SONGS

Title	Artist	Style	Tempo	Seeker-Sensitivity Rating
Audience of One	*Willow Creek Music*	*Power ballad*	*Slow*	8
Strength in You	*Willow Creek Music*	*MOR pop*	*Slow/mid*	10
Treasure	**Gary Chapman**	**Acoustic ballad**	**Slow**	9

Title	Artist	Style	Tempo	Seeker-Sensitivity Rating

Worship Choruses

Title	Artist	Style	Tempo	Seeker-Sensitivity Rating

MOVIE CLIPS

Title: _____

Topic: _____

Description: _____

Start Time: _____

Start Cue: _____

End Time: _____

End Cue: _____

Comments: _____

_____

_____

Regret

See also: **Guilt**

MESSAGE TITLES

- ❏ Life without Regret
- ❏ Resolving Regrets
- ❏ *Telling the Truth:* Expressing Positive Emotions

DRAMAS

Title	Tone	Characters	Topics
The Angry Woman	Serious	2 males, 3 females, 1 narrator	The roots of anger
The Boy Who Never Got Dirty	Humorous	1 male, 1 female, 1 narrator	Service; Risk taking
The Brow Beater	Mixed, mostly serious	1 male, 1 female	Self-esteem; Failures; Forgiveness
December the 27th		1 male, 1 female	Overcoming regret; Pace of life at Christmas; Finances
Just Below the Jetta	Serious	1 female	Valuing people
A Nice Guy	Serious	2 males	Regret; Admitting failures; Effects of sin; Confession
The Painful Process	Serious	1 female	Abortion

SONGS

Title	Artist	Style	Tempo	Seeker-Sensitivity Rating
Cat's in the Cradle	Harry Chapin; Ricky Skaggs	Folk	Mid	10
Hunger for Healing	*Willow Creek Music*	*Folk ballad*	*Slow*	*10*
If I Had Only Known	Reba McEntire	Ballad	Slow	10
The Living Years	Mike & the Mechanics	Pop	Mid/up	10
Mercy for the Memories	Geoff Moore & the Distance	Folk pop ballad	Slow	9
Only Here for a Little While	Billy Dean	Country	Mid/up	10
Seize the Day	**Carolyn Arends**	**Folk pop, in 3**	**Mid**	**8**

Worship Choruses

Title	Artist	Style	Tempo	Seeker-Sensitivity Rating

MOVIE CLIPS

Title: 8 Seconds

Topic: Regret; Communicating love

Description: A father, whose son has recently died in a rodeo accident, breaks down in remorse over not telling his son that he loved him. This short clip probably needs to be set up.

Start Time: 1:27:22

Start Cue: Pallbearers carry the casket out of the church.

End Time: 1:28:44

End Cue: The mother puts her hands on the father's shoulders.

Comments: _____

Title: Dad

Topic: Parenting; Father-son relationships

Description: Ted Danson and Jack Lemmon play a father and son. Lemmon is dying in a hospital bed, and they have a very poignant exchange, ending with Danson crawling into bed with his dad.

Start Time: 1:46:20

Start Cue: "How you feeling?"

End Time: 1:50:35

End Cue: "I must have done something right." End after wide shot.

Comments: _____

_____

Title: Rudy

Topic: Quitting; Perseverance

Description: Rudy decides to quit the football team. Fortune, his friend and former boss, challenges him because he used to play for Notre Dame and quit.

Start Time: 1:29:10

Start Cue: Just before "What're you doing here?"

End Time: 1:31:20

End Cue: "Do you hear me clear enough?"

Comments: The words *crap* and *hell* are used.

_____

_____

Title: The Shawshank Redemption

Topic: Regret; Consequences of sin

Description: Red, a forty-year inmate, stands before the parole board and talks about his regret over forty years lost.

Start Time: 2:05:30

Start Cue: Bars slide open and door opens to parole board room.

End Time: 2:07:34

End Cue: Stop immediately after "I gotta live with that."

Comments: There is profanity immediately following the end cue.

_____

_____

Title: _____

Topic: _____

Description: _____

Start Time: _____

Start Cue: _____

End Time: _____

End Cue: _____

Comments: _____

_____

Risk Taking

Might also include: *Apathy*

See also: **Fear**

MESSAGE TITLES

- ❏ Opportunity Knocks
- ❏ The Rewards of Spiritual Risk Taking
- ❏ Seizing Spiritual Opportunities
- ❏ *Games We Play:* Risk
- ❏ *Life's Too Short* . . . to Play It Safe
- ❏ *Living with an Attitude:* The Attitude of Living Now
- ❏ *Making Life Work:* Take Initiative

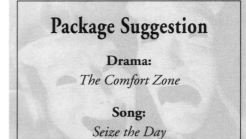

Package Suggestion

Drama:
The Comfort Zone

Song:
Seize the Day

DRAMAS

Title	Tone	Characters	Topics
The Boy Who Never Got Dirty	Humorous	1 male, 1 female, 1 narrator	Service; Risk taking
Character Test	Mixed, moving	2 males, 1 female	Promptings from God; Obedience; Power of encouragement
The Comfort Zone	Humorous	1 male, 2 females (1 TV announcer on tape)	Risk taking
Conversations	Serious	2 males, 1 female, 1 offstage female voice	Self-esteem; Self-criticism; Failure
The Fence-Sitter	Mixed	4 males, 1 female	Indecision; Getting involved in ministry; Deciding to become a Christian
Mr. X, Mr. Y, and Mr. Z	Humorous	4 males, 1 female, 1 narrator	Friendship; Intimacy
The Next Step	Humorous	2 males	Authentic community; Positive relational risk taking; Men's relationships
The Speculators	Humorous	2 males, 1 female	Risk taking; Missed opportunities

Title	Tone	Characters	Topics
Straight-Jacketed	Serious	1 male	Bondage to past and to sin; Anger at God
The Waiting Room	Mixed	2 males, 2 females	Fear of decision making; Need to take risks
War and Peace	Serious	2 males, 2 females	Relationships; Taking risks
___	___	___	___
___	___	___	___
___	___	___	___
___	___	___	___

SONGS

Title	Artist	Style	Tempo	Seeker-Sensitivity Rating
Desperado	Eagles	Ballad	Slow	10
Dive	**Steven Curtis Chapman**	**Pop/rock**	**Up**	**9**
For the Sake of the Call	Steven Curtis Chapman	Anthemic pop	Up	3
Life Means So Much	**Chris Rice**	**Folk pop**	**Mid**	**7**
Live Out Loud	**Steven Curtis Chapman**	**Pop**	**Up**	**9**
Seize the Day	**Carolyn Arends**	**Folk pop, in 3**	**Mid**	**8**
Take My Hand	The Kry	Acoustic ballad	Mid/slow	9
___	___	___	___	___
___	___	___	___	___
___	___	___	___	___
___	___	___	___	___
___	___	___	___	___

Worship Choruses

Title	Artist	Style	Tempo	Seeker-Sensitivity Rating
___	___	___	___	___
___	___	___	___	___
___	___	___	___	___
___	___	___	___	___

MOVIE CLIPS

Title: Dead Poet's Society

Topic: Risk taking

Description: Robin Williams plays a teacher who encourages his students to "seize the day."

Start Time: 0:13:42

Start Cue: Student reads, "Gather ye rosebuds while ye may."

End Time: 0:16:25

End Cue: "Make your lives extraordinary."

Comments: _____

_____

_____

Title: The Matrix

Topic: Decision making; Spiritual seeking

Description: Metaphors abound in this clip, which shows Morpheus explaining the matrix to Neo. He offers him the choice to stay in the bondage of the world he's in (the matrix) or to know the truth and be set free. Should he take the blue pill or the red pill (the truth)? Neo chooses the red pill.

Start Time: 0:25:42

Start Cue: Neo enters the room where Morpheus is.

End Time: 0:29:50

End Cue: "Follow me."

Comments: The clip probably needs explaining but could easily be used in a sermon to illustrate the choice we make to be free of the slavery of sin through choosing Christ.

_____

_____

_____

Title: _____

Topic: _____

Description: _____

Start Time: _____

Start Cue: _____

End Time: _____

End Cue: _____

Comments: _____

_____

_____

_____

Selfishness/Pride

Selfishness and pride are somewhat different but arise from the same issue—being centered on ourselves.

Might also include: *Humility*

See also: **Lordship of Christ, Obeying God**

MESSAGE TITLES

- ❏ The Altar of Ego
- ❏ An Audience of One
- ❏ The Blessedness of Brokenness
- ❏ A Check-up from the Neck Up
- ❏ Humility for High-Flying Achievers
- ❏ *Christianity's Toughest Competition:* Individualism
- ❏ *Truths That Transform:* Look Not to Your Interests Only, but to the Interests of Others as Well
- ❏ *Understanding the Times:* The '80s
- ❏ *What Money Can't Buy:* Humility

DRAMAS

Title	Tone	Characters	Topics
Am I Missing Something?	Serious	3 males, 2 females	Attitudes in serving; Giving; Self-deception; Rationalizing
Any Time?	Mixed, mostly serious	1 male	Making time for God
Credit Due	Mixed	2 males, 2 females, 2 children's voices offstage	When others use you
Hard to Be Humble	Humorous	4 males or females	Evangelism; Fruit of the Spirit; World's view vs. Christianity
Improving Your Lie	Humorous	1 male, 1 female	Truth telling; Marriage
Truthful Words	Serious	1 male, 1 female	Leadership; Pride; Truth telling
You Cramp My Style	Serious	1 male, 1 female, 1 either male or female	Reasons people don't believe; Society's view of God

Title	Tone	Characters	Topics

SONGS

Title	Artist	Style	Tempo	Seeker-Sensitivity Rating
Altar of Ego	Carolyn Arends	Folk pop	Mid/up	6
At the Foot of the Cross	*Willow Creek Music*	*Pop*	*Mid*	*7*
Audience of One	*Willow Creek Music*	*Power ballad*	*Slow*	*8*
Call of the Wild	Susan Ashton	Country	Mid	10
Ever Devoted	*Willow Creek Music*	*Ballad*	*Slow*	*6*
If That's What It Takes	*Willow Creek Music*	*MOR pop*	*Mid/slow*	*5*
In Christ Alone	**Michael English**	**Power ballad**	**Slow**	**8**
Miracle of Mercy	Steven Curtis Chapman	Acoustic ballad	Slow	4
Strength in You	*Willow Creek Music*	*MOR pop*	*Slow/mid*	*10*
What if I?	*Willow Creek Music*	*Piano ballad*	*Slow/mid*	*8*

Worship Choruses

Title	Artist	Style	Tempo	Seeker-Sensitivity Rating

MOVIE CLIPS

Title: Remember the Titans

Topic: Leadership; Respecting authority; Pride; Racism

Description: The Titans' star player confronts the coach and tries to lay down the law about who will play, based on color. The coach puts him in his place.

Start Time: 0:14:21/DVD Ch. 5

Start Cue: The coach starts to walk to the bus.

End Time: 0:16:57

End Cue: "Fix that tie, son." Close-up of the coach.

Comments: If you are using this clip for a message on racism, you may want to use the next minute or so, which shows the coach integrating the two buses.

_____

_____

_____

Title: _____

Topic: _____

Description: _____

Start Time: _____

Start Cue: _____

End Time: _____

End Cue: _____

Comments: _____

_____

_____

Values

Refers specifically to what we believe and what is important to us—what we value.

See also: **Moral Issues, Christian Character**

Package Suggestion

Drama:
Richard: 1992

Song:
Time to Return

MESSAGE TITLES

❑ The Upside-Down Priorities
❑ *Life's Defining Moments:* Defining Our Beliefs
❑ *Making Life Work:* Do Goodness
❑ *What Money Can't Buy:* Conviction
❑ **Defining Family Values:** Origin of Values • Transmitting Values • Endangered Values

DRAMAS

Title	Tone	Characters	Topics
The Big Sell	Humorous	3 males, 2 females	Obsession with sex in society; Effect of the media
Driven	Serious	1 male, 1 female	Workaholism; Marriage
Family Snapshots—Take II	Humorous	2 males, 2 females, 1 junior high boy	Families; Values; Priorities
Getting the Nod	Mixed	2 males, 1 either male or female	Honesty; Integrity; Business ethics; Handling failure
It's Only a Movie	Humorous	2 males, 2 females, 1 offstage voice	The power of media; The effects of what we see; Male/female differences
Just Below the Jetta	Serious	1 female	Valuing people
Just Looking	Mixed, light	1 male, 1 female	Eye causing you to stumble; Purity of thoughts
Mere Technicality	Serious	1 male, 1 female	Living together; The cost of taking a stand for Christ
Mixed Signals	Mixed	1 male, 1 boy	Encouragement; Fathers; Priorities

Title	Tone	Characters	Topics
Richard: 1968	Mixed	2 males, 2 females	Youthful idealism; Changing societal values; Generation gap; The '60s
Richard: 1992	Serious	2 males, 1 female	Anger; Rebellion; Decay of the family
The Right Thing	Serious	1 male	Costly obedience; Christian character; Persecution

SONGS

Title	Artist	Style	Tempo	Seeker-Sensitivity Rating
Life Means So Much	**Chris Rice**	**Folk pop**	**Mid**	7
Man of God	*Greg Ferguson*	*Pop/rock*	*Mid/up*	*7*
There Is a Line	Susan Ashton	Folk pop	Mid	6
Time to Return	*Willow Creek Music*	*Ballad*	*Slow*	*7*
The Urgency of the Generally Insignificant	Wayne Watson	Pop/rock	Up	9
You've Got to Stand for Something	Aaron Tippin	Country	Up	10

Worship Choruses

Title	Artist	Style	Tempo	Seeker-Sensitivity Rating

MOVIE CLIPS

Title: _____

Topic: _____

Description: _____

Start Time: _____

Start Cue: _____

End Time: _____

End Cue: _____

Comments: _____

_____

_____

_____

Women's Issues

See also: **Mother's Day**

MESSAGE TITLES

- ❏ *The Amazing American Stereotype:* The Amazing American Female
- ❏ *The Amazing American Stereotype:* The Amazing American Wife
- ❏ *Changing Times:* The Changing American Female
- ❏ *Fanning the Flames of Marriage:* Wisdom for Wives
- ❏ *Marriagewerks:* Loving a Man without Losing Yourself
- ❏ *Taking Care of Business:* How Much Should Mothers Work?

_____

_____

_____

_____

_____

DRAMAS

Title	Tone	Characters	Topics
Maternal Measures	Humorous	3 females	Mother's Day; Pressure on women to measure up
The Rest Room	Humorous	1 female, offstage voices: 1 male, 2 children	Boundaries; Taking better care of yourself; Motherhood
Watching from the Window	Serious	1 female, 1 child	Stress of life; Challenge of motherhood; Draining relationships

SONGS

Title	Artist	Style	Tempo	Seeker-Sensitivity Rating
Charm Is Deceitful	Kim Hill	Ballad	Slow	5

Worship Choruses

Title	Artist	Style	Tempo	Seeker-Sensitivity Rating

MOVIE CLIPS

Title:

Topic:

Description:

Start Time:

Start Cue:

End Time:

End Cue:

Comments:

Work Issues

Marketplace Pressures

Might also include: *Christians in the Marketplace*

MESSAGE TITLES

❑ Christians in the Marketplace
❑ A Day in the Life of a Christian
❑ Keeping Your Head Up When Your Job Gets You Down

DRAMAS

Title	Tone	Characters	Topics
Call Waiting	Mixed; Serious ending	2 males	Marketplace pressures; Search for significance; Mid-life crisis
A Day in the Life	Humorous	5 males	Christians in the marketplace; New Christian
Driven	Serious	1 male, 1 female	Workaholism; Marriage
It's No Picnic	Humorous	3 males, 3 females	Work stress; Surface relationships
No Clue	Humorous	2 males, 1 female, 1 voice-over	Gender sensitivity; Male/female workplace issues
Pastor General: Consultant Visit	Humorous	2 males, 4 females	Leadership; Oppressive managers; Communication
The Plate Spinner	Humorous	5 males, 4 females, 1 narrator	Pace of life; Being in control
Tired When Needed	Humorous	1 male, 1 female	Burnout; Boundaries; Saying "no"
Up on the Roof	Mixed	1 male, 1 female	Emotional refueling; Building compassion

Title	Tone	Characters	Topics

SONGS

Title	Artist	Style	Tempo	Seeker-Sensitivity Rating
I'm in a Hurry (and Don't Know Why)	Alabama	Country pop	Up	10
King of the Jungle	Steven Curtis Chapman	Pop shuffle with African touches	Mid/up	9
On My Knees	*Willow Creek Music*	*Acoustic guitar ballad*	*Slow*	*5*

Worship Choruses

Title	Artist	Style	Tempo	Seeker-Sensitivity Rating

MOVIE CLIPS

Title: _____

Topic: _____

Description: _____

Start Time: _____

Start Cue: _____

End Time: _____

End Cue: _____

Comments: _____

Success

Might also include: *Ambition, Fame*
See also: **Fulfillment**

MESSAGE TITLES

- ❏ Achievement's Shadow
- ❏ Essential Ingredients for Successful Living
- ❏ Humility for High-Flying Achievers
- ❏ *Life's Defining Moments:* Defining Our Personal Aspirations
- ❏ *Taking Care of Business:* Called or Driven?
- ❏ *Understanding the Times:* The '80s
- ❏ *What Jesus Would Say to . . .* Bill Gates
- ❏ *What Jesus Would Say to . . .* Tiger Woods

_____

_____

_____

DRAMAS

Title	Tone	Characters	Topics
Driven	Serious	1 male, 1 female	Workaholism; Marriage
Lifetime Deal	Serious	2 males	Workaholism
Make It Happen	Humorous	5 males, 1 female (numerous extras for attendees and security)	Taking responsibility for change; The limits of self-help seminars
Maybe Someday	Mixed, mostly serious	2 males	Evangelism; Success that leaves us empty; Going back to church
One Step Up, One Step Down	Serious	4 males (1 can be female)	Ambition; Priorities
_____	_____	_____	_____
_____	_____	_____	_____
_____	_____	_____	_____
_____	_____	_____	_____

SONGS

Title	Artist	Style	Tempo	Seeker-Sensitivity Rating
Audience of One	*Willow Creek Music*	*Power ballad*	*Slow*	*8*
Busy Man	Steven Curtis Chapman	Pop	Mid/up	10
Cat's in the Cradle	Harry Chapin; Ricky Skaggs	Folk	Mid	10
In Christ Alone	**Michael English**	**Power ballad**	**Slow**	**8**
The Measure of a Man	4Him	Pop	Up	6
Strength in You	*Willow Creek Music*	*MOR pop*	*Slow/mid*	*10*
Treasure	**Gary Chapman**	**Acoustic ballad**	**Slow**	**9**
Unimportant Things	**Paul Smith**	**Ballad**	**Slow**	**7**

Worship Choruses

Title	Artist	Style	Tempo	Seeker-Sensitivity Rating

MOVIE CLIPS

Title: Cool Runnings

Topic: Success; Ambition

Description: A bobsledder asks his coach why he cheated twenty years ago in the Olympics. The answer has a lot to say about the trap of success and its ultimate lack of fulfillment.

Start Time:	1:25:15
Start Cue:	Coach enters hotel room.
End Time:	1:27:15
End Cue:	"When you cross that finish line, you'll know."
Comments:	_____

Title:	Searching for Bobby Fischer
Topic:	Success; Fear of failure
Description:	Josh Waitzkin, a chess prodigy, has a late-night talk with his dad about the possibility of losing. Shows the pressure of staying on top.
Start Time:	1:01:30
Start Cue:	Josh's dad is reading him a story.
End Time:	1:03:50
End Cue:	"Maybe it's better not to be the best. Then you can lose and it's O.K."
Comments:	_____

Title:	Searching for Bobby Fischer
Topic:	Fatherhood; Failure; Destructive parenting
Description:	Eight-year-old Josh loses a chess match, and his dad angrily confronts him about losing. Illustrates a dad who has too much invested in his son's success.
Start Time:	1:06:30
Start Cue:	Shot of clock tower. "Seven moves" is first line.
End Time:	1:08:20
End Cue:	"Sorry."
Comments:	_____

Title:	She's Having a Baby
Topic:	Life in suburbia; Emptiness of suburban life/American dream
Description:	Funny parody of suburban life shows men in bad clothes dancing with lawnmowers while their wives dance around them with refreshments.
Start Time:	0:53:00
Start Cue:	Start after the bicyclist leaves.
End Time:	0:54:30
End Cue:	End when music stops.
Comments:	_____

Title:	_____
Topic:	_____
Description:	_____
Start Time:	_____
Start Cue:	_____
End Time:	_____
End Cue:	_____
Comments:	_____

Work/Marketplace Issues

This is a general category. For more specific topics, see: **Leadership, Marketplace Pressures, Success, Workaholism**

Might also include: *Labor Day*

MESSAGE TITLES

❑ Achievement's Shadow
❑ Driven: What Fuels You?
❑ Four Advantages Christians Have at Work
❑ Humility for High-Flying Achievers
❑ Keeping Your Head Up When Your Job Gets You Down
❑ Your Work Matters to God
❑ *Facing New Realities:* The Changing American Workplace
❑ *Life's Too Short . . .* to Work All the Time
❑ **Christians in the Workplace:** The Value of Human Labor • The Secret of Job Satisfaction • Missionaries in the Marketplace • Women in the Workplace • Profits or People • Please Pass the Paycheck
❑ **Loving Mondays:** Discovering Your Vocational Calling • Optimizing Your Vocational Potential • Increasing Your Impact
❑ **Taking Care of Business:** The Rewards of Human Labor • Keys to Job Satisfaction • How Much Should Mothers Work? • What Drives the Workaholic? • The Character Crisis • Called or Driven?

DRAMAS

Title	Tone	Characters	Topics
The Brotherhood	Humorous	2 males, 4 either males or females	Workaholism; Balancing your life
Call Waiting	Mixed; Serious ending	2 males	Marketplace pressures; Search for significance; Mid-life crisis
Credit Due	Mixed	2 males, 2 females, 2 children's voices offstage	When others use you
A Day in the Life	Humorous	5 males	Christians in the marketplace; New Christian

Title	Tone	Characters	Topics
Don't Mention It	Mixed, mostly humorous	2 males, 2 females	Unemployment; Being open about problems
The Do-Over	Humorous	1 male, 1 female	Longing for second chances; The importance of good choices
Driven	Serious	1 male, 1 female	Workaholism; Marriage
Getting the Nod	Mixed	2 males, 1 either male or female	Honesty; Integrity; Business ethics; Handling failures
An Hour on Wednesday	Mixed; Serious ending	1 male, 1 female	Marriage; Damaging effects of a fast-paced life
It's No Picnic	Humorous	3 males, 3 females	Work stress; Surface relationships
Labor of Love	Mixed, mostly serious	2 males, 1 female	Finding a career that fits; Sacrifices parents make for the next generation
Lifetime Deal	Serious	2 males	Workaholism
Lightening Leadership	Humorous	2 males, 1 female	Leadership; Work
No Clue	Humorous	2 males, 1 female, 1 voice-over	Gender sensitivity; Male/female workplace issues
One Step Up, One Step Down	Serious	4 males (1 can be female)	Ambition; Priorities
One Sunday in the Parking Lot	Humorous	4 males or females	Pace of life; Making changes
Parlor Talk	Mixed	3 males, 2 females	Making a difference with your life; Death; Workaholism
Pastor General: Consultant Visit	Humorous	2 males, 4 females	Leadership; Oppressive managers; Communication
Quality Time	Serious	1 male, 1 female, 2 teenage girls	Fatherhood; Workaholism
Richard: 1985	Serious	2 males	Workaholism; Materialism vs. idealism
Shop Talk	Mixed	2 males, 2 females	Failure; Adversity; Small groups
Tired When Needed	Humorous	1 male, 1 female	Burnout; Boundaries; Saying "no"
Up on the Roof	Mixed	1 male, 1 female	Emotional refueling; Building compassion
Wasted	Mixed	2 males	Job satisfaction; Christians and work

SONGS

Title	Artist	Style	Tempo	Seeker-Sensitivity Rating
Audience of One	*Willow Creek Music*	*Power ballad*	*Slow*	*8*
Busy Man	Steven Curtis Chapman	Pop	Mid/up	10
Cat's in the Cradle	Harry Chapin; Ricky Skaggs	Folk	Mid	10
I'm in a Hurry (and Don't Know Why)	Alabama	Country pop	Up	10
King of the Jungle	**Steven Curtis Chapman**	**Pop shuffle with African touches**	**Mid/up**	**9**
Only Here for a Little While	Billy Dean	Country	Mid/up	10
Only You	*Willow Creek Music*	*Ballad*	*Slow*	*9*
Strength in You	*Willow Creek Music*	*MOR pop*	*Slow/mid*	*10*
Treasure	**Gary Chapman**	**Acoustic ballad**	**Slow**	**9**
_____	_____	_____	_____	___
_____	_____	_____	_____	___
_____	_____	_____	_____	___
_____	_____	_____	_____	___
_____	_____	_____	_____	___
_____	_____	_____	_____	___

Worship Choruses

Title	Artist	Style	Tempo	Seeker-Sensitivity Rating
_____	_____	_____	_____	___
_____	_____	_____	_____	___
_____	_____	_____	_____	___
_____	_____	_____	_____	___
_____	_____	_____	_____	___
_____	_____	_____	_____	___

MOVIE CLIPS

Title: Chariots of Fire

Topic: Being true to the person God made you to be; Honoring God with your gifts

Description: Eric Liddell talks to his sister, who wants him to forsake running to be a missionary. Eric talks about the fact that God made him fast, and when he runs, he can feel God's pleasure.

Start Time: 0:58:20

Start Cue: First line is "I've decided . . . I'm going back to China."

End Time: 0:59:15

End Cue: "To win is to honor Him."

Comments: _____

_____

_____

Title: Cool Runnings

Topic: Success; Ambition

Description: A bobsledder asks his coach why he cheated twenty years ago in the Olympics. The answer has a lot to say about the trap of success and its ultimate lack of fulfillment.

Start Time: 1:25:15

Start Cue: Coach enters hotel room.

End Time: 1:27:15

End Cue: "When you cross that finish line, you'll know."

Comments: _____

_____

_____

Title: _____

Topic: _____

Description: _____

Start Time: _____

Start Cue: _____

End Time: _____

End Cue: _____

Comments: _____

_____

_____

Workaholism

This is different from **Pace of Life,** in that it deals specifically with work.

MESSAGE TITLES

❑ Balance in Your Life
❑ It All Goes Back in the Box
❑ Profession or Obsession
❑ *Signs of the Times:* Reduce Speed
❑ *Taking Care of Business:* What Drives the Workaholic?
❑ *What Jesus Would Say to . . .* Bill Gates

_____

_____

_____

_____

DRAMAS

Title	Tone	Characters	Topics
The Brotherhood	Humorous	2 males, 4 either males or females	Workaholism; Balancing your life
Driven	Serious	1 male, 1 female	Workaholism; Marriage
An Hour on Wednesday	Mixed; Serious ending	1 male, 1 female	Marriage; Damaging effects of a fast-paced life
It's No Picnic	Humorous	3 males, 3 females	Work stress; Surface relationships
Lifetime Deal	Serious	2 males	Workaholism
The Mirror Thought of It	Mixed	1 male, 1 female, 1 offstage voice	Materialism; Workaholism; Striving for more
One Step Up, One Step Down	Serious	4 males (1 can be female)	Ambition; Priorities
One Sunday in the Parking Lot	Humorous	4 males or females	Pace of life; Making changes
Parlor Talk	Mixed	3 males, 2 females	Making a difference with your life; Death; Workaholism
Quality Time	Serious	1 male, 1 female, 2 teenage girls	Fatherhood; Workaholism

Title	Tone	Characters	Topics
Richard: 1985	Serious	2 males	Workaholism; Materialism vs. idealism
Vince Bueller's Day Off	Humorous	1 male, 1 female, 1 boy	Workaholism; Importance of rest/leisure

SONGS

Title	Artist	Style	Tempo	Seeker-Sensitivity Rating
Busy Man	Steven Curtis Chapman	Pop	Mid/up	10
Cat's in the Cradle	Harry Chapin; Ricky Skaggs	Folk	Mid	10
I'm in a Hurry (and Don't Know Why)	Alabama	Country pop	Up	10
King of the Jungle	**Steven Curtis Chapman**	**Pop shuffle with African touches**	**Mid/up**	**9**
The Measure of a Man	4Him	Pop	Up	6
Only Here for a Little While	Billy Dean	Country	Mid/up	10
Strength in You	*Willow Creek Music*	*MOR pop*	*Slow/mid*	*10*
Unimportant Things	Paul Smith	Ballad	Slow	7

Worship Choruses

Title	Artist	Style	Tempo	Seeker-Sensitivity Rating

MOVIE CLIPS

Title: _____

Topic: _____

Description: _____

Start Time: _____

Start Cue: _____

End Time: _____

End Cue: _____

Comments: _____

_____

_____

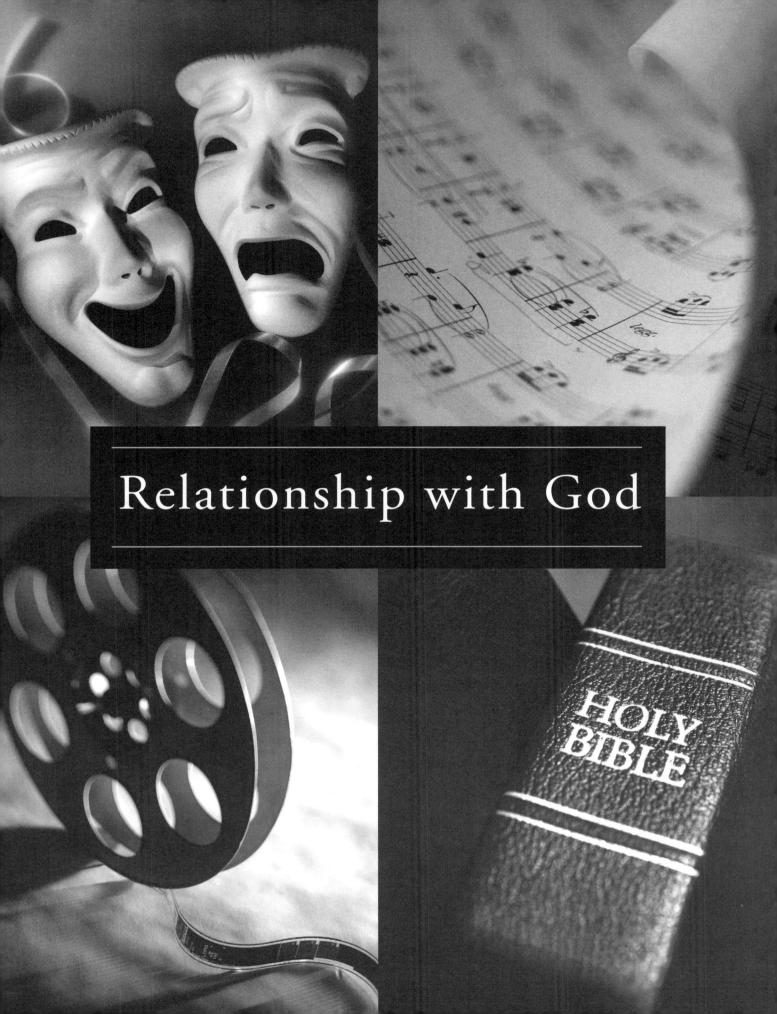

Relationship with God

Anger toward God

MESSAGE TITLES

- ❏ When I'm Mad at God
- ❏ Why Did This Happen to Me?
- ❏ *The Power of Prayer:* The Mystery of Unanswered Prayer
- ❏ **Disappointment with God:** What Causes Disappointment? • Where Is God When You Need Him?
  • When God Seems Silent

DRAMAS

Title	Tone	Characters	Topics
Another Day at the Bus Stop	Mixed	1 male, 1 female	Our relationship with God; Self-esteem
Great Expectations	Mixed; Very serious ending	1 male, 2 females	Unanswered prayer
Straight-Jacketed	Serious	1 male	Bondage to past and to sin; Anger toward God

SONGS

*No songs specifically about anger toward God. Look at **Anger** or **Doubting**.

Title	Artist	Style	Tempo	Seeker-Sensitivity Rating

Worship Choruses

Title	Artist	Style	Tempo	Seeker-Sensitivity Rating
_____	_____	_____	____	____
_____	_____	_____	____	____
_____	_____	_____	____	____
_____	_____	_____	____	____

MOVIE CLIPS

Title: Shadowlands

Topic: Suffering; Pain; Why does God allow bad things to happen?

Description: C. S. Lewis delivers a speech about why God allows suffering.

Start Time: 0:10:00

Start Cue: "Yesterday I received a letter."

End Time: 0:11:40

End Cue: "Thank you very much."

Comments: The last line is a bit hard to understand.

_____

_____

_____

Title: _____

Topic: _____

Description: _____

Start Time: _____

Start Cue: _____

End Time: _____

End Cue: _____

Comments: _____

_____

_____

Changed Life

MESSAGE TITLES

- ❑ *The Case for Christianity:* The Case for Life-Change
- ❑ *Faith Has Its Reasons:* Reasons for Believing in Jesus Christ
- ❑ *God's Outrageous Claims:* Unleashing Our Potential
- ❑ *Seven Wonders of the Spiritual World:* God Transforms Me

DRAMAS

Title	Tone	Characters	Topics
First-Day Jitters	Humorous	1 female	New Christian; Obeying God
The Lane of Life	Serious; Mime	5 either males or females, 1 offstage narrator	Salvation; Our value to God; Self-esteem
Measuring Up	Mixed; Mime	2 males, 1 female, 1 either male or female	God's acceptance of us; Self-esteem
Milestones	Mixed	1 male	Baptism; New Christian
Sitters, Strivers, Standers, and Saints	Mixed	4 either males or females, 1 narrator	God changing lives; God completing us
Take Heart	Mixed; Mime	2 males, 2 females	God heals the brokenhearted; Disappointment
"X" Marks the Spot	Serious; Mime	1 male, 1 female, 3 either males or females	Sin; Redemption; Forgiveness; Guilt

SONGS

Title	Artist	Style	Tempo	Seeker-Sensitivity Rating
All Things New	Watermark	Folk pop	Mid	8
Change in My Life	John Pagano	Gospel	Mid/up	9
Cross Medley	*Willow Creek Music*	*Ballad medley—hymns*	*Slow*	*7*
Evidence	*Willow Creek Music*	*Folk pop*	*Mid*	*10*
I Found Myself in You	Clay Crosse	Gospel ballad	Mid/slow	10
I Will Never Be	Hillsongs	Worship power ballad	Slow	4
I'm Amazed	*Willow Creek Music*	*Ballad*	*Slow*	*7*
I've Been Released	*Willow Creek Music*	*Pop/rock—Chicago sound*	*Up*	*9*
Love That Will Not Let Me Go	**Steve Camp**	**Ballad**	**Slow**	**10**
Mind, Body, Heart and Soul	Bob Carlisle	Pop/rock	Up	9
Never Be an Angel	Margaret Becker	Pop	Mid	4
Only by Grace	*Willow Creek Music*	*Pop/rock*	*Mid*	*10*
Remember Your Chains	Steven Curtis Chapman	Acoustic MOR	Mid	2
River God	Nicole Nordeman	Piano ballad	Slow	6
Speechless	**Steven Curtis Chapman**	**Acoustic rock**	**Mid/up**	**7**
There Is a Love	Michael English	Pop	Up	9
What a Ride	*Willow Creek Music*	*Pop/rock*	*Up*	*9*
Why Me?	*Willow Creek Music*	*Ballad*	*Slow*	*9*

Worship Choruses

Title	Artist	Style	Tempo	Seeker-Sensitivity Rating
Happy Song	Delirious	Country rockabilly	Up	5
I Live to Know You	Hillsongs	Worship power ballad	Slow	3
I Will Never Be	Hillsongs	Worship ballad	Slow/mid	3

Title	Artist	Style	Tempo	Seeker-Sensitivity Rating
Jesus, Lover of My Soul	Hillsongs	Pop worship	Up	3
Jesus, What a Beautiful Name	Hillsongs	Worship ballad—in 6/8	Slow/mid	6
Mourning into Dancing	Tommy Walker	Pop	Up	5
My Redeemer Lives	Hillsongs	Pop/rock	Up	3
_____	_____	_____	_____	_____
_____	_____	_____	_____	_____
_____	_____	_____	_____	_____
_____	_____	_____	_____	_____

 MOVIE CLIPS

Title: _____

Topic: _____

Description: _____

Start Time: _____

Start Cue: _____

End Time: _____

End Cue: _____

Comments: _____

_____

_____

—Commitment to Christ—

Refers not to the point of salvation, but to a believer's covenant to serve and walk with Christ.
See also: **Being Salt and Light**

MESSAGE TITLES

- ❏ Arresting Spiritual Drift
- ❏ Be There!
- ❏ Becoming Fully-Devoted Followers
- ❏ Cosmetic Christianity
- ❏ Living a Life of Passion
- ❏ Redefining Commitment
- ❏ Unmasking Your Master
- ❏ *Living Excellent Lives:* Spiritually
- ❏ *Living with an Attitude:* The Attitude of Commitment
- ❏ *Making Life Work:* Develop Discipline
- ❏ *Seasons of Spiritual Life:* Spiritual Adulthood
- ❏ *What Money Can't Buy:* Loyalty

DRAMAS

Title	Tone	Characters	Topics
Impressions, Inc.	Humorous	2 males, 1 female	Skin-deep Christianity
Mere Technicality	Serious	1 male, 1 female	Living together; The cost of taking a stand for Christ
The Right Thing	Serious	1 male	Costly obedience; Christian character; Persecution
Unaverage Joe	Mixed	2 males, 1 female	Christmas; Obeying God's call

SONGS

*Many of these songs work well in response to topics like **Hypocrisy** and **Sin.***

Title	Artist	Style	Tempo	Seeker-Sensitivity Rating
All I Ever Wanted	Margaret Becker	Pop/rock ballad	Slow/mid	4
Casual Christian	**DeGarmo & Key**	**Power ballad**	**Slow**	**6**
Ever Devoted	*Willow Creek Music*	*Ballad*	*Slow*	*6*
Everything (Apron Full of Stains)	The Normals	Pop/rock	Mid/up	10
Facts Are Facts	Steven Curtis Chapman	Rock/pop	Up	4
For the Sake of the Call	Steven Curtis Chapman	Anthemic pop	Up	3
From the Heart	**Scott Krippayne**	**Pop/rock**	**Up/mid**	**7**
Give Me Jesus	**Willow Creek Music**	**Ballad**	**Slow**	**7**
Heart's Cry	Steven Curtis Chapman	Acoustic ballad	Mid/slow	7
Highest Honor	**Chris Eaton**	**Ballad**	**Slow**	**7**
I Choose to Follow	Al Denson	Ballad	Slow	5
I Will Never Be	Hillsongs	Worship power ballad	Slow	4
If That's What It Takes	*Willow Creek Music*	*MOR pop*	*Mid/slow*	*5*
In Christ Alone	**Michael English**	**Power ballad**	**Slow**	**8**
It Will Be Worth It All	Tommy Walker	Guitar ballad	Slow	4
Just Say the Word	*Willow Creek Music*	*Gospel pop, in 3*	*Mid/up*	*4*
Let's Stand Together	The Kry	Rock	Mid/up	1
Live Out Loud	**Steven Curtis Chapman**	**Pop**	**Up**	**9**
Lord, I Want to Be Like Jesus	Fernando Ortega	Ballad	Slow	5
Man of God	*Greg Ferguson*	*Pop/rock*	*Mid/up*	*7*
Mind, Body, Heart and Soul	Bob Carlisle	Pop/rock	Up	9
No Better Place	Steven Curtis Chapman	Pop/folk rock	Up	7
No More Pretending	**Scott Krippayne**	**Pop ballad**	**Slow**	**7**
Only You	*Willow Creek Music*	*Ballad*	*Slow*	*9*
Own Me	Ginny Owens	Ballad	Slow	6
Power of a Moment	Chris Rice	Folk pop	Up	8
Promise	*Willow Creek Music*	*Pop*	*Mid/up*	*6*
Revive Us	Anointed	R & B/gospel	Up	3

Title	Artist	Style	Tempo	Seeker-Sensitivity Rating
Show Yourselves to Be	Steven Curtis Chapman	Acoustic ballad	Slow/mid	4
There Is a Line	Susan Ashton	Folk pop	Mid	6
Treasure	**Gary Chapman**	**Acoustic ballad**	**Slow**	**9**
Turn It All Over	*Greg Ferguson*	*Motown-ish pop*	*Up*	8
Whatever	Steven Curtis Chapman	Rock/pop	Up	8
Whatever You Ask	Steve Camp	Power ballad	Slow	5
_____	_____	_____	_____	____
_____	_____	_____	_____	____
_____	_____	_____	_____	____
_____	_____	_____	_____	____

Worship Choruses

Title	Artist	Style	Tempo	Seeker-Sensitivity Rating
Bend My Knee	*Student Impact*	*Rock worship*	*Up*	5
Better Than	Vineyard	Pop/rock worship	Up	6
Cry of My Heart	Terry Butler	Pop	Up	4
Everyday	Student Impact/Sonlight Band	Rock worship	Up	6
Everything I Am	*Willow Creek Music*	*Pop/rock*	*Up*	7
From the Start of the Day	*Willow Creek Music*	*Pop*	*Mid*	4
Heart of Worship	Matt Redman	Worship ballad	Slow	2
Here I Am Again	Tommy Walker/ Willow Creek Music	Pop shuffle	Up	3
How Could I But Love You?	Tommy Walker	Worship ballad	Slow	3
I Do Believe	*Willow Creek Music*	*Pop*	*Up*	3
I Give You My Heart	Hillsongs	Worship ballad	Slow	4
I Surrender All	None	Worship ballad	Slow	4
Just Say the Word	*Willow Creek Music*	*Gospel pop, in 3*	*Mid/up*	4
Lord, I Believe in You	Tommy Walker	Worship power ballad	Slow/mid	4
Lord of All	Hillsongs	Worship power ballad	Slow	3
Lord, Reign in Me	Vineyard	Rock/pop worship	Up	5
More Love More Power	Jude Del Herro	Worship ballad	Slow	3
Potter's Hand	Hillsongs	Worship ballad	Slow/mid	3

Title	Artist	Style	Tempo	Seeker-Sensitivity Rating
Reach Down Deep	*Willow Creek Music*	*Pop*	*Up*	5
Spirit of the Living God	NA	Traditional worship song	Slow	4
Step by Step	Rich Mullins	Folk worship	Mid	3
Take My Life and Let It Be	Paul Baloche	Worship ballad	Mid/slow	3
Undivided Heart	*Willow Creek Music*	*Folk pop worship ballad*	*Slow*	*3*
With Our Hearts	Lenny LeBlanc	Pop worship, in 3	Mid/up	3
You Alone	Passion	Folk pop worship, in 6/8	Mid	4
You Mean the World to Me	*Willow Creek Music*	*Worship ballad*	*Slow/mid*	*2*
Your Love	Hillsongs	Worship ballad	Slow	4
You've Won My Affection	Curt Coffield	Worship ballad	Slow	4
_____	_____	_____	_____	_____
_____	_____	_____	_____	_____
_____	_____	_____	_____	_____
_____	_____	_____	_____	_____

 MOVIE CLIPS

Title: Chariots of Fire

Topic: Integrity; Standing up for what you believe in; The Sabbath

Description: Eric Liddell refuses to run on the Sabbath. The English Olympic Committee tries to make him compromise, but he stands firm.

Start Time: 1:28:15

Start Cue: "We decided to invite you in for a little chat."

End Time: 1:30:00

End Cue: "But I can't make that sacrifice."

Comments: _____

_____

Title: _____

Topic: _____

Description: _____

Start Time: _____

Start Cue: _____

End Time: _____

End Cue: _____

Comments: _____

Confession

Might also include: *Conviction of Sin*
See also: **Communion, Sin**

MESSAGE TITLES

- ❑ *Do You Have What It Takes to Grow?:* Tell Somebody
- ❑ *Games We Play:* Sorry
- ❑ *The "S" Word:* Sin in a No-Fault Society

DRAMAS

Title	Tone	Characters	Topics
A Nice Guy	Serious	2 males	Regret; Admitting failures; Effects of sin; Confession

SONGS

Title	Artist	Style	Tempo	Seeker-Sensitivity Rating
At Jesus' Feet	Billy & Sarah Gaines	Ballad	Slow	6
Forgive Me	*Willow Creek Music*	*Ballad*	*Slow*	*3*
I Am the Man	*Greg Ferguson*	*Piano ballad*	*Slow*	*8*
I Stand, I Fall	*Greg Ferguson*	*Piano ballad*	*Slow*	*7*
Miracle of Mercy	Steven Curtis Chapman	Acoustic ballad	Slow	4
Never Be an Angel	Margaret Becker	Pop	Mid	4
No More Pretending	**Scott Krippayne**	**Pop ballad**	**Slow**	**7**

Title	Artist	Style	Tempo	Seeker-Sensitivity Rating

Worship Choruses

Title	Artist	Style	Tempo	Seeker-Sensitivity Rating
Create in Me	*Willow Creek Music*	*Ballad*	*Slow*	*3*

MOVIE CLIPS

Title:	Dead Man Walking
Topic:	Confession of sin; Grace
Description:	Death row inmate Matthew Poncelet confesses to a rape and murder he had previously been denying. This acknowledgment of sin was his last barrier to receiving grace. His friend Sister Helen Prejean tells him that he is a "son of God" because of his ownership of his sin.
Start Time:	1:35:12
Start Cue:	"The boy . . . Walter? I killed him."
End Time:	1:37:28
End Cue:	"Thank you for loving me." Close-up of Sister Prejean.
Comments:	This clip is a bit risky because of the subject matter. The sister asks if he killed a boy and raped a girl, and he says yes. But, especially as a companion to the other "Dead Man Walking" clip listed, it is potentially a powerful illustration of the need to acknowledge our sin and the grace that follows.

Title:	
Topic:	
Description:	
Start Time:	
Start Cue:	
End Time:	
End Cue:	
Comments:	

Discipleship

Refers to a person committed to *following* Christ
See also: **Obeying God**

MESSAGE TITLES

- ❑ Arresting Spiritual Drift
- ❑ Becoming Fully-Devoted Followers
- ❑ Habits of Highly Ineffective Christians
- ❑ Heart-Building Habits
- ❑ How Do You Recognize a Disciple?
- ❑ How to Be Strong When It Counts
- ❑ The Marks of a Mature Christian
- ❑ Ordinary Folks Make Great Disciples
- ❑ Spiritual Pathways
- ❑ Walking with God
- ❑ Windows of the Soul
- ❑ *Developing a Daring Faith:* Following God
- ❑ *A Faith That Works—The Book of James:* Doers or Hearers
- ❑ *Life at Its Best:* You at Your Best
- ❑ *Living Excellent Lives:* Spiritually
- ❑ *Living with an Attitude:* The Attitude of Commitment
- ❑ *Making Life Work:* Develop Discipline
- ❑ *Seasons of a Spiritual Life:* Spiritual Adulthood
- ❑ *Truths That Transform:* Think Excellent Thoughts
- ❑ *Truths That Transform:* To Live Is Christ . . . to Die Is Gain

DRAMAS

Title	Tone	Characters	Topics
First-Day Jitters	Humorous	1 female	New Christian; Obeying God
I Don't Want to Fight You Anymore	Serious	1 female	Relationship with God; Giving up control; Our value to God
Monday Night Meeting	Humorous	4 males	New Christian; Joy of Christian life; Discipleship

Title	Tone	Characters	Topics
The Mystery of Robert Richardson	Mixed	3 males, 2 females, 1 narrator	Living the Christian life
One Sunday in the Parking Lot	Humorous	4 males or females	Pace of life; Making changes
Quiet Time?	Humorous	1 female	Prayer
The Right Thing	Serious	1 male	Costly obedience; Christian character; Persecution
A Second Chance	Mixed, more serious	3 males, 1 female	Decision making; Father-son relationships
Seeing Is Believing	Humorous	1 male, 1 female, 1 narrator	A Savior you can trust; Easy faith
Unaverage Joe	Mixed	2 males, 1 female	Christmas; Obeying God's call

SONGS

Title	Artist	Style	Tempo	Seeker-Sensitivity Rating
All I Ever Wanted	Margaret Becker	Pop/rock ballad	Slow/mid	4
Casual Christian	**DeGarmo & Key**	**Power ballad**	**Slow**	**6**
Dive	**Steven Curtis Chapman**	**Pop/rock**	**Up**	**9**
Fill Me, Lord	DeGarmo & Key	Ballad	Slow	2
For the Sake of the Call	Steven Curtis Chapman	Anthemic pop	Up	3
From the Heart	**Scott Krippayne**	**Pop/rock**	**Up/mid**	**7**
Give Me Jesus	**Willow Creek Music**	**Ballad**	**Slow**	**7**
The Great Adventure	Steven Curtis Chapman	Pop/rock	Up	5
Great Expectations	Steven Curtis Chapman	Pop/rock	Mid	8
Growing	Wayne Watson	Ballad	Slow	5
Highest Honor	**Chris Eaton**	**Ballad**	**Slow**	**7**
Hunger and Thirst	Susan Ashton	Folk pop	Mid/up	6
I Choose to Follow	Al Denson	Ballad	Slow	5
I Stand, I Fall	*Greg Ferguson*	*Piano ballad*	*Slow*	*7*

Title	Artist	Style	Tempo	Seeker-Sensitivity Rating
I Will Never Be	Hillsongs	Worship power ballad	Slow	4
If That's What It Takes	Willow Creek Music	MOR pop	Mid/slow	5
It Will Be Worth It All	Tommy Walker	Guitar ballad	Slow	4
Just Say the Word	Willow Creek Music	Gospel pop, in 3	Mid/up	4
Knockin' on Heaven's Door	Avalon	Pop	Up	9
Let Us Pray	Steven Curtis Chapman	Pop/rock	Up	7
Life Means So Much	Chris Rice	Folk pop	Mid	7
Live Out Loud	Steven Curtis Chapman	Pop	Up	9
Man of God	Greg Ferguson	Pop/rock	Mid/up	7
Mind, Body, Heart and Soul	Bob Carlisle	Pop/rock	Up	9
No More Pretending	Scott Krippayne	Pop ballad	Slow	7
On My Knees	Willow Creek Music	Acoustic guitar ballad	Slow	5
Own Me	Ginny Owens	Ballad	Slow	6
Power of a Moment	Chris Rice	Folk pop	Up	8
Promise	Willow Creek Music	Pop	Mid/up	6
River God	Nicole Nordeman	Piano ballad	Slow	6
Show Yourselves to Be	Steven Curtis Chapman	Acoustic ballad	Slow/mid	4
Surrender Medley	Willow Creek Music	Ballad medley duet	Slow	6
Take My Hand	The Kry	Acoustic ballad	Mid/slow	9
These Things Are True of You	Tommy Walker & the CA Worship Band	Ballad duet	Slow	9
Treasure	Gary Chapman	Acoustic ballad	Slow	9
Turn It All Over	Greg Ferguson	Motown-ish pop	Up	8
Unimportant Things	Paul Smith	Ballad	Slow	7
What if I?	Willow Creek Music	Piano ballad	Slow/mid	8
Whatever	Steven Curtis Chapman	Rock/pop	Up	8
Whatever You Ask	Steve Camp	Power ballad	Slow	5
_____	_____	_____	____	____
_____	_____	_____	____	____
_____	_____	_____	____	____
_____	_____	_____	____	____

Worship Choruses

Title	Artist	Style	Tempo	Seeker-Sensitivity Rating
Bend My Knee	*Student Impact*	*Rock worship*	*Up*	*5*
Better Than	Vineyard	Pop/rock worship	Up	6
Come Let Us Bow Down	Dennis Jernigan	Worship ballad	Slow/mid	3
Cry of My Heart	Terry Butler	Pop	Up	4
Everyday	Student Impact/Sonlight Band	Rock worship	Up	6
Everything I Am	*Willow Creek Music*	*Pop/rock*	*Up*	*7*
From the Start of the Day	*Willow Creek Music*	*Pop*	*Mid*	*4*
He Loves Me	Tommy Walker	Worship ballad	Slow	6
Heart of Worship	Matt Redman	Worship ballad	Slow	2
High and Exalted	Bob Fitts	Pop worship	Slow/mid	2
Holy Spirit, Take Control	*Willow Creek Music*	*Ballad*	*Slow*	*2*
How Could I But Love You?	Tommy Walker	Worship ballad	Slow	3
I Give You My Heart	Hillsongs	Worship ballad	Slow	4
I Surrender All	None	Worship ballad	Slow	4
I Wanna Learn More	Curt Coffield, Ed Kerr	Folk pop worship	Mid	5
I Will Never Be	Hillsongs	Worship ballad	Slow/mid	3
Jesus, Draw Me Close	*Willow Creek Music*	*Worship ballad*	*Slow*	*3*
Just Say the Word	*Willow Creek Music*	*Gospel pop, in 3*	*Mid/up*	*4*
Let the Peace of God Reign	Hillsongs	Worship ballad	Slow	3
Lord of All	Hillsongs	Worship power ballad	Slow	3
Lord, Reign in Me	Vineyard	Rock/pop worship	Up	5
Potter's Hand	Hillsongs	Worship ballad	Slow/mid	3
Power of Your Love	Hillsongs	Worship ballad	Slow	6
A Pure Heart	Rusty Nelson	Worship ballad	Slow	4
Reach Down Deep	*Willow Creek Music*	*Pop*	*Up*	*5*
Spirit of the Living God	NA	Traditional worship song	Slow	4
Step by Step	Rich Mullins	Folk worship	Mid	3
Take My Life and Let It Be	Paul Baloche	Worship ballad	Mid/slow	3
These Things Are True of You	Tommy Walker & the CA Worship Band	Ballad duet	Slow	9
Undivided Heart	*Willow Creek Music*	*Folk pop worship ballad*	*Slow*	*3*

Title	Artist	Style	Tempo	Seeker-Sensitivity Rating

MOVIE CLIPS

Title: Chariots of Fire

Topic: Christian life; Endurance

Description: Eric Liddell gives a sermonette about running the race of faith.

Start Time: 0:25:35

Start Cue: "You came to see a race today."

End Time: 0:27:20

End Cue: "That is how you run a straight race."

Comments: _____

_____

Title: Chariots of Fire

Topic: Integrity; Standing up for what you believe in; The Sabbath

Description: Eric Liddell refuses to run on the Sabbath. The English Olympic Committee tries to make him compromise, but he stands firm.

Start Time: 1:28:15

Start Cue: "We decided to invite you in for a little chat."

End Time: 1:30:00

End Cue: "But I can't make that sacrifice."

Comments: _____

_____

Title: The Karate Kid

Topic: Discipleship

Description: Daniel-San, fed up with having to do all of Mr. Myagi's chores, gets mad at Myagi for not teaching him anything. Myagi shows him that the chores actually taught him the motions he would need for karate. This clip can be used as a metaphor for discipleship. The little things we do to grow in discipleship, no matter how mundane or difficult they may seem, prepare us spiritually to follow God when it gets difficult. It's all about the training.

Start Time: 1:14:30

Start Cue: "Daniel-San . . . come here."

End Time: 1:17:35

End Cue: "Come back tomorrow." Close-up of Daniel.

Comments: There is profanity immediately before this clip, so make sure your start point is right.

Title: _____

Topic: _____

Description: _____

Start Time: _____

Start Cue: _____

End Time: _____

End Cue: _____

Comments: _____

_____

_____

_____

Title: _____

Topic: _____

Description: _____

Start Time: _____

Start Cue: _____

End Time: _____

End Cue: _____

Comments: _____

_____

_____

Doubting

See also: **Apologetics, Faith**

MESSAGE TITLES

- ❑ Can I Trust a Silent God?
- ❑ Doubters Welcome
- ❑ I Have My Doubts
- ❑ *Faith on Trial:* A Skeptic's Surprise
- ❑ *I Have a Friend Who* Has Doubts about God
- ❑ *The Power of Prayer:* The Mystery of Unanswered Prayer

DRAMAS

Title	Tone	Characters	Topics
Great Expectations	Mixed; Very serious ending	1 male, 2 females	Unanswered Prayer
Mistaken Identity	Mixed	3 males, 2 females, 1 young girl	Christmas; Doubting
On the Outside	Serious	1 female or male	Being salt and light; Negative church experiences
Plane Talk	Humorous	2 males, 1 offstage voice (pilot)	Doubt; Skepticism; God's presence
Reason Enough	Mixed, mostly serious	1 male, 1 female	Importance of faith grounded in reason

SONGS

Title	Artist	Style	Tempo	Seeker-Sensitivity Rating
Big Enough	Chris Rice	Folk ballad, in 6/8	Slow/mid	10
Dear God	**Midge Ure**	**Rock**	**Mid/up**	**10**
Hold On to Jesus	Steven Curtis Chapman	Ballad	Slow	8
I Choose to Follow	Al Denson	Ballad	Slow	5
Naïve	Chris Rice	Folk pop	Mid	8

Worship Choruses

Title	Artist	Style	Tempo	Seeker-Sensitivity Rating
Be Still My Soul	*Willow Creek Music*	*Worship ballad*	*Slow/mid*	*4*
I Am Here	*Willow Creek Music*	*Worship ballad*	*Slow*	*8*
Jesus, You're the Answer	Tommy Walker	Soulish worship ballad	Slow	5
Lord, I Believe in You	Tommy Walker	Worship power ballad	Slow/mid	4
Reaching for You	*Willow Creek Music*	*Rock/pop*	*Up*	*10*
Still I Will Worship You	*Willow Creek Music*	*Pop/rock worship*	*Up*	*3*

MOVIE CLIPS

Title: Shadowlands

Topic: Suffering; Pain; Why does God allow bad things to happen?

Description: C. S. Lewis delivers a speech about why God allows suffering.

Start Time: 0:10:00

Start Cue: "Yesterday I received a letter."

End Time: 0:11:40

End Cue: "Thank you very much."

Comments: The last line is a bit hard to understand.

_____
_____
_____

Title: _____

Topic: _____

Description: _____

Start Time: _____

Start Cue: _____

End Time: _____

End Cue: _____

Comments: _____

_____
_____

Faith

Might also include: *Trusting God*
See also: **God's Faithfulness**

MESSAGE TITLES

- ❏ Can I Trust a Silent God?
- ❏ Developing a Daring Faith
- ❏ Faith's First Steps
- ❏ Mind-Expanding Faith
- ❏ *Making Life Work:* Trust God
- ❏ *Seven Wonders of the Spiritual World:* God Can Be Trusted
- ❏ *What Money Can't Buy:* Conviction
- ❏ **Faith Has Its Reasons:** Reasons for Believing in God • Reasons for Believing in the Bible • Reasons for Believing in Jesus Christ • Reasons for Believing in the Resurrection • Reasons for Believing in Heaven and Hell

Package Suggestion

Drama:
Straight-Jacketed

Song:
Take My Hand

DRAMAS

Title	Tone	Characters	Topics
In . . . We Trust	Serious, not heavy	1 male	Trust; Difficulty trusting God
Just in Case	Humorous	1 male, 1 female	Trusting God; God's faithfulness
Plane Talk	Humorous	2 males, 1 offstage voice (pilot)	Doubt; Skepticism; God's presence
The Quagmire	Serious	1 male or female	Failure; Self-esteem; Being "stuck"; Trusting God
Reason Enough	Mixed, mostly serious	1 male, 1 female	Importance of faith grounded in reason
Seeing Is Believing	Humorous	1 male, 1 female, 1 narrator	A Savior you can trust; Easy faith
Straight-Jacketed	Serious	1 male	Bondage to past and to sin; Anger toward God

SONGS

Title	Artist	Style	Tempo	Seeker-Sensitivity Rating
All the Faith You Need	*Greg Ferguson*	*Bluesy rock*	*Up*	*10*
Dive	**Steven Curtis Chapman**	**Pop/rock**	**Up**	**9**
Facts Are Facts	Steven Curtis Chapman	Rock/pop	Up	4
Found a Way	*Greg Ferguson*	*Ballad*	*Slow*	*9*
God Is in Control	Twila Paris	Pop/rock	Up	1
I Choose to Follow	Al Denson	Ballad	Slow	5
In My Father's Hands	Susan Ashton	Folk pop	Mid	9
Live Out Loud	**Steven Curtis Chapman**	**Pop**	**Up**	**9**
Seize the Day	**Carolyn Arends**	**Folk pop, in 3**	**Mid**	**8**
Take My Hand	The Kry	Acoustic ballad	Mid/slow	9
There Is a Love	Michael English	Pop	Up	9
_____	_____	_____	_____	_____
_____	_____	_____	_____	_____

Worship Choruses

Title	Artist	Style	Tempo	Seeker-Sensitivity Rating
All the Power You Need	Hillsongs	Pop worship	Up	5
Be Still My Soul	*Willow Creek Music*	*Worship ballad*	*Slow/mid*	*4*
I Will Bless You, Lord	Hillsongs	Worship ballad, in 3	Mid	3
Jesus, You're the Answer	Tommy Walker	Soulish worship ballad	Slow	5
Joy, Joy, Joy	Tommy Walker	Rock shuffle	Up	5
Lord, I Believe in You	Tommy Walker	Worship power ballad	Slow/mid	4
My Redeemer Lives	Hillsongs	Pop/rock	Up	3
Still I Will Worship You	*Willow Creek Music*	*Pop/rock worship*	*Up*	*3*
With Our Hearts	Lenny LeBlanc	Pop worship, in 3	Mid/up	3
You Are Worthy of My Praise	Passion	Rock/pop	Up	3
_____	_____	_____	_____	_____
_____	_____	_____	_____	_____

MOVIE CLIPS

Title: Chariots of Fire

Topic: Christian life; Endurance

Description: Eric Liddell gives a sermonette about running the race of faith.

Start Time: 0:25:35

Start Cue: "You came to see a race today."

End Time: 0:27:20

End Cue: "That is how you run a straight race."

Comments: _____

_____

_____

Title: Indiana Jones and the Last Crusade

Topic: Faith; Trusting God when circumstances are confusing

Description: Indiana Jones faces a seemingly uncrossable chasm but takes a "leap of faith" and steps onto an invisible bridge. Illustrates faith, believing what can't be seen.

Start Time: 1:46:50

Start Cue: Indiana Jones walks through cave to the chasm.

End Time: 1:48:45

End Cue: Indy throws sand on bridge to mark it (can be cut earlier).

Comments: _____

_____

_____

Title: _____

Topic: _____

Description: _____

Start Time: _____

Start Cue: _____

End Time: _____

End Cue: _____

Comments: _____

_____

_____

Freedom in Christ

Might also include: *Freedom from Sin*
See also: **The Joy of the Christian Life**

MESSAGE TITLES

❏ A Better Kind of Freedom

DRAMAS

Title	Tone	Characters	Topics
Measuring Up	Mixed; Mime	2 males, 1 female, 1 either male or female	God's acceptance of us; Self-esteem
The Prisoner	Serious	3 males, 1 female	Easter; Freedom from sin; New Christian
The Stickholders	Serious	3 males, 1 female, 1 narrator	Relationship with God; Freedom from rules

SONGS

Title	Artist	Style	Tempo	Seeker-Sensitivity Rating
Ball and Chain	Susan Ashton	Folk pop	Mid	9
Change in My Life	John Pagano	Gospel	Mid/up	9
Free	Ginny Owens	Folk pop	Mid/up	8
I've Been Released	*Willow Creek Music*	*Pop/rock—Chicago sound*	*Up*	9
Remember Your Chains	Steven Curtis Chapman	Acoustic MOR	Mid	2

Title	Artist	Style	Tempo	Seeker-Sensitivity Rating

Worship Choruses

Title	Artist	Style	Tempo	Seeker-Sensitivity Rating
Mourning into Dancing	Tommy Walker	Pop	Up	5

MOVIE CLIPS

Title: _____

Topic: _____

Description: _____

Start Time: _____

Start Cue: _____

End Time: _____

End Cue: _____

Comments: _____

_____

_____

Glorifying God

Refers to honoring God in our words and deeds

MESSAGE TITLES

❏ **Secret Christianity: An Audience of One** • Secret Giving • Secret Praying • Secret Fasting

_____

_____

_____

DRAMAS

Title	Tone	Characters	Topics
Mr. Hibbs' Day Off	Mixed; Mime	3 males, 1 female, 1 child	Serving others; Self-denial; Being used by God
The Mystery of Robert Richardson	Mixed	3 males, 2 females, 1 narrator	Living the Christian life
Parlor Talk	Mixed	3 males, 2 females	Making a difference with your life; Death; Workaholism
10	Humorous	3 males, 2 females	First commandment
_____	_____	_____	_____
_____	_____	_____	_____
_____	_____	_____	_____

SONGS

Title	Artist	Style	Tempo	Seeker-Sensitivity Rating
All I Ever Wanted	Margaret Becker	Pop/rock ballad	Slow/mid	4
Always before Me	Steven Curtis Chapman	Worship ballad, in 3	Slow/mid	1
Audience of One	_Willow Creek Music_	_Power ballad_	_Slow_	_8_

Title	Artist	Style	Tempo	Seeker-Sensitivity Rating
Casual Christian	**DeGarmo & Key**	**Power ballad**	**Slow**	**6**
Heart's Cry	Steven Curtis Chapman	Acoustic ballad	Mid/slow	7
Highest Honor	Chris Eaton	Ballad	Slow	7
In Christ Alone	**Michael English**	**Power ballad**	**Slow**	**8**
Keep My Mind	Margaret Becker	Pop/rock	Up	8
Live Out Loud	**Steven Curtis Chapman**	**Pop**	**Up**	**9**
No More Pretending	**Scott Krippayne**	**Pop ballad**	**Slow**	**7**
Power of a Moment	Chris Rice	Folk pop	Up	8
Promise	*Willow Creek Music*	*Pop*	*Mid/up*	*6*
_____	_____	_____	_____	_____
_____	_____	_____	_____	_____
_____	_____	_____	_____	_____
_____	_____	_____	_____	_____
_____	_____	_____	_____	_____

Worship Choruses

Title	Artist	Style	Tempo	Seeker-Sensitivity Rating
Awesome in This Place	Dave Billington	Worship ballad	Slow	2
Be Magnified	Don Moen	Ballad	Slow	2
Blessed Be the Name	Vineyard	Worship ballad	Slow	4
Celebrate the Lord of Love	Paul Baloche	Pop worship	Up	5
Come Let Us Bow Down	Dennis Jernigan	Worship ballad	Slow/mid	3
Cry of My Heart	Terry Butler	Pop	Up	4
Doxology	Tommy Walker	Pop/rock	Mid	6
From the Rising of the Sun	Paul Deming	Ballad	Slow	3
From the Start of the Day	*Willow Creek Music*	*Pop*	*Mid*	*4*
Got the Need	The Parachute Band	Funky R & B/pop	Up	4
He Is Exalted	Twila Paris	Pop worship, in 3	Mid	3
High and Exalted	Bob Fitts	Pop worship	Slow/mid	2
Holy and Anointed One	Vineyard	Worship ballad	Slow	3

Title	Artist	Style	Tempo	Seeker-Sensitivity Rating
Holy, Holy, Holy (Gary Oliver)	Alvin Slaughter/ Willow Creek Music	Gospel pop	Up	5
I Give You My Heart	Hillsongs	Worship ballad	Slow	4
I Love You, Lord	Maranatha!/Laurie Klein	Worship ballad	Slow	4
I Will Bless You, Lord	Hillsongs	Worship ballad, in 3	Mid	3
Let Everything That Has Breath	Matt Redman	Pop/rock worship	Up	4
Let It Rise	Praise Band	Rock worship	Up	5
Lift Up Your Heads	Tommy Walker	Rock/pop worship	Up	2
Lord, I Lift Your Name on High	Maranatha!/Praise Band	Pop worship	Up	6
Lord Most High	Willow Creek Music	MOR worship	Mid	3
Lord of All	Hillsongs	Worship power ballad	Slow	3
The Lord's Prayer	*Willow Creek Music*	*U2-ish rock/pop*	*Up*	*9*
More Love More Power	Jude Del Herro	Worship ballad	Slow	3
My Glorious	Student Impact	Rock	Mid/up	4
O for a Thousand Tongues	*Willow Creek Music*	*Contemporary arrangement of hymn*	*Up*	*3*
Open the Eyes of My Heart	Paul Baloche	Pop/rock worship	Up	5
Shout to the Lord	Hillsongs	Worship power ballad	Slow	3
Te Alabamos	Tommy Walker	Latin pop worship	Mid/up	4
Unto the King	Don Moen	Worship ballad, in 3	Slow/mid	3
You Are Holy	Hillsongs	Worship ballad	Slow	3
You Are Worthy of My Praise	Passion	Rock/pop	Up	3
You Have Been Given	Willow Creek Music	Worship ballad, in 3	Slow	3
_____	_____	_____	_____	_____
_____	_____	_____	_____	_____
_____	_____	_____	_____	_____
_____	_____	_____	_____	_____
_____	_____	_____	_____	_____
_____	_____	_____	_____	_____

MOVIE CLIPS

Title:	Chariots of Fire
Topic:	Being true to the person God made you to be; Honoring God with your gifts
Description:	Eric Liddell talks to his sister, who wants him to forsake running to be a missionary. Eric talks about the fact that God made him fast, and when he runs, he can feel God's pleasure.
Start Time:	0:58:20
Start Cue:	First line is "I've decided . . . I'm going back to China."
End Time:	0:59:15
End Cue:	"To win is to honor Him."
Comments:	_____
	_____
	_____
	_____

Title:	_____
Topic:	_____
Description:	_____
Start Time:	_____
Start Cue:	_____
End Time:	_____
End Cue:	_____
Comments:	_____
	_____
	_____
	_____

—God's Acceptance of Us—

Addresses the belief of many seekers that they are beyond salvation

MESSAGE TITLES

- ❑ Come as You Are
- ❑ *Private Conversations:* Jesus Talks to a Sinner
- ❑ *What Jesus Would Say to . . .* O. J. Simpson

DRAMAS

Title	Tone	Characters	Topics
Another Day at the Bus Stop	Mixed	1 male, 1 female	Our relationship with God; Self-esteem
I Know What You Want	Serious	2 males, 2 females	God's love; Dysfunctional families
Measuring Up	Mixed; Mime	2 males, 1 female, 1 either male or female	God's acceptance of us; Self-esteem

SONGS

Title	Artist	Style	Tempo	Seeker-Sensitivity Rating
Change in My Life	John Pagano	Gospel	Mid/up	9
Enough	*Willow Creek Music*	*Piano ballad*	*Slow*	*7*
Farther Than Your Grace Can Reach	**Jonathan Pierce**	**Ballad**	**Slow**	**9**
Free	Ginny Owens	Folk pop	Mid/up	8
If I Could Look through Your Eyes	*Willow Creek Music*	*Piano ballad*	*Slow*	*10*
In My Heart	*Greg Ferguson*	*Celtic worship ballad*	*Slow*	*9*

Title	Artist	Style	Tempo	Seeker-Sensitivity Rating
Jesus Loves Me	Whitney Houston	R & B/pop	Slow/mid	8
Love Is Always There	Carolyn Arends	Folk pop	Up	9
A Picture of Grace	*Willow Creek Music*	*Medley of ballads*	*Slow*	*9*
There Is a Love	Michael English	Pop	Up	9
Who Am I?	Margaret Becker	Power ballad	Slow	7
Who Am I? (Grace Flows Down)	**Watermark**	**Folk pop**	**Mid/slow**	**8**

Worship Choruses

Title	Artist	Style	Tempo	Seeker-Sensitivity Rating
Amen	Tommy Walker	Worship shuffle	Up	5
Come, Now is the Time to Worship	Vineyard	Pop/rock	Up	5
How Could I But Love You?	Tommy Walker	Worship ballad	Slow	3
In Your Hands	Hillsongs	Worship ballad	Slow/mid	4
Meet with Me	Ten Shekel Shirt	Modern worship	Up	7
You Are My King	Passion	Worship ballad	Slow	4

MOVIE CLIPS

Title:

Topic:

Description:

Start Time:

Start Cue:

End Time:

End Cue:

Comments:

God's Laws

The Ten Commandments work well as a series. For ideas on individual listings on commandments, look up a related topic—for example, tenth commandment **(Contentment, Materialism/Greed).**

See also: **God's Wisdom, Obeying God**

MESSAGE TITLES

❑ The Benefits of God's Laws
❑ Laws That Liberate
❑ **The Ten Commandments:** Honor God as God • Refuse to Reduce God • Revere the Name of God • Remember the Sabbath Day • Honor Your Parents • Respect Human Life • Restrain Sexual Desires • Respect the Property of Others • Refuse to Lie • Restrain Material Desires

DRAMAS

Title	Tone	Characters	Topics
Everything's Relative	Humorous	3 males, 1 female	God's holiness; Benefits of God's laws
10	Humorous	3 males, 2 females	First commandment
A Thief's Carol	Mixed	3 males, 2 females	Stealing; Eighth commandment

SONGS

Title	Artist	Style	Tempo	Seeker-Sensitivity Rating
Only by Grace	*Willow Creek Music*	*Pop/rock*	*Mid*	*10*
There Is a Line	Susan Ashton	Folk pop	Mid	6

Title	Artist	Style	Tempo	Seeker-Sensitivity Rating

Worship Choruses

Title	Artist	Style	Tempo	Seeker-Sensitivity Rating

MOVIE CLIPS

Title: Chariots of Fire

Topic: Integrity; Standing up for what you believe in; The Sabbath

Description: Eric Liddell refuses to run on the Sabbath. The English Olympic Committee tries to make him compromise, but he stands firm.

Start Time: 1:28:15

Start Cue: "We decided to invite you in for a little chat."

End Time: 1:30:00

End Cue: "But I can't make that sacrifice."

Comments: _____

_____

Title: _____

Topic: _____

Description: _____

Start Time: _____

Start Cue: _____

End Time: _____

End Cue: _____

Comments: _____

_____

Heaven

See also: **Death, Salvation**

MESSAGE TITLES

- ❏ Hang On for Heaven
- ❏ Reasons for Believing in Heaven and Hell
- ❏ *Facing Up to Fear:* The Fear of Death

_____

_____

_____

DRAMAS

Title	Tone	Characters	Topics
After Life	Mixed; Serious ending, sober	1 male	The afterlife; Heaven and hell
Security Check	Mixed	1 male, 1 female, 1 offstage voice	Salvation; Works vs. grace

SONGS

Title	Artist	Style	Tempo	Seeker-Sensitivity Rating
Another Time, Another Place	Sandi Patti (with Wayne Watson)	Power ballad	Slow	8
He Won't Let You Go	**The Kry**	**Piano ballad**	**Slow**	**10**
Healing River	*Willow Creek Music*	*Ballad*	*Slow/mid*	*9*
I Will Be Free	Cindy Morgan	Ballad	Slow	7

Title	Artist	Style	Tempo	Seeker-Sensitivity Rating
If You Could See Me Now	Truth	Ballad	Slow	5
It Will Be Worth It All	Tommy Walker	Guitar ballad	Slow	4
Reaching	Carolyn Arends	Ballad	Slow	6
There's a Reason	*Willow Creek Music*	*Pop/rock*	*Up*	*9*
What a Day It Will Be	*Greg Ferguson*	*Flowing ballad*	*Slow/mid*	*8*

Worship Choruses

Title	Artist	Style	Tempo	Seeker-Sensitivity Rating
Did You Feel the Mountains Tremble?	Passion	Pop/rock	Mid/up	2
Never Gonna Stop	Tommy Walker/ Willow Creek Music	Pop/rock	Up	3
Praise God on High	*Willow Creek Music*	*Worship ballad*	*Slow*	*5*

MOVIE CLIPS

Title: _____

Topic: _____

Description: _____

Start Time: _____

Start Cue: _____

End Time: _____

End Cue: _____

Comments: _____

_____

_____

Lordship of Christ

Refers to the rightful place of Christ as Lord in the life of a believer; also encompasses the commandment "You shall have no other Gods before me"

MESSAGE TITLES

❏ Unmasking Your Master
❏ *First Commandment:* Honor God as God
❏ *God Has Feelings Too:* What Makes God Jealous
❏ *What Jesus Would Say to . . .* Oprah Winfrey

_____

_____

_____

DRAMAS

Title	Tone	Characters	Topics
I Don't Want to Fight You Anymore	Serious	1 female	Relationship with God; Giving up control; Our value to God
A Serf's Tale	Humorous	1 male, 1 female	Serving two masters; Materialism
10	Humorous	3 males, 2 females	First commandment

SONGS

Title	Artist	Style	Tempo	Seeker-Sensitivity Rating
All I Ever Wanted	Margaret Becker	Pop/rock ballad	Slow/mid	4
But if Not	*Student Impact*	*Acoustic ballad*	*Slow*	*5*

Title	Artist	Style	Tempo	Seeker-Sensitivity Rating
Ever Devoted	*Willow Creek Music*	*Ballad*	*Slow*	*6*
Foundations	Geoff Moore & the Distance	Folk pop ballad	Slow/mid	8
From the Heart	**Scott Krippayne**	**Pop/rock**	**Up/mid**	**7**
God Is in Control	Twila Paris	Pop/rock	Up	1
Hold Me, Jesus	Rich Mullins	Ballad	Slow	7
I Choose to Follow	Al Denson	Ballad	Slow	5
I Found Myself in You	Clay Crosse	Gospel ballad	Mid/slow	10
I Go to the Rock	Dottie Rambo; Whitney Houston	Swing/big band	Mid	7
If That's What It Takes	*Willow Creek Music*	*MOR pop*	*Mid/slow*	*5*
In Christ Alone	**Michael English**	**Power ballad**	**Slow**	**8**
In My Father's Hands	Susan Ashton	Folk pop	Mid	9
In My Heart	*Greg Ferguson*	*Celtic worship ballad*	*Slow*	*9*
Just Say the Word	*Willow Creek Music*	*Gospel pop, in 3*	*Mid/up*	*4*
King of the Jungle	**Steven Curtis Chapman**	**Pop shuffle with African touches**	**Mid/up**	**9**
Own Me	Ginny Owens	Ballad	Slow	6
Power of a Moment	Chris Rice	Folk pop	Up	8
Promise	*Willow Creek Music*	*Pop*	*Mid/up*	*6*
Strength in You	*Willow Creek Music*	*MOR pop*	*Slow/mid*	*10*
This Is My Father's World	Fernando Ortega	Folk ballad	Slow/mid	8
Turn It All Over	*Greg Ferguson*	*Motown-ish pop*	*Up*	*8*
Unimportant Things	**Paul Smith**	**Ballad**	**Slow**	**7**
We Believe in God	Amy Grant	Acoustic ballad	Slow	3
Whatever	Steven Curtis Chapman	Rock/pop	Up	8
Whatever You Ask	Steve Camp	Power ballad	Slow	5
_____	_____	_____	_____	_____
_____	_____	_____	_____	_____
_____	_____	_____	_____	_____
_____	_____	_____	_____	_____

Worship Choruses

Title	Artist	Style	Tempo	Seeker-Sensitivity Rating
The Beauty of Holiness	Steve Camp	Worship ballad, in 3	Slow	3
Bend My Knee	*Student Impact*	*Rock worship*	*Up*	5
Better Than	Vineyard	Pop/rock worship	Up	6
Build Your Church into My Heart	*Greg Ferguson/ Willow Creek Music*	*Pop*	*Up*	2
But if Not	*Student Impact*	*Acoustic ballad*	*Slow*	5
Celebrate the Lord of Love	Paul Baloche	Pop worship	Up	5
Come Let Us Bow Down	Dennis Jernigan	Worship ballad	Slow/mid	3
Come, Now Is the Time to Worship	Vineyard	Pop/rock	Up	5
Cry of My Heart	Terry Butler	Pop	Up	4
Everyday	Student Impact/Sonlight Band	Rock worship	Up	6
Everything I Am	*Willow Creek Music*	*Pop/rock*	*Up*	7
From the Start of the Day	*Willow Creek Music*	*Pop*	*Mid*	4
He Is Exalted	Twila Paris	Pop worship, in 3	Mid	3
He Loves Me	Tommy Walker	Worship ballad	Slow	6
Heart of Worship	Matt Redman	Worship ballad	Slow	2
High and Exalted	Bob Fitts	Pop worship	Slow/mid	2
Holy and Anointed One	Vineyard	Worship ballad	Slow	3
Holy Spirit, Take Control	*Willow Creek Music*	*Ballad*	*Slow*	2
How Could I But Love You?	Tommy Walker	Worship ballad	Slow	3
I Give You My Heart	Hillsongs	Worship ballad	Slow	4
I Love You, Lord	Maranatha!/Laurie Klein	Worship ballad	Slow	4
I See the Lord	Chris Falson, Maranatha! Singers/Willow Creek Music	Worship ballad	Slow/mid	2
I Surrender All	None	Worship ballad	Slow	4
Joy, Joy, Joy	Tommy Walker	Rock shuffle	Up	5
Just Say the Word	*Willow Creek Music*	*Gospel pop, in 3*	*Mid/up*	4
Let It Rise	Praise Band	Rock worship	Up	5
Lift Up Your Heads	Tommy Walker	Rock/pop worship	Up	2
Lord of All	Hillsongs	Worship power ballad	Slow	3
Lord, Reign in Me	Vineyard	Rock/pop worship	Up	5
The Lord's Prayer	*Willow Creek Music*	*U2-ish rock/pop*	*Up*	9

Title	Artist	Style	Tempo	Seeker-Sensitivity Rating
More Love More Power	Jude Del Herro	Worship ballad	Slow	3
Potter's Hand	Hillsongs	Worship ballad	Slow/mid	3
Shout to the Lord	Hillsongs	Worship power ballad	Slow	3
Shout to the North	Student Impact	Rock, in 3	Up	4
Spirit of the Living God	NA	Traditional worship song	Slow	4
Step by Step	Rich Mullins	Folk worship	Mid	3
Still I Will Worship You	*Willow Creek Music*	*Pop/rock worship*	*Up*	*3*
Take My Life and Let It Be	Paul Baloche	Worship ballad	Mid/slow	3
Undivided Heart	*Willow Creek Music*	*Folk pop worship ballad*	*Slow*	*3*
We Fall Down	Passion	Worship ballad	Slow/mid	3
We Praise Your Name	*Willow Creek Music*	*Worship ballad*	*Slow/mid*	*4*
What the Lord Has Done	Hillsongs	Worship ballad, in 3	Slow/mid	2
With Our Hearts	Lenny LeBlanc	Pop worship, in 3	Mid/up	3
You Alone	Passion	Folk pop worship, in 6/8	Mid	4
You Are Holy	Hillsongs	Worship ballad	Slow	3
You Mean the World to Me	*Willow Creek Music*	*Worship ballad*	*Slow/mid*	*2*
Your Love for Me	Integrity Songwriters	Pop worship	Up	4
You've Won My Affection	Curt Coffield	Worship ballad	Slow	4
___	___	___	___	___
___	___	___	___	___
___	___	___	___	___
___	___	___	___	___

MOVIE CLIPS

Title: _____

Topic: _____

Description: _____

Start Time: _____

Start Cue: _____

End Time: _____

End Cue: _____

Comments: _____

_____

Obeying God

See also: **Commitment to Christ**

MESSAGE TITLES

- ❏ Life in the Comfort Zone
- ❏ Living by Dying
- ❏ Unmasking Your Master
- ❏ *Developing a Daring Faith:* Obeying God
- ❏ *Leadings from God:* Obeying God's Leadings
- ❏ *Living Excellent Lives:* Spiritually
- ❏ *Seasons of a Spiritual Life:* Spiritual Adulthood

_____

_____

_____

_____

_____

DRAMAS

Title	Tone	Characters	Topics
The Advisory Board	Mixed	3 males, 2 females (some characters not gender specific)	Decision making; Finding the will of God; Voices in our heads
Character Test	Mixed, moving	2 males, 1 female	Promptings from God; Obedience; Power of encouragement
A Failure Tale	Mixed	5 males, 1 narrator	Failing; Obeying rules
First-Day Jitters	Humorous	1 female	New Christian; Obeying God
The Gardeners	Humorous	1 male, 1 female	New Age movement
I Don't Want to Fight You Anymore	Serious	1 female	Relationship with God; Giving up control; Our value to God
Impressions, Inc.	Humorous	2 males, 1 female	Skin-deep Christianity
Mere Technicality	Serious	1 male, 1 female	Living together; The cost of taking a stand for Christ

Title	Tone	Characters	Topics
The Mystery of Robert Richardson	Mixed	3 males, 2 females, 1 narrator	Living the Christian life
The Right Thing	Serious	1 male	Costly obedience; Christian character; Persecution
10	Humorous	3 males, 2 females	First commandment

SONGS

Title	Artist	Style	Tempo	Seeker-Sensitivity Rating
All I Ever Wanted	Margaret Becker	Pop/rock ballad	Slow/mid	4
But if Not	*Student Impact*	*Acoustic ballad*	*Slow*	*5*
Casual Christian	**DeGarmo & Key**	**Power ballad**	**Slow**	**6**
Dive	**Steven Curtis Chapman**	**Pop/rock**	**Up**	**9**
Ever Devoted	*Willow Creek Music*	*Ballad*	*Slow*	*6*
Everything (Apron Full of Stains)	The Normals	Pop/rock	Mid/up	10
Fill Me, Lord	DeGarmo & Key	Ballad	Slow	2
For the Sake of the Call	Steven Curtis Chapman	Anthemic pop	Up	3
From the Heart	**Scott Krippayne**	**Pop/rock**	**Up/mid**	**7**
Heart's Cry	Steven Curtis Chapman	Acoustic ballad	Mid/slow	7
Highest Honor	**Chris Eaton**	**Ballad**	**Slow**	**7**
Hold Me, Jesus	Rich Mullins	Ballad	Slow	7
I Choose to Follow	Al Denson	Ballad	Slow	5
If That's What It Takes	*Willow Creek Music*	*MOR pop*	*Mid/slow*	*5*
In My Heart	*Greg Ferguson*	*Celtic worship ballad*	*Slow*	*9*
It Will Be Worth It All	Tommy Walker	Guitar ballad	Slow	4
Just Say the Word	*Willow Creek Music*	*Gospel pop, in 3*	*Mid/up*	*4*
Keep My Mind	Margaret Becker	Pop/rock	Up	8

Title	Artist	Style	Tempo	Seeker-Sensitivity Rating
Man of God	*Greg Ferguson*	*Pop/rock*	*Mid/up*	7
Mind, Body, Heart and Soul	Bob Carlisle	Pop/rock	Up	9
Never Be an Angel	Margaret Becker	Pop	Mid	4
Own Me	Ginny Owens	Ballad	Slow	6
Power of a Moment	Chris Rice	Folk pop	Up	8
Promise	*Willow Creek Music*	*Pop*	*Mid/up*	6
Show Yourselves to Be	Steven Curtis Chapman	Acoustic ballad	Slow/mid	4
Stranger to Holiness	Steve Camp	Ballad	Slow/mid	2
Surrender Medley	*Willow Creek Music*	*Ballad medley duet*	*Slow*	6
There Is a Line	Susan Ashton	Folk pop	Mid	6
Turn It All Over	*Greg Ferguson*	*Motown-ish pop*	*Up*	8
Unimportant Things	**Paul Smith**	**Ballad**	**Slow**	7
Whatever	Steven Curtis Chapman	Rock/pop	Up	8
Whatever You Ask	Steve Camp	Power ballad	Slow	5
Would I Know You?	Wayne Watson	Ballad	Slow	3
_____	_____	_____	_____	_____
_____	_____	_____	_____	_____
_____	_____	_____	_____	_____
_____	_____	_____	_____	_____
_____	_____	_____	_____	_____

Worship Choruses

Title	Artist	Style	Tempo	Seeker-Sensitivity Rating
Bend My Knee	*Student Impact*	*Rock worship*	*Up*	5
But if Not	*Student Impact*	*Acoustic ballad*	*Slow*	5
Create in Me	*Willow Creek Music*	*Ballad*	*Slow*	3
Cry of My Heart	Terry Butler	Pop	Up	4
Everyday	Student Impact/Sonlight Band	Rock worship	Up	6
Everything I Am	*Willow Creek Music*	*Pop/rock*	*Up*	7
From the Start of the Day	*Willow Creek Music*	*Pop*	*Mid*	4
Heart of Worship	Matt Redman	Worship ballad	Slow	2

Title	Artist	Style	Tempo	Seeker-Sensitivity Rating
Holy Spirit, Take Control	*Willow Creek Music*	*Ballad*	*Slow*	*2*
I Give You My Heart	Hillsongs	Worship ballad	Slow	4
I Surrender All	None	Worship ballad	Slow	4
In My Heart	*Greg Ferguson*	*Celtic worship ballad*	*Slow*	*9*
Jesus, Draw Me Close	*Willow Creek Music*	*Worship ballad*	*Slow*	*3*
Just Say the Word	*Willow Creek Music*	*Gospel pop, in 3*	*Mid/up*	*4*
Lord of All	Hillsongs	Worship power ballad	Slow	3
Lord, Reign in Me	Vineyard	Rock/pop worship	Up	5
Potter's Hand	Hillsongs	Worship ballad	Slow/mid	3
Spirit of the Living God	NA	Traditional worship song	Slow	4
Step by Step	Rich Mullins	Folk worship	Mid	3
Take My Life and Let It Be	Paul Baloche	Worship ballad	Mid/slow	3
Undivided Heart	*Willow Creek Music*	*Folk pop worship ballad*	*Slow*	*3*
Your Love for Me	Integrity Songwriters	Pop worship	Up	4

MOVIE CLIPS

Title: Chariots of Fire

Topic: Integrity; Standing up for what you believe in; The Sabbath

Description: Eric Liddell refuses to run on the Sabbath. The English Olympic Committee tries to make him compromise, but he stands firm.

Start Time: 1:28:15

Start Cue: "We decided to invite you in for a little chat."

End Time: 1:30:00

End Cue: "But I can't make that sacrifice."

Comments:

Title: Indiana Jones and the Last Crusade

Topic: Faith; Trusting God when circumstances are confusing

Description: Indiana Jones faces a seemingly uncrossable chasm but takes a "leap of faith" and steps onto an invisible bridge. Illustrates faith, believing what can't be seen.

Start Time: 1:46:50

Start Cue: Indiana Jones walks through cave to the chasm.

End Time: 1:48:45

End Cue: Indy throws sand on bridge to mark it (can be cut earlier).

Comments: _____
_____
_____

Title: _____

Topic: _____

Description: _____

Start Time: _____

Start Cue: _____

End Time: _____

End Cue: _____

Comments: _____
_____
_____

Praise and Worship

MESSAGE TITLES

_____

_____

_____

DRAMAS

*No dramas for this topic. See **God's Character, General,** or various attributes of God, like **God's Faithfulness,** for ideas.

_____   _____   _____   _____

_____   _____   _____   _____

_____   _____   _____   _____

SONGS

Title	Artist	Style	Tempo	Seeker-Sensitivity Rating
Almighty	Wayne Watson	Praise & worship/pop	Up	2
Always before Me	Steven Curtis Chapman	Worship ballad, in 3	Slow/mid	1
Awesome God	Rich Mullins	Pop anthem	Mid/up	1
The Beauty of Holiness	Steve Camp	Ballad	Slow	1
Change in My Life	John Pagano	Gospel	Mid/up	9
God of Wonders	**Various**	**Folk rock**	**Mid**	**7**
He Knows My Name	**Tommy Walker/Helena**	**Worship ballad**	**Slow**	**9**
He's Been Faithful	Brooklyn Tabernacle Choir	Ballad with choir	Slow	6
Here in the Quiet	*Willow Creek Music*	*Ballad*	*Slow*	*4*
Holy One	*Helena*	*Ballad*	*Slow*	*7*

Title	Artist	Style	Tempo	Seeker-Sensitivity Rating
I Will Never Be	**Hillsongs**	**Worship power ballad**	**Slow**	**4**
I Will Worship You	**Matthew Ward**	**Ballad**	**Slow**	**5**
I'm Amazed	*Willow Creek Music*	*Ballad*	*Slow*	*7*
In My Heart	*Greg Ferguson*	*Celtic worship ballad*	*Slow*	*9*
Listen to Our Hearts	Geoff Moore & the Distance (with Steven Curtis Chapman)	Acoustic ballad duet	Slow/mid	5
Lord, I Want to Be Like Jesus	**Fernando Ortega**	**Ballad**	**Slow**	**5**
The Love of God	*Willow Creek Music*	*A cappella vocal group*	*Slow*	*6*
More Than Words	Steven Curtis Chapman	Acoustic guitar ballad	Mid/slow	4
My Redeemer Is Faithful and True	**Steven Curtis Chapman**	**Ballad**	**Slow**	**9**
Praise the King	**Cindy Morgan**	**Ballad**	**Slow**	**4**
Reaching for You	*Willow Creek Music*	*Rock/pop*	*Up*	*10*
Speechless	**Steven Curtis Chapman**	**Acoustic rock**	**Mid/up**	**7**
We Believe in God	Amy Grant	Acoustic ballad	Slow	3
Who Am I?	Margaret Becker	Power ballad	Slow	7
_____	_____	_____	_____	_____
_____	_____	_____	_____	_____
_____	_____	_____	_____	_____
_____	_____	_____	_____	_____

Worship Choruses

Title	Artist	Style	Tempo	Seeker-Sensitivity Rating
Amen	Tommy Walker	Worship shuffle	Up	5
As We Worship You	Tommy Walker	Worship ballad	Slow	1
Awesome in This Place	Dave Billington	Worship ballad	Slow	2
Be Magnified	Don Moen	Ballad	Slow	2
The Beauty of Holiness	Steve Camp	Worship ballad, in 3	Slow	3
Blessed Be the Name	Vineyard	Worship ballad	Slow	4
Celebrate Jesus Celebrate	Alleluia Music	Pop	Up	6
Celebrate the Lord of Love	Paul Baloche	Pop worship	Up	5
Come Let Us Bow Down	Dennis Jernigan	Worship ballad	Slow/mid	3

Title	Artist	Style	Tempo	Seeker-Sensitivity Rating
Come, Now Is the Time to Worship	Vineyard	Pop/rock	Up	5
Did You Feel the Mountains Tremble?	Passion	Pop/rock	Mid/up	2
Don't Forget His Benefits	Tommy Walker & the CA Worship Band	Rock/pop	Up	4
Doxology	Tommy Walker	Pop/rock	Mid	6
Everyone Arise	Tommy Walker	Pop/rock	Up	3
Everything I Am	*Willow Creek Music*	*Pop/rock*	*Up*	*7*
For the Beauty of the Earth	*Willow Creek Music*	*Worship ballad*	*Slow*	*5*
From the Rising of the Sun	Paul Deming	Ballad	Slow	3
From the Start of the Day	*Willow Creek Music*	*Pop*	*Mid*	*4*
God of Wonders	**Various**	**Folk rock**	**Mid**	**7**
Hallelujah (Your Love Is Amazing)	Vineyard—Brenton Brown	Rock/pop worship	Up	4
Happy Song	Delirious	Country rockabilly	Up	5
He Is Exalted	Twila Paris	Pop worship, in 3	Mid	3
Heart of Worship	Matt Redman	Worship ballad	Slow	2
Here I Am Again	Tommy Walker/ Willow Creek Music	Pop shuffle	Up	3
High and Exalted	Bob Fitts	Pop worship	Slow/mid	2
Holy and Anointed One	Vineyard	Worship ballad	Slow	3
Holy, Holy, Holy (Gary Oliver)	Alvin Slaughter/ Willow Creek Music	Gospel pop	Up	5
Holy, Holy, Holy (traditional)	*Willow Creek Music*	*Traditional hymn*	*Mid*	*5*
How Could I But Love You?	Tommy Walker	Worship ballad	Slow	3
How Good and Pleasant	Tommy Walker	Pop/rock	Up	5
I Could Sing of Your Love Forever	Passion	Rock/pop worship	Mid	4
I Give You My Heart	Hillsongs	Worship ballad	Slow	4
I Live to Know You	Hillsongs	Worship power ballad	Slow	3
I Love You, Lord	Maranatha!/Laurie Klein	Worship ballad	Slow	4
I See the Lord	Chris Falson, Maranatha! Singers/Willow Creek Music	Worship ballad	Slow/mid	2
I Will Bless You, Lord	Hillsongs	Worship ballad, in 3	Mid	3
In My Heart	*Greg Ferguson*	*Celtic worship ballad*	*Slow*	*6*
Jesus, Draw Me Close	Willow Creek Music	Worship ballad	Slow	3

Title	Artist	Style	Tempo	Seeker-Sensitivity Rating
Let Everything That Has Breath	Matt Redman	Pop/rock worship	Up	4
Let It Rise	Praise Band	Rock worship	Up	5
Lift Up Your Heads	Tommy Walker	Rock/pop worship	Up	2
Lord, I Lift Your Name on High	Maranatha!/Praise Band	Pop worship	Up	6
Lord Most High	*Willow Creek Music*	*MOR worship*	*Mid*	*3*
Lord of All	Hillsongs	Worship power ballad	Slow	3
The Lord's Prayer	*Willow Creek Music*	*U2-ish rock/pop*	*Up*	*9*
Love You So Much	Hillsongs	Worship ballad	Slow	5
More Love More Power	Jude Del Herro	Worship ballad	Slow	3
More Precious Than Silver	Don Moen	Worship ballad	Slow	5
My Heart Sings Praises	Hillsongs	Pop worship	Mid	4
My Jesus, I Love You	*Willow Creek Music*	*Worship ballad*	*Slow*	*3*
Never Gonna Stop	*Tommy Walker/ Willow Creek Music*	*Pop/rock*	*Up*	*3*
No Greater Love	Tommy Walker	Pop/rock	Up	6
O for a Thousand Tongues	*Willow Creek Music*	*Contemporary arrangement of hymn*	*Up*	*3*
Pour Out My Heart	Vineyard	Worship shuffle	Mid	4
Praise God on High	*Willow Creek Music*	*Worship ballad*	*Slow*	*5*
Reach Down Deep	*Willow Creek Music*	*Pop*	*Up*	*5*
Revelation 19	Student Impact	Worship ballad	Slow/mid	4
Shout to the Lord	Hillsongs	Worship power ballad	Slow	3
Shout to the North	Student Impact	Rock, in 3	Up	4
Still I Will Worship You	*Willow Creek Music*	*Pop/rock worship*	*Up*	*3*
Te Alabamos	Tommy Walker	Latin pop worship	Mid/up	4
That's Why We Praise Him	Tommy Walker	Rock/pop worship	Mid	5
There Is None Like You	Lenny LeBlanc	Worship ballad	Slow/mid	6
Unto the King	Don Moen	Worship ballad, in 3	Slow/mid	3
We Fall Down	Passion	Worship ballad	Slow/mid	3
We Praise Your Name	*Willow Creek Music*	*Worship ballad*	*Slow/mid*	*4*
What the Lord Has Done	Hillsongs	Worship ballad, in 3	Slow/mid	2
Where You Are	Tommy Walker	Pop worship	Mid	5

Title	Artist	Style	Tempo	Seeker-Sensitivity Rating
Who Is Like Our God?	Vineyard	Rock/pop worship	Mid	3
You Are Holy	Hillsongs	Worship ballad	Slow	3
You Are Worthy of My Praise	Passion	Rock/pop	Up	3
You Have Been Given	*Willow Creek Music*	*Worship ballad, in 3*	*Slow*	*3*
You've Won My Affection	Curt Coffield	Worship ballad	Slow	4

MOVIE CLIPS

Title: _____

Topic: _____

Description: _____

Start Time: _____

Start Cue: _____

End Time: _____

End Cue: _____

Comments: _____

_____

_____

Prayer

Might also include: *Quiet Time*

MESSAGE TITLES

- ❏ Does God Still Listen?
- ❏ Does God Still Speak?
- ❏ Practicing the Presence of God
- ❏ Prayer Busters
- ❏ Two-Way Prayer
- ❏ *A Faith That Works—The Book of James:* Just Pray
- ❏ *I Have a Friend Who* Wonders If Prayer Works
- ❏ *Truths That Transform:* Don't Worry . . . Pray
- ❏ *What Jesus Would Say to . . .* Bart Simpson
- ❏ **The Power of Prayer:** Amazing Answers to Prayer • God's Attitude toward Prayer • How to Pray Authentically • Practicing the Presence of God • Prayer, Our Last Resort • Mountain-Moving Prayer • The Mystery of Unanswered Prayer
- ❏ **Prayer:** Why I Gave Up on Prayer • Pray at Your Own Risk • Praying for One Another
- ❏ **The Privilege of Prayer:** The Privilege of Prayer • Painfully Honest Prayers • Prayer Abuse • Dangerous Prayers

Package Suggestion

Movie Clip:
Meet the Parents

Drama:
Prayer Perplexity

Song:
Open Up

DRAMAS

Title	Tone	Characters	Topics
Great Expectations	Mixed; Very serious ending	1 male, 2 females	Unanswered prayer
Just the Two of Us	Serious	1 male, 2 females	Infertility; Unanswered prayer
No Interruptions	Humorous	1 male	Quiet time; Prayer
Plane Talk	Humorous	2 males, 1 offstage voice (pilot)	Doubt; Skepticism; God's presence
Prayer Despair	Mixed	1 male, 2 females	Waiting for answers to prayer; Marriage; Process of change
Prayer Group Therapy	Humorous	2 males, 3 females	Prayer

Title	Tone	Characters	Topics
Prayer Perplexity	Humorous	2 males, 2 females	Prayer; The Lord's Prayer
Quiet Time?	Humorous	1 female	Prayer
Snow Job	Humorous	2 males, 1 female	Prayer abuse
The Warrior	Mixed, light	1 female	Prayer; Taking God with you throughout the day
_____	_____	_____	_____
_____	_____	_____	_____
_____	_____	_____	_____
_____	_____	_____	_____

SONGS

Title	Artist	Style	Tempo	Seeker-Sensitivity Rating
At Jesus' Feet	Billy and Sarah Gaines	Ballad	Slow	6
Great Expectations	Steven Curtis Chapman	Pop/rock	Mid	8
Here in the Quiet	*Willow Creek Music*	*Ballad*	*Slow*	*4*
He's My Son	Mark Schultz	Ballad	Slow	9
I Can Hear You	Carolyn Arends	Folk pop	Mid/up	8
Knockin' on Heaven's Door	**Avalon**	**Pop**	**Up**	**9**
Let Us Pray	**Steven Curtis Chapman**	**Pop/rock**	**Up**	**7**
More Than Words	Steven Curtis Chapman	Acoustic guitar ballad	Mid/slow	4
On My Knees	*Willow Creek Music*	*Acoustic guitar ballad*	*Slow*	*5*
Open Up	*Willow Creek Music*	*Hip-Hop/R & B*	*Up*	*9*
Prayer Medley	*Willow Creek Music*	*Ballad medley trio*	*Slow*	*7*
Sometimes He Calms the Storms	Scott Krippayne	Ballad	Slow/mid	6
Still Listening	**Steven Curtis Chapman**	**Acoustic ballad**	**Slow/mid**	**7**
_____	_____	_____	_____	_____
_____	_____	_____	_____	_____
_____	_____	_____	_____	_____
_____	_____	_____	_____	_____

Worship Choruses

Title	Artist	Style	Tempo	Seeker-Sensitivity Rating
The Lord's Prayer	*Willow Creek Music*	*U2-ish rock/pop*	*Up*	*9*
Meet with Me	Ten Shekel Shirt	Modern worship	Up	7
____	____	____	____	____
____	____	____	____	____
____	____	____	____	____
____	____	____	____	____
____	____	____	____	____
____	____	____	____	____

MOVIE CLIPS

Title: Meet the Parents

Topic: Prayer

Description: Robert DeNiro's character asks Greg, his daughter's boyfriend, to pray before dinner. The results are hilarious!

Start Time: 0:24:27

Start Cue: "Greg, would you like to say grace?"

End Time: 0:26:14

End Cue: "Thank you, Greg. That was interesting too."

Comments: _____
_____
_____

Title: Shadowlands

Topic: Prayer

Description: A very short clip in which C. S. Lewis's friend tells him he knows God has answered his prayers for Joy's healing. Lewis's answer is a profound statement about prayer.

Start Time: 1:29:30

Start Cue: "Jack, what news?"

End Time: 1:30:00

End Cue: "It doesn't change God; it changes me."

Comments: May be too short, except as a sermon illustration.
_____
_____
_____

Title: Sister Act

Topic: Prayer

Description: Sister Mary Clarence is asked to pray at dinner, and the results are humorous.

Start Time: 0:23:15

Start Cue: Sister Mary Patrick raises her hand.

End Time: 0:24:15

End Cue: Nuns echo, "Amen."

Comments: _____

_____

_____

Title: Sister Act

Topic: Prayer abuse

Description: The nuns need a free helicopter ride to Reno to save Mary Clarence. When the pilot refuses, they start to pray very manipulative prayers.

Start Time: 1:21:15

Start Cue: "It's $1,500 for the run to Reno."

End Time: 1:22:15

End Cue: Nuns in helicopter.

Comments: _____

_____

_____

Title: _____

Topic: _____

Description: _____

Start Time: _____

Start Cue: _____

End Time: _____

End Cue: _____

Comments: _____

_____

_____

—Relationship with God,— General

Refers to the general idea of having a relationship with God, and that God desires a relationship with us

See also: **Prayer**

MESSAGE TITLES

- ❑ The Benefits of Knowing God
- ❑ Does God Still Listen?
- ❑ Does God Still Speak?
- ❑ Listening to God
- ❑ Ordering Your Spiritual World
- ❑ When God Comes Near
- ❑ Windows of the Soul
- ❑ *A Faith That Works—The Book of James:* All Things Are Possible
- ❑ *A Faith That Works—The Book of James:* Religion According to God
- ❑ *No Fear:* Should I Be Afraid of God?
- ❑ *The Relationship You've Always Wanted:* The Ultimate Relationship
- ❑ *Truths That Transform:* I Can Do All Things
- ❑ *Truths That Transform:* To Live Is Christ . . . to Die Is Gain
- ❑ *28 Days of Truth Telling:* Telling the Truth to God
- ❑ **Developing a Daring Faith:** Dialoging with God • Obeying God • Following God
- ❑ **Seven Wonders of the Spiritual World:** God Loves Me • God Can Be Trusted • God Forgives My Failures • God Transforms Me • God Guides Me • God Uses Me • God Satisfies Me

DRAMAS

Title	Tone	Characters	Topics
Another Day at the Bus Stop	Mixed	1 male, 1 female	Our relationship with God; Self-esteem
Any Time?	Mixed, mostly serious	1 male	Making time for God

Title	Tone	Characters	Topics
The Big Question	Mixed, mostly humorous	1 male, 1 female, 1 child	The existence of God
The Black Hole	Serious but light	2 males, 1 female, 1 narrator	Filling the void; Contentment; God's love
Good Friday Medley	Serious	1 male, 4 females (though some roles are interchangeable)	Good Friday; How we view Jesus
Guess Which God	Humorous	4 males, offstage male and female voices	Confusion about God; The nature of God
I Don't Want to Fight You Anymore	Serious	1 female	Relationship with God; Giving up control; Our value to God
Impressions, Inc.	Humorous	2 males, 1 female	Skin-deep Christianity
Plane Talk	Humorous	2 males, 1 offstage voice (pilot)	Doubt; Skepticism; God's presence
Quiet Time?	Humorous	1 female	Prayer
Seeing Is Believing	Humorous	1 male, 1 female, 1 narrator	A Savior you can trust; Easy faith
Sitters, Strivers, Standers, and Saints	Mixed	4 either males or females, 1 narrator	God changing lives; God completing us
The Stickholders	Serious	3 males, 1 female, 1 narrator	Relationship with God; Freedom from rules
Take Heart	Mixed; Mime	2 males, 2 females	God heals the brokenhearted; Disappointment
Tom, Dick, and Mary	Serious	3 males, 1 female, 1 narrator	Hearing God's voice; Crowding God out of your life
The Warrior	Mixed, light	1 female	Prayer; Taking God with you throughout the day
You Cramp My Style	Serious	1 male, 1 female, 1 either male or female	Reasons people don't believe; Society's view of God

SONGS

Title	Artist	Style	Tempo	Seeker-Sensitivity Rating
All Things New	Watermark	Folk pop	Mid	8
At Jesus' Feet	Billy & Sarah Gaines	Ballad	Slow	6
Can't Live a Day without You	Avalon	Pop ballad	Slow/mid	8
Could You Believe?	Scott Krippayne	Pop	Up	9
Dive	**Steven Curtis Chapman**	**Pop/rock**	**Up**	9
Enough	*Willow Creek Music*	*Piano ballad*	*Slow*	7
Every Season	**Nicole Nordeman**	**Ballad**	**Slow**	8
Found a Way	*Greg Ferguson*	*Ballad*	*Slow*	9
God of Wonders	**Various**	**Folk rock**	**Mid**	7
Great Expectations	Steven Curtis Chapman	Pop/rock	Mid	8
Greater Than	**Riley Armstrong**	**Alternative pop/rock**	**Up**	8
He Knows My Name	**Tommy Walker/Helena**	**Worship ballad**	**Slow**	9
Heart's Cry	**Steven Curtis Chapman**	**Acoustic ballad**	**Mid/slow**	7
Heirlooms	Amy Grant	Ballad	Slow	8
Here in My Heart	Susan Ashton	Folk rock	Up	8
Here in the Quiet	*Willow Creek Music*	*Ballad*	*Slow*	4
Highest Honor	**Chris Eaton**	**Ballad**	**Slow**	7
Hunger and Thirst	Susan Ashton	Folk pop	Mid/up	6
I Can Hear You	Carolyn Arends	Folk pop	Mid/up	8
I Don't Know Why/Found a Way	*Willow Creek Music*	*Ballad*	*Slow*	8
I Go to the Rock	Dottie Rambo; Whitney Houston	Swing/big band	Mid	7
I'm Amazed	*Willow Creek Music*	*Ballad*	*Slow*	7
In Christ Alone	Michael English	Power ballad	Slow	8
In My Heart	*Greg Ferguson*	*Celtic worship ballad*	*Slow*	9
Jesus, King of Angels	**Fernando Ortega**	**Ballad**	**Slow**	6
Jesus Loves Me	Whitney Houston	R & B/pop	Slow/mid	8
Knockin' on Heaven's Door	**Avalon**	**Pop**	**Up**	9
Let Us Pray	**Steven Curtis Chapman**	**Pop/rock**	**Up**	7

Title	Artist	Style	Tempo	Seeker-Sensitivity Rating
Life Support	*Greg Ferguson*	*R & B/pop*	*Mid/up*	9
Man of God	*Greg Ferguson*	*Pop/rock*	*Mid/up*	7
Mind, Body, Heart and Soul	Bob Carlisle	Pop/rock	Up	9
More Than Words	Steven Curtis Chapman	Acoustic guitar ballad	Mid/slow	4
No One Knows My Heart	Susan Ashton	Folk pop ballad	Slow/mid	9
On My Knees	*Willow Creek Music*	*Acoustic guitar ballad*	*Slow*	5
Open Up	*Willow Creek Music*	*Hip-Hop/R & B*	*Up*	9
Own Me	Ginny Owens	Ballad	Slow	6
Power of a Moment	Chris Rice	Folk pop	Up	8
Prayer Medley	*Willow Creek Music*	*Ballad medley trio*	*Slow*	7
Reaching for You	*Willow Creek Music*	*Rock/pop*	*Up*	10
Speechless	**Steven Curtis Chapman**	**Acoustic rock**	**Mid/up**	7
Still Listening	Steven Curtis Chapman	Acoustic ballad	Slow/mid	7
There Is a God	**Tommy Walker**	**Ballad duet**	**Slow**	**8**
Turn It All Over	*Greg Ferguson*	*Motown-ish pop*	*Up*	8
We Believe in God	Amy Grant	Acoustic ballad	Slow	3
What a Ride	*Willow Creek Music*	*Pop/rock*	*Up*	9
Who Am I? (Grace Flows Down)	**Watermark**	**Folk pop**	**Mid/slow**	**8**
Would I Know You?	Wayne Watson	Ballad	Slow	3
You Brought My Heart to Life	*Willow Creek Music*	*Ballad*	*Slow*	9
_____	_____	_____	_____	_____
_____	_____	_____	_____	_____
_____	_____	_____	_____	_____
_____	_____	_____	_____	_____

Worship Choruses

Title	Artist	Style	Tempo	Seeker-Sensitivity Rating
Amen	Tommy Walker	Worship shuffle	Up	5
And That My Soul Knows Very Well	Hillsongs	Worship ballad	Slow	5
Beautiful God	Vineyard	Pop	Up	5
Better Is One Day	Matt Redman/Passion	Folk worship	Mid	4

Title	Artist	Style	Tempo	Seeker-Sensitivity Rating
Better Than	Vineyard	Pop/rock worship	Up	6
Breathe	Michael W. Smith	Worship ballad	Slow	3
Can't Stop Talkin'	Hillsongs	Pop worship	Up	6
Cry of My Heart	Terry Butler	Pop	Up	4
Everyday	Student Impact/Sonlight Band	Rock worship	Up	6
Everything I Am	*Willow Creek Music*	*Pop/rock*	*Up*	*7*
Faithful to Me	Curt Coffield	Pop worship	Mid	6
From the Start of the Day	*Willow Creek Music*	*Pop*	*Mid*	*4*
God of Wonders	**Various**	**Folk rock**	**Mid**	**7**
Great Is Thy Faithfulness	NA	Traditional worship/ hymn	Slow	5
He Knows My Name	Tommy Walker	Worship ballad	Slow	7
He Loves Me	Tommy Walker	Worship ballad	Slow	6
I Could Sing of Your Love Forever	Passion	Rock/pop worship	Mid	4
I Live to Know You	Hillsongs	Worship power ballad	Slow	3
I Wanna Learn More	Curt Coffield, Ed Kerr	Folk pop worship	Mid	5
In Your Hands	Hillsongs	Worship ballad	Slow/mid	4
In Your Loving Arms	*Willow Creek Music*	*Ballad*	*Slow*	*4*
Jesus, Draw Me Close	*Willow Creek Music*	*Worship ballad*	*Slow*	*3*
Jesus, Lover of My Soul	Hillsongs	Pop worship	Up	3
Jesus, You're the Answer	Tommy Walker	Soulish worship ballad	Slow	5
Joy, Joy, Joy	Tommy Walker	Rock shuffle	Up	5
Let the Peace of God Reign	Hillsongs	Worship ballad	Slow	3
Love You So Much	Hillsongs	Worship ballad	Slow	5
Meet with Me	Ten Shekel Shirt	Modern worship	Up	7
Nothing Is as Wonderful	Vineyard	Worship ballad	Slow	3
Open the Eyes of My Heart	Paul Baloche	Pop/rock worship	Up	5
Pour Out My Heart	Vineyard	Worship shuffle	Mid	4
Power of Your Love	Hillsongs	Worship ballad	Slow	6
Reach Down Deep	*Willow Creek Music*	*Pop*	*Up*	*5*
Step by Step	Rich Mullins	Folk worship	Mid	3

Title	Artist	Style	Tempo	Seeker-Sensitivity Rating
Think about His Love	NA	Worship ballad	Slow	6
What the Lord Has Done	Hillsongs	Worship ballad, in 3	Slow/mid	2
Where You Are	Tommy Walker	Pop worship	Mid	5
Your Love	Hillsongs	Worship ballad	Slow	4
You've Won My Affection	Curt Coffield	Worship ballad	Slow	4

MOVIE CLIPS

Title: Chariots of Fire

Topic: Christian life; Endurance

Description: Eric Liddell gives a sermonette about running the race of faith.

Start Time: 0:25:35

Start Cue: "You came to see a race today."

End Time: 0:27:20

End Cue: "That is how you run a straight race."

Comments: _____

Title: _____

Topic: _____

Description: _____

Start Time: _____

Start Cue: _____

End Time: _____

End Cue: _____

Comments: _____

Sanctification/ Growing in Christ

Refers to the process of becoming like Christ

Might also include: *Growing in Christ, Spiritual Development*

MESSAGE TITLES

- ❑ Building Bigger Hearts
- ❑ Do You Have What It Takes to Grow?
- ❑ *Truths That Transform:* He Who Began a Good Work in You Will Complete It
- ❑ *When God Shows Up:* The Ordinary Become Extraordinary
- ❑ **For Mature Audiences Only:** How to Stunt Your Spiritual Growth • The Marks of a Mature Christian • Myths about Maturing • What Motivates Mature Christians
- ❑ **The Seasons of a Spiritual Life:** The Season of Spiritual Seeking • The Season of Spiritual Infancy • The Season of Spiritual Adolescence • The Season of Spiritual Adulthood

DRAMAS

Title	Tone	Characters	Topics
The Knowing Years	Mixed	3 females	Spiritual adolescence; Adolescence
Make It Happen	Humorous	5 males, 1 female (numerous extras for attendees and security)	Taking responsibility for change; The limits of self-help seminars
Monday Night Meeting	Humorous	4 males	New Christian; Joy of Christian life; Discipleship
One Sunday in the Parking Lot	Humorous	4 males or females	Pace of life; Making changes
A Perspective on Spring	Humorous	1 male	Optimistic/pessimistic views of life; Spring; The spiritual season of spring
Prayer Despair	Mixed	1 male, 2 females	Waiting for answers to prayer; Marriage; Process of change

Title	Tone	Characters	Topics
Sitters, Strivers, Standers, and Saints	Mixed	4 either males or females, 1 narrator	God changing lives; God completing us
Welcome to the Family	Humorous	2 males, 1 female	New Christian; Growing in Christ

SONGS

Title	Artist	Style	Tempo	Seeker-Sensitivity Rating
All I Ever Wanted	Margaret Becker	Pop/rock ballad	Slow/mid	4
Clumsy	**Chris Rice**	**Pop**	**Mid/up**	**8**
Every Season	**Nicole Nordeman**	**Ballad**	**Slow**	**8**
Evidence	*Willow Creek Music*	*Folk pop*	*Mid*	*10*
Growing	Wayne Watson	Ballad	Slow	5
Heart's Cry	**Steven Curtis Chapman**	**Acoustic ballad**	**Mid/slow**	**7**
I Stand, I Fall	*Greg Ferguson*	*Piano ballad*	*Slow*	*7*
If That's What It Takes	*Willow Creek Music*	*MOR pop*	*Mid/slow*	*5*
Lord, I Want to Be Like Jesus	**Fernando Ortega**	**Ballad**	**Slow**	**5**
Never Be an Angel	Margaret Becker	Pop	Mid	4
Own Me	Ginny Owens	Ballad	Slow	6
Power of a Moment	Chris Rice	Folk pop	Up	8
River God	**Nicole Nordeman**	**Piano ballad**	**Slow**	**6**
Stranger to Holiness	Steve Camp	Ballad	Slow/mid	2
Take My Hand	The Kry	Acoustic ballad	Mid/slow	9
These Things Are True of You	**Tommy Walker & the CA Worship Band**	**Ballad duet**	**Slow**	**9**

Worship Choruses

Title	Artist	Style	Tempo	Seeker-Sensitivity Rating
Create in Me	*Willow Creek Music*	*Ballad*	*Slow*	*3*
Power of Your Love	Hillsongs	Worship ballad	Slow	6
Spirit of the Living God	NA	Traditional worship song	Slow	4
Take My Life and Let It Be	Paul Baloche	Worship ballad	Mid/slow	3
These Things Are True of You	Tommy Walker & the CA Worship Band	Ballad duet	Slow	9

MOVIE CLIPS

Title: _____

Topic: _____

Description: _____

Start Time: _____

Start Cue: _____

End Time: _____

End Cue: _____

Comments: _____
_____
_____

Sin

See also: **God's Forgiveness of Us, Grace, Guilt, Self-Control**

MESSAGE TITLES

- ❏ *A Faith That Works—The Book of James:* Destructive Desires
- ❏ *A Faith That Works—The Book of James:* No More! The Power to Stop
- ❏ *A Faith That Works—The Book of James:* The Power of Confession
- ❏ *Learning through Life's Crises:* Learning through Falling
- ❏ *Signs of the Times:* Dead-End Road
- ❏ *When God Shows Up:* The Wayward Find Mercy
- ❏ **Modern Day Madness:** The Agony of Escapism • The Pornography Problem • Hope for the Homosexual • Unwanted Pregnancies
- ❏ **The "S" Word:** Sin in a No-Fault Society • The High Cost of a Cheap Thrill • The Other "S" Word (Salvation)

<table>
<tr><td colspan="2">

Package Suggestion

Drama:
A Nice Guy

Song:
Face of Forgiveness

</td></tr>
</table>

DRAMAS

Title	Tone	Characters	Topics
All Gummed Up	Serious	1 male, 1 female, 1 offstage male voice	Adultery; Dealing with past hurts; The pain of lies
Attractive Deal	Serious	1 male, 1 female	Convictions; Adultery; Temptation
Because I Love You	Serious	1 male, 1 female	Adultery; The consequences of sin
A Failure Tale	Mixed	5 males, 1 narrator	Failing; Obeying rules
Forgive Again?	Serious	1 male, 1 female	Forgiving others
Forgiven	Serious	2 females	Forgiving others; God's forgiveness
The Gardeners	Humorous	1 male, 1 female	New Age movement
Investment at Risk	Serious	2 males, 1 female, 1 child	Convictions; Adultery
It's Not My Fault	Humorous	3 males, 4 females	Sin; Taking responsibility for our sin; Excuses
Man of the Year	Serious	5 males, 1 female	Moralism; Our need for Christ

Title	Tone	Characters	Topics
A Nice Guy	Serious	2 males	Regret; Admitting failures; Effects of sin; Confession
Straight-Jacketed	Serious	1 male	Bondage to past and to sin; Anger at God
Taking Step Four	Humorous	1 female	Self-examination; Self-delusion; Confession of Sin
"X" Marks the Spot	Serious; Mime	1 male, 1 female, 3 either males or females	Sin; Redemption; Forgiveness; Guilt

SONGS

Title	Artist	Style	Tempo	Seeker-Sensitivity Rating
Ball and Chain	Susan Ashton	Folk pop	Mid	9
Behind Every Fantasy	*Willow Creek Music*	*Country pop*	*Up*	*10*
Between You and Me	**DC Talk**	**Pop/rock**	**Mid**	**10**
Blind Side	Susan Ashton	Folk rock	Up	9
Call of the Wild	Susan Ashton	Country	Mid	10
Casual Christian	**DeGarmo & Key**	**Power ballad**	**Slow**	**6**
Clumsy	Chris Rice	Pop	Mid/up	8
Cross Medley	*Willow Creek Music*	*Ballad medley—hymns*	*Slow*	*7*
Face of Forgiveness	*Willow Creek Music*	*Ballad*	*Slow*	*10*
Farther Than Your Grace Can Reach	**Jonathan Pierce**	**Ballad**	**Slow**	**9**
Forgive Me	*Willow Creek Music*	*Ballad*	*Slow*	*3*
The Great Divide	Point of Grace	Power ballad	Slow	9
Healing Song	Curt Coffield	Ballad, in 3	Slow/mid	7
I Am the Man	*Greg Ferguson*	*Piano ballad*	*Slow*	*8*
I Stand, I Fall	*Greg Ferguson*	*Piano ballad*	*Slow*	*7*
I Will Never Be	Hillsongs	Worship power ballad	Slow	4
Keep My Mind	Margaret Becker	Pop/rock	Up	8
Mercy for the Memories	**Geoff Moore & the Distance**	**Folk pop ballad**	**Slow**	**9**

Title	Artist	Style	Tempo	Seeker-Sensitivity Rating
My Life Is Yours	*Willow Creek Music*	*Acoustic ballad*	*Slow*	*10*
No More Pretending	**Scott Krippayne**	**Pop ballad**	**Slow**	**7**
A Picture of Grace	*Willow Creek Music*	*Medley of ballads*	*Slow*	*9*
Remember Your Chains	Steven Curtis Chapman	Acoustic MOR	Mid	2
Stranger to Holiness	Steve Camp	Ballad	Slow/mid	2

Worship Choruses

Title	Artist	Style	Tempo	Seeker-Sensitivity Rating
Be Magnified	Don Moen	Ballad	Slow	2
The Beauty of Holiness	Steve Camp	Worship ballad, in 3	Slow	3
Create in Me	*Willow Creek Music*	*Ballad*	*Slow*	*3*
Healing Song	Curt Coffield	Ballad, in 3	Slow/mid	7
Holy Spirit, Take Control	*Willow Creek Music*	*Ballad*	*Slow*	*2*
I Will Never Be	Hillsongs	Worship ballad	Slow/mid	3
The Lord Is Gracious and Compassionate	Vineyard	Worship ballad	Mid/slow	5
My Jesus, I Love You	*Willow Creek Music*	*Worship ballad*	*Slow*	*3*
Power of Your Love	Hillsongs	Worship ballad	Slow	6
A Pure Heart	Rusty Nelson	Worship ballad	Slow	4

MOVIE CLIPS

Title: Dead Man Walking

Topic: Salvation; Redemption; Acknowledgment of sin

Description: A nun visits a death row inmate with whom she has been working. She asks him if he has been reading his Bible and essentially inquires about his relationship with God. He misunderstands redemption as a "free admission ticket" in which he plays no part. Her point is that he must acknowledge his sin before grace can cover him.

Start Time: 1:12:09

Start Cue: "I was able to arrange for a lie detector test."

End Time: 1:14:11

End Cue: The inmate stares blankly, looking troubled.

Comments: _____

_____

_____

Title: Dead Man Walking

Topic: Confession of sin; Grace

Description: Death row inmate Matthew Poncelet confesses to a rape and murder he had previously been denying. This acknowledgment of sin was his last barrier to receiving grace. His friend Sister Helen Prejean tells him that he is a "son of God" because of his ownership of his sin.

Start Time: 1:35:12

Start Cue: "The boy . . . Walter? I killed him."

End Time: 1:37:28

End Cue: "Thank you for loving me." Close-up of Sister Prejean.

Comments: This clip is a bit risky because of the subject matter. The sister asks if he killed a boy and raped a girl, and he says yes. But, especially as a companion to the other "Dead Man Walking" clip listed, it is potentially a powerful illustration of the need to acknowledge our sin and the grace that follows.

_____

_____

_____

Title: The Shawshank Redemption

Topic: Regret; Consequences of sin

Description: Red, a forty-year inmate, stands before the parole board and talks about his regret over forty years lost.

Start Time: 2:05:30

Start Cue: Bars slide open and door opens to parole board room.

End Time: 2:07:34

End Cue: Stop immediately after "I gotta live with that."

Comments: There is profanity immediately following the end cue.

Title: _____

Topic: _____

Description: _____

Start Time: _____

Start Cue: _____

End Time: _____

End Cue: _____

Comments: _____

_____

_____

Relationships

Comforting Others

See also: **Hardship**

MESSAGE TITLES

❑ *A Faith That Works—The Book of James:* The Power of Words
❑ *Love of Another Kind:* Comforting Love

DRAMAS

Title	Tone	Characters	Topics
Attack of the Well-Meaners	Mixed, mostly humorous	1 male, 2 females	Dealing with crisis; Friendship
The Breakfast Club	Mixed, mostly serious	4 males, 1 female	Friendship; Small groups; Friends in crisis
Don't Mention It	Mixed, mostly humorous	2 males, 2 females	Unemployment; Being open about problems
Mr. Hibbs' Day Off	Mixed; Mime	3 males, 1 female, 1 child	Serving others; Self-denial; Being used by God
Shop Talk	Mixed	2 males, 2 females	Failure; Adversity; Small groups
What Now?	Serious	2 males, 4 females	Coping with a crisis; Dealing with death

SONGS

Title	Artist	Style	Tempo	Seeker-Sensitivity Rating
Helping Hand	Amy Grant	Pop	Mid/up	10
Let the Lord Love You	*Willow Creek Music*	*Acoustic guitar ballad*	*Slow*	*9*
A Place to Call Home	*Greg Ferguson/ Willow Creek Music*	*Gospel ballad*	*Slow, in 3*	*10*
A Rose Is a Rose	Susan Ashton	Piano ballad	Slow	9
___	___	___	___	___
___	___	___	___	___
___	___	___	___	___
___	___	___	___	___

Worship Choruses

Title	Artist	Style	Tempo	Seeker-Sensitivity Rating
___	___	___	___	___
___	___	___	___	___
___	___	___	___	___

MOVIE CLIPS

Title: _____

Topic: _____

Description: _____

Start Time: _____

Start Cue: _____

End Time: _____

End Cue: _____

Comments: _____
_____
_____

Communication

See also: **Truth Telling**

MESSAGE TITLES

- ❏ *The Age of Rage:* Expressing Anger Appropriately
- ❏ *The Age of Rage:* Responding to the Anger of Others
- ❏ *The Lost Art of Loving:* Please Speak My Language
- ❏ *Telling the Truth:* Expressing Positive Emotions
- ❏ *Telling the Truth:* Games People Play

DRAMAS

Title	Tone	Characters	Topics
The Luncheon	Serious	3 females	Mother-daughter conflict; Honesty in relationships
Pastor General: Consultant Visit	Humorous	2 males, 4 females	Leadership; Oppressive managers; Communication
A Problem of Perspective	Humorous	1 male, 1 female, 1 either male or female	Marriage; Marital conflict
Thanks for Listening	Humorous	1 male, 1 female, 1 male and 1 female teenager	Family; Listening

SONGS

Title	Artist	Style	Tempo	Seeker-Sensitivity Rating
If I Had Only Known	Reba McEntire	Ballad	Slow	10
Only Here for a Little While	Billy Dean	Country	Mid/up	10
Words	Kim Hill	Pop/rock	Up	10

Worship Choruses

Title	Artist	Style	Tempo	Seeker-Sensitivity Rating
Let the Walls Fall Down	Student Impact	Pop worship	Up	6

MOVIE CLIPS

Title: 8 Seconds

Topic: Regret; Communicating love

Description: A father, whose son has recently died in a rodeo accident, breaks down in remorse over not telling his son that he loved him. This short clip probably needs to be set up.

Start Time: 1:27:22

Start Cue: Pallbearers carry the casket out of the church.

End Time: 1:28:44

End Cue: The mother puts her hands on the father's shoulders.

Comments: _____

Title: Forrest Gump

Topic: Gratitude; Friendship

Description: Dan thanks Forrest for saving his life.

Start Time: 1:37:15

Start Cue: "Forrest . . . I never thanked you for saving my life."

End Time: 1:37:50

End Cue: Dan swims away.

Comments: May be too short for use.

Title: Remember the Titans

Topic: Truth telling; Racism; Leadership; Friendship

Description: The Titans' two star defensive players, one white and one black, confront each other on their effort and leadership, respectively. They become best friends later in the movie.

Start Time: 0:29:09/DVD Ch. 9

Start Cue: Gary bumps into Julius. "Okay, man, listen. I'm Gary, you're Julius."

End Time: 0:30:48

End Cue: "Attitude reflects leadership, Captain."

Comments: The two scenes following this one are also very strong, and the three scenes combined, though long, would be a great example of leadership and breaking down racial barriers. Gary says "shiver push," and it sounds like profanity because it goes by fast, but it's not.

Title: Shrek

Topic: Friendship; Truth telling

Description: Donkey confronts Shrek about being selfish and being mean to him. This clip has some great statements about friendship and forgiveness.

Start Time: 1:11:28/DVD Ch. 16

Start Cue: Shrek comes out of his house. "Donkey, what are you doing?"

End Time: 1:13:45

End Cue: "Friends?" "Friends."

Comments: One caution: Shrek refers to Donkey as a "jackass," which is technically true because he is a donkey, but it might be offensive to some. Also, Shrek goes into an outhouse.

Title: _____

Topic: _____

Description: _____

Start Time: _____

Start Cue: _____

End Time: _____

End Cue: _____

Comments: _____

Community

Different from **Small Groups** in that this topic speaks of the whole church, or groups of people within the church, knowing, loving, and caring for one another— *being* the church to one another.

See also: **The Church, Small Groups**

MESSAGE TITLES

- ❑ Discovering Community
- ❑ Making God's Dream (Community) Happen
- ❑ Nobody Stands Alone
- ❑ Only Community Is Forever
- ❑ The Reward for Relational Authenticity
- ❑ *A Faith That Works—The Book of James:* Relational Fundamentals
- ❑ *Living Excellent Lives:* Relationally
- ❑ *Living with an Attitude:* The Attitude of Community
- ❑ *Making Life Work:* Choose Friends Wisely
- ❑ *Making Life Work:* Speak Truth
- ❑ *The Power of Love:* Being a Friend
- ❑ *Relational Intelligence:* To Know and Be Known
- ❑ *Restoring Weary Souls:* Life-Restoring Relationships

DRAMAS

Title	Tone	Characters	Topics
The Breakfast Club	Mixed, mostly serious	4 males, 1 female	Friendship; Small groups; Friends in crisis
.COMmunity	Humorous	1 male	True community; The Internet; Relationships
Don't Mention It	Mixed, mostly humorous	2 males, 2 females	Unemployment; Being open about problems
Just an Acquaintance	Mixed	2 males, 2 females	Relationships between men; Superficial relationships
Kind of Rare	Mixed	3 males, 3 females	Confronting in love; Friendship; Marriage; Character flaws

Title	Tone	Characters	Topics
Lifeline	Mixed, touching	1 male, 2 females, 1 small child (no lines)	Serving the church; Life in community; Aging
Mr. X, Mr. Y, and Mr. Z	Humorous	4 males, 1 female, 1 narrator	Friendship; Intimacy
The Neighborhood	Mixed	3 males, 3 females	Small Groups; Relationships; Getting deeper; Authenticity
The Next Step	Humorous	2 males	Authentic Community; Positive relational risk taking; Men's relationships
Shop Talk	Mixed	2 males, 2 females	Failure; Adversity; Small groups
Something in Common	Mixed	1 male, 3 females	Starting relationships
Unknown	Serious	1 male, 4 females	Friendship; Loneliness; Small groups
___	___	___	___
___	___	___	___
___	___	___	___
___	___	___	___

SONGS

Title	Artist	Style	Tempo	Seeker-Sensitivity Rating
At the Foot of the Cross	*Willow Creek Music*	*Pop*	*Mid*	*7*
Between You and Me	**DC Talk**	**Pop/rock**	**Mid**	**10**
Bridge between Two Hearts	Bob Carlisle	Pop	Up	9
Circle of Friends	Point of Grace	Pop	Mid	9
Gather at the River	Point of Grace	Pop	Up	8
I Will Be Your Friend	Amy Grant	Pop	Up	10
Let's Stand Together	The Kry	Rock	Mid/up	1
Love Can Build a Bridge	**The Judds**	**Ballad**	**Slow**	**10**
Somebody Make Me Laugh	Patti Austin	Ballad	Slow	10
Take My Hand	**Russ Taff**	**Folk/rock**	**Mid**	**9**
Undivided	First Call	Ballad trio	Slow	5
Wanna Be Loved	**DC Talk**	**Funky pop**	**Up**	**10**
We All Need	Aaron Jeoffrey	Pop	Mid/up	9

Title	Artist	Style	Tempo	Seeker-Sensitivity Rating
_____	_____	_____	_____	_____
_____	_____	_____	_____	_____
_____	_____	_____	_____	_____
_____	_____	_____	_____	_____

Worship Choruses

Title	Artist	Style	Tempo	Seeker-Sensitivity Rating
Faith, Hope, and Love Remain	_Willow Creek Music_	_Bluesy pop_	_Up_	_10_
How Good and Pleasant	Tommy Walker	Pop/rock	Up	5
Let the Walls Fall Down	Student Impact	Pop worship	Up	6
_____	_____	_____	_____	_____
_____	_____	_____	_____	_____
_____	_____	_____	_____	_____
_____	_____	_____	_____	_____

MOVIE CLIPS

Title: Forrest Gump

Topic: Love; Friendship

Description: Forrest, driving a shrimp boat, sees his friend Lieutenant Dan and jumps off the boat to greet him.

Start Time: 1:31:10

Start Cue: Shot of Forrest's hands steering the boat.

End Time: 1:32:50

End Cue: "That's my boat." Can end earlier.

Comments: _____

_____

_____

Title: Remember the Titans

Topic: Truth telling; Racism; Leadership; Friendship

Description: The Titans' two star defensive players, one white and one black, confront each other on their effort and leadership, respectively. They become best friends later in the movie.

Start Time: 0:29:09/DVD Ch. 9

Start Cue: Gary bumps into Julius. "Okay, man, listen. I'm Gary, you're Julius."

End Time: 0:30:48

End Cue: "Attitude reflects leadership, Captain."

Comments: The two scenes following this one are also very strong, and the three scenes combined, though long, would be a great example of leadership and breaking down racial barriers. Gary says "shiver push," and it sounds like profanity because it goes by fast, but it's not.

_____

_____

_____

Title: Remember the Titans

Topic: Racism; Friendship

Description: Julius comes to visit his friend Gary, who has been paralyzed in a car accident. The scene is a poignant example of friendship and breaking down racial barriers.

Start Time: 1:26:18/DVD Ch. 25

Start Cue: Julius walks into the hospital.

End Time: 1:29:25

End Cue: "Left side. Strong side." The boys clasp hands.

Comments: _____

_____

_____

Title: Shrek

Topic: Friendship; Truth telling

Description: Donkey confronts Shrek about being selfish and being mean to him. This clip has some great statements about friendship and forgiveness.

Start Time: 1:11:28/DVD Ch. 16

Start Cue: Shrek comes out of his house. "Donkey, what are you doing?"

End Time: 1:13:45

End Cue: "Friends?" "Friends."

Comments: One caution: Shrek refers to Donkey as a "jackass," which is technically true because he is a donkey, but it might be offensive to some. Also, Shrek goes into an outhouse.

_____

_____

_____

Title: _____

Topic: _____

Description: _____

Start Time: _____

Start Cue: _____

End Time: _____

End Cue: _____

Comments: _____

_____

_____

Control Issues

MESSAGE TITLES

❏ *Love of Another Kind:* Love Busters

_____

_____

_____

_____

Package Suggestion

Drama:
Let Me Go

Song:
Let Me Go

DRAMAS

Title	Tone	Characters	Topics
Hungry Children	Very serious	1 male, 1 female, 1 boy, 1 teenage girl	Abusive parenting; Anger; Control issues
Let Me Go	Mixed	2 females	Parenting; Letting go of adult children
The Plate Spinner	Humorous	5 males, 4 females, 1 narrator	Pace of life; Being in control
Speak for Yourself	Humorous	3 males, 3 females	Being an enabler; Insecurity
Terminal Visit	Serious	3 females	Resurrecting relationships; Family conflict

SONGS

Title	Artist	Style	Tempo	Seeker-Sensitivity Rating
In My Father's Hands	Susan Ashton	Folk pop	Mid	9
Let Me Go	Susan Ashton	Folk ballad	Slow	10

Title	Artist	Style	Tempo	Seeker-Sensitivity Rating
_____	_____	_____	_____	_____
_____	_____	_____	_____	_____
_____	_____	_____	_____	_____
_____	_____	_____	_____	_____

Worship Choruses

*No worship choruses specifically about control issues: See _Lordship of Christ_ and _Obeying God_ for ideas.

Title	Artist	Style	Tempo	Seeker-Sensitivity Rating
_____	_____	_____	_____	_____
_____	_____	_____	_____	_____
_____	_____	_____	_____	_____
_____	_____	_____	_____	_____

MOVIE CLIPS

Title: Shadowlands

Topic: Control issues; Intimacy

Description: Joy confronts Jack with the fact that he has set his world up so that nobody can touch him—he has blocked intimacy by surrounding himself with people he can control.

Start Time: 1:05:55

Start Cue: "So what do you do here . . . think great thoughts?"

End Time: 1:07:37

End Cue: "You just don't like it. Nor do I."

Comments: _____
_____

Title: _____

Topic: _____

Description: _____

Start Time: _____

Start Cue: _____

End Time: _____

End Cue: _____

Comments: _____
_____

—Draining Relationships—

MESSAGE TITLES

- ❑ *The Lost Art of Loving:* People Who Love Too Much
- ❑ *Love of Another Kind:* Loving Hard-to-Love People
- ❑ *Restoring Weary Souls:* Building Better Boundaries

DRAMAS

Title	Tone	Characters	Topics
The Angry Woman	Serious	2 males, 3 females, 1 narrator	The roots of anger
Best Friends	Humorous	2 males, 2 females	Friendship; Insecurity; Needy people
Brother's Keeper	Serious	3 males	Unhealthy dependencies
Just a Little Different	Mixed, mostly serious	1 male, 2 females	Loving the unlovely; The story behind people we don't like
Kind of Rare	Mixed	3 males, 3 females	Confronting in love; Friendship; Marriage; Character flaws
No Thanks Giving	Serious	3 females	Truth telling; Family dynamics
Parents on the Sidelines	Humorous	2 males, 2 females	Evangelism
Six Happy Hearts	Mixed	6 males or females	Laughter; A sour spirit affects others
Watching from the Window	Serious	1 female, 1 child	Stress of life; Challenge of motherhood; Draining relationships
What Are Friends For?	Serious	1 male, 2 females	Friendship; Truth telling

SONGS

*No songs specifically about draining relationships. Look at **Our Value to God**, **Compassion**, *and* **Relational Conflict**.*

Title	Artist	Style	Tempo	Seeker-Sensitivity Rating

Worship Choruses

Title	Artist	Style	Tempo	Seeker-Sensitivity Rating

MOVIE CLIPS

Title: _____

Topic: _____

Description: _____

Start Time: _____

Start Cue: _____

End Time: _____

End Cue: _____

Comments: _____

_____

_____

Family Relationships

Decay of the Family

Might also include: *Broken Families, Dysfunctional Families*
See also: **Divorce**

MESSAGE TITLES

❏ *Defining Family Values:* Endangered Values
❏ *Facing the Family Challenge:* Fragile: Handle with Care

Package Suggestion

Drama:
Richard: 1992

Song:
Time to Return

DRAMAS

Title	Tone	Characters	Topics
All Gummed Up	Serious	1 male, 1 female, 1 offstage male voice	Adultery; Dealing with past hurts; The pain of lies
Hungry Children	Very serious	1 male, 1 female, 1 boy, 1 teenage girl	Abusive parenting; Anger; Control issues
I Know What You Want	Serious	2 males, 2 females	God's love; Dysfunctional families
The Intruder	Serious	1 male, 1 female	Self-image; Destructive parenting; God's love in spite of failure
Missing	Serious	3 males, 1 female	Generational barriers; The church's failure to reach Gen-X
No Thanks Giving	Serious	3 females	Truth telling; Family dynamics
Richard: 1992	Serious	2 males, 1 female	Anger; Rebellion; Decay of the family
Straight-Jacketed	Serious	1 male	Bondage to past and to sin; Anger at God
Tired of Trying	Serious	1 male, 2 females	Dealing with the anger of others; Confronting injustice

Title	Tone	Characters	Topics

SONGS

*Many of the above dramas leave the audience in a tender, vulnerable place. Responding with a song of **Healing** or **God's Love**, such as "A Place to Call Home," often works well.*

Title	Artist	Style	Tempo	Seeker-Sensitivity Rating
Cat's in the Cradle	Harry Chapin; Ricky Skaggs	Folk	Mid	10
Time to Return	*Willow Creek Music*	*Ballad*	*Slow*	*7*

Worship Choruses

Title	Artist	Style	Tempo	Seeker-Sensitivity Rating

MOVIE CLIPS

Title: City Slickers

Topic: Dysfunctional families; Friendship

Description: Three friends share the best and worst days of their lives.

Start Time: 1:12:45

Start Cue: "All right, I got one."

End Time: 1:14:50

End Cue: "Same day."

Comments: Could start earlier, but Billy Crystal swears briefly during his worst-day description.

Title: Dead Poet's Society

Topic: Destructive parenting

Description: Todd, a boarding school student, shares with a friend that his parents sent him the same birthday present they gave him the previous years. Illustrates disconnected parenting.

Start Time: 1:05:40

Start Cue: "Todd?"

End Time: 1:07:30

End Cue: "You'll get another one next year."

Comments: _____

Title: Forrest Gump

Topic: Child abuse; Bondage to the past

Description: Jenny and Forrest walk by the house where Jenny was abused as a child. She throws rocks at it.

Start Time: 1:45:30

Start Cue: After "Jenny, most of the times was real quiet."

End Time: 1:46:50

End Cue: "Sometimes, there just aren't enough rocks."

Comments: _____

Title: Parenthood

Topic: Parenting; Absent fathers

Description: Funny, bittersweet scene where young Gil is taken to a baseball game by his father and then left with an usher. We find out it's actually a combination of memories of his strained childhood.

Start Time: 0:00:05

Start Cue: Start at fade-in. This is the opening scene.

End Time: 0:02:28

End Cue: "Strong, happy, confident kids."

Comments: Profanity immediately follows cutoff point.

Title: The Story of Us

Topic: Marriage; Family conflict

Description: A typical suburban family sits down to dinner and shares the high and low points of their day, a family tradition. When the kids leave, it's clear the parents are putting on a front for the kids regarding their marriage, which is in trouble.

Start Time: 0:02:47

Start Cue: "Now, high/low—who wants to go first?"

End Time: 0:04:30

End Cue: "Just as long as the kids see us leaving together and coming home together."

Comments: This is sort of a bittersweet clip. The "high/low" idea is a great one, which many families have adopted because of this movie. But it's a sad clip because such a seemingly stable family is really falling apart.

_____
_____

Title: _____

Topic: _____

Description: _____

Start Time: _____

Start Cue: _____

End Time: _____

End Cue: _____

Comments: _____

Destructive Parenting

MESSAGE TITLES

❏ Fixing Broken Relationships
❏ *Facing the Family Challenge:* Fragile: Handle with Care
❏ *Parenthood:* Mistakes Parents Make

Package Suggestion

Drama:
Hungry Children

Song:
Peace Be Still

_____
_____
_____
_____

DRAMAS

Title	Tone	Characters	Topics
Expectations of the Expecting	Mixed	1 male, 1 female	Parenting; Affirming personality differences
Hungry Children	Very serious	1 male, 1 female, 1 boy, 1 teenage girl	Abusive parenting; Anger; Control issues
The Intruder	Serious	1 male, 1 female	Self-image; Destructive parenting; God's love in spite of failure
Reason Enough	Mixed, mostly serious	1 male, 1 female	Importance of faith grounded in reason
Richard: 1992	Serious	2 males, 1 female	Anger; Rebellion; Decay of the family
Tired of Trying	Serious	1 male, 2 females	Dealing with the anger of others; Confronting injustice
Wonderfully Made	Serious	2 males, 2 females, 1 narrator	Affirming a child's uniqueness

SONGS

*For more songs for this topic, see **God's Love**, **Healing**, and **Our Value to God**.*

Title	Artist	Style	Tempo	Seeker-Sensitivity Rating
Peace Be Still	Al Denson	Ballad	Slow	10

Worship Choruses

Title	Artist	Style	Tempo	Seeker-Sensitivity Rating

MOVIE CLIPS

Title: City Slickers

Topic: Dysfunctional families; Friendship

Description: Three friends share the best and worst days of their lives.

Start Time: 1:12:45

Start Cue: "All right, I got one."

End Time: 1:14:50

End Cue: "Same day."

Comments: Could start earlier, but Billy Crystal swears briefly during his worst-day description.

Title: Dead Poet's Society

Topic: Destructive parenting

Description: Todd, a boarding school student, shares with a friend that his parents sent him the same birthday present they gave him the previous years. Illustrates disconnected parenting.

Start Time: 1:05:40

Start Cue: "Todd?"

End Time: 1:07:30

End Cue: "You'll get another one next year."

Comments: _____

Title: Forrest Gump

Topic: Child abuse; Bondage to the past

Description: Jenny and Forrest walk by the house where Jenny was abused as a child. She throws rocks at it.

Start Time: 1:45:30

Start Cue: After "Jenny, most of the times was real quiet."

End Time: 1:46:50

End Cue: "Sometimes, there just aren't enough rocks."

Comments: _____

Title: Indiana Jones and the Last Crusade

Topic: Father-son relationships

Description: Indiana Jones mildly confronts his father about the lack of a relationship between them.

Start Time: 1:13:45

Start Cue: "Remember the last time we had a quiet drink?"

End Time: 1:15:05

End Cue: "I can't think of anything."

Comments: Conversation is over a drink. May be offensive to some churches.

Title: Kramer vs. Kramer

Topic: The effect of divorce on children

Description: Dustin Hoffman's character reads a letter to his little boy from Meryl Streep's character, telling him why she left. The effects on the child are what is left after divorce.

Start Time: 0:21:50

Start Cue: Just before "Hey, Billy!"

End Time: 0:23:45

End Cue: Scene ends with Billy staring at the TV.

Comments:

Title: Parenthood

Topic: Parenting; Absent fathers

Description: Funny, bittersweet scene where young Gil is taken to a baseball game by his father and then left with an usher. We find out it's actually a combination of memories of his strained childhood.

Start Time: 0:00:05

Start Cue: Start at fade-in. This is the opening scene.

End Time: 0:02:28

End Cue: "Strong, happy, confident kids."

Comments: Profanity immediately follows cutoff point.

Title: Parenthood

Topic: Controlling parents; Unrealistic expectations of children

Description: Funny clip about parents' unrealistic expectations of their kids. Two parents lecture their daughter about not putting enough effort into her studies. At the end, we realize she's three years old.

Start Time: 0:12:40

Start Cue: "Oh listen, Julie got 1291..."

End Time: 0:13:45

End Cue: "That's all I ask."

Comments:

Title: Searching for Bobby Fischer

Topic: Fatherhood; Failure; Destructive parenting

Description: Eight-year-old Josh loses a chess match, and his dad angrily confronts him about losing. Illustrates a dad who has too much invested in his son's success.

Start Time: 1:06:30

Start Cue: Shot of clock tower. "Seven moves" is first line.

End Time: 1:08:20

End Cue: "Sorry."

Comments: _____
_____

Title: _____

Topic: _____

Description: _____

Start Time: _____

Start Cue: _____

End Time: _____

End Cue: _____

Comments: _____
_____
_____

Family Conflict

See also: **Relational Conflict**

MESSAGE TITLES

❑ Fixing Broken Relationships
❑ *Facing the Family Challenge:* Fragile: Handle with Care

Package Suggestion

Drama:
Terminal Visit

Song:
Beyond Justice to Mercy

_____
_____
_____
_____
_____

DRAMAS

Title	Tone	Characters	Topics
Anything but Religion	Mixed, mostly serious	2 males, 2 females	Denominational differences; Families alienated because of religion
Brother's Keeper	Serious	3 males	Unhealthy dependencies
Christmas Lite	Serious	3 males (2 teens/preteens), 1 female	Christmas; Faith; Family under stress; Dealing with crisis
Distancing	Mixed, mostly serious	1 male, 1 female	Good marriages take work; Demands of life
Finding Evidence	Serious	2 males, 1 female	Trust; Jumping to conclusions
Grandma's Recipe	Serious	1 male, 2 females, 2 children	Family struggle during holidays
Hungry Children	Very serious	1 male, 1 female, 1 boy, 1 teenage girl	Abusive parenting; Anger; Control issues
The Intruder	Serious	1 male, 1 female	Self-image; Destructive parenting; God's love in spite of failure
The Luncheon	Serious	3 females	Mother-daughter conflict; Honesty in relationships
Misjudged Love	Serious	2 males, 1 female	Homosexuality; AIDS; Father-son relationships
Missing	Serious	3 males, 1 female	Generational barriers; The church's failure to reach Gen-X
No Thanks Giving	Serious	3 females	Truth telling; Family dynamics
Remembrances	Serious	1 male, 1 female	Parent-child relationships; Forgiveness
Richard: 1992	Serious	2 males, 1 female	Anger; Rebellion; Decay of the family
Sister Act	Serious	2 females	Dysfunctional families; Wounds
Terminal Visit	Serious	3 females	Resurrecting relationships; Family conflict
Tired of Trying	Serious	1 male, 2 females	Dealing with the anger of others; Confronting injustice
Unacceptable	Mixed	2 females (1 older teen)	Dealing with adolescence
Watching from the Window	Serious	1 female, 1 child	Stress of life; Challenge of motherhood; Draining relationships
_____	_____	_____	_____
_____	_____	_____	_____
_____	_____	_____	_____

SONGS

Title	Artist	Style	Tempo	Seeker-Sensitivity Rating
Beyond Justice to Mercy	**Susan Ashton**	**Ballad**	**Slow**	**10**
Bridge between Two Hearts	Bob Carlisle	Pop	Up	9
Healing Song	Curt Coffield	Ballad, in 3	Slow/mid	7
The Last Song	Elton John	Ballad	Slow	10
The Living Years	Mike & the Mechanics	Pop	Mid/up	10
Love Conquers All	Pam Thum	Pop	Up	10
Meet in the Middle	Diamond Rio	Country	Mid/up	10
Sticks and Stones	Wes King	Rock/pop	Up	9
That's What Love Is For	Amy Grant	Power ballad	Slow	10

Worship Choruses

Title	Artist	Style	Tempo	Seeker-Sensitivity Rating
Healing Song	Curt Coffield	Ballad, in 3	Slow/mid	7
Let the Walls Fall Down	Student Impact	Pop worship	Up	6

MOVIE CLIPS

Title: Hoosiers

Topic: Unconditional love; Forgiveness

Description: Dennis Hopper's character, a recovering alcoholic, is in the hospital drying out. His son visits him and tells him he loves him.

Start Time: 1:30:15

Start Cue: "No school this small . . ."

End Time: 1:32:30

End Cue: "Anyway, no school this small has ever been in the state championship!"

Comments: Needs some setup for those who haven't seen the movie.

Title: October Sky

Topic: Parent-child relationships; Father-son relationships

Description: Homer Hikam, a young aspiring rocket scientist comes to his dad's coal mine to talk to him. His dad makes a sarcastic comment about Homer meeting his "hero," Dr. Wernher von Braun. Homer speaks inspiring words to his dad about the man he is and, without saying the words, lets his dad know that he is Homer's real hero.

Start Time: 1:33:00

Start Cue: "Will you let me out?" Homer runs to meet his dad.

End Time: 1:35:08

End Cue: Homer's dad turns his mining light on as he watches Homer walk away.

Comments: Can be ended sooner than the end cue listed above. It can also be extended to show Homer's rocket launch, for which his dad unexpectedly shows up.

Title: The Story of Us

Topic: Marriage; Family conflict

Description: A typical suburban family sits down to dinner and shares the high and low points of their day, a family tradition. When the kids leave, it's clear the parents are putting on a front for the kids regarding their marriage, which is in trouble.

Start Time: 0:02:47

Start Cue: "Now, high/low—who wants to go first?"

End Time: 0:04:30

End Cue: "Just as long as the kids see us leaving together and coming home together."

Comments: This is sort of a bittersweet clip. The "high/low" idea is a great one, which many families have adopted because of this movie. But it's a sad clip because such a seemingly stable family is really falling apart.

Title: _____

Topic: _____

Description: _____

Start Time: _____

Start Cue: _____

End Time: _____

End Cue: _____

Comments: _____

Family Relationships, General

MESSAGE TITLES

- ❏ *Facing New Realities:* The Post-Walton Family
- ❏ *Making Life Work:* Forge Strong Families
- ❏ *The Relationship You've Always Wanted:* The Relatives Are Coming!
- ❏ **Defining Family Values:** Origin of Values • Transmitting Values • Endangered Values
- ❏ **Facing the Family Challenge:** Fragile: Handle with Care • Traits of a Healthy Family • Forming a Spiritual Foundation • The Future of the Family
- ❏ **Turning Houses into Homes:** The Home as a Filling Station • The Home as a Training Center • The Home as a Trauma Center • The Home as a Seminary

DRAMAS

Title	Tone	Characters	Topics
The Best Gift	Humorous, touching	3 males, 4 females	Christmas; Gift-giving
Buy One, Get One Free	Mixed, moving	1 male, 1 female	The joy of giving
Changes	Mixed, mostly serious	2 males, 2 females	Reparenting parents; Family; Aging parents
Character Test	Mixed, moving	2 males, 1 female	Promptings from God; Obedience; Power of encouragement
Christmas Story	Mixed; End is moving	4 males, 4 females, 12-year-old boy, 10-year-old girl	Christmas; Family
Distancing	Mixed, mostly serious	1 male, 1 female	Good marriages take work; Demands of life
Doomed	Humorous	1 male, 1 female, 2 children	Thanksgiving
The Family Meeting (Parts 1 and 2)	Humorous	1 male, 1 female, 3 children	Family; Discipline; Parenting

Title	Tone	Characters	Topics
Family Snapshots—Take I	Humorous	3 males, 2 females, 1 junior high boy	Family; Communication
Family Snapshots—Take II	Humorous	2 males, 2 females, 1 junior high boy	Families; Values; Priorities
Family Snapshots—Take III	Mixed, touching	1 male, 1 female	Parent-child relationships; Helping kids through hard times
Family Snapshots—Take IV	Serious	2 males, 3 females, 1 junior high boy	Family; Self-sacrifice
First Thing First	Humorous	1 male, 1 female, 1 female infant	New parents; Balancing children and marriage
Fishin'	Mixed, touching	2 males	Expressing positive emotions; Father-son relationships
For Better or Worse—Part VI	Mixed	3 males, 3 females	Family; Marriage
Hungry Children	Very serious	1 male, 1 female, 1 boy, 1 teenage girl	Abusive parenting; Anger; Control issues
I Always Will	Mixed, very moving	3 males, 3 females	Father's Day; Father-daughter relationships
I Know What You Want	Serious	2 males, 2 females	God's love; Dysfunctional families
If These Walls Could Speak	Serious, touching	3 females	Mother's Day; Family traditions
The Intruder	Serious	1 male, 1 female	Self-image; Destructive parenting; God's love in spite of failure
Masterpiece	Mixed, touching	1 male, 1 female, 2 teenage females	Self-esteem; Parenting
No Thanks Giving	Serious	3 females	Truth telling; Family dynamics
Reflections	Mixed	1 male, 2 females, 2 children either males or females	Motherhood
Remembrances	Serious	1 male, 1 female	Parent-child relationships; Forgiveness
Sister Act	Serious	2 females	Dysfunctional families; Wounds
The Speculators	Humorous	2 males, 1 female	Risk taking; Missed opportunities
Suit Yourself	Humorous	1 male, 2 females	Parenting; Letting kids make their own decisions
Thanks for Listening	Humorous	1 male, 1 female, 1 male and 1 female teenager	Family; Listening
Wings	Mixed	2 males, 1 female, 1 teen, 1 preteen	Christmas; Family
Worth Keeping	Mixed, touching	1 male, 2 females	The nobility of motherhood; Single parenting

Title	Tone	Characters	Topics

SONGS

Title	Artist	Style	Tempo	Seeker-Sensitivity Rating
Cat's in the Cradle	**Harry Chapin; Ricky Skaggs**	**Folk**	**Mid**	**10**
Heirlooms	Amy Grant	Ballad	Slow	8
How Could I Ask for More?	**Cindy Morgan**	**Piano ballad**	**Slow**	**9**
I Want to Be Just Like You	**Phillips, Craig and Dean**	**MOR**	**Mid/slow**	**9**
If I Had Only Known	Reba McEntire	Ballad	Slow	10
Let Me Go	Susan Ashton	Folk ballad	Slow	10
The Living Years	Mike & the Mechanics	Pop	Mid/up	10
Only Here for a Little While	Billy Dean	Country	Mid/up	10

Worship Choruses

Title	Artist	Style	Tempo	Seeker-Sensitivity Rating
Faith, Hope, and Love Remain	*Willow Creek Music*	*Bluesy pop*	*Up*	*10*
For the Beauty of the Earth	*Willow Creek Music*	*Worship ballad*	*Slow*	*5*

MOVIE CLIPS

Title: 8 Seconds

Topic: Regret; Communicating love

Description: A father, whose son has recently died in a rodeo accident, breaks down in remorse over not telling his son that he loved him. This short clip probably needs to be set up.

Start Time: 1:27:22

Start Cue: Pallbearers carry the casket out of the church.

End Time: 1:28:44

End Cue: The mother puts her hands on the father's shoulders.

Comments: _____

_____

_____

_____

Title: Dad

Topic: Parenting; Father-son relationships

Description: Ted Danson and Jack Lemmon play a father and son. Lemmon is dying in a hospital bed, and they have a very poignant exchange, ending with Danson crawling into bed with his dad.

Start Time: 1:46:20

Start Cue: "How you feeling?"

End Time: 1:50:35

End Cue: "I must have done something right." End after wide shot.

Comments: _____

_____

_____

_____

Title: Father of the Bride

Topic: Parenthood; Father-daughter relationships

Description: Steve Martin's character plays basketball with his daughter as "My Girl" plays in the background. Shows the warmth and fun of their relationship.

Start Time: 0:14:55

Start Cue: "Suppose you're not in the mood for a little one-on-one?"

End Time: 0:17:00

End Cue: Steve Martin's character and his daughter walk off together.

Comments: _____

_____

_____

_____

_____

Title: Parenthood

Topic: Parenting; Absent fathers

Description: Funny, bittersweet scene where young Gil is taken to a baseball game by his father and then left with an usher. We find out it's actually a combination of memories of his strained childhood.

Start Time: 0:00:05

Start Cue: Start at fade-in. This is the opening scene.

End Time: 0:02:28

End Cue: "Strong, happy, confident kids."

Comments: Profanity immediately follows cutoff point.

_____
_____
_____
_____

Title: The Story of Us

Topic: Marriage; Family conflict

Description: A typical suburban family sits down to dinner and shares the high and low points of their day, a family tradition. When the kids leave, it's clear the parents are putting on a front for the kids regarding their marriage, which is in trouble.

Start Time: 0:02:47

Start Cue: "Now, high/low—who wants to go first?"

End Time: 0:04:30

End Cue: "Just as long as the kids see us leaving together and coming home together."

Comments: This is sort of a bittersweet clip. The "high/low" idea is a great one, which many families have adopted because of this movie. But it's a sad clip because such a seemingly stable family is really falling apart.

_____
_____
_____
_____

Title: _____

Topic: _____

Description: _____

Start Time: _____

Start Cue: _____

End Time: _____

End Cue: _____

Comments: _____
_____
_____
_____

Generation Gap

See also: **Relational Conflict**

MESSAGE TITLES

- ❏ Bridging the Generation Gap
- ❏ Bridging the Generational Divide
- ❏ Intergenerational Community
- ❏ *Understanding the Times:* The '60s

_____

_____

_____

_____

_____

_____

_____

DRAMAS

Title	Tone	Characters	Topics
Caught in the Middle	Humorous	1 male, 2 females (1 teen)	Raising teenagers in today's world; The challenge of parenting
Finding Evidence	Serious	2 males, 1 female	Trust; Jumping to conclusions
Missing	Serious	3 males, 1 female	Generational barriers; The church's failure to reach Gen-X
Richard: 1968	Mixed	2 males, 2 females	Youthful idealism; Changing societal values; Generation gap; The '60s

SONGS

Title	Artist	Style	Tempo	Seeker-Sensitivity Rating
Art in Me	Jars of Clay	Alternative rock	Mid/up	9
The Living Years	Mike & the Mechanics	Pop	Mid/up	10
When We Fail Love	**Grover Levy**	**Piano ballad**	**Slow**	**9**

Worship Choruses

Title	Artist	Style	Tempo	Seeker-Sensitivity Rating
Healing Song	Curt Coffield	Ballad, in 3	Slow/mid	7

MOVIE CLIPS

Title: _____

Topic: _____

Description: _____

Start Time: _____

Start Cue: _____

End Time: _____

End Cue: _____

Comments: _____

_____

Parent-Child Relationships

This refers both to relationships between parents and their adult children and to parents with children still in the home. This deals less with the challenges and "to do's" of parenthood and more with the relationships.

MESSAGE TITLES

❑ The Launching Pad of Loving
❑ Leaving a Living Legacy
❑ Phantom Fathers
❑ Unforgettable Fathers
❑ *Facing the Family Challenge:* The Future of the Family
❑ *Fifth Commandment:* Honor Your Parents
❑ *Parenthood:* Reparenting Parents

DRAMAS

Title	Tone	Characters	Topics
Caught in the Middle	Humorous	1 male, 2 females (1 teen)	Raising teenagers in today's world; The challenge of parenting
Changes	Mixed, mostly serious	2 males, 2 females	Reparenting parents; Family; Aging parents
Definitely Safe	Serious, heartwarming	2 males, 1 female	Father's Day; Prodigal son; Unconditional love
Empty Nest		1 male, 1 female	Empty nesters; Parenting
Family Snapshots—Take I	Humorous	3 males, 2 females, 1 junior high boy	Family; Communication
Family Snapshots—Take III	Mixed, touching	1 male, 1 female	Parent-child relationships; Helping kids through hard times
Finding Evidence	Serious	2 males, 1 female	Trust; Jumping to conclusions
Fishin'	Mixed, touching	2 males	Expressing positive emotions; Father-son relationships
Giving a Blessing Vignettes	Mixed	2 males	Father's Day; Parenting; Giving blessings

Title	Tone	Characters	Topics
I Always Will	Mixed, very moving	3 males, 3 females	Father's Day; Father-daughter relationships
In the Dark	Serious	1 male, 1 female	Death of a child; Grief
The Intruder	Serious	1 male, 1 female	Self-image; Destructive parenting; God's love in spite of failure
Labor of Love	Mixed, mostly serious	2 males, 1 female	Finding a career that fits; Sacrifices parents make for the next generation
Let Me Go	Mixed	2 females	Parenting; Letting go of adult children
Lucky Day at the Ballpark	Mixed	2 males, 1 boy	Father's Day; Proper priorities
The Luncheon	Serious	3 females	Mother-daughter conflict; Honesty in relationships
Masterpiece	Mixed, touching	1 male, 1 female, 2 teenage females	Self-esteem; Parenting
Misjudged Love	Serious	2 males, 1 female	Homosexuality; AIDS; Father-son relationships
Missing	Serious	3 males, 1 female	Generational barriers; The church's failure to reach Generation X
Mixed Signals	Mixed	1 male, 1 boy	Encouragement; Fathers; Priorities
Model Behavior	Humorous	1 male, 3 boys (8-year-old, 12-year-old, and 16-year-old)	Fathering; The shortness of the parenting years
A Mother's Day	Mixed	1 male, 2 females	Mother's Day
The Night Light	Mixed	2 females	Mother's Day; Parenting
No Thanks Giving	Serious	3 females	Truth telling; Family dynamics
The Piano Recital	Humorous	2 males, 4 females, 2 children	Singleness; Adult parent-child tension
Playing God	Serious	1 male	Aging parent; Right to die
Quality Time	Serious	1 male, 1 female, 2 teenage girls	Fatherhood; Workaholism
Reflections	Mixed	1 male, 2 females, 2 children	Motherhood
Remembrances	Serious	1 male, 1 female	Parent-child relationships; Forgiveness
Richard: 1992	Serious	2 males, 1 female	Anger; Rebellion; Decay of the family
A Second Chance	Mixed, more serious	3 males, 1 female	Decision making; Father-son relationships
Self-list Giving	Mixed	2 males, 2 females	Disappointment
Stepping In	Touching	1 male, 2 females	Caring for parents; Aging

Title	Tone	Characters	Topics
Suit Yourself	Humorous	1 male, 2 females	Parenting; Letting kids make their own decisions
This Side of Heaven	Touching	1 male, 2 females	Growing old; Taking care of aging parents
Time Flies	Mixed	2 males, 1 female, 1 young girl	Honoring parents
Unacceptable	Mixed	2 females (1 older teen)	Dealing with adolescence
Wings	Mixed	2 males, 1 female, 1 teen, 1 preteen	Christmas; Family
Worth Keeping	Mixed, touching	1 male, 2 females	The nobility of motherhood; Single parenting
You and Me	Mixed	2 females	Mother's Day; Family; Rebuilding after divorce; Navigating life's challenges

SONGS

Title	Artist	Style	Tempo	Seeker-Sensitivity Rating
Because You Loved Me	Celine Dion	Pop ballad	Slow	10
Butterfly Kisses	Bob Carlisle	Pop ballad	Slow	10
Cat's in the Cradle	**Harry Chapin; Ricky Skaggs**	**Folk**	**Mid**	**10**
I Want to Be Just Like You	**Phillips, Craig and Dean**	**MOR**	**Mid/slow**	**9**
The Last Song	Elton John	Ballad	Slow	10
Let Me Go	Susan Ashton	Folk ballad	Slow	10
The Living Years	Mike & the Mechanics	Pop	Mid/up	10
Nothing You Could Do	*Willow Creek Music*	*Ballad*	*Slow*	*10*
When You Come Home	**Mark Schultz**	**Country-tinged ballad**	**Slow/mid**	**9**

Worship Choruses

Title	Artist	Style	Tempo	Seeker-Sensitivity Rating
_____	_____	_____	_____	_____
_____	_____	_____	_____	_____
_____	_____	_____	_____	_____

MOVIE CLIPS

Title: 8 Seconds

Topic: Regret; Communicating love

Description: A father, whose son has recently died in a rodeo accident, breaks down in remorse over not telling his son that he loved him. This short clip probably needs to be set up.

Start Time: 1:27:22

Start Cue: Pallbearers carry the casket out of the church.

End Time: 1:28:44

End Cue: The mother puts her hands on the father's shoulders.

Comments: _____

_____

Title: Dad

Topic: Parenting; Father-son relationships

Description: Ted Danson and Jack Lemmon play a father and son. Lemmon is dying in a hospital bed, and they have a very poignant exchange, ending with Danson crawling into bed with his dad.

Start Time: 1:46:20

Start Cue: "How you feeling?"

End Time: 1:50:35

End Cue: "I must have done something right." End after wide shot.

Comments: _____

_____

Title: Dead Poet's Society

Topic: Destructive parenting

Description: Todd, a boarding school student, shares with a friend that his parents sent him the same birthday present they gave him the previous years. Illustrates disconnected parenting.

Start Time: 1:05:40

Start Cue: "Todd?"

End Time: 1:07:30

End Cue: "You'll get another one next year."

Comments: _____

_____

Title:	Father of the Bride
Topic:	Parenthood; Letting go of adult children
Description:	Steve Martin's character's daughter tells him she's getting married, and he sees her as a little girl telling him. Very short clip.
Start Time:	0:09:30
Start Cue:	"I met somebody in Rome."
End Time:	0:10:45
End Cue:	Little girl says, "We're getting married."
Comments:	Might be used in conjunction with the song "Watercolour Ponies" by Wayne Watson.

Title:	Father of the Bride
Topic:	Parenthood; Father-daughter relationships
Description:	Steve Martin's character plays basketball with his daughter as "My Girl" plays in the background. Shows the warmth and fun of their relationship.
Start Time:	0:14:55
Start Cue:	"Suppose you're not in the mood for a little one-on-one?"
End Time:	0:17:00
End Cue:	Steve Martin's character and his daughter walk off together.
Comments:	

Title:	Indiana Jones and the Last Crusade
Topic:	Father-son relationships
Description:	Indiana Jones mildly confronts his father about the lack of a relationship between them.
Start Time:	1:13:45
Start Cue:	"Remember the last time we had a quiet drink?"
End Time:	1:15:05
End Cue:	"I can't think of anything."
Comments:	Conversation is over a drink. May be offensive to some churches.

Title:	October Sky
Topic:	Parent-child relationships; Father-son relationships
Description:	Homer Hikam, a young aspiring rocket scientist comes to his dad's coal mine to talk to him. His dad makes a sarcastic comment about Homer meeting his "hero," Dr. Wernher von Braun. Homer speaks inspiring words to his dad about the man he is and, without saying the words, lets his dad know that he is Homer's real hero.
Start Time:	1:33:00
Start Cue:	"Will you let me out?" Homer runs to meet his dad.
End Time:	1:35:08
End Cue:	Homer's dad turns his mining light on as he watches Homer walk away.
Comments:	Can be ended sooner than the end cue listed above. It can also be extended to show Homer's rocket launch, for which his dad unexpectedly shows up.

Title:	Parenthood
Topic:	Parenting; Absent fathers
Description:	Funny, bittersweet scene where young Gil is taken to a baseball game by his father and then left with an usher. We find out it's actually a combination of memories of his strained childhood.
Start Time:	0:00:05
Start Cue:	Start at fade-in. This is the opening scene.
End Time:	0:02:28
End Cue:	"Strong, happy, confident kids."
Comments:	Profanity immediately follows cutoff point.

Title:	
Topic:	
Description:	
Start Time:	
Start Cue:	
End Time:	
End Cue:	
Comments:	

Parenting

Refers primarily, though not exclusively, to parents with children still in the home.

MESSAGE TITLES

- ❑ Formula for a Successful Family (Ephesians 6:1–4)
- ❑ Mindful Motherhood
- ❑ *Making Life Work:* Forge Strong Families
- ❑ *Making the Most of Your Marriage:* . . . And Then We Had Kids
- ❑ **Parenthood:** To Be or Not to Be • Raising Whole Children • Affirming Each Child's Uniqueness • Mistakes Parents Make • Reparenting Parents
- ❑ **Turning Houses into Homes:** The Home as a Filling Station • The Home as a Training Center • The Home as a Trauma Center • The Home as a Seminary

Package Suggestion

Drama:
I Always Will

Song:
Nothing You Could Do

DRAMAS

Title	Tone	Characters	Topics
Baby Talk	Humorous	2 males, 2 females	Decision making; Parenting; Decision to have children
Caught in the Middle	Humorous	1 male, 2 females (1 teen)	Raising teenagers in today's world; The challenge of parenting
Distancing	Mixed, mostly serious	1 male, 1 female	Good marriages take work; Demands of life
Empty Nest		1 male, 1 female	Empty nesters; Parenting
Expectations of the Expecting	Mixed	1 male, 1 female	Parenting; Affirming personality differences
The Family Meeting (Parts 1 and 2)	Humorous	1 male, 1 female, 3 children	Family; Discipline; Parenting
Fat Chance	Mixed, mostly humorous	1 female	Parenting
Finding Evidence	Serious	2 males, 1 female	Trust; Jumping to conclusions
First Thing First	Humorous	1 male, 1 female, 1 female infant	New parents; Balancing children and marriage
Giving a Blessing Vignettes	Mixed	2 males	Father's Day; Parenting; Giving Blessings
Hungry Children	Very serious	1 male, 1 female, 1 boy, 1 teenage girl	Abusive parenting; Anger; Control issues
I Always Will	Mixed, very moving	3 males, 3 females	Father's Day; Father-daughter relationships
I Know What You Want	Serious	2 males, 2 females	God's love; Dysfunctional families
In the Dark	Serious	1 male, 1 female	Death of a child; Grief
The Intruder	Serious	1 male, 1 female	Self-image; Destructive parenting; God's love in spite of failure
Just the Two of Us	Serious	1 male, 2 females	Infertility; Unanswered prayer
Labor of Love	Mixed, mostly serious	2 males, 1 female	Finding a career that fits; Sacrifices parents make for the next generation
Let Me Go	Mixed	2 females	Parenting; Letting go of adult children
Little What's His Face	Mixed	3 males, 3 females	Christmas; Parenting
Lucky Day at the Ballpark	Mixed	2 males, 1 boy	Father's Day; Proper priorities
Masterpiece	Mixed, touching	1 male, 1 female, 2 teenage females	Self-esteem; Parenting
Misjudged Love	Serious	2 males, 1 female	Homosexuality; AIDS; Father-son relationships

Title	Tone	Characters	Topics
Mixed Signals	Mixed	1 male, 1 boy	Encouragement; Fathers; Priorities
Model Behavior	Humorous	1 male, 3 boys (8-year-old, 12-year-old, and 16-year-old)	Fathering; The shortness of the parenting years
The Night Light	Mixed	2 females	Mother's Day; Parenting
No More Womb	Mixed	1 male, 1 female	State of the world; Fear of the unknown
On Track	Serious	2 males, 1 female	Forcing people into molds; Character building
One Day at the Zoo	Humorous	1 narrator, 3 males, 2 females, and some offstage voices	Fatherhood
Out of Control	Humorous	2 males, 1 female	Fatherhood; Parenting
Quality Time	Serious	1 male, 1 female, 2 teenage girls	Fatherhood; Workaholism
Reflections	Mixed	1 male, 2 females, 2 children	Motherhood
Remembrances	Serious	1 male, 1 female	Parent-child relationships; Forgiveness
Suit Yourself	Humorous	1 male, 2 females	Parenting; Letting kids make their own decisions
Unacceptable	Mixed	2 females (1 older teen)	Dealing with adolescence
Wings	Mixed	2 males, 1 female, 1 teen, 1 preteen	Christmas; Family
Wonderfully Made	Serious	2 males, 2 females, 1 narrator	Affirming a child's uniqueness
Worth Keeping	Mixed, touching	1 male, 2 females	The nobility of motherhood; Single parenting
_____	_____	_____	_____
_____	_____	_____	_____
_____	_____	_____	_____
_____	_____	_____	_____
_____	_____	_____	_____
_____	_____	_____	_____

SONGS

Title	Artist	Style	Tempo	Seeker-Sensitivity Rating
Because You Loved Me	Celine Dion	Pop ballad	Slow	10
Butterfly Kisses	Bob Carlisle	Pop ballad	Slow	10
Cat's in the Cradle	**Harry Chapin; Ricky Skaggs**	**Folk**	**Mid**	**10**
Father's Love	Bob Carlisle	Ballad	Slow	8
He's My Son	Mark Schultz	Ballad	Slow	9
I Want to Be Just Like You	**Phillips, Craig and Dean**	**MOR**	**Mid/slow**	**9**
Let Me Go	Susan Ashton	Folk ballad	Slow	10
Nothing You Could Do	*Willow Creek Music*	*Ballad*	*Slow*	*10*
Only Here for a Little While	Billy Dean	Country	Mid/up	10
Somewhere in the World	Wayne Watson	Acoustic ballad	Slow	3
When You Come Home	Mark Schultz	Country-tinged ballad	Slow/mid	9
_____	_____	_____	_____	___
_____	_____	_____	_____	___
_____	_____	_____	_____	___
_____	_____	_____	_____	___
_____	_____	_____	_____	___
_____	_____	_____	_____	___

Worship Choruses

Title	Artist	Style	Tempo	Seeker-Sensitivity Rating
_____	_____	_____	_____	___
_____	_____	_____	_____	___
_____	_____	_____	_____	___
_____	_____	_____	_____	___
_____	_____	_____	_____	___
_____	_____	_____	_____	___

MOVIE CLIPS

Title: Dad

Topic: Parenting; Father-son relationships

Description: Ted Danson and Jack Lemmon play a father and son. Lemmon is dying in a hospital bed, and they have a very poignant exchange, ending with Danson crawling into bed with his dad.

Start Time: 1:46:20

Start Cue: "How you feeling?"

End Time: 1:50:35

End Cue: "I must have done something right." End after wide shot.

Comments: _____

Title: Dead Poet's Society

Topic: Destructive parenting

Description: Todd, a boarding school student, shares with a friend that his parents sent him the same birthday present they gave him the previous years. Illustrates disconnected parenting.

Start Time: 1:05:40

Start Cue: "Todd?"

End Time: 1:07:30

End Cue: "You'll get another one next year."

Comments: _____

Title: Father of the Bride

Topic: Parenthood; Letting go of adult children

Description: Steve Martin's character's daughter tells him she's getting married, and he sees her as a little girl telling him. Very short clip.

Start Time: 0:09:30

Start Cue: "I met somebody in Rome."

End Time: 0:10:45

End Cue: Little girl says, "We're getting married."

Comments: Might be used in conjunction with the song "Watercolour Ponies" by Wayne Watson.

Title: Father of the Bride

Topic: Parenthood; Father-daughter relationships

Description: Steve Martin's character plays basketball with his daughter as "My Girl" plays in the background. Shows the warmth and fun of their relationship.

Start Time: 0:14:55

Start Cue: "Suppose you're not in the mood for a little one-on-one?"

End Time: 0:17:00

End Cue: Steve Martin's character and his daughter walk off together.

Comments: _____

Title: Indiana Jones and the Last Crusade

Topic: Father-son relationships

Description: Indiana Jones mildly confronts his father about the lack of a relationship between them.

Start Time: 1:13:45

Start Cue: "Remember the last time we had a quiet drink?"

End Time: 1:15:05

End Cue: "I can't think of anything."

Comments: Conversation is over a drink. May be offensive to some churches.

Title: Kramer vs. Kramer

Topic: Challenges of parenthood; Rebellion

Description: The son of the character played by Dustin Hoffman refuses to eat his dinner and goes to eat ice cream instead. High identification for parents.

Start Time: 0:35:40

Start Cue: Begin at "It's Salisbury steak."

End Time: 0:37:15

End Cue: Billy puts spoon in his mouth.

Comments: Don't go past the cutoff point—the father spanks his son, and it is not necessary to see it. Can be used to show the challenges of parenthood or to illustrate our rebellious nature.

Title: Kramer vs. Kramer

Topic: The effect of divorce on children

Description: Dustin Hoffman's character reads a letter to his little boy from Meryl Streep's character, telling him why she left. The effects on the child are what is left after divorce.

Start Time: 0:21:50

Start Cue: Just before "Hey, Billy!"

End Time: 0:23:45

End Cue: Scene ends with Billy staring at the TV.

Comments: _____

Title: Kramer vs. Kramer

Topic: Divorce; Effects of divorce on children

Description: Billy tells his dad that he thinks his mom left because he (Billy) was bad. The dad, played by Dustin Hoffman, explains why he thinks she left. Very moving clip.

Start Time: 0:39:10

Start Cue: Billy turns on the light and says, "Daddy . . ."

End Time: 0:41:40

End Cue: The father closes the door.

Comments: Video is dark, and audio is mostly whispered. This clip's effectiveness may vary, depending on the quality of your equipment.

Title: October Sky

Topic: Parent-child relationships; Father-son relationships

Description: Homer Hikam, a young aspiring rocket scientist comes to his dad's coal mine to talk to him. His dad makes a sarcastic comment about Homer meeting his "hero," Dr. Wernher von Braun. Homer speaks inspiring words to his dad about the man he is and, without saying the words, lets his dad know that he is Homer's real hero.

Start Time: 1:33:00

Start Cue: "Will you let me out?" Homer runs to meet his dad.

End Time: 1:35:08

End Cue: Homer's dad turns his mining light on as he watches Homer walk away.

Comments: Can be ended sooner than the end cue listed above. It can also be extended to show Homer's rocket launch, for which his dad unexpectedly shows up.

Title: Parenthood

Topic: Parenthood

Description: Very short, funny clip shows the "joys" of parenthood. The daughter of the character played by Steve Martin throws up on him.

Start Time: 0:06:45

Start Cue: "Hi, Daddy"

End Time: 0:07:12

End Cue: "Waiting for her head to spin around."

Comments: _____

Title: Parenthood

Topic: Controlling parents; Unreasonable expectations of children

Description: Funny clip about parents' unrealistic expectations of their kids. Two parents lecture their daughter about not putting enough effort into her studies. At the end, we realize she's three years old.

Start Time: 0:12:40

Start Cue: "Oh listen, Julie got 1291..."

End Time: 0:13:45

End Cue: "That's all I ask."

Comments: _____

Title: Parenthood

Topic: Joys of parenthood

Description: Short but heartwarming clip in which a boy tells his dad he wants to work where he does someday so they can still see each other every day.

Start Time: 1:03:25

Start Cue: Mom says, "Good night, sweetheart."

End Time: 1:04:10

End Cue: End before "Hubba Hubba."

Comments: _____

Title: Parenthood

Topic: Frustrations of parenting

Description: While looking for their son's retainer, two parents talk about how difficult it is to know how to parent their son. Steve Martin's characters says some profound things about the reality of parenting.

Start Time: 1:13:30

Start Cue: Steve Martin looking through garbage for retainer.

End Time: 1:15:15

End Cue: "Then they grow up to be like . . . me."

Comments: _____

_____

Title: Parenthood

Topic: Parenting

Description: Funny scene. Steve Martin's character has his son play second base and has a daydream of his son graduating from college as valedictorian. When his son loses the game, he has a daydream of his son being a mad sniper shooting up the college, yelling, "You made me play second base."

Start Time: 0:42:15

Start Cue: "We're gonna need a new second baseman."

End Time: 0:46:50

End Cue: "It's important to be supportive."

Comments: _____

_____

Title: Parenthood

Topic: Parenting; Ups and downs of parenting

Description: Steve Martin's character and his wife argue about having another child. His grandma comes in and tells a story about a roller coaster, which is a thinly veiled analogy to parenting.

Start Time: 1:48:40

Start Cue: Steve Martin's character says, "I love you."

End Time: 1:51:15

End Cue: "Well, I'll be seeing you in the car." Could also end at "If she's so brilliant, how come she's in the neighbor's car?"

Comments: _____

_____

Title: Searching for Bobby Fischer

Topic: Fatherhood; Failure; Destructive parenting

Description: Eight-year-old Josh loses a chess match, and his dad angrily confronts him about losing. Illustrates a dad who has too much invested in his son's success.

Start Time: 1:06:30

Start Cue: Shot of clock tower. "Seven moves" is first line.

End Time: 1:08:20

End Cue: "Sorry."

Comments: _____

_____

Title: She's Having a Baby

Topic: Parenthood; Fear of parenthood

Description: Jake's (Kevin Bacon) wife tells him she stopped taking her birth control pills. He screams and has a vision of being strapped to a speeding train car and crashing into a brick wall.

Start Time: 0:57:45/0:58:45

Start Cue: "Are you mad?" / "If I tell you something, will you promise. . . ?"

End Time: 0:59:30

End Cue: Jake crashes into the wall.

Comments: _____

_____

Title: The Story of Us

Topic: Marriage; Family conflict

Description: A typical suburban family sits down to dinner and shares the high and low points of their day, a family tradition. When the kids leave, it's clear the parents are putting on a front for the kids regarding their marriage, which is in trouble.

Start Time: 0:02:47

Start Cue: "Now, high/low—who wants to go first?"

End Time: 0:04:30

End Cue: "Just as long as the kids see us leaving together and coming home together."

Comments: This is sort of a bittersweet clip. The "high/low" idea is a great one, which many families have adopted because of this movie. But it's a sad clip because such a seemingly stable family is really falling apart.

_____

_____

Title: _____

Topic: _____

Description: _____

Start Time: _____

Start Cue: _____

End Time: _____

End Cue: _____

Comments: _____

_____

Friendship

MESSAGE TITLES

- ☐ Relationship Management
- ☐ The Rewards of Relationships
- ☐ Superficial or Significant?
- ☐ *A Faith That Works—The Book of James:* Relational Fundamentals
- ☐ *Living Excellent Lives:* Relationally
- ☐ *Making Life Work:* Choose Friends Wisely
- ☐ *The Power of Love:* Being a Friend
- ☐ *Restoring Weary Souls:* Life-Restoring Relationships
- ☐ *What Money Can't Buy:* Loyalty
- ☐ **Enriching Your Relationships:** Enriching Your Relationships
  • A Formula for Friendship • Relational Viruses • The Secret to Lasting Friendships
- ☐ **Relational Intelligence:** Forming Great Relationships • Reading People Like a Book • To Know and Be Known
- ☐ **The Lost Art of Loving:** Why Aren't You Normal Like Me? • Please Speak My Language • Resurrecting Dying Loves • The Launching Pad of Love • People Who Love Too Much

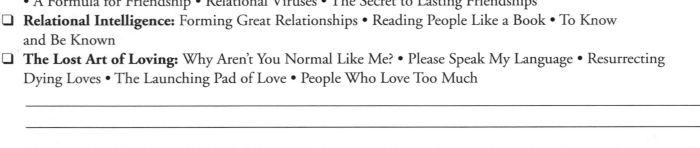

Package Suggestions

Drama:
Don't Mention It

Song:
Love Can Build a Bridge

Drama:
Character Test

Song:
Highest Honor

DRAMAS

Title	Tone	Characters	Topics
Attack of the Well-Meaners	Mixed, mostly humorous	1 male, 2 females	Dealing with crisis; Friendship
Best Friends	Humorous	2 males, 2 females	Friendship; Insecurity; Needy people
The Breakfast Club	Mixed, mostly serious	4 males, 1 female	Friendship; Small groups; Friends in crisis
Can't Live Without 'Em	Mixed, mostly humorous	2 males, 2 females	Relationships; Unconditional love
Character Test	Mixed, moving	2 males, 1 female	Promptings from God; Obedience; Power of encouragement
.COMmunity	Humorous	1 male	True community; The Internet; Relationships

Title	Tone	Characters	Topics
Don't Mention It	Mixed, mostly humorous	2 males, 2 females	Unemployment; Being open about problems
For Better or Worse—Part VI	Mixed	3 males, 3 females	Family; Marriage
It's No Picnic	Humorous	3 males, 3 females	Work stress; Surface relationships
Just an Acquaintance	Mixed	2 males, 2 females	Relationships between men; Superficial relationships
Lifeline	Mixed, touching	1 male, 2 females, 1 small child (no lines)	Serving the church; Life in community; Aging
Mr. X, Mr. Y, and Mr. Z	Humorous	4 males, 1 female, 1 narrator	Friendship; Intimacy
The Neighborhood	Mixed	3 males, 3 females	Small groups; Relationships; Getting deeper; Authenticity
The Next Step	Humorous	2 males	Authentic community; Positive relational risk taking; Men's relationships
Shop Talk	Mixed	2 males, 2 females	Failure; Adversity; Small groups
Something in Common	Mixed	1 male, 3 females	Starting relationships
Unknown	Serious	1 male, 4 females	Friendship; Loneliness; Small groups
The Vacationers—Parts 1 and 2	Humorous	2 males, 2 females	Personality differences; Friendships; Accepting others
War and Peace	Serious	2 males, 2 females	Relationships; Taking risks
What Are Friends For?	Serious	1 male, 2 females	Friendship; Truth telling
What Now?	Serious	2 males, 4 females	Coping with a crisis; Dealing with death

SONGS

Title	Artist	Style	Tempo	Seeker-Sensitivity Rating
Between You and Me	**DC Talk**	**Pop/rock**	**Mid**	**10**
Bridge between Two Hearts	Bob Carlisle	Pop	Up	9
Circle of Friends	Point of Grace	Pop	Mid	9
Faith, Hope, and Love Remain	*Willow Creek Music*	*Bluesy pop*	*Up*	*10*

Title	Artist	Style	Tempo	Seeker-Sensitivity Rating
Highest Honor	**Chris Eaton**	**Ballad**	**Slow**	7
How Could I Ask for More?	**Cindy Morgan**	**Piano ballad**	**Slow**	9
I Will Be Your Friend	Amy Grant	Pop	Up	10
Love Can Build a Bridge	**The Judds**	**Ballad**	**Slow**	10
Only Here for a Little While	Billy Dean	Country	Mid/up	10
Somebody Make Me Laugh	Patti Austin	Ballad	Slow	10
Take My Hand	**Russ Taff**	**Folk/rock**	**Mid**	9
Tell It Like It Is	**Scott Krippayne**	**Funky pop**	**Up**	9
That's What Love Is For	Amy Grant	Power ballad	Slow	10
Wanna Be Loved	**DC Talk**	**Funky pop**	**Up**	10
We All Need	Aaron Jeoffrey	Pop	Mid/up	9
When We Fail Love	**Grover Levy**	**Piano ballad**	**Slow**	9

Worship Choruses

Title	Artist	Style	Tempo	Seeker-Sensitivity Rating
Faith, Hope, and Love Remain	*Willow Creek Music*	*Bluesy pop*	*Up*	*10*
For the Beauty of the Earth	*Willow Creek Music*	*Worship ballad*	*Slow*	*5*
How Good and Pleasant	Tommy Walker	Pop/rock	Up	5

MOVIE CLIPS

Title: Beaches

Topic: Friendship; Truth telling

Description: Two friends, estranged for years, come back together and confront each other. Truth is spoken.

Start Time: 1:09:20

Start Cue: "Well, look who's here."

End Time: 1:12:00

End Cue: "No, it was our fault."

Comments: Three objectionable words may need to be bleeped.

Title: City Slickers

Topic: Dysfunctional families; Friendship

Description: Three friends share the best and worst days of their lives.

Start Time: 1:12:45

Start Cue: "All right, I got one."

End Time: 1:14:50

End Cue: "Same day."

Comments: Could start earlier, but Billy Crystal swears briefly during his worst-day description.

Title: Finding Forrester

Topic: Friendship; Keeping promises

Description: William, a reclusive author, comes to the aid of his young friend Jamal, who has been accused of cheating at a writing contest. In coming out of his seclusion, a very big step for him, he clears Jamal's name and honors a promise Jamal kept to him.

Start Time: 1:58:04/DVD Ch. 26

Start Cue: "Professor Crawford, may I read a few words?"

End Time: 2:02:35 or 2:04:02

End Cue: "I didn't write them. . . . Jamal Wallace did" (applause). Or William and Jamal leave together to applause.

Comments:

Title: Forrest Gump

Topic: Friendship; Laying your life down for a friend

Description: Forrest goes back into the jungle of Vietnam to find his fallen friend, Bubba, and runs him out of the battle zone.

Start Time: 0:53:30

Start Cue: "I gotta find Bubba!"

End Time: 0:55:00

End Cue: Forrest runs out of frame, with the jungle exploding behind him. Can also end at "That's all I have to say about that."

Comments: _____

_____

_____

Title: Forrest Gump

Topic: Love; Friendship

Description: Forrest, driving a shrimp boat, sees his friend Lieutenant Dan and jumps off the boat to greet him.

Start Time: 1:31:10

Start Cue: Shot of Forrest's hands steering the boat.

End Time: 1:32:50

End Cue: "That's my boat." Can end earlier.

Comments: _____

_____

_____

Title: Forrest Gump

Topic: Gratitude; Friendship

Description: Dan thanks Forrest for saving his life.

Start Time: 1:37:15

Start Cue: "Forrest . . . I never thanked you for saving my life."

End Time: 1:37:50

End Cue: Dan swims away.

Comments: May be too short for use.

_____

_____

Title: Hoosiers

Topic: Friendship; Belief in each other

Description: Rudy's friend Pete gives him a Notre Dame jacket, symbolizing his belief in his friend's dream.

Start Time: 0:12:25

Start Cue: "What is today?"

End Time: 0:14:25

End Cue: Rudy blows out "candle," smiles at Pete.

Comments: Pete lights a cigarette in the clip. Some people may be uncomfortable with that.

_____

_____

_____

Title: Men of Honor

Topic: Courage; Friendship; Inspiring others to succeed

Description: Carl Brashear, a navy master diver who lost a leg in an accident, in order to be reinstated to full duty, must walk twelve paces in a very heavy diving suit. At a court hearing, his former drill sergeant, a former antagonist, pushes him and challenges him to do it.

Start Time: 1:55:11

Start Cue: Wide shot of the courtroom.

End Time: 2:00:30

End Cue: Courtroom erupts in applause.

Comments: There is brief profanity in this clip that must be bleeped, but the power of the clip is worth the extra work.

_____
_____
_____
_____

Title: Remember the Titans

Topic: Truth telling; Racism; Leadership; Friendship

Description: The Titans' two star defensive players, one white and one black, confront each other on their effort and leadership, respectively. They become best friends later in the movie.

Start Time: 0:29:09/DVD Ch. 9

Start Cue: Gary bumps into Julius. "Okay, man, listen. I'm Gary, you're Julius."

End Time: 0:30:48

End Cue: "Attitude reflects leadership, Captain."

Comments: The two scenes following this one are also very strong, and the three scenes combined, though long, would be a great example of leadership and breaking down racial barriers. Gary says "shiver push," and it sounds like profanity because it goes by fast, but it's not.

_____
_____
_____
_____

Title: Remember the Titans

Topic: Racism; Friendship

Description: Julius comes to visit his friend Gary, who has been paralyzed in a car accident. The scene is a poignant example of friendship and breaking down racial barriers.

Start Time: 1:26:18/DVD Ch. 25

Start Cue: Julius walks into the hospital.

End Time: 1:29:25

End Cue: "Left side. Strong side." The boys clasp hands.

Comments: _____
_____
_____
_____
_____

Title: Shadowlands

Topic: Control issues; Intimacy

Description: Joy confronts Jack with the fact that he has set his world up so that nobody can touch him—he has blocked intimacy by surrounding himself with people he can control.

Start Time: 1:05:55

Start Cue: "So what do you do here . . . think great thoughts?"

End Time: 1:07:37

End Cue: "You just don't like it. Nor do I."

Comments: _____

_____

_____

Title: Shrek

Topic: Friendship; Truth telling

Description: Donkey confronts Shrek about being selfish and being mean to him. This clip has some great statements about friendship and forgiveness.

Start Time: 1:11:28/DVD Ch. 16

Start Cue: Shrek comes out of his house. "Donkey, what are you doing?"

End Time: 1:13:45

End Cue: "Friends?" "Friends."

Comments: One caution: Shrek refers to Donkey as a "jackass," which is technically true because he is a donkey, but it might be offensive to some. Also, Shrek goes into an outhouse.

_____

_____

_____

Title: _____

Topic: _____

Description: _____

Start Time: _____

Start Cue: _____

End Time: _____

End Cue: _____

Comments: _____

_____

_____

Love

See also: **God's Love**

MESSAGE TITLES

- ❑ Building Bigger Hearts
- ❑ Building Compassionate Hearts
- ❑ Loving Your Enemies
- ❑ *A Faith That Works—The Book of James:* Who Matters?
- ❑ **Giving and Receiving Love:** Gentleness • Trust • Sacrificial Love
- ❑ **Graduate-Level Loving:** The Supremacy of Love • The Essence of Love • The Effort of Love • When Love Breaks Down
- ❑ **The Lost Art of Loving:** Why Aren't You Normal Like Me? • Please Speak My Language • Resurrecting Dying Loves • The Launching Pad of Love • People Who Love Too Much
- ❑ **Love of Another Kind:** The Supremacy of Love • Bold Love • Loving Hard-to-Love People • Comforting Love • No Greater Love • When Love Breaks Down • The Sexual Side of Love • Love Busters • Love Never Fails
- ❑ **Loving Lessons:** Loving Lessons • Tender Love • Tough Love • Sacrificial Love • Steadfast Love • More about Tough Love • Radical Love
- ❑ **The Power of Love:** Being a Friend • Romantic Love • God's Love

DRAMAS

Title	Tone	Characters	Topics
Buy One, Get One Free	Mixed, moving	1 male, 1 female	The joy of giving
Can't Live Without 'Em	Mixed, mostly humorous	2 males, 2 females	Relationships; Unconditional love
Character Test	Mixed, moving	2 males, 1 female	Promptings from God; Obedience; Power of encouragement
I Know What You Want	Serious	2 males, 2 females	God's love; Dysfunctional families
Just Below the Jetta	Serious	1 female	Valuing people
Reflections	Mixed	1 male, 2 females, 2 children	Motherhood

Title	Tone	Characters	Topics
The Story of Rachel	Serious	3 females	Care for the poor; Compassion
Terminal Visit	Serious	3 females	Resurrecting relationships; Family conflict

SONGS

Title	Artist	Style	Tempo	Seeker-Sensitivity Rating
Art in Me	Jars of Clay	Alternative rock	Mid/up	9
Because You Loved Me	Celine Dion	Pop ballad	Slow	10
Bridge between Two Hearts	Bob Carlisle	Pop	Up	9
Desperado	Eagles	Ballad	Slow	10
Everything (Apron Full of Stains)	The Normals	Pop/rock	Mid/up	10
Faith, Hope, and Love Remain	*Willow Creek Music*	*Bluesy pop*	*Up*	*10*
Father's Love	Bob Carlisle	Ballad	Slow	8
Forever's as Far as I'll Go	Alabama	Country ballad	Slow	10
Helping Hand	Amy Grant	Pop	Mid/up	10
His Love Is Strong	Clay Crosse	Pop	Up	10
How Could I Ask for More?	**Cindy Morgan**	**Piano ballad**	**Slow**	**9**
If I Had Only Known	Reba McEntire	Ballad	Slow	10
Love Can Build a Bridge	**The Judds**	**Ballad**	**Slow**	**10**
Love Conquers All	Pam Thum	Pop	Up	10
Meet in the Middle	Diamond Rio	Country	Mid/up	10
Nothing You Could Do	*Willow Creek Music*	*Ballad*	*Slow*	*10*
Tell It Like It Is	Scott Krippayne	Funky pop	Up	9
There Is a Love	Michael English	Pop	Up	9
Wanna Be Loved	**DC Talk**	**Funky pop**	**Up**	**10**
We All Need	Aaron Jeoffrey	Pop	Mid/up	9

Title	Artist	Style	Tempo	Seeker-Sensitivity Rating

Worship Choruses

Title	Artist	Style	Tempo	Seeker-Sensitivity Rating
Faith, Hope, and Love Remain	*Willow Creek Music*	*Bluesy pop*	*Up*	*10*
For the Beauty of the Earth	*Willow Creek Music*	*Worship ballad*	*Slow*	*5*

MOVIE CLIPS

Title: 8 Seconds

Topic: Regret; Communicating love

Description: A father, whose son has recently died in a rodeo accident, breaks down in remorse over not telling his son that he loved him. This short clip probably needs to be set up.

Start Time: 1:27:22

Start Cue: Pallbearers carry the casket out of the church.

End Time: 1:28:44

End Cue: The mother puts her hands on the father's shoulders.

Comments: _____

Title: A Beautiful Mind

Topic: Love; Marriage

Description: John Nash, in his acceptance speech for the Nobel Prize, acknowledges that his wife's love and support have made him who he is.

Start Time: 2:05:12

Start Cue: Screen reads "Nobel Prize Ceremony."

End Time: 2:07:25

End Cue: Wide shot of the stage as John Nash walks off.

Comments: _____

Title: Forrest Gump

Topic: Friendship; Laying your life down for a friend

Description: Forrest goes back into the jungle of Vietnam to find his fallen friend, Bubba, and runs him out of the battle zone.

Start Time: 0:53:30

Start Cue: "I gotta find Bubba!"

End Time: 0:55:00

End Cue: Forrest runs out of frame, with the jungle exploding behind him. Can also end at "That's all I have to say about that."

Comments: _____

_____

Title: Forrest Gump

Topic: Love; Friendship

Description: Forrest, driving a shrimp boat, sees his friend Lieutenant Dan and jumps off the boat to greet him.

Start Time: 1:31:10

Start Cue: Shot of Forrest's hands steering the boat.

End Time: 1:32:50

End Cue: "That's my boat." Can end earlier.

Comments: _____

_____

Title: Hoosiers

Topic: Unconditional love; Forgiveness

Description: Dennis Hopper's character, a recovering alcoholic, is in the hospital drying out. His son visits him and tells him he loves him.

Start Time: 1:30:15

Start Cue: "No school this small . . ."

End Time: 1:32:30

End Cue: "Anyway, no school this small has ever been in the state championship!"

Comments: Needs some setup for those who haven't seen the movie.

_____

_____

Title: Remember the Titans

Topic: Racism; Friendship

Description: Julius comes to visit his friend Gary, who has been paralyzed in a car accident. The scene is a poignant example of friendship and breaking down racial barriers.

Start Time: 1:26:18/DVD Ch. 25

Start Cue: Julius walks into the hospital.

End Time: 1:29:25

End Cue: "Left side. Strong side." The boys clasp hands.

Comments: _____

_____

Title: _____

Topic: _____

Description: _____

Start Time: _____

Start Cue: _____

End Time: _____

End Cue: _____

Comments: _____

_____

_____

_____

Title: _____

Topic: _____

Description: _____

Start Time: _____

Start Cue: _____

End Time: _____

End Cue: _____

Comments: _____

_____

_____

_____

──Marriage and Dating──

Adultery

See also: **Purity, Sex**

MESSAGE TITLES

- ❏ The High Cost of a Cheap Thrill
- ❏ Looking, Lusting, or Loving?
- ❏ *Seventh Commandment:* Restrain Sexual Desires

Package Suggestion

Drama:
Because I Love You

Song:
Can't We Try?

DRAMAS

Title	Tone	Characters	Topics
All Gummed Up	Serious	1 male, 1 female, 1 offstage male voice	Adultery; Dealing with past hurts; The pain of lies
Attractive Deal	Serious	1 male, 1 female	Convictions; Adultery; Temptation
Because I Love You	Serious	1 male, 1 female	Adultery; The consequences of sin
Investment at Risk	Serious	2 males, 1 female, 1 child	Convictions; Adultery
Richard: 1992	Serious	2 males, 1 female	Anger; Rebellion; Decay of the family

SONGS

Title	Artist	Style	Tempo	Seeker-Sensitivity Rating
Behind Every Fantasy	*Willow Creek Music*	*Country pop*	*Up*	*10*
Call of the Wild	Susan Ashton	Country	Mid	10
Can't We Try?	Dan Hill & Vonda Shepard	Pop ballad duet	Slow	10
Faithless Heart	Amy Grant	Ballad	Slow/mid	10
Walk On By	Susan Ashton	Folk pop	Mid/up	8

Worship Choruses

Title	Artist	Style	Tempo	Seeker-Sensitivity Rating

MOVIE CLIPS

Title: City Slickers

Topic: Adultery; Temptation

Description: Billy Crystal's character's friend asks him if he would cheat on his wife if no one would ever know. His answer shows integrity.

Start Time: 0:44:38

Start Cue: "What if you could have great sex . . ."

End Time: 0:45:30

End Cue: "I wouldn't like myself . . . that's all."

Comments: May be too straightforward for some. Profanity precedes the clip.

Title:	_____
Topic:	_____
Description:	_____
Start Time:	_____
Start Cue:	_____
End Time:	_____
End Cue:	_____
Comments:	_____
	_____

Dating

See also: **Love, Fulfillment,** and **Marriage**

MESSAGE TITLES

- ❑ How to Pick a Partner
- ❑ The Payoff for Sexual Purity
- ❑ *Fit to Be Tied:* Exposing the Marriage Myth
- ❑ *Fit to Be Tied:* The Keys to Compatibility
- ❑ *Fit to Be Tied:* Making Your Courtship Count
- ❑ *I Have a Friend Who* Struggles with Being Single
- ❑ *Making Life Work:* Marry Well
- ❑ *Making the Most of Your Marriage:* Picking a Partner
- ❑ *The Power of Love:* Romantic Love

DRAMAS

Title	Tone	Characters	Topics
Date of the Weak	Humorous	2 males, 3 females	Judging others; The "game" of dating
Don Juan De Schaumburg	Humorous	3 males, 1 female	False views of Christians; Dating
For Better or Worse—Part I	Humorous	3 males, 3 females (offstage male and female voices)	Marriage

Title	Tone	Characters	Topics
For Better or Worse—Part II	Humorous	2 males, 2 females	Marriage; Personality differences
For Better or Worse—Part III	Mixed	1 male, 1 female, 1 either male or female	Marriage; Dating
Hands Off	Humorous	1 male, 1 female	Dating; Sex; Temptation
Me, Myself, and Chris	Mixed	2 males, 1 female	Dating; Sex; Temptation
Mere Technicality	Serious	1 male, 1 female	Living together; The cost of taking a stand for Christ
The Piano Recital	Humorous	2 males, 4 females, 2 children	Singleness; Adult parent-child tension
Premarital Flutter	Humorous	3 males	Marriage expectations
A Real Man	Humorous	4 males, 1 female	The American male; Finding the right man
Single?	Mixed	1 male, 1 female	Singleness; Loneliness; Fear of living alone

SONGS

Title	Artist	Style	Tempo	Seeker-Sensitivity Rating
When Love Finds You	Vince Gill	Country ballad, in 3	Slow/mid	10

Worship Choruses

Title	Artist	Style	Tempo	Seeker-Sensitivity Rating

MOVIE CLIPS

Title: She's Having a Baby

Topic: Marriage; Reality of marriage

Description: A young couple is at the altar. During the vows, the groom (played by Kevin Bacon) spaces out and hears the minister giving vows that are closer to reality. Very funny.

Start Time: 0:07:55

Start Cue: "Kristen, wilt thou have . . ."

End Time: 0:09:15

End Cue: "I will."

Comments: _____

_____

Title: _____

Topic: _____

Description: _____

Start Time: _____

Start Cue: _____

End Time: _____

End Cue: _____

Comments: _____

Divorce

MESSAGE TITLES

❑ Divorce and Remarriage
❑ *Fanning the Flames of Marriage:* The Keys to Conflict Resolution
❑ *Fit to Be Tied:* Now That I Married the Wrong Person
❑ *Making the Most of Your Marriage:* When Forever Doesn't Last
❑ *The Relationship You've Always Wanted:* When Marriage Ends

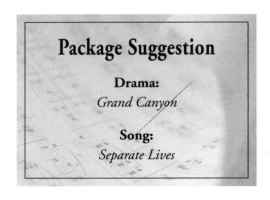

Package Suggestion

Drama:
Grand Canyon

Song:
Separate Lives

_____

_____

_____

DRAMAS

Title	Tone	Characters	Topics
All Gummed Up	Serious	1 male, 1 female, 1 offstage male voice	Adultery; Dealing with past hurts; The pain of lies
Grand Canyon	Serious	1 male, 1 female	Marital breakdown
Missing	Serious	3 males, 1 female	Generational barriers; The church's failure to reach Generation X
Richard: 1992	Serious	2 males, 1 female	Anger; Rebellion; Decay of the family
You and Me	Mixed	2 females	Mother's Day; Family; Rebuilding after divorce; Navigating life's challenges

SONGS

Title	Artist	Style	Tempo	Seeker-Sensitivity Rating
Behind Every Fantasy	*Willow Creek Music*	*Country pop*	*Up*	*10*
Call of the Wild	Susan Ashton	Country	Mid	10
Can't We Try?	Dan Hill & Vonda Shepard	Pop ballad duet	Slow	10
Healing Song	Curt Coffield	Ballad, in 3	Slow/mid	7
Separate Lives	Phil Collins & Marilyn White	Power ballad duet	Slow	10
When We Fail Love	**Grover Levy**	**Piano ballad**	**Slow**	**9**

Worship Choruses

Title	Artist	Style	Tempo	Seeker-Sensitivity Rating

MOVIE CLIPS

Title: Kramer vs. Kramer

Topic: Divorce

Description: Joanna (Meryl Streep) tells Ted (Dustin Hoffman) she's leaving him.

Start Time: 0:04:35

Start Cue: Door knock.

End Time: 0:07:15

End Cue: Elevator door closes.

Comments: Very real, painful clip showing the moment of separation. Might be very difficult for divorced people to watch.

Title: Kramer vs. Kramer

Topic: The effect of divorce on children

Description: Dustin Hoffman's character reads a letter to his little boy from Meryl Streep's character, telling him why she left. The effects on the child are what is left after divorce.

Start Time: 0:21:50

Start Cue: Just before "Hey, Billy!"

End Time: 0:23:45

End Cue: Scene ends with Billy staring at the TV.

Comments: _____

Title: Kramer vs. Kramer

Topic: Divorce; Effects of divorce on children

Description: Billy tells his dad that he thinks his mom left because he (Billy) was bad. The dad, played by Dustin Hoffman, explains why he thinks she left. Very moving clip.

Start Time: 0:39:10

Start Cue: Billy turns on the light and says, "Daddy . . ."

End Time: 0:41:40

End Cue: The father closes the door.

Comments: Video is dark, and audio is mostly whispered. This clip's effectiveness may vary, depending on the quality of your equipment.

Title: The Story of Us

Topic: Marriage; Family conflict

Description: A typical suburban family sits down to dinner and shares the high and low points of their day, a family tradition. When the kids leave, it's clear the parents are putting on a front for the kids regarding their marriage, which is in trouble.

Start Time: 0:02:47

Start Cue: "Now, high/low—who wants to go first?"

End Time: 0:04:30

End Cue: "Just as long as the kids see us leaving together and coming home together."

Comments: This is sort of a bittersweet clip. The "high/low" idea is a great one, which many families have adopted because of this movie. But it's a sad clip because such a seemingly stable family is really falling apart.

_____

_____

Title: The Story of Us

Topic: Marital breakdown

Description: Brief clip that shows the distancing that can happen in a marriage when life is hectic. It's very short but is a good picture of what commonly happens when marriages go untended.

Start Time: 0:45:42

Start Cue: "Over the years, there were less and less moments . . ."

End Time: 0:46:25

End Cue: ". . . if we faced each other there'd be nothing there."

Comments: _____

Title: _____

Topic: _____

Description: _____

Start Time: _____

Start Cue: _____

End Time: _____

End Cue: _____

Comments: _____

_____

Intimacy

Refers to the kind of knowing and being known that marriage was designed to produce

MESSAGE TITLES

❑ Marathon Marriages
❑ Superficial or Significant?
❑ *Loving Lessons:* Steadfast Love
❑ *The Power of Love:* Romantic Love

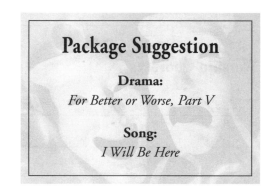

Package Suggestion

Drama:
For Better or Worse, Part V

Song:
I Will Be Here

_____

_____

_____

DRAMAS

Title	Tone	Characters	Topics
All Gummed Up	Serious	1 male, 1 female, 1 offstage male voice	Adultery; Dealing with past hurts; The pain of lies
For Better or Worse—Part V	Mixed	1 male, 1 female	Marriage; Romance
Grand Canyon	Serious	1 male, 1 female	Marital breakdown
An Hour on Wednesday	Mixed; serious ending	1 male, 1 female	Marriage; Damaging effects of a fast-paced life
Just Say It!	Humorous	1 male, 1 female, 1 either male or female	Marriage communication; Importance of saying "I love you"

SONGS

Title	Artist	Style	Tempo	Seeker-Sensitivity Rating
I Will Be Here	**Steven Curtis Chapman**	**Ballad**	**Slow**	**10**
Love and Learn	Steven Curtis Chapman	Pop folk	Mid/slow	9
When I Said I Do	*Willow Creek Music*	*Ballad*	*Slow*	*10*

Worship Choruses

Title	Artist	Style	Tempo	Seeker-Sensitivity Rating

MOVIE CLIPS

Title: Shadowlands

Topic: Control issues; Intimacy

Description: Joy confronts Jack with the fact that he has set his world up so that nobody can touch him—he has blocked intimacy by surrounding himself with people he can control.

Start Time: 1:05:55

Start Cue: "So what do you do here . . . think great thoughts?"

End Time: 1:07:37

End Cue: "You just don't like it. Nor do I."

Comments: _____
_____

Title: Shadowlands

Topic: Death; Sharing the dying process

Description: Jack and Joy talk about her imminent death. She makes a couple of profound statements about sharing the dying process.

Start Time: 1:45:30

Start Cue: "I don't want to be somewhere else anymore."

End Time: 1:47:55

End Cue: Jack and Joy kiss.

Comments: _____
_____

Title: The Story of Us

Topic: Marital breakdown

Description: Brief clip that shows the distancing that can happen in a marriage when life is hectic. It's very short but is a good picture of what commonly happens when marriages go untended.

Start Time: 0:45:42

Start Cue: "Over the years, there were less and less moments . . ."

End Time: 0:46:25

End Cue: ". . . if we faced each other there'd be nothing there."

Comments: _____
_____

Title: _____

Topic: _____

Description: _____

Start Time: _____

Start Cue: _____

End Time: _____

End Cue: _____

Comments: _____

Male-Female Differences

See also: **Personality Differences**

MESSAGE TITLES

❏ Bridging the Gender Divide
❏ Loving a Man without Losing Yourself
❏ When a Man Loves a Woman
❏ *The Amazing American Stereotype:* The Amazing American Female
❏ *The Amazing American Stereotype:* The Amazing American Male
❏ *Changing Times:* The Changing American Female
❏ *Changing Times:* The Changing American Male

_____

_____

_____

_____

DRAMAS

Title	Tone	Characters	Topics
Feeling Opposition	Humorous	1 male, 1 female	Thinkers vs. feelers
For Better or Worse—Part V	Mixed	1 male, 1 female	Marriage; Romance
It's Only a Movie	Humorous	2 males, 2 females, 1 offstage voice	The power of media; The effects of what we see; Male-female differences
Just Looking	Mixed, light	1 male, 1 female	Eye causing you to stumble; Purity of thoughts
No Clue	Humorous	2 males, 1 female, 1 voice-over	Gender sensitivity, Male-female workplace issues
_____	_____	_____	_____
_____	_____	_____	_____
_____	_____	_____	_____
_____	_____	_____	_____

SONGS

Title	Artist	Style	Tempo	Seeker-Sensitivity Rating
Meet in the Middle	Diamond Rio	Country	Mid/up	10

Worship Choruses

Title	Artist	Style	Tempo	Seeker-Sensitivity Rating

MOVIE CLIPS

Title: City Slickers

Topic: Differences between men and women

Description: Discussion about why men loving baseball reveals some differences between men and women.

Start Time: 1:05:33

Start Cue: "Will you stop with Roberto Clemente?" or "So, do you hate baseball?"

End Time: 1:07:20

End Cue: "That was real."

Comments: _____

_____

Title: _____

Topic: _____

Description: _____

Start Time: _____

Start Cue: _____

End Time: _____

End Cue: _____

Comments: _____

Marriage, General

MESSAGE TITLES

- How to Pick a Partner
- *Making Life Work:* Marry Well
- *The Power of Love:* Romantic Love
- *The Relationship You've Always Wanted:* The Relatives Are Coming!
- *The Relationship You've Always Wanted:* When Marriage Begins
- **Fanning the Flames of Marriage:** Why Fires Burn Low • Help for Husbands • Wisdom for Wives • Keys to Conflict Resolution • Whatever Happened to Romance?
- **Fit to Be Tied:** Exposing the Marriage Myth • Keys to Compatibility • Making Your Courtship Count • Now That I Married the Wrong Person • Keeping Romance Alive • Strengthening Family Ties
- **Making the Most of Your Marriage:** Picking a Partner • The Love of Your Life • The Myths of Marriage • . . . And Then We Had Kids • When Forever Doesn't Last
- **Marriagewerks:** Demystifying Marriage • When a Man Loves a Woman • Loving a Man without Losing Yourself • Marathon Marriages • Surviving a Spiritual Mismatch
- **When the Honeymoon's Over:** The Legacy of Love • Love the Second Time Around • Investing in Your Spouse • Surviving a Marital Mismatch • The Making of a Marriage

> ## Package Suggestion
>
> **Drama:**
> *For Better or Worse, Part IV*
>
> **Song:**
> *I Will Be Here*

DRAMAS

Title	Tone	Characters	Topics
All Gummed Up	Serious	1 male, 1 female, 1 offstage male voice	Adultery; Dealing with past hurts; The pain of lies
Baby Talk	Humorous	2 males, 2 females	Decision making; Parenting; Decision to have children
A Change of Life	Mixed	1 male, 1 female	Marriage; Change
Distancing	Mixed, mostly serious	1 male, 1 female	Good marriages take work; Demands of life
Driven	Serious	1 male, 1 female	Workaholism; Marriage
First Thing First	Humorous	1 male, 1 female, 1 female infant	New parents; Balancing children and marriage
For Better or Worse—Part I	Humorous	3 males, 3 females (offstage male and female voices)	Marriage

Title	Tone	Characters	Topics
For Better or Worse—Part II	Humorous	2 males, 2 females	Marriage; Personality differences
For Better or Worse—Part III	Mixed	1 male, 1 female, 1 either male or female	Marriage; Dating
For Better or Worse—Part IV	Mixed, mostly serious	1 male, 1 female	Marriage
For Better or Worse—Part V	Mixed	1 male, 1 female	Marriage; Romance
For Better or Worse—Part VI	Mixed	3 males, 3 females	Family; Marriage
Forgive Again?	Serious	1 male, 1 female	Forgiving others
Grand Canyon	Serious	1 male, 1 female	Marital breakdown
Grandma's Recipe	Serious	1 male, 2 females, 2 children	Family struggle during the holidays
An Hour on Wednesday	Mixed; serious ending	1 male, 1 female	Marriage; Damaging effects of a fast-paced life
Improving Your Lie	Humorous	1 male, 1 female	Truth telling; Marriage
Just Say It!	Humorous	1 male, 1 female, 1 either male or female	Marriage communication; Importance of saying "I love you"
Prayer Despair	Mixed	1 male, 2 female	Waiting for answers to prayer; Marriage; Process of change
Premarital Flutter	Humorous	3 males	Marriage expectations
A Problem of Perspective	Humorous	1 male, 1 female, 1 either male or female	Marriage; Marital conflict
Trying Time	Serious	1 male, 2 females	Marriage; Spiritual mismatch

SONGS

Title	Artist	Style	Tempo	Seeker-Sensitivity Rating
Can't We Try?	Dan Hill & Vonda Shepard	Pop ballad duet	Slow	10
Faithless Heart	Amy Grant	Ballad	Slow/mid	10
Forever's as Far as I'll Go	Alabama	Country ballad	Slow	10
Go There with You	Steven Curtis Chapman	MOR	Mid	10
I Just Never Say It Enough	Wayne Watson	Ballad, in 3	Slow	8

Title	Artist	Style	Tempo	Seeker-Sensitivity Rating
I Will Be Here	**Steven Curtis Chapman**	**Ballad**	**Slow**	**10**
If You Could See What I See	Geoff Moore & the Distance	Folk ballad	Slow	10
Love and Learn	Steven Curtis Chapman	Pop folk	Mid/slow	9
Love Conquers All	Pam Thum	Pop	Up	10
Meet in the Middle	Diamond Rio	Country	Mid/up	10
Separate Lives	Phil Collins & Marilyn White	Power ballad duet	Slow	10
That's What Love Is For	Amy Grant	Power ballad	Slow	10
When I Said I Do	*Willow Creek Music*	*Ballad*	*Slow*	*10*
When Love Finds You	**Vince Gill**	**Country ballad, in 3**	**Slow/mid**	**10**
_____	_____	_____	_____	____
_____	_____	_____	_____	____
_____	_____	_____	_____	____

Worship Choruses

Title	Artist	Style	Tempo	Seeker-Sensitivity Rating
Faith, Hope, and Love Remain	*Willow Creek Music*	*Bluesy pop*	*Up*	*10*
_____	_____	_____	_____	____
_____	_____	_____	_____	____
_____	_____	_____	_____	____
_____	_____	_____	_____	____

MOVIE CLIPS

Title: 8 Seconds

Topic: Regret; Communicating love

Description: A father, whose son has recently died in a rodeo accident, breaks down in remorse over not telling his son that he loved him. This short clip probably needs to be set up.

Start Time: 1:27:22

Start Cue: Pallbearers carry the casket out of the church.

End Time: 1:28:44

End Cue: The mother puts her hands on the father's shoulders.

Comments: _____

_____

Title: A Beautiful Mind

Topic: Love; Marriage

Description: John Nash, in his acceptance speech for the Nobel Prize, acknowledges that his wife's love and support have made him who he is.

Start Time: 2:05:12

Start Cue: Screen reads "Nobel Prize Ceremony."

End Time: 2:07:25

End Cue: Wide shot of the stage as John Nash walks off.

Comments: _____

_____

Title: She's Having a Baby

Topic: Marriage; Reality of marriage

Description: A young couple is at the altar. During the vows, the groom (played by Kevin Bacon) spaces out and hears the minister giving vows that are closer to reality. Very funny.

Start Time: 0:07:55

Start Cue: "Kristen, wilt thou have . . ."

End Time: 0:09:15

End Cue: "I will."

Comments: _____

_____

Title: The Story of Us

Topic: Marriage; Family conflict

Description: A typical suburban family sits down to dinner and shares the high and low points of their day, a family tradition. When the kids leave, it's clear the parents are putting on a front for the kids regarding their marriage, which is in trouble.

Start Time: 0:02:47

Start Cue: "Now, high/low—who wants to go first?"

End Time: 0:04:30

End Cue: "Just as long as the kids see us leaving together and coming home together."

Comments: This is sort of a bittersweet clip. The "high/low" idea is a great one, which many families have adopted because of this movie. But it's a sad clip because such a seemingly stable family is really falling apart.

_____

_____

Title: The Story of Us

Topic: Marital breakdown

Description: Brief clip that shows the distancing that can happen in a marriage when life is hectic. It's very short but is a good picture of what commonly happens when marriages go untended.

Start Time: 0:45:42

Start Cue: "Over the years, there were less and less moments . . ."

End Time: 0:46:25

End Cue: ". . . if we faced each other there'd be nothing there."

Comments: _____

Title:	_____
Topic:	_____
Description:	_____
Start Time:	_____
Start Cue:	_____
End Time:	_____
End Cue:	_____
Comments:	_____
	_____

Sex

See also: **Purity, Self-Control**

MESSAGE TITLES

- ❏ Christians in a Sex-Crazed Culture
- ❏ The Difference between Looking and Lusting
- ❏ Looking, Lusting, or Loving?
- ❏ The Payoff for Sexual Purity
- ❏ *Facing New Realities:* The Sexual Ethic
- ❏ *A Faith That Works: The Book of James:* Destructive Desires
- ❏ *Money, Sex, and Power:* Sex
- ❏ *Seventh Commandment:* Restrain Sexual Desires
- ❏ *Three Things God Loves (That Most People Don't Think He Does):* Lovemaking

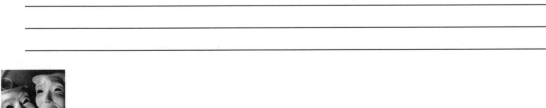

Package Suggestion

Drama:
The Big Sell

Song:
Walk On By

DRAMAS

Title	Tone	Characters	Topics
All Gummed Up	Serious	1 male, 1 female, 1 offstage male voice	Adultery; Dealing with past hurts; The pain of lies
Attractive Deal	Serious	1 male, 1 female	Convictions; Adultery; Temptation

Title	Tone	Characters	Topics
Because I Love You	Serious	1 male, 1 female	Adultery; The consequences of sin
The Big Sell	Humorous	3 males, 2 females	Obsession with sex in society; Effect of the media
For Better or Worse—Part V	Mixed	1 male, 1 female	Marriage; Romance
Hands Off	Humorous	1 male, 1 female	Dating; Sex; Temptation
Investment at Risk	Serious	2 males, 1 female, 1 child	Convictions; Adultery
Just Looking	Mixed, light	1 male, 1 female	Eye causing you to stumble; Purity of thoughts
Me, Myself, and Chris	Mixed	2 males, 1 female	Sex; Temptation; Dating

 # SONGS

Title	Artist	Style	Tempo	Seeker-Sensitivity Rating
Behind Every Fantasy	*Willow Creek Music*	*Country pop*	*Up*	*10*
Blind Side	Susan Ashton	Folk rock	Up	9
Call of the Wild	Susan Ashton	Country	Mid	10
I Am the Man	*Greg Ferguson*	*Piano ballad*	*Slow*	*8*
Keep My Mind	Margaret Becker	Pop/rock	Up	8
Strength in You	*Willow Creek Music*	*MOR pop*	*Slow/mid*	*10*
Walk On By	Susan Ashton	Folk pop	Mid/up	8

Worship Choruses

Title	Artist	Style	Tempo	Seeker-Sensitivity Rating
I Will Never Be	Hillsongs	Worship ballad	Slow/mid	3

MOVIE CLIPS

Title: City Slickers

Topic: Adultery; Temptation

Description: Billy Crystal's character's friend asks him if he would cheat on his wife if no one would ever know. His answer shows integrity.

Start Time: 0:44:38

Start Cue: "What if you could have great sex . . ."

End Time: 0:45:30

End Cue: "I wouldn't like myself . . . that's all."

Comments: May be too straightforward for some. Profanity precedes the clip.

Title:

Topic:

Description:

Start Time:

Start Cue:

End Time:

End Cue:

Comments:

—Personality Differences—

Refers to the way God "wired us up"—"thinkers" vs. "feelers," etc.

MESSAGE TITLES

❑ Affirming Your Uniqueness
❑ *The Lost Art of Loving:* Why Aren't You Normal Like Me?
❑ *Negotiating the Maze of Life:* Thinkers, Feelers, and Procrastinators
❑ **Discovering the Way God Wired You Up:** Temperament • Emotions • Sexuality • Physically • Spiritually

_____

_____

_____

DRAMAS

Title	Tone	Characters	Topics
Expectations of the Expecting	Mixed	1 male, 1 female	Parenting; Affirming personality differences
Feeling Opposition	Humorous	1 male, 1 female	Thinkers vs. feelers
For Better or Worse—Part II	Humorous	2 males, 2 females	Marriage; Personality differences
Oh, What a Feeling!	Humorous	2 males, 1 female	Decision making; Self-control; Money management
On Track	Serious	2 males, 1 female	Forcing people into molds; Character building
A Problem of Perspective	Humorous	1 male, 1 female, 1 either male or female	Marriage; Marital conflict
The Vacationers—Parts 1 and 2	Humorous	2 males, 2 females	Personality differences; Friendships; Accepting others
Wonderfully Made	Serious	2 males, 2 females, 1 narrator	Affirming a child's uniqueness
_____	_____	_____	_____
_____	_____	_____	_____
_____	_____	_____	_____
_____	_____	_____	_____

SONGS

Title	Artist	Style	Tempo	Seeker-Sensitivity Rating
Art in Me	Jars of Clay	Alternative rock	Mid/up	9
Bridge between Two Hearts	Bob Carlisle	Pop	Up	9
Undivided	First Call	Ballad trio	Slow	5
_____	_____	_____	_____	___
_____	_____	_____	_____	___
_____	_____	_____	_____	___
_____	_____	_____	_____	___

Worship Choruses

Title	Artist	Style	Tempo	Seeker-Sensitivity Rating
Let the Walls Fall Down	Student Impact	Pop worship	Up	6
_____	_____	_____	_____	___
_____	_____	_____	_____	___
_____	_____	_____	_____	___
_____	_____	_____	_____	___

MOVIE CLIPS

Title: _____

Topic: _____

Description: _____

Start Time: _____

Start Cue: _____

End Time: _____

End Cue: _____

Comments: _____

_____

_____

——Relational Conflict——

Forgiveness is a major theme here, though this listing deals with the entire process involved in resolving relational conflict.

See also: **God's Forgiveness of Us, Grace, Truth Telling**

Package Suggestion

Drama:
Terminal Visit

Song:
Beyond Justice to Mercy

MESSAGE TITLES

❏ The Keys to Resolving Conflict
❏ *Enriching Your Relationships:* Relational Viruses
❏ *A Faith That Works—The Book of James:* The Power of Words
❏ *A Faith That Works—The Book of James:* War and Peace
❏ *The God of the Second Chance:* Giving Second Chances
❏ *Life's Too Short . . .* for Unresolved Bitterness
❏ *The Lost Art of Loving:* Resurrecting Dying Loves
❏ *Making Life Work:* Speak Truth
❏ *Relationships in the Kingdom:* Fixing Broken Relationships
❏ *Relationships in the Kingdom:* Loving Your Enemies
❏ *Strength for the Storms of Life:* Betrayal
❏ *Telling the Truth:* Games People Play

DRAMAS

Title	Tone	Characters	Topics
Famous Lost Words	Humorous	4 males, 1 female	Turning the other cheek; Boundaries
Finding Evidence	Serious	2 males, 1 female	Trust; Jumping to conclusions
Forgive Again?	Serious	1 male, 1 female	Forgiving others
Forgiven	Serious	2 females	Forgiving others; God's forgiveness
In . . . We Trust	Serious; not heavy	1 male	Trust; Difficulty trusting God
Kind of Rare	Mixed	3 males, 3 females	Confronting in love; Friendship; Marriage; Character flaws
The Luncheon	Serious	3 females	Mother-daughter conflict; Honesty in relationships

Title	Tone	Characters	Topics
No Accident	Mixed, mostly serious	2 females	Forgiveness; Love your enemies; Growing in Christlikeness
No Thanks Giving	Serious	3 females	Truth telling; Family dynamics
Only Child	Serious	1 male, 2 females	Grace; Outrageous forgiveness; Doctrine of adoption
A Problem of Perspective	Humorous	1 male, 1 female, 1 either male or female	Marriage; Marital conflict
Sister Act	Serious	2 females	Dysfunctional families; Wounds
Terminal Visit	Serious	3 females	Resurrecting relationships; Family conflict
War and Peace	Serious	2 males, 2 females	Relationships; Taking risks
What Are Friends For?	Serious	1 male, 2 females	Friendship; Truth telling
_____	_____	_____	_____
_____	_____	_____	_____
_____	_____	_____	_____

SONGS

Title	Artist	Style	Tempo	Seeker-Sensitivity Rating
Between You and Me	**DC Talk**	**Pop/rock**	**Mid**	**10**
Beyond Justice to Mercy	**Susan Ashton**	**Ballad**	**Slow**	**10**
Bridge between Two Hearts	Bob Carlisle	Pop	Up	9
Gather at the River	Point of Grace	Pop	Up	8
Healing Song	Curt Coffield	Ballad, in 3	Slow/mid	7
Love Can Build a Bridge	**The Judds**	**Ballad**	**Slow**	**10**
Love Conquers All	Pam Thum	Pop	Up	10
Meet in the Middle	Diamond Rio	Country	Mid/up	10
Sticks and Stones	Wes King	Rock/pop	Up	9
Tell It Like It Is	**Scott Krippayne**	**Funky pop**	**Up**	**9**
That's What Love Is For	Amy Grant	Power ballad	Slow	10
Undivided	First Call	Ballad trio	Slow	5
When We Fail Love	**Grover Levy**	**Piano ballad**	**Slow**	**9**
Words	Kim Hill	Pop/rock	Up	10

Title	Artist	Style	Tempo	Seeker-Sensitivity Rating

Worship Choruses

Title	Artist	Style	Tempo	Seeker-Sensitivity Rating
Healing Song	Curt Coffield	Ballad, in 3	Slow/mid	7
Let the Walls Fall Down	Student Impact	Pop worship	Up	6

MOVIE CLIPS

Title: Beaches

Topic: Friendship; Truth telling

Description: Two friends, estranged for years, come back together and confront each other. Truth is spoken.

Start Time: 1:09:20

Start Cue: "Well, look who's here."

End Time: 1:12:00

End Cue: "No, it was our fault."

Comments: Three objectionable words may need to be bleeped.

Title: Hoosiers

Topic: Unconditional love; Forgiveness

Description: Dennis Hopper's character, a recovering alcoholic, is in the hospital drying out. His son visits him and tells him he loves him.

Start Time: 1:30:15

Start Cue: "No school this small . . ."

End Time: 1:32:30

End Cue: "Anyway, no school this small has ever been in the state championship!"

Comments: Needs some setup for those who haven't seen the movie.

Title: Les Misérables

Topic: Grace; Forgiveness

Description: In the first scene of the movie, ex-convict Jean Valjean is welcomed into a church for food and shelter. He steals some silverware, is caught, and in order to model the grace of God to him, the bishop forgives Valjean and gives the silver to him and gives him candlesticks in addition.

Start Time: 0:6:22

Start Cue: Jean Valjean creeps down the stairs.

End Time: 0:9:53

End Cue: "Now I give you back to God." Close-up of Valjean, fade to black.

Comments: Valjean strikes the bishop. It is a bit violent but adds to the power of the bishop's forgiveness of Valjean. One of the bishop's statements sounds as if he bought Valjean's soul, but more likely he is saying that he used the silver essentially to buy him out of the evil he had done so that he could be presented to God. A great picture of grace.

_____

_____

_____

Title: Shrek

Topic: Friendship; Truth telling

Description: Donkey confronts Shrek about being selfish and being mean to him. This clip has some great statements about friendship and forgiveness.

Start Time: 1:11:28/DVD Ch. 16

Start Cue: Shrek comes out of his house. "Donkey, what are you doing?"

End Time: 1:13:45

End Cue: "Friends?" "Friends."

Comments: One caution: Shrek refers to Donkey as a "jackass," which is technically true because he is a donkey, but it might be offensive to some. Also, Shrek goes into an outhouse.

_____

_____

_____

Title: _____

Topic: _____

Description: _____

Start Time: _____

Start Cue: _____

End Time: _____

End Cue: _____

Comments: _____

_____

_____

_____

Small Groups

See also: **Friendship**

MESSAGE TITLES

❑ Jesus Forms a Small Group
❑ *Making Life Work:* Speak Truth
❑ **Benefits of Brotherhood:** Overcoming Independence • Superficial or Significant • The Cost of Commitment • The Rewards of Relationships
❑ **Enlisting in Little Platoons:** The Purpose of Little Platoons • Picking Platoon Members • Problems in Little Platoons • The Rewards of Little Platoons • War Stories

_____

_____

_____

DRAMAS

Title	Tone	Characters	Topics
The Breakfast Club	Mixed, mostly serious	4 males, 1 female	Friendship; Small groups; Friends in crisis
Just an Acquaintance	Mixed	2 males, 2 females	Relationships between men; Superficial relationships
Kind of Rare	Mixed	3 males, 3 females	Confronting in love; Friendship; Marriage; Character flaws
The Neighborhood	Mixed	3 males, 3 females	Small groups; Relationships; Getting deeper; Authenticity
Shop Talk	Mixed	2 males, 2 females	Failure; Adversity; Small groups
Something in Common	Mixed	1 male, 3 females	Starting relationships

SONGS

*No songs specifically on small groups. See **Friendship** and **Community** for ideas.*

Title	Artist	Style	Tempo	Seeker-Sensitivity Rating
_____	_____	_____	_____	_____
_____	_____	_____	_____	_____
_____	_____	_____	_____	_____

Worship Choruses

Title	Artist	Style	Tempo	Seeker-Sensitivity Rating
_____	_____	_____	_____	_____
_____	_____	_____	_____	_____
_____	_____	_____	_____	_____

MOVIE CLIPS

Title: Forrest Gump

Topic: Friendship; Laying your life down for a friend

Description: Forrest goes back into the jungle of Vietnam to find his fallen friend, Bubba, and runs him out of the battle zone.

Start Time: 0:53:30

Start Cue: "I gotta find Bubba!"

End Time: 0:55:00

End Cue: Forrest runs out of frame, with the jungle exploding behind him. Can also end at "That's all I have to say about that."

Comments: _____
_____

Title: _____

Topic: _____

Description: _____

Start Time: _____

Start Cue: _____

End Time: _____

End Cue: _____

Comments: _____

Truth Telling

Refers to speaking the truth in love
See also: **Communication, Relational Conflict**

MESSAGE TITLES

❑ Simple Truth Telling
❑ *Life's Too Short . . .* for Unresolved Bitterness
❑ *Loving Lessons:* Tough Love
❑ *Making Life Work:* Speak Truth
❑ *28 Days of Truth Telling:* Telling the Truth Every Day
❑ *28 Days of Truth Telling:* Telling the Truth to Each Other
❑ **Telling the Truth:** Secret Conversations • Five Deadly Lies • Truth or Consequences • Games People Play • Expressing Positive Emotions • Learning How to Hear the Truth

DRAMAS

Title	Tone	Characters	Topics
For Image Sake	Humorous	3 males, 1 female	Honesty; Pretense
Kind of Rare	Mixed	3 males, 3 females	Confronting in love; Friendship; Marriage; Character flaws
The Luncheon	Serious	3 females	Mother-daughter conflict; Honesty in relationships
No Thanks Giving	Serious	3 females	Truth telling; Family dynamics
Truthful Words	Serious	1 male, 1 female	Leadership; Pride; Truth telling
War and Peace	Serious	2 males, 2 females	Relationships; Taking risks
What Are Friends For?	Serious	1 male, 2 females	Friendship; Truth telling

SONGS

Title	Artist	Style	Tempo	Seeker-Sensitivity Rating
Between You and Me	**DC Talk**	**Pop/rock**	**Mid**	**10**
The Living Years	Mike & the Mechanics	Pop	Mid/up	10
Only Here for a Little While	Billy Dean	Country	Mid/up	10
Tell It Like It Is	Scott Krippayne	Funky pop	Up	9

Worship Choruses

Title	Artist	Style	Tempo	Seeker-Sensitivity Rating

MOVIE CLIPS

Title: Beaches

Topic: Friendship; Truth telling

Description: Two friends, estranged for years, come back together and confront each other. Truth is spoken.

Start Time: 1:09:20

Start Cue: "Well, look who's here."

End Time: 1:12:00

End Cue: "No, it was our fault."

Comments: Three objectionable words may need to be bleeped.

Title: Remember the Titans

Topic: Truth telling; Racism; Leadership; Friendship

Description: The Titans' two star defensive players, one white and one black, confront each other on their effort and leadership, respectively. They become best friends later in the movie.

Start Time: 0:29:09/DVD Ch. 9

Start Cue: Gary bumps into Julius. "Okay, man, listen. I'm Gary, you're Julius."

End Time: 0:30:48

End Cue: "Attitude reflects leadership, Captain."

Comments: The two scenes following this one are also very strong, and the three scenes combined, though long, would be a great example of leadership and breaking down racial barriers. Gary says "shiver push," and it sounds like profanity because it goes by fast, but it's not.

_____

_____

_____

Title: Shrek

Topic: Friendship; Truth telling

Description: Donkey confronts Shrek about being selfish and being mean to him. This clip has some great statements about friendship and forgiveness.

Start Time: 1:11:28/DVD Ch. 16

Start Cue: Shrek comes out of his house. "Donkey, what are you doing?"

End Time: 1:13:45

End Cue: "Friends?" "Friends."

Comments: One caution: Shrek refers to Donkey as a "jackass," which is technically true because he is a donkey, but it might be offensive to some. Also, Shrek goes into an outhouse.

_____

_____

_____

Title: _____

Topic: _____

Description: _____

Start Time: _____

Start Cue: _____

End Time: _____

End Cue: _____

Comments: _____

_____

_____

Seeker Issues

Apologetics

Refers to defending the faith

Might also include: *Atheism, Evolution vs. Creation, Evidence for Christianity, Reasons People Don't Believe*

MESSAGE TITLES

- ❑ Doubters Welcome
- ❑ Spiritual Sticking Points
- ❑ The Surprise of Truth
- ❑ Where Does the Evidence Point?
- ❑ *I Have a Friend Who* Thinks All Religions Are the Same
- ❑ *What Jesus Would Say to . . .* Rob Sherman (a local atheist)
- ❑ **Believing the Unbelievable:** The Odds for Evolution • The Case for Creation • Myths or Miracles? • Are Science and Christianity Compatible?
- ❑ **The Case for Christ:** The Credibility of Christ's Claims • The Reality of the Resurrection • The Relevance of the Resurrection
- ❑ **The Case for Christianity:** The Case for God • The Case for the Bible • The Case for Christ • The Case for Life-Change
- ❑ **Faith Has Its Reasons:** Reasons for Believing in God • Reasons for Believing in the Bible • Reasons for Believing in Jesus Christ • Reasons for Believing in the Resurrection • Reasons for Believing in Heaven and Hell
- ❑ **Faith on Trial:** A Skeptic's Surprise • Barriers to Belief

DRAMAS

Title	Tone	Characters	Topics
D-Day	Humorous	2 males, 1 female	Misconceptions about Christianity; Becoming a Christian
Don Juan De Schaumburg	Humorous	3 males, 1 female	False views of Christians; Dating
The Fence-Sitter	Mixed	4 males, 1 female	Indecision; Getting involved in ministry; Deciding to become a Christian
Getting Directions	Humorous	2 males	Not all paths lead to God; Christianity's exclusive claims

Title	Tone	Characters	Topics
Guess Which God	Humorous	4 males, offstage male and female voices	Confusion about God; The nature of God
I Am	Serious	4 readers, male or female	Who is Jesus Christ?
Is "Nothing" Sacred?	Humorous	3 males, and at least 4 others in group	Evolution vs. creation; Modern science
Mistaken Identity	Mixed	3 males, 2 females, 1 young girl	Christmas; Doubting
On the Outside	Serious	1 male or female	Being salt and light; Negative church experiences
Pastor General	Humorous	2 males, 2 females	Leadership; Church life; Serving others
Reason Enough	Mixed, mostly serious	1 male, 1 female	Importance of faith grounded in reason
A Visitor	Serious	2 males, 1 female	Wolves in sheep's clothing; Discernment; Spiritual manipulation
Wait 'Til Half-Time	Mixed	1 male, 1 female	Eternity; Heaven and hell; Evangelism
You Cramp My Style	Serious	1 male, 1 female, 1 either male or female	Reasons people don't believe; Society's view of God
___	___	___	___
___	___	___	___
___	___	___	___
___	___	___	___

SONGS

*For more song ideas, see **Changed Life.**

Title	Artist	Style	Tempo	Seeker-Sensitivity Rating
Big Enough	Chris Rice	Folk ballad, in 6/8	Slow/mid	10
Dear God	**Midge Ure**	**Rock**	**Mid/up**	**10**
Evidence	*Willow Creek Music*	*Folk pop*	*Mid*	*10*
He Was	*Willow Creek Music*	*Pop/rock, in 6/8*	*Mid*	*10*
Naïve	Chris Rice	Folk pop	Mid	8
There Is a God	**Tommy Walker**	**Ballad duet**	**Slow**	**8**
This Is My Father's World	Fernando Ortega	Folk ballad	Slow/mid	8

Title	Artist	Style	Tempo	Seeker-Sensitivity Rating

Worship Choruses

Title	Artist	Style	Tempo	Seeker-Sensitivity Rating
All Around	Curt Coffield	Caribbean pop	Up	7
I Am Here	*Willow Creek Music*	*Worship ballad*	*Slow*	*8*
Lord, I Believe in You	Tommy Walker	Worship power ballad	Slow/mid	4

MOVIE CLIPS

Title: Sister Act

Topic: The church; Reasons people don't go to church

Description: Humorous clip of a boring preacher and a horrible choir, illustrating a couple of reasons why people don't go to church.

Start Time: 0:30:25

Start Cue: "We are a small congregation this morning . . ."

End Time: 0:32:25

End Cue: Whoopi Goldberg's character winces.

Comments: _____

_____

_____

_____

Title: Shadowlands

Topic: Suffering; Pain; Why does God allow bad things to happen?

Description: C. S. Lewis delivers a speech about why God allows suffering.

Start Time: 0:10:00

Start Cue: "Yesterday I received a letter."

End Time: 0:11:40

End Cue: "Thank you very much."

Comments: The last line is a bit hard to understand.

_____
_____
_____

Title: _____

Topic: _____

Description: _____

Start Time: _____

Start Cue: _____

End Time: _____

End Cue: _____

Comments: _____
_____
_____

──Basics of Christianity──

Grace

A difficult concept for some seekers to understand because it is so foreign to human nature. This goes beyond the topic of **God's Forgiveness of Us** to understanding the heart of a God who would die in our place.

Package Suggestion

Drama:
Security Check

Song:
Only by Grace

MESSAGE TITLES

- ❑ Amazed by Grace
- ❑ The Core Idea
- ❑ The Difference Grace Makes
- ❑ The Grace of God
- ❑ Never Ending Grace
- ❑ Radical Love
- ❑ What's So Amazing about Grace?
- ❑ Why They Call Grace Amazing
- ❑ The Wonder of Grace
- ❑ *A Faith That Works—The Book of James:* How Good Is Good Enough?
- ❑ *Illustrating the Identity of God:* Our Gracious God
- ❑ *When God Shows Up:* The Wayward Find Mercy
- ❑ *Yeah God:* For Being Gracious
- ❑ **Amazing Grace:** The God of Grace • The Gifts of Grace • Gracious Fathers
- ❑ **The God of the Second Chance:** Getting a Second Chance • Giving Second Chances

DRAMAS

Title	Tone	Characters	Topics
Acting the Part		1 male, 2 females	Legalism; Living out our Christianity
The Book of Life	Energetic mime; Mixed	3 males, 3 females	Baptism; Faith; Basic Christianity; Eternal life
A Clean Slate	Serious	1 male, 2 or 3 males or females	Forgiveness; Redemption; Guilt

Title	Tone	Characters	Topics
Keeping Tabs	Humorous	1 male, 1 female	Gifts of grace; Undeserved love
Measuring Up	Mixed; Mime	2 males, 1 female, 1 either male or female	God's acceptance of us; Self-esteem
Only Child	Serious	1 male, 2 females	Grace; Outrageous forgiveness; Doctrine of adoption
The Prisoner	Serious	3 males, 1 female	Easter; Freedom from sin; New Christian
Security Check	Mixed	1 male, 1 female, 1 offstage voice	Salvation; Works vs. grace
"X" Marks the Spot	Serious; Mime	1 male, 1 female, 3 either males or females	Sin; Redemption; Forgiveness; Guilt
_____	_____	_____	_____
_____	_____	_____	_____
_____	_____	_____	_____
_____	_____	_____	_____

SONGS

Title	Artist	Style	Tempo	Seeker-Sensitivity Rating
All Things New	Watermark	Folk pop	Mid	8
Clumsy	Chris Rice	Pop	Mid/up	8
Could You Believe?	Scott Krippayne	Pop	Up	9
Cross Medley	*Willow Creek Music*	*Ballad medley—hymns*	*Slow*	*7*
Face of Forgiveness	*Willow Creek Music*	*Ballad*	*Slow*	*10*
Farther Than Your Grace Can Reach	**Jonathan Pierce**	**Ballad**	**Slow**	**9**
Forgive Me	*Willow Creek Music*	*Ballad*	*Slow*	*3*
The Great Divide	Point of Grace	Power ballad	Slow	9
I Stand, I Fall	*Greg Ferguson*	*Piano ballad*	*Slow*	*7*
I'm Amazed	*Willow Creek Music*	*Ballad*	*Slow*	*7*
I've Been Released	*Willow Creek Music*	*Pop/rock—Chicago sound*	*Up*	*9*
Jesus Loves Me	Whitney Houston	R & B/pop	Slow/mid	8
Love Is Always There	Carolyn Arends	Folk pop	Up	9
The Love of God	*Willow Creek Music*	*A cappella vocal group*	*Slow*	*6*

Title	Artist	Style	Tempo	Seeker-Sensitivity Rating
Mercy for the Memories	Geoff Moore & the Distance	Folk pop ballad	Slow	9
Miracle of Mercy	Steven Curtis Chapman	Acoustic ballad	Slow	4
My Life Is Yours	*Willow Creek Music*	*Acoustic ballad*	*Slow*	*10*
Only by Grace	*Willow Creek Music*	*Pop/rock*	*Mid*	*10*
A Picture of Grace	*Willow Creek Music*	*Medley of ballads*	*Slow*	*9*
Speechless	**Steven Curtis Chapman**	**Acoustic rock**	**Mid/up**	**7**
There Is a Love	Michael English	Pop	Up	9
Who Am I?	Margaret Becker	Power ballad	Slow	7
Who Am I? (Grace Flows Down)	**Watermark**	**Folk pop**	**Mid/slow**	**8**
Why Me?	*Willow Creek Music*	*Ballad*	*Slow*	*9*
Your Grace Still Amazes Me	Phillips, Craig and Dean	Pop ballad	Slow	7

Worship Choruses

Title	Artist	Style	Tempo	Seeker-Sensitivity Rating
The Cross Has Said It All	Matt Redman	Worship ballad	Mid/slow	2
Everyone Arise	Tommy Walker	Pop/rock	Up	3
He Loves Me	Tommy Walker	Worship ballad	Slow	6
The Lord Is Gracious and Compassionate	Vineyard	Worship ballad	Mid/slow	5
My Redeemer Lives	Hillsongs	Pop/rock	Up	3
Still Amazing	Danny Chambers	Worship ballad	Slow	5
Thank You for Saving Me	Delirious	Folk rock worship ballad	Slow/mid	3
Thank You, Lord	Hillsongs	Worship ballad, in 3	Mid	3
When I Survey the Wondrous Cross	NA	Updated traditional	Slow	3
You Are My King	Passion	Worship ballad	Slow	4

MOVIE CLIPS

Title: Dead Man Walking

Topic: Salvation; Redemption; Acknowledgment of sin

Description: A nun visits a death row inmate with whom she has been working. She asks him if he has been reading his Bible and essentially inquires about his relationship with God. He misunderstands redemption as a "free admission ticket" in which he plays no part. Her point is that he must acknowledge his sin before grace can cover him.

Start Time: 1:12:09

Start Cue: "I was able to arrange for a lie detector test."

End Time: 1:14:11

End Cue: The inmate stares blankly, looking troubled.

Comments: _____

_____

Title: Dead Man Walking

Topic: Confession of sin; Grace

Description: Death row inmate Matthew Poncelet confesses to a rape and murder he had previously been denying. This acknowledgment of sin was his last barrier to receiving grace. His friend Sister Helen Prejean tells him that he is a "son of God" because of his ownership of his sin.

Start Time: 1:35:12

Start Cue: "The boy . . . Walter? I killed him."

End Time: 1:37:28

End Cue: "Thank you for loving me." Close-up of Sister Prejean.

Comments: This clip is a bit risky because of the subject matter. The sister asks if he killed a boy and raped a girl, and he says yes. But, especially as a companion to the other "Dead Man Walking" clip listed, it is potentially a powerful illustration of the need to acknowledge our sin and the grace that follows.

_____

_____

Title: Les Misérables

Topic: Grace; Forgiveness

Description: In the first scene of the movie, ex-convict Jean Valjean is welcomed into a church for food and shelter. He steals some silverware, is caught, and in order to model the grace of God to him, the bishop forgives Valjean and gives the silver to him and gives him candlesticks in addition.

Start Time: 0:6:22

Start Cue: Jean Valjean creeps down the stairs.

End Time: 0:9:53

End Cue: "Now I give you back to God." Close-up of Valjean, fade to black.

Comments: Valjean strikes the bishop. It is a bit violent but adds to the power of the bishop's forgiveness of Valjean. One of the bishop's statements sounds as if he bought Valjean's soul, but more likely he is saying that he used the silver essentially to buy him out of the evil he had done so that he could be presented to God. A great picture of grace.

_____

_____

Title:	_____
Topic:	_____
Description:	_____
Start Time:	_____
Start Cue:	_____
End Time:	_____
End Cue:	_____
Comments:	_____
	_____

Grace vs. Works/Legalism

Might also include: *Legalism*

Refers to the fact that eternal life cannot be earned but is a free gift through Christ alone. This is an issue that keeps many seekers from faith and keeps many believers from experiencing real freedom and joy.

MESSAGE TITLES

❏ Averting Your Worst Nightmare
❏ The Difference Grace Makes
❏ Show Me the Way
❏ What's So Amazing about Grace?
❏ *Christianity's Toughest Competition:* Moralism
❏ *A Faith That Works: The Book of James:* How Good Is Good Enough?

> ## Package Suggestion
>
> **Drama:**
> *The Stickholders*
>
> **Song:**
> *If I Could Look through Your Eyes*

DRAMAS

Title	Tone	Characters	Topics
Acting the Part		1 male, 2 females	Legalism; Living out our Christianity
The Book of Life	Energetic mime; Mixed	3 males, 3 females	Baptism; Faith; Basic Christianity; Eternal life
A Clean Slate	Serious	1 male, 2 or 3 males or females	Forgiveness; Redemption; Guilt

Title	Tone	Characters	Topics
Keeping Tabs	Humorous	1 male, 1 female	Gifts of grace; Undeserved love
Security Check	Mixed	1 male, 1 female, 1 offstage male voice	Salvation; Works vs. Grace
The Stickholders	Serious	3 males, 1 female, 1 narrator	Relationship with God; Freedom from rules

SONGS

Title	Artist	Style	Tempo	Seeker-Sensitivity Rating
He Won't Let You Go	**The Kry**	**Piano ballad**	**Slow**	**10**
If I Could Look through Your Eyes	*Willow Creek Music*	*Piano ballad*	*Slow*	*10*
My Life Is Yours	*Willow Creek Music*	*Acoustic ballad*	*Slow*	*10*
Only by Grace	*Willow Creek Music*	*Pop/rock*	*Mid*	*10*
The Great Divide	Point of Grace	Power ballad	Slow	9
What a Ride	*Willow Creek Music*	*Pop/rock*	*Up*	*9*

Worship Choruses

Title	Artist	Style	Tempo	Seeker-Sensitivity Rating

MOVIE CLIPS

Title: _____

Topic: _____

Description: _____

Start Time: _____

Start Cue: _____

End Time: _____

End Cue: _____

Comments: _____

_____

Our Need for Christ

Refers to recognizing the need for a relationship with Christ

See also: **Guilt, Relationship with God, General**

MESSAGE TITLES

❑ Averting Your Worst Nightmare
❑ Just What You're Looking For
❑ Settling Life's Biggest Issue
❑ _Ordering Your Private World:_ Ordering Your Spiritual World

DRAMAS

Title	Tone	Characters	Topics
After Life	Mixed; Serious ending, sober	1 male	The afterlife; Heaven and hell
Any Time?	Mixed, mostly serious	1 male	Making time for God

Title	Tone	Characters	Topics
The Black Hole	Serious but light	2 males, 1 female, 1 narrator	Filling the void; Contentment; God's love
Lizzy and Leroy	Humorous	1 male, 1 female, piano player (optional)	Life fulfillment; Material things don't satisfy
Man of the Year	Serious	5 males, 1 female	Moralism; Our need for Christ
Maybe Someday	Mixed, mostly serious	2 males	Evangelism; Success that leaves us empty; Going back to church
Richard: 1992	Serious	2 males, 1 female	Anger; Rebellion; Decay of the family
The Safe	Mixed	1 male, 1 female, 3 either males or females	Inner strength; Needing God's strength
These Parts	Mixed	2 males, 1 female, 3 either males or females, 1 child, 1 narrator	The resurrection; Our need for Christ; Easter
Wait 'Til Half-Time	Mixed	1 male, 1 female	Eternity; Heaven and hell; Evangelism
What about Life?	Mixed, mostly humorous	1 male, 1 female	Finding meaning to life; The empty void inside
What's the Ticket?	Mixed	2 females, 4 either males or females	Need for Christ; Contentment; Needs and wants
"X" Marks the Spot	Serious; Mime	1 males, 1 females, 3 either males or females	Sin; Redemption; Forgiveness; Guilt
You Cramp My Style	Serious	1 male, 1 female, 1 either male or female	Reasons people don't believe; Society's view of God
___	___	___	___
___	___	___	___
___	___	___	___
___	___	___	___

SONGS

Title	Artist	Style	Tempo	Seeker-Sensitivity Rating
Ball and Chain	Susan Ashton	Folk pop	Mid	9
Can't Live a Day without You	Avalon	Pop ballad	Slow/mid	8
Desperado	Eagles	Ballad	Slow	10
Forgive Me	*Willow Creek Music*	*Ballad*	*Slow*	*3*
Give Me Jesus	**Willow Creek Music**	**Ballad**	**Slow**	**7**

Title	Artist	Style	Tempo	Seeker-Sensitivity Rating
He Was	*Willow Creek Music*	*Pop/rock, in 6/8*	*Mid*	*10*
Heaven in the Real World	Steven Curtis Chapman	Pop/rock	Up	7
Hole Hearted	**Extreme**	**Rock**	**Up**	**10**
I'll Find You There	The Kry	Folk rock ballad	Slow	9
Jesus Will Still Be There	Point of Grace	Ballad	Slow	9
Leave a Light On	*Greg Ferguson*	*Ethereal pop ballad*	*Slow/mid*	*8*
Life Support	*Greg Ferguson*	*R & B/pop*	*Mid/up*	*9*
Love That Will Not Let Me Go	**Steve Camp**	**Ballad**	**Slow**	**10**
Mercy for the Memories	Geoff Moore & the Distance	Folk pop ballad	Slow	9
Only by Grace	*Willow Creek Music*	*Pop/rock*	*Mid*	*10*
A Place to Call Home	*Greg Ferguson/ Willow Creek Music*	*Gospel ballad*	*Slow, in 3*	*10*
Reaching for You	*Willow Creek Music*	*Rock/pop*	*Up*	*10*
Strength in You	*Willow Creek Music*	*MOR pop*	*Slow/mid*	*10*
Time to Return	*Willow Creek Music*	*Ballad*	*Slow*	*7*
Wanna Be Loved	**DC Talk**	**Funky pop**	**Up**	**10**
We Believe in God	Amy Grant	Acoustic ballad	Slow	3
Who Am I? (Grace Flows Down)	**Watermark**	**Folk pop**	**Mid/slow**	**8**
_____	_____	_____	_____	_____
_____	_____	_____	_____	_____
_____	_____	_____	_____	_____
_____	_____	_____	_____	_____

Worship Choruses

Title	Artist	Style	Tempo	Seeker-Sensitivity Rating
Better Is One Day	Matt Redman/Passion	Folk worship	Mid	4
Breathe	Michael W. Smith	Worship ballad	Slow	3
I Am Here	*Willow Creek Music*	*Worship ballad*	*Slow*	*8*
In My Heart	*Greg Ferguson*	*Celtic worship ballad*	*Slow*	*9*
Meet with Me	Ten Shekel Shirt	Modern worship	Up	7
Open the Eyes of My Heart	Paul Baloche	Pop/rock worship	Up	5
Pour Out My Heart	Vineyard	Worship shuffle	Mid	4

Title	Artist	Style	Tempo	Seeker-Sensitivity Rating
___	___	___	___	___
___	___	___	___	___
___	___	___	___	___
___	___	___	___	___

MOVIE CLIPS

Title: _____

Topic: _____

Description: _____

Start Time: _____

Start Cue: _____

End Time: _____

End Cue: _____

Comments: _____

_____

_____

Our Value to God

Refers to the essential truth that people matter to God

See also: **God's Love, Self-Esteem**

MESSAGE TITLES

❏ Measuring How Much You Matter to God

❏ People Matter to God

❏ *Seven Wonders of the Spiritual World:* God Loves Me

_____

_____

_____

DRAMAS

Title	Tone	Characters	Topics
Another Day at the Bus Stop	Mixed	1 male, 1 female	Our relationship with God; Self-esteem
The Intruder	Serious	1 male, 1 female	Self-image; Destructive parenting; God's love in spite of failure
The Lane of Life	Serious; Mime	5 either males or females, 1 offstage narrator	Salvation; Our value to God; Self-esteem
Measuring Up	Mixed; Mime	2 males, 1 female, 1 either male or female	God's acceptance of us; Self-esteem
Wonderfully Made	Serious	2 males, 2 females, 1 narrator	Affirming a child's uniqueness

SONGS

Title	Artist	Style	Tempo	Seeker-Sensitivity Rating
Art in Me	Jars of Clay	Alternative rock	Mid/up	9
He Knows My Name	**Tommy Walker/Helena**	**Worship ballad**	**Slow**	**9**
His Eyes	Steven Curtis Chapman	Acoustic guitar ballad	Mid/slow	9
I Don't Know Why/Found a Way	*Willow Creek Music*	*Ballad*	*Slow*	8
If I Could Look through Your Eyes	*Willow Creek Music*	*Piano ballad*	*Slow*	10
Jesus Loves Me	Whitney Houston	R & B/pop	Slow/mid	8
Let the Lord Love You	*Willow Creek Music*	*Acoustic guitar ballad*	*Slow*	9
Love Is Always There	Carolyn Arends	Folk pop	Up	9
The Love of God	*Willow Creek Music*	*A cappella vocal group*	*Slow*	6
A Place to Call Home	*Greg Ferguson/ Willow Creek Music*	*Gospel ballad*	*Slow, in 3*	10
There Is a Love	Michael English	Pop	Up	9
Treasure of You	Steven Curtis Chapman	Driving rock	Up	10
What I Wouldn't Give	*Willow Creek Music*	*Acoustic ballad*	*Slow*	10

Title	Artist	Style	Tempo	Seeker-Sensitivity Rating
Who Am I? (Grace Flows Down)	**Watermark**	**Folk pop**	**Mid/slow**	**8**
Why Me?	*Willow Creek Music*	*Ballad*	*Slow*	*9*

Worship Choruses

Title	Artist	Style	Tempo	Seeker-Sensitivity Rating
Above All	Paul Baloche/Lenny LeBlanc	Worship ballad	Slow	5
Amen	Tommy Walker	Worship shuffle	Up	5
He Loves Me	Tommy Walker	Worship ballad	Slow	6

 MOVIE CLIPS

Title: Forrest Gump

Topic: Love; Friendship

Description: Forrest, driving a shrimp boat, sees his friend Lieutenant Dan and jumps off the boat to greet him.

Start Time: 1:31:10

Start Cue: Shot of Forrest's hands steering the boat.

End Time: 1:32:50

End Cue: "That's my boat." Can end earlier.

Comments: _____
_____

Title: _____

Topic: _____

Description: _____

Start Time: _____

Start Cue: _____

End Time: _____

End Cue: _____

Comments: _____

Salvation

MESSAGE TITLES

- ❑ Averting Your Worst Nightmare
- ❑ Christianity 101
- ❑ Cliff's Notes on Christianity
- ❑ The Core Idea
- ❑ The Doorway to Heaven
- ❑ How to Become a Christian
- ❑ Plain-English Christianity
- ❑ Settling Life's Biggest Issue
- ❑ Show Me the Way
- ❑ *A Faith That Works—The Book of James:* How Good Is Good Enough?
- ❑ *Private Conversations:* Jesus Talks to a Sinner
- ❑ *The "S" Word:* The Other "S" Word (Salvation)
- ❑ *A Taste of Christianity:* A Better Kind of Confidence
- ❑ *When God Shows Up:* The Wayward Find Mercy
- ❑ **Your Ever After:** Heaven • Hell • The Crimson Thread • One Eye on Eternity

DRAMAS

Title	Tone	Characters	Topics
The Black Hole	Serious but light	2 males, 1 female, 1 narrator	Filling the void; Contentment; God's love
The Book of Life	Energetic mime; Mixed	3 males, 3 females	Baptism; Faith; Basic Christianity; Eternal life
A Clean Slate	Serious	1 male, 2 or 3 males or females	Forgiveness; Redemption; Guilt
D-Day	Humorous	2 males, 1 female	Misconceptions about Christianity; Becoming a Christian
Getting Directions	Humorous	2 males	Not all paths lead to God; Christianity's exclusive claims
The Lane of Life	Serious; Mime	5 either males or females, 1 offstage narrator	Salvation; Our value to God; Self-esteem

Title	Tone	Characters	Topics
Maybe Someday	Mixed, mostly serious	2 males	Evangelism; Success that leaves us empty; Going back to church
Measuring Up	Mixed; Mime	2 males, 1 female, 1 either male or female	God's acceptance of us; Self-esteem
Only Child	Serious	1 male, 2 females	Grace; Outrageous forgiveness; Doctrine of adoption
The Prisoner	Serious	3 males, 1 female	Easter; Freedom from sin; New Christian
Security Check	Mixed	1 male, 1 female, 1 offstage voice	Salvation; Works vs. grace
These Parts	Mixed	2 males, 1 female, 3 either males or females, 1 child, 1 narrator	The resurrection; Our need for Christ; Easter
Wait 'Til Half-Time	Mixed	1 male, 1 female	Eternity; Heaven and hell; Evangelism
"X" Marks the Spot	Serious; Mime	1 male, 1 female, 3 either males or females	Sin; Redemption; Forgiveness; Guilt
_____	_____	_____	_____
_____	_____	_____	_____
_____	_____	_____	_____

SONGS

Title	Artist	Style	Tempo	Seeker-Sensitivity Rating
All the Faith You Need	*Greg Ferguson*	*Bluesy rock*	*Up*	*10*
Change in My Life	John Pagano	Gospel	Mid/up	9
Cross Medley	*Willow Creek Music*	*Ballad medley—hymns*	*Slow*	*7*
Free	Ginny Owens	Folk pop	Mid/up	8
Give Me Jesus	**Willow Creek Music**	**Ballad**	**Slow**	7
Good News	**Chris Rice**	**Pop**	**Up**	**9**
The Great Divide	Point of Grace	Power ballad	Slow	9
He Was	*Willow Creek Music*	*Pop/rock, in 6/8*	*Mid*	*10*
He Won't Let You Go	The Kry	Piano ballad	Slow	10
I Found Myself in You	Clay Crosse	Gospel ballad	Mid/slow	10
I've Been Released	*Willow Creek Music*	*Pop/rock—Chicago sound*	*Up*	*9*
Love Is Always There	Carolyn Arends	Folk pop	Up	9

Title	Artist	Style	Tempo	Seeker-Sensitivity Rating
The Love of God	*Willow Creek Music*	*A cappella vocal group*	*Slow*	6
Love That Will Not Let Me Go	Steve Camp	Ballad	Slow	10
Mercy for the Memories	Geoff Moore & the Distance	Folk pop ballad	Slow	9
More Than Words	Steven Curtis Chapman	Acoustic guitar ballad	Mid/slow	4
My Life Is Yours	*Willow Creek Music*	*Acoustic ballad*	*Slow*	10
Only by Grace	*Willow Creek Music*	*Pop/rock*	*Mid*	10
A Place to Call Home	*Greg Ferguson/ Willow Creek Music*	*Gospel ballad*	*Slow, in 3*	10
Speechless	**Steven Curtis Chapman**	**Acoustic rock**	**Mid/up**	**7**
There Is a God	**Tommy Walker**	**Ballad duet**	**Slow**	**8**
There Is a Love	Michael English	Pop	Up	9
What a Good God	**Tommy Walker**	**Worship ballad**	**Slow**	**7**
What I Wouldn't Give	*Willow Creek Music*	*Acoustic ballad*	*Slow*	10
Why Me?	*Willow Creek Music*	*Ballad*	*Slow*	9
Wonderful Merciful Savior	Susan Ashton	Acoustic ballad, 6/8 feel	Mid/slow	9
You Brought My Heart to Life	*Willow Creek Music*	*Ballad*	*Slow*	9
Your Grace Still Amazes Me	Phillips, Craig and Dean	Pop ballad	Slow	7
_____	_____	_____	_____	_____
_____	_____	_____	_____	_____
_____	_____	_____	_____	_____

Worship Choruses

Title	Artist	Style	Tempo	Seeker-Sensitivity Rating
Amazing Love	*Student Impact*	*Rock worship*	*Mid/up*	6
Can't Stop Talkin'	Hillsongs	Pop worship	Up	6
The Cross Has Said It All	Matt Redman	Worship ballad	Mid/slow	2
Do You Know?	Tommy Walker	Worship ballad	Slow/mid	2
Don't Forget His Benefits	Tommy Walker & the CA Worship Band	Rock/pop	Up	4
Great Is Thy Faithfulness	NA	Traditional worship/hymn	Slow	5
Happy Song	Delirious	Country rockabilly	Up	5
He Loves Me	Tommy Walker	Worship ballad	Slow	6
Jesus, What a Beautiful Name	Hillsongs	Worship ballad—in 6/8	Slow/mid	6

Title	Artist	Style	Tempo	Seeker-Sensitivity Rating
Lift Up Your Heads	Tommy Walker	Rock/pop worship	Up	2
Lord, I Lift Your Name on High	Maranatha!/Praise Band	Pop worship	Up	6
My Jesus, I Love You	*Willow Creek Music*	*Worship ballad*	*Slow*	*3*
My Redeemer Lives	Hillsongs	Pop/rock	Up	3
Never Gonna Stop	Tommy Walker/ Willow Creek Music	Pop/rock	Up	3
No Greater Love	Tommy Walker	Pop/rock	Up	6
O for a Thousand Tongues	*Willow Creek Music*	*Contemporary arrangement of hymn*	*Up*	*3*
Still Amazing	Danny Chambers	Worship ballad	Slow	5
Thank You for Saving Me	Delirious	Folk rock worship ballad	Slow/mid	3
Thank You, Lord	Hillsongs	Worship ballad, in 3	Mid	3
That's Why We Praise Him	Tommy Walker	Rock/pop worship	Mid	5
What a Good God You've Been	Tommy Walker	Worship ballad	Slow	7
What the Lord Has Done	Hillsongs	Worship ballad, in 3	Slow/mid	2
When I Survey the Wondrous Cross	NA	Updated traditional	Slow	3
You Are My King	Passion	Worship ballad	Slow	4
You Have Been Given	Willow Creek Music	Worship ballad, in 3	Slow	3
You've Won My Affection	Curt Coffield	Worship ballad	Slow	4
_____	_____	_____	_____	____
_____	_____	_____	_____	____
_____	_____	_____	_____	____

MOVIE CLIPS

Title: Amistad

Topic: The gospel; Salvation

Description: Powerful telling of the gospel from the standpoint of a wrongly imprisoned slave who has learned the story from pictures in a Bible.

Start Time: 1:35:45

Start Cue: Prisoner is reading the Bible. Cinque says, "You don't have to pretend to be interested in that."

End Time: 1:39:36

End Cue: "It doesn't look so bad." Picture of three crosses.

Comments: _____

_____

Title: Dead Man Walking

Topic: Salvation; Redemption; Acknowledgment of sin

Description: A nun visits a death row inmate with whom she has been working. She asks him if he has been reading his Bible and essentially inquires about his relationship with God. He misunderstands redemption as a "free admission ticket" in which he plays no part. Her point is that he must acknowledge his sin before grace can cover him.

Start Time: 1:12:09

Start Cue: "I was able to arrange for a lie detector test."

End Time: 1:14:11

End Cue: The inmate stares blankly, looking troubled.

Comments: _____

_____

Title: Dead Man Walking

Topic: Confession of sin; Grace

Description: Death row inmate Matthew Poncelet confesses to a rape and murder he had previously been denying. This acknowledgment of sin was his last barrier to receiving grace. His friend Sister Helen Prejean tells him that he is a "son of God" because of his ownership of his sin.

Start Time: 1:35:12

Start Cue: "The boy . . . Walter? I killed him."

End Time: 1:37:28

End Cue: "Thank you for loving me." Close-up of Sister Prejean.

Comments: This clip is a bit risky because of the subject matter. The sister asks if he killed a boy and raped a girl, and he says yes. But, especially as a companion to the other "Dead Man Walking" clip listed, it is potentially a powerful illustration of the need to acknowledge our sin and the grace that follows.

_____

_____

Title: Indiana Jones and the Last Crusade

Topic: Faith; Trusting God when circumstances are confusing

Description: Indiana Jones faces a seemingly uncrossable chasm but takes a "leap of faith" and steps onto an invisible bridge. Illustrates faith, believing what can't be seen.

Start Time: 1:46:50

Start Cue: Indiana Jones walks through cave to the chasm.

End Time: 1:48:45

End Cue: Indy throws sand on bridge to mark it (can be cut earlier).

Comments: _____

_____

Title: _____

Topic: _____

Description: _____

Start Time: _____

Start Cue: _____

End Time: _____

End Cue: _____

Comments: _____

Fulfillment

Until we come to Christ, there is a void in our souls that we try desperately to fill. Nothing ultimately satisfies but a relationship with God.

MESSAGE TITLES

- ❏ Filling the Void
- ❏ *Seven Wonders of the Spiritual World:* God Satisfies Me
- ❏ *Surprised by God:* Surprised by God's Satisfaction
- ❏ **Money, Sex, and Power:** Money • Sex • Power

DRAMAS

Title	Tone	Characters	Topics
The Black Hole	Serious but light	2 males, 1 female, 1 narrator	Filling the void; Contentment; God's love
Call Waiting	Mixed; Serious ending	2 males	Marketplace pressures; Search for significance; Mid-life crisis
In Pursuit of Happiness	Mixed	1 male, 1 female	Contentment; Possessions
Lizzy and Leroy	Humorous	1 male, 1 female, piano player (optional)	Life fulfillment; Material things don't satisfy
The Lures of Life	Mixed, light; Mime	5 males, 1 female	Adventurism; Life fulfillment
Maybe Someday	Mixed, mostly serious	2 males	Evangelism; Success that leaves us empty; Going back to church
Wasted	Mixed	2 males	Job satisfaction; Christians and work
What about Life?	Mixed, mostly humorous	1 male, 1 female	Finding meaning to life; The empty void inside
What's the Ticket?	Mixed	2 females, 4 either males or females	Need for Christ; Contentment; Needs and wants

SONGS

Title	Artist	Style	Tempo	Seeker-Sensitivity Rating
Give Me Jesus	**Willow Creek Music**	**Ballad**	**Slow**	7
He Was	*Willow Creek Music*	*Pop/rock, in 6/8*	*Mid*	*10*
Heaven in the Real World	Steven Curtis Chapman	Pop/rock	Up	7
Hole Hearted	**Extreme**	**Rock**	**Up**	**10**
I Found Myself in You	Clay Crosse	Gospel ballad	Mid/slow	10
Leave a Light On	*Greg Ferguson*	*Ethereal pop ballad*	*Slow/mid*	*8*
Love That Will Not Let Me Go	**Steve Camp**	**Ballad**	**Slow**	**10**
Only You	*Willow Creek Music*	*Ballad*	*Slow*	*9*
A Place to Call Home	*Greg Ferguson/ Willow Creek Music*	*Gospel ballad*	*Slow, in 3*	*10*
Somebody Make Me Laugh	Patti Austin	Ballad	Slow	10
Strength in You	*Willow Creek Music*	*MOR pop*	*Slow/mid*	*10*
Treasure	**Gary Chapman**	**Acoustic ballad**	**Slow**	9
What a Ride	*Willow Creek Music*	*Pop/rock*	*Up*	*9*
_____	_____	_____	_____	___
_____	_____	_____	_____	___
_____	_____	_____	_____	___

Worship Choruses

Title	Artist	Style	Tempo	Seeker-Sensitivity Rating
I Am Here	*Willow Creek Music*	*Worship ballad*	*Slow*	*8*
Jesus, You're the Answer	Tommy Walker	Soulish worship ballad	Slow	5
Let Your Love Pour	*Student Impact*	*MOR worship*	*Mid*	*4*
More Precious Than Silver	Don Moen	Worship ballad	Slow	5
Reaching for You	*Willow Creek Music*	*Rock/pop*	*Up*	*10*
_____	_____	_____	_____	___
_____	_____	_____	_____	___

MOVIE CLIPS

Title: City Slickers

Topic: Disillusionment; Life fulfillment

Description: Billy Crystal's character speaks at his son's school. Disillusioned with life in general, he gives a very funny, very depressing discourse on the stages of life.

Start Time: 0:44:38

Start Cue: "As Danny said . . ."

End Time: 0:45:30

End Cue: "Any questions?"

Comments: _____

_____

Title: Cool Runnings

Topic: Success; Ambition

Description: A bobsledder asks his coach why he cheated twenty years ago in the Olympics. The answer has a lot to say about the trap of success and its ultimate lack of fulfillment.

Start Time: 1:25:15

Start Cue: Coach enters hotel room.

End Time: 1:27:15

End Cue: "When you cross that finish line, you'll know."

Comments: _____

_____

Title: She's Having a Baby

Topic: Life in suburbia; Emptiness of suburban life/American dream

Description: Funny parody of suburban life shows men in bad clothes dancing with lawnmowers while their wives dance around them with refreshments.

Start Time: 0:53:00

Start Cue: Start after the bicyclist leaves.

End Time: 0:54:30

End Cue: End when music stops.

Comments: _____

_____

Title: _____

Topic: _____

Description: _____

Start Time: _____

Start Cue: _____

End Time: _____

End Cue: _____

Comments: _____

Life Foundation

Refers to the biblical rock vs. sand analogy; asks the question "What are you building your life on?"
See also: **God's Faithfulness**

MESSAGE TITLES

❏ A Better Kind of Confidence
❏ Finding Your Place in the World
❏ Unmasking Your Master
❏ *Strength for the Storms of Life:* Staying Steady in the Storm
❏ *A Taste of Christianity:* Defining Our Beliefs
❏ *What Jesus Would Say to . . .* Bill Gates (or use the name of another very wealthy person)
❏ *What Would You Ask God?* What Is the Purpose of Life?

_____

_____

_____

DRAMAS

Title	Tone	Characters	Topics
After Life	Mixed; Serious ending, sober	1 male	The afterlife; Heaven and hell
Chameleon	Mixed	3 males	Controlling our emotions; God's presence in our lives
The Game of Life	Humorous	1 male, 1 female, 1 narrator	Decision making; Search for meaning
Is "Nothing" Sacred?	Humorous	3 males, and at least 4 others in group	Evolution vs. creation; Modern science
Lifetime Deal	Serious	2 males	Workaholism
Lizzy and Leroy	Humorous	1 male, 1 female, piano player (optional)	Life fulfillment; Material things don't satisfy
The Lures of Life	Mixed, light; Mime	5 males, 1 female	Adventurism; Life fulfillment
Maybe Someday	Mixed, mostly serious	2 males	Evangelism; Success that leaves us empty; Going back to church

Title	Tone	Characters	Topics
One Step Up, One Step Down	Serious	4 males (1 can be female)	Ambition; Priorities
Richard: 1985	Serious	2 males	Workaholism; Materialism vs. idealism
The Safe	Mixed	1 male, 1 female, 3 either males or females	Inner strength; Needing God's strength
Security Check	Mixed	1 male, 1 female, 1 offstage voice	Salvation; Works vs. grace
What about Life?	Mixed, mostly humorous	1 male, 1 female	Finding meaning to life; The empty void inside
_____	_____	_____	_____
_____	_____	_____	_____
_____	_____	_____	_____
_____	_____	_____	_____

SONGS

Title	Artist	Style	Tempo	Seeker-Sensitivity Rating
Ever Devoted	*Willow Creek Music*	*Ballad*	*Slow*	6
Foundations	Geoff Moore & the Distance	Folk pop ballad	Slow/mid	8
Give Me Jesus	**Willow Creek Music**	**Ballad**	**Slow**	7
Heaven in the Real World	Steven Curtis Chapman	Pop/rock	Up	7
His Love Is Strong	Clay Crosse	Pop	Up	10
Hold On to Jesus	Steven Curtis Chapman	Ballad	Slow	8
Hole Hearted	Extreme	Rock	Up	10
I Found Myself in You	Clay Crosse	Gospel ballad	Mid/slow	10
I Go to the Rock	Dottie Rambo; Whitney Houston	Swing/big band	Mid	7
In My Father's Hands	Susan Ashton	Folk pop	Mid	9
Life Support	*Greg Ferguson*	*R & B/pop*	*Mid/up*	*9*
Love That Will Not Let Me Go	**Steve Camp**	**Ballad**	**Slow**	10
No Better Place	Steven Curtis Chapman	Pop/folk rock	Up	7
A Place to Call Home	*Greg Ferguson/ Willow Creek Music*	*Gospel ballad*	*Slow, in 3*	10
Strength in You	*Willow Creek Music*	*MOR pop*	*Slow/mid*	10

Title	Artist	Style	Tempo	Seeker-Sensitivity Rating
Thy Word	Amy Grant	Ballad	Slow	4
Treasure	**Gary Chapman**	**Acoustic ballad**	**Slow**	**9**
Unimportant Things	**Paul Smith**	**Ballad**	**Slow**	**7**
What a Ride	*Willow Creek Music*	*Pop/rock*	*Up*	*9*

Worship Choruses

Title	Artist	Style	Tempo	Seeker-Sensitivity Rating
Jesus, What a Beautiful Name	Hillsongs	Worship ballad—in 6/8	Slow/mid	6
Jesus, You're the Answer	Tommy Walker	Soulish worship ballad	Slow	5

 MOVIE CLIPS

Title: _____

Topic: _____

Description: _____

Start Time: _____

Start Cue: _____

End Time: _____

End Cue: _____

Comments: _____

_____

_____

Misconceptions of Christianity

Many people don't believe because they have a distorted view of God or of the Christian life.
See also: **Grace vs. Works/Legalism, Identity of God—General, The Joy of the Christian Life**

MESSAGE TITLES

- ❏ Five Deadly Lies
- ❏ Fully Informed Followers
- ❏ *Faith on Trial:* Barriers to Belief
- ❏ *A Taste of Christianity:* A Better Kind of Freedom
- ❏ *What Jesus Would Say to . . .* Oprah Winfrey
- ❏ **Three Things God Loves (That Most People Think He Doesn't):** Leisure • Laughter • Love Making

DRAMAS

Title	Tone	Characters	Topics
Acting the Part		1 male, 2 females	Legalism; Living out our Christianity
D-Day	Humorous	2 males, 1 female	Misconceptions about Christianity; Becoming a Christian
Don Juan De Schaumburg	Humorous	3 males, 1 female	False views of Christians; Dating
Guess Which God	Humorous	4 males, offstage male and female voices	Confusion about God; The nature of God
"It"	Humorous	2 males, 1 female	Becoming a Christian doesn't mean no problems; Vulnerability of new believers
The Lures of Life	Mixed, light; Mime	5 males, 1 female	Adventurism; Life fulfillment
Monday Night Meeting	Humorous	4 males	New Christian; Joy of Christian life; Discipleship
A Problem of Perception	Humorous	3 males, 1 female	Misconceptions about Christianity; Christian life

Title	Tone	Characters	Topics
Pulpit Talk	Humorous	3 males, 2 females	Stereotypical church experiences; Sermons; Introduction to Sermon on the Mount
Will the Real God Please Stand Up?	Humorous	3 males, 1 female	God's character; Second commandment; What is God like?
_____	_____	_____	_____
_____	_____	_____	_____
_____	_____	_____	_____

SONGS

Title	Artist	Style	Tempo	Seeker-Sensitivity Rating
He Was	*Willow Creek Music*	*Pop/rock, in 6/8*	*Mid*	*10*
No Better Place	Steven Curtis Chapman	Pop/folk rock	Up	7
Only by Grace	*Willow Creek Music*	*Pop/rock*	*Mid*	*10*
What a Ride	*Willow Creek Music*	*Pop/rock*	*Up*	*9*
_____	_____	_____	_____	____
_____	_____	_____	_____	____
_____	_____	_____	_____	____

Worship Choruses

Title	Artist	Style	Tempo	Seeker-Sensitivity Rating
_____	_____	_____	_____	____
_____	_____	_____	_____	____
_____	_____	_____	_____	____

MOVIE CLIPS

Title: _____

Topic: _____

Description: _____

Start Time: _____

Start Cue: _____

End Time: _____

End Cue: _____

Comments: _____

New Christians

Refers to the specific issues that face brand-new or young believers
See also: **Baptism**

MESSAGE TITLES

❑ *Seasons of a Spiritual Life:* Spiritual Infancy

_____

_____

_____

_____

DRAMAS

Title	Tone	Characters	Topics
A Day in the Life	Humorous	5 males	Christians in the marketplace; New Christian
Call of the Wild	Mixed	1 male, 1 female	Serving God; Serving in a place consistent with your gifts and temperament
First-Day Jitters	Humorous	1 female	New Christian; Obeying God
"It"	Humorous	2 males, 1 female	Becoming a Christian doesn't mean no problems; Vulnerability of new believers
Milestones	Mixed	1 male	Baptism; New Christian
Monday Night Meeting	Humorous	4 males	New Christian; Joy of Christian life; Discipleship
The Prisoner	Serious	3 males, 1 female	Easter; Freedom from sin; New Christian
Welcome to the Family	Humorous	2 males, 1 female	New Christian; Growing in Christ
_____	_____	_____	_____
_____	_____	_____	_____
_____	_____	_____	_____
_____	_____	_____	_____

SONGS

Title	Artist	Style	Tempo	Seeker-Sensitivity Rating
All the Faith You Need	*Greg Ferguson*	*Bluesy rock*	*Up*	*10*
From This Moment On	Newsong	Ballad	Slow	8
He Won't Let You Go	**The Kry**	**Piano ballad**	**Slow**	**10**
I Found Myself in You	Clay Crosse	Gospel ballad	Mid/slow	10
I'm Amazed	*Willow Creek Music*	*Ballad*	*Slow*	*7*
I've Been Released	*Willow Creek Music*	*Pop/rock—Chicago sound*	*Up*	*9*
My Life Is Yours	*Willow Creek Music*	*Acoustic ballad*	*Slow*	*10*
Take My Hand	The Kry	Acoustic ballad	Mid/slow	9
Who Am I? (Grace Flows Down)	**Watermark**	**Folk pop**	**Mid/slow**	**8**

Worship Choruses

Title	Artist	Style	Tempo	Seeker-Sensitivity Rating
Jesus, You're the Answer	Tommy Walker	Soulish worship ballad	Slow	5
Thank You for Saving Me	Delirious	Folk rock worship ballad	Slow/mid	3

MOVIE CLIPS

Title: _____

Topic: _____

Description: _____

Start Time: _____

Start Cue: _____

End Time: _____

End Cue: _____

Comments: _____

Other Religions

This includes cults, and I've also included Catholicism here, because of some of the methodological, and sometimes theological differences between Catholics and Protestants.

MESSAGE TITLES

❑ Religions Gone Awry
❑ What Catholics Can Learn from Protestants
❑ What Protestants Can Learn from Catholics
❑ *Facing New Realities:* Smorgasbord Spirituality
❑ *I Have a Friend Who* Thinks All Religions Are the Same
❑ **Alternatives to Christianity:** The New Age Movement • Contemporary Cults • Major World Religions
❑ **The Rise of Satanism:** The Secret World of Satan Worship • A Biography of Satan • Overcoming Satanic Opposition

DRAMAS

Title	Tone	Characters	Topics
Anything but Religion	Mixed, mostly serious	2 males, 2 females	Denominational differences; Families alienated because of religion
The Conversion	Serious	2 males, 1 female	Hinduism
Differences	Humorous	2 males, 1 female	Catholicism vs. Protestantism
Faith in Jeopardy	Mixed	2 males, 2 females	Mormonism
Family Values	Serious	2 males; 2 females	Cults; Broken families
The Gardeners	Humorous	1 male, 1 female	New Age movement
Getting Directions	Humorous	2 males	Not all paths lead to God; Christianity's exclusive claims
Is "Nothing" Sacred?	Humorous	3 males, and at least 4 others in group	Evolution vs. creation; Modern science

Title	Tone	Characters	Topics
Jeopardized Religion	Humorous	3 males, 1 female	World religions; People's ignorance of ideas other than their own
Make It Happen	Humorous	5 males, 1 female (numerous extras for attendees and security)	Taking responsibility for change; The limits of self-help seminars
Nothing to It	Mixed	2 males, 2 females	Satanism; Spiritual warfare
Winning Strategy	Mixed	2 males, 4 males or females	Good vs. evil; Busyness

SONGS

*It is difficult to pin down specific songs for this topic, but with theological issues, it often works well to use songs that affirm who God is. See **Apologetics, God's Character—General, Lordship of Christ.***

Title	Artist	Style	Tempo	Seeker-Sensitivity Rating

Worship Choruses

Title	Artist	Style	Tempo	Seeker-Sensitivity Rating
Bend My Knee	*Student Impact*	*Rock worship*	*Up*	*5*

MOVIE CLIPS

Title: _____

Topic: _____

Description: _____

Start Time: _____

Start Cue: _____

End Time: _____

End Cue: _____

Comments: _____

_____

_____

Spiritual Seeking

This topic seeks to affirm and encourage the seeking process.

MESSAGE TITLES

- ❏ The Benefits of Being a Seeker
- ❏ Cliffs Notes on Christianity
- ❏ Doubters Welcome
- ❏ The Rewards of Spiritual Risk Taking
- ❏ Settling Life's Biggest Issue
- ❏ Show Me the Way
- ❏ *Seasons of a Spiritual Life:* Spiritual Seeking
- ❏ *What Jesus Would Say to . . .* Peter Jennings

Package Suggestion

Drama:
Reason Enough

Song:
A Place to Call Home

Song:
Dear God

Drama:
Maybe Someday

Song:
Leave a Light On

DRAMAS

Title	Tone	Characters	Topics
After Life	Mixed; Serious ending, sober	1 male	The afterlife; Heaven and hell
The Big Question	Mixed, mostly humorous	1 male, 1 female, 1 child	The existence of God
D-Day	Humorous	2 males, 1 female	Misconceptions about Christianity; Becoming a Christian
The Fence-Sitter	Mixed	4 males, 1 female	Indecision; Getting involved in ministry; Deciding to become a Christian
The Game of Life	Humorous	1 male, 1 female, 1 narrator	Decision making; Search for meaning
Getting Directions	Humorous	2 males	Not all paths lead to God; Christianity's exclusive claims
Guess Which God	Humorous	4 males, offstage male and female voices	Confusion about God; The nature of God

Title	Tone	Characters	Topics
Is "Nothing" Sacred?	Humorous	3 males and at least 4 others in group	Evolution vs. creation; Modern science
Jeopardized Faith	Humorous	3 males, 1 female	The Bible
The Lures of Life	Mixed, light; Mime	5 males, 1 female	Adventurism; Life fulfillment
Maybe Someday	Mixed, mostly serious	2 males	Evangelism; Success that leaves us empty; Going back to church
Reason Enough	Mixed, mostly serious	1 male, 1 female	Importance of faith grounded in reason
Wait 'Til Half-Time	Mixed	1 male, 1 female	Eternity; Heaven and hell; Evangelism
What about Life?	Mixed, mostly humorous	1 male, 1 female	Finding meaning to life; The empty void inside

SONGS

Title	Artist	Style	Tempo	Seeker-Sensitivity Rating
All the Faith You Need	*Greg Ferguson*	*Bluesy rock*	*Up*	*10*
Big Enough	Chris Rice	Folk ballad, in 6/8	Slow/mid	10
Could You Believe?	Scott Krippayne	Pop	Up	9
Dear God	**Midge Ure**	**Rock**	**Mid/up**	**10**
Evidence	*Willow Creek Music*	*Folk pop*	*Mid*	*10*
The Great Divide	Point of Grace	Power ballad	Slow	9
He Was	*Willow Creek Music*	*Pop/rock, in 6/8*	*Mid*	*10*
Heaven in the Real World	Steven Curtis Chapman	Pop/rock	Up	7
Hole Hearted	Extreme	Rock	Up	10
I Found Myself in You	Clay Crosse	Gospel ballad	Mid/slow	10
In My Heart	*Greg Ferguson*	*Celtic worship ballad*	*Slow*	*9*
Leave a Light On	*Greg Ferguson*	*Ethereal pop ballad*	*Slow/mid*	*8*
A Place to Call Home	*Greg Ferguson/ Willow Creek Music*	*Gospel ballad*	*Slow, in 3*	*10*

Title	Artist	Style	Tempo	Seeker-Sensitivity Rating
Reaching for You	*Willow Creek Music*	*Rock/pop*	*Up*	*10*
Treasure	**Gary Chapman**	**Acoustic ballad**	**Slow**	**9**

Worship Choruses

Title	Artist	Style	Tempo	Seeker-Sensitivity Rating
I Am Here	*Willow Creek Music*	*Worship ballad*	*Slow*	*8*
In My Heart	*Greg Ferguson*	*Celtic worship ballad*	*Slow*	*9*
Jesus, You're the Answer	Tommy Walker	Soulish worship ballad	Slow	5
Lord, I Believe in You	Tommy Walker	Worship power ballad	Slow/mid	4
Meet with Me	Ten Shekel Shirt	Modern worship	Up	7
Open the Eyes of My Heart	Paul Baloche	Pop/rock worship	Up	5
Reaching for You	*Willow Creek Music*	*Rock/pop*	*Up*	*10*

MOVIE CLIPS

Title: Amistad

Topic: The gospel; Salvation

Description: Powerful telling of the gospel from the standpoint of a wrongly imprisoned slave who has learned the story from pictures in a Bible.

Start Time: 1:35:45

Start Cue: Prisoner is reading the Bible. Cinque says, "You don't have to pretend to be interested in that."

End Time: 1:39:36

End Cue: "It doesn't look so bad." Picture of three crosses.

Comments: _____

_____

Title: The Matrix

Topic: Decision making; Spiritual seeking

Description: Metaphors abound in this clip, which shows Morpheus explaining the matrix to Neo. He offers him the choice to stay in the bondage of the world he's in (the matrix) or to know the truth and be set free. Should he take the blue pill or the red pill (the truth)? Neo chooses the red pill.

Start Time: 0:25:42

Start Cue: Neo enters the room where Morpheus is.

End Time: 0:29:50

End Cue: "Follow me."

Comments: The clip probably needs explaining but could easily be used in a sermon to illustrate the choice we make to be free of the slavery of sin through choosing Christ.

_____
_____
_____

Title: _____

Topic: _____

Description: _____

Start Time: _____

Start Cue: _____

End Time: _____

End Cue: _____

Comments: _____
_____
_____

Social Issues

Abortion

MESSAGE TITLES

- ❏ *Modern Day Madness:* Unwanted Pregnancies
- ❏ *Our Modern Moral Trifecta:* Abortion

DRAMAS

Title	Tone	Characters	Topics
Catch 22	Serious	2 females	Abortion
The Painful Process	Serious	1 female	Abortion

SONGS

*Songs of tenderness and compassion work well with these dramas. See **God as a Refuge, God's Love, God's Tenderness, Our Value to God.**

Title	Artist	Style	Tempo	Seeker-Sensitivity Rating
Lay Your Burdens Down	*Willow Creek Music*	*Ballad*	*Slow*	*9*
Peace Be Still	Al Denson	Ballad	Slow	10

Worship Choruses

Title	Artist	Style	Tempo	Seeker-Sensitivity Rating

MOVIE CLIPS

Title: _____

Topic: _____

Description: _____

Start Time: _____

Start Cue: _____

End Time: _____

End Cue: _____

Comments: _____

_____

_____

———Caring for the Poor———

See also: **Compassion**

MESSAGE TITLES

- ❏ Practicing Compassion
- ❏ *Becoming a Contagious Christian:* Compassion
- ❏ *A Faith That Works—The Book of James:* Religion according to God
- ❏ *A Faith That Works—The Book of James:* Who Matters?
- ❏ *Making Life Work:* Cultivate Compassion
- ❏ *Making Life Work:* Do Goodness
- ❏ *What Jesus Would Say to . . .* Mother Teresa

DRAMAS

Title	Tone	Characters	Topics
Am I Missing Something?	Serious	3 males, 2 females	Attitudes in serving; Giving; Self-deception; Rationalizing
Buy One, Get One Free	Mixed, moving	1 male, 1 female	The joy of giving
Everybody Needs	Mixed	1 female	Being impressed with externals
Fourth of July	Mixed	1 male, 2 females, 1 child	Fourth of July; The homeless
Heart Failure	Humorous	1 male	Giving
Here to Help	Mixed	6 females	Helping those less fortunate; Not giving up; Dealing with difficult people
No Accident	Mixed, mostly serious	2 females	Forgiveness; Love your enemies; Growing in Christlikeness
Simple Gifts	Humorous but touching	2 males (1 teen), 3 females (1 teen and 1 girl)	Caring for others less fortunate; Materialism
The Story of Rachel	Serious	3 females	Care for the poor; Compassion
Suit and Volly	Humorous	2 males, 2 females	Motives in serving others

SONGS

Title	Artist	Style	Tempo	Seeker-Sensitivity Rating
Broadway	Sherri Youngward	Ballad	Slow	7
Everything (Apron Full of Stains)	**The Normals**	**Pop/rock**	**Mid/up**	**10**
Giving Thing	**Truth**	**Pop**	**Mid/up**	**8**
Heaven in the Real World	Steven Curtis Chapman	Pop/rock	Up	7
Helping Hand	Amy Grant	Pop	Mid/up	10
Not Too Far from Here	**Kim Boyce**	**Pop ballad**	**Slow**	**8**
We Can Make a Difference	**Jaci Velasquez**	**Pop**	**Up**	**8**
_____	_____	_____	_____	_____
_____	_____	_____	_____	_____
_____	_____	_____	_____	_____

Worship Choruses

Title	Artist	Style	Tempo	Seeker-Sensitivity Rating
_____	_____	_____	_____	_____
_____	_____	_____	_____	_____
_____	_____	_____	_____	_____

MOVIE CLIPS

Title: _____

Topic: _____

Description: _____

Start Time: _____

Start Cue: _____

End Time: _____

End Cue: _____

Comments: _____

_____

_____

Homosexuality

Might also include: *AIDS*

MESSAGE TITLES

- ❏ Hope for the Homosexual
- ❏ The Truth about Homosexuality
- ❏ *Our Modern Moral Trifecta:* Homosexuality

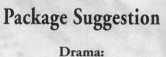

Package Suggestion

Drama:
Misjudged Love

Song:
The Last Song

DRAMAS

Title	Tone	Characters	Topics
Just as I Am	Serious	1 male	Homosexuality
Misjudged Love	Serious	2 males, 1 female	Homosexuality; AIDS; Father-son relationships

SONGS

Title	Artist	Style	Tempo	Seeker-Sensitivity Rating
The Last Song	**Elton John**	**Ballad**	**Slow**	**10**

Worship Choruses

Title	Artist	Style	Tempo	Seeker-Sensitivity Rating

MOVIE CLIPS

Title: _____

Topic: _____

Description: _____

Start Time: _____

Start Cue: _____

End Time: _____

End Cue: _____

Comments: _____
_____
_____
_____

—The Power of the Media—

MESSAGE TITLES

❑ Sources for Values
❑ Spiritual Eyesight
❑ *What Jesus Would Say to* . . . Murphy Brown
❑ *What Jesus Would Say to* . . . Oprah Winfrey
❑ *What Jesus Would Say to* . . . Rush Limbaugh

_____

_____

_____

DRAMAS

Title	Tone	Characters	Topics
The Big Sell	Humorous	3 males, 2 females	Obsession with sex in society; Effect of the media
Confessions of an Ad-aholic	Humorous	1 male, 1 female	Materialism; Power of the media; The American dream
It's Only a Movie	Humorous	2 males, 2 females, 1 offstage voice	The power of media; The effects of what we see; Male-female differences

SONGS

Title	Artist	Style	Tempo	Seeker-Sensitivity Rating
Couch Potato	Billy Crockett	Acoustic pop	Up	10
Words	**Kim Hill**	**Pop/rock**	**Up**	**10**

Title	Artist	Style	Tempo	Seeker-Sensitivity Rating

Worship Choruses

Title	Artist	Style	Tempo	Seeker-Sensitivity Rating

MOVIE CLIPS

Title: _____

Topic: _____

Description: _____

Start Time: _____

Start Cue: _____

End Time: _____

End Cue: _____

Comments: _____

Racism

MESSAGE TITLES

- ❏ Bridging the Racial Divide
- ❏ *Our Modern Moral Trifecta:* Racism

DRAMAS

Title	Tone	Characters	Topics
Face Value	Serious	1 male, 2 females	Racial prejudice; September 11
Half-Baked	Humorous	1 male, 2 females	Racism; Prejudice

SONGS

Title	Artist	Style	Tempo	Seeker-Sensitivity Rating
At the Foot of the Cross	*Willow Creek Music*	*Pop*	*Mid*	*7*
Love Can Build a Bridge	**The Judds**	**Ballad**	**Slow**	**10**
Someday	Grover Levy	Pop	Mid/up	8

Worship Choruses

Title	Artist	Style	Tempo	Seeker-Sensitivity Rating
Let the Walls Fall Down	Student Impact	Pop worship	Up	6

MOVIE CLIPS

Title: Remember the Titans

Topic: Leadership; Respecting authority; Pride; Racism

Description: The Titans' star player confronts the coach and tries to lay down the law about who will play, based on color. The coach puts him in his place.

Start Time: 0:14:21/DVD Ch. 5

Start Cue: The coach starts to walk to the bus.

End Time: 0:16:57

End Cue: "Fix that tie, son." Close-up of the coach.

Comments: If you are using this clip for a message on racism, you may want to use the next minute or so, which shows the coach integrating the two buses.

Title: Remember the Titans

Topic: Truth telling; Racism; Leadership; Friendship

Description: The Titans' two star defensive players, one white and one black, confront each other on their effort and leadership, respectively. They become best friends later in the movie.

Start Time: 0:29:09/DVD Ch. 9

Start Cue: Gary bumps into Julius. "Okay, man, listen. I'm Gary, you're Julius."

End Time: 0:30:48

End Cue: "Attitude reflects leadership, Captain."

Comments: The two scenes following this one are also very strong, and the three scenes combined, though long, would be a great example of leadership and breaking down racial barriers. Gary says "shiver push," and it sounds like profanity because it goes by fast, but it's not.

Title: Remember the Titans

Topic: Racism; Friendship

Description: Julius comes to visit his friend Gary, who has been paralyzed in a car accident. The scene is a poignant example of friendship and breaking down racial barriers.

Start Time: 1:26:18/DVD Ch. 25

Start Cue: Julius walks into the hospital.

End Time: 1:29:25

End Cue: "Left side. Strong side." The boys clasp hands.

Comments: _____

_____

_____

Title: The Man without a Face

Topic: Prejudice; Racism

Description: Mel Gibson plays a disfigured man who recites a portion of Shakespeare's *Merchant of Venice* about prejudice against Jews. The clip is all the more poignant because of his disfigured face.

Start Time: 0:49:30

Start Cue: "I hold the world but as the world . . ."

End Time: 0:50:40

End Cue: "Shall we not revenge?"

Comments: Last line is pretty harsh, though honest.

_____

_____

_____

Title: _____

Topic: _____

Description: _____

Start Time: _____

Start Cue: _____

End Time: _____

End Cue: _____

Comments: _____

_____

_____

——The State of the World——

Refers to the decay of our society. This topic also includes many elements used in the wake of the events of September 11, 2001.

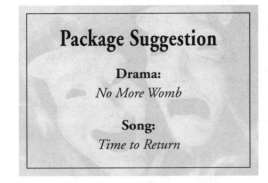

Package Suggestion

Drama:
No More Womb

Song:
Time to Return

MESSAGE TITLES

❏ *Understanding the Times:* The '90s
❏ **Changing Times:** The Changing American Male • The Changing American Female • The Changing American Child • The Changing American Sexuality • The Changing American Dream • The Changing American Church
❏ **Facing New Realities:** Life.com • The Post-Walton Family • The Sexual Ethic • The Changing American Workplace • Smorgasbord Spirituality

_____
_____
_____
_____
_____

DRAMAS

Title	Tone	Characters	Topics
Everybody Needs	Mixed	1 female	Being impressed with externals
Face Value	Serious	1 male, 2 females	Racial prejudice; September 11
No More Womb	Mixed	1 male, 1 female	State of the world; Fear of the unknown

SONGS

Title	Artist	Style	Tempo	Seeker-Sensitivity Rating
Dear God	**Midge Ure**	**Rock**	**Mid/up**	**10**
Good News	**Chris Rice**	**Pop**	**Up**	**9**
Have No Fear	*Willow Creek Music*	*Piano ballad*	*Slow*	*9*
Healing Song	Curt Coffield	Ballad, in 3	Slow/mid	7
Heaven in the Real World	Steven Curtis Chapman	Pop/rock	Up	7
Hold On	*Willow Creek Music*	*Acoustic rock/pop ballad*	*Slow/mid*	*10*
Naïve	**Chris Rice**	**Folk pop**	**Mid**	**8**
Not Too Far from Here	Kim Boyce	Pop ballad	Slow	8
Someday	Grover Levy	Pop	Mid/up	8
Time to Return	*Willow Creek Music*	*Ballad*	*Slow*	*7*
We Can Make a Difference	Jaci Velasquez	Pop	Up	8
You Are with Me Still	*Willow Creek Music*	*Acoustic ballad*	*Slow*	*9*
_____	_____	_____	_____	_____
_____	_____	_____	_____	_____
_____	_____	_____	_____	_____

Worship Choruses

Title	Artist	Style	Tempo	Seeker-Sensitivity Rating
As We Worship You	Tommy Walker	Worship ballad	Slow	1
Build Your Church into My Heart	*Greg Ferguson/ Willow Creek Music*	*Pop*	*Up*	*2*
Healing Song	Curt Coffield	Ballad, in 3	Slow/mid	7
Show Your Power	Kevin Prosch, Vineyard	Rock/pop worship	Up	3
Still I Will Worship You	*Willow Creek Music*	*Pop/rock worship*	*Up*	*3*
You Are with Me Still	*Willow Creek Music*	*Acoustic ballad*	*Slow*	*9*
_____	_____	_____	_____	_____
_____	_____	_____	_____	_____
_____	_____	_____	_____	_____

MOVIE CLIPS

Title: _____

Topic: _____

Description: _____

Start Time: _____

Start Cue: _____

End Time: _____

End Cue: _____

Comments: _____

_____

_____

Song Index

Specials

All I Ever Wanted
Artist: Margaret Becker
Album/Label: Simple House/Sparrow
Style: Pop/rock ballad
Tempo: Slow/mid
Seeker-Sensitivity Rating: 4
Themes: Statement of devotion to Christ

*All the Faith You Need
Artist: Greg Ferguson
Album/Label: Leave a Light On/Willow Creek Music
Style: Bluesy rock
Tempo: Up
Seeker-Sensitivity Rating: 10
Themes: Faith; Affirmation of seeking process
Comments: Strong opener, especially for evangelistic services

All Things New
Artist: Watermark
Album/Label: All Things New/Rocketown
Style: Folk pop
Tempo: Mid
Seeker-Sensitivity Rating: 8
Themes: God's renewing power; Redemption

Almighty
Artist: Wayne Watson
Album/Label: Home Free/Word
Style: Praise & worship/pop
Tempo: Up
Seeker-Sensitivity Rating: 2
Themes: Praise & worship; God's power
Comments: Older song that might still work as a worship chorus in some churches

Altar of Ego
Artist: Carolyn Arends
Album/Label: I Can Hear You/Reunion
Style: Folk pop
Tempo: Mid/up
Seeker-Sensitivity Rating: 6
Themes: Pride; Ego; Thinking more highly of ourselves than we ought to
Comments: Clever writing—may be a bit hard to catch and track the words. Great hook phrase—could be used in a sermon

Always before Me
Artist: Steven Curtis Chapman
Album/Label: Coram Deo 2/Sparrow
Style: Worship ballad, in 3
Tempo: Slow/mid

Seeker-Sensitivity Rating: 1
Themes: Worship; Holding God above all else

Another Time, Another Place
Artist: Sandi Patti (with Wayne Watson)
Album/Label: Another Time, Another Place/Word
Style: Power ballad
Tempo: Slow
Seeker-Sensitivity Rating: 8
Themes: Heaven; Longing for heaven

Art in Me
Artist: Jars of Clay
Album/Label: Jars of Clay/Essential
Style: Alternative rock
Tempo: Mid/up
Seeker-Sensitivity Rating: 9
Themes: Our uniqueness; Self-worth

Ask Me
Artist: Amy Grant
Album/Label: Heart in Motion/Myrrh
Style: Pop
Tempo: Mid
Seeker-Sensitivity Rating: 9
Themes: Child abuse
Comments: Very volatile subject, and some of the images in this song may be overwhelming—handle with extreme care

At Jesus' Feet
Artist: Billy and Sarah Gaines
Album/Label: Love's the Key/Benson
Style: Ballad
Tempo: Slow
Seeker-Sensitivity Rating: 6
Themes: Relationship with God; Being in God's presence
Comments: Has worked in Willow Creek seeker services as a picture of a relationship with God

*At the Foot of the Cross
Artist: Willow Creek Music
Album/Label: None
Style: Pop
Tempo: Mid
Seeker-Sensitivity Rating: 7
Themes: Equality in Christ; Unity
Comments: Can be used as a worship chorus

*Audience of One
Artist: Willow Creek Music
Album/Label: A Place to Call Home/Word; Maranatha!

Style: Power ballad
Tempo: Slow
Seeker-Sensitivity Rating: 8
Themes: Pleasing God, not men; Ministry motives
Comments: Strong statement of ministry/personal motives

Away in a Manger
Artist: Steven Curtis Chapman
Album/Label: Sparrow Christmas/Sparrow
Style: Folk pop
Tempo: Mid
Seeker-Sensitivity Rating: 10
Themes: Christmas

Awesome God
Artist: Rich Mullins
Album/Label: Winds of Heaven . . . Stuff of Earth/Reunion
Style: Pop anthem
Tempo: Mid/up
Seeker-Sensitivity Rating: 1
Themes: God's power; Praise & worship

Ball and Chain
Artist: Susan Ashton
Album/Label: Wakened by the Wind/Sparrow
Style: Folk pop
Tempo: Mid
Seeker-Sensitivity Rating: 9
Themes: Freedom from sin; Salvation
Comments: Poetic lyrics—might be tough to track lyrically in some settings. Strong images

*Be Not Afraid
Artist: Bridgeway Community Church
Album/Label: From the Cradle to the Cross/none
Style: Ballad
Tempo: Slow
Seeker-Sensitivity Rating: 9
Themes: Christmas; Christ overcoming sin and shame
Comments: Beautiful Christmas song. The church's website is www.bridgewaycommunitychurch.com.

*Be Still and Know
Artist: Tommy Walker & the CA Worship Band
Album/Label: Live at Home/Get Down Records
Style: Rock/pop, in 6/8

Tempo: Mid
Seeker-Sensitivity Rating: 5
Themes: God as a refuge; God's help in troubled times
Comments: Can be used as a worship song or a special

A Beautiful Place
Artist: Wayne Watson
Album/Label: A Beautiful Place/Dayspring
Style: MOR ballad
Tempo: Mid/slow
Seeker-Sensitivity Rating: 9
Themes: Romans 8:28; The benefits of trials

The Beauty of Holiness
Artist: Steve Camp
Album/Label: Mercy in the Wilderness/Warner Alliance
Style: Ballad
Tempo: Slow
Seeker-Sensitivity Rating: 1
Themes: Worship; God's holiness

Because You Loved Me
Artist: Celine Dion
Album/Label: Falling into You/Sony
Style: Pop ballad
Tempo: Slow
Seeker-Sensitivity Rating: 10
Themes: Love; Parenting; Believing in people
Comments: A bit sappy but still moves people

*Behind Every Fantasy
Artist: Willow Creek Music
Album/Label: A Place to Call Home/Word; Maranatha!
Style: Country pop
Tempo: Up
Seeker-Sensitivity Rating: 10
Themes: Temptation; Consequences of sin
Comments: "Behind every fantasy is a harsh reality" is the "hook" and basic message of the song.

Between You and Me
Artist: DC Talk
Album/Label: Jesus Freak/Forefront
Style: Pop/rock
Tempo: Mid
Seeker-Sensitivity Rating: 10
Themes: Reconciliation; Broken relationships; Relational breakdown
Comments: Had some secular radio airplay—might be familiar to your congregation

Beyond Justice to Mercy
Artist: Susan Ashton
Album/Label: Wakened by the Wind/Sparrow
Style: Ballad
Tempo: Slow
Seeker-Sensitivity Rating: 10
Themes: Relational breakdown; Forgiveness
Comments: Powerful song—follows several dramas well

*Big Enough
Artist: Chris Rice
Album/Label: Past the Edges/Rocketown
Style: Folk ballad, in 6/8
Tempo: Slow/mid
Seeker-Sensitivity Rating: 10
Themes: Doubt; Questioning God

*Blind Side
Artist: Susan Ashton
Album/Label: A Distant Call/Sparrow
Style: Folk rock
Tempo: Up
Seeker-Sensitivity Rating: 9
Themes: Sin; Temptation

Bound to Come Some Trouble
Artist: Rich Mullins
Album/Label: Never Picture Perfect/Reunion
Style: Ballad
Tempo: Slow
Seeker-Sensitivity Rating: 10
Themes: Hardship—Jesus understands; Jesus will be there
Comments: Can also work as a female solo

Bridge between Two Hearts
Artist: Bob Carlisle
Album/Label: Bob Carlisle/Sparrow
Style: Pop
Tempo: Up
Seeker-Sensitivity Rating: 9
Themes: Relationships; God's love joining peoples' hearts
Comments: Key might need to be lowered

*Broadway
Artist: Sherri Youngward
Album/Label: Faces, Memories, Places/5 Minute Walk
Style: Ballad
Tempo: Slow
Seeker-Sensitivity Rating: 7
Themes: Caring for the poor and needy

Busy Man
Artist: Steven Curtis Chapman
Album/Label: For the Sake of the Call/Sparrow
Style: Pop
Tempo: Mid/up
Seeker-Sensitivity Rating: 10
Themes: Pace of life; Materialism

But if Not
Artist: Student Impact
Album/Label: Alive/Willow Creek Music
Style: Acoustic ballad
Tempo: Slow
Seeker-Sensitivity Rating: 5
Theme: Worshiping God regardless of circumstances; Hardship
Comments: Can be done as a special or as a worship chorus

Butterfly Kisses
Artist: Bob Carlisle
Album/Label: Butterfly Kisses (Shades of Grace)/Brentwood

Style: Pop ballad
Tempo: Slow
Seeker-Sensitivity Rating: 10
Themes: Father-daughter relationships
Comments: Get out the Kleenex!

Call of the Wild
Artist: Susan Ashton
Album/Label: Susan Ashton/Sparrow
Style: Country
Tempo: Mid
Seeker-Sensitivity Rating: 10
Themes: Faithfulness in marriage; Consequences of sin
Comments: Story song—needs to be communicated well to avoid loss of focus. Could be enhanced by drama or video

*Can't Live a Day without You
Artist: Avalon
Album/Label: In a Different Light/Sparrow
Style: Pop ballad
Tempo: Slow/mid
Seeker-Sensitivity Rating: 8
Themes: Our need for Christ

Can't We Try?
Artist: Dan Hill and Vonda Shepard
Album/Label: Dan Hill's Greatest Hits/Columbia
Style: Pop ballad duet
Tempo: Slow
Seeker-Sensitivity Rating: 10
Themes: Marital breakdown; Marital healing
Comments: Older song but still a good song to follow a drama showing marital conflict.

Casual Christian
Artist: DeGarmo & Key
Album/Label: Commander Sozo . . ./Frontline; Benson
Style: Power ballad
Tempo: Slow
Seeker-Sensitivity Rating: 6
Themes: Authenticity; Commitment to Christ
Comments: May be out of print—great song that still holds up

Cat's in the Cradle
Artist: Harry Chapin; Ricky Skaggs
Album/Label: Harry Chapin Anthology/Elektra; Solid Ground/WEA; Atlantic
Style: Folk
Tempo: Mid
Seeker-Sensitivity Rating: 10
Themes: Parenting; Having time for your kids; Regret
Comments: The opening guitar riff alone provokes an emotional response. This is still a very strong song. Ricky Skaggs's version also has a strong video companion.

*Change in My Life
Artist: John Pagano
Album/Label: Leap of Faith Soundtrack/MCA
Style: Gospel

Tempo: Mid/up
Seeker-Sensitivity Rating: 9
Themes: Testimonial—changed life
Comments: Works best with a medium-large vocal group but can be done with smaller group. Great testimonial song

Charm Is Deceitful
Artist: Kim Hill
Album/Label: Talk about Life/Reunion
Style: Ballad
Tempo: Slow
Seeker-Sensitivity Rating: 5
Themes: Proverbs 13 woman
Comments: Language is a little Christian for an unchurched audience but can still work

Circle of Friends
Artist: Point of Grace
Album/Label: Life, Love and Other Mysteries/Word
Style: Pop
Tempo: Mid
Seeker-Sensitivity Rating: 9
Themes: Friendship
Comments: Great to have vocalists who are close friends or who are in a small group sing this together.

Clumsy
Artist: Chris Rice
Album/Label: Deep Enough to Dream/Rocketown
Style: Pop
Tempo: Mid/up
Seeker-Sensitivity Rating: 8
Themes: Personal failure; God's unending love; Sanctification

Couch Potato
Artist: Billy Crockett
Album/Label: The Basic Stuff/Urgent
Style: Acoustic pop
Tempo: Up
Seeker-Sensitivity Rating: 10
Themes: TV; Sloth
Comments: Funny song about the negative effects of TV—especially fun with a vocalist who can play the guitar

*Could You Believe?
Artist: Scott Krippayne
Album/Label: More/Word
Style: Pop
Tempo: Up
Seeker-Sensitivity Rating: 9
Themes: God's love; Grace

Cross Medley
Artist: Willow Creek Music
Album/Label: None/Willow Creek Music
Style: Ballad medley—hymns
Tempo: Slow
Seeker-Sensitivity Rating: 7
Themes: The cross; Atonement; Grace
Comments: Combines "How Great Thou Art," "It Is Well," "Nothing but the Blood," and "Jesus Paid It All"

Dear God
Artist: Midge Ure
Album/Label: Answers to Nothing: If I Was: The Very Best of Midge Ure and Ultravox/Chrysalis
Style: Rock
Tempo: Mid/up
Seeker-Sensitivity Rating: 10
Themes: Doubt; State of the world; Does God exist?
Comments: Powerful song from a secular writer and the perspective of a nonbeliever

Desperado
Artist: Eagles
Album/Label: Eagles Live: Greatest Hits, 1971–1976—Desperado/Asylum
Style: Ballad
Tempo: Slow
Seeker-Sensitivity Rating: 10
Themes: Decision song—get off the fence
Comments: The Eagles' live version is great—a lot of passion.

*Dive
Artist: Steven Curtis Chapman
Album/Label: Speechless/Sparrow
Style: Pop/rock
Tempo: Up
Seeker-Sensitivity Rating: 9
Themes: Discipleship; Risk taking in our relationship with God; Going deeper
Comments: Great, fun song! We have done this with footage of skydivers and also with a home video of the guys singing the song jumping into a swimming pool fully clothed!

Dust in the Wind
Artist: Kansas
Album/Label: Point of Know Return/Columbia
Style: Acoustic ballad
Tempo: Slow/mid
Seeker-Sensitivity Rating: 10
Themes: Brevity of life
Comments: Classic rock song that has a powerful message and still connects

Eleanor Rigby
Artist: Beatles
Album/Label: Revolver/Capitol
Style: Acoustic ballad
Tempo: Slow/mid
Seeker-Sensitivity Rating: 10
Themes: Loneliness
Comments: We did this with an acoustic guitar accompaniment and a slower tempo—very effective

*Enough
Artist: Willow Creek Music
Album/Label: Enough/Willow Creek Music
Style: Piano ballad
Tempo: Slow
Seeker-Sensitivity Rating: 7
Themes: Sufficiency of Christ; God's acceptance of us as we are

Ever Devoted
Artist: Willow Creek Music
Album/Label: Ever Devoted/Willow Creek Music
Style: Ballad
Tempo: Slow
Seeker-Sensitivity Rating: 6
Themes: Devotion to God; Emptiness without God

*Every Season
Artist: Nicole Nordeman
Album/Label: This Mystery/Sparrow
Style: Ballad
Tempo: Slow
Seeker-Sensitivity Rating: 8
Themes: Seeing God in the changing seasons; Seasons of life

*Every Single Tear
Artist: Scott Krippayne
Album/Label: Bright Star, Blue Sky/Spring Hill
Style: Ballad
Tempo: Slow
Seeker-Sensitivity Rating: 10
Themes: God's love for the hurting; God as a refuge

*Everything (Apron Full of Stains)
Artist: The Normals
Album/Label: Better Than This/EMD; Chordant
Style: Pop/rock
Tempo: Mid/up
Seeker-Sensitivity Rating: 10
Themes: Love; Loving the lonely and broken; Being fully devoted
Comments: Works great with some of the lyrics acted out as sort of a "live music video"

*Evidence
Artist: Willow Creek Music
Album/Label: Enough/Willow Creek Music
Style: Folk pop
Tempo: Mid
Seeker-Sensitivity Rating: 10
Themes: Apologetics; Life change as evidence for Christ

*Face of Forgiveness
Artist: Willow Creek Music
Album/Label: Enough/Willow Creek Music
Style: Ballad
Tempo: Slow
Seeker-Sensitivity Rating: 10
Themes: Grace; Forgiveness

Facts Are Facts
Artist: Steven Curtis Chapman
Album/Label: Heaven in the Real World/Sparrow
Style: Rock/pop
Tempo: Up
Seeker-Sensitivity Rating: 4
Themes: God fulfills his promises; Call to commitment

*Faith, Hope, and Love Remain
Artist: Willow Creek Music

Album/Label: Enough/Willow Creek Music
Style: Bluesy pop
Tempo: Up
Seeker-Sensitivity Rating: 10
Themes: 1 Corinthians 13; Love
Comments: Can be done as a worship chorus or as a special

Faithless Heart
   Artist: Amy Grant
   Album/Label: Lead Me On/Myrrh
   Style: Ballad
   Tempo: Slow/mid
   Seeker-Sensitivity Rating: 10
   Themes: Marriage; Staying faithful

*Farther Than Your Grace Can Reach
   Artist: Jonathan Pierce
   Album/Label: Mission/Curb
   Style: Ballad
   Tempo: Slow
   Seeker-Sensitivity Rating: 9
   Themes: God's forgiveness; Grace

*Father's Love
   Artist: Bob Carlisle
   Album/Label: Stories from the Heart/Benson; BMG
   Style: Ballad
   Tempo: Slow
   Seeker-Sensitivity Rating: 8
   Themes: Fatherhood; God's love

Fill Me, Lord
   Artist: DeGarmo & Key
   Album/Label: Mission of Mercy/Benson; Forefront
   Style: Ballad
   Tempo: Slow
   Seeker-Sensitivity Rating: 2
   Themes: Obedience; Yieldedness
   Comments: From an older album that may be hard to locate—but a great ballad that still holds up

*For the Sake of the Call
   Artist: Steven Curtis Chapman
   Album/Label: For the Sake of the Call/Sparrow
   Style: Anthemic pop
   Tempo: Up
   Seeker-Sensitivity Rating: 3
   Themes: Commitment to the cause of Christ; Answering the call
   Comments: Would be great with a strong choir

For Who He Really Is
   Artist: Steven Curtis Chapman
   Album/Label: Real Life Conversations/Sparrow
   Style: Folk pop ballad
   Tempo: Mid/slow
   Seeker-Sensitivity Rating: 1
   Themes: Spiritual authenticity; Lifestyle evangelism

Forever's as Far as I'll Go
   Artist: Alabama

Album/Label: Pass It On Down: Greatest Hits, Vol. 3/RCA
Style: Country ballad
Tempo: Slow
Seeker-Sensitivity Rating: 10
Themes: Marriage; Love; Marital commitment

*Forgive Me
   Artist: Willow Creek Music
   Album/Label: Still I Will Worship You: Live Worship at Willow Creek/Willow Creek Music
   Style: Ballad
   Tempo: Slow
   Seeker-Sensitivity Rating: 3
   Themes: Prayer for forgiveness; Our need for God's grace
   Comments: Works well in communion services. Might also work as a worship chorus

*Found a Way
   Artist: Greg Ferguson
   Album/Label: Leave a Light On/Willow Creek Music
   Style: Ballad
   Tempo: Slow
   Seeker-Sensitivity Rating: 9
   Themes: God's faithfulness; God's activity in our lives

Foundations
   Artist: Geoff Moore & the Distance
   Album/Label: Foundations/Sparrow
   Style: Folk pop ballad
   Tempo: Slow/mid
   Seeker-Sensitivity Rating: 8
   Themes: Christ as the foundation of life; Rock vs. sand

*Free
   Artist: Ginny Owens
   Album/Label: Without Condition/Rocketown
   Style: Folk pop
   Tempo: Mid/up
   Seeker-Sensitivity Rating: 8
   Themes: Freedom in Christ; God's acceptance of us

*From the Heart
   Artist: Scott Krippayne
   Album/Label: More/Myrrh; Word
   Style: Pop/rock
   Tempo: Up/mid
   Seeker-Sensitivity Rating: 7
   Themes: Authenticity; Integrity

From This Moment On
   Artist: Newsong
   Album/Label: All Around the World/Benson
   Style: Ballad
   Tempo: Slow
   Seeker-Sensitivity Rating: 8
   Themes: Encouraging a new Christian

Gather at the River
   Artist: Point of Grace

Album/Label: The Whole Truth/Word
Style: Pop
Tempo: Up
Seeker-Sensitivity Rating: 8
Themes: Forgiving others

Give Me Jesus
   Artist: Willow Creek Music
   Album/Label: To Know You More/Willow Creek Music
   Style: Ballad
   Tempo: Slow
   Seeker-Sensitivity Rating: 7
   Themes: Sufficiency of Christ; Need for Christ
   Comments: Beautiful Fernando Ortega arrangement of an old spiritual

*Giving Thing
   Artist: Truth
   Album/Label: One/Integrity
   Style: Pop
   Tempo: Mid/up
   Seeker-Sensitivity Rating: 8
   Themes: Caring for the poor and needy; Servanthood

Go There with You
   Artist: Steven Curtis Chapman
   Album/Label: The Great Adventure/Sparrow
   Style: MOR
   Tempo: Mid
   Seeker-Sensitivity Rating: 10
   Themes: Marriage; Commitment in marriage

*God Is in Control
   Artist: Twila Paris
   Album/Label: Beyond a Dream/Star Song
   Style: Pop/rock
   Tempo: Up
   Seeker-Sensitivity Rating: 1
   Themes: God's sovereignty
   Comments: Encouraging praise anthem

*God of Wonders
   Artist: Various
   Album/Label: City on a Hill/Essential; BMG
   Style: Folk rock
   Tempo: Mid
   Seeker-Sensitivity Rating: 7
   Themes: The majesty and holiness of God
   Comments: Can be done as a worship chorus or as a special

*Good News
   Artist: Chris Rice
   Album/Label: Deep Enough to Dream/Rocketown; Word
   Style: Pop
   Tempo: Up
   Seeker-Sensitivity Rating: 9
   Themes: The gospel in the face of hardship; State of the world

The Great Adventure
   Artist: Steven Curtis Chapman

Album/Label: The Great
Adventure/Sparrow
Style: Pop/rock
Tempo: Up
Seeker-Sensitivity Rating: 5
Themes: The adventure of the Christian life
Comments: Works well coming out of the "yee-hah" scene in *City Slickers*

The Great Divide
Artist: Point of Grace
Album/Label: The Whole Truth/Word
Style: Power ballad
Tempo: Slow
Seeker-Sensitivity Rating: 9
Themes: Salvation; The cross

*Great Expectations
Artist: Steven Curtis Chapman
Album/Label: Speechless/Sparrow
Style: Pop/rock
Tempo: Mid
Seeker-Sensitivity Rating: 8
Themes: Relationship with God; The adventure of the Christian life; Prayer

*Greater Than
Artist: Riley Armstrong
Album/Label: Riley Armstrong/Flicker; Chordant
Style: Alternative pop/rock
Tempo: Up
Seeker-Sensitivity Rating: 8
Themes: Greatness of God

*Growing
Artist: Wayne Watson
Album/Label: The Way Home/Word
Style: Ballad
Tempo: Slow
Seeker-Sensitivity Rating: 5
Themes: Spiritual growth/sanctification; Discipleship

*Hark Medley
Artist: Willow Creek Music
Album/Label: None
Style: Christmas carol medley
Tempo: Up
Seeker-Sensitivity Rating: 10
Themes: Christmas
Comments: Combines "Hark! the Herald Angels Sing," "Joy to the World," "The First Noel," and "O Come, All Ye Faithful." Available only at www.willowcharts.com

*Have No Fear
Artist: Willow Creek Music
Album/Label: Enough/Willow Creek Music
Style: Piano ballad
Tempo: Slow
Seeker-Sensitivity Rating: 9
Themes: Fear; Comfort for the hurting; God's presence in the midst of tragedy; September 11; Psalm 23
Comments: Written the day after September 11 and performed for the service that evening

*He Knows My Name
Artist: Tommy Walker/Helena
Album/Label: Never Gonna Stop/Integrity; Honestly/Willow Creek Music
Style: Worship ballad
Tempo: Slow
Seeker-Sensitivity Rating: 9
Themes: God's love; God knows me; Intimacy with God
Comments: Great worship song that seekers can sing as well. The Helena version is a duet that works great as a special.

*He Was
Artist: Willow Creek Music
Album/Label: Enough, Willow Creek Music
Style: Pop/rock, in 6/8
Tempo: Mid
Seeker-Sensitivity Rating: 10
Themes: Jesus; Person of Christ; Misconceptions of Christ

He Won't Let You Go
Artist: The Kry
Album/Label: You/Freedom; Malaco
Style: Piano ballad
Tempo: Slow
Seeker-Sensitivity Rating: 10
Themes: God's faithful love; Assurance—God will never leave nor forsake you
Comments: Poignant song, great "moment" potential

*Healing River
Artist: Willow Creek Music
Album/Label: A Place to Call Home/Word; Maranatha!
Style: Ballad
Tempo: Slow/mid
Seeker-Sensitivity Rating: 9
Themes: Healing; Heaven

*Healing Song
Artist: Curt Coffield
Album/Label: Let the World See/Independent
Style: Ballad, in 3
Tempo: Slow/mid
Seeker-Sensitivity Rating: 7
Themes: Need for healing
Comments: Can be done as a special or as a worship song. Written by Curt after a trip to the former Yugoslavia. Available at www.reslife.org

*Heart's Cry
Artist: Steven Curtis Chapman
Album/Label: The Great Adventure/Sparrow
Style: Acoustic ballad
Tempo: Mid/slow
Seeker-Sensitivity Rating: 7
Themes: Desire to be like Christ
Comments: Works in seeker services as a testimonial, an opportunity to eavesdrop on a committed Christian

Heaven in the Real World
Artist: Steven Curtis Chapman

Album/Label: Heaven in the Real World/Sparrow
Style: Pop/rock
Tempo: Up
Seeker-Sensitivity Rating: 7
Themes: Need for Christ; Need for hope

Heirlooms
Artist: Amy Grant
Album/Label: Christmas Album/Myrrh
Style: Ballad
Tempo: Slow
Seeker-Sensitivity Rating: 8
Themes: Christmas; Family; Relationship with Christ

Helping Hand
Artist: Amy Grant
Album/Label: House of Love/Myrrh
Style: Pop
Tempo: Mid/up
Seeker-Sensitivity Rating: 10
Themes: Helping others; Servanthood
Comments: We've used this to a mixed response.

Here in My Heart
Artist: Susan Ashton
Album/Label: Angels of Mercy/Sparrow
Style: Folk rock
Tempo: Up
Seeker-Sensitivity Rating: 8
Themes: God's faithful love
Comments: Great groove, though the message may be hard to catch in a one-time hearing. Solid opener for a Baby Buster–oriented service.

Here in the Quiet
Artist: Willow Creek Music
Album/Label: None
Style: Ballad
Tempo: Slow
Seeker-Sensitivity Rating: 4
Themes: Worship; Desire for intimacy with God

He's All You Need
Artist: Steve Camp
Album/Label: One On One: Doing My Best, Vol. 1/Sparrow
Style: Ballad
Tempo: Slow
Seeker-Sensitivity Rating: 7
Themes: Sufficiency of Christ; Grace
Comments: Second verse is a little closer to a believer's experience than that of a seeker but can still relate.

He's Been Faithful
Artist: Brooklyn Tabernacle Choir
Album/Label: Live . . . Again/Word
Style: Ballad with choir
Tempo: Slow
Seeker-Sensitivity Rating: 6
Themes: God's faithfulness
Comments: Great testimony song—might sound a bit dated, but still powerful with a big choir

*He's My Son
    Artist: Mark Schultz
    Album/Label: Mark Schultz, Word
    Style: Ballad
    Tempo: Slow
    Seeker-Sensitivity Rating: 9
    Themes: Prayer for the healing of a sick child

Hiding Place
    Artist: Steven Curtis Chapman
    Album/Label: First Hand/Sparrow
    Style: Pop ballad
    Tempo: Mid/slow
    Seeker-Sensitivity Rating: 9
    Themes: God as a refuge

*Highest Honor
    Artist: Chris Eaton
    Album/Label: What Kind of Love/Cadence
    Style: Ballad
    Tempo: Slow
    Seeker-Sensitivity Rating: 7
    Themes: Honoring God; Decision making
    Comments: Works great as a male or female solo

His Eyes
    Artist: Steven Curtis Chapman
    Album/Label: Real Life Conversations/Sparrow
    Style: Acoustic guitar ballad
    Tempo: Mid/slow
    Seeker-Sensitivity Rating: 9
    Themes: God's omnipresence; God's care of us; Diversity in the character of Christ

His Love Is Strong
    Artist: Clay Crosse
    Album/Label: Time to Believe/Reunion
    Style: Pop
    Tempo: Up
    Seeker-Sensitivity Rating: 10
    Themes: God's love
    Comments: Great opener. Can also be done as a female solo, one step up

His Strength Is Perfect
    Artist: Steven Curtis Chapman
    Album/Label: Real Life Conversations/Sparrow
    Style: Ballad
    Tempo: Slow
    Seeker-Sensitivity Rating: 9
    Themes: God's strength in our weakness
    Comments: Works well as a female solo also, with key change

*Hold Me, Jesus
    Artist: Rich Mullins
    Album/Label: Best of Rich Mullins: A Liturgy, a Legacy and a Ragamuffin Band/Reunion
    Style: Ballad
    Tempo: Slow
    Seeker-Sensitivity Rating: 7
    Themes: Hardship; Surrendering to Christ

*Hold On
    Artist: Willow Creek Music

    Album/Label: Enough/Willow Creek Music
    Style: Acoustic rock/pop ballad
    Tempo: Slow/mid
    Seeker-Sensitivity Rating: 10
    Themes: Hardship; September 11; Holding on to God
    Comments: Powerful song written after the attacks of September 11; performed the weekend following

*Hold On to Jesus
    Artist: Steven Curtis Chapman
    Album/Label: Signs of Life/Sparrow
    Style: Ballad
    Tempo: Slow
    Seeker-Sensitivity Rating: 8
    Themes: Christ as a refuge; Strength for the storms of life

Hole Hearted
    Artist: Extreme
    Album/Label: Pornograffiti/A and M
    Style: Rock
    Tempo: Up
    Seeker-Sensitivity Rating: 10
    Themes: God-shaped void; Fulfillment in life; Need for God
    Comments: Older secular song that still holds up well

*Holy Flame
    Artist: Ken Medema
    Album/Label: Little Pictures/Brier Patch
    Style: Gospel shuffle
    Tempo: Mid
    Seeker-Sensitivity Rating: 3
    Themes: Pentecost; Call for God to revive the church
    Comments: Done with a dance—the combination is powerful. Video can be seen at www.willowcharts.com. CD available at www.kenmedema.com

*Holy King
    Artist: Willow Creek Music
    Album/Label: None
    Style: Ballad
    Tempo: Slow
    Seeker-Sensitivity Rating: 8
    Themes: Christmas
    Comments: Available only at www.willowcharts.com

Holy One
    Artist: Helena
    Album/Label: The Healing/Willow Creek Music
    Style: Ballad
    Tempo: Slow
    Seeker-Sensitivity Rating: 7
    Themes: The tenderness of Christ; God's love for us
    Comments: Works as a worship special or as a chorus.

How Could I Ask for More?
    Artist: Cindy Morgan
    Album/Label: Real Life/Word
    Style: Piano ballad

    Tempo: Slow
    Seeker-Sensitivity Rating: 9
    Themes: Thanksgiving for the simple pleasures of life
    Comments: We've used the original recording with a video, showing stills and moving footage of families.

Hunger and Thirst
    Artist: Susan Ashton
    Album/Label: Angels of Mercy/Sparrow
    Style: Folk pop
    Tempo: Mid/up
    Seeker-Sensitivity Rating: 6
    Themes: Hunger for God

Hunger for Healing
    Artist: Willow Creek Music
    Album/Label: None
    Style: Folk ballad
    Tempo: Slow
    Seeker-Sensitivity Rating: 10
    Themes: Need for wholeness; Healing
    Comments: Available only at www.willowcharts.com

*I Am the Man
    Artist: Greg Ferguson
    Album/Label: Leave a Light On/Willow Creek Music
    Style: Piano ballad
    Tempo: Slow
    Seeker-Sensitivity Rating: 8
    Themes: Conviction of sin; God's forgiveness

*I Can Hear You
    Artist: Carolyn Arends
    Album/Label: I Can Hear You/Reunion
    Style: Folk pop
    Tempo: Mid/up
    Seeker-Sensitivity Rating: 8
    Themes: God's presence; God speaking to us

I Choose to Follow
    Artist: Al Denson
    Album/Label: The Extra Mile/Benson
    Style: Ballad
    Tempo: Slow
    Seeker-Sensitivity Rating: 5
    Themes: Commitment; Discipleship

*I Don't Know Why/Found a Way
    Artist: Willow Creek Music
    Album/Label: None
    Style: Ballad
    Tempo: Slow
    Seeker-Sensitivity Rating: 8
    Themes: God's activity in our lives; Relationship with God; God's pursuit of us
    Comments: Powerful combination of two of Greg Ferguson's songs. Arrangement available only at www. willowcharts.com

I Found Myself in You
    Artist: Clay Crosse
    Album/Label: Time to Believe/Reunion
    Style: Gospel ballad
    Tempo: Mid/slow
    Seeker-Sensitivity Rating: 10

Themes: Salvation; Search for meaning
Comments: The title line may need to be set up for clarity, and the key may need to be lowered. Strong song

I Go to the Rock
Artist: Dottie Rambo; Whitney Houston
Album/Label: Songs for Sunday/Benson
Style: Swing/big band
Tempo: Mid
Seeker-Sensitivity Rating: 7
Themes: Life foundation; Stability of Christ
Comments: Old song that might still work for a change of pace with either a big band or black gospel treatment

I Just Never Say It Enough
Artist: Wayne Watson
Album/Label: Home Free/Word
Style: Ballad, in 3
Tempo: Slow
Seeker-Sensitivity Rating: 8
Themes: Marriage; Speaking love to spouse
Comments: A touching song from husband to wife

*I Stand, I Fall
Artist: Greg Ferguson
Album/Label: Leave a Light On/Willow Creek Music
Style: Piano ballad
Tempo: Slow
Seeker-Sensitivity Rating: 7
Themes: Sanctification; Failure; Grace
Comments: Very transparent song; allows people to see the reality of the Christian growth process

I Want to Be Just Like You
Artist: Phillips, Craig and Dean
Album/Label: Lifeline/Star Song
Style: MOR
Tempo: Mid/slow
Seeker-Sensitivity Rating: 9
Themes: Parenthood
Comments: Great song on fatherhood. We have used slides of families in conjunction with a live performance.

I Will Be Free
Artist: Cindy Morgan
Album/Label: Reason to Live/Word
Style: Ballad
Tempo: Slow
Seeker-Sensitivity Rating: 7
Themes: Heaven; Healing; Freedom

I Will Be Here
Artist: Steven Curtis Chapman
Album/Label: More to This Life/Sparrow
Style: Ballad
Tempo: Slow
Seeker-Sensitivity Rating: 10
Themes: Marriage; Commitment to spouse
Comments: Beautiful statement of marital commitment

*I Will Be Your Friend
Artist: Amy Grant

Album/Label: Behind the Eyes/Word
Style: Pop
Tempo: Up
Seeker-Sensitivity Rating: 10
Themes: Friendship; Commitment to friends

I Will Never Be
Artist: Hillsongs
Album/Label: Shout to the Lord/Integrity
Style: Worship ballad
Tempo: Slow/mid
Seeker-Sensitivity Rating: 3
Themes: Changed life; Desire to be pure
Comments: Works as a special or as a worship song

*I Will Rest in You
Artist: Jaci Velasquez
Album/Label: Streams/Word
Style: Ballad
Tempo: Slow
Seeker-Sensitivity Rating: 8
Themes: God as a refuge; God watching over us

*I Will Worship You
Artist: Matthew Ward
Album/Label: Even Now/Discovery House
Style: Ballad
Tempo: Slow
Seeker-Sensitivity Rating: 5
Themes: God's character, attributes; Worship

If I Could Look through Your Eyes
Artist: Willow Creek Music
Album/Label: Ever Devoted/Willow Creek Music
Style: Piano ballad
Tempo: Slow
Seeker-Sensitivity Rating: 10
Themes: Self-esteem; Our value to God; God's view of us
Comments: Great song on our value to God

If I Had Only Known
Artist: Reba McEntire
Album/Label: 8 Seconds Soundtrack/MCA
Style: Ballad
Tempo: Slow
Seeker-Sensitivity Rating: 10
Themes: Regret for unspoken love
Comments: We have used the recorded version in conjunction with the movie clip from 8 Seconds—very motivating.

If That's What It Takes
Artist: Willow Creek Music
Album/Label: Ever Devoted/Willow Creek Music
Style: MOR pop
Tempo: Mid/slow
Seeker-Sensitivity Rating: 5
Themes: Willingness to be broken; Desire to be like Christ

*If This World
Artist: Jaci Velasquez
Album/Label: Heavenly Place/Word

Style: Pop
Tempo: Up
Seeker-Sensitivity Rating: 9
Themes: Loneliness; God meets us in our need; God's love

If You Could See Me Now
Artist: Truth
Album/Label: Something to Hold On To/Integrity
Style: Ballad
Tempo: Slow
Seeker-Sensitivity Rating: 5
Themes: Heaven; Death of a loved one
Comments: Lyrics are very specific—from the voice of a Christian who was in great physical pain and is now in heaven. Must be used carefully

If You Could See What I See
Artist: Geoff Moore & the Distance
Album/Label: Evolution/Forefront
Style: Folk ballad
Tempo: Slow
Seeker-Sensitivity Rating: 10
Themes: Marriage; Self-esteem
Comments: Song from a husband to his wife, stating the beauty he sees in her, in spite of what she sees in herself

*I'll Find You There
Artist: The Kry
Album/Label: I'll Find You There/Freedom; Malaco
Style: Folk rock ballad
Tempo: Slow
Seeker-Sensitivity Rating: 9
Themes: God's faithfulness; God meets our needs
Comments: Has an alternative, anthemic feel. Especially good for Baby Buster-oriented services

I'm Amazed
Artist: Willow Creek Music
Album/Label: Ever Devoted/Willow Creek Music
Style: Ballad
Tempo: Slow
Seeker-Sensitivity Rating: 7
Themes: God's amazing love and goodness
Comments: Can be used in a number of contexts—a real "moment" song

I'm in a Hurry (and Don't Know Why)
Artist: Alabama
Album/Label: American Pride/RCA
Style: Country pop
Tempo: Up
Seeker-Sensitivity Rating: 10
Themes: Pace of life
Comments: Works well out of "Plate Spinners" drama or as a fun opener

In Christ Alone
Artist: Michael English
Album/Label: Michael English/Warner Alliance
Style: Power ballad

Tempo: Slow
Seeker-Sensitivity Rating: 8
Themes: Sufficiency of Christ; Giving God the glory

In the Light
Artist: DC Talk
Album/Label: Jesus Freak/Forefront
Style: Alternative pop/rock
Tempo: Up
Seeker-Sensitivity Rating: 8
Themes: Desire to follow Christ; Frustration with our own depravity; Walking with God
Comments: Great arrangement of Charlie Peacock song works great with a wide age range. Very compelling song

In My Father's Hands
Artist: Susan Ashton
Album/Label: Wakened by the Wind/Sparrow
Style: Folk pop
Tempo: Mid
Seeker-Sensitivity Rating: 9
Themes: God is able; Trusting God; Letting God have control

*In My Heart
Artist: Greg Ferguson
Album/Label: Leave a Light On/Willow Creek Music
Style: Celtic worship ballad
Tempo: Slow
Seeker-Sensitivity Rating: 9
Themes: Coming to Christ to worship just as we are
Comments: Works as a special or as a worship chorus

*It Will Be Worth It All
Artist: Tommy Walker
Album/Label: Live Worship with Tommy Walker and the CA Worship Band/Maranatha!
Style: Guitar ballad
Tempo: Slow
Seeker-Sensitivity Rating: 4
Themes: Difficulty of Christian life; Heaven

*I've Been Released
Artist: Willow Creek Music
Album/Label: A Place to Call Home/Word; Maranatha!
Style: Pop/rock—Chicago sound
Tempo: Up
Seeker-Sensitivity Rating: 9
Themes: Freedom from sin

*Jesus, King of Angels
Artist: Fernando Ortega
Album/Label: The Breaking of the Dawn/Word
Style: Ballad
Tempo: Slow
Seeker-Sensitivity Rating: 6
Themes: God's protection; God as a refuge; God's peace

*Jesus Loves Me
Artist: Whitney Houston

Album/Label: Bodyguard Soundtrack/Arista
Style: R & B/pop
Tempo: Slow/mid
Seeker-Sensitivity Rating: 8
Themes: God's love

Jesus Will Still Be There
Artist: Point of Grace
Album/Label: Point of Grace/Word
Style: Ballad
Tempo: Slow
Seeker-Sensitivity Rating: 9
Themes: God's love for the brokenhearted

*Just Say the Word
Artist: Willow Creek Music
Album/Label: None
Style: Gospel pop, in 3
Tempo: Mid/up
Seeker-Sensitivity Rating: 4
Themes: Commitment to Christ; Obedience
Comments: Available only at www.willowcharts.com. Can be used as a special or as a worship chorus

*Keep My Mind
Artist: Margaret Becker
Album/Label: Soul/Sparrow
Style: Pop/rock
Tempo: Up
Seeker-Sensitivity Rating: 8
Themes: Purity; Temptation; Honoring God

*King of the Jungle
Artist: Steven Curtis Chapman
Album/Label: Heaven in the Real World/Sparrow
Style: Pop shuffle with African touches
Tempo: Mid/up
Seeker-Sensitivity Rating: 9
Themes: Pace of life; God's sovereignty
Comments: Fun song—may be too light musically for some churches

*Knockin' on Heaven's Door
Artist: Avalon
Album/Label: A Maze of Grace/Sparrow
Style: Pop
Tempo: Up
Seeker-Sensitivity Rating: 9
Themes: Prayer

Land of Opportunity
Artist: Steven Curtis Chapman
Album/Label: Signs of Life/Sparrow
Style: Pop/rock
Tempo: Mid/up
Seeker-Sensitivity Rating: 6

The Last Song
Artist: Elton John
Album/Label: The One/MCA
Style: Ballad
Tempo: Slow
Seeker-Sensitivity Rating: 10
Themes: AIDS; Father-son relationships

*Lay Your Burdens Down
Artist: Willow Creek Music

Album/Label: Enough/Willow Creek Music
Style: Ballad
Tempo: Slow
Seeker-Sensitivity Rating: 9
Themes: Hardship; "Come to me, all who are weary . . ."

*Leave a Light On
Artist: Greg Ferguson
Album/Label: Leave a Light On/Willow Creek Music
Style: Ethereal pop ballad
Tempo: Slow/mid
Seeker-Sensitivity Rating: 8
Themes: Seeking God
Comments: Great song from a seeker's perspective aimed at the church, asking, "Is there a place for me?"

Let Me Go
Artist: Susan Ashton
Album/Label: Angels of Mercy/Sparrow
Style: Folk ballad
Tempo: Slow
Seeker-Sensitivity Rating: 10
Themes: Letting go of adult children; Parenting
Comments: The drama "Let Me Go" was written to precede this song.

*Let the Lord Love You
Artist: Willow Creek Music
Album/Label: A Place to Call Home/Word; Maranatha!
Style: Acoustic guitar ballad
Tempo: Slow
Seeker-Sensitivity Rating: 9
Themes: Self-esteem; God's love
Comments: Works well after self-esteem—oriented dramas.

Let Us Pray
Artist: Steven Curtis Chapman
Album/Label: Signs of Life/Sparrow
Style: Pop/rock
Tempo: Up
Seeker-Sensitivity Rating: 7
Themes: Prayer

*Let's Stand Together
Artist: The Kry
Album/Label: I'll Find You There/Freedom; Malaco
Style: Rock
Tempo: Mid/up
Seeker-Sensitivity Rating: 1
Themes: Commitment; Unity
Comments: Strong anthemic call to commitment. Might be a little "edgy" for some churches

*Life Means So Much
Artist: Chris Rice
Album/Label: Smell the Color 9/Rocketown; Word
Style: Folk pop
Tempo: Mid
Seeker-Sensitivity Rating: 7
Themes: Making the most of our days

*Life Support
  Artist: Greg Ferguson
  Album/Label: Leave a Light On/Willow Creek Music
  Style: R & B/pop
  Tempo: Mid/up
  Seeker-Sensitivity Rating: 9
  Themes: Need for Christ; "I am the vine, you are the branches"; Healing

Lion and the Lamb
  Artist: Maranatha! Singers; Crystal Lewis
  Album/Label: Praise 14/Maranatha!; Beauty for Ashes/Myrrh
  Style: Ballad trio
  Tempo: Slow
  Seeker-Sensitivity Rating: 4
  Themes: Character, person of Christ
  Comments: The Crystal Lewis version works great as a male-female duet; it is more of a power ballad than the Maranatha! version.

Listen to Our Hearts
  Artist: Geoff Moore & the Distance (with Steven Curtis Chapman)
  Album/Label: A Friend Like U/Forefront
  Style: Acoustic ballad duet
  Tempo: Slow/mid
  Seeker-Sensitivity Rating: 5
  Themes: Praise & worship; Love for God

Live Out Loud
  Artist: Steven Curtis Chapman
  Album/Label: Declaration/Sparrow
  Style: Pop
  Tempo: Up
  Seeker-Sensitivity Rating: 9
  Themes: Living out our faith boldly

The Living Years
  Artist: Mike & the Mechanics
  Album/Label: The Living Years/Atlantic
  Style: Pop
  Tempo: Mid/up
  Seeker-Sensitivity Rating: 10
  Themes: Regret over unspoken words to a father
  Comments: Works best with a large vocal group, especially a mixture of children and adults

*Lord, I Want to Be Like Jesus
  Artist: Fernando Ortega
  Album/Label: In a Welcome Field/Urgent
  Style: Ballad
  Tempo: Slow
  Seeker-Sensitivity Rating: 5
  Themes: Worship; Sanctification

*Lord of All
  Artist: First Call
  Album/Label: Something Takes Over/Dayspring
  Style: Ballad trio
  Tempo: Slow
  Seeker-Sensitivity Rating: 6
  Themes: Praise & worship; God's sovereignty, majesty

  Comments: Older song that may be hard to find but is still powerful. The songbook has all three vocal parts written out.

*Love and Learn
  Artist: Steven Curtis Chapman
  Album/Label: Heaven in the Real World/Sparrow
  Style: Folk pop
  Tempo: Mid/slow
  Seeker-Sensitivity Rating: 9
  Themes: Working through marital difficulty

Love Can Build a Bridge
  Artist: The Judds
  Album/Label: Love Can Build a Bridge/Curb; RCA
  Style: Ballad
  Tempo: Slow
  Seeker-Sensitivity Rating: 10
  Themes: Relationships; Love
  Comments: Works especially well with a choir, though not necessary

Love Conquers All
  Artist: Pam Thum
  Album/Label: Faithful/Benson
  Style: Pop
  Tempo: Up
  Seeker-Sensitivity Rating: 10
  Themes: Power of love to break down walls; God's love

*Love Is Always There
  Artist: Carolyn Arends
  Album/Label: I Can Hear You/Reunion
  Style: Folk pop
  Tempo: Up
  Seeker-Sensitivity Rating: 9
  Themes: Nobody is beyond salvation
  Comments: Try it with an "unplugged" feel and look.

*The Love of God
  Artist: Willow Creek Music
  Album/Label: None
  Style: A cappella vocal group
  Tempo: Slow
  Seeker-Sensitivity Rating: 6
  Themes: God's love
  Comments: A cappella treatment of this hymn has been one of our strongest moments at a seeker service. Available only at www.willowcharts.com

Love That Will Not Let Me Go
  Artist: Steve Camp
  Album/Label: Justice: Doing My Best, Vol. 1/Sparrow
  Style: Ballad
  Tempo: Slow
  Seeker-Sensitivity Rating: 10
  Themes: God's steadfast love
  Comments: A great song. The title is a great phrase to work into a message.

*Man of God
  Artist: Greg Ferguson
  Album/Label: Leave a Light On/Willow Creek Music

  Style: Pop/rock
  Tempo: Mid/up
  Seeker-Sensitivity Rating: 7
  Themes: A man's commitment to integrity

Mary, Did You Know?
  Artist: Michael English
  Album/Label: Michael English/Warner Brothers
  Style: Pop ballad
  Tempo: Slow
  Seeker-Sensitivity Rating: 7
  Themes: Christmas

The Measure of a Man
  Artist: 4Him
  Album/Label: The Message/Benson
  Style: Pop
  Tempo: Up
  Seeker-Sensitivity Rating: 6
  Themes: What makes a man a man; Inner life

Meet in the Middle
  Artist: Diamond Rio
  Album/Label: Diamond Rio/Arista
  Style: Country
  Tempo: Mid/up
  Seeker-Sensitivity Rating: 10
  Themes: Marriage; Relational conflict

Mercy for the Memories
  Artist: Geoff Moore & the Distance
  Album/Label: Foundations/Sparrow
  Style: Folk pop ballad
  Tempo: Slow
  Seeker-Sensitivity Rating: 9
  Themes: Forgiveness; Healing of the past
  Comments: Older song with an acoustic feel that still holds up

Mighty Lord
  Artist: Kathy Troccoli; Ashley Cleveland
  Album/Label: Portfolio/Reunion; Lesson of Love/Reunion
  Style: Funky pop
  Tempo: Up
  Seeker-Sensitivity Rating: 8
  Themes: God's power; God's character
  Comments: The Ashley Cleveland version is only a couple of years old and is a bit more bluesy.

Mind, Body, Heart and Soul
  Artist: Bob Carlisle
  Album/Label: Bob Carlisle/Sparrow
  Style: Pop/rock
  Tempo: Up
  Seeker-Sensitivity Rating: 9
  Themes: Testimony—changed life; Commitment to Christ
  Comments: As with all Bob Carlisle songs, it should probably be lowered to make it singable for almost any male.

Miracle of Mercy
  Artist: Steven Curtis Chapman
  Album/Label: Heaven in the Real World/Sparrow

Style: Acoustic ballad
Tempo: Slow
Seeker-Sensitivity Rating: 4
Themes: God's grace; Our weakness—flesh vs. spirit

*Money Is a Powerful Thing
  Artist: Willow Creek Music
  Album/Label: None
  Style: Motown/pop
  Tempo: Up
  Seeker-Sensitivity Rating: 10
  Themes: Power of money

More Than Words
  Artist: Steven Curtis Chapman
  Album/Label: More to This Life/Sparrow
  Style: Acoustic guitar ballad
  Tempo: Mid/slow
  Seeker-Sensitivity Rating: 4
  Themes: Progression from prayer to God's Word to the fact that who God is goes beyond our words to the fact that Christ's sacrifice backed up his words with action.
  Comments: Beautifully crafted, wonderfully complex song—may be hard to nail down to a specific topic

*My Life Is Yours
  Artist: Willow Creek Music
  Album/Label: None
  Style: Acoustic ballad
  Tempo: Slow
  Seeker-Sensitivity Rating: 10
  Themes: Substitutionary atonement; Grace
  Comments: Available only at www.willowcharts.com. Great "decision" song

My Redeemer Is Faithful and True
  Artist: Steven Curtis Chapman
  Album/Label: First Hand/Sparrow
  Style: Ballad
  Tempo: Slow
  Seeker-Sensitivity Rating: 9
  Themes: God's faithfulness
  Comments: Strong song. The term "redeemer" may need to be explained to a seeker audience.

*Naïve
  Artist: Chris Rice
  Album/Label: Past the Edges/Rocketown; Word
  Style: Folk pop
  Tempo: Mid
  Seeker-Sensitivity Rating: 8
  Themes: State of the world; God's patience with the world's depravity

Never Be an Angel
  Artist: Margaret Becker
  Album/Label: Simple House/Sparrow
  Style: Pop
  Tempo: Mid
  Seeker-Sensitivity Rating: 4
  Themes: Desire to change, to be like Christ
  Comments: Probably works best with a thirty-five and under audience

No Better Place
  Artist: Steven Curtis Chapman
  Album/Label: For the Sake of the Call/Sparrow
  Style: Folk pop rock
  Tempo: Up
  Seeker-Sensitivity Rating: 7
  Themes: Fulfillment; Joy of the Christian life

*No More Pretending
  Artist: Scott Krippayne
  Album/Label: More/Myrrh; Word
  Style: Pop ballad
  Tempo: Slow
  Seeker-Sensitivity Rating: 7
  Themes: Authenticity; Confession; Desire to honor God

No One Knows My Heart
  Artist: Susan Ashton
  Album/Label: Wakened by the Wind/Sparrow
  Style: Folk pop ballad
  Tempo: Slow/mid
  Seeker-Sensitivity Rating: 9
  Themes: God knows us and loves us; Yieldedness

Not Too Far from Here
  Artist: Kim Boyce
  Album/Label: By Faith/Warner Brothers
  Style: Pop ballad
  Tempo: Slow
  Seeker-Sensitivity Rating: 8
  Themes: Hurting People; Compassion

*Nothing You Could Do
  Artist: Willow Creek Music
  Album/Label: None
  Style: Ballad
  Tempo: Slow
  Seeker-Sensitivity Rating: 10
  Themes: Parenting; Unconditional love
  Comments: Available only at www.willowcharts.com

*Now That You're Gone
  Artist: Fernando Ortega
  Album/Label: Night of Your Return/Brentwood
  Style: Piano ballad
  Tempo: Slow/mid
  Seeker-Sensitivity Rating: 10
  Themes: Death; Losing a loved one; Grief
  Comments: Heartbreaking song about a brother dying

*On My Knees
  Artist: Willow Creek Music
  Album/Label: A Place to Call Home/Word; Maranatha!
  Style: Acoustic guitar ballad
  Tempo: Slow
  Seeker-Sensitivity Rating: 5
  Themes: Prayer; Intimacy with God
  Comments: Can work in a seeker context as a demonstration of the inner life of a believer

*Only by Grace
  Artist: Willow Creek Music
  Album/Label: A Place to Call Home/Word; Maranatha!
  Style: Pop/rock
  Tempo: Mid
  Seeker-Sensitivity Rating: 10
  Themes: Grace vs. works
  Comments: Works well for "target weekends" to explain that you can't earn your way to heaven, but that God offers the grace gift of salvation

Only Here for a Little While
  Artist: Billy Dean
  Album/Label: Young Man/Capitol; SBK
  Style: Country
  Tempo: Mid/up
  Seeker-Sensitivity Rating: 10
  Themes: Make the most of your time on earth

*Only You
  Artist: Willow Creek Music
  Album/Label: None
  Style: Ballad
  Tempo: Slow
  Seeker-Sensitivity Rating: 9
  Themes: Fulfillment in Christ

*Open Up
  Artist: Willow Creek Music
  Album/Label: Enough/Willow Creek Music
  Style: Hip-Hop/R & B
  Tempo: Up
  Seeker-Sensitivity Rating: 9
  Themes: Prayer; Does prayer work?
  Comments: Destiny's Child-inspired song that works great as a female group, male group, or mixed group.

*Own Me
  Artist: Ginny Owens
  Album/Label: Without Condition/Rocketown
  Style: Ballad
  Tempo: Slow
  Seeker-Sensitivity Rating: 6
  Themes: Desire to be changed by God; Legalism vs. a relationship with God; Surrendering to Christ

Peace Be Still
  Artist: Al Denson
  Album/Label: Al Denson/Benson
  Style: Ballad
  Tempo: Slow
  Seeker-Sensitivity Rating: 10
  Themes: God's peace; Comfort for the hurting
  Comments: Great song to come out of a drama that ends with a hurting character

*A Picture of Grace
  Artist: Willow Creek Music
  Album/Label: None
  Style: Medley of ballads
  Tempo: Slow
  Seeker-Sensitivity Rating: 9

Themes: Grace; Unconditional love
Comments: Combines "Face of Forgiveness," "If I Could Look through Your Eyes," "His Grace Is Greater," and "I Stand, I Fall." Available only at www.willowcharts.com

*A Place to Call Home
Artist: Greg Ferguson/Willow Creek Music
Album/Label: Leave a Light On/Willow Creek Music; A Place to Call Home/Word; Maranatha!
Style: Gospel ballad
Tempo: Slow, in 3
Seeker-Sensitivity Rating: 10
Themes: Filling the void; Salvation; Healing
Comments: Works well with several dramas, especially those ending with a character who feels lost. The *Leave a Light On* version is slower and a bit more tender. The *A Place to Call Home* version has more of a gospel feel and gets bigger.

Power of a Moment
Artist: Chris Rice
Album/Label: Past the Edges/Rocketown
Style: Folk pop
Tempo: Up
Seeker-Sensitivity Rating: 8
Themes: Surrender to God's will; Following God; Yieldedness to God

*Praise the King
Artist: Cindy Morgan
Album/Label: The Loving Kind/Word; Sony
Style: Ballad
Tempo: Slow
Seeker-Sensitivity Rating: 4
Themes: Worship; Praising God for who he is

*Prayer Medley
Artist: Willow Creek Music
Album/Label: To Know You More/Willow Creek Music
Style: Ballad medley trio
Tempo: Slow
Seeker-Sensitivity Rating: 7
Themes: Prayer; Relationship with God
Comments: Includes "On My Knees," "In His Sanctuary," and "Here in the Quiet"

*Promise
Artist: Willow Creek Music
Album/Label: Enough/Willow Creek Music
Style: Pop
Tempo: Mid/up
Seeker-Sensitivity Rating: 6
Themes: Commitment to Christ; Following Christ

Reaching
Artist: Carolyn Arends
Album/Label: I Can Hear You/Reunion
Style: Ballad
Tempo: Slow
Seeker-Sensitivity Rating: 6
Themes: Longing for heaven

Comments: Very poignant song. Be careful not to use it out of context.

Reaching for You
Artist: Willow Creek Music
Album/Label: None
Style: Rock/pop
Tempo: Up
Seeker-Sensitivity Rating: 10
Themes: Seeking God; Relationship with God; Asking God to meet us where we are
Comments: Intended as a seeker-sensitive worship chorus. Available only at www.willowcharts.com

Remember Your Chains
Artist: Steven Curtis Chapman
Album/Label: Heaven in the Real World/Sparrow
Style: Acoustic MOR
Tempo: Mid
Seeker-Sensitivity Rating: 2
Themes: Remembering life before Christ; Freedom from sin

*Revive Us
Artist: Anointed
Album/Label: Anointed/Myrrh
Style: R & B/gospel
Tempo: Up
Seeker-Sensitivity Rating: 3
Themes: Prayer for God to revive the church and reignite our joy and passion for him

*River God
Artist: Nicole Nordeman
Album/Label: Wide Eyed/Sparrow
Style: Piano ballad
Tempo: Slow
Seeker-Sensitivity Rating: 6
Themes: Sanctification; God changing us
Comments: Beautiful, very poetic song. If you have the ability to have the lyrics on video during the song, it would probably enhance the audience's experience.

A Rose Is a Rose
Artist: Susan Ashton
Album/Label: Susan Ashton/Sparrow
Style: Piano ballad
Tempo: Slow
Seeker-Sensitivity Rating: 9
Themes: Encouragement—stay true to who you are
Comments: May need contextual setup to work

*Seize the Day
Artist: Carolyn Arends
Album/Label: I Can Hear You/Reunion
Style: Folk pop, in 3
Tempo: Mid
Seeker-Sensitivity Rating: 8
Themes: Risk taking; Following your dreams
Comments: Strong song—might work with a scene from *Dead Poets' Society*

Separate Lives
Artist: Phil Collins and Marilyn White

Album/Label: White Nights Soundtrack/Atco
Style: Power ballad duet
Tempo: Slow
Seeker-Sensitivity Rating: 10
Themes: Marital breakdown; Divorce
Comments: Older duet that can still be a powerful song following a drama like "Grand Canyon"

Show Yourselves to Be
Artist: Steven Curtis Chapman
Album/Label: For the Sake of the Call/Sparrow
Style: Acoustic ballad
Tempo: Slow/mid
Seeker-Sensitivity Rating: 4
Themes: John 15; Bearing fruit; Being connected to Christ

Silent Night/All Is Well
Artist: Willow Creek Music
Album/Label: None
Style: A cappella vocal group ballad
Tempo: Slow
Seeker-Sensitivity Rating: 10
Themes: Christmas
Comments: Gorgeous arrangement by Greg Ferguson. Available only at www. willowcharts.com

*Small Enough
Artist: Nicole Nordeman
Album/Label: This Mystery/Sparrow
Style: Ballad duet
Tempo: Slow
Seeker-Sensitivity Rating: 6
Themes: Prayer for God to be near
Comments: Very well-written song that includes a lot of references to Bible characters—might need a setup for a nonchurched audience

*Smellin' Coffee
Artist: Chris Rice
Album/Label: Past the Edges/Rocketown; Word
Style: Pop/rock
Tempo: Up
Seeker-Sensitivity Rating: 8
Themes: Love for life; The goodness of God

Somebody Make Me Laugh
Artist: Patti Austin
Album/Label: That Secret Place/MCA; GRP
Style: Ballad
Tempo: Slow
Seeker-Sensitivity Rating: 10
Themes: Fulfillment; Longing for more
Comments: First part of first verse seems a little out of place in church, but a powerful song. We have used the original recording in conjunction with drama.

Someday
Artist: Grover Levy
Album/Label: Grover Levy/Myrrh; Word

Style: Pop
Tempo: Mid/up
Seeker-Sensitivity Rating: 8
Themes: Racism

*Sometimes He Calms the Storms
   Artist: Scott Krippayne
   Album/Label: Wild Imagination/Myrrh;
   Word
   Style: Ballad
   Tempo: Slow/mid
   Seeker-Sensitivity Rating: 6
   Themes: Unanswered prayer; Healing;
   Learning from pain

Somewhere in the World
   Artist: Wayne Watson
   Album/Label: Giants in the Land/Dayspring
   Style: Acoustic ballad
   Tempo: Slow
   Seeker-Sensitivity Rating: 3
   Themes: Parenthood; Prayer for son's future
   wife

*Speechless
   Artist: Steven Curtis Chapman
   Album/Label: Speechless/Sparrow
   Style: Acoustic rock
   Tempo: Mid/up
   Seeker-Sensitivity Rating: 7
   Themes: The wonder of God's grace

Sticks and Stones
   Artist: Wes King
   Album/Label: Sticks and Stones/Word
   Style: Rock/pop
   Tempo: Up
   Seeker-Sensitivity Rating: 9
   Themes: Destructive power of words

*Still Listening
   Artist: Steven Curtis Chapman
   Album/Label: Heaven in the Real
   World/Sparrow
   Style: Acoustic ballad
   Tempo: Slow/mid
   Seeker-Sensitivity Rating: 7
   Themes: Prayer

A Strange Way to Save the World
   Artist: 4Him
   Album/Label: A Strange Way to Save the
   World/Benson
   Style: Ballad
   Tempo: Slow
   Seeker-Sensitivity Rating: 7
   Themes: Christmas—in light of salvation

*Stranger to Holiness
   Artist: Steve Camp
   Album/Label: Shake Me to Wake
   Me/Sparrow
   Style: Ballad
   Tempo: Slow/mid
   Seeker-Sensitivity Rating: 2
   Themes: Our sinfulness; How unlike God
   we are
   Comments: Key may need to be lowered;
   may be a bit dated but strong lyrics

*Strength in You
   Artist: Willow Creek Music
   Album/Label: A Place to Call Home/Word;
   Maranatha!
   Style: MOR pop
   Tempo: Slow/mid
   Seeker-Sensitivity Rating: 10
   Themes: Foundation of life

Surrender Medley
   Artist: Willow Creek Music
   Album/Label: Ever Devoted/Willow Creek
   Music
   Style: Ballad medley duet
   Tempo: Slow
   Seeker-Sensitivity Rating: 6
   Themes: Submission to Christ
   Comments: Includes "My Life Is in Your
   Hands," "Holy Spirit, Take Control,"
   "Living Sacrifice," "Take My Life"

Take My Hand
   Artist: The Kry
   Album/Label: You/Freedom; Malaco
   Style: Acoustic ballad
   Tempo: Mid/slow
   Seeker-Sensitivity Rating: 9
   Themes: Trusting God in faith—taking a
   step
   Comments: Compelling song. Having two
   strong male vocalists helps but is not critical

*Take My Hand
   Artist: Russ Taff
   Album/Label: The Way Home/Myrrh;
   Word
   Style: Folk rock
   Tempo: Mid
   Seeker-Sensitivity Rating: 9
   Themes: Friendship; Desire for community

*Take You at Your Word
   Artist: Avalon
   Album/Label: In a Different Light/Sparrow
   Style: Pop
   Tempo: Up
   Seeker-Sensitivity Rating: 8
   Themes: The Bible
   Comments: Takes a good vocal group to pull
   it off, but a really good song

*Tell It Like It Is
   Artist: Scott Krippayne
   Album/Label: All of Me/Spring Hill
   Style: Funky pop
   Tempo: Up
   Seeker-Sensitivity Rating: 9
   Themes: Truth telling; Navigating the
   relational tunnel of chaos
   Comments: Really fun song

Thankful
   Artist: Willow Creek Music
   Album/Label: Ever Devoted/Willow Creek
   Music
   Style: Pop
   Tempo: Up
   Seeker-Sensitivity Rating: 7
   Themes: Thanksgiving; God's faithfulness
   and goodness

Comments: Older song that might still work
with an updated arrangement

That's What Love Is For
   Artist: Amy Grant
   Album/Label: Heart in Motion/Myrrh
   Style: Power ballad
   Tempo: Slow
   Seeker-Sensitivity Rating: 10
   Themes: Love overcoming relational or
   marital conflict

*There Is a God
   Artist: Tommy Walker
   Album/Label: None/Get Down Records
   Style: Ballad duet
   Tempo: Slow
   Seeker-Sensitivity Rating: 8
   Themes: Existence of God; Relationship
   with God
   Comments: Great song that has not yet been
   recorded. Chart available at
   www.willowcharts.com

There Is a Line
   Artist: Susan Ashton
   Album/Label: Susan Ashton/Sparrow
   Style: Folk pop
   Tempo: Mid
   Seeker-Sensitivity Rating: 6
   Themes: No compromise; Statement of
   commitment to integrity
   Comments: May be a bit hard to track
   lyrically

There Is a Love
   Artist: Michael English
   Album/Label: Hope/Warner Alliance
   Style: Pop
   Tempo: Up
   Seeker-Sensitivity Rating: 9
   Themes: God's love for the brokenhearted;
   God's love

*There's a Reason
   Artist: Willow Creek Music
   Album/Label: None
   Style: Pop/rock
   Tempo: Up
   Seeker-Sensitivity Rating: 9
   Themes: Hardship; Heaven
   Comments: Available only at
   www.willowcharts.com

*These Things Are True of You
   Artist: Tommy Walker and the CA Worship
   Band
   Album/Label: Yes, We All Agree/Get Down
   Records
   Style: Ballad duet
   Tempo: Slow
   Seeker-Sensitivity Rating: 9
   Themes: God's character, attributes; Desire
   to be like God
   Comments: Available at
   www.getdownrecords.com

This Is My Father's World
   Artist: Fernando Ortega

Album/Label: Night of Your Return/Brentwood
Style: Folk ballad
Tempo: Slow/mid
Seeker-Sensitivity Rating: 8
Themes: God the creator; God's sovereignty
Comments: Beautiful arrangement of an old hymn

Thy Word
Artist: Amy Grant
Album/Label: Straight Ahead/Myrrh
Style: Ballad
Tempo: Slow
Seeker-Sensitivity Rating: 4
Themes: God's Word; Guidance
Comments: Oldie but goody that might still work in some worship contexts

*Time to Return
Artist: Willow Creek Music
Album/Label: None
Style: Ballad
Tempo: Slow
Seeker-Sensitivity Rating: 7
Themes: Decaying world; Need for Christ
Comments: Available only at www.willowcharts.com

*Treasure
Artist: Gary Chapman
Album/Label: The Light Inside/Reunion
Style: Acoustic ballad
Tempo: Slow
Seeker-Sensitivity Rating: 9
Themes: Fulfillment in Christ
Comments: Already great song was recently improved with slightly updated treatment.

*Treasure of You
Artist: Steven Curtis Chapman
Album/Label: Heaven in the Real World/Sparrow
Style: Driving rock
Tempo: Up
Seeker-Sensitivity Rating: 10
Themes: Our value to God
Comments: Great statement to seekers. May be too edgy musically for some churches

*Turn It All Over
Artist: Greg Ferguson
Album/Label: Leave a Light On/Willow Creek Music
Style: Motown-ish pop
Tempo: Up
Seeker-Sensitivity Rating: 8
Themes: Obedience; Lordship of Christ
Comments: Fun, catchy song with a great message

Undivided
Artist: First Call
Album/Label: Undivided/Dayspring
Style: Ballad trio
Tempo: Slow
Seeker-Sensitivity Rating: 5
Themes: Unity in the body of Christ

Comments: More church-oriented, dealing with denominational differences, but can work in a seeker context when talking about unity

Unimportant Things
Artist: Paul Smith
Album/Label: Extra Measure
Style: Ballad
Tempo: Slow
Seeker-Sensitivity Rating: 7
Themes: Materialism; Priorities

*The Urgency of the Generally Insignificant
Artist: Wayne Watson
Album/Label: The Way Home/Word
Style: Pop/rock
Tempo: Up
Seeker-Sensitivity Rating: 9
Themes: Pace of life

Via Dolorosa
Artist: Sandi Patti
Album/Label: Songs from the Heart/Impact; Benson
Style: Inspirational ballad
Tempo: Slow
Seeker-Sensitivity Rating: 7
Themes: Easter; Suffering of Christ
Comments: Older but still powerful song that might work well in a slightly more traditional Easter service

*Walk On By
Artist: Susan Ashton
Album/Label: Angels of Mercy/Sparrow
Style: Folk pop
Tempo: Mid/up
Seeker-Sensitivity Rating: 8
Themes: Temptation

*Wanna Be Loved
Artist: DC Talk
Album/Label: Supernatural/Forefront; Virgin
Style: Funky pop
Tempo: Up
Seeker-Sensitivity Rating: 10
Themes: Our need for love
Comments: Not easy to sing but a fun song

*We All Need
Artist: Aaron Jeoffrey
Album/Label: After the Rain/StarSong; Chordant
Style: Pop
Tempo: Mid/up
Seeker-Sensitivity Rating: 9
Themes: Need for friends in difficult times

We Believe in God
Artist: Amy Grant
Album/Label: Songs from the Loft/Reunion
Style: Acoustic ballad
Tempo: Slow
Seeker-Sensitivity Rating: 3
Themes: Creed; Need for Christ

*We Can Make a Difference
Artist: Jaci Velasquez

Album/Label: Jaci Velasquez/Word; Sony
Style: Pop
Tempo: Up
Seeker-Sensitivity Rating: 8
Themes: Impacting lives; Impacting the world

Weary Soul
Artist: Helena
Album/Label: The Healing/Willow Creek Music
Style: Tender ballad
Tempo: Slow
Seeker-Sensitivity Rating: 9
Themes: Healing; God's tenderness

*Welcome to Our World
Artist: Chris Rice
Album/Label: Deep Enough to Dream/Rocketown; Word
Style: Ballad
Tempo: Slow
Seeker-Sensitivity Rating: 9
Themes: Christmas; Birth of Christ

*What a Day It Will Be
Artist: Greg Ferguson
Album/Label: Leave a Light On/Willow Creek Music
Style: Flowing ballad
Tempo: Slow/mid
Seeker-Sensitivity Rating: 8
Themes: Healing longtime pain; Heaven

*What a Good God
Artist: Tommy Walker
Album/Label: Praise Band 8: I Walk by Faith/Maranatha!; There Is a Rock/Get Down Ministries
Style: Worship ballad
Tempo: Slow
Seeker-Sensitivity Rating: 7
Themes: God's goodness; God's blessings
Comments: Can be done as a special or as a worship chorus. *There Is a Rock* is available at www.getdownministries.com.

*What a Ride
Artist: Willow Creek Music
Album/Label: A Place to Call Home/Word; Maranatha!
Style: Pop/rock
Tempo: Up
Seeker-Sensitivity Rating: 9
Themes: Joy of the Christian life
Comments: Very fun song live

What I Wouldn't Give
Artist: Willow Creek Music
Album/Label: None
Style: Acoustic ballad
Tempo: Slow
Seeker-Sensitivity Rating: 10
Themes: Our value to God
Comments: From Christ's perspective, so it probably needs some kind of a setup

*What If I?
Artist: Willow Creek Music

Album/Label: Enough/Willow Creek Music
Style: Piano ballad
Tempo: Slow/mid
Seeker-Sensitivity Rating: 8
Themes: Humility

*Whatever
Artist: Steven Curtis Chapman
Album/Label: Speechless/Sparrow
Style: Rock/pop
Tempo: Up
Seeker-Sensitivity Rating: 8
Themes: Obedience; Doing God's will

Whatever You Ask
Artist: Steve Camp
Album/Label: After God's Own Heart: Doing My Best, Vol. 1/Sparrow
Style: Power ballad
Tempo: Slow
Seeker-Sensitivity Rating: 5
Themes: Obedience; Commitment
Comments: Strong song of desired obedience. There is also an updated version on Generation Y's debut album, with a female lead.

*When I Said I Do
Artist: Willow Creek Music
Album/Label: None
Style: Ballad
Tempo: Slow
Seeker-Sensitivity Rating: 10
Themes: Marriage
Comments: Available only at www.willowcharts.com

*When Love Came Down
Artist: Point of Grace
Album/Label: A Christmas Story/Word
Style: Pop
Tempo: Up
Seeker-Sensitivity Rating: 10
Themes: Christmas; Birth of Christ; God's love

When Love Finds You
Artist: Vince Gill
Album/Label: When Love Finds You/MCA
Style: Country ballad, in 3
Tempo: Slow/mid
Seeker-Sensitivity Rating: 10
Themes: Love; Marriage
Comments: Fun song about romantic love

*When We Fail Love
Artist: Grover Levy
Album/Label: Grover Levy/Myrrh
Style: Piano ballad
Tempo: Slow
Seeker-Sensitivity Rating: 9
Themes: Failure in relationships; Forgiveness
Comments: Poignant song

When You Are a Soldier
Artist: Steven Curtis Chapman
Album/Label: For the Sake of the Call/Sparrow
Style: Keyboard ballad

Tempo: Slow/mid
Seeker-Sensitivity Rating: 4
Themes: The Christian life is hard; God will be there

*When You Come Home
Artist: Mark Schultz
Album/Label: Mark Schultz/Word
Style: Country-tinged ballad
Tempo: Slow/mid
Seeker-Sensitivity Rating: 9
Themes: Mother-son relationships; Death of a parent

Where Would I Be Now?
Artist: Willow Creek Music
Album/Label: None
Style: Ballad, Broadway feel
Tempo: Slow
Seeker-Sensitivity Rating: 6
Themes: Good Friday; Atonement
Comments: Powerful song for a Good Friday service

Who Am I?
Artist: Margaret Becker
Album/Label: The Reckoning: Steps of Faith/Sparrow
Style: Power ballad
Tempo: Slow
Seeker-Sensitivity Rating: 7
Themes: Grace; God's unconditional love

*Who Am I? (Grace Flows Down)
Artist: Watermark
Album/Label: All Things New/Rocketown
Style: Folk pop
Tempo: Mid/slow
Seeker-Sensitivity Rating: 8
Themes: God's grace; God's amazing love

*Why Me?
Artist: Willow Creek Music
Album/Label: A Place to Call Home/Word; Maranatha!
Style: Ballad
Tempo: Slow
Seeker-Sensitivity Rating: 9
Themes: God's undeserved, sacrificial love
Comments: Works well for Good Friday

*Wonderful Merciful Savior
Artist: Susan Ashton
Album/Label: Listen to Our Hearts, Vol. 1/Sparrow
Style: Acoustic ballad, 6/8 feel
Tempo: Mid/slow
Seeker-Sensitivity Rating: 9
Themes: Christmas; Jesus

Words
Artist: Kim Hill
Album/Label: Brave Heart/Myrrh
Style: Pop/rock
Tempo: Up
Seeker-Sensitivity Rating: 10
Themes: The tongue; Slander
Comments: This song is an older one but still sounds very current musically

Would I Know You?
Artist: Wayne Watson
Album/Label: Watercolour Ponies/Word
Style: Ballad
Tempo: Slow
Seeker-Sensitivity Rating: 3
Themes: Spiritual authenticity
Comments: Strong message of self-examination—very convicting

*You Are with Me Still
Artist: Willow Creek Music
Album/Label: None
Style: Acoustic ballad
Tempo: Slow
Seeker-Sensitivity Rating: 9
Themes: God's presence in the midst of hardship
Comments: Can be used as a special or worship chorus. Written after September 11. Available only at www.willowcharts.com

You Brought My Heart to Life
Artist: Willow Creek Music
Album/Label: None
Style: Ballad
Tempo: Slow
Seeker-Sensitivity Rating: 9
Themes: God's love; Healing a life; Salvation
Comments: Can work as a male or female song

*You Have Been Good (Krippayne)
Artist: Scott Krippayne
Album/Label: Bright Star Blue Sky/Spring Hill
Style: Pop ballad
Tempo: Slow
Seeker-Sensitivity Rating: 6
Themes: God's goodness

*Your Grace Still Amazes Me
Artist: Phillips, Craig and Dean
Album/Label: Let My Words Be Few/Sparrow
Style: Pop ballad
Tempo: Slow
Seeker-Sensitivity Rating: 7
Themes: God's grace, mercy

Your Love Stays with Me
Artist: Gary Chapman
Album/Label: Everyday Man/Reunion
Style: Piano ballad
Tempo: Slow
Seeker-Sensitivity Rating: 10
Themes: God's unfailing, faithful love
Comments: Album may be out of print. Great song if you can find it.

You've Got to Stand for Something
Artist: Aaron Tippin
Album/Label: You've Got to Stand for Something/BMG; RCA
Style: Country
Tempo: Up
Seeker-Sensitivity Rating: 10
Themes: Integrity

Worship Choruses

Individual music charts are available at www.willowcharts.com for all of the worship choruses listed.

Above All
Artist: Paul Baloche/Lenny LeBlanc
Album/Label: Open the Eyes of My Heart/Integrity; Above All/Integrity
Style: Worship ballad
Tempo: Slow
Seeker-Sensitivity Rating: 5
Themes: God's supremacy; God's love for us; God's sacrifice for us
Comments: Can be done as a special or as a worship chorus

All Around
Artist: Curt Coffield/Resurrection Life Church
Album/Label: Let the World See/Independent
Style: Caribbean pop
Tempo: Up
Seeker-Sensitivity Rating: 7
Themes: God's love; The evidence of God in creation
Comments: Available at www.reslife.org

All the Power You Need
Artist: Hillsongs
Album/Label: Shout to the Lord/Integrity
Style: Pop worship
Tempo: Up
Seeker-Sensitivity Rating: 5
Themes: God's power; Trusting in God's strength

All Things Are Possible
Artist: Hillsongs
Album/Label: All Things Are Possible/Integrity
Style: Pop worship
Tempo: Up
Seeker-Sensitivity Rating: 5
Themes: God's strength in our weakness

Amazing Love
Artist: Student Impact
Album/Label: Alive/Willow Creek Music
Style: Rock worship
Tempo: Mid/up
Seeker-Sensitivity Rating: 6
Themes: God's love

Amen
Artist: Tommy Walker
Album/Label: Live at Home/Get Down Records
Style: Worship shuffle
Tempo: Up
Seeker-Sensitivity Rating: 5
Themes: Response to God's love for us
Comments: Available at www.getdownrecords.com

And That My Soul Knows Very Well
Artist: Hillsongs

Album/Label: God Is in the House/Integrity
Style: Worship ballad
Tempo: Slow
Seeker-Sensitivity Rating: 5
Themes: God's protection, strength

As We Worship You
Artist: Tommy Walker
Album/Label: Live at Home/Get Down Records
Style: Worship ballad
Tempo: Slow
Seeker-Sensitivity Rating: 1
Themes: Worship evangelism; Desire for people to know Christ
Comments: Available at www.getdownrecords.com

Awesome in This Place
Artist: Dave Billington
Album/Label: Awesome in This Place/Alleluia; Integrity
Style: Worship ballad
Tempo: Slow
Seeker-Sensitivity Rating: 2
Themes: God's majesty, power

Be Magnified
Artist: Don Moen
Album/Label: Worship with Don Moen/Integrity
Style: Ballad
Tempo: Slow
Seeker-Sensitivity Rating: 2
Themes: Confession; Glorifying God; Underestimating God

Be Still My Soul
Artist: Willow Creek Music
Album/Label: Still I Will Worship You: Live Worship at Willow Creek/Willow Creek Music
Style: Worship ballad
Tempo: Slow/mid
Seeker-Sensitivity Rating: 4
Themes: Reminder of God's strength in hard times; Putting our hope in God

Beautiful God
Artist: Vineyard
Album/Label: Winds of Worship 12: Live from London/Vineyard Music
Style: Pop
Tempo: Up
Seeker-Sensitivity Rating: 5
Themes: God's beauty; Relationship with God

The Beauty of Holiness
Artist: Steve Camp
Album/Label: Mercy in the Wilderness/Warner Brothers

Style: Worship ballad, in 3
Tempo: Slow
Seeker-Sensitivity Rating: 3
Themes: God's holiness; Being broken before God

Bend My Knee
Artist: Student Impact
Album/Label: Alive/Willow Creek Music
Style: Rock worship
Tempo: Up
Seeker-Sensitivity Rating: 5
Themes: Worshiping God only

Better Is One Day
Artist: Matt Redman/Passion
Album/Label: The Friendship and the Fear/Worship Together; Better Is One Day/Sparrow
Style: Folk worship
Tempo: Mid
Seeker-Sensitivity Rating: 4
Themes: The goodness of being in God's presence

Better Than
Artist: Vineyard
Album/Label: Touching the Father's Heart #34: You Shelter Me/Vineyard Music
Style: Pop/rock worship
Tempo: Up
Seeker-Sensitivity Rating: 6
Themes: God's love; Desire to be close to God

Blessed Be the Name
Artist: Vineyard
Album/Label: Touching the Father's Heart #24: Blessed Be the Name/Vineyard Music
Style: Worship ballad
Tempo: Slow
Seeker-Sensitivity Rating: 4
Themes: Praise to God; His presence during hard times

Breathe
Artist: Michael W. Smith
Album/Label: Worship/Reunion
Style: Worship ballad
Tempo: Slow
Seeker-Sensitivity Rating: 3
Themes: Our need for Christ

Build Your Church into My Heart
Artist: Greg Ferguson/Willow Creek Music
Album/Label: None
Style: Pop
Tempo: Up
Seeker-Sensitivity Rating: 2
Themes: The church; The church is the hope of the world
Comments: Available only at www.willowcharts.com

But if Not
Artist: Student Impact
Album/Label: Alive/Willow Creek Music
Style: Acoustic ballad
Tempo: Slow
Seeker-Sensitivity Rating: 5
Themes: Worshiping God regardless of circumstances; Hardship
Comments: Can be done as a special or as a worship chorus

Can't Stop Talkin'
Artist: Hillsongs
Album/Label: All Things Are Possible/Integrity
Style: Pop worship
Tempo: Up
Seeker-Sensitivity Rating: 6
Themes: Testimonial; What God has done for us

Celebrate Jesus Celebrate
Artist: Alleluia Music
Album/Label: Celebrate Jesus/Integrity; Alleluia
Style: Pop
Tempo: Up
Seeker-Sensitivity Rating: 6
Themes: The resurrection

Celebrate the Lord of Love
Artist: Paul Baloche
Album/Label: Open the Eyes of My Heart/Integrity
Style: Pop worship
Tempo: Up
Seeker-Sensitivity Rating: 5
Themes: Celebrating what God has done; God's love

Come Let Us Bow Down
Artist: Dennis Jernigan
Album/Label: Celebrate Living/Heart Cry; Word
Style: Worship ballad
Tempo: Slow/mid
Seeker-Sensitivity Rating: 3
Themes: Lordship of Christ

Come, Now Is the Time to Worship
Artist: Vineyard
Album/Label: Winds of Worship 12: Live from London/Vineyard Music
Style: Pop/rock
Tempo: Up
Seeker-Sensitivity Rating: 5
Themes: Call to worship; God's acceptance of us as we are; Praise & worship

Create in Me
Artist: Willow Creek Music
Album/Label: Still I Will Worship You: Live Worship at Willow Creek Music/Willow Creek Music
Style: Ballad
Tempo: Slow
Seeker-Sensitivity Rating: 3
Themes: Confession; Prayer for cleansing

The Cross Has Said It All
Artist: Matt Redman
Album/Label: The Friendship and the Fear/Sparrow
Style: Worship ballad
Tempo: Mid/slow
Seeker-Sensitivity Rating: 2
Themes: The cross; Redemption; Salvation

Cry of My Heart
Artist: Terry Butler
Album/Label: Wow Worship Green/Integrity
Style: Pop
Tempo: Up
Seeker-Sensitivity Rating: 4
Themes: Desire to be close to God and to follow him

Did You Feel the Mountains Tremble?
Artist: Passion
Album/Label: Live Worship from the 268 Generation/Sparrow
Style: Pop/rock
Tempo: Mid/up
Seeker-Sensitivity Rating: 2
Themes: God's power, majesty; People worshiping Jesus

Do You Know?
Artist: Tommy Walker
Album/Label: Yes, We All Agree/Get Down Records
Style: Worship ballad
Tempo: Slow/mid
Seeker-Sensitivity Rating: 2
Themes: Blood of Christ; Salvation; Thanksgiving
Comments: Available at www.getdownrecords.com

Don't Forget His Benefits
Artist: Tommy Walker & the CA Worship Band
Album/Label: Live Worship with Tommy Walker & the CA Worship Band/Maranatha!
Style: Rock/pop
Tempo: Up
Seeker-Sensitivity Rating: 4
Themes: Being grateful for all that God has done

Doxology
Artist: Tommy Walker
Album/Label: Live at Home/Get Down Records
Style: Pop/rock
Tempo: Mid
Seeker-Sensitivity Rating: 6
Themes: Praise & worship
Comments: Great modern arrangement of the Doxology. Available at www.getdownrecords.com

Everyday
Artist: Student Impact/Sonlight Band
Album/Label: Alive; Walk with You/Willow Creek Music
Style: Rock worship

Tempo: Up
Seeker-Sensitivity Rating: 6
Themes: Following Christ; Living for God
Comments: This song is from Hillsong's youth ministry. The two versions listed above are slightly different, and both are a lot of fun.

Everyone Arise
Artist: Tommy Walker
Album/Label: Live at Home/Get Down Records
Style: Pop/rock
Tempo: Up
Seeker-Sensitivity Rating: 3
Themes: Letting your life shine to others; Praise
Comments: Available at www.getdownrecords.com

Everything I Am
Artist: Willow Creek Music
Album/Label: To Know You More/Willow Creek Music
Style: Pop/rock
Tempo: Up
Seeker-Sensitivity Rating: 7
Themes: Bringing all we are to God; Call to worship

Faith, Hope, and Love Remain
Artist: Willow Creek Music
Album/Label: Enough/Willow Creek Music
Style: Bluesy pop
Tempo: Up
Seeker-Sensitivity Rating: 10
Themes: Love; 1 Corinthians 13
Comments: 1 Corinthians 13 put to a call and response chorus—a lot of fun

Faithful to Me
Artist: Curt Coffield
Album/Label: Let the World See/Independent
Style: Pop worship
Tempo: Mid
Seeker-Sensitivity Rating: 6
Themes: God's faithfulness

For the Beauty of the Earth
Artist: Willow Creek Music
Album/Label: Still I Will Worship You: Live Worship at Willow Creek/Willow Creek Music
Style: Worship ballad
Tempo: Slow
Seeker-Sensitivity Rating: 5
Themes: Praising God for creation and for his blessings and work in our lives
Comments: Lyrics of the hymn put to a new melody

From the Rising of the Sun
Artist: Paul Deming
Album/Label: Come and Worship: Top 200 Songbook/Integrity
Style: Ballad
Tempo: Slow
Seeker-Sensitivity Rating: 3
Themes: God's praise shall be unceasing

From the Start of the Day
  Artist: Willow Creek Music
  Album/Label: None
  Style: Pop
  Tempo: Mid
  Seeker-Sensitivity Rating: 4
  Themes: Praising God with our daily lives; God is worthy to be praised
  Comments: Available only at www.willowcharts.com

God of Wonders
  Artist: Various
  Album/Label: City on a Hill/Essential; BMG
  Style: Folk rock
  Tempo: Mid
  Seeker-Sensitivity Rating: 7
  Themes: God's majesty; Holiness; Creation
  Comments: Can be done as a special or as a worship chorus

Got the Need
  Artist: The Parachute Band
  Album/Label: Adore; Always and Forever/Here to Him
  Style: Funky R & B/pop
  Tempo: Up
  Seeker-Sensitivity Rating: 4
  Themes: Responding to what God has done for us
  Comments: Get info at www.heretohim.com

Great Is Thy Faithfulness
  Artist: NA
  Album/Label: NA
  Style: Traditional worship/hymn
  Tempo: Slow
  Seeker-Sensitivity Rating: 5
  Themes: God's faithfulness
  Comments: Works great with rhythm section

Hallelujah (Your Love Is Amazing)
  Artist: Vineyard—Brenton Brown
  Album/Label: Wow Worship Green/Integrity
  Style: Rock/pop worship
  Tempo: Up
  Seeker-Sensitivity Rating: 4
  Themes: God's love

Happy Song
  Artist: Delirious
  Album/Label: Cutting Edge/Sparrow
  Style: Country rockabilly
  Tempo: Up
  Seeker-Sensitivity Rating: 5
  Themes: Joy of the Christian life; Thankfulness for salvation
  Comments: We sometimes leave out the bridge when we do this.

He Is Exalted
  Artist: Twila Paris
  Album/Label: Wow Worship Green/Integrity
  Style: Pop worship, in 3
  Tempo: Mid

Seeker-Sensitivity Rating: 3
Themes: Lifting up God

He Knows My Name
  Artist: Tommy Walker
  Album/Label: Never Gonna Stop/Integrity
  Style: Worship ballad
  Tempo: Slow
  Seeker-Sensitivity Rating: 7
  Themes: God knows us and loves us; God as our Father

He Loves Me
  Artist: Tommy Walker
  Album/Label: Yes, We All Agree/Get Down Records
  Style: Worship ballad
  Tempo: Slow
  Seeker-Sensitivity Rating: 6
  Themes: God's love, our response
  Comments: Available at www.getdownrecords.com

Healing Song
  Artist: Curt Coffield
  Album/Label: Let the World See/Independent
  Style: Ballad, in 3
  Tempo: Slow/mid
  Seeker-Sensitivity Rating: 7
  Themes: Need for healing
  Comments: Can be done as a special or as a worship song. Written by Curt after a trip to the former Yugoslavia. Available at www.reslife.org

Heart of Worship
  Artist: Matt Redman
  Album/Label: Heart of Worship/Worship Together; EMI
  Style: Worship ballad
  Tempo: Slow
  Seeker-Sensitivity Rating: 2
  Themes: Worship; Bringing God all that we are

Here I Am Again
  Artist: Tommy Walker/Willow Creek Music
  Album/Label: There Is a Rock/Get Down Ministries; Still I Will Worship You: Live Worship at Willow Creek/Willow Creek Music
  Style: Pop shuffle
  Tempo: Up
  Seeker-Sensitivity Rating: 3
  Themes: Finding a way to tell God how much we love him
  Comments: Tommy's version is available at www.getdownministries.com

He's Here
  Artist: Student Impact
  Album/Label: Alive/Willow Creek Music
  Style: Worship ballad
  Tempo: Slow
  Seeker-Sensitivity Rating: 7
  Themes: God's presence; God's love

High and Exalted
  Artist: Bob Fitts

Album/Label: He Will Save You/Integrity
  Style: Pop worship
  Tempo: Slow/mid
  Seeker-Sensitivity Rating: 2
  Themes: God's power and majesty, our response; God's holiness; Lifting up God

Holy and Anointed One
  Artist: Vineyard
  Album/Label: Isn't He?: Acoustic Worship/Vineyard Music
  Style: Worship ballad
  Tempo: Slow
  Seeker-Sensitivity Rating: 3
  Themes: Jesus; Holiness of God

Holy, Holy, Holy (Gary Oliver)
  Artist: Alvin Slaughter/Willow Creek Music
  Album/Label: God Can/Integrity; Still I Will Worship You: Live Worship at Willow Creek/Willow Creek Music
  Style: Gospel pop
  Tempo: Up
  Seeker-Sensitivity Rating: 5
  Themes: God's holiness; Lifting up God
  Comments: Alvin's version is fun. The Willow Creek version is the last part of a three-song medley that includes "I See the Lord" and the traditional "Holy, Holy, Holy."

Holy, Holy, Holy (Traditional)
  Artist: Willow Creek Music
  Album/Label: Still I Will Worship You: Live Worship at Willow Creek/Willow Creek Music
  Style: Traditional hymn
  Tempo: Mid
  Seeker-Sensitivity Rating: 5
  Themes: God's holiness
  Comments: We did this on the CD as the middle song of a three-song medley featuring "I See the Lord," this song, and Gary Oliver's "Holy, Holy, Holy."

Holy Spirit, Take Control
  Artist: Willow Creek Music
  Album/Label: Ever Devoted/Willow Creek Music
  Style: Ballad
  Tempo: Slow
  Seeker-Sensitivity Rating: 2
  Themes: Holy Spirit; Yielding to God; Conviction of sin

How Could I But Love You?
  Artist: Tommy Walker
  Album/Label: Never Gonna Stop/Integrity
  Style: Worship ballad
  Tempo: Slow
  Seeker-Sensitivity Rating: 3
  Themes: We love God because he first loved us

How Good and Pleasant
  Artist: Tommy Walker
  Album/Label: Never Gonna Stop/Integrity
  Style: Pop/rock
  Tempo: Up

Seeker-Sensitivity Rating: 5
Themes: Unity; Community; Worshiping God together

How Good You Are
Artist: Willow Creek Music
Album/Label: None
Style: Pop worship
Tempo: Mid/up
Seeker-Sensitivity Rating: 3
Themes: God's goodness; Thankfulness
Comments: Available only at www.willowcharts.com

I Am Here
Artist: Willow Creek Music
Album/Label: None
Style: Worship ballad
Tempo: Slow
Seeker-Sensitivity Rating: 8
Themes: Seeking God
Comments: Song simply says, "I am here; meet me here." Allows a seeker to simply ask God to meet him or her. Available only at www.willowcharts.com

I Could Sing of Your Love Forever
Artist: Passion
Album/Label: Live Worship from the 268 Generation/Sparrow
Style: Rock/pop worship
Tempo: Mid
Seeker-Sensitivity Rating: 4
Themes: God's love
Comments: This was originally a Delirious song.

I Do Believe
Artist: Willow Creek Music
Album/Label: None
Style: Pop
Tempo: Up
Seeker-Sensitivity Rating: 3
Themes: What we believe; Creed
Comments: Written by Rory Noland. Available only at www.willowcharts.com

I Give You My Heart
Artist: Hillsongs
Album/Label: God Is in the House/Integrity
Style: Worship ballad
Tempo: Slow
Seeker-Sensitivity Rating: 4
Themes: Honoring God; Surrendering to Christ

I Live to Know You
Artist: Hillsongs
Album/Label: All Things Are Possible/Integrity
Style: Worship power ballad
Tempo: Slow
Seeker-Sensitivity Rating: 3
Themes: Desire to know God; Response to the change God has made in our lives

I Love You, Lord
Artist: Maranatha!/Laurie Klein
Album/Label: Wow! Worship Blue/Integrity
Style: Worship ballad

Tempo: Slow
Seeker-Sensitivity Rating: 4
Themes: Expression of love to God

I See the Lord
Artist: Chris Falson, Maranatha! Singers/Willow Creek Music
Album/Label: I See the Lord/Maranatha!; Still I Will Worship You: Live Worship at Willow Creek/Willow Creek Music
Style: Worship ballad
Tempo: Slow/mid
Seeker-Sensitivity Rating: 2
Themes: God's holiness; Book of Isaiah
Comments: The Willow Creek version is the first song in a medley also featuring the traditional "Holy, Holy, Holy" and the Gary Oliver "Holy, Holy, Holy." We also do it as a stand-alone in our worship services.

I Surrender All
Artist: None
Album/Label: None
Style: Worship ballad
Tempo: Slow
Seeker-Sensitivity Rating: 4
Themes: Surrendering to Christ; Obedience
Comments: Traditional worship song. An old Deniece Williams version can be found on "So Good to Know" (Sparrow). A chart for our version of this song is available at www.willowcharts.com.

I Wanna Learn More
Artist: Curt Coffield, Ed Kerr
Album/Label: None
Style: Folk pop worship
Tempo: Mid
Seeker-Sensitivity Rating: 5
Themes: God's Word; Wanting to know more about God
Comments: Written by Curt and Ed for Willow Creek's Old Testament Challenge series

I Will Bless You, Lord
Artist: Hillsongs
Album/Label: Touching Heaven, Changing Earth/Integrity
Style: Worship ballad, in 3
Tempo: Mid
Seeker-Sensitivity Rating: 3
Themes: Desire to bless God

I Will Never Be
Artist: Hillsongs
Album/Label: Shout to the Lord/Integrity
Style: Worship ballad
Tempo: Slow/mid
Seeker-Sensitivity Rating: 3
Themes: Changed life; Desire to be pure

In My Heart
Artist: Greg Ferguson
Album/Label: Leave a Light On/Willow Creek Music
Style: Celtic-style worship ballad
Tempo: Slow
Seeker-Sensitivity Rating: 6

Themes: Worshiping God and praying to him right where we are spiritually
Comments: Can be done as a special or as a worship chorus

In Your Hands
Artist: Hillsongs
Album/Label: All Things Are Possible/Integrity
Style: Worship ballad
Tempo: Slow/mid
Seeker-Sensitivity Rating: 4
Themes: God's healing hands; The security of a relationship with God—assurance

In Your Loving Arms
Artist: Willow Creek Music
Album/Label: None
Style: Ballad
Tempo: Slow
Seeker-Sensitivity Rating: 4
Themes: God's love; Desire to be close to God
Comments: Written by Rory Noland. Available only at www.willowcharts.com

Jesus, Draw Me Close
Artist: Willow Creek Music
Album/Label: To Know You More/Willow Creek Music
Style: Worship ballad
Tempo: Slow
Seeker-Sensitivity Rating: 3
Themes: Desire to be close to God; Obedience

Jesus, Lover of My Soul
Artist: Hillsongs
Album/Label: Shout to the Lord/Integrity
Style: Pop worship
Tempo: Up
Seeker-Sensitivity Rating: 3
Themes: Changed life; Friendship with God; God's love

Jesus, What a Beautiful Name
Artist: Hillsongs
Album/Label: God Is in the House/Integrity
Style: Worship ballad, in 6/8
Tempo: Slow/mid
Seeker-Sensitivity Rating: 6
Themes: Jesus—the beauty of Christ
Comments: Might work as a Christmas chorus if you're focusing on the person of Christ

Jesus, You're the Answer
Artist: Tommy Walker
Album/Label: There Is a Rock/Get Down Ministries
Style: Soulish worship ballad
Tempo: Slow
Seeker-Sensitivity Rating: 5
Themes: Seeking God; God is our hope and strength
Comments: Available at www.getdownrecords.com

Joy, Joy, Joy
Artist: Tommy Walker

Album/Label: Live at Home/Get Down Records
Style: Rock shuffle
Tempo: Up
Seeker-Sensitivity Rating: 5
Themes: Joy of the Christian life
Comments: Fun song! Available at www.getdownrecords.com

Just Say the Word
Artist: Willow Creek Music
Album/Label: None
Style: Pop shuffle, in 3
Themes: Mid
Seeker-Sensitivity Rating: 3
Themes: Obeying God; Discipleship
Comments: Written by Greg Ferguson. Available only at www.willowcharts.com

Let Everything That Has Breath
Artist: Matt Redman
Album/Label: The Heart of Worship/Sparrow; Worship Together; EMI
Style: Pop/rock worship
Tempo: Up
Seeker-Sensitivity Rating: 4
Themes: Praising God without end

Let It Rise
Artist: Praise Band
Album/Label: Praise Band 7/Maranatha!
Style: Rock worship
Tempo: Up
Seeker-Sensitivity Rating: 5
Themes: God's glory; Praising God

Let the Peace of God Reign
Artist: Hillsongs
Album/Label: Shout to the Lord/Integrity
Style: Worship ballad
Tempo: Slow
Seeker-Sensitivity Rating: 3
Themes: God's peace; God's healing power; Desire to be closer to God

Let the Walls Fall Down
Artist: Student Impact
Album/Label: Draw Me Close/Willow Creek Music
Style: Pop worship
Tempo: Up
Seeker-Sensitivity Rating: 6
Themes: Unity in Christ; The church
Comments: Also on one of the early Maranatha! Praise Band recordings

Let Your Love Pour
Artist: Student Impact
Album/Label: Draw Me Close/Willow Creek Music
Style: MOR worship
Tempo: Mid
Seeker-Sensitivity Rating: 4
Themes: Prayer for God to fill us, heal us

Let Your Word Go Forth
Artist: Willow Creek Music
Album/Label: None
Style: Pop worship

Tempo: Up
Seeker-Sensitivity Rating: 2
Themes: The power of God's Word

Lift Up Your Heads
Artist: Tommy Walker
Album/Label: Live at Home/Get Down Records
Style: Rock/pop worship
Tempo: Up
Seeker-Sensitivity Rating: 2
Themes: Majesty of Jesus; Glorifying God
Comments: Available at www.getdownrecords.com

Lord, I Believe in You
Artist: Tommy Walker
Album/Label: Yes, We All Agree/Get Down Records
Style: Worship power ballad
Tempo: Slow/mid
Seeker-Sensitivity Rating: 4
Themes: Faith—believing in God by faith
Comments: Crystal Lewis did this as a solo on her Gold CD. Tommy's version is available at www.getdownrecords.com.

Lord, I Lift Your Name on High
Artist: Maranatha!/Praise Band
Album/Label: Top 25 Praise Songs/Maranatha!; Best of Praise Band/Maranatha!
Style: Pop worship
Tempo: Up
Seeker-Sensitivity Rating: 6
Themes: Lifting up God; Praising God for salvation

The Lord Is Gracious and Compassionate
Artist: Vineyard
Album/Label: Winds of Worship 12: Live from London/Vineyard Music
Style: Worship ballad
Tempo: Mid/slow
Seeker-Sensitivity Rating: 5
Themes: God's grace and love

Lord Most High
Artist: Willow Creek Music
Album/Label: To Know You More/Willow Creek Music
Style: MOR worship
Tempo: Mid
Seeker-Sensitivity Rating: 3
Themes: Praise; Magnifying God
Comments: Split male-female song

Lord of All
Artist: Hillsongs
Album/Label: All Things Are Possible/Integrity
Style: Worship power ballad
Tempo: Slow
Seeker-Sensitivity Rating: 3
Themes: Glorifying God with our lives; Surrender; Worship

Lord, Reign in Me
Artist: Vineyard

Album/Label: Winds of Worship 12: Live in London/Vineyard Music
Style: Rock/pop worship
Tempo: Up
Seeker-Sensitivity Rating: 5
Themes: Surrendering to God; Lordship of Christ

The Lord's Prayer
Artist: Willow Creek Music
Album/Label: Still I Will Worship You: Live Worship at Willow Creek/Willow Creek Music
Style: U2-ish rock/pop
Tempo: Up
Seeker-Sensitivity Rating: 9
Themes: Lord's prayer

Love You So Much
Artist: Hillsongs
Album/Label: Shout to the Lord/Integrity
Style: Worship ballad
Tempo: Slow
Seeker-Sensitivity Rating: 5
Themes: Thankfulness; Love for God; Longing for God

Meet with Me
Artist: Ten Shekel Shirt
Album/Label: Much/Vertical; Integrity
Style: Modern worship
Tempo: Up
Seeker-Sensitivity Rating: 7
Themes: Longing to connect with God
Comments: Can be done as a worship chorus or as a special

More Love More Power
Artist: Jude Del Herro
Album/Label: Wow Worship Blue/Integrity
Style: Worship ballad
Tempo: Slow
Seeker-Sensitivity Rating: 3
Themes: Longing for more of God; Worshiping God with all that we are

More Precious Than Silver
Artist: Don Moen
Album/Label: God in Us/Integrity
Style: Worship ballad
Tempo: Slow
Seeker-Sensitivity Rating: 5
Themes: The value, worth of God

Mourning into Dancing
Artist: Tommy Walker
Album/Label: Pray for Each Other/Get Down Records
Style: Pop
Tempo: Up
Seeker-Sensitivity Rating: 5
Themes: Changed life
Comments: Available at www.getdownrecords.com

My Glorious
Artist: Student Impact
Album/Label: Alive/Willow Creek Music
Style: Rock

Tempo: Mid/up
Seeker-Sensitivity Rating: 4
Themes: The glory of God

My Heart Sings Praises
Artist: Hillsongs
Album/Label: God Is in the House/Integrity
Style: Pop worship
Tempo: Mid
Seeker-Sensitivity Rating: 4
Themes: Praise; God is our strength

My Jesus, I Love You
Artist: Willow Creek Music
Album/Label: To Know You More/Willow Creek Music
Style: Worship ballad
Tempo: Slow
Seeker-Sensitivity Rating: 3
Themes: Worship; Response to God's love

My Redeemer Lives
Artist: Hillsongs
Album/Label: By Your Side/Integrity; Wow Worship Green/Integrity
Style: Pop/rock
Tempo: Up
Seeker-Sensitivity Rating: 3
Themes: Redemption; Salvation

Never Gonna Stop
Artist: Tommy Walker/Willow Creek Music
Album/Label: Never Gonna Stop/Integrity; Still I Will Worship You: Live Worship at Willow Creek/Willow Creek Music
Style: Pop/rock
Tempo: Up
Seeker-Sensitivity Rating: 3
Themes: Praising God for eternity; Thankfulness

No Greater Love
Artist: Tommy Walker
Album/Label: We Say Yes/Get Down Records
Style: Pop/rock
Tempo: Up
Seeker-Sensitivity Rating: 6
Themes: God's love
Comments: Available at www.getdownrecords.com

Nothing Is as Wonderful
Artist: Vineyard
Album/Label: The Very Best of Touching the Father's Heart/Vineyard Music
Style: Worship ballad
Tempo: Slow
Seeker-Sensitivity Rating: 3
Themes: Desire to know Christ

O for a Thousand Tongues
Artist: Willow Creek Music
Album/Label: None
Style: Contemporary arrangement of hymn
Tempo: Up
Seeker-Sensitivity Rating: 3
Themes: Praise; Salvation
Comments: Available only at www.willowcharts.com

O Most High
Artist: Mark Altrogge
Album/Label: Hosanna! Music Songbook 5/Integrity
Style: Pop
Tempo: Up
Seeker-Sensitivity Rating: 3
Themes: God as a refuge
Comments: Video clip of this song is available at www.willowcharts.com.

Open the Eyes of My Heart
Artist: Paul Baloche
Album/Label: Open the Eyes of My Heart/Integrity
Style: Pop/rock worship
Tempo: Up
Seeker-Sensitivity Rating: 5
Themes: Desire to see and know God; Praise

Potter's Hand
Artist: Hillsongs
Album/Label: Wow Worship Green/Integrity
Style: Worship ballad
Tempo: Slow/mid
Seeker-Sensitivity Rating: 3
Themes: Doing God's will; Yielding our lives to God

Pour Out My Heart
Artist: Vineyard
Album/Label: Touching the Father's Heart #16/Vineyard Music
Style: Worship shuffle
Tempo: Mid
Seeker-Sensitivity Rating: 4
Themes: Expression of love to God; Worship

Power of Your Love
Artist: Hillsongs
Album/Label: Shout to the Lord/Integrity
Style: Worship ballad
Tempo: Slow
Seeker-Sensitivity Rating: 6
Themes: God's love

Praise God on High
Artist: Willow Creek Music
Album/Label: None
Style: Worship ballad
Tempo: Slow
Seeker-Sensitivity Rating: 5
Themes: Heaven—all tears will be dried, pain will be gone, etc.
Comments: Written by Rory Noland. Available only at www.willowcharts.com

A Pure Heart
Artist: Rusty Nelson
Album/Label: Take the City/Integrity
Style: Worship ballad
Tempo: Slow
Seeker-Sensitivity Rating: 4
Themes: Purity; Discipleship

Reach Down Deep
Artist: Willow Creek Music
Album/Label: None

Style: Pop
Tempo: Up
Seeker-Sensitivity Rating: 5
Themes: Giving God our deepest worship
Comments: Written by Greg Ferguson. Available only at www.willowcharts.com

Reaching for You
Artist: Willow Creek Music
Album/Label: None
Style: Rock/pop
Tempo: Up
Seeker-Sensitivity Rating: 9
Themes: Seeking God
Comments: Written as a seeker-sensitive congregational chorus by Greg Ferguson. Available only at www.willowcharts.com

Revelation 19
Artist: Student Impact
Album/Label: Alive/Willow Creek Music
Style: Worship ballad
Tempo: Slow/mid
Seeker-Sensitivity Rating: 4
Themes: Worship; God's glory and power
Comments: Great antiphonal chorus—has three different parts going at the same time

Shout to the Lord
Artist: Hillsongs
Album/Label: Shout to the Lord/Integrity
Style: Worship power ballad
Tempo: Slow
Seeker-Sensitivity Rating: 3
Themes: Praise & worship; The wonder of Christ

Shout to the North
Artist: Student Impact
Album/Label: Alive/Willow Creek Music
Style: Rock, in 3
Tempo: Up
Seeker-Sensitivity Rating: 4
Themes: Praise; The lordship of Christ

Show Your Power
Artist: Kevin Prosch, Vineyard
Album/Label: Winds of Worship 1/Vineyard Music
Style: Rock/pop worship
Tempo: Up
Seeker-Sensitivity Rating: 3
Themes: Prayer for God to show his power

Spirit of the Living God
Artist: NA
Album/Label: None
Style: Traditional worship song
Tempo: Slow
Seeker-Sensitivity Rating: 4
Themes: Yielding our lives to God

Step by Step
Artist: Rich Mullins
Album/Label: The World as Best as I Remember It, Vol. 1/Reunion
Style: Folk worship
Tempo: Mid
Seeker-Sensitivity Rating: 3
Themes: Lordship of Christ; Following God

Still Amazing
Artist: Danny Chambers
Album/Label: Hosanna! Music Songbook 7/Integrity
Style: Worship ballad
Tempo: Slow
Seeker-Sensitivity Rating: 5
Themes: God's grace
Comments: Video clip of this song is available at www.willowcharts.com.

Still I Will Worship You
Artist: Willow Creek Music
Album/Label: Still I Will Worship You: Live Worship at Willow Creek/Willow Creek Music
Style: Pop/rock worship
Tempo: Up
Seeker-Sensitivity Rating: 3
Themes: Praising God even when we don't understand his work in our lives; Worship in the face of difficult circumstances

Take My Life and Let It Be
Artist: Paul Baloche
Album/Label: God of Wonders/Hosanna!; Integrity
Style: Worship ballad
Tempo: Mid/slow
Seeker-Sensitivity Rating: 3
Themes: Yielding our lives to God

Te Alabamos
Artist: Tommy Walker
Album/Label: Live at Home/Get Down Records
Style: Latin pop worship
Tempo: Mid/up
Seeker-Sensitivity Rating: 4
Themes: Praise; Expression of love to God
Comments: Chorus is in Spanish—very fun! Available at www.getdownrecords.com

Thank You for Saving Me
Artist: Delirious
Album/Label: Cutting Edge/Sparrow
Style: Folk rock worship ballad
Tempo: Slow/mid
Seeker-Sensitivity Rating: 3
Themes: Salvation; Thanksgiving

Thank You, Lord
Artist: Hillsongs
Album/Label: God Is in the House/Integrity
Style: Worship ballad, in 3
Tempo: Mid
Seeker-Sensitivity Rating: 3
Themes: Thankfulness for being saved

That's Why We Praise Him
Artist: Tommy Walker
Album/Label: Live at Home/Get Down Records
Style: Rock/pop worship
Tempo: Mid
Seeker-Sensitivity Rating: 5
Themes: We praise God because of what he has done for us
Comments: Great song! Available at www.getdownrecords.com

There Is None Like You
Artist: Lenny LeBlanc
Album/Label: Above All/Integrity
Style: Worship ballad
Tempo: Slow/mid
Seeker-Sensitivity Rating: 6
Themes: God's uniqueness

These Things Are True of You
Artist: Tommy Walker and the CA Worship Band
Album/Label: Yes, We All Agree/Get Down Records
Style: Ballad duet
Tempo: Slow
Seeker-Sensitivity Rating: 9
Themes: God's attributes; Desire to be like God
Comments: Available at www.getdownrecords.com. Can be done as a special or as a worship chorus

Think about His Love
Artist: NA
Album/Label: Wow Worship Green/Integrity
Style: Worship ballad
Tempo: Slow
Seeker-Sensitivity Rating: 6
Themes: God's love and goodness

Turn Your Eyes upon Jesus
Artist: Hillsongs
Album/Label: The Secret Place/Integrity
Style: Worship ballad
Tempo: Slow
Seeker-Sensitivity Rating: 3
Themes: Fixing our eyes on Christ

Undivided Heart
Artist: Willow Creek Music
Album/Label: None
Style: Folk pop worship ballad
Tempo: Slow
Seeker-Sensitivity Rating: 3
Themes: Devotion to Christ; Discipleship
Comments: Written by Greg Ferguson and Matt Shepardson. Available at www.willowcharts.com

Unto the King
Artist: Don Moen
Album/Label: Best of Don Moen, Vol. 1/Integrity
Style: Worship ballad, in 3
Tempo: Slow/mid
Seeker-Sensitivity Rating: 3
Themes: Giving God honor and glory

Unto the King
Artist: Tommy Walker
Album/Label: Live at Home/Get Down Records
Style: Rock shuffle
Tempo: Up
Seeker-Sensitivity Rating: 4
Themes: Glorifying and honoring God
Comments: Available at www.getdownrecords.com

We Fall Down
Artist: Passion
Album/Label: Wow Worship Green/Integrity
Style: Worship ballad
Tempo: Slow/mid
Seeker-Sensitivity Rating: 3
Themes: God's holiness; Worship

We Praise Your Name
Artist: Willow Creek Music
Album/Label: Still I Will Worship You: Live Worship at Willow Creek/Willow Creek Music
Style: Worship ballad
Tempo: Slow/mid
Seeker-Sensitivity Rating: 4
Themes: There is no one like God; Worship

What a Good God You've Been
Artist: Tommy Walker
Album/Label: Praise Band 8: I Walk by Faith/Maranatha!; There Is a Rock/Get Down Ministries
Style: Worship ballad
Tempo: Slow
Seeker-Sensitivity Rating: 7
Themes: God's goodness; God's blessings
Comments: Can be done as a special or as a worship chorus. *There Is a Rock* is available at www.getdownministries.com.

What the Lord Has Done
Artist: Hillsongs
Album/Label: Touching Heaven, Changing Earth/Integrity
Style: Worship ballad, in 3
Tempo: Slow/mid
Seeker-Sensitivity Rating: 2
Themes: Praising God for all that he has done

When I Survey the Wondrous Cross
Artist: NA
Album/Label: None
Style: Updated traditional
Tempo: Slow
Seeker-Sensitivity Rating: 3
Themes: The cross; Jesus' sacrifice on the cross
Comments: Arrangement available at www.willowcharts.com

Where You Are
Artist: Tommy Walker
Album/Label: Never Gonna Stop/Integrity
Style: Pop worship
Tempo: Mid
Seeker-Sensitivity Rating: 5
Themes: God's presence; Desire to be close to God

Who Is Like Our God?
Artist: Vineyard
Album/Label: Winds of Worship 12: Live from London/Vineyard Music
Style: Rock/pop worship
Tempo: Mid
Seeker-Sensitivity Rating: 3
Themes: God's character

With Our Hearts
Artist: Lenny LeBlanc
Album/Label: Pure Heart/Integrity
Style: Pop worship, in 3
Tempo: Mid/up
Seeker-Sensitivity Rating: 3
Themes: Faith; Lordship of Christ

You Alone
Artist: Passion
Album/Label: Live Worship from the 268 Generation/Sparrow
Style: Folk pop worship, in 6/8
Tempo: Mid
Seeker-Sensitivity Rating: 4
Themes: God's uniqueness; God as a Father; God's goodness

You Are Holy
Artist: Hillsongs
Album/Label: Touching Heaven, Changing Earth/Integrity
Style: Worship ballad
Tempo: Slow
Seeker-Sensitivity Rating: 3
Themes: God's holiness

You Are My King
Artist: Passion
Album/Label: One Day—Live/Sparrow
Style: Worship ballad
Tempo: Slow
Seeker-Sensitivity Rating: 4
Themes: God's amazing love; The sacrifice of Christ

You Are with Me Still
Artist: Willow Creek Music
Album/Label: None

Style: Acoustic ballad
Tempo: Slow
Seeker-Sensitivity Rating: 9
Themes: God is with us even in the darkness
Comments: Written after the September 11 tragedy. Available only at www.willowcharts.com

You Are Worthy of My Praise
Artist: Passion
Album/Label: Better Is One Day/Sparrow
Style: Rock/pop
Tempo: Up
Seeker-Sensitivity Rating: 3
Themes: Praise & worship; God deserves our worship

You Have Been Given
Artist: Willow Creek Music
Album/Label: To Know You More/Willow Creek Music
Style: Worship ballad, in 3
Tempo: Slow
Seeker-Sensitivity Rating: 3
Themes: The name of Christ; Worship

You Mean the World to Me
Artist: Willow Creek Music
Album/Label: None
Style: Worship ballad
Tempo: Slow/mid
Seeker-Sensitivity Rating: 2
Themes: Desire for others to know Christ
Comments: Written by Joe Horness. Available only at www.willowcharts.com

Your Everlasting Love
Artist: Student Impact

Album/Label: Draw Me Close/Willow Creek Music
Style: Rock worship
Tempo: Up
Seeker-Sensitivity Rating: 6
Themes: God's love
Comments: Also available on one of the early Maranatha! Praise Band CDs

Your Love
Artist: Hillsongs
Album/Label: All Things Are Possible/Integrity
Style: Worship ballad
Tempo: Slow
Seeker-Sensitivity Rating: 4
Themes: God's love

Your Love for Me
Artist: Integrity Songwriters
Album/Label: Rock of Refuge/Integrity
Style: Pop worship
Tempo: Up
Seeker-Sensitivity Rating: 4
Themes: God's love and mercy; Serving God

You've Won My Affection
Artist: Curt Coffield
Album/Label: Let the World See/Independent
Style: Worship ballad
Tempo: Slow
Seeker-Sensitivity Rating: 4
Themes: Response of love to God's sacrifice
Comments: Beautiful song. Available at www.reslife.org

Drama Index

ACTING THE PART by Sharon Sherbondy

Carol is having a difficult time putting her faith into action. Specifically, she is driving her husband crazy with her list of "don'ts." Like many sincere but misinformed believers, she has an exaggerated view of how God calls us to live.

Suggested Topics: Legalism; Living out Christianity
Characters: 1 male, 2 females

ADULTEROUS WOMAN/SOLDIER AT THE CROSS by Judson Poling

(These are two monologues, either of which could stand alone.) The first story is told by the woman caught in adultery (John 8), though it is some time after the fact. She has just witnessed Jesus' crucifixion, especially ironic because there was nothing she could do to help him even though his encounter with her spared her life. She recounts the shame of that day, the travesty of justice, and the tenderness of Jesus, who not only treated her with dignity and saved her life, but also forgave her sin. She knows that even though he is now dead, she will see him again; and until that day she will always hold in her heart the freedom and new start he gave her.

Suggested Topics: Good Friday; Grace; God's tenderness; The woman caught in adultery
Characters: 1 female

The second monologue recounts the experience of one of the soldiers at the cross. He has mixed feelings about the whole ordeal, wondering why Rome has taken to killing off such apparently harmless victims. When he wrestles with what he has done, especially in light of Jesus' readiness to forgive all who hurt him, he blurts out to the heavens that he had to do it—he had orders. Maybe this guy was the Messiah, maybe not. But God should have made it more obvious. He should have sent someone who at least looked more impressive so everybody would know.

Suggested Topics: Good Friday; Skeptical reactions to Jesus
Characters: 1 male

THE ADVISORY BOARD by Judson Poling

Don is trying to make an important decision about whether or not to take a new job and relocate. But as he thinks about the pros and cons, his "advisory board"—the voices in his head—leaves him reeling in confusion. First is his Mother, whose image of him as a doctor has never been realized. Next is the Motivator, always enthusiastic but not very realistic. Then comes the Calculator, crunching the numbers, trying to anticipate every contingency. Finally, there's Superstitious Voice, trying to attach significance to everyday, random occurrences. In the end making a decision is hard when all the voices in his head are talking at once.

Suggested Topics: Decision making; Finding the will of God; Voices in our heads
Characters: 3 males, 2 females (some characters not gender specific)

AFTER LIFE by Mark Demel

In this monologue a man talks about planning his own funeral. He wants it to be a festive affair—no organ music or formal dress. He wants balloons, party mix, casual attire—all the things that were part of his happiest moments in life. Yet when he thinks about what really happens after life, he is confused because there are so many points of view from which to choose. He ends on a sobering note: He is really scared of what might happen to him when he dies—scared as hell.

Suggested Topics: The afterlife; Heaven and hell
Characters: 1 male

ALL GUMMED UP by Judson Poling

It's fifteen minutes before Jennifer's wedding, and she is sitting outside at the bus stop talking to an old man. She is attempting to sort out her feelings of mistrust toward her father. When she was twelve she discovered her father was having an affair, and she still hasn't recovered. Now she wonders if she can trust her fiancé. The old man encourages her to see her fiancé for who he is, not for who her father was.

Suggested Topics: Adultery; Dealing with past hurts; The pain of lies
Characters: 1 male, 1 female, 1 offstage male voice

ALL I WANT FOR CHRISTMAS by Judson Poling

This sketch examines the difficulty people have in restraining their material desires. The setting is a shopping mall at Christmas time. Parents are trying to convince their daughter that adding a seventh Barbie doll to her collection isn't necessary. Through a brief series of events, she ends up talking to two other adults, and ironically, she is able to poignantly explain how she is trying to be less greedy.

Suggested Topics: Greed; Desire to acquire possessions
Characters: 3 males, 2 females, 1 female child

AM I MISSING SOMETHING? by Donna Lagerquist

When amiable businessman and city council candidate Robert Dibbons is honored as the "Giver of the Week" by a local newspaper, everyone is thrilled! However, one employee soon begins to question her boss's sincerity. She recounts a painful memory of her father giving her leftover presents from work; items that cost him nothing monetarily or emotionally. In a frustrating conclusion Mr. Dibbons fails to see the harm in something being "mutually beneficial." We know, however, that he volunteers to promote himself and gives only out of his excess.

Suggested Topics: Attitudes in serving; Giving; Self-deception; Rationalizing
Characters: 3 males, 2 females

THE ANGRY WOMAN by Judson Poling

As we look back over Jean's life, several episodes of disappointment and humiliation show us why she is an angry woman: nagging from her mother, embarrassment from a teacher, being dumped by a boyfriend, and disparagement from her alcoholic husband. She "never said what she needed to say," which has kept her from expressing her true feelings—she has bottled them up so that now they leak out in the wrong places, leaving her angry and lonely. "Because she didn't say what she needed to say, she has said what she didn't want to say—and now doesn't know what to say."

Suggested Topics: The roots of anger
Characters: 2 males, 3 females, 1 narrator

ANOTHER DAY AT THE BUS STOP by Judson Poling

A modern retelling of the story of the woman at the well from John 4. A "woman of the evening" meets a stranger at a bus stop, who not only shows her kindness, but even asks for a sip of her Coke. She is unaccustomed to being treated as a person, but the stranger amazes her even more by claiming to be Jesus. Though she is skeptical, his ability to sympathetically describe so many details about her life convinces her he is real—and as he leaves, she haltingly expresses her desire to talk with him again.

Suggested Topics: Our relationship with God; Self-esteem
Characters: 1 male, 1 female

ANY TIME? by Sharon Sherbondy

In this sketch we see how an "everyman" character responds to God's desire to be a part of his life. In his college years he is too busy with studies and asks God to come back when he is more settled. In his early adulthood he has too many responsibilities but this time asks God to come back when he is retired. In his retirement he is glad to see God but isn't prepared for the challenge of meeting with him regularly.

Suggested Topics: Making time for God
Characters: 1 male

ANYTHING BUT RELIGION by Sharon Sherbondy

Ruth and Hank are on their way to visit their daughter, Cheryl, and her husband, Brian. All are hoping to have a "nice" evening, but it's unlikely because no matter how hard they try, they end up fighting over religion. The reason: Ruth and Hank are Catholic, and Cheryl has left the church and has become a Protestant like her husband. The sketch honestly presents the misunderstandings and hurt feelings that often result from this very common family tension.

Suggested Topics: Denominational differences; Families alienated because of religion
Characters: 2 males, 2 females

ATTACK OF THE WELL-MEANERS by Various Authors

When Gwen's father takes ill, two of her friends fly in to console her. The comedy occurs as they attempt to help Gwen deal with this tragedy and fail completely to offer what Gwen really needs.

Suggested Topics: Dealing with crisis; Friendship
Characters: 1 male, 2 females

ATTRACTIVE DEAL by Mark Demel

(*Note:* This script serves as Part 1 to "Investment at Risk")
Brett returns to his office late on a Friday night and is surprised to find his administrative assistant, Sharon, who is still there working late. He is elated because his business trip was a success and credits her with playing a key role. As he praises her work and tries to convince her that she will be compensated for her effort, it becomes clear each finds the other more than attractive. Both hoped they would find the other one there after hours. After Brett finds out his wife is staying at her parents' house that evening, he and Sharon decide to celebrate their success—and propose a toast "to us."

Suggested Topics: Convictions; Adultery; Temptation
Characters: 1 male, 1 female

BABY TALK by Mark Demel

Two couples are having dinner in a Chinese restaurant. The fun conversation of these good friends turns to the subject of children. One couple has children. The other couple, Mike and Allison, are at odds over the issue. While Allison is ready to start a family, Mike is unsure. In fact, he is taking an informal survey of everyone he meets, asking, "Why did you have kids?" Allison is embarrassed by his approach and frustrated by his seeming inability to make a decision. When Mike seeks rational answers from Maureen and Terry, he is unsatisfied because their decision to have kids seemed like the next thing to do after buying a house. The sketch ends in a playful manner, but it is clear that Mike is no closer to a decision, much to his wife's dismay.

Suggested Topics: Decision making; Parenting; Decision to have children
Characters: 2 males, 2 females

BECAUSE I LOVE YOU by Sharon Sherbondy

Michelle has planned a romantic dinner for Eric only to have it spoiled by a piece of junk mail. Michelle had an affair four years earlier with a man who worked at the company that sent the letter. Suddenly the romantic evening turns into a major argument, as Eric

reveals his deep hurt and continual lack of trust, even after four years. The sketch ends with the couple alienated and hurting.

Suggested Topics: Adultery; The consequences of sin
Characters: 1 male, 1 female

BEST FRIENDS by Sharon Sherbondy

The kids are off camping, and a husband and wife are looking forward to a romantic weekend alone. They are interrupted by the neighbors who come loaded down with games, munchies, and sleeping bags determined to keep the couple company. The neighbors are actually a very needy couple whose complaints and insensitivity lead to a delightfully comic resolution.

Suggested Topics: Friendship; Insecurity; Needy people
Characters: 2 males, 2 females

THE BEST GIFT by Donna Lagerquist

It's Christmas day, and four grown siblings are exchanging gifts. The mood is fun and playful as one receives a gift certificate, another an item of clothing, and another a "singing fish." Finally, it's Kim's turn, but she has to qualify her gift. Because she has been unemployed for some time, she couldn't afford to buy something big and expensive. Instead, she chooses to present her brother with the "gift of words." Using an item she "found around the house" as her gift, she lovingly tells her brother how a whistle reminds her of his "ability to rally the troops." She tells the story of a time when his ability to cheer her up made such a difference to her. The rest of the group agrees that this inexpensive gift was the most precious of all.

Suggested Topic: Christmas
Characters: 2 males, 3 females

THE BIG QUESTION by Sharon Sherbondy

Brian and Lisa are in a panic as they decide how to explain the "facts of life" to their young daughter, Amy. Much to their surprise, Amy doesn't have questions about sex, but about the existence of God. She wants to know where God lives and if he is good. As a result of the conversation, Brian and Lisa begin questioning whether they believe in God and what they know about him.

Suggested Topic: The existence of God
Characters: 1 male, 1 female, 1 child

THE BIG SELL by Sharon Sherbondy and Steve Pederson

An ad agency is contracted to devise an ad campaign for a new soft-drink product, "Rejuven-ade." The product manager comes in just as the team is thinking up ways to make the beverage sell. True to Madison Avenue, the ideas quickly turn toward sexual themes, and instead of extolling the family values the product manager wanted, the campaign's slogan becomes "Don't drink it 'cause you're thirsty, drink it 'cause you're hot." On a roll, though oblivious to the fact the product manager left because he didn't like it, they move to their next account, "Catalina Gourmet Cat Food." Within seconds the ideas have turned to—you guessed it—"erotic."

Suggested Topics: Obsession with sex in society; Effect of the media
Characters: 3 males, 2 females

THE BLACK HOLE by Various Authors

Joe, an average guy, and Jane, an average girl, were created by God, and he loved them very much. Like all of us, they have a definite need for him, but typically they try to fill the "black hole" with relationships, status, and possessions. Until they ask God's forgiveness and are filled by him, they live empty lives.

Suggested Topics: Contentment; God's love; Filling the void
Characters: 2 males, 1 female, 1 narrator

THE BOOK OF LIFE by Donna Lagerquist

An energetic mime that shows how—and how not—to have one's name written in the Book of Life and thus obtain entrance into heaven. In this parable a bicyclist ponders his/her flat tire and

becomes a witness to several people (of varied occupations/backgrounds) getting "called" by a Maître D' (God) to enter through a door (heaven). Whenever the door is open, there's the sound of a great party. When the Maître D' finds a person's name in the Book of Life, that person is allowed to enter through the door. The bicyclist tries to enter, but his/her name is not in the book. The Maître D' tries to explain that in order for people to have their name in the book, they must give him their heart. Not satisfied with that, the bicyclist tries money, good deeds, and even sneaking into heaven before finally trusting his/her heart to God.
Suggested Topics: Baptism; Faith; Basic Christianity; Eternal life
Characters: 3 females, 3 males

THE BOY WHO NEVER GOT DIRTY by Various Authors

A lighthearted tale of a boy named LeRoy Boskowitz. He never got dirty, took risks, or helped others because he was afraid of getting hurt. He remained this way into adulthood until his wife, Stella, got fed up and devised a plan that led LeRoy to experience the joy of serving others.
Suggested Topics: Service; Risk taking
Characters: 1 male, 1 female, 1 narrator

THE BREAKFAST CLUB by Sharon Sherbondy

The cost of building relationships can be high, but the rewards can be just as great. A group of four men meet together once a week to hold one another accountable, encourage one another, and share in one another's lives. In a busy world one meeting a week can be an inconvenience, but when a crisis occurs that investment can really pay off.
Suggested Topics: Friendship; Friends in crisis; Small groups
Characters: 4 males, 1 female

THE BROTHERHOOD by Various Authors

We have an exaggerated view of a serious problem when the local chapter of the International Order of the Brotherhood of Fellow Workaholics meets. Their motto is "Work hard, die young, and leave a haggard-looking corpse." One of the members shares his "testimony" of how he came dangerously close to becoming a well-balanced person.
Suggested Topics: Workaholism; Balancing your life
Characters: 2 males, 4 either males or females

BROTHER'S KEEPER by Various Authors

How would you handle someone wanting to be included in every part of your life? This sketch shows us how Larry deals with his needy brother, Jack. Larry's frustrations finally bring him to a confrontation with Jack. At first we think Jack understands the point, but he simply has refocused his attention elsewhere.
Suggested Topics: Unhealthy dependencies
Characters: 3 males

THE BROW BEATER by Various Authors

Norman just can't seem to forget his past failures, and just in case he might, he carries with him a "Brow Beater's Book." This comprehensive guide to all of his failures reminds him that he is a second-class citizen and keeps him in his place. His date for the evening tries to explain the freeing power of forgiveness and how that can change his outlook on life.
Suggested Topics: Self-esteem; Failures; Forgiveness
Characters: 1 male, 1 female

BUY ONE, GET ONE FREE by Donna Lagerquist

Karen comes home from the grocery store loaded down with bags of groceries. "Buy one, get one free," she explains to her husband, Rob. She is actually planning to give away half of the groceries to her sister's family, who has had a spell of bad luck. Just then she receives a phone call saying she has won a minivan in a local

contest. As she and Rob get excited, she realizes the people who really need it are her sister Kris and her family. Rob picks up the phone and calls Kris to tell her about their good fortune but surprises Karen by telling Kris she is getting the car. Karen is moved by Rob's unselfishness and glad he wanted to do the very thing she wanted to do.
Suggested Topic: The joy of giving
Characters: 1 male, 1 female

CALL OF THE WILD by Sharon Sherbondy

Charlie is in for a shock when Marla comes home from church. She heard a message on taking a step of faith and letting God have complete charge of the direction of our lives. The night before, she saw a special on needy people in Africa, and now she is convinced that God has called her there. Marla ignores that her personality and skills are completely out of sync with a ministry in Africa and that her own community is a more suitable mission field.
Suggested Topics: Serving God
Characters: 1 male, 1 female

CALL WAITING by Judson Poling

Two men in an office anticipate a reprimand for their failure to get the loan the company needs for expansion. Though they tease each other good-naturedly about what they will have to endure, Allan is having deeper questions about his significance to the company—and in reality, his significance as a person. His income has not matched his hopes, and he has had to watch others rise higher and faster in the corporate structure. He is having, in the words of Chris, a poorly timed "mid-life crisis." Chris decides to go and hide out from the dreaded call. Now left alone, Allan sits in his office contemplating the conversation and whether he should quit or stay. The phone rings. He stares at it as the lights fade.
Suggested Topics: Mid-life crisis; Marketplace pressures; Search for significance
Characters: 2 males

CAN'T LIVE WITHOUT 'EM by Donna Lagerquist

A sweeping look at the various relationships that affect us throughout life. An on-stage narrator and actors recreate scenes from childhood, high school, college, and marriage that illustrate in a comic way the many frustrations of living with imperfect people. Clothes, brains, beauty, neatness, even store-bought rather than homemade cakes—all affect whether we're accepted or rejected. The difficulty of loving others unconditionally is contrasted with words from the Sermon on the Mount (and other passages) that show Christianity's striking—and challenging—countercultural stance.
Suggested Topics: Relationships; Unconditional love
Characters: 2 males, 2 females

CATALOG-ITIS by Judson Poling

This is an exaggerated look at one family's struggle with compulsive shopping. Arn and Peggy are unable to control their desire for more possessions and confuse wants with needs. Their attempt to buy a legitimate household necessity turns into a mad frenzy for more, more, more!
Suggested Topics: Self-control; Contentment
Characters: 1 male, 1 female, 2 junior high girls

CATCH 22 by Sharon Sherbondy

A woman contemplating an abortion confides in a friend. The ensuing dialogue explores the difficulty, agony, and emotions associated with this issue. In a surprise twist the friend admits that she has had an abortion herself—and still suffers from the guilt. There are no pat answers here, but no one will miss the power of this real-life drama.
Suggested Topics: Abortion
Characters: 2 females

CAUGHT IN THE MIDDLE by Sharon Sherbondy

Hank, Ronda, and teenage daughter Kendra are shopping for a prom dress. Not only are the styles more risqué than Hank is comfortable with, but Kendra is talking about a post-prom sleepover with three other couples at the summer home of one of the teen's parents. Kendra is trying to maintain that there is nothing to worry about, but Hank cannot see it—especially because he was a teenage boy once! The argument ultimately comes down to trust: Do the parents trust their daughter's word that sex is not part of the party? The parents agree to reconsider but only if Kendra will also reconsider her choice for her prom dress—one that's more modest. She agrees but immediately heads off to pick out a bikini for the "swim prom" party!

Suggested Topics: Raising teenagers in today's world; The challenge of parenting

Characters: 1 male, 2 females (1 teen)

THE CENTERPIECE by Donna Lagerquist

This comic, fun sketch focuses on the idea of people refusing to admit the reality of Christ even though they are confronted with much evidence. The evidence, in this case, is a huge cross that has come through the roof and crashed through the dining room table. It is Easter Sunday, and a family is having dinner but refuses to even acknowledge the obvious. A friend from Dad's work arrives for dinner and can't believe what he sees and cannot fathom why nobody speaks of it. When he finally mentions the word "cross," the family rebukes him. The friend discovers this has happened before—frequently at Easter and Christmas. But the family has learned that if they don't mention the cross, it will disappear—until next time.

Suggested Topics: Easter; Denial; Not dealing with reality

Characters: 2 males, 3 females, 2 children

CHAMELEON by Sharon Sherbondy

Jeff is taken by surprise when his father's behavior is determined by the happenings around him. One minute Jeff's father is affectionate and singing his praises, but as soon as Dad receives bad news, he verbally attacks Jeff and questions his motives. Jeff is exhausted when this happens twice in a short period of time.

Suggested Topics: God's presence in our lives; Controlling our emotions

Characters: 3 males

A CHANGE OF LIFE by Donna Lagerquist

As Holly enters the living room with a basket of clothes that need folding, her husband, Pete, complains that his favorite breakfast cereal has been "ruined" by the company's attempt to add a new flavor. We identify with the challenge in their relationship—Pete has been on reserve with his employer for two weeks, and Holly isn't used to her normally absent husband's presence. Pete is trying to help around the house but has thrown off Holly's rhythm. It's not that she doesn't love having him around more, she explains, it's just that change is difficult for her. Pete agrees and then, by suggesting a small change in the way she does the laundry, illustrates that sometimes "change can be a good thing."

Suggested Topics: Marriage; Change

Characters: 1 male, 1 female

CHANGES by Sharon Sherbondy

Karen and Russ are having dinner with Karen's parents. For some reason, during this visit she is struck with the aging of her parents. A combination of their helplessness and Karen's memories of past times together makes her sad, yet at the same time she is filled with a love for these two special people in her life.

Suggested Topics: Reparenting parents; Family

Characters: 2 males, 2 females

CHARACTER TEST by Mark Demel

Mark begins the day by talking on the phone with his very nervous brother, Scott, who is about to take his doctoral oral exam. After hanging up, Mark realizes he wanted to say more—to be a better encourager. He calls Scott back, but he has already left. As the day wears on, Mark realizes he needs to make the two-hour drive to wish his brother well. He does so and arrives just in the nick of time. Scott is shocked but pleased. They are able to share a quick but meaningful moment before the exam starts, and when it is over, Mark is glad he obeyed the prompting from God to step out and serve his brother.

Suggested Topics: Promptings from God; Obedience; Power of encouragement

Characters: 2 males, 1 female

CHECK MATES by Sharon Sherbondy

The subject of finances brings fear to the heart of Rob and excitement to Judy. In the midst of trying to balance their checkbook, Judy and Rob discover that their significant debt is a shared problem. To correct the situation, they decide to get rid of all their credit cards. When they actually try to do it, however, they rationalize and end up keeping most of the cards and destroying only two.

Suggested Topics: Personal finances; Debt

Characters: 1 male, 1 female

CHRISTMAS LITE by Sharon Sherbondy

Jodie calls her family to a special dinner during a Christmas of uncertainty for this family—her husband, Vic, has been out of work for six months. Jodie announces it will be the end of the macaroni and cheese they have been eating lately, and they are going to put the Christmas tree up tonight. The kids aren't very enthused when they hear there won't be many gifts under the tree. Vic is upset: "Why are you putting up a tree? I thought we agreed it would just make things worse." As the conflict mounts between Jodie and Vic, the kids duck out to the kitchen. When they return, they are able to defuse the situation a bit as the family does its best to hold out hope for a change in their situation. A mixture of honest doubt, frustration, and hope characterizes this drama as faith is stretched and relationships are challenged.

Suggested Topics: Christmas; Faith; Family under stress; Dealing with crisis

Characters: 3 males (2 teens/preteens), 1 female

CHRISTMAS STORY by Donna Lagerquist

An extended half-hour sketch. A young couple, Renee and Kurt, decide to host this year's extended family Christmas celebration. They have an infant son, and they are hoping to put in place some meaningful Christmas traditions. Renee would like to have the Christmas story read at some point during the night. Kurt would like to have some substantive conversations with members of the family. The rest of this sketch is a somewhat comical look at how these plans go awry. The other family members arrive, mostly with quirky peculiarities, and all with expectations that don't match with Renee and Kurt's. By the end of the night, much has transpired, but the Christmas story is never read and in-depth conversations never materialize. In the quiet of the now-empty home, Renee and Kurt settle on the couch with their baby, and Kurt finally reads the Christmas story. It has been a far-from-perfect night, but this young family is making its own tradition stick even if the rest of the family isn't with them.

Suggested Topics: Christmas; Family

Characters: 4 males, 4 females, 12-year-old boy, 10-year-old girl

A CLEAN SLATE by Various Authors

An "everyman" character delivers three brief monologues. After each one, two or three guilt figures with small black slates mark down his "sins" while saying, "God is gonna get you for that!" Guilt ridden "everyman" has finally had enough, and he cries out to God only to discover that instead of "getting him," God forgives him. The guilt figures disappear, and "everyman" discovers in their place a large clean slate.

Suggested Topics: Forgiveness; Redemption; Guilt
Characters: 1 male, 2 or 3 either males or females

CLEARING THINGS UP by Mark Demel

This comical sketch is a look at how the red tape of organization can get in the way of the true passion of ministry. Bob is nervous. His assistant is leaving the office for a minute as he tries to prepare for his boss's pending visit. She reminds him he'll have to answer his own phone and tries to reassure him. Of course, as soon as she leaves, the phone starts ringing. In quick succession he gets three calls from people at his church—none of whom seems to know the other is calling. Each person needs something from him: information, a lunch appointment, participation in a committee. As Bob humorously tries to avoid committing more of his time, he also exchanges emails with a seeker friend. Bob's ultimate choice to keep on his calendar the things that are most important gives this predominantly comical sketch a touching finish.

Suggested Topics: Balancing life; Priorities
Characters: 5 males or females

THE COMFORT ZONE by Judson Poling

Ken and Karla spend another "comfortable" night at home. Their lives are always very comfortable, a fact to which they repeatedly refer. Any disturbance either by way of TV, career opportunity from a friend, intruding neighbors—even a life-threatening piece of popcorn stuck in Karla's throat—is met with their same commitment to remain . . . comfortable. This comic sketch shows that in the end the desire to avoid risks can actually mean death, not life.

Suggested Topics: Risk taking
Characters: 1 male, 2 females (1 TV announcer on tape)

.COMmunity by Various Authors

Jim comes home from work to an empty apartment. He does what a lot of lonely people do: he turns on his computer. He begins by "chatting" with a woman he has a date with later that night. (*Note:* The audience reads the entire dialogue on side screens.) She comes up with a flimsy excuse and cancels. Now with no plans for the night, he decides to visit a few chat rooms. Through humorous situations, each fails to give Jim what he is looking for. Finally, he finds a new website designed for lonely people and selects "Bob, the Internet Friend" to interact with. We see a video of Bob trying to carry on a conversation with Jim, but this virtual friend is clearly not making any real connection. He eventually gets Jim to hug his computer—causing a power surge that erases all his files. A great metaphor for how pseudo-community leaves you empty.

Suggested Topics: True community; The Internet; Relationships
Characters: 1 male

CONFESSIONS OF AN AD-AHOLIC by Judson Poling

Al and Alice are "ad-aholics," individuals addicted to advertisements. They explain how the addiction started, progressed, and eventually ruined their lives. This satire shows how chasing the American dream of having more can be a nightmare.

Suggested Topics: American dream; Power of the media; Materialism
Characters: 1 male, 1 female

CONVERSATIONS by Judson Poling

Phil, accompanied by another man, is waiting to talk to his boss. We quickly find out this other person is a personified critical voice, heard and seen only by Phil but always there. As the conversation with Barb, his boss, gets going, the critical voice constantly interrupts, making Phil say things he really doesn't want to. He eventually must excuse himself, knowing the voice has won again and has convinced him he is a failure. As Phil exits, Barb comments to herself on Phil's erratic behavior—only to be shamed by her own critical voice!

Suggested Topics: Self-esteem; Self-criticism; Failure
Characters: 2 males, 1 female, 1 offstage female voice

CONVERSATIONS IN A FIELD by Judson Poling

Two lilies and two ravens become discontent with their lot. After worrying themselves into a frenzy, they realize that God created them to enjoy being lilies and ravens, and that he will care for their needs.

Suggested Topics: Anxiety; Worry; God's providence
Characters: 2 males, 2 females

THE CONVERSION by Judson Poling

Todd, an appealing college student, discusses with his parents his recent conversion to Hinduism. Todd's dad doesn't understand how he could "turn his back on his country and his family's faith." Todd feels they don't know enough about Hinduism to make a judgment.

Suggested Topics: Hinduism
Character: 2 males, 1 female

CREDIT DUE by Donna Lagerquist

Miss Patsy is the host of a local television show for children but definitely has some problems liking her job—and kids. Norah, a make-up person on the set, offers some helpful ideas for the show. Though Miss Patsy appears to disdain Norah, she uses her idea anyway, without giving her credit. It isn't the first time she has done something like this; and in the end, Norah knows she is being used but doesn't know what to do.

Suggested Topics: When others use you
Characters: 2 males, 2 females, 2 offstage children's voices

DATE OF THE WEAK by Judson Poling

The premise of this sketch is a television show called "Date of the Weak," in which two "sportscasters," a male and a female, provide a play-by-play of a dinner date between Mike and LuAnne. Using typical sportscaster language, they assess every action and response of the dating couple. Much of the time, Mike doesn't "execute on the fundamentals," while LuAnne makes all the "points." A major turnaround—"What a swing in momentum!"—brings a delightful end in which Mike scores an "amazing recovery" and shows his "champion" form. This very fun sketch takes a lighthearted look at the challenge of dating but also warns against judging by appearances.

Suggested Topics: Judging others; The "game" of dating
Characters: 2 males, 3 females

A DAY IN THE LIFE by Judson Poling

This unique drama is really a series of short, interconnected vignettes that illustrate in a humorous way a new Christian going about his first day at work after his conversion. To perform this sketch, the pastor must actually interact with the actor playing the new Christian, interspersing his message throughout the vignettes. As the new believer faces a hectic morning commute, an obnoxious coworker, and the temptation to lie to keep a sale, the scenes cover three broad topics of interest for new Christians: making time for God in the midst of a busy schedule, forgiving those who wrong you, and steering through ethical dilemmas in the workplace.

Suggested Topics: New Christians; Basic Christian lifestyle; Christians in the marketplace
Characters: 5 males (or adapted for females)

D–DAY by Sharon Sherbondy

Humorous sketch about a businessman, Rob, whose wife and coworker find his calendar at work filled with thrill-seeking activities up until a day marked "D–Day"—then there's nothing scheduled after it. They first think he's going through a mid-life crisis, then fear he is going to die. When Rob comes into his office, he informs them that "D–Day" refers to the "decision" to become a Christian. He has filled his calendar with fun things, because once "D–Day" arrives, "it's all over!"

Suggested Topics: Misconceptions about Christianity; Becoming a Christian

Characters: 2 males, 1 female

DECEMBER THE 27TH by Sharon Sherbondy

Paul and Beth are recovering from hosting Christmas at their house with a total of "twenty-eight people and three stray dogs." Combining two extended families and their quirkiness made it a crazy time—egg yolks with smiley faces in the eggnog, creme de menthe glazing on the turkey, White Castle stuffing, and a flashing Santa nose ring on one of the nephews. On top of all that, the VISA bill that came today was so thick it needed extra postage. How can they rescue themselves from the commercialism and exhausting family demands of the season? Just as they resolve to make a change, the phone rings. Aunt Lilly's flight got overbooked, and she needs a place to stay the night. The lights fade as Paul and Beth look at each other, wondering what to do.

Suggested Topics: Overcoming regret; Pace of life at Christmas; Finances

Characters: 1 male, 1 female

DEFINITELY SAFE by Donna Lagerquist

It's Father's Day, and a college-age son and father are talking on the back porch of the family home. The son, Mark, has been sensing his mother's anger toward him and finally gets the explanation: Both parents are disappointed in Mark because he has lied to them about dropping out of school. Mark confesses readily and verbally beats himself up for being such a failure, especially compared to his successful older sister. The father, though angry, wants Mark to move back home so they can work things out. Mark marvels at his dad's patience. As they play a quick baseball skirmish, the father calls his son "safe—definitely safe." The obvious double entendre of his words touch us with the never-ending love of a committed father.

Suggested Topics: Father's Day; Prodigal son; Unconditional love

Characters: 2 males, 1 female

DIFFERENCES by Donna Lagerquist

A bag lady innocently and humorously opens up the otherwise "sensitive" topic of Catholicism versus Protestantism when she happens upon two ministers—one of each denomination—on a street corner and wrongly assumes they are friends. With childlike wonder, she questions them on topics such as confession, communion, and why they wear what they do. Despite her lightheartedness and attempts at bringing them together, friction between the two men remains obvious and unresolved.

Suggested Topics: Catholicism vs. Protestantism; Friction among believers

Characters: 2 males, 1 female

DISTANCING by Sharon Sherbondy

Paul and Liz are in the middle of marriage, kids, work, and life, and busyness is beginning to separate them. Liz has shut down because of Paul's absence. The scene we witness is a discussion between them during the mad rush of the morning—kids demanding attention and appointments pending. First, each tries to justify his/her own position. Then Paul takes a step of vulnerability and admits he is worried because this is the course his parents were on as they headed to divorce. There is little time to resolve the issue but enough time for them to take a small step forward.

Suggested Topics: Good marriages take work; Demands of life

Characters: 1 male, 1 female

DON JUAN DE SCHAUMBURG by Judson Poling

Don, a very pagan, single man has fallen for Donna, a "fox in sheep's clothing" as he calls his Christian heartthrob. He is determined to do whatever it takes to get her, so he consults with three friends to find out how to woo a "born-again type" woman. Among the suggestions that Don adopts are carrying a big Bible, saying "Praise the Lord" (especially when he finds out the bars are still open!), and quoting Rush Limbaugh. These and other misconceptions add up to a ridiculously superficial (though laughable) portrait of what people commonly think it means to be a Christ-follower.

Suggested Topics: False views of Christians; Dating

Characters: 3 males, 1 female

DON'T MENTION IT by Donna Lagerquist

An evening together for two couples is strained because one of the men is unemployed. While the host wife is (comically) going overboard trying to be sensitive to the unemployed couple's embarrassment, the unemployed man just wishes he could stay at home so he wouldn't have to deal with other people and their reaction to his condition. Finally, the two husbands speak openly about the situation, with the host husband confessing he too was unemployed for a while and went through all the feelings associated with that time of hardship. The sketch ends on a light note with the two men realizing it's better to "mention it"—instead of hiding the need to talk about what is really going on.

Suggested Topics: Unemployment; Being open about problems; Community

Characters: 2 males, 2 females

DONUTS AND DEADBEATS by Sharon Sherbondy

Joyce is on a diet again, but Dick is paying the price. As he describes it, after ten minutes on the diet, she becomes "cranky and neurotic and even suicidal." So they make a deal: He will be her support and encouragement as long as his food intake remains the same. Can Joyce handle temptation? Will Dick cheer her on? The ending is very true to the "real world" we all live in.

Suggested Topics: Physical health; Self-control

Characters: 1 male, 1 female

DOOMED by Sharon Sherbondy

As the family prepares for a quiet Thanksgiving dinner, Mom gives each family member an envelope and instructs him or her to leave it sealed until she has finished explaining the contents. Unable to withstand the mystery, the family members open their envelopes. Enclosed are pictures of relatives. Dad and the kids learn that each one of them is assigned to entertain the relative whose picture he or she has. Shocked and disappointed that Mom has broken her promise never to have the relatives over again, they recount the tragedies of last year's Thanksgiving fiasco. Mom confesses she folded under the pressure. Mom reminds Dad and the kids that she will rescue them when it gets to be too much to handle. All they need to do is signal her like they did last year. As the discussion escalates and kids protest, the doorbell rings, signaling impending doom. With the battle ahead, they unite and affirm their love for one another—no matter what happens!

Suggested Topic: Thanksgiving

Characters: 1 male, 1 female, 2 children

THE DO-OVER by Judson Poling

John shows up for a job interview and greets the secretary. Just as he arrives, he sneezes—into his hand! A bell rings and the scene freezes then resets. The exact entrance scene is replayed, but this time John sneezes into a tissue. The sketch continues like this: embarrassing event followed by a reset and the same situation played out with a chance for John to "do over" each moment. Sometimes it takes several tries for him to get it right. The scene ends with John finally being allowed in for the interview, ironically telling himself, "You only get one chance to do it right!" (*Note:* This sketch follows a similar formula to the movie *Groundhog Day* and was also inspired by a short play entitled "Sure Thing" by David Ives.)

Suggested Topics: Longing for second chances; The importance of good choices

Characters: 1 male, 1 female

DRIVEN by Donna Lagerquist

In the car on the way to an awards banquet for his being salesman of the year, Doug and Nancy get in a fight. She is becoming more and more frightened of the man he is becoming as he claws his way to success. He can't see the way both he and his family are paying a price for his drivenness. He also can't see how part of his problem is his trying to please his deceased father's wishes for him. In the end Nancy gets out of the car and leaves Doug to his success act. As the lights fade, Doug lays on the horn, frustrated and alone.

Suggested Topics: Workaholism; Marriage

Characters: 1 male, 1 female

EARLY ONE MORNING JUST AFTER THE DAWN OF HISTORY AS WE KNOW IT by Judson Poling

Two cavemen stumble upon each other and immediately establish their respective territories. They quickly discover this is not enough to satisfy their need to feel superior, so they begin a one-upmanship game that starts with a stone rock for a chair and ends with a La-Z-Boy recliner! Just when you think things couldn't be weirder, another caveman shows up—with a cellular phone! He outdoes the other two hands down! This entire sketch is done without any dialog—just actions, props, and "grunts."

Suggested Topics: Materialism; Keeping up with the Joneses

Characters: 3 males

EASTER SNAPSHOTS by Donna Lagerquist

This sketch looks at three broad areas of life: family, work, and church. Six short scenes confront us with the stark contrast between relationships rooted in love and mutual respect and those driven by self-interest. Two family scenes contrast a family enjoying the making of memories and the free flow of trust with one in which trust has been broken by unfaithfulness and addiction. One of the workplace scenes depicts the enthusiasm of two friends embarking on a business partnership, while the other scene shows the once trust-filled partnership dissolving in bankruptcy, bitterness, and blame. Two church scenes contrast the healing impact of a church filled with love with a church that damages people by preaching graceless morality and judgment. This sketch is uniquely suited to an interactive format, allowing for each scene to be presented at a strategic point during a message. (At Willow Creek this was presented on Easter 2000.)

Suggested Topics: Easter; Love vs. selfishness

Characters: Multiple, flexible

EMPTY NEST by Donna Lagerquist and Steve Pederson

Paul and Nancy have just returned from dropping off their daughter at college. As they face the evening home alone without a teenager, it's a bittersweet moment. They're glad to have the peace and quiet, but it's hard to make the transition from their active parenting role to living without being needed. As Nancy says, "I feel like I got fired from my job as a mom." Still, Paul points out that they made the transition to parenting, so they can make the transition to being empty nesters. We see his calm exterior evaporate when the phone rings and he thinks it may be his daughter.

Suggested Topics: Empty nesters; Parenting

Characters: 1 male, 1 female

EVERYBODY NEEDS by Mark Demel

In this monologue a woman laments her inability to resolve the problems of the world. Her busy schedule—all perfectly legitimate and needful activities—leaves her exhausted with little time or energy to make a dent in world hunger. Even her trips to the shopping mall create despair as she encounters a homeless woman there. She is left frustrated, complaining, "Even if I make a difference, it won't make a difference."

Suggested Topic: Being impressed with externals

Characters: 1 female

EVERYTHING'S RELATIVE by Judson Poling

Sid's pleas for a break don't move the policeman giving him a ticket. Instead, a lecture ensues on the importance of upholding the law. Once at home, Sid falls asleep and dreams of being burglarized. In the dream the policeman and thief merely echo Sid's earlier lines to the policeman concerning how to show "mercy." When Sid wakes up, he has a new appreciation for a standard of right and wrong.

Suggested Topics: God's holiness; Benefit of God's laws

Characters: 3 males, 1 female

EXPECTATIONS OF THE EXPECTING by Judson Poling

Dirk and Claire are expecting their first child, but they're finding out just how much they're expecting of that child. Dirk, the perfectionist, has a life of education and achievement all laid out; Claire is mostly laid back about it. The soon-to-be-parents are copies of their own parents' expectations, and they're only now realizing how different those expectations are. The sketch ends on a positive note as both affirm the differences in each other that together will help bring about balance in their child's life.

Suggested Topics: Parenting; Affirming personality differences

Characters: 1 male, 1 female

FACE VALUE by Donna Lagerquist

This sketch was written following the September 11 attack and focuses on the issue of racial prejudice. Ken returns home from work and asks his wife, Erin, if the insurance adjuster showed up. Erin says yes but confesses she didn't let him look at the roof—"He was Middle Eastern!" Ken is frustrated by her reaction—"They aren't all terrorists"—and Erin is largely embarrassed. A friend, Sandy, enters to pick up her girls, who are playing with Erin's girls. She has a darker skin color and recounts a story of prejudice she has just experienced in the grocery store. Erin responds sympathetically to her friend and fully realizes that she, too, has judged a stranger based solely on the color of his skin.

Suggested Topics: Racial prejudice; September 11

Characters: 1 male, 2 females

A FAILURE TALE by Donna Lagerquist

Once upon a time there was a kingdom that was ruled by a very kind and loving king. We see what happens when the king confronts three of the subjects who have violated the rule of making firearms. How will they react to deliberately disobeying rules that create serious consequences not only for themselves but for those around them? You can expect denial, admission, and forgiveness at the conclusion of the tale.

Suggested Topics: Failing; Obeying rules

Characters: 5 males, 1 narrator

FAITH IN JEOPARDY by Cathy Peters

Two couples get together for an evening and through a game of Jeopardy discover where their faith lies. Bruce and Annette, a semi-churched couple, find out Jim and Carol have recently made a commitment to the Mormon Church. At first there doesn't seem to be any major difference in what they believe, but as the game goes on, it reveals some alarming aspects of Mormon theology.

Suggested Topics: Mormonism

Characters: 2 males, 2 females

THE FAMILY MEETING (PARTS 1 AND 2) by Donna Lagerquist

Part 1: It's the start of the new year, and the parents in this sketch are laying down some ground rules. Their three children have been running their lives, and it is now time to take back control! First off, the kids have to turn in their cell phones and Game Boys. In addition they are informed that anything left on the floor will be confiscated. The new rules are not popular with the kids, but the parents are energized and excited about the prospects for the new year.

Part 2: A week has passed, and another family meeting is in progress. This time the parents are exhausted because the rules they set in place have backfired. The children, dressed in old clothing that is too small, have had all their clothes taken because they were left on the floor. They have also lost all their "toys" for the same reason. The kids are difficult to deal with, bored with nothing to do. The parents find themselves in a worse place than before and end up giving in to their children. The question is, "Who's in charge?"
Suggested Topics: Family; Discipline; Parenting
Characters: 1 male, 1 female, 3 children

FAMILY SNAPSHOTS—TAKE I by Sharon Sherbondy

The first of five sketches involving a typical family. Linda, the mother, is visiting with an old friend when the kids come home. Chaos breaks out as the children (Chris, a typical eighth-grade boy; Jenny, a high school student; and Ned, who is home visiting from college) get Linda more and more embarrassed at the impression they are making on her friend. When the father arrives, a decision is made that things have to change.
Suggested Topics: Family; Communication
Characters: 3 males, 2 females, 1 junior high boy

FAMILY SNAPSHOTS—TAKE II by Sharon Sherbondy

In an effort to get closer, the family has decided to spend the evening playing Scruples (a board game asking the players how they would react to specific situations). The game reveals that the time parents invest in teaching children values and priorities is well worth it.
Suggested Topics: Values; Priorities
Characters: 2 males, 2 females, 1 junior high boy

FAMILY SNAPSHOTS—TAKE III by Sharon Sherbondy

This touching sketch looks at the special relationship between parent and child, particularly father and daughter. Mike is distracted with work and surprised when Jenny says she feels neglected. After talking about a sensitive issue Jenny is dealing with, Mike recommits himself to being available to her.
Suggested Topics: Parent-child relationships; Helping kids through hard times
Characters: 1 male, 1 female

FAMILY SNAPSHOTS—TAKE IV by Sharon Sherbondy

The family has decided to take in a teenage friend of Jenny's whose family asked her to leave when they discovered she was pregnant. The characters learn that "integrity and concern for your fellow man" takes sacrifice.
Suggested Topics: Family; Self-sacrifice
Characters: 2 males, 3 females, 1 junior high boy

FAMILY SNAPSHOTS—TAKE V: CHRISTMAS EVE by Sharon Sherbondy

It's Christmas Eve and the family is getting ready for church when they receive a phone call saying the service has been canceled because of the heavy snow. Mom comes up with the idea that the family do their own version of the Christmas story. Despite the older children's moanings and humorous interpretations, the scene ends with a touching moment when Dad reads the story of Christ's birth.
Suggested Topics: Christmas
Characters: 2 males, 2 females, 1 junior high boy

FAMILY VALUES by Judson Poling

Paula and her mom meet after what appears to have been a long separation. Her mother wants her to come home with her, but Paula indicates she wants to stay. We finally discover that Paula has joined some kind of cult. As Mom describes the life she wants Paula to come home to, we realize that a party-hearty brother and Mom's on-again, off-again romance make for a less than appealing home life. Still the control of the cult group makes us see that Paula has been brainwashed. A member of the group enters to escort Paula back. Paula decides to go with him, and Mom is left calling for her daughter in an empty room.
Suggested Topics: Cults; Broken families
Characters: 2 females, 2 males

FAMOUS LOST WORDS by Judson Poling

Turn the other cheek? Give to anyone who asks? Are these commands meant to be taken literally? In this "drama within a drama," the actors break from reading Jesus' words when one of them confesses he is skeptical. The words sound noble enough, but nobody he knows really lives them. Two brief scenes recounted from the actors' lives show in a lighthearted way the extremes of, on the one hand, allowing yourself to be walked on and, on the other hand, setting up inflexible boundaries. Can either of these be right? What did Jesus really mean? The sketch ends without resolution, the actors—and the audience—left with the unanswered question.
Suggested Topics: Turning the other cheek; Healthy boundaries/unhealthy submission
Characters: 4 males, 1 female

FAT CHANCE by Sharon Sherbondy

Sharon is trying to get a few minutes alone to talk to God about her struggles as a parent. However, the kids (heard only by her) are constantly interrupting outside the bedroom door. We witness the typical parental tension between wanting to do the right things and fearing doing the wrong things. The sketch takes a lighthearted, but also poignant, look at every parent's struggle.
Suggested Topics: Parenting
Characters: 1 female

FEELING OPPOSITION by Donna Lagerquist

Phil and Kate visit their lawyer friend to draw up a will. Kate becomes very emotional as she envisions the will being needed (i.e., herself or Phil dying). Phil, being "practical," tries to convince Kate she is overreacting (as usual). As they comically reach the point of actually signing the will, Phil gets a little surprise that releases an "overreaction" on his part—much to Kate's delight.
Suggested Topics: Thinkers vs. feelers
Characters: 1 male, 1 female

THE FENCE-SITTER by Donna Lagerquist

A man is literally sitting on a fence on the stage. Through vignettes reenacted from the past, we see how, all his life, he has been keeping his options open and avoiding commitment. As a kid, he never committed to a sport; as a man he refused to marry the girl of his dreams; now he doesn't want to have to get involved in church. In the end he remains where he has always been—sitting up on the fence of life, alone and unfulfilled.
Suggested Topics: Indecision; Getting involved in ministry; Deciding to become a Christian
Characters: 4 males, 1 female

FINDING EVIDENCE by Sharon Sherbondy

Vicki and Russ come across a bag of cocaine in their son's room. They confront him with assumptions and accusations before he has had a chance to explain. He is angry that they have jumped to conclusions and informs them that he took the bag away from a friend who is trying to kick the habit. Russ's response is one of disbelief. The audience is left to decide for themselves whom to believe.

Suggested Topics: Recognizing the truth; Jumping to conclusions; Trust
Characters: 2 males, 1 female

FIRST-DAY JITTERS by Sharon Sherbondy

Over the weekend, Claire has made a decision to accept Christ as her Savior. It's Monday morning and she is having a conversation with God about how she expects her day to go. Claire has gone to some unnecessary extremes, like an oversized Bible and saying "Praise the Lord" often, to demonstrate her changed life. God impresses upon her the need to die to her old nature.

Suggested Topics: New Christians; Obeying God; Witnessing
Characters: 1 female

FIRST THING FIRST by Sharon Sherbondy

This sketch takes a humorous look at the home that allows children to become the central focus. Kathy and Greg have been parents for ten months, and their lives have changed drastically. Kathy is especially finding it difficult to adapt to the new demands of a baby and still maintain a marriage.

Suggested Topics: New parents; Priorities; Balancing children and marriage
Characters: 1 male, 1 female, 1 female infant

FISHIN' by Steve Pederson

It's not easy for some of us to say, "I love you and appreciate what you do for me." That's the case with this father and son. They accomplish little fishing, but they do manage to break the ice and share how they really feel about each other.

Suggested Topics: Expressing positive emotions; Father-son relationships
Characters: 2 males

FOR BETTER OR WORSE—PART I by Sharon Sherbondy

Paula and Marsha have dragged their husbands to ballroom dance lessons in hopes of doing something fun and exciting for their marriages. Joining them are Paula's sister, Lisa, and her fiancé, Dan. Lisa and Dan's gushy demonstrations of their love totally turn off Steve and Kurt. Paula and Marsha on the other hand remind them that they used to be just like that—"but then they had to go and get married."

Suggested Topics: Marriage
Characters: 3 males, 3 females (offstage male and female voices)

FOR BETTER OR WORSE—PART II by Sharon Sherbondy

Dan and Lisa are coming to Steve and Paula's house for the evening. Steve is not very excited about the idea until Paula mentions that Dan and Lisa have never had a fight. Suddenly Steve is bringing out the cards, and together they begin setting up the young lovers' doom. Except things don't exactly turn out as planned—or do they?

Suggested Topics: Marriage; Personality differences
Characters: 2 males, 2 females

FOR BETTER OR WORSE—PART III by Donna Lagerquist

The sketch opens with Marsha and Kurt in their first marriage counseling session. The sketch is a mix of humor and soberness as the two reveal the story of their courtship. The conclusion leaves the audience with the idea that a healthy marriage begins before the wedding day.

Suggested Topics: Courtship; Marriage
Characters: 1 male, 1 female, 1 either male or female

FOR BETTER OR WORSE—PART IV by Sharon Sherbondy

Dan and Lisa have been married for a while, and love is still in the air—or so Lisa tells Paula over the phone. Lisa also talks of her anger and frustration with her dad's controlling and authoritative personality. When Dan comes home, Lisa's happy marriage slowly begins to unravel as she sees clearly for the first time that she has married a man just like her father.

Suggested Topics: Marriage
Characters: 1 male, 1 female

FOR BETTER OR WORSE—PART V by Sharon Sherbondy

It's 11:15 P.M. Steve is asleep on the couch. Paula heads for bed when suddenly Steve wakes up and wants to "you know." Paula becomes furious. What ensues is an honest look at the pain Paula has in feeling like "the last thought of the day."

Suggested Topics: Marriage
Characters: 1 male, 1 female

FOR BETTER OR WORSE—PART VI by Donna Lagerquist

The three couples introduced to the audience in Part I are reunited at a Christmas party. The scene opens with the group watching home movies. A few of the characters share childhood memories, impressing us with the importance of family relationships. The sketch closes with Marsha and Kurt sharing the news of their pregnancy. We see how each of the couples has worked and is continuing to work on their marriage and the blessings they receive.

Suggested Topics: Marriage; Family; Family of God; The importance of friends
Characters: 3 males, 3 females

FOR IMAGE SAKE by Cathy Peters

Bob will do anything to get ahead, and now he is paying the price. He has lied to everyone at work about his family and possessions. Bob comically scrambles to make things appear true when his boss invites himself to dinner in order to meet his family.

Suggested Topics: Honesty; Pretense
Characters: 3 males, 1 female

FORGIVE AGAIN? by Sharon Sherbondy

Susan is furious. She has just spent another evening humiliated by her husband Jerry's stories. It seems that every time they are with friends she becomes the brunt of Jerry's jokes. And this time she has had it. She is not going to be so quick to forgive as she has in the past.

Suggested Topics: Forgiving others
Characters: 1 male, 1 female

FORGIVEN by Donna Lagerquist

Rita and Nancy run into each other at the grocery store. They used to be close friends but have lost touch. Nancy seems anxious to continue her shopping, but Rita wants to say something. She tells Nancy she forgives her. Years before, Nancy had an affair with a friend's husband and broke up a close group of friends. Rita wants Nancy to know that although she wasn't the offended party, she still wants to forgive her and wants to remind her that God forgives her too. Nancy cannot accept that right now—she has done too much damage and been too damaged to dare hope that forgiveness is possible. Rita insists they get together sometime, and Nancy reluctantly agrees. Nancy is left alone on stage, a slip of paper in hand with Rita's phone number on it. She begins to weep as the lights fade.

Suggested Topics: Forgiving others; God's forgiveness
Characters: 2 females

FOURTH OF JULY by Donna Lagerquist

A family watching fireworks is joined by the likable bag lady Vivian. The son, Elliott, takes a real liking to her, but his parents are naturally standoffish. Elliott can't understand why she doesn't have the benefits associated with living in America, the land of opportunity, especially when Vivian is truly patriotic (in her eccentric sort of way). The sketch ends as the parents awkwardly decide to move to a different spot to get away from her in spite of Elliott's protest.

Suggested Topics: Fourth of July; The homeless
Characters: 1 male, two females, one child

FREEDOM CELEBRATION by Sharon Sherbondy

Dave and Stacey are dragging themselves and their two teenage children to a fireworks display on the Fourth of July. There is much comic conflict among them, but they do it because "this is what one does on the Fourth of July." They begin talking and listening to Bill, a World War II pilot. He helps to reorient their thinking concerning the freedom they have taken for granted.

Suggested Topics: Fourth of July; Freedom; Patriotism
Characters: 2 females, 2 males, 1 male and 1 female teenager

FULL SERVICE STATIONS AND OTHER MYTHS
by Donna Lagerquist

Jane has to deliver a company presentation on the importance and benefits of service. Instead, she reviews her frustrating experiences with a gas station attendant, an answering service operator, a night watchman, and the police department. She is left pondering, "Whatever happened to the idea of one person serving another?"

Suggested Topics: Serving
Characters: 1 male, 1 female

FUNNY GIRL by Donna Lagerquist

Margo, the "funny girl," tells her story of being overweight from her youth. As a child, she is teased by her brother, in high school she learns how to generate laughter from embarrassment, and by college she has discovered that making people laugh is the only way to get them to notice her and like her. She even tries a stint as a stand-up comic—though in the end, as she huddles in a closet with a Twinkie, she still feels lost in the crowd.

Suggested Topics: Being an outsider; Need for acceptance
Characters: 1 male, 2 females (multiple roles for one man and woman)

THE GAME OF LIFE by Steve Pederson and Judson Poling

This sketch is a parody on the board game "The Game of Life." An "everyman" character spins the wheel and begins the game. He is confronted along the way with choices that will determine the game's outcome. He loses, but when the narrator gets ready to put the game away, the man's wife stops him. She thinks that if the right choices are made, she'll do better.

Suggested Topics: Search for meaning; Spiritual seeking; Decision making
Characters: 1 male, 1 female, 1 narrator

THE GARDENERS by Judson Poling

To explain the New Age movement, this sketch goes back to the Garden of Eden. Similar to those following the New Age philosophy, Adam and Eve want to be gods and control their own destiny. Through humor, aspects of the New Age are exposed.

Suggested Topics: New Age movement
Characters: 1 male, 1 female

GETTING DIRECTIONS by Judson Poling

A parable about Jesus being the only way to heaven. A bicyclist stops to ask directions from a roadside beverage vendor. He wants to get to the top of Stone Mountain. When the vendor points out the one road to get there, the man is put off by the limits imposed by having only one route available. Surely there must be other ways. He keeps trying to suggest alternatives, even getting to the point of proposing ridiculous means, but each is met with warnings about how it won't get him there. Determined to prove a point, he takes

off down the wrong road anyway. The vendor offers a free bottle of water—not because he is giving in, but because he knows the cyclist will need it for the trip back to the only safe and certain road.

Suggested Topics: Not all paths lead to God; Christianity's exclusive claims
Characters: 2 males

GETTING THE NOD by Judson Poling

Doug and Mark have two different ways of viewing and handling failure. Mark plays the corporate game but finds out Doug's honesty earns him the respect of his boss. It also earns him the opportunity at a second chance.

Suggested Topics: Honesty; Integrity; Handling failures; Business ethics
Characters: 2 males, 1 either male or female

GIVING A BLESSING VIGNETTES by Judson Poling

(*Note:* This sketch is actually a series of three sequential—but not contiguous—scenes, which work well as illustrations placed within a message.) Part 1: Dad comes home to his fifteen-year-old son, Ryan, playing a computer game. Dad wants Ryan to bring in the trash cans, but Ryan is defensive. With persistence and sensitivity, Dad uncovers Ryan's real issue—anxiety about the upcoming basketball tryouts. Part 2: Dad is going through a litany of Ryan's poor use of time. Ryan sneezes, and when Dad offhandedly says, "God bless you," Ryan challenges. How does a "blessing" come so easily when Dad is in the middle of berating him? Part 3: Dad approaches Ryan with sensitivity and humor, wanting to talk to him "man to man." Ryan jokes that he already knows where babies come from, but a tender moment ensues as Dad struggles to tell Ryan that he is proud of him and is trying to do better with Ryan than his own dad did with him. The sketch ends with them affirming their love for each other.

Suggested Topics: Father's Day; Parenting; Giving blessings
Characters: 2 males

GOOD FRIDAY MEDLEY by Various Authors

(*Note:* This series of five monologues centers around people grappling with the significance of the cross and Christ's sacrifice. At Willow Creek we used a very large cross that appeared to have crashed through the roof of the church and into the lives of these people.) #1: A woman is perplexed because she understands Jesus' death on a cross but struggles with appropriating his sacrifice for her personally. She says, "God so loved the world," but questions if that means her. #2: A woman is confronted by her husband's request for a divorce and is in great pain. She wonders where God is when life really stinks. The words of a song strike her: "Jesus loves the brokenhearted because his heart was broken too." Jesus understands and cares; she experiences the depth of his love at a time when she needs it the most. #3: A woman recounts a time when her college roommate entered their room in tears. The roommate tells her she was just in a Bible study and she questioned where her friend was going when she died. The woman is touched by her roommate's concern and asks, "What makes someone care that much?" #4: An encounter with a woman at K-Mart causes another woman, a Christian, to sense she should start a conversation with her. Through the course of the conversation, she finds out the woman is trying to find a place to live so she can get her baby back. Moved by the story, the Christian reaches out, offering help and hope. #5: At a time when his life feels out of control, a man sits in quiet on a pier at a lake. He pours out his thoughts and frustrations to God. When he is done, he stands in silence and is suddenly overwhelmed with a feeling of peace. He senses that God knows his struggles and imagines God challenging him with the simple question, "Am I enough?"

Suggested Topics: Good Friday; How we view Jesus
Characters: 1 male, 4 females (though some roles are interchangeable)

GOOD FRIDAY 1990 by Steve Pederson and Judson Poling

Included are two short sketches. The first one features Mary Magdalene and Judas, the second one Mary Magdalene and Joseph of Arimathea. Mary encounters Judas as he is leaving the upper room to betray Christ. Not realizing his intentions, Mary tells Judas she has been sent by Joseph (a member of the Sanhedrin but a follower of Christ) to warn Jesus of impending danger. Eventually Mary realizes what Judas is about to do. The second sketch takes place outside the high priest's chamber where Jesus is being interrogated by the Sanhedrin. Joseph has left because he can no longer tolerate what is going on. He meets Mary, who awaits news; together they reflect on what Jesus means to them, fully realizing what will likely happen to their Master.

Suggested Topics: Good Friday
Characters: 2 males, 1 female

GOOD FRIDAY 1991, SCENE I by Steve Pederson and Judson Poling

This sketch and the following one both portray Jesus and the disciples in a very human, touching, and even at times humorous light. The emphasis is on trying to make the gospel accounts contemporary without dating them, and on wanting the audience to see the characters and identify with them. Jesus is the Son of God, but his role as Servant is stressed in these sketches. The sketch focuses on the foot-washing episode. Peter, John, and Mary prepare the upper room, discussing the imminent danger Jesus faces. The supper begins, but Jesus immediately explains his mission among them through the act of washing their feet. The scene ends with Jesus admonishing them to "serve others, even as I have served you." (*Note:* This sketch can be used with or without Scene II.)

Suggested Topics: Good Friday; Serving others
Characters: Jesus character, 12 disciples, 2 females

GOOD FRIDAY 1991, SCENE II by Judson Poling

This second sketch picks up later in the "Last Supper" scene. Thomas expresses concern that Jesus didn't exploit the opportunities the masses' enthusiasm offered him. Mary agrees, adding the warning that word on the street is that he is soon to be betrayed. Jesus, of course, knows all this but takes it one step further—one of them will be the betrayer. After all deny this (Peter most vehemently), Jesus explains their need to abide in him to bear fruit. Tension breaks out between Peter and Thomas over the "number two spot," but Jesus adds to his prediction of his betrayal the warning to Peter that he will deny Jesus. Once again Jesus returns to the "servant" theme and ends with the establishment of the Eucharist as Judas slips out to seal both their fates. (*Note:* This sketch can be used with or without Scene I.)

Suggested Topics: Good Friday
Characters: Jesus character, 12 disciples, 2 females

GRAND CANYON by Daniel S. Johnson

In a doleful poetic style, a husband and wife tell the story of disillusionment and deterioration within their relatively short marriage. Expectations haven't been met, and both aren't sure they can go on. Options of a divorce and an affair look enticing. In a surprise twist the story ends with the wife receiving a doctor's report: "I have good news for you."

Suggested Topics: Marital breakdown
Characters: 1 male, 1 female

GRANDMA'S RECIPE by Sharon Sherbondy

It's Christmas Eve, and the family returns home from church discussing favorite parts of the service. Grandma is visiting, but there is no masking the tension between parents Gina and Brent. They can't seem to agree on anything. Left alone when Brent takes the kids to the kitchen, Grandma tells her daughter she has noticed "that look" in her eyes and prods her until she opens up. Gina confides that she and Brent are "a mess" and counseling hasn't helped. Grandma tries to console her daughter, but Gina dismisses her perspective. Nevertheless, Grandma proceeds to tell her daughter about a time in her life when she hated her own marriage. In a nonsimplistic way she tells Gina that there is hope; through determination and prayer, things turned around. When Brent and the kids return to the living room, Gina's suggestion that maybe Dad was right about opening a gift tonight offers a glimmer of hope for a merry Christmas.

Suggested Topic: Family struggle during holidays
Characters: 1 male, 2 females, 2 children

GREAT EXPECTATIONS by Sharon Sherbondy

It seems as if Kathy and Greg's long-awaited prayer has finally been answered. In a few hours they will be parents. Unexpectedly, the birth mother changes her mind about the adoption. Kathy and Greg are again left childless and broken, wondering why God hasn't answered their prayers.

Suggested Topics: Unanswered prayer
Characters: 1 male, 2 females

GUESS WHICH GOD by Judson Poling

The contestants on the game show "To Tell the Truth, I Don't Know What's My Line," have to determine which one of the three guests is the real God. The first God fixates on his brute strength—an Arnold Schwarzenegger type. The second is a rage-filled biker type—hostile and thundering (thunder is literally heard every time he speaks!). The third is a meek, flower-child type—sprouting ethereal words of wisdom that frankly don't make any sense. In the end none of these gods is the real one. The game show host then shifts out of character and addresses the audience, challenging them from the Scriptures to discard their stereotypes of God and to reexamine who he really is as taught in the Bible.

Suggested Topics: Confusion about God; Nature of God
Characters: 4 males, offstage male and female voices

HALF-BAKED by Donna Lagerquist

In this light comedy a woman becomes frustrated at the bakery because they can't find her cheesecake order, and the clerk behind the counter doesn't speak English well. The woman expresses her frustration to her friend who is with her, and the friend is surprised at the borderline racist comments she makes. As the woman finally slams her receipt on the counter and demands her money back, the clerk points out that she'll have to go to another bakery—because that's where she ordered her cheesecake!

Suggested Topics: Racism; Prejudice
Characters: 1 male, 2 females

HANDS OFF by Sharon Sherbondy

The sketch opens with dating couple Randy and Lana enjoying a romantic dinner for two. The rest of the evening takes a comical twist as we watch this couple keep true to their "decision to not . . . you know. . . ." They are hit from all sides of our culture—radio, magazines, TV, movies, and peers. The audience will be laughing as they watch this couple avoid these snares but will be left with a real picture of the struggles singles face.

Suggested Topics: Sex; Dating; Temptation
Characters: 1 male, 1 female

HAPPY EASTER by Donna Lagerquist

Through short vignettes, we see the confusion about the meaning of Easter. A ten-year-old struggles to accept her silly looking polka-dot Easter dress made by Grandma, which matches her mom's. When Dad enters, he is wearing a polka-dot tie and lapel hankie made from the same cloth! In the next scene two moms cheer on their kids at an

Easter egg hunt. A dad enters dressed up as the "Easter Barney" (the costume store was out of bunny costumes; only Barney the dinosaur was available). Other than candy, eggs, and prizes, no one has a clue as to what Easter is all about. Finally, a grad student daughter and her mother argue about going to a family gathering at Aunt Fran's. The daughter wants to head for Florida to avoid the hassles of having to explain her broken engagement to the rest of the family and painfully reminds her mother of the shame of her recent divorce. She laments the scorn she will receive because of how she "can't keep a man around, just like my mother." The on-stage narrator sums up at the end that despite the obvious lack of personal happiness for many, it is the empty tomb that gives us hope.

Suggested Topics: Easter
Characters: 3 males, 5 females, 1 ten-year-old girl (by double casting, all adult parts can be played by two women and two men)

HARD TO BE HUMBLE by Various Authors

When a large-volume beverage client threatens to pull its business, an advertising executive gathers a group of interesting "creatives" to an emergency meeting to brainstorm a new ad pitch. After several lame attempts to come up with something new and fresh, they land on a theme with promise—humility. One of them asks, "Humility sells soda?" But desperation forces them to seriously consider this idea, even going so far as to select a famous, deceased spokesperson who embodies humility. They clearly don't understand the true meaning of humility, however, as the exec bemoans the missed opportunity: "Too bad; we could have made her famous."

Suggested Topics: Evangelism; Fruit of the Spirit; World's view vs. Christianity
Characters: 4 males or females

HEART FAILURE by Judson Poling

In this humorous but easily identifiable monologue, "Terry Tightwad" tells of his transformation from a cold-hearted miser into a kind and charitable person—then back again! After he makes a resolution to be more generous, he discovers there is no end to people and organizations that have their hand out for donations. When he comes down hard on his own daughter selling Girl Scout Cookies, he realizes he has been stretched too thin. But he doesn't know what to do—how can you be kind to others without going broke? The monologue ends with him asking the audience for answers—and silence. A great setup for a talk on giving.

Suggested Topic: Giving
Characters: 1 male

HERE TO HELP by Sharon Sherbondy

A group of women who work together have agreed to help clean up an old building that is being transformed into a free clinic. Although they mean well, their middle-class values and experiences show—and hinder the work. One woman, the martyr, makes sure everyone understands how much she has sacrificed for the cause. Another, the complainer, has allergies and is afraid to get hives. One woman's cell phone keeps ringing, and so she keeps getting distracted. Still another didn't even dress appropriately because she has never had to clean anything so dirty. There is also the controller, who tries to take over the project. In the end the driver of the van that brought them has an emergency at work and has to leave, and they all must go with her. The only one left is the woman who organized the effort. She turns up the radio and, with a sigh, dives in to do the work alone.

Suggested Topics: Helping those less fortunate; Not giving up; Dealing with difficult people
Characters: 6 females

HEROIC DELUSION by Judson Poling

This comic sketch is a broad look at how people sometimes fail to see their blind spots. A woman is held up by a mugger. As she reluctantly complies with the mugger's request, suddenly Superman appears. Only this is not the young, virile hero from the comic books, but a middle-aged Superman. When the mugger runs off, the woman is relieved and leaves. Once Superman is alone, he collapses, wheezing. The mugger returns—not to threaten anyone, but because he is an actor the aging superhero has hired to fake holdups! The mugger complains the "act" is getting ridiculous. Superman counters that he has still got it. But his physique and the erosion of his superpowers make it clear that he is past his prime.

Suggested Topic: Self-delusion
Characters: 2 males, 1 female

HOLY WEEK by Judson Poling

A family is preparing to go to church. Each of the three characters is answering questions from a little girl unseen and unheard by the audience. The first is the mother, who is asked about what is meant by "Holy Week" and "Palm Sunday." She doesn't want to be bothered with "complex spiritual questions" for which she obviously doesn't have good answers, even though she claims to believe. The next is ditzy Aunt Eunice, who confusedly wraps together Easter, Christmas, the three bears, and the tooth fairy! Then comes cynical Uncle Walter, who confesses the whole resurrection thing is probably made up, a good story that "more educated people"—like him—smile at but don't really believe. The little girl—and the audience—are left with more questions than answers about the meaning of Holy Week.

Suggested Topics: Holy Week; Palm Sunday; Easter; The resurrection
Characters: 1 male, 2 females, offstage girl's voice

HONESTLY SPEAKING by Debra Poling

We all struggle with allowing God to recreate and redefine us despite our insecurities and past failures. It's hard to stop telling ourselves things we have become so accustomed to hearing in our own head: "I'm dumb!" "No one really likes me." "I'm worthless." A dinner party becomes a very awkward situation when Penny's negative self-talk overwhelms her.

Suggested Topics: Positive self-talk, Self-esteem
Characters: 3 males, 3 females

AN HOUR ON WEDNESDAY by Sharon Sherbondy

Chris and Laura are a couple living in the fast track. Their highly scheduled existence leaves them little time for each other. When Laura reveals she is pregnant, Chris's machine-like response is "February is a bad month." Laura ends up hurt by his insensitivity. While much of the sketch is comic, it moves toward a very poignant ending.

Suggested Topics: Marriage; Damaging effects of a fast-paced life
Characters: 1 male, 1 female

HUNGRY CHILDREN by Donna Lagerquist

A sobering look at the destructive effects of careless family communication. As a family eats their supper, Dad's sour, hostile attitude takes its toll on Mom and the kids. He is critical and complaining, and no one escapes his attacks. When he picks on his teenage daughter for how she is starving herself, she runs out of the room exasperated. Her little brother wants to go "give her something," but Dad insists no one should cater to her. But the brother doesn't want to give her food—he wants to give her a hug.

Suggested Topics: Abusive Parenting; Poor family communication; Anger; Control issues
Characters: 1 male, 1 female, 1 boy, 1 teenage girl

HUNTING FOR EASTER by Donna Lagerquist

A family gathers at home after the Easter morning church service. There is a flurry of activity as Grandma completes her preparation for the lunchtime feast. In the midst of this, little Amy asks a lot of questions about the meaning of various Easter traditions—and gets some humorously skewed replies. Some questions are simple, like "Why do we have ham on Easter?" "Because it's pink," replies Grandma. Some questions are of a more profound nature, regarding the empty tomb. Laura, Amy's aunt, uses some plastic eggs filled with items representing different aspects of the holiday to explain the message of Easter to the family.

Suggested Topic: Easter
Characters: 2 males, 3 females, 2 preteens

I ALWAYS WILL by Mark Demel

The reception is over and the mother and father of the bride are getting ready to leave. Something is bothering Dad. His "little girl" didn't say good-bye—at least not personally. Dad reminisces about how he would tuck her in and they would act out the phrase "I love you so much you don't know, and I always will, no matter what you do" with hand motions. But that was long ago, and it's tough to see things change, even if for the better. Just then, the bride and groom return because they forgot her bag. She starts to leave again without saying a special good-bye to dad. Unexpectedly, she signals Mom to get Dad's attention, and when he looks at her from across the room, she uses the old hand motions to signal their special daddy-daughter love phrase. Dad accompanies her motions in sync, and she blows him a kiss as she leaves.

Suggested Topic: Father's Day; Father-daughter relationships
Characters: 3 males, 3 females

I AM by Mark Demel

Four actors read passages out of the Gospels that illustrate Jesus' unique claims, centering around the many "I am's," such as "I am the good shepherd," "I am the bread of life," "I am the way," etc. These readings are a sharp contrast to usual "slice of life" dramas found in this catalog, but their creative juxtaposition paints a compelling—and uncompromising—portrait of the unique, controversial, and comforting claims of Jesus Christ.

Suggested Topic: Who is Jesus Christ?
Characters: 4 readers, male or female

I DON'T WANT TO FIGHT YOU ANYMORE by Debra Poling

This monologue eavesdrops on a conversation between a woman and God. She describes her frustration at obeying God in an effort to be a new creation He desires. He demands a lot. She reminds God that she lacked a loving father role model. She felt controlled by her father and now isn't sure she is willing to let God control her life. But she is tired of fighting and needs to make a decision.

Suggested Topics: Relationship with God; Giving up control; Our value to God
Characters: 1 female

I KNOW WHAT YOU WANT by Judson Poling

Using a combination of two dramatic styles—choral speaking and short monologue—four characters representing the child roles of a dysfunctional family (i.e., superachiever, clown, scapegoat, and lost child) reflect on learning the rules of life's most important game: "I know what you want." They each relate the formative experiences from their childhood that taught them how to relate to other's expectations. As adults, they now believe they have it all figured out, but then God shows up with totally foreign expectations. Having never experienced this kind of unconditional love, they are now left pondering, "I wonder what he wants."

Suggested Topics: Evangelism; God's love; Dysfunctional families
Characters: 2 males, 2 females

IF THESE WALLS COULD SPEAK by Donna Lagerquist

This portrayal of the emotional connection among three generations of women opens with a mild argument between Jane and her daughter, Heather. Heather, anticipating liberation by her upcoming wedding, complains about the constraints of living at home. Her mother, however, reminds her of their commitment to take care of Grandma this morning. Heather reluctantly agrees to spend time with her mentally failing grandmother in the next room. As Heather tries to paint her grandmother's nails, Grandma takes Heather's hands and begins singing the tune to a familiar finger-play game. Recognizing the tune, Heather responds with the remainder of the verses. Excitedly, Heather calls her mother into the room. Jane tearfully and tenderly recounts how the game has passed through the generations. In this touching moment we are moved by the bond of love among these three women.

Suggested Topics: Mother's Day; Family traditions
Characters: 3 females

IMPRESSIONS, INC. by Judson Poling

With spiritual makeovers as his specialty, Dr. P. W. Donnenuff "assists" a new customer at his Impressions, Inc. consulting firm. From knee-expanders that give the impression of having spent hours in prayer to onion ring "glasses" that keep the wearer's eyes in a perpetual state of tears of repentance, Dr. Donnenuff remakes his clients so they "look" like spiritual giants ("without any thyroid complications"). This is a humorous spoof of applying Christianity from the outside in—with minimal cost at a fraction of the effort.

Suggested Topics: Skin-deep Christianity; Christian in appearance only
Characters: 2 males, 1 female

IMPROVING YOUR LIE by Sharon Sherbondy

Doing some paperwork on a Saturday morning, Jamie is surprised when her husband suddenly arrives home. She thought he was with his brothers playing their monthly golf game and can't understand why they didn't pick him up. She surmises he must have cheated on his score the last time they played. He denies it at first, but when she forces the issue, he finally admits it. She encourages him to talk to his brothers as soon as possible. The embarrassment of admitting his lie to Jamie diminishes his desire to confess to his brothers, but he finally accepts that he must. Mike then notices Jamie has been less than honest about her weight on an insurance form she wants him to sign and confronts her. She counters this confrontation by threatening to add to his list of household projects. He quickly heads off to fix the shower door!

Suggested Topics: Truth telling; Marriage
Characters: 1 male, 1 female

IN THE DARK by Donna Lagerquist

As a couple prepares to go out with friends, the wife tries to rerecord the answering machine message. In doing so she hears a previously unheard message from her husband and young daughter. She is visibly moved. Painfully, we realize her daughter is dead. The husband reenters, and the two come once again to an apparently oft-repeated place of grief and anger. In the end she can't go out with the friends as planned, and the lights fade as she hugs her daughter's picture.

Suggested Topics: Death of a child; Grief
Characters: 1 male, 1 female

IN PURSUIT OF HAPPINESS by Sharon Sherbondy

Janice seems to have everything she needs, but she can't keep up with everything she wants. Her husband thinks she expects too much out of life. That scares and saddens Janice, because nothing seems to fill the emptiness she is feeling.

Suggested Topics: Contentment; Possessions
Characters: 1 male, 1 female

IN . . . WE TRUST by Judson Poling

In this monologue a man struggles with trust in the everyday relationships of life. His son has had a recent accident, so he is reluctant to trust his driving. His wife has embarrassed him in front of some coworkers as well as upset his placid marriage with demands he be more sensitive and meet her needs. Every relationship in his life, he confesses, boils down to somebody "using" somebody else, a point with which he bluntly stabs the audience. And then there's trust in God, a whole different subject. Or is it?

Suggested Topics: Trust; Difficulty trusting God; Father/husband role
Characters: 1 male

THE INTRUDER by Sharon Sherbondy

A woman is studying for a nursing exam when the voice of her father comes back to haunt her. His criticisms, sneers, and lack of support verbalized over the years are now virtually resident in her even though he has been dead for two years. He steps out onto the stage, and the two continue talking though he is only a phantom. He calls attention to her failed marriage and supposed neglect of her kids, all intended to make her feel inadequate. Even her newfound relationship with God is fodder for his belittling comments. The sketch ends with his final jeer: "Who knows you better than your father?"

Suggested Topics: Self-image; Destructive parenting; God's love in spite of failure
Characters: 1 male, 1 female

INVESTMENT AT RISK by Mark Demel

(*Note:* This script serves as Part 2 to "Attractive Deal.")
Sharon is readying a hotel room with flowers and music when Brett walks in. She offers him a drink when it becomes clear that Brett is agitated. He tells her he can't stay. Sharon is upset when Brett starts talking about cutting off their affair. She offers other options: "What about next week?" But he expresses the challenge of maintaining a double life. Just then, Brett's young daughter walks into the room. She has innocently defied his order to "sit in the chair by the elevator" to ask him something. After sending her back out of the room, Brett apologizes to Sharon and leaves for good.

Suggested Topics: Convictions; Adultery
Characters: 2 males, 1 female, 1 child

IS "NOTHING" SACRED? by Judson Poling

Sam is invited by his friend Mark to a meeting of a new religious group that combines faith with science. As the meeting begins, Sam realizes this is a bizarre group. The "Nihilo Master" leads the members in the ritual, and he unveils the meaning behind all of life and the source of everything that is—a big zero. Everything has come from nothing; everything is going toward nothing; therefore everyone and everything are nothing. This is the message of modern scientific "religion," and this humorous satire leaves the audience laughingly aware of the logical outcome of this prevailing worldview.

Suggested Topics: Evolution; Creation; Modern science
Characters: 3 males and at least 4 others in a group

"IT" by Judson Poling

This parody shows how people become deceived into believing that a relationship with Christ will keep away much of the suffering and pain of life. "Real Life" catches up with a happy couple and dumps a "load" of problems on them. They try to make Real Life go away by threatening to have "It" get after him. They come to find that they have only made themselves easier targets by ignoring Real Life.

Suggested Topics: Dealing with problems; Vulnerability of new believers
Characters: 2 males, 1 female

IT'S NO PICNIC by Donna Lagerquist

When Al brings a cooler containing his laptop computer and files to his company picnic, his wife, Cindy, tries to explain to him how ridiculous he is acting. Al is confident that his boss will only talk "work" and wants to be prepared. However, Cindy shows Al the invitation to the picnic, which contains a stipulation: No "work talk" will be allowed. Instead of relaxing with that information, Al's paranoia increases as he wonders what he'll talk about to people he barely recognizes away from the office! Once they find a group of "picnickers" and join them, Al's fears become humorously valid. The group has a very difficult time talking about anything other than work issues. It's a sad commentary on the types of relationships Al has at work. Sadder still (yet quite funny), in the end we find out that Al and Cindy are in the wrong place and thus have joined the wrong company picnic.

Suggested Topics: Work stress; Surface relationships; Our sin
Characters: 3 males, 3 females

IT'S NOT MY FAULT by Donna Lagerquist

In the setting of a high school principal's office, we see a humorous portrayal of people "passing the buck" for their wrongdoing. When her daughter is caught smoking in the school bathroom, Mrs. Randall sets out to prove that it was not her daughter's fault. In defense attorney-style, she calls various people "forward" (to the principal's desk) and accuses them of their part in the "crime." Each character pleads innocence by pointing at another, who in turn does the same. In the end we find a roomful of flustered people, none of whom is willing to take responsibility for his or her offense.

Suggested Topics: Sin; Taking responsibility for our sin
Characters: 3 males, 4 females

IT'S ONLY A MOVIE by Judson Poling

Gina and Bruce are getting ready for a night out with friends. When Lori and Eric arrive, all are concerned it's too cold to go out, so they decide to rent a movie. The problem is they can't agree on what kind to get, and their interests divide strictly along gender lines. The women want romance and adventure—a "chick flick"— while the men want fast cars and guns. They decide to all go together to find something at the video store they can agree on. In the second part of the drama, the women are watching the last few minutes of *Dr. Zhivago*, Kleenex in hand, as the men come upstairs from watching their movie, *Die Hard 2: Die Harder*. Earlier the women chided the men on the effect movies have on their testosterone levels, but the men now point out how the women have been taken in. The men are smug about their ability to stay in control of their feelings despite what they watch. After Eric and Lori leave, however, we hear Eric yelling offstage at someone who cuts him off as he drives away. Bruce also yells at the guy outside. Gina gives him a cold stare, and he sheepishly realizes he too has been affected by what he sees.

Suggested Topics: The effects of what we see; Male-female differences; Power of the media
Characters: 2 males, 2 females, 1 offstage male voice

JEOPARDIZED RELIGION by Judson Poling

(*Note:* This sketch has a format similar to the drama "Faith in Jeopardy," which highlights people's misunderstanding about the Bible.)
The emphasis in this sketch is people's confusion about world religions. On a TV game show three bumbling contestants try to answer simple questions about world religions. Among their many misconceptions, they think Aladdin is the founding prophet of Islam, Buddha never would have eaten SlimFast, Charlton Heston presented the Ten Commandments, and the holiday that celebrates a religion's dead-founder-come-back-to-life is Groundhog's Day. This hilarious and disarming sketch causes us to agree that most of us are a bit ignorant about basic religious beliefs in our modern culture.

Suggested Topics: World religions; People's ignorance of ideas other than their own
Characters: 3 males, 1 female

JUST AN ACQUAINTANCE by Donna Lagerquist

Julie surprises her fiancé, Gary, by dropping by the restaurant where he is waiting to meet his out-of-town friend, Andy. As the subject of the best man is broached, Gary seems defensive. He has no best friend—"it's a girl thing." Julie points out that Andy would qualify, though Gary thinks his brother should do it because he "owes him." Just then Andy comes by, and Julie has to leave. As Gary and Andy get reacquainted, it is obvious their lives are going in separate directions. Gary is embarrassed when Andy finds out that he is a waiter at the restaurant they're at. Instead of drawing closer, the two talk about sports and other superficialities, and in the end, when Andy is off making a call, Gary tells his waitress Andy is merely "a guy I went to college with . . . just an acquaintance."

Suggested Topics: Relationships between men; Superficial relationships
Characters: 2 males, 2 females

JUST AS I AM by Various Authors

In this monologue (based on the true experience of a homosexual) a man openly and honestly addresses a church congregation. He recounts his struggle, including the lack of understanding by his friends and his father. The rejection caused him to seek solace in bars and alcohol, but the experience left him empty. He is thinking of turning his struggles over to Christ but wonders if the church is ready for the likes of him.

Suggested Topics: Homosexuality
Characters: 1 male

JUST BELOW THE JETTA by Mark Demel

In this monologue a woman reminisces about a fellow employee, Marsha, with whom she sat at last year's Christmas party. Although Marsha worked in the mailroom and didn't have the same rank in the company, the woman had a good time with her. She wrote down her name to call her sometime on a list of things to do—just below taking in the Jetta for emissions testing. But just like so many important, but not urgent, things, she never called Marsha, and last summer Marsha died of an overdose. She had had a chemical imbalance and was now gone forever. The woman was left wondering what she might have done, what possibilities now are impossible. She keeps the "to do" list as a reminder of what ought to be her priorities in life.

Suggested Topic: Valuing people
Characters: 1 female

JUST IN CASE by Various Authors

Margaret is accosted by a high-pressure salesman promising her assurance if God should fail her. This "Just in Case Kit" (parodies Ephesians 6) includes items like the "knee pads of pessimism," the "shield of fallacy," the "helmet of humanism," and the "almighty machete." This ridiculous sketch confronts us with our own level of trust in God.

Suggested Topics: Trusting God; God's faithfulness
Characters: 1 male, 1 female

JUST A LITTLE DIFFERENT by Donna Lagerquist

Newlyweds Julie and David drop by to visit Julie's Aunt Lorraine. She is a quirky woman, going on incessantly about her diabetes and ignoring the conversation while watching *Wheel of Fortune*. When they finally leave, David mutters a comment about how his mother also has diabetes but doesn't sit around feeling sorry for herself all day. Julie knows Aunt Lorraine is hard to like but tries to give perspective—Aunt Lorraine's husband and daughter were killed in a car accident eighteen years ago. David can only whisper "Wow" as they walk off, leaving Aunt Lorraine alone watching her TV.

Suggested Topics: Loving the unlovely; The story behind people we don't like
Characters: 1 male, 2 females

JUST LOOKING by Sharon Sherbondy

A wife confronts her husband with shocking news: She has "found something" in their teenage son's room. When she pulls out the swimsuit issue of a sports magazine, the husband shrugs it off as nothing to be concerned about. Her anxiety about their son's sexual purity takes a surprising turn as she reveals the hurt she has felt all these years about how her husband notices other women. She is embarrassed—and scared. She is not getting any younger, and she wants to know her husband won't be lured by another woman's beauty. For the first time, he sees what his careless gazes cost his wife. At the conclusion, he vows, "There's only one woman for me—" but he is good-naturedly chased off when he teases, "and she's right here on page 23; did you see her?"

Suggested Topics: Eye causing you to stumble; Purity of thoughts
Characters: 1 male, 1 female

JUST SAY IT! by Donna Lagerquist

In an attempt to get her husband to say he loves her, Terri installs a subliminal message system. This machine gets Ed to say all those things she has been longing to hear. However, Terri discovers they don't satisfy her because Ed isn't saying them on his own.

Suggested Topics: Marriage communication; Importance of saying "I love you"
Characters: 1 male, 1 female, 1 either male or female

JUST THE TWO OF US by Donna Lagerquist

After a visit by her friend Jan and her three kids, Kathy struggles with her own infertility. Here is Jan, busy raising her brood, and Kathy is still waiting for number one. What adds to the irony is that Kathy took a pregnancy test just this morning, and found out—again—it was negative. Her husband, Jack, tries to console her, but it's just too painful. He suggests that after he gets back from the office, they go out together—"just the two of us." Kathy repeats to herself when alone, "just the two of us."

Suggested Topics: Infertility; Unanswered prayer
Characters: 1 male, 2 females

KEEPING TABS by Sharon Sherbondy

Nancy is so compulsive in her need not to be obligated to anyone that she keeps tabs on everything she and her husband receive. She believes that nothing is given without something being expected in return. Anonymously, flowers arrive and Nancy threatens to call the florist to find out who she "owes." When her husband confesses that he sent them "just because he loves her," she thinks it is because he wants something.

Suggested Topics: Gifts of grace; Undeserved love
Characters: 1 male, 1 female

THE KILLING SPREE by Sharon Sherbondy

Most of us believe we have nothing to worry about when it comes to the sixth commandment. But this sketch helps us take a comical look at the murder we commit with our mouth. During a conversation, Jane enters the "Twilight Zone," where consequences of her caustic tongue are deadly. It's too late when Jane realizes the lesson—she has already "killed" her best friend, her dog, her daughter, and a solicitor.

Suggested Topics: Sixth commandment; Gossip; Murder
Characters: 1 male, 3 females

KIND OF RARE by Mark Demel

Three couples are enjoying a backyard barbecue. Ted, the host, is a nice guy, but his evasive and somewhat hostile answer to a simple question causes Penny to confront him. She is tired of the group saying, "That's just Ted." As the group negotiates an uncomfortable situation, Ted's wife, Lisa, begins to cry. She shares with the group that she has tried to confront him, but he always manages to turn it around on her. At last, with others having experienced his abrasive behavior and bringing up the issue, Ted begins to face the fact that he may have a problem.

Suggested Topics: Confronting in love; Friendship; Marriage; Character flaws

Characters: 3 males, 3 females

THE KNOWING YEARS by Donna Lagerquist

This sketch looks at the season of omniscience, adolescence. Ruthie, Kate, and Mandy are three high school cheerleaders who think they know more about life and what matters than the adults around them.

Suggested Topics: Spiritual adolescence; adolescence

Characters: 3 females

LABOR OF LOVE by Mark Demel

Tim, a recent college grad, and his mother are talking at a backyard barbecue. Conversation turns to his job search. His mother seems worried he hasn't found anything, but Tim is determined to find the right job, not just the first thing to come along. Comparisons are made to how hard his dad worked even though he didn't like his job, but Tim doesn't want to dread his work—he wants to be proud of his accomplishments. Just then, Dad enters, and there is some awkwardness. Dad defends doing what he didn't like to do so he could provide for his family, though he admits sometimes wishing he'd taken risks to find a better fit. In the end Tim expresses appreciation for his dad's sacrifice, which made his own career possibilities a reality.

Suggested Topics: Finding a career that fits; Sacrifices parents make for the next generation

Characters: 2 males, 1 female

THE LANE OF LIFE by Deb Poling

A mime with narration. A person walking down life's lane hears and believes what others are saying: "You're ugly!" "You're stupid!" "You're worthless." But a kindly stranger offers a new perspective: "You matter to God!" At first unconvinced, the person gradually comes to believe this wonderful news and reaches out to share it with others.

Suggested Topics: Salvation; Evangelism; Self-esteem; Our value to God

Characters: 5 either males or females, 1 offstage narrator
(*Note:* This sketch is very similar to a later version of this sketch titled "You Matter to God.")

THE LEGACY by Donna Lagerquist

Miriam, the town librarian, has just returned from her retirement celebration with her adult daughter, Laura. Miriam is somewhat quiet. Laura asks how she is feeling about the new library being named after the man who donated the land instead of her, the person who built the library up from nothing. Miriam—with typical humility—says she feels the honor should go to the land owner, but we know she feels somewhat hurt. Just then, a man named Clay Barnes, who was a student years ago in that town, stops by. Miriam had encouraged him to read and even helped him discover and find help for his dyslexia. He has now written a book, *Teaching Your Children to Love Literature,* and dedicated it to Miriam. She is deeply touched by the realization that she has invested her life in a significant way. He signs the book for her, and they embrace as the lights fade.

Suggested Topics: Parenting; Character; Heroes; Christians at work; Making a difference; Serving others

Characters: 1 male, 2 females

LET ME GO by Judson Poling

A mom is visiting her "twentysomething" daughter who has just moved into her first apartment on her own. Mom has been organizing the house all day when Deb comes home from work. She is put off by all the changes her mother has made to her living space, though Mom shrugs it off, thinking she has been doing Deb a favor. Alphabetizing her soup cans is one thing, but when Deb discovers her mom has also interfered with a romantic relationship, she explodes. After some harsh words, Mom weakens, hurt that her role as mother is no longer needed (she has also just recently been widowed). Deb tries to apologize and explains she wants a mother, not a caretaker. But Mom is uncertain how she can be one without being the other.

Suggested Topics: Parenting; Letting go of adult children

Characters: 2 females

LIFE CYCLE by Sharon Sherbondy

Two women find themselves next to each other on exercise bikes at the health club. They begin conversing and discover they are both worn-out moms who use the health club as an escape—anything "to get out of the house." Almost by accident, Linda tells Ann that she is also in a Bible study group. When she realizes Ann is nonchurched, Linda gets nervous, pedals faster, and somewhat self-consciously talks about a few practical dimensions of her faith. By the time Ann leaves, it's clear that the women enjoy an affinity that will likely result in future deeper conversations.

Suggested Topics: Evangelism; Making a difference; Starting new relationships

Characters: 2 females

LIFELINE by Donna Lagerquist

An elderly man and woman work in a K-Mart together. We soon discover they and their spouses have been friends for years, and the four of them served in their local church. Now, however, Ed's wife has died and Doris's husband is in the hospital. A young woman and her daughter come into the store, and she recognizes Doris as her vacation Bible school teacher. It turns out that Doris and her husband and Ed and his wife made a big impression on her spiritually years ago, one that continues to impact her life today. As Doris and Ed take their coffee break, they both recognize the value of their service to others over the years and the blessing of lifelong friendships.

Suggested Topics: Serving the church; Life in community; Aging

Characters: 1 male, 2 females, 1 small child (no lines)

LIFESTYLES OF THE OBSCURE AND INDEBTED by Cathy Peters

This sketch takes an exaggerated look at how people mismanage money in order to "keep up with the Joneses." It begins when Stanley and Henrietta Havemore notice a new car in Charlie Contendo's driveway. We see a chain reaction of spending spread throughout the neighborhood. When Charlie finally enters the scene at the end, everyone is in for a surprise.

Suggested Topics: Coveting; Materialism

Characters: 4 males, 3 females

LIFETIME DEAL by Brian Svenkeson, Steve Pederson, and Mark Demel

Jack and David have negotiated to sell the company they have worked ten years to build. Jack is elated at the nine-million-dollar offer an investment group has proposed, but David can only find fault. As they try to decide what they're going to do, Jack challenges David on his overcommitment to his business. When David defensively answers that he has invested his life here, Jack agrees: "You've invested your life; I've invested my time." Jack leaves, pleading with David to consider the offer. After Jack is gone, David calls his wife and unexpectedly tells her that the deal fell through and that he is planning to buy Jack out.

Suggested Topics: Work; Workaholism

Characters: 2 males

LIGHTENING LEADERSHIP by Judson Poling

Apprehensively, Jeff attends the "Lightning Leadership" Institute on the recommendation of his management team. His trainers take him through typical work scenarios to test his leadership style. The institute uses a unique training technique that requires Jeff to wear an electronic collar. Each time Jeff deals with a work scenario incorrectly, he gets zapped like a dog trying to cross an invisible electronic fence. After numerous unsuccessful attempts at properly dealing with leadership issues, Jeff reaches his maximum tolerance for electric shock therapy.

Suggested Topics: Leadership; Work

Characters: 2 males, 1 female

A LITTLE CHARITY by Judson Poling

Four members of a church committee are meeting at a restaurant where they discuss plans for a homeless shelter. The hardworking waitress arrives with their food, but they obliviously ask her to perform finicky tasks for them: a new knife for one, more crackers for another, and hot water for yet another (who brought her own tea bag to save money!). Treating her as a servant, they continue to focus on their agenda, missing the fact that they are ignoring a person because they need to figure out how to share the love of Christ with others. When it comes time to go, they leave her a paltry tip and a Bible tract—smug that they are "sharing Christ's love" with her. After they've gone, the waitress reads the tract, which promises a great eternity. Frankly, she doesn't want any part of an eternity with people like that!

Suggested Topics: Evangelism; Christian character

Characters: 2 males, 3 females

LITTLE WHAT'S HIS FACE by Sharon Sherbondy

A young couple still in the hospital try to name their infant son born just before Christmas. Extended family members get involved in the debate, and finally a decision is made. The second half of this drama focuses on the father, who performs a monologue telling his infant son what he promises to give him for Christmas. The father confesses that someday he'll fail his son, but the Savior never will.

Suggested Topics: Christmas; Parenting

Characters: 3 males, 3 females

LIZZIE AND LEROY by Sharon Sherbondy

This is a familiar tale of how "things" don't provide ultimate fulfillment. The melodramatic Southern belle, Lizzie, tells the tragic story of how her husband's promotion in a chicken ranch ultimately provided them with everything they wanted, except happiness. LeRoy eventually leaves Lizzie in search of "it." Lizzie ends up alone, hoping LeRoy will return with news of what he has discovered.

Suggested Topics: Only God satisfies; Material goods don't provide ultimate happiness

Characters: 1 male, 1 female, piano player (optional)

LONELY AT THE TOP by Judson Poling

An obviously overworked politician talks on the phone with his assistant about delegates from a political action committee who dropped by unexpectedly. He manages to stall them for a few minutes, during which he laments the incessant demands on him to please and appease. He also vilifies those around him who constantly want to use him. In fact, just recently he was forced to get rid of a group's political enemy when he himself found the man rather harmless, if not a bit interesting. As he musters up the energy to meet the delegation in his waiting room, he can't understand what crisis could be so urgent—he got rid of their enemy on Friday, so why do they have to bother him on Sunday morning? As he walks out, we realize Pilate—dressed in a modern suit—is about to find out about the resurrection of Jesus.

Suggested Topics: The perils of power; A leader's need for divine help; Easter

Characters: 1 male

LUCKY DAY AT THE BALLPARK by Sharon Sherbondy

Josh (about thirteen) and his grandfather are at a Cubs ball game. Josh has been anxiously waiting for his dad to arrive, but he doesn't appear until the game is almost finished. The grandfather is upset with his son's seeming insensitivity to Josh's needs. In spite of marriage problems that plague the father, the grandfather tells him that he is the most important person in Josh's life and that he needs to "be there" for him. It's obvious the grandfather's challenge has been heard, because the father changes some future plans to accommodate his son. The sketch ends with Josh catching a fly ball, which he then gives to his dad.

Suggested Topics: Father's Day; Proper priorities

Characters: 2 males, 1 boy

THE LUNCHEON by Sharon Sherbondy

This sketch painfully portrays a deteriorating mother-daughter relationship. From the moment they are seated in the restaurant, Susan begins defensively fielding her mom's disapproving comments. When Susan can take it no more, she lets her mother know how she really feels. To Susan's surprise, her mom has some dissatisfied and hurt feelings too. The scene ends with the two ready to try some changes.

Suggested Topics: Motherhood; Family relationships; Honesty

Characters: 3 females

THE LURES OF LIFE by Debra Poling

This mime features Charlie Chaplin and the Keystone Cops. Charlie illegally gets money and experiences the pleasure money can buy—a girlfriend, a cruise, world travels—but not before having to outwit the Keystone Cops. With the cops off his trail, he and his girlfriend are free to pursue pleasure. Chaplin eventually realizes, however, the emptiness of this lifestyle and walks away from it all.

Suggested Topics: Adventurism; The pleasures of the world don't satisfy

Characters: 5 males, 1 female

MAKE IT HAPPEN by Judson Poling

Phil is attending a personal growth seminar at the request of his friend. The speaker, Jerry Wilson—a dynamic, high-energy type— teaches that we need to "make it happen" as the answer to challenges in the workplace. Although there's lots of hype—even to the point of the ridiculous—Wilson offers no practical help to the seminar attendees. Phil sees through the scam and challenges Wilson's empty philosophy. Security people end up "escorting" Phil out of the room, while devotees chant "Make it happen!"

Suggested Topics: Taking responsibility for change; The limits of self-help seminars

Characters: 5 males, 1 female (numerous extras for attendees and security)

MAN OF THE YEAR by Judson Poling

Richard Hanson is honored as "Man of the Year," yet as he begins to give his speech, memories of his past come back to haunt him. Though his outward appearance seems noble enough, the realities of the other side of his life show him up for the sinner he is—even the man of the year needs a Savior from moral imperfections.

Suggested Topics: Moralism; Our need for grace

Characters: 5 males, 1 female,

MASTERPIECE by Sharon Sherbondy

A family getting ready to leave for the grandparents' house experiences the usual hassle trying to get out the door. What's

different this time is that Mom and her teenage daughter stay behind to talk about the daughter's struggles with self-esteem. Mom is able to reaffirm her daughter's beauty and uniqueness—she is a "masterpiece."
Suggested Topics: Self-esteem; Parenting
Characters: 1 male, 1 female, 2 teenage females

MATERNAL MEASURES by Donna Lagerquist

A lighthearted look at how women—especially young moms—feel pressure to compare themselves with others. On the advice of her husband, Meg takes a walk in the park to try to cheer herself up. She meets Joanne, a mother of four—three of whom are triplets (on "leashes" that lead offstage). Just one baby tires Meg out—how can Joanne seem to do so well with four? Then Judy comes by. She is even more the "perfect mom." Three weeks since her delivery, she is back in shape and teaching aerobics. She is also carting around her preschooler to daily gymnastics, swimming, and interactive play workshops. The more Judy and Joanne talk, the more Meg feels inadequate. As Judy and Joanne go off to break up a fight between their kids, Meg sarcastically mutters to herself about what an encouragement it was to go to the park!
Suggested Topics: Mother's Day; Pressure on women to measure up
Characters: 3 females

MAYBE SOMEDAY by Sharon Sherbondy

Mike is a successful businessman, father, and husband who has been finding himself driving around at night and ending up in the church parking lot. Tonight he actually gets out of the car and meets up with the church choir director, Ron, leaving after a potluck dinner. As the men chat, Mike's growing restlessness about something missing from his otherwise perfect life becomes apparent. Ron is a good listener and encourages Mike to come back and actually attend a service. "Maybe someday," he replies. Ron has to leave, but the sketch ends with Mike choosing to stay, pondering his need and the possibility that this church might hold some answers.
Suggested Topics: Evangelism; Success that leaves us empty; Going back to church
Characters: 2 males

ME, MYSELF, AND CHRIS by Sharon Sherbondy

Bill and his alter ego battle over the temptation of premarital sex. Bill's alter ego tries every possible tactic and argument but to no avail, Bill sticks to his principles.
Suggested Topics: Sex; Temptation; Dating
Characters: 2 males, 1 female

MEASURING UP by Judson Poling

In this mime a boy discovers early in life what others think of him. His friends don't let him play with them—he doesn't "measure up." They show this graphically by pulling out measuring tapes and laughing as they shake their heads and leave their tapes around his neck. When he goes home as a teenager, his family has their measuring tapes too and intimidate him with them. He enters adulthood with his failed attempts at measuring up still around his neck. Even in business he can't seem to keep up with peers who make it clear that he doesn't measure up. Finally, he is ready to hang himself with the tapes he has collected over the years, but God breaks through. God tells him that someone else has already measured up for him—Jesus died so he wouldn't have to keep trying to make the grade. At God's behest, the man shreds the tape measures that have choked him his whole life and gratefully begins the relationship God has initiated.
Suggested Topics: God's acceptance of us; Self-esteem
Characters: 2 males, 1 female, 1 other male or female

MERE TECHNICALITY by Sharon Sherbondy

Mark comes home and announces to Karen that they're going on a trip together to Cancun, compliments of his business. Karen is not exactly overjoyed, and Mark thinks it's because of the fight they had that morning. It turns out that she is uncomfortable with the fact that they are living together but aren't married. She has been going back to church, and although she loves him, she wants the relationship to be right. Mark is angry Karen is taking her religion so seriously and goes upstairs in a huff. Karen is left alone and curls up with a blanket to sleep on the couch.
Suggested Topics: Living together vs. marriage; The cost of taking a stand for Christ
Characters: 1 male, 1 female

MILESTONES by Donna Lagerquist and Mark Demel

A monologue. A man reflects on the various milestones in his life, from childhood to the present. In a box first given to him by his mother, he has collected various mementos of those milestones. Today he is getting baptized, so he is including in the collection a small bottle of water to remind him of the day he went "public" about his commitment to Christ. He hopes to keep adding objects to his box—but from now on the emphasis will be on what God is doing in his life.
Suggested Topics: Baptism; New Christian
Characters: 1 male

THE MIRROR THOUGHT OF IT by Donna Lagerquist

Norm Anderson is being shown a home in the prestigious neighborhood of Beachwood Hills Estates. His eccentric realtor, Mrs. Foley, extols the value of the home and the neighborhood. When she leaves the room for a few minutes, he begins to measure to see if his bed will fit—and hears a voice. It's the mirror talking to him. Norm thinks it's a friend playing a practical joke, but the mirror's detailed knowledge of his life quickly convinces him the voice is in fact the mirror image of his life. The mirror questions Norm's motives for wanting to move and makes him think about his restlessness and compulsion to want more. When Mrs. Foley returns, he leaves, convinced he doesn't need the "tropic-simulated greenhouse." She is bewildered—but then hears the mirror call her name.
Suggested Topics: Materialism; Workaholism; Striving for more
Characters: 1 male, 1 female, 1 offstage voice

MISJUDGED LOVE by Brian Svenkeson and Steve Pederson

As an older man enters a hospital room, we learn from his conversation with the nurse that he is here to visit his adult son. Eddie, his son, is obviously quite sick. As the conversation continues, the awful truth comes out: He has AIDS. The dad has had trouble accepting both the illness and the lifestyle that produced it. But when all is said and done, Eddie is his son, the son he loves, the son he will stand with till the end.
Suggested Topics: Father's Day; Homosexuality; AIDS
Characters: 2 males, 1 female

MISSING by Donna Lagerquist

Three generations of the Elsberg family are having their picture taken for the church directory. At different times during the sitting, the scene freezes and each person talks to the audience. Mavis is the matriarch. She has watched her son, John, grow up and become a successful businessman, though she had to do it alone as the widow of a Korean War soldier killed in action. John, her son, works hard and wishes the family appreciated his efforts on their behalf—even though it cost him his marriage. William is the Generation-X son—aimless, cynical, and determined not to be like his dad. When the sitting is over, Mavis wants the names of her ex-daughter-in-law and granddaughter included along with her son's and grandson's. But she is the only one in the whole family who even attends the church—everyone else is "missing."

Suggested Topics: Generational barriers; The church's failure to reach Generation X

Characters: 3 males, 1 female

MISTAKEN IDENTITY by Donna Lagerquist

A park district production of the Christmas story causes one woman to question what she believed when she was a girl. She remembers celebrating Christ's birth and then three months later being confused when celebrating his death and resurrection. How did he grow up so fast? Did events happen the way the Bible says? This sketch provides an opportunity to recognize the questions of those who are not regular attendees.

Suggested Topics: Christmas

Characters: 3 males, 2 females, 1 young girl

MIXED SIGNALS by Mark Demel

During Liam's Little League baseball game, his father is trying his best to encourage him by giving him pointers on his batting technique. But Liam's confidence is shaky, and he is nervous as he is called to take his turn at the plate. As Liam bats "offstage," we watch his dad and hear the action. Liam finally gets on base, even if it is by getting hit by the pitch. However, he very quickly gets "picked off," causing the third out for his team. As we watch Liam head out to his position in the field, it's obvious that Dad's encouragement isn't making a dent. Suddenly his father marches out on the field next to him, interrupting the game. Liam's dad tells him, "The game can wait a minute—this is important," as he clarifies to his son that it's not his performance that matters, but his attitude and his willingness to give it his very best.

Suggested Topics: Encouragement; Fathers; Priorities

Characters: 1 male, 1 boy

MODEL BEHAVIOR by Mike Muhr

A father returning home from work is greeted by his eight-year-old son. The father agrees to build a model spaceship with the boy. As they start to work, the son goes into the kitchen but comes out as a twelve-year-old. The dad is naturally shocked, but the now-older son doesn't realize anything has happened. When the boy goes into the kitchen again, he comes out a sixteen-year-old. Now the dad is completely dumbfounded. The son goes into the kitchen a final time but comes out as the original eight-year-old. The dad is greatly relieved and realizes the preciousness of the time he has with his son.

Suggested Topics: Fathering; Shortness of the parenting years

Characters: 1 male, 3 boys (8-year-old, 12-year-old, and 16-year-old)

MONDAY NIGHT MEETING by Judson Poling

Wally, a new Christian, struggles with how to act out his faith. In an effort to be godly, he overspiritualizes everything and eliminates leisure from his life. Three of the guys from his small group (Bible study) try to explain and demonstrate that a serious commitment to God doesn't negate fun and enjoyment in life.

Suggested Topics: New Christians; Realistic expectations; Discipleship

Characters: 4 males

A MOTHER'S DAY by Donna Lagerquist

It's Mother's Day, and Julie is disappointed and a little angry that her mother (an actress in California) isn't able to stay with her and her newborn son while her husband is out of town. Julie reluctantly agrees to her husband's idea of hiring a nanny to come and help while he is gone. When the foreign nanny, Sophie, arrives, Julie is pleasantly surprised by her homey touches, despite a heavy accent and comical mannerisms. However, as time passes, Sophie's homey touches seem all too familiar to what Julie experienced as a child.

Finally, to Julie's great surprise, Sophie removes her disguise and reveals her true identity—Julie's mom.

Suggested Topics: Mother's Day

Characters: 1 male, 2 females

MR. HIBBS' DAY OFF by Various Authors

This simple but effective mime tells the story of a man whose day off goes differently than he planned. While on his way to the zoo, Mr. Hibbs is confronted by many needy people: a young girl upset over her lost balloon, a woman who has just been robbed, and a hungry, homeless man. Mr. Hibbs stops and helps each person, buying a balloon for the girl, giving his coat to the woman, and providing lunch for the man. When Mr. Hibbs finally gets to the zoo, it is closed. He is upset, even angry. On his way home, however, he is reminded how meaningful his day has been when the kindness he had earlier demonstrated is returned to him.

Suggested Topics: Serving others; Self-denial; Being used by God

Characters: 3 males, 1 female, 1 child

MR. P. NOCCHIO by Judson Poling

A man with a very large nose enters a therapist's office. He complains of problems going back to his childhood that have become worse in recent months. At first the therapist thinks he must be talking about self-esteem issues from his big nose. But the client explains that his nose is a symptom; the real problem is that he keeps stretching the truth. He is, in fact, Pinocchio—now grown up. The therapist tries to be sympathetic but alternates between believing Mr. Nocchio's story and wondering if this guy is just plain nuts. The therapist concludes the time with the promise of a quick cure—a lie that causes his nose to suddenly grow as well!

Suggested Topics: Honesty

Characters: 2 males or 1 male and 1 female

MR. PEEPERS GOES TO SLEEP by Donna Lagerquist

Lisa wants to know why Mr. Peepers, her pet bird, won't move anymore. When her dad says the bird is dead, Lisa demands that he make it "undead." Lisa's mom feels that Lisa isn't old enough to understand death. Lisa's grandmother believes that most people don't understand or accept death. A young child's first experience with death forces the adults in her life to examine their own fears and beliefs.

Suggested Topics: Death; Facing the truth

Characters: 1 male, 2 females, 1 either male or female child

MR. X, MR. Y, AND MR. Z by Judson Poling

Three superficially related neighbors maintain their space and protect themselves from intimacy. Mr. Z, however, is changed by a newcomer, Mr. Smith ("the one with the funny name"), who helps him see the joys of stepping out of his comfort zone. Through experiencing some embarrassment and then returning to his protective environment, Mr. Z finds that it is a new beginning—a true friendship has been born, and Mr. Z will never be the same.

Suggested Topics: Friendship; Intimacy

Characters: 4 males, 1 female, 1 narrator

THE MYSTERY OF ROBERT RICHARDSON by Judson Poling

This sketch is comprised of five different monologues that all comment on the character of Robert Richardson through various stages of his life. The stories told make us realize that Robert was a person who lived a Christ-glorifying life.

Suggested Topics: Living the Christian life

Characters: 3 males, 2 females, 1 narrator

THE NATURE OF LIFE by Sharon Sherbondy

This two-part drama shows a family of four going camping. In the first part the family is setting up camp, but the kids with their headphones and blow-dryers aren't exactly in the camping mood, and Dad wonders why they even bothered to come. The second part opens later that night with Dad looking through his telescope. At first no one else is interested, but then the son sees a shooting star. Within a few minutes, father and son end up in a shared moment, marveling at God's creation.

Suggested Topics: Family; Wonder of creation

Characters: 2 males, 2 females

THE NEIGHBORHOOD by Donna Lagerquist

Three couples are sitting in lawn chairs in a driveway, a regular get-together for this group of neighbors. The conversation flows freely around typical topics of suburban families: dogs, minivans, work, houses, and yards, with only hints at deeper struggles. Everything is friendly but not very personal or authentic. Then the scene freezes, and one of the characters, Ed, speaks to the audience. He finds the whole thing depressing. He wants deeper relationships—especially because he knows people are hurting and really need support. Whenever conversation gets more substantial, he complains, someone changes the subject. In the end Ed doesn't know what to do to make it different.

Suggested Topics: Small groups; Relationships; Getting deeper; Authenticity

Characters: 3 males, 3 females

NEW BALL GAME by Mark Demel

Greg is having a tough time getting over his brother's death. Three flashback vignettes show their sometimes feisty but always friendly relationship during the past few years. First, Greg tells Jeff about his upcoming marriage. The second scene shows them interacting about Greg's soon-to-be father status. Third, Greg reacts to the news that his brother has cancer. The scene shifts to the present. Greg's wife comes in pleading with Greg to get over his loss and get on with his life. But Greg is stuck in sadness and despair.

(*Note:* This drama was followed by the song "Now That You're Gone" by Elaine Rubenstein and Fernando Ortega, recorded on Ortega's album *Night of Your Return,* published by Randolf Productions, Inc.)

Suggested Topics: Death; Meaning in life after sorrow

Characters: 2 males, 1 female

THE NEXT STEP by Mark Demel and Rod Armentrout

This comic sketch is a delightful look at how challenging it is to develop a strong friendship—especially for men! The scene takes place in a diner where Ron is returning Sam's drill bits. Ron is hurt because Sam borrowed someone else's ladder, not his. Their conversation sounds like it is between two people romantically involved, but these are two masculine tool guys! At first, Sam tries to rationalize his actions but finally admits his "infidelity" and pleads with his friend, "It meant nothing! You've got to believe me!" But Ron is not sure he can. In the end Sam risks it all by telling Ron he wants to take the next step in their relationship and borrow . . . his mower! Ron is stunned by Sam's request (after all, his mower is a "Deere") as they exchange a "manly" and hilarious good-bye.

Suggested Topics: Authentic community; Positive relational risk taking; Men's relationships

Characters: 2 males

A NICE GUY by Donna Lagerquist

Glen was recently hired to teach fifth grade and brought along a friend, Bill, to help set up the room. Coincidently, this was Bill's alma mater, and Bill shares some funny stories from those years. The mood abruptly changes, however, when Bill discovers the room's radiator still has a bend in it from when he was there. In that spot a boy in his class, Bobby Heaver, was tied to the radiator and had his pants pulled down in front of the class. Bill feels the guilt of

his participation that day—also knowing Bobby later committed suicide. Bill knows everyone thinks he is a nice guy on the outside, but his capacity to hurt another human being haunts him. When left alone for a few minutes, Bill tries to apologize to Bobby.

Suggested Topics: Admitting failures; Effects of sin; Confession

Characters: 2 males

NICE TO HAVE AROUND by Donna Lagerquist

This mime demonstrates how the Bible is sometimes viewed as just a nice "item" to have in a household. The narrative shows a woman encountering her Bible at various stages of her life: infancy, childhood, adolescence, marriage, midlife, and eventually at her death. Though the encounters and uses for her Bible are numerous, never once do they involve opening it and reading it.

Suggested Topics: Attitudes toward the Bible

Characters: 2 males, 1 female

THE NIGHT LIGHT by Donna Lagerquist

This drama contains three separate scenes that chronicle the relationship of a mom and her daughter. In the first scene the daughter, Claire, is an infant, and mom is getting up with her in the middle of the night. She sings "You Are My Sunshine," which puts her back to sleep. In the next scene Claire is grown up and home from college. Her independence is hard for Mom to cope with, and a fight ensues. They both realize this is not how they want their relationship to be and apologize. In the final scene Claire is a young mom herself and calls her mom for help with her newborn. Mom is understanding, and although Claire is scared, Mom reassures her she will make it. When the baby won't quiet down, Mom suggests Claire hold the phone to her ear, and she sings "You Are My Sunshine" to her granddaughter. Just as years ago with Claire, the song puts the baby to sleep.

Suggested Topics: Mother's Day; Parenting

Characters: 2 females

NO ACCIDENT by Donna Lagerquist

Two women are involved in a fender bender. After they exchange information, the sketch progresses to their conversations over the ensuing days, and we learn that one woman has fallen on hard times and is trying to avoid her responsibility to the woman she hit. She has no insurance and can't afford to pay for the repairs the first woman needs. The offended woman is anxious for recompense and threatens to involve the police. She softens, however, when she comes across Jesus' words to go the second mile and love your enemies. As a result, she sends a letter to the woman who hit her and forgives the debt—and encloses a check so the struggling woman can get proper insurance.

Suggested Topics: Forgiveness; Loving your enemies; Growing in Christlikeness

Characters: 2 females

NO CLUE by Judson Poling

Lou Loughetti is leading a corporate seminar about gender sensitivity. He sets up some role-play situations that illustrate various dilemmas. His first scene involves a man and a woman approaching a door at the same time. Should the man hold the door? Should the woman? Should anybody? The next scene involves a man and a woman at a business lunch. Who should pick up the tab? This is especially problematic, considering the woman is the man's supervisor! In the final scenario a man and woman meet in the hallway. What is the appropriate greeting, and how much should be said about appearance? At the end of each scenario, Lou leaves his clients in a quandary because all his suggestions are ridiculous—comically highlighting the complexity of knowing the "right way" for men and women to behave toward one another in today's workplace.

Suggested Topics: Gender sensitivity; Male-female workplace issues

Characters: 2 males, 1 female, 1 voice-over

NO INTERRUPTIONS by Sharon Sherbondy

This monologue describes one man's struggle with a quiet time. He has evaluated his life and assessed a lack of balance and a need for replenishing. So he has instructed his wife and children that he is not to be interrupted for any reason while he is praying. As the sketch progresses, we see he is more than willing to be interrupted.

Suggested Topics: Quiet time; Prayer

Characters: 1 male

NO MORE WOMB by Donna Lagerquist

This sketch takes both a comic and serious look at the issues facing children today. The scene begins inside the womb, where our two characters—a set of fraternal twins—discuss the things they are most looking forward to. As the discussion progresses, they talk about that which they are most afraid of—not being accepted by their peers, not doing well academically, being abducted or abused.

Suggested Topics: The world children face today; Fear of the unknown

Characters: 1 male, 1 female

NO THANKS GIVING by Donna Lagerquist

The scene opens with Terri busily placing name cards around her dining room table set for ten. A friend stops by to encourage her not to get too caught up in pleasing others. Then Terri sits and "preenacts" what she thinks will happen during the meal. Via a tape, we hear the voices of various family members complaining or needing something, especially Terri's mother, finding fault in just about everything Terri does. Overwhelmed, she cries out about how tired she is of taking care of everyone else and of pretending that everything is "nice," and she decides things will be different this year. Terri is caught off guard when her mother enters the dining room and immediately begins "altering" the seating assignments and centerpiece. The confidence Terri had gained moments earlier falls to the wayside in her mother's presence.

Suggested Topics: Truth telling; Needy people

Characters: 3 females

NOTHING TO IT by Donna Lagerquist

After a Halloween party, two couples wind down chatting about what they believe to be "harmless" demonic activities. Three of them wear ghoulish costumes and one is dressed as Bo Peep. "Bo" is uncomfortable with the topic of conversation, yet the others coax her on, saying she is making a big deal out of nothing. They continue by reminiscing about Ouija boards, rabbit's feet, and childhood voodoo spells, and they decide to reenact one of their slumber party levitations. Bo resists this too, yet in predictable repetition, the others remind her once again, "There's nothing to it!"

Suggested Topics: Satanism; Spiritual warfare

Characters: 2 males, 2 females

THE OFFERING by Judson Poling

It's time for the offering, and four people express their reasons for giving. The first chooses not to give because he believes his tithe could be used more wisely by himself. The second gives because of the recognition he might receive. The third hates giving because she feels God is never satisfied with what she offers. The fourth enjoys giving because it is his opportunity to say thanks to God.

Suggested Topics: Tithing

Characters: 3 males, 1 female

OH, WHAT A FEELING! by Debra Poling

A husband and wife are out to buy a car—a stripped-down, bottom-of-the-line model. He cautions her to not get carried away with the emotional appeal of the salesman, but to let him be in charge of making the deal. He winds up getting "lost in the feeling" and buying a loaded, top-of-the-line model.

Suggested Topics: Decision making; Self-control; Money management

Characters: 2 males, 1 female

THE OLD MAN AND THE LAUNDROMAT by Donna Lagerquist

John, in his sixties, was recently widowed and is now having to do his laundry at the laundromat. Through the course of a conversation with a woman there, he shares his grief, anger, and struggles to do anything—even the laundry—since his wife's death. While helping John "sort," the woman uncovers an inflatable Christmas ornament, a memento of his wife, which he keeps because "she blew it up." When the woman's daughter innocently unplugs the ornament, John yells out and replugs it. Once left alone, he realizes he must let go and slowly lets the air out gently against his cheek.

Suggested Topics: Letting go; Grieving; Dealing with death

Characters: 1 male, 1 female, 1 child

ON THE OUTSIDE by Donna Lagerquist

In this monologue a woman sitting on a park bench across from a church recounts her experience growing up when every week she sat in church "third row, left of center." Her happy Christian family illusion was shattered one day when her mother announced she and her father were getting a divorce. Now, the "divorcée and her kids" sat in the back of the church, outcasts and unwelcome. She angrily recounts her disappointment at how little those who were supposed to be the "light of the world, salt of the earth" did for her during those difficult years. When she grew up, the woman left the church—and hasn't been back. The closest she gets is "the second park bench, left of the sidewalk."

Suggested Topics: Being salt and light; Negative church experiences

Characters: 1 female

ON TRACK by Judson Poling

Don and Ruth are having a tough time understanding their son Kevin's attraction to computers. They want him to be involved with sports because of the friends he'll make and the experience it will bring. Computers "can't build character." What they fail to see is Kevin's uniqueness and how best to encourage him.

Suggested Topics: Character building; Forcing people into a mold

Characters: 2 males, 1 female

ON VACATION by Judson Poling

Peter and Nancy are on a plane to a much-needed vacation in Colorado. Peter, however, has a hard time relaxing. A combination of guilt (he'll miss his small group Bible study), burnout, and another passenger's attempts to witness to him eventually push him over the edge.

Suggested Topics: Guilt; Leisure time; Inability to slow down

Characters: 2 males, 1 female, 1 either male or female

ONE DAY AT THE ZOO by Judson Poling

This sketch takes a humorous look at a futuristic view of a zoo that houses some endangered species and one of the last examples of a paternal *normalus* (father) now residing in a zoo. The father interacts with automated facsimiles of his predators: *office dictatorus* (boss), *secretaria hot-to-trotus* (seductress), *neighborous influencius* (friend), and *nagus ad infinitum* (wife).

Suggested Topics: Father's Day

Characters: 3 males, 2 females, 1 narrator, and some offstage voices

ONE STEP UP, ONE STEP DOWN by Judson Poling

In this narrated mime an everyman character faces ambition and the high price it solicits. To be at the top costs him family, friendships, and integrity, but he is left with wealth, a big office, and acceptance. Everyman has difficulty feeling the satisfaction he thought success would bring.

Suggested Topics: Ambition; Priorities
Characters: 4 males

ONE SUNDAY IN THE PARKING LOT by Judson Poling

If cars in a church parking lot could talk, what would they say? This lighthearted sketch answers that question as four cars—an Escort, a BMW, a Celebrity, and a Honda—come to life. One car in particular laments being "driven" all the time and wonders if it's worth it to go on. The key to longevity? Making changes, especially before things get so bad. In regard to the need for preventative maintenance, the cars' needs are no different than ours. The sketch ends on a humorous note as the cars play their favorite game, "Parking Lot Shuffle," and move to another spot to confuse their owners.

Suggested Topics: Pace of life
Characters: 4 males

ONLY CHILD by Donna Lagerquist

Elise is at her college friend Andy's home while Andy's mom is preparing supper. While they make small talk, Mom looks at a package that has arrived in the mail—and is shocked. It's addressed to her deceased son, Jason, who was killed by a drunk driver four years earlier. Andy finally enters, and Mom leaves upset. Andy must finish telling the story about how a crazy kid in a stolen car killed Jason and didn't even have to go to prison. Instead, the family adopted him. Elise suddenly understands—Andy is the one who hit and killed Jason four years ago, and who was brought into the family and raised as their own.

Suggested Topics: Grace; Outrageous forgiveness; The doctrine of adoption
Characters: 1 male, 2 females

OUT OF CONTROL by Sharon Sherbondy

Steve has the afternoon to prove that he is not a P.O.P. (Push Over Parent). The outcome is that Nick, his son, easily manipulates and controls his father.

Suggested Topics: Father's Day; Parenting
Characters: 2 males and 1 female

THE PAINFUL PROCESS by Donna Lagerquist

In this monologue a woman recounts her struggle to overcome the pain of her abortion. As she remembers the events of that day, she compares the descriptions others gave her to dry cleaning—to having a spot removed. But although that's what she was told it was like, she feels lied to. Yes, there was some physical pain, but that passed fairly quickly. What followed—and haunts her—is the emotional pain. "They told me lots of women have abortions and never think about it again. I'm not one of them." She bluntly tells the audience, "I didn't just remove a spot."

Suggested Topics: Abortion
Characters: 1 female

PARALYZED by Sharon Sherbondy

The typical family rush before Chris's high school basketball game is interrupted when Doug, Chris's father, comes in the door from work. His wife, Nancy, tries to spur him on to eat and change quickly while his son, Chris, makes clear the importance of this game. None of it seems to have any affect on Doug, however, as he tells his family he can't muster the energy to go. After Nancy sends the kids off to the game in the other car, she confronts Doug about how he is letting Chris down by not going and how he is letting down Nancy by not fighting against his depression. "We can't keep living like this," she says. He understands her frustration and tries to give her insight into how he is feeling but admits he is "paralyzed" by it and that even his prayers don't seem to help.

Suggested Topics: Depression; Prayer; Relationship with God; Family in crisis
Characters: 2 males (1 adult, 1 teen), 2 females (1 adult, 1 teen)

PARENTS ON THE SIDELINES by Sharon Sherbondy

This humorous depiction of "awkward evangelism" opens with two couples arriving at a soccer game to watch their seven-year-old daughters play. As the game progresses, Lee loudly criticizes his daughter's playing, while Roger attempts to be more encouraging of his daughter. Lee asks Roger how he manages to remain so controlled. Faced with the unexpected challenge to share his faith, Roger panics and spits out the salvation message in rapid-fire fashion, leaving Lee a little confused and in need of a repeat. Instead, Roger finds himself inviting Lee and his wife over to his house after the game for a cookout. The invitation is enthusiastically accepted. Just then, Roger's daughter helps Lee's daughter score the team's first goal of the season. As the parents celebrate, we see a friendship in the making and know that this will be the basis for a more comfortable sharing of faith.

Suggested Topic: Evangelism
Characters: 2 males, 2 females

PARLOR TALK by Donna Lagerquist

Bill and Ray meet at a funeral parlor—where they are the ones who have died. Ray's wake is heavily attended, mostly by business associates. Bill recently moved from out of town, so only his wife, Elaine, is there. As she sits alone and Bill tries in vain to talk to her, Bill's doctor comes in. She tells Elaine about the profound impact Bill's life had, especially on another cancer patient, a little boy named Joey. Despite the small showing at his funeral, Bill's life was a testimony to caring for others, while Ray, although popular even in death, laments he poured his life into his business and "never even got a gold watch!"

Suggested Topics: Death; Living for others; Workaholism; Making a difference
Characters: 3 males, 2 females

PASTOR GENERAL by Judson Poling

Dave and Penny have an appointment with the pastor of the church they recently visited for the first time. He comes off somewhat firm at first, though he does impress them by remembering their names. They soon discover his military-like style is just the tip of the iceberg; he is a virtual dictator in his church. He "goes by the book"—which is the book he wrote. He has a church organizational chart that pictures him at the top in a big box and everybody else in a small box under him. When he forces his aging secretary to give him twenty push-ups for forgetting to bring cream for the coffee, Dave and Penny flee. This is a broad, satirical look at controlling-style leadership—which for some is painfully too close to reality!

Suggested Topics: Leadership; Church life; Serving others
Characters: 2 males, 2 females

PASTOR GENERAL: CONSULTANT VISIT by Judson Poling

Ms. Flanners is a consultant working with three very frightened employees. We finally understand their intimidation when their boss, the infamous Pastor Howitzer, arrives. As they enjoy their refreshments of bread and water, Ms. Flanners suggests they do some role playing with Pastor Howitzer to discover better ways to interact. All the employees are terrified, but after Ms. Flanners skillfully leads them through some tough situations, Howitzer explodes. Ms. Flanners points out that the main problem Howitzer's employees have is him. Insulted, he demands they do push-ups for penance. She refuses and storms out; so to save face, Howitzer insists his employees pay for her insolence—illustrating, he says, the "rich doctrine of substitutionary atonement."

Suggested Topics: Leadership; Oppressive managers; Communication
Characters: 2 males, 4 females

PASTOR GENERAL: EVALUATION TIME by Judson Poling

A church programming/worship team is getting ready for its weekly evaluation of the weekend service. As the members discuss the service, their pastor, Pastor Howitzer, wants to listen in. They continue the evaluation, but Pastor Howitzer can't help but speak up. He starts friendly enough but is soon expressing outrage over a bad drama, a crazy idea involving birds in the sanctuary, and offertory music that was so loud people had their hands over their ears. Howitzer makes the whole team give him twenty push-ups. In his words, if they're going to work in the vineyard, he wants grapes, not lemons!

Suggested Topics: Authoritarian leadership; How not to do program evaluations; Church programming/worship teams

Characters: 4 males, 2 females

PASTOR GENERAL: RESOURCE ALLOCATION by Judson Poling

Pastor Howitzer, a military-style commander, leads a staff meeting, and the church is in trouble. Fund-raising efforts have failed. People are leaving. Worse, the faithful few who remain are under-resourced. But Pastor Howitzer offers some creative—though inadequate—solutions. Instead of that new word processor, he produces a package of pens; instead of a data-base, three-by-five cards. People just need to work harder, he barks. Just then, his secretary, Eunice, comes in carrying a weed whacker that she just broke. Pastor Howitzer insists she do twenty push-ups. Turning to the rest of his staff, he asks if there are any other resource needs. Everyone shakes his or her head no. Meeting adjourned! A broad, humorous look at the difficulties of resourcing church leaders and volunteers.

Suggested Topics: Providing for volunteers; Bad leadership styles

Characters: 4 males, 2 females

PERMANENT SOLUTION by Sharon Sherbondy

Mary Ann has a tough career decision to make, so she heads to her hair dresser's for some respected advice. Before she can get that, she is bombarded with "advice" from two other women who base their wisdom on talk shows, gossip magazines, and fortune-tellers.

Suggested Topics: Decision-making, Whom to listen to

Characters: 4 females

A PERSPECTIVE ON SPRING by Judson Poling

In this short, comic monologue, a groundhog interrupts the service to "set up" the topic of spring (one of the four "Seasons of the Soul"). He is talking on the phone with his agent about landing a movie deal for the sequel to *Groundhog Day* but quickly turns to the audience and laments how unpredictable spring is. In his words spring is "a meteorological manifestation of Murphy's Law . . . it's 'winter-lite': half the calories, all the headache." What has he learned from spring? Sunny days aren't proof of anything, because a blizzard could hit you the day after you put your snow blower away. So "get it in writing"!

Suggested Topics: Optimistic/pessimistic views of life

Characters: 1 male

THE PIANO RECITAL by Donna Lagerquist

At the end of a children's music recital, the instructor, Pam, thanks everyone for coming and directs them to refreshments. She is surprised to see her mother there with a friend. As she tries to excuse herself to go meet some of the parents, including "that guy in the ten-gallon hat," Pam discovers the reason they're there is to set her up with the friend's son, Robert—the guy with the hat! Pam can't believe her mother! Setting her up on another blind date? Here—at her recital?! When Robert approaches, allowing the meddling parents to escape, Pam takes out her wrath on him. He totally agrees! He has had enough of this too. In fact, he tells her, "I've resorted to this little outfit here to ward off any future dates as quickly as possible." At the end of the sketch, their vulnerable frustration about being seen as "broken" gives this mostly comical sketch a thought-provoking finish.

Suggested Topics: Singleness; Adult parent-child tension

Characters: 2 males, 4 females, 2 children

PLANE TALK by Judson Poling

Dan, a nervous, talkative passenger, engages Bill, a seasoned business traveler, on a plane trip. The conversation turns to spiritual matters when Bill casually observes he saw Dan pray before his meal. Bill expresses his skepticism about God's involvement in the everyday affairs of life—at the very moment the captain announces an engine failure! Bill suddenly becomes panic stricken, and all his poised confidence gives way to desperate (and comical) pleas for God to help. When the captain announces the crisis has passed and they will be landing soon, Bill goes back to his "got-it-all-together" facade, as if nothing has happened. The saying "There are no atheists in foxholes" finds an amusing, contemporary counterpart in this sketch.

Suggested Topics: God's presence; Faith; God's feelings; Doubt; Skepticism

Characters: 2 males, 1 (narrator) pilot

THE PLATE SPINNER by Donna Lagerquist

In this narrated story (the narrator is the only speaking part), Hank Spinner finds his life is becoming overwhelming. At first, everything is "Hunkey-Dorey." He keeps his boss, Mr. Hunkey, and his wife, Dorey, quite happy (represented by him spinning imaginary plates on wooden poles each character holds). He is further challenged when Peachy, his daughter, and Keen, a new account, require his attention. Add to those obligations Oakey, a health club membership, Dokey, a counselor, and his aging parents, Nitty and Gritty, and Hank now has a Hunkey-Dorey, Peechy Keen, Oakey-Dokey, Nitty-Gritty life. Keeping all those plates spinning has him on the edge of a breakdown!

Suggested Topics: Pace of life; Being in control

Characters: 5 males, 4 females, 1 offstage narrator

PLAYING GOD by Donna Lagerquist

In this monologue a man struggles with knowing his ailing father could be put out of his misery by a simple overdose. It seems so right—an end to pain, not having to watch his father live at such a low-functioning level. He has been so vibrant and active but is now hooked up to machines and must be cared for twenty-four hours a day. A few extra pills, and Dad's life and pain would be over. The man is torn, knowing that, although his father's care is a heavy load, playing God would be an overwhelming load to bear.

Suggested Topics: Aging parent; Right to die

Characters: 1 male

PRAYER DESPAIR by Judson Poling

When JoAnn complains about her husband's lack of interest in her, Valerie questions whether she has asked God to change Glenn. JoAnn replies she has, "but nothing happens, he is still the same." In the end we discover it is JoAnn who is insensitive to the change taking place in Glenn.

Suggested Topics: Waiting for answers to prayer; Marriage

Characters: 1 male, 2 females

PRAYER GROUP THERAPY by Donna Lagerquist

Four would-be pray-ers meet for group therapy. In this case each member has some sort of common prayer dysfunction. Doug is into "holy language," and his prayers are full of outbursts and alleluias that disrupt the others. Margaret uses prayer as a vehicle for gossip. Amy is timid and uses only memorized or formula prayers. Jay doesn't really pray at all, because he has concluded that God knows everything, so he certainly doesn't need any prayers to inform him of a request. Karen, the facilitator, tries to get everyone to participate in a simple time of prayer, but as each person's warped perspective on prayer kicks in, the results are disastrous—in an outlandishly comical way!

Suggested Topics: Prayer
Characters: 2 males, 3 females

PRAYER PERPLEXITY by Judson Poling

Several brief scenes illustrate comically the confusion in our culture about prayer. In the first scene a group of people pray fervently—to rip off the heads of the opposing team! Then a child's nighttime prayer becomes a confusing theology lesson from mom who doesn't really understand why we pray. Next, a man prays for a meal and puts on a holy-sounding prayer voice complete with religious vocabulary. A teenager prays for justice on her ex-friend who stole her boyfriend. A shipwrecked man promises God anything but backs out of it all when rescued. A memorized mealtime prayer doesn't quite fit—at a funeral! Finally, a committee trying to update prayer goes to ridiculous lengths. In the end the actors paraphrase the Lord's Prayer, and we see the wonderful simplicity of Jesus' model.

Suggested Topics: The Lord's Prayer; Prayer
Characters: 2 males, 2 females, (all play multiple roles)

PREMARITAL FLUTTER by Judson Poling

On his wedding day Jim begins to second guess his decision to marry Ann. He finds himself torn between his desire to be with her and the reality that their relationship has changed during the engagement. He turns to his married friends, Ben and Carl. They assure Jim that Ann's altered behavior is due to "premarital flutter"—something all couples experience. Ben and Carl lead Jim to believe that after the wedding the fights will soon end, the money problems will disappear, and sex will be one wild night of pleasure after another. Jim is now more excited than ever, but when he leaves the room, one of his buddies says to the other, "Are you gonna tell him?" "No way," answers the other. "Nobody told me!"

Suggested Topic: Marriage expectations
Characters: 3 males

THE PRISONER by Donna Lagerquist

A three-part drama. In the first scene we meet Joey, a prisoner. He receives an unexpected visit from the warden, who tells him the governor has granted him clemency. The scene ends with him dazed in joyous disbelief. In the next scene a janitor drops by. He can't understand why Joey is still in his cell playing cards. Joey is actually more comfortable staying there—it's what he is used to. In the third scene Joey's sister has arrived to take him home. Although it doesn't make sense, Joey's not sure he can leave. The scene ends as his sister takes his hand and literally walks him into the freedom of his new life.

Suggested Topics: Easter; New Christians; Freedom from sin
Characters: 3 males, 1 female

A PROBLEM OF PERCEPTION by Sharon Sherbondy

Did you know that Christians always wear black? And they never mow the lawn on Wednesdays? This sketch takes a comical look at three people's misconceptions of what the Christian life is like.

Suggested Topics: The Christian life; Misconceptions about Christianity
Characters: 3 males, 1 female

A PROBLEM OF PERSPECTIVE by Judson Poling

A tired husband returns home at the end of a work day to his equally tired wife. In the few moments as they talk, their exhaustion and unmet needs create a tense (but comical) exchange. The scene freezes and a counselor appears and explains that he'd like to hear what happened from each of their perspectives. The scene is replayed twice, once from each point of view, and it's hard to believe they're describing the same situation!

Suggested Topics: Marital conflict; Truth telling
Characters: 1 male, 1 female, 1 either male or female

PULPIT TALK by Donna Lagerquist and Steve Pederson

In this broadly comic sketch, a narrator introduces us to a pulpit, wondering what our reaction to it is. With the help of other characters, we experience a variety of sermons that could be found in an average church on a typical Sunday: the Sominex, the Terminex, and the Feel-Good. But none of these compare to the greatest sermon of all known as the Sermon on the Mount, and this drama ends with the opening lines of that sermon. If a broader emphasis is desired, an alternate ending of Scripture verses is provided that focuses on the power of God's Word.

Suggested Topics: Introduction to the Sermon on the Mount; Stereotypical church experiences; How does God speak?
Characters: 3 males, 2 females

THE QUAGMIRE by Various Authors

An "everyman" character explains to the audience his reasons for heading to the Quagmire. It isn't a pleasant place; in fact, most people there are miserable, but it's attractive because it's an escape. Halfway through this sketch, God reminds the character that he loves him and will guide him through to higher ground.

Suggested Topics: Failure; Self-esteem; Trusting God
Characters: 1 male or female, 1 offstage voice

QUALITY TIME? by Judson Poling

This sketch takes a look at the philosophy of "quality time" between parents and children. We see a father who has a difficult time controlling his preoccupation with business and keeping up with his daughters' lives. The daughters contemplate a friend's situation whose parents are divorced and wonder if her one afternoon a week with her dad isn't better than the "quality time" they have each day.

Suggested Topics: Fathers
Characters: 1 male, 1 female, 2 teenage girls

QUIET TIME? by Sharon Sherbondy

This sketch focuses on the difficulty so many have in giving God their complete attention during their devotional time. A new mom unsuccessfully tries to combat the distractions and situational demands surrounding her. This comical sketch has application to many.

Suggested Topics: Prayer
Characters: 1 female

THE QUITTER by Judson Poling

Warren has been unemployed for seven months and has been having a tough struggle. To get everyone "off his back," he decided to tell them he had a new job and for a week has been hanging out at the shopping mall from nine to five. When the truth comes out, Warren and everyone else have a hard time with the fact he quit trying.

Suggested Topics: Quitting; Failure
Characters: 2 male, 1 female

A REAL MAN by Judson Poling

One evening Cheryl decides to list the qualities she is looking for in a "real man." Much to her surprise, her dreams come true and she is faced with three men; a rugged individualist, a twenty-first-century entrepreneur, and a poetic type. After seeing their strengths and weaknesses, she rejects them all and concludes she needs a man who can make her laugh.

Suggested Topics: The American male; Finding the right man
Characters: 4 males, 1 female

REASON ENOUGH by Sharon Sherbondy

During her weekly counseling session, Susan discusses everything from what's on television to whether she believes in God. Susan doesn't believe in God but not because she doesn't want to. Growing up she wasn't given any reasons for believing, and now as an adult she doesn't know where to go for answers.

Suggested Topics: Importance of faith grounded in reason
Characters: 1 male, 2 females

REFLECTIONS by Sharon Sherbondy

It's Mother's Day again, and Lois takes a look back at her years as a mother. Her reflecting reveals the pain, humor, and joy she experienced. She concludes that motherhood is a privilege and has added to her life.

Suggested Topics: Mother's Day; Mother-child relationships
Characters: 1 male, 2 females, 2 children either males or females

REMEMBRANCES by Judson Poling

While helping their mother move, Jerry and Sue talk about their father, who has recently died. Jerry is angry because, although he had access to his father's property (boat, car, money), he felt his father was never there for him. Later he is alone and stumbles across some letters he wrote to his father. While reading one, he painfully becomes aware that at one time there was a significant relationship between them.

Suggested Topics: Parent-child relationships; Forgiveness; Fifth commandment
Characters: 1 male, 1 female

THE REST ROOM by Donna Lagerquist

In this lighthearted sketch a woman has barricaded herself in the bathroom in an attempt to protect herself from the onslaught of all the people who put demands on her. Her father is calling from the retirement home, her husband just came home from work and wants his supper before he leaves for an evening meeting, her kids need socks mended, her friend wants her to make designer scrapbooks out of her family photos, and her boss wants her to work on some files. In the end she surrenders and heads out of her "bunker." Clearly, she needs some help learning how to make time for herself.

Suggested Topics: Boundaries; Taking better care of yourself; Motherhood
Characters: 1 female, offstage voices: 1 male, 2 children

RICHARD: 1968 by Donna Lagerquist

(The first sketch in a four-part series.) Richard, a hippie-type college student is invited home to meet Mr. and Mrs. Matson, the parents of his girlfriend, "M.A." It is the classic but comical encounter of radical values versus mainstream, conservative America. As the father grills Richard about his eating—and "weed" consumption—habits, Richard counters with concerns about the war in Vietnam. With both parents in the kitchen, he and M.A. talk about how trapped the older generation seems. Richard leaves on an angry note, challenging M.A. to choose which side she'll be on, quoting "The Times They Are a-Changin'."

Suggested Topics: Youth idealism; Changing societal values; Generation gap
Characters: 2 males, 2 females

RICHARD: 1974 by Sharon Sherbondy

(The second sketch in a four-part series.) Richard is sitting in a bar on the night of President Nixon's resignation. He and others around him lament the jobs they don't have. M.A., his wife, comes in looking for him. His pride is wounded, both because of his unemployment and because he is a Vietnam veteran with no respect or appreciation from society. His situation is doubly ironic because he opposed the war but was drafted and forced to serve. In the end

a friendly bartender—a vet himself—counsels Richard, and the two fellow soldiers share some moments of identification. The bartender encourages Richard to go back to his wife and consider the job offer from his much-hated father-in-law. Richard reluctantly takes the advice, and the two part with a nostalgic military salute.

Suggested Topics: Dillusionment; Crumbling dreams
Characters: 5 males, 1 female

RICHARD: 1985 by Judson Poling

(The third sketch in a four-part series.) After coming home late at night, Richard finds himself looking down the barrel of his father-in-law's rifle, who thinks he is a prowler. Once they settle down, their conversation turns to the changes in Richard's life: his growing interest in making money, his extensive time commitments at work, and the loss of his youthful idealism. The father-in-law knows all too well how short life is, especially now that he has lost his own wife. He finally decides to go to bed, "warning" Richard he may kidnap his ten-year-old and play hooky with him the next day. Richard calls out after him not to "corrupt" his boy, but as he considers why he is so concerned, he realizes he is not sure the path of college and career will truly make his son happy.

Suggested Topics: Workaholism; Materialism vs. idealism; Fathers
Characters: 2 males

RICHARD: 1992 by Donna Lagerquist

(The last sketch in a four-part series.) Richard's college-age son, Zach, enters the living room just as Richard settles in with a late-night snack. Tension fills the air: Zach got thrown out of his mother's house. Richard is now divorced, and Zach has grown up to be a rebellious, troubled young man. Richard chastises his son for having a girlfriend in his room—as his own live-in girlfriend enters. Awkward greetings are exchanged and she exits. The conversation now crescendos as father and son express their lifetime of rage. After all is said and done, Zach angrily sums up: "We sure don't have much, do we, Dad?"

Suggested Topics: Anger; Rebellion; Decay of the family
Characters: 2 males, 1 female

THE RIGHT THING by Various Authors

A reflective monologue set in front of the home of a man who was just fired from his job as a reporter because he chose to help someone in need and missed his story. We hear him struggle with how to tell his wife and children and to understand why doing the right thing in God's eyes can sometimes be very difficult. (Suggestion: Follow with verses pertaining to the Christian struggle or God's seeing what is done in secret.)

Suggested Topics: Christian character; Costly obedience; Persecution
Characters: 1 male

THE SAFE by Judson Poling

An "everyman" character demonstrates to the audience how a safe that contains all of his inborn and personal resources can solve anything that comes his way. We see how he effectively handles the IRS, employees, and health problems, but to his surprise the resources in his safe won't subdue a spiritual "crisis" as easily.

Suggested Topics: Inner strength; Needing God's strength
Characters: 1 male, 1 female, 3 either males or females

A SECOND CHANCE by Sharon Sherbondy

Al and Marge have made a difficult and seemingly illogical decision to let Al's father, Earl, move in with them. Both feel strongly that God has led them to this decision, and even when challenged by another believer and Earl's difficult personality, they plan to trust in God's leading.

Suggested Topics: Decision making; Father-son relationships
Characters: 3 males, 1 female

SECURITY CHECK by Sharon Sherbondy

Roy is nervously pacing at what appears to be an airport terminal. Sue joins him, and in the course of their conversation, we discover they have died and are now on the outskirts of heaven waiting for their name to be called. Roy is counting on his duffel bag "trophies," his life's accomplishments, as his ticket to get in. Sue is counting on the fact that the price has been paid "already." In the end Sue's name is called, and Roy is left clutching his trophies.

Suggested Topics: Salvation; Works vs. grace
Characters: 1 male, 1 female, voice on tape

SEEING IS BELIEVING by Various Authors

A commercial for the "Bonco-God-O-Matic" causes two typical people, Bob and Jane, to replace Christ with a tangible, "comfortable" god. Thus, they avoid church, prayer, worship, and serving. This god is easy, but will he provide help for the problems of life?

Suggested Topics: A Savior you can trust; The emptiness of an easy faith
Characters: 1 male, 1 female, 1 narrator

SELF-LIST GIVING by Judson Poling

Todd and Diane, a young married couple, are opening Christmas presents with Todd's parents. Gradually, it becomes apparent that each person has given a gift he or she would rather have received. Todd receives another tool from his father, as well as the inherent pressure to be "Mr. Fix-It" like his dad. Diane receives an espresso maker from her mother-in-law, who wants Diane to be more domestic. Todd and Diane are frustrated with their parents' inconsiderate gifts, but they also demonstrate similar insensitivity in what they choose to give. In the end each person has gravitated toward the gift he or she gave rather than the one he or she received.

Suggested Topics: Meeting needs; Expressing value; Expectations; Disappointment
Characters: 2 males, 2 females

A SERF'S TALE by Judson Poling

In this zany sketch a medieval serf and his wife recount their botched attempt at grabbing for the "good life." In their longing to break out of their mere peasant's existence, they hatch a plan for the husband to be indentured to two lords—strictly forbidden by the law of the land, which says "one lord only." For a while the plan works, but in his exhaustion, the serf's duplicity is discovered and the lords both banish them. In the end they share the simple but stinging moral of their saga: "You cannot serf two masters."

Suggested Topics: Serving two masters; Materialism
Characters: 1 male, 1 female

SHOP TALK by Donna Lagerquist

Vic has lost the family business. When friends come by to comfort him, he finds it hard to receive their help. He can't get it out of his mind that he destroyed the business started by his grandfather seventy-three years earlier. His pain and anger with himself keep him from benefiting from the help they are trying to offer. They continue to stand with him and in the end affirm one more time, "We're here for you . . . all of us."

Suggested Topics: Unemployment; Adversity; Small groups
Characters: 2 males, 2 females

SIMPLE GIFTS by Sharon Sherbondy

Jane has invited over a single mom and her young daughter for dinner. The house is a panic as Jane's two kids and husband help prepare for the visit in the middle of math assignments and clothes selection for their daughter, Christine's, senior picture. Christine is especially irritable because she has "nothing to wear"—and a big pile of clothes to prove it. The single mom and daughter arrive and share the good news that she has a job interview, but other than jeans and a waitress outfit, she literally has nothing to wear. Christine has been watching, somewhat aloof, but suddenly chimes in and offers one of her outfits, which is actually quite nice. Her generosity is touching—though she quickly reverts to threatening to poke out her brother's eyes.

Suggested Topics: Caring for others less fortunate; Materialism
Characters: 2 males (1 teen), 3 females (1 teen and 1 girl)

SINGLE? by Donna Lagerquist

Two old acquaintances meet on a chairlift at a ski slope. They engage in small talk by use of one-word questions and answers. The conversation reveals a lot more than either intend, specifically their feelings about being single.

Suggested Topics: Singleness; Loneliness; Fear of living alone
Characters: 1 male, 1 female

SISTER ACT by Donna Lagerquist

Lisa has just moved out of her ex-boyfriend's apartment when big sister Betsy stops by with a pizza to console her. Betsy and the family had disapproved of Lisa's immoral relationship, but Betsy is trying not to say, "I told you so." Still, there is unresolved tension surrounding the family's general lack of support for Lisa over the years, and it causes an argument. Lisa has always felt like the black sheep of the family and continues to feel hurt over violations of trust and her failed attempts at trying to be understood. The discussion ends in a stalemate, and Betsy leaves. Lisa opens the pizza and discovers it's pepperoni—even though she told everyone six years ago she was a vegetarian!

Suggested Topics: Dysfunctional families; Wounds
Characters: 2 females

SITTERS, STRIVERS, STANDERS, AND SAINTS by Judson Poling

An underachiever ("Sitter"), an overachiever ("Striver"), and an opinionated analyzer ("Stander") receive a visit from God. Each person discovers he or she is living in some excess and finds he or she needs some quality another person possesses. When each makes a move according to God's gentle nudge, he or she becomes a more balanced, fulfilled person.

Suggested Topics: God completing us; God changing lives
Characters: 4 either males or females, 1 narrator

SIX HAPPY HEARTS by Donna Lagerquist

A mime based on Proverbs 17:22: "A cheerful heart is good medicine, but a downcast spirit dries up the bones." Six friends drive their cars (chairs) to a place they all choose to rendezvous for laughter and fun. However, one of the friends is obviously unhappy. One by one, his downcast spirit affects each of his friends. The chairs are used to create the different places these friends go; a movie theater, roller coaster, restaurant, and living room. In the end the six friends return to their homes—all negatively affected by the one, downcast spirit.

Suggested Topics: Laughter; A sour spirit affects others
Characters: 6 males or females

SNOW JOB by Donna Lagerquist

Mr. and Mrs. Kneely use—rather, abuse—prayer in order to get things done that they'd rather not do themselves. They send their daughter off to the store just minutes before her new boyfriend arrives at their house. The boyfriend then becomes prey to the Kneelys' dramatic prayers for God to send someone into their life to shovel the snow, take out the garbage, etc. Organ music, threats, and bribery are all a part of their outlandish prayers. The exaggerated situation presents a humorous look at the sad reality of people who abuse prayer.

Suggested Topics: Prayer abuse
Characters: 2 males, 1 female

SOMEBODY'S GOT TO DO IT by Sharon Sherbondy

Somehow the word has been spread that in order to serve God and the church, you have to suffer doing it or it doesn't count. That's why Paul is avoiding Reverend Roper's phone call. But to the surprise of Paul, and Shirley, his wife, he discovers a new word in serving: *joy!*

Suggested Topics: Spiritual gifts; Serving
Characters: 1 male, 1 female

SOMETHING IN COMMON by Donna Lagerquist and Steve Pederson

How does a friendship start? What does it take to build significant relationships? In this sketch we see four complete strangers develop a "platoon." Over the weeks, while watching their girls in gymnastics, common interests, risk-taking, and time become keys to developing close friendships.

Suggested Topics: Starting relationships
Characters: 3 females, 1 male

SPEAK FOR YOURSELF by Donna Lagerquist

Vicki has always been quiet, but things have gotten ridiculous. Joe, her husband, does all the talking for her. Some mutual friends confront Joe about his enabling Vicki to stay in her comfort zone. They agree that the rest of the evening Joe will only speak for himself and allow his wife to talk. Everyone is pleasantly surprised at Vicki's reaction.

Suggested Topics: Insecurity; Being an enabler
Characters: 3 males, 3 females

THE SPECULATORS by Various Authors

Alfred, Cora, and their daughter, Tammy, have made thinking about living an end in itself. Humorously they verbalize the possibilities of their day without actually doing anything. Tammy encourages her parents to consider having a weekly family time. However, when Alfred and Cora realize this will necessitate taking action to make some changes in their lives, they decide they would rather not think about it.

Suggested Topics: Risk taking, Missed opportunities
Characters: 2 males, 1 female

STEPPING IN by Donna Lagerquist

Patti and her husband, Bill, are struggling to adjust to the new reality that Grace, Bill's aging mother, is moving in with them. Grace, too, has her concerns. Even simple things like answering the phone are a challenge to Grace as she tries to adjust to this major change. In her forgetfulness she left the stove on and went out to water some flowers. Patti decides that she needs to encourage Grace to help in simple ways, like sweeping the floor with her. This sketch is a touching look at the fears and challenges associated with caring for aging parents.

Suggested Topics: Caring for parents; Aging
Characters: 1 male, 2 females

THE STICKHOLDERS by Debra Poling

This mime takes a creative look at how we tend to view God as all "rules and regulations" rather than as someone who wants a relationship with us. The "everyman" character soon learns that if he obeys life's rules, he'll get along just fine. But when he disobeys, the consequences are answering to the Stickholders. But God's stick, a shepherd's staff, is different. The man learns he can lean on the staff and rest from his rules.

Suggested Topics: Relationship with God; Resting from rules
Characters: 3 males, 1 female, 1 narrator

STOLEN JESUS by Donna Lagerquist

The setting for this Christmas-season drama is a vandalized nativity scene in the middle of a large city. All that remains of the nativity is the stable, hay, and manger. A woman, Barbara, is frustrated with the holidays and in particular a home in turmoil. While carrying just-bought gifts home, she breaks the heel on her shoe, sits on a park bench, and encounters Vivian, a bag lady. Vivian has taken up residency in the "stable." Through the course of their conversation, Barbara moves from fear and disgust to actually confiding in and having true compassion for Vivian. Vivian's homespun wisdom and quiet simple view of Jesus deeply touch Barbara—and the audience.

Suggested Topics: Christmas
Characters: 2 females

THE STORY OF RACHEL by Donna Lagerquist

Three women tell the same story from their own perspective. One day, while feeding ducks in the park, Mary Pat has her bag of bread crumbs stolen by Rachel, a street girl. The scene is witnessed by Jean. Their descriptions of what happened are interwoven throughout, showing how the three women view Rachel's poverty—and theft—in totally different ways. Rachel sees it as her only way to survive; Mary Pat, though Rachel's target, sees past her offense and tries to reach out to help her—first, practically, and then in personal ways; and Jean watches all this and thinks it foolishness for anyone to reach out to a street urchin.

Suggested Topics: Care for the poor; Compassion
Characters: 3 females

STRAIGHT-JACKETED by Various Authors

A man in a straight-jacket talks to the audience about his painful past. He has chosen his life of bondage because it keeps him from having to get vulnerable. His constriction keeps him safe. His father was an alcoholic and beat his mom, his wife left him, and now he stays in his cocoon. Even if he did want to be free, he observes without emotion, "I don't know how to get out."

Suggested Topics: Bondage to sin and our past; Anger toward God
Characters: 1 male

SUIT AND VOLLY by Donna Lagerquist

Vivian the bag lady explains to her fellow homeless friend Earl that two people she names "Suit" and "Volly" are the soup servers today at the soup kitchen and that they make her angry. Suit always wears his suit and makes sure he lets everyone know he is a prominent lawyer who takes time to do community service. Volly prides herself on her dedication to volunteer anywhere and everywhere. Earl eventually convinces Vivian to join him, and once at the kitchen, Suit and Volly live up to their nicknames. Suit soon leaves to get back to the office; Volly goes off to volunteer somewhere else. Finally, Earl serves Vivian her meal, for the right reasons with the right heart.

Suggested Topics: Genuine commitment; Service
Characters: 2 males, 2 females

SUIT YOURSELF by Donna Lagerquist

Dan has just returned home from shopping for a bathing suit with his daughter Tracey. Marlene stayed home, dreading the annual argument over what is modest enough for parents but stylish enough for a teenager. While Tracey visits outside with the neighbor kids, Dan and Marlene discuss the shopping trip. Tracey bought a suit, but Dan hasn't seen it, deciding instead to trust his daughter's judgment after expressing his concerns. Marlene considers his deference to Tracey a cop-out and worries about what others will think of them as parents if Tracey shows up at church camp in a string bikini. Just then a neighbor brings in the shopping bag Tracey left outside. What kind of suit did Tracey buy? The drama ends as both parents lunge for the bag to find out.

Suggested Topics: Parenting; Letting kids make their own decisions
Characters: 1 male, 2 females

THE SURPRISED PARTY by Donna Lagerquist

It's Dennis's birthday, and he is sure that his wife has organized a surprise party for him. While with a friend, Larry, he repeatedly tries to get him to break down and admit that a surprise party is in the works. Larry is unsuccessful in convincing Dennis that he knows nothing about a party. Once home, both Dennis and Larry are surprised! There is a party—but it's for Larry! In the end, when his wife finds him off by himself, Dennis reluctantly shares his embarrassment and disappointment.

Suggested Topics: Disappointments are a part of life
Characters: 2 males, 1 female

TAKE HEART by Debra Poling

This solo mime shows a woman in three different stages of life; as a child, a teenager, and a woman in the workplace. In each stage the narrative demonstrates how the woman essentially suffers a broken heart. In the end it is God who not only mends her heart, but returns it to her full and strong.

Suggested Topics: God heals the brokenhearted; Disappointment
Characters: 2 males, 2 females

TAKING STEP FOUR by Sharon Sherbondy

In this lighthearted monologue a women reads from the book *Hunger for Healing* about taking Step 4 (from 12-step programs). She has prepared herself to "take a searching and fearless moral inventory" with paper, pen, Kleenex . . . and food. As she begins, she humorously retreats to blaming others and missing the whole point of the step. The need for honesty in self-examination comes through powerfully—yet in a disarmingly funny way.

Suggested Topics: Self-delusion; Confession of sin; Self-examination
Characters: 1 female

"10" by Judson Poling

To introduce a series on the Ten Commandments and to present the First Commandment—"Honor God as God"—the audience meets the character "10." In this sketch "10" is an on-the-street reporter quizzing people on their knowledge of the Ten Commandments. He also speaks directly to the audience concerning impressions that the Ten Commandments are dated and nitpicky.

(*Note:* "10" also appears in other dramas.)
Suggested Topics: First commandment
Characters: 3 males, 2 females

TERMINAL VISIT by Debra Poling

Two grown sisters meet in an airport. Their relationship has become superficial, and now their inability to communicate about hidden hurts has built a wall. Instead of feeling close and supported, they experience disappointment in each other.

Suggested Topics: Resurrecting relationships; Family conflict
Characters: 3 females

THANKS FOR LISTENING by Sharon Sherbondy

A family decides to picnic outside although it's quite cold. As they engage in typical "busy family" dinner conversation, Mark, the teenage son, tries to talk about his baseball game. He is interrupted throughout his story. Several times he is asked to begin again, only to be ignored repeatedly. In the end everyone complains that it is too cold, so they head back in. Mark is left at the table alone. He decides to finish his story, talking enthusiastically as if everyone was still there. He thanks them all for listening, though he sits with no one left to hear.

Suggested Topics: Family, Listening
Characters: 1 male, 1 female, 1 male and 1 female teenager

THESE PARTS by Judson Poling

In the land of "These Parts," where everyone has only part sight, part hearing, and one arm, a Stranger appears who tells a family they can be whole. After consulting the experts, the Stranger is rejected and killed. But he returns to life and again offers to give them sight, hearing, and use of both arms. When the family consults the experts, they say it's impossible. Only the child remains, and only the child receives . . . "a hug with both arms."

Suggested Topics: The resurrection; Our need for Christ; Easter
Characters: 2 males, 1 female, 3 either males or females, 1 child, 1 narrator

A THIEF'S CAROL by Sharon Sherbondy

In the spirit of Dickens's *Christmas Carol,* our character "10" (see the script "10") pays a visit to Rouge (a Scrooge-like character). During the night, "10" escorts three people from Rouge's past, whom he has stolen from, deceived, and defrauded. By the end of the evening, Rouge is ready to change his life and make restitution for his wrongdoings.

Suggested Topics: Eighth commandment; Stealing
Characters: 3 males, 2 females

THIS SIDE OF HEAVEN by Sharon Sherbondy

Annie is admitting her elderly father into a nursing home. He has fallen at home and broken his wrist, and it's time that he live where he can receive more watchful care. He grumbles about the transition, though in a touching and poignant way. He feels he has turned into a burden—it's not easy getting old. Tenderly, his daughter explains she loves him, and after all he has done for her, she doesn't consider him a burden.

Suggested Topics: Growing old; Taking care of aging parents
Characters: 1 male, 2 females

TIME FLIES by Donna Lagerquist

Two elderly men are swatting flies outside their retirement home. They have an ongoing contest to see who can get the most. They talk about the simple routines of their week: basically, what food is being served on what days. The scene cuts to a mother and a daughter who are planning to visit the dad/grandfather as they do every week, though the granddaughter doesn't want to go. The scene cuts back to the men now wondering if they are going to receive a visit from the family. The scene cuts to the mother on the phone to her husband, who was supposed to join them but can't. She doesn't want to go without him, so she decides to call her dad and cancel. The final scene cuts back to the men, talking about the ambulance that came last night for someone who died. It's a regular occurrence that doesn't seem to phase them much. At least when there's a funeral, they can count on getting some cake.

Suggested Topic: Honoring parents
Characters: 2 males, 1 female, 1 young girl

TIRED OF TRYING by Donna Lagerquist

Kate tries to make the best of the dilemma she faces when her son invites his grandfather (her father) to his birthday party. He is a "miserable man." At first Kate stifles her anger toward him as she has all her life. However, when forced to protect her son from emotional abuse from his grandfather, she ends up honestly and powerfully confronting her father.

Suggested Topics: Dealing with the anger of others; Confronting injustice
Characters: 1 male, 2 females

TIRED WHEN NEEDED by Sharon Sherbondy

Mr. Watson has locked himself up in a motel room to get away from people and their demands on his time. Mrs. Willoughby, however, has tracked him down to request his involvement in just one more worthy cause. He tries reason, but even a direct no doesn't work with Mrs. Willoughby—until he cracks!

Suggested Topics: Burnout; Saying no; Boundaries
Characters: 1 male, 1 female

TOM, DICK, AND MARY by Judson Poling

Sometimes the noise in people's lives prevents them from hearing God's message of love. Tom couldn't hear God because he was always on his soap box. Dick's ears were filled with the sound of his money machine. And Mary filled her world with the television, the radio, and the walkman. When their lives are quieted, all three discover they are miserable and very much alone.

Suggested Topics: Crowding out God; Hearing God's voice
Characters: 3 males, 1 female, 1 narrator

TRUTHFUL WORDS by Mark Demel

Marge, the secretary at St. John's Church, is getting some refreshments for an elder meeting in the boardroom. As she passes through the empty sanctuary, she discovers Greg—her boss and the pastor of the church—"laying down thinking, not praying." The elder meeting is about him and whether or not he should be fired for using "descriptive" words. Greg tries to elicit empathy from this partner in ministry about his predicament and the necessity of speaking the truth. Marge, however, compassionately shares her own truthful words about what seems to be his main concern in the situation—how he is being perceived. Eventually, Greg asks her for something to do to take his mind off the waiting. The task she gives him is demeaning and similar to Jesus' washing of feet and, combined with the words she has spoken to him, finally breaks his attitude of pride.

Suggested Topics: Leadership; Pride; Truth telling
Characters: 1 male, 1 female

TRYING TIME by Donna Lagerquist

Paula is a believer and Marty is not. While shopping, they meet a friend, Connie, who enthusiastically tells Paula that her son has just become a Christian. When she leaves, Paula and Marty have a hard conversation because Marty can't share Paula's enthusiasm for spiritual things. He knows she is not happy with him the way he is, and she knows he is angry that she has changed since they got married. Both are frustrated that, though they love each other, a major area of life is a constant sore spot.

Suggested Topics: Marriage; Beloved unbeliever; Evangelism
Characters: 1 male, 2 females

UNACCEPTABLE by Sharon Sherbondy

Mom comes into the bedroom of her teenage daughter, Jennie, with a basket of clean laundry. The exchange is terse but not too unpleasant. Mom, however, discovers that Jennie pierced her nose that afternoon, and she is appalled. This becomes just one more in a long series of arguments over Jennie's behavior. There are no easy answers about how to deal with teenagers who are still dependent economically yet who can—and should—be making decisions for themselves even when parents disagree.

Suggested Topic: Dealing with adolescence
Characters: 2 females (1 older teen)

UNAVERAGE JOE by Sharon Sherbondy

This sketch is a lighthearted retelling of the angel's visit to Joseph before he attempted to divorce Mary. In a contemporary setting (complete with stereotypical Jewish accents), a good Jewish boy, Joseph, awakens his good Jewish parents in the middle of the night to tell them that he has had an encounter with an angel. His wife to be, Mary, is pregnant and will have a child, God's Son—or so says the angel. Mom and Dad can't believe it. They argue, with each other and with Joseph, and in the end they admit they will try to stay open but that it will be hard to accept the loss of honor to their family name. Joseph replies that this willingness to sacrifice reputation is not merely for the love of a woman, it is for the love of his God. He can do no other.

Suggested Topics: Christmas; Obeying God's call
Characters: 2 males, 1 female

UNKNOWN by Sharon Sherbondy

Four women who have been friends for years meet for lunch to celebrate Dana's birthday. As she unwraps her presents, each woman brings the topic of conversation back to herself. The birthday girl—supposedly at the center of the celebration—gets forgotten in the self-centered chatter. At the end, Dana talks directly to the audience about how she wishes the relationships could go deeper and how she wishes these women would take a more sincere interest in her life.

Suggested Topics: Friendship; Loneliness; Small groups
Characters: 1 male, 4 females

UP ON THE ROOF by Donna Lagerquist

Stressed-out Wally is sent up to the roof of his office building to check on his boss's TV reception, and he discovers a real problem. A bag lady is using the antenna for a clothesline while she retreats to the roof to "get away from it all." However, through the course of lighthearted conversation with the lady, in which she shares her homespun wisdom, Wally discovers a problem more serious than the antenna debris. His personal life has become overwhelming and he is exhausted. Just as Wally begins to absorb the peaceful rooftop environment, his boss interrupts by calling on Wally's cordless phone. Wally hurries to return back to work but has obviously been touched by the woman's concern for him and her words of wisdom to visit the roof as often as he needs in order to handle life one little battle at a time.

Suggested Topics: Emotional refueling; Building compassion
Characters: 1 male, 1 female

THE VACATIONERS—PARTS 1 AND 2 by Judson Poling

This is a two-part sketch that takes a comedic look at how two couples survive the planning of a mutual vacation. The couples come to the realization that they have some very different ideas on how to plan and enjoy their time together. While on the vacation, the reality of the couples' differences seems like a nightmare. As they calm down, they realize there is no right or wrong way to do things, just different preferences.

Suggested Topics: Personality differences; Friendships; Accepting others
Characters: 2 males, 2 females

VINCE BUELLER'S DAY OFF by Sharon Sherbondy

This is Vince's first day off in two weeks. He vowed to spend the day relaxing but ends up driving his wife crazy by "fixing" everything he sets his eyes on.

Suggested Topics: Workaholism; Importance of rest/leisure
Characters: 1 male, 1 female, 1 boy

A VISITOR by Sharon Sherbondy

Howard, a recent widower, is visited in his home by Mr. Kendall from Tree of Life ministries. When Howard's adult daughter Penny drops by to bring supper, she begins to question Mr. Kendall about his "ministry" and finds him evasive. As she continues to press him, it becomes clear her father is being duped into giving a large contribution, manipulated by his own emotional vulnerability and Mr. Kendall's connivery. Penny finally insists Mr. Kendall leave, and as he goes, bids him, "Happy hunting!"

Suggested Topics: Discernment; Spiritual manipulation; Wolves in sheep's clothing
Characters: 2 males, 1 female

WAIT 'TIL HALF-TIME by Sharon Sherbondy

Larry is into the Bulls basketball game when Beth comes in suggesting they do something more social for the evening. When she suggests inviting over another couple, Craig and Robin, he becomes especially disinterested. He doesn't like their Christianity, while she finds them interesting, caring people. The exchange is mostly lighthearted until the end when she expresses concern for his eternal well-being. He quips about burial in "asbestos underwear" to try to fend her off. In his mind eternity can wait until half-time.
Suggested Topics: Evangelism; Heaven and hell
Characters: 1 male, 1 female

THE WAITING ROOM by Donna Lagerquist

Four characters mysteriously end up in a "waiting room" with a phone at the center. An older woman is waiting for her sister to call. They had a falling out twelve years ago and haven't spoken since. A younger woman is waiting to figure out what to do with the rest of her life—and she wants someone to guarantee her future before she takes a step to go to college. Another man has been laid off because of explosive anger but wants the company to call him up and ask him back to work—even though he hasn't taken any concrete steps to get at the root of his rage. Finally, a man is waiting to be sure before he takes the step into marriage—he needs to know he won't ever get divorced. That man, the newest arrival to the waiting room, asks how often the phone rings so he can get an idea of when he'll get his answer. But none of the people there has ever heard it ring.
Suggested Topics: Fear of decision making; Need to take risks
Characters: 2 males, 2 females

THE WALL by Donna Lagerquist

The setting is the Vietnam War Memorial. At one end of the Wall, two army buddies reminisce about a friend they lost in the war and how he had personally affected their lives. Further down the Wall a woman talks to and remembers her brother, whose name is also on the Wall. A warm, reflective mood is broken when a "vacationing" family invades the area, taking pictures and making insensitive comments. The family soon learns the difference between touring monuments and visiting/remembering loved ones.
Suggested Topics: Significance of remembering, i.e., communion
Characters: 3 males, 2 females, 1 child

WAR AND PEACE by Sharon Sherbondy

Steve and Ronda take a risk and confront Tim and Barb about the uncontrollable behavior of Tim and Barb's two hyperactive daughters. Steve is reluctant to do so, but Ronda insists that someone has to tell Tim and Barb their daughters are making it hard for anyone to want to be around them. Unfortunately, the situation explodes, and Tim and Barb leave in a huff. Steve tries to keep his sense of humor, but Ronda is hurt and determines that in the future she is not going to make a friend's problem her own. This sketch shows the cost of taking risks and how in the short run things may get harder when people decide to be more honest with each other.
Suggested Topics: Relationships; Taking risks
Characters: 2 males, 2 females

THE WARRIOR by Donna Lagerquist

Marlene is a maid cleaning one of her customer's homes. She has devised a clever way to remind herself to pray for various concerns: items in the house trigger her recollection of people or events she promised to pray for. A candy dish reminds her to pray for a little girl who needs to be "sweeter." Plugging in her vacuum cleaner reminds her of a friend going through hard times, someone who needs God's "power"; and when she unplugs it, it reminds her to pray her friend can "shut down" and get rest. People think she is just a maid doing housecleaning. But she is really a prayer warrior on the front lines every day. A touching story at the end explains why this woman is so committed to prayer on behalf of others.
Suggested Topics: Prayer; Taking God with you throughout the day
Characters: 1 female

WASTED by Judson Poling

Cliff, a janitor, is showing Brett, a new employee, the ropes. Brett is a student intent on moving ahead and dreams of someday working in an office like the one they're cleaning. The scene changes, and now Brett does work there, and Cliff stops by on his way out to a fishing trip. Brett is harried and envies Cliff's freedom. The scene changes again to a night at the office: Brett has moved up the ladder and is working late again. He is confronted by Cliff and explains that Cliff doesn't understand the pressure of a man in Brett's position. Cliff confesses that he envies what Brett has done with his life. Both realize neither career has been perfect, and neither knows what to do. We're left knowing both white collar and blue collar jobs have difficulties—but how to cope is left unspecified.
Suggested Topics: Christians and work; Job satisfaction
Characters: 2 males

WATCHING FROM THE WINDOW by Sharon Sherbondy

Carol is standing in front of her house with a suitcase in her hand. She is contemplating walking out on her family. At first she seems somewhat cold and hard, but gradually our empathy is aroused because we realize that she has been beaten down by the people in her life who take from her but give nothing back.
Suggested Topics: Draining relationships; Challenge of motherhood; Stress of life
Characters: 1 female, 1 child

WELCOME TO THE FAMILY by Sharon Sherbondy

Judy and Fred are overwhelmed by a pushy salesman offering them a "Lifestyle for God" package. They are new Christians, both confused and vulnerable, and while wanting to grow in their faith, they are unsure how to respond to the salesman's offer.
Suggested Topics: Growing in Christ; Spiritual infancy and/or gullibility
Characters: 2 males, 1 female

WHAT ABOUT LIFE? by Sharon Sherbondy

Carl sneaks into bed late one night with a snack. His wife, Nicole, sleepily asks what's the matter. Something is bothering him, but he just doesn't know what it is. At first, Nicole thinks it's her and apologizes for whatever she may have done. That's not it. So then she thinks Carl is heading into a mid-life crisis. But that's not it either. There should be something more to life, he asserts. But Nicole assures him that they're educated, Internet-connected, middle-class, Baby Boomers. If there was supposed to be more to life, they'd know it—right? Carl decides to try and sleep, leaving Nicole snacking in the dark, wondering what's missing.
Suggested Topics: Finding meaning to life; The empty void inside
Characters: 1 male, 1 female

WHAT ARE FRIENDS FOR? by Sharon Sherbondy

Wayne has just arrived home from work and greets Joan, who doesn't really seem to hear him. She is preoccupied with thoughts of her recent conversation with her friend Sue. Sue is coming over to "talk" because she needs it. Wayne is tired of Sue and her problems and finds an excuse to leave. Sue has marital and family problems that require professional counseling, but she won't go. Joan doesn't know how to tell Sue the truth, because she is afraid Sue will feel hurt. In the meantime these "talks" have caused a strain in Joan's marriage. Finally, Joan has a difficult but truthful conversation with Sue, once again suggesting she see a counselor. Sue feels betrayed. The telephone rings, and Sue hands the phone to Joan as she exits. "Relax, it's not me!"

Suggested Topics: Friendship; Truth telling
Characters: 1 male, 2 females

WHAT IF . . . by Donna Lagerquist

In this lighthearted sketch a man nervously tries to get to sleep, anxious about a variety of concerns. He goes in and out of dreams where his boss, a doctor, his wife, and even two movers show up to torment him. All the characters come back at the end and talk directly to the audience, quoting the familiar words from the Sermon on the Mount about being anxious for nothing and seeking first the kingdom. Easier said than done!

Suggested Topics: Worry
Characters: 3 males, 1 female

WHAT NOW? by Sharon Sherbondy

This sketch opens with a group of friends reminiscing about the good times they've shared. Slowly the audience discovers that the reason they gathered is to support their friend after the sudden death of her husband. She has caring friends and family to support her, but that isn't enough. She doesn't know how she'll face the challenges of being a widow and single parent.

Suggested Topics: Coping with a crisis; Dealing with death
Characters: 2 males, 4 females

WHAT'S THE TICKET? by Sharon Sherbondy

Joyce is frustrated with her lack of contentment. She lives her life with determination when it comes to getting what she wants and thinks she needs. Each year she searches out her Christmas present from her husband, unwraps it, and takes it back to get what she really wants. She is also dedicated to trying to win the lottery so she can get the things she needs (new wardrobe, new furniture) to go along with her color scheme.

Suggested Topics: Need for Christ; Contentment; Needs and wants
Characters: 2 females, 4 either males or females

WHEEL OF POWER by Cathy Peters

This sketch exemplifies the "wheel of power" or pecking order people experience today. We watch how people misuse the power they've been given or have taken.

Suggested Topics: Power
Characters: 4 males, 1 female, 1 child

WILL THE REAL GOD PLEASE STAND UP? by Sharon Sherbondy

On her thirty-fifth birthday Ginger is plagued by a series of nagging questions, and at the top of the list is "What happens when I die?" Three characters appear representing different views of God she has been taught at various stages in her life. The sheriff who keeps track of everything, the mechanic who fixes things, and the grandfather who just wants her to feel good. None of them represents the true complete view of God.

Suggested Topics: Second commandment; What is God like?
Characters: 3 males, 1 female

WINGS by Donna Lagerquist

A family is eagerly awaiting the return of their eldest son, Chuck, from flight training school. According to Chuck, the training center closed early for Christmas. When he arrives home, he dazzles everyone with stories of flight school and simulation training. When his mother and siblings leave the room, Chuck confesses to his father that he was actually thrown out of the program for breaking the rules. His father, also a commercial pilot, is

disappointed. Chuck feels like he is ruining Christmas with his presence. When the rest of the family returns, they assure him that home is where he belongs, and they pledge to stand by him.

Suggested Topics: Christmas; Family
Characters: 2 males, 1 female, 1 teen, 1 preteen

WINNING STRATEGY by Various Authors

At what appears to be a high-level corporate board meeting, officers discuss plans for expansion. It gradually becomes apparent these people are really demons planning to enslave humanity. A unique idea is suggested by a relatively low-ranking participant: make people self-reliant, busy—in a word, "successful." Tragedies make people recognize their need, but preoccupation with gain keeps them away from God. The new idea is received warmly, and all get to work.

Suggested Topics: Good vs. evil
Characters: 2 males, 4 either males or females

WONDERFULLY MADE by Donna Lagerquist

A creative interpretation of the statement in Psalm 139 of how God knits us together in our mother's womb and has a plan for our life. We see a child, Elizabeth, assigned qualities by God while in her mother's womb. She is to be a dancer, a left-handed painter, an introvert, and strong-willed. She knows she is loved and made just right. However, once she is born, these feelings change because her parents' aspirations for her are quite different than what she was "told" in the womb. Her father replaces ballet shoes with soccer shoes. Her mother makes her keep her left hand behind her back so that her penmanship doesn't look funny. Their "redirection" through the years physically and emotionally stifles who Elizabeth was meant to be, and she grows up a very sad and confused child.

Suggested Topics: Affirming each child's uniqueness
Characters: 2 females, 2 males, 1 narrator

WORTH KEEPING by Donna Lagerquist

Moving into a new home sets the scene for a touching encounter between Dan, a newly hired Major League baseball player, and his mother, who raised him alone. When Dan leaves to move the truck, his mother shares her box of memories with Dan's wife. Among the Little League snapshots and trophies, there is also an afghan that she knitted during his high school games. Dan had spoken of it but doesn't know his mother has kept it until the box is unpacked. As Dan and his mother continue to sort through the box, Dan realizes the major role his mother played in his achievement of becoming a Major League player.

Suggested Topics: Mother's Day; Single parenting
Characters: 1 male, 2 females

"X" MARKS THE SPOT by Judson Poling and Steve Pederson

This mime takes a look at people's efforts to get rid of their sin: "X." Our characters meet three people who claim to have the answer to their problem. The first tries to make it go away, the second tries to hide it, and the last offers the only hope, the cross. The score that accompanied this mime is not available; however, we have provided comments so you can create your own.

Suggested Topics: Sin; Redemption; Forgiveness; Guilt
Characters: 1 male, 1 female, and 3 either males or females

YOU AND ME by Donna Lagerquist

Sarah, a college-aged woman, is talking on the phone, her arm in a sling. Her mother stops by with some sandwiches. As they talk, Sarah reveals that she has made a tough decision to leave dental hygienist school. Her injury will put her too far behind. Her mother tries to stay upbeat, but Sarah can't see a way out. Her recently divorced mother stands with her, promising whatever assistance she can, financially and personally, because they "are family." They end on a hopeful note, with Mom encouraging Sarah to talk to her professor and not throw out her books. Mom also surprises Sarah with a bottle of her favorite shampoo from childhood, with a promise to help her wash her hair just like she used to back then.

Suggested Topics: Mother's Day; Family; Rebuilding after divorce; Navigating life's challenges

Characters: 2 females

YOU CRAMP MY STYLE by Donna Lagerquist

Three people, who are very much individuals, give three monologues that are intercut with each other. The first is a too-busy businessman in his car on his car phone. The second is a woman in an airport phone booth on her way to a new life in a new location. The third is an energetic DJ processing music requests in his studio. One by one we see each of them receive a phone call from God. And one by one we see each of them explain why they have no need of him.

Suggested Topics: Reasons people don't believe; How society views God

Characters: 1 male, 1 female, 1 either male or female

Keep your heart healthy with Willow Creek Resources™

The Heart of the Artist

*A Character-Building Guide
for You and Your Ministry Team*
Rory Noland

Find wisdom and encouragement that can help you survive the challenges and reap the rich joys of a ministry in the arts.

Written for artists by an artist, this frank, knowledgeable book deals head-on with issues every person in an arts ministry faces. With passion and conviction that come from personal experience, Rory Noland, music director for Willow Creek Community Church, addresses topics such as:

- Servanthood Versus Stardom
- The Artist in Community
- Excellence Versus Perfectionism
- Jealousy and Envy
- Managing Your Emotions
- The Spiritual Disciplines of the Artist

Between pride and self-abasement lies true humility—just one aspect of the balanced character God wants to instill in you as an actor, a musician, a visual artist, or other creative person involved in ministry. He's interested in your art *and* your heart.

Softcover: 0-310-22471-3

Find The Heart of the Artist ***at your local Christian bookstore.***

Get dramatic results with Willow Creek Resources®

Drama Ministry
Practical Help for Making Drama
a Vital Part of Your Church
Steve Pederson

Whether you're a drama director, part of a drama team, or a pastor interested in developing drama ministry in your church, *Drama Ministry* will ignite your vision for church drama and help you produce material that grabs your congregation's attention—and heart—from the beginning.

Veteran drama director Steve Pederson of Willow Creek Community Church's renowned drama department takes you into the workings of powerful and effective drama ministry. Drawing on his vast experience as a world-class drama director and instructor, Pederson shares expert advice on every aspect of drama—powerful, hands-on insights you can apply today. Here's everything you need to know and do to:

- Assemble a drama team
- Train a drama team
- Make your team last
- Write a winning sketch
- Direct effectively

Drama Ministry includes a CD-ROM that provides a video demonstration of directing techniques. And it's punctuated with personal testimonies and stories from audiences and actors that reveal the power and impact of drama.

Softcover: 0-310-21945-0

Find Drama Ministry ***at your local Christian bookstore.***

GRAND RAPIDS, MICHIGAN 49530 USA

Willow Creek Association
Vision, Training, Resources for Prevailing Churches

This resource was created to serve you and to help you in building a local church that prevails!

Since 1992, the Willow Creek Association (WCA) has been linking like-minded, action-oriented churches with each other and with strategic vision, training, and resources. Now a worldwide network of over 6,400 churches from more than ninety denominations, the WCA works to equip Member Churches and others with the tools needed to build prevailing churches. Our desire is to inspire, equip, and encourage Christian leaders to build biblically functioning churches that reach increasing numbers of unchurched people, not just with innovations from Willow Creek Community Church in South Barrington, Illinois, but from any church in the world that has experienced God-given breakthroughs.

WILLOW CREEK CONFERENCES

Each year, thousands of local church leaders, staff and volunteers—from WCA Member Churches and others—attend one of our conferences or training events. Conferences offered on the Willow Creek campus in South Barrington, Illinois, include:

Prevailing Church Conference: Foundational training for staff and volunteers working to build a prevailing local church.

Prevailing Church Workshops: More than fifty strategic, day-long workshops covering seven topic areas that represent key characteristics of a prevailing church; offered twice each year.

Promiseland Conference: Children's ministries; infant through fifth grade.

Student Ministries Conference: Junior and senior high ministries.

Willow Creek Arts Conference: Vision and training for Christian artists using their gifts in the ministries of local churches.

Leadership Summit: Envisioning and equipping Christians with leadership gifts and responsibilities; broadcast live via satellite to eighteen cities across North America.

Contagious Evangelism Conference: Encouragement and training for churches and church leaders who want to be strategic in reaching lost people for Christ.

Small Groups Conference: Exploring how developing a church *of* small groups can play a vital role in developing authentic Christian community that leads to spiritual transformation.

PREVAILING CHURCH REGIONAL WORKSHOPS

Each year the WCA team leads several, two-day training events in select cities across the United States. Some twenty day-long workshops are offered in topic areas including leadership, next-generation ministries, small groups, arts and worship, evangelism, spiritual gifts, financial stewardship, and spiritual formation. These events make quality training more accessible and affordable to larger groups of staff and volunteers.

To find out more about Prevailing Church Regional Workshops, visit our website at www.willowcreek.com.

WILLOW CREEK RESOURCES™

Churches can look to Willow Creek Resources™ for a trusted channel of ministry tools in areas of leadership, evangelism, spiritual gifts, small groups, drama, contemporary music, financial stewardship, spiritual transformation, and more. For ordering information, call (800) 570-9812 or visit our website at www.willowcreek.com.

WCA MEMBERSHIP

Membership in the Willow Creek Association as well as attendance at WCA Conferences is for churches, ministries, and leaders who hold to a historic, orthodox understanding of biblical Christianity. The annual church membership fee of $249 provides substantial discounts for your entire team on all conferences and Willow Creek Resources, networking opportunities with other outreach-oriented churches, a bimonthly newsletter, a subscription to the *Defining Moments* monthly audio journal for leaders, and more.

Willow Creek Association
P.O. Box 3188, Barrington, IL 60011-3188
Phone: (800) 570-9812 or (847) 765-0070
Fax (888) 922-0035 or (847) 765-5046
Web: www.willowcreek.com